The Lewis and Clark Journals

An American Epic of Discovery

The Abridgment of
the Definitive Nebraska Edition

Meriwether Lewis,
William Clark, and Members of
the Corps of Discovery

Edited and with an introduction
by Gary E. Moulton

University of Nebraska Press
Lincoln and London

WINGATE UNIVERSITY LIBRARY

© 2003 by the Board of Regents of the University of Nebraska
All rights reserved
Manufactured in the United States of America
First Nebraska paperback printing: 2004

LIBRARY OF CONGRESS CATALOGING-IN-PUBLICATION DATA
The Lewis and Clark journals : an American epic of discovery :
the abridgment of the definitive Nebraska edition / Meriwether
Lewis, William Clark, and members of the Corps of Discovery ;
edited and with an introduction by Gary E. Moulton.
p. cm. Includes index. ISBN 0-8032-2950-x (cloth : alk. paper)
1. Lewis and Clark Expedition (1804-1806) 2. West (U.S.) –
Discovery and exploration. 3. West (U.S.) – Description and
travel. 4. Lewis, Meriwether, 1774-1809 – Diaries. 5. Clark, William, 1770-1838 – Diaries. 6. Explorers – West (U.S.) – Diaries.
I. Lewis, Meriwether, 1774-1809. II. Clark, William, 1770-1838.
III. Moulton, Gary E. IV. Journals of the Lewis and Clark
Expedition.   F592.4 2003 917.804'2 – dc21 2002028526

ISBN 0-8032-8039-4 (pbk.)

Portions of the introduction and afterword were previously
published in the introductions to the volumes of the *Journals of
the Lewis and Clark Expedition,* written in conjunction with
Thomas W. Dunlay; in a publication for the Nebraska Humani-
ties Council and the Center for Great Plains Studies, University
of Nebraska–Lincoln, *American Encounters: Lewis and Clark,
the People, and the Land*; and in an anonymously written work
for Chelsea House Publishers.

Jacket and chapter-opening details are reproduced from the
journals of Lewis and Clark held at the American Philosophical
Society, the Frederick W. and Carrie S. Beinecke Collection of
Western Americana at Yale University, and the Eleanor Glasgow
Voorhis Collection at the Missouri Historical Society.

To my grandchildren   Jeremy and Daniel
                           Natalie and Nicholas
                           Kaitlyn and Grace
                           Jacquelyn, Allessandra,
                           and Christian

May all your explorations lead to great discoveries.

Contents

Illustrations

Preface

Instructed by President Jefferson to keep meticulous records bearing upon the geography, ethnology, and natural history of the trans-Mississippi West, Lewis and Clark filled hundreds of notebook pages with observations during their expedition. Some of the enlisted men—those who were literate—did the same. The result is a national treasure: a complete look at the Great Plains, the Rocky Mountains, and the Pacific Northwest, reported by men who were intelligent and well prepared, at a time when Easterners knew almost nothing about those regions so newly acquired in the Louisiana Purchase. Getting at the actual words of the explorers, however, is either a formidable task (the party's diarists wrote more than one million words) or a disappointment, because existing condensations of the men's writings are outdated and incomplete.

A narrative based on the journals was prepared first by Nicholas Biddle and published in 1814. The journals themselves, most of which were deposited in the American Philosophical Society in Philadelphia by Jefferson, lay largely unused and almost forgotten for nearly a century, until an edition of known materials was published in 1904–5. This first comprehensive edition of the journals, Reuben Gold Thwaites's *Original Journals of the Lewis and Clark Expedition, 1804–1806*, was a superb tool for scholars and laypersons in its time. It had, however, suffered the various kinds of erosion that beset all such works: new manuscripts were discovered, much new information was available with which to annotate the journals, and documentary editing procedures had undergone profound changes. These deficiencies led to the project to publish an entirely new comprehensive edition of the journals. That effort, begun in 1979 and completed in 2001, was published as *The Journals of the Lewis and Clark Expedition* in thirteen volumes by the University of Nebraska Press under the direction of the editor of this volume. However, that massive undertaking, targeted primarily at scholars and research institutions, does not reach a public who wants a less weighty introduction to the party's diaries. This book seeks to bring these important words to a wider audience in a compact form: an accessible one-volume abridgment based on a reliable source with pertinent clarifying information.

Thwaites lacked both the time and knowledge to interpret fully the wondrous variety of raw materials produced by the explorers—ranging from reflections on Indian tribal customs to speculations on geological and ecological phenomena. Most important, documents were omitted from his edition because the material was either unknown or unavailable. These valuable resources include a journal kept by Lewis and later Clark as they traveled down the Ohio and up the Mississippi on the first leg of the expedition in 1803; a journal kept by Sergeant John Ordway, an intelligent soldier whose observations cover the entire expedition; Clark's rough field notes discovered in a Minnesota attic in the 1950s, which provide rich new data of a hitherto obscure period of the expedition; an extended copy of a journal kept by Private Joseph Whitehouse, not discovered until the 1960s (Thwaites had only a portion of the original); a number of Clark's original maps and a trove of historic copies, some replacing lost originals; and more than two hundred botanical items preserved from the expedition, many of them type specimens. Existing one-volume abridgments of the journals are all based on the limited Thwaites edition.

The abridged edition presented here proposes to overcome the inadequacies of Thwaites which were carried into current one-volume treatments. The new selections and annotations are made from the full corpus of journal materials, including those discovered since Thwaites's time and the important diaries of the enlisted men. Present condensations largely ignore the subordinates' diaries and miss the important collateral information that they provide. The captains' relations with and studies of the Native Americans with whom they came in contact is a major focus of the new selected edition. The men's extensive passages concerning American Indians are incorporated into this book in order to provide the fullest treatment possible. The natural history work of the party forms the second most prominent place in the selection process. Few other matters were so extensively noticed by the men. Finally, the exciting story the diaries tell is not neglected. The diarists observed, considered, and recorded it all.

If the Lewis and Clark expedition were a closed matter—an event that happened, made its contribution, and then was forgotten—a new selected edition of the journals would be less pressing. Few events in American history are more alive today. Serious scholars have produced a number of significant books relating to the expedition in the last decades, books eagerly purchased by an interested public. The work of scholars has been greatly aided by the new edition, and it has been universally praised for its faithful transcriptions and valuable annotation. Indeed, the volumes of the new edition have already influenced new areas of scholarship and the reinterpretation of traditional themes. These scholars' works and scores of other books, articles, pamphlets, essays, scientific studies, film works, musical compositions, and artistic endeavors have relied on the new edition of the journals. This abridgment is based on that comprehensive edition. I hope it finds a ready reception and brings new enthusiasts to the words of the Corps of Discovery.

A number of persons and institutions have been supportive of my efforts in this work. Dr. Stephen E. Ambrose, Helena, Montana, provided the financial assistance that freed me to begin work on this book and develop general guidelines for the editing. I received a Faculty Development Fellowship from the University of Nebraska–Lincoln in the fall of 1998 during which time I completed the first two chapters. Additional editing work was carried out while I was a scholar-in-residence at Fort Clatsop National Memorial, Astoria, Oregon, in the summer of 1999. I was able to make great headway on the work during the academic year of 2000–2001 while under a grant from the National Historical Publications and Records Commission, Washington DC, that released me from teaching duties in Lincoln. In the spring of 2001 I spent a productive and enjoyable six weeks working on the book while a Resident Fellow at the International Center for Jefferson Studies, Monticello, Charlottesville, Virginia. I very much appreciate the assistance and generosity of Steve Ambrose and the many people who represent these acclaimed institutions where I carried out the work preparing this book. Having my wife, Faye, nearby during all this time lessened the tedium such a work inevitably brings and made life more pleasant and worthwhile altogether.

Introduction

The president awoke at his residence in the White House on the morning of May 14, 1804, tired and sore from the previous day's journey. It had been a very exhausting trip from Monticello to the capital city for Jefferson, and he called it "the most fatiguing journey I have experienced for a great many years" over a "laborious road as could be travelled." The night's sleep had not entirely rested him and he still felt the aches of the final fifty-five miles by horseback on his six-feet-two-inch frame of sixty-one years. He promised daughter Martha that he would not forget his age before setting out on a similar trip. In Jefferson's day such cross-country trips required the vigor of youth. Transcontinental travel demanded much more.

Half a continent away, the president's explorers, Meriwether Lewis and William Clark, readied themselves for such a trip. Having spent a winter in camp across from the mouth of the Missouri River in Illinois, the young army officers were anxious to set out. Indeed, Lewis must have viewed the day as the culmination of a decade of delay, for he later called the undertaking a "da[r]ling project of mine for the last ten years." The winter had not been a period of inactivity. At Camp Dubois the officers selected and disciplined their troops and molded a disparate group of men into the Corps of Discovery. They also began to sharpen their skills at the many tasks they would perform over the next twenty-eight months. They made their initial efforts at scientific descriptions and astronomical observations, tested and retested their equipment, visited with Indians, gained advice from seasoned river travelers, and recorded events in rough journal notes. Camp Dubois can fittingly be called the proving ground of the Lewis and Clark expedition. The final days were spent in checking out equipment, packing goods, and adjusting loading. Some experimental trips were even made up and down the Mississippi in laded boats. Clark's journal entries grew shorter as excitement mounted to get underway. Finally, on the morning of departure, May 14, 1804, he briskly penned, "fixing for a Start."

Meriwether Lewis And William Clark

Jefferson's choice of Meriwether Lewis to head this important mission grew out of confidence formed from a lifelong acquaintance. Lewis was born in 1774 at the family's plantation, Locust Hill, in Albemarle County, Virginia, a short distance from Monticello. After the death of his father, William, and his mother's remarriage to John Marks, the family moved to Georgia but returned to Locust Hill after Lucy was widowed once more. During his youth Lewis received rudimentary education and seems to have had a keen interest in natural history. Like others of his generation he found his first calling in military service—for young Lewis, militia duty during the Whiskey Rebellion in 1794. Within a year he joined the regular army as ensign, equivalent to a modern lieutenant, and the next year was transferred to the First Infantry Regiment. By 1800, at age twenty-six, he had risen to the rank of captain and probably saw for himself a career in military service. During these years he moved about on various assignments, with no apparent combat experience, but with exposure to command, the frontier, and to Indians. It was also during this period that he met fellow soldier William Clark, four years his senior and his superior officer for a time. Little is known of that encounter, but it is certain that they struck a deep friendship and it lasted their lifetimes.

Shortly before assuming the presidency Jefferson called Lewis from military duty to become his private secretary, allowing the captain to retain his army rank. It now seems possible that Jefferson selected the young officer not only to groom him for western exploration, but also to use Lewis's knowledge of military personnel in order to remove weak links in the officer ranks. During his stay with Jefferson, Lewis had the president's magnificent library at his disposal and he used the opportunity to prepare himself. What Jefferson wanted for the expedition, he confided to a friend, was a person "perfectly skilled in botany, natural history, mineralogy, astronomy, with at the same time the necessary firmness of body & mind, habits of living in the woods & familiarity with the Indian character." He knew that no such person existed, but that Lewis filled the latter requirements perfectly and could be sufficiently trained in the former to carry out such duties in the field. With that in mind he sent Lewis to study in Philadelphia with some of the leading scientists of the young republic.

During the return trip to Washington, Lewis took time to ask Clark to join him as co-commander of the expedition "in it's fatigue, it's dangers and it's honors." Delays in the mail caused some frustration for Lewis, to the point that he had invited another officer, Lieutenant Moses Hooke, to accompany him in case Clark declined. In fact, Clark replied enthusiastically the day after getting Lewis's letter, saying that "no man lives whith whome I would perfur to undertake Such a Trip."

The red-haired Clark was born in Caroline County, Virginia, in 1770. His older brother, George Rogers Clark, was a Revolutionary War hero whose fame might have eclipsed William's were it not for the expedition. Apparently, Jefferson did not know the younger Clark but was well acquainted with his family, in spite of which he consistently spelled the name "Clarke." When Clark was fourteen the family moved to the site of today's Louisville, Kentucky. From there he enlisted in the militia, transferring to the regular army in 1791. He saw actual combat during campaigns in the Ohio valley and rose to the rank of captain, ahead of his junior officer, Lewis. Clark resigned his military commission in 1796 and returned home to Kentucky to help his family. In 1803 he joined George Rogers and moved across the Ohio River from Louisville and built a cabin near modern Clarksville, Indiana. There he met Lewis as he came down the Ohio.

Clark eagerly accepted the appointment Lewis offered, but a mix-up in Washington denied him a captain's rank. An aggravated Lewis told Clark that his "grade has no effect upon your compensation, which G—d, shall be equal to my own." The leaders hid the fact of Clark's lower rank from their men and throughout the trip shared the command equally. After the expedition Clark brusquely returned the commission. While Lewis signed orders as captain of the first regiment, Clark occasionally endorsed himself as captain of a Corps of Discovery. Writers have tended to emphasize and even exaggerate the apparent differences in the men's personalities. Lewis appears as the moody, sensitive intellectual, Clark as the pragmatic, less literate frontiersman. These contrasts may be valid and are somewhat borne out in the record, but can be overstated. In spite of the differences, in the twenty-eight months of the expedition, there is no hint of disagreement between them.

Lewis performed most of the expedition's scientific tasks, principally as the party's naturalist and astronomer, and he tended to be absent from the party on intellectual quests. His writing is more technical than Clark's and he had something of a literary flair. Clark worked primarily as the party's surveyor and his writing is more matter-of-fact. His eccentric spelling, grammar, and punctuation, resulting from a lack of formal education and the loose rules of that era, have accentuated his reputation as a backwoodsman. Yet his vocabulary and phrasing are hardly those of an illiterate man and his prose can be as stirring as Lewis's, if less poetic.

Expedition Underway

The morning of May 14, 1804, dawned cloudy and cool and rain began at nine o'clock, but by afternoon the temperature had climbed to the mid-60s and the weather turned fair. At four o'clock, with nearby settlers there to cheer them off, the men fired the keelboat's swivel gun and set out, all in high spirits, according to Clark. The sail was hoisted on the keelboat and the two pirogues fell in as they crossed the Mississippi and started up the Missouri. Lewis was in St. Louis making final arrangements and would ride overland to meet them at St. Charles, a few miles up the river. No great distance was covered that first day; it was a shakedown run and the party traveled less than five miles.

It is unclear how many men were with the expedition at the outset. The captains' apparent indifference to the number of temporary hands may explain discrepancies in the records. These Frenchmen, called *engagés* (engaged men), were professional boatmen who enlisted to pole and pull the heavy keelboat and two pirogues up the Missouri as far as the first winter post. Altogether it appears that forty-two men left Camp Dubois with Clark, organized into three squads of permanent soldiers and two units of temporary personnel. Interpreter George Drouillard was ahead and, like Lewis, would catch up at St. Charles. The permanent party manned the keelboat for the most part, the French *engagés* were in the larger, red pirogue, while the return detachment took the smaller, white pirogue. Alterations were made along the way and in difficult situations everyone helped out where needed.

The party arrived at St. Charles on May 16. The loading in the boats was shifted again, some last-minute supplies were purchased, and other final preparations were attended to. Extra boatmen were also added, including the Frenchmen Pierre Cruzatte and François Labiche, who enlisted as privates in the permanent party, although they may have been with the Corps earlier. Both were of mixed-blooded heritage, perhaps part Omaha Indian, so they could assist with interpreting Indian languages as well as translating French. Both were also expert Missouri boatmen. Cruzatte is remembered for his fiddle playing that entertained soldiers and Indians alike, while Labiche took charge of the boats at several critical junctures.

Here, too, at St. Charles was the last chance for social pursuits among townspeople. The men entertained the villagers aboard the keelboat and were welcomed to parties in return. Some of the men went too far in their carousing, so that Clark called a court-martial and charged three of the men for misbehavior. About twenty of the more sober celebrants attended Mass on Sunday, the twentieth. Lewis came in that same evening and the men set out the next afternoon, to the cheers of townsfolk lining the banks. On May 26 the party passed La Charette, a tiny cluster of cabins and the last white settlement on the river. From there they moved into the wilderness, meeting occasional parties of traders heading downriver for St. Louis.

The first stage of the journey, as far as present north-central North Dakota, was through country already explored to some extent. Indeed, the captains carried reliable maps of the Missouri to that point. Moreover, some of the French engagés had been that far on previous trading ventures and could name incoming streams and prominent landmarks. Curiously, there are no records of daily events by Lewis for this period, from May 1804 to April 1805, except for two short fragments of two days each. Lewis seems to have contented himself with writing scientific notes from his observations. Whether he failed to keep a diary of daily events for the period or whether such notes are lost has never been wholly resolved.

The journey up the Missouri against the current was slow and laborious. Occasionally the men raised the keelboat's sail under a favorable wind, but more often they poled the huge craft or pulled the boats with a tow rope, called a cordelle. Toiling in the increasing summer heat, the men were plagued by boils, diarrhea, mosquitoes, and sandbars. Despite their heavy work, the land appeared lush and beautiful to the working hands and expedition diarists universally reported high spirits and enthusiasm. The party reached the mouth of the Kansas River on June 26, and on

July 21 they came to the Platte River, a point they had anticipated for some time. The Corps was now six hundred and forty-two miles up the Missouri by their reckoning, and over two months out of Camp Dubois, averaging about ten river miles a day. Here the captains decided to spend several days to refresh the men, dry out wet gear, take celestial readings, and bring their maps and journals up to date. They also hoped to meet nearby Indians, but the Otoes and Pawnees were away on buffalo hunts and no conferences were held.

A little over a week later the party had its first meeting with Indians in council. On July 30 in a small grove of trees on some prairie high ground, the expedition formed a camp. They called the site Council Bluff, from the meeting held there with Indians over the next few days. The site is near the town of Fort Calhoun, Nebraska, about fifteen miles north of Omaha. At sunset on August 2 the captains arranged to comply with Jefferson's instructions regarding Indians. That evening a resident trader came into the Council Bluff camp with six Otoe and Missouria chiefs and a meeting was arranged for the next day. Lewis and Clark began the formalities by parading the men, then they passed a ceremonial pipe, demonstrated their weapons, and gave gifts to Indian dignitaries. Lewis brought along an air gun to display American technology, since the weapon could fire off several rounds without reloading. It was a continued source of amazement to Indians across the continent. Out of their trunks came Indian presents—red leggings, fancy dress coats, and blue blankets; ball and powder, tobacco, and whiskey were also handed out. Lewis and Clark also distributed printed commissions for acknowledging chiefs and, of course, Indian peace medals, which were especially prized by the recipients. Indians presented food, tobacco, and native handicrafts.

After the exchanges one of the captains delivered a speech announcing American sovereignty over the new lands, then pled for peace among the Indian tribes, promised increased trade, explained the purposes of the expedition, and requested Indian emissaries to journey to the capital. Now the Indians rose to respond. They apparently approved of what they had heard and promised to heed the good advice. Lewis and Clark perfected such rituals over countless meetings across the continent, but Council Bluff became the initial test of Indian diplomacy, and it apparently went well. At four o'clock that afternoon the party moved on.

Hard physical labor and distance from settlement temptations did not guarantee an end to disciplinary problems. In fact this period marked the most serious breach of order when one of the men deserted. Prior to reaching Council Bluff and finding Indians, the captains dispatched one of the Frenchmen, La Liberté, to find natives and invite chiefs to a council. The Otoes and Missourias arrived, but without La Liberté. After the conference and as the expedition moved upriver, Private Moses B. Reed requested permission to return to the area to reclaim a lost knife. Several days later, with both Reed and La Liberté still out, the captains sent a detachment to apprehend the missing men.

Reed's desertion was a serious offense, punishable by death; La Liberté's action, though not technically desertion since he was a civilian, set a poor example if not treated seriously. Wholesale quitting could endanger the success of the endeavor, if not the very lives of the men if attacked. On August 18 the search party returned with Reed. La Liberté had been captured but true to his name had escaped and was seen no more. Reed was tried, convicted, and expelled. He was also forced to run the gauntlet four times as the men flogged his bare back. Considering the era's military discipline, his sentence was lenient. Some weeks later Private John Newman was arrested for "mutinous expression," tried, punished with seventy-five lashes, and dishonorably discharged. Both men were repentant but were never reinstated to the Corps. Nonetheless, they continued with the party until the following spring, doing hard labor, since it would have been virtually a death sentence to cast them adrift in the wilderness.

Near present Sioux City, Iowa, on August 20, a loss of another sort occurred. Sergeant Charles Floyd died, apparently of a ruptured appendix. He was the only member to die on the expedition. His comrades buried him on a bluff and commemorated him by naming Floyd's River in his honor. The medical treatment given him by the captains—probably bleeding with lancets and purging with strong laxatives—was the accepted practice of the day, and a remedy that Lewis learned from Dr. Benjamin Rush in Philadelphia. If used here it would have weakened the sergeant and hastened his death. Patrick Gass was elected sergeant in Floyd's place.

The Middle Missouri

As the men moved on into present South Dakota, they became increasingly concerned about George Shannon, the youngest member of the

Corps, who had been missing for several days, when he separated to find stray horses. Believing the boats were ahead of him, Shannon hurried on trying to catch up, when in fact the party was behind him. Not until September 11 did they overtake the young man, now weak from hunger after being out more than two weeks. A relieved Clark reflected, "thus a man had like to have Starved to death in a land of Plenty for the want of Bullets or Something to kill his meat."

In late September, the Corps arrived in the vicinity of present Pierre, South Dakota. Here they encountered a band of the Teton Sioux, or Lakota, Indians, and for the first time their meeting with natives was less than cordial. The Tetons regularly charged tolls of Missouri River traders and now tried their bullying tactics on Lewis and Clark. After some conversation and exchange of gifts, the Indians became surly, demanded more presents, and would not allow Clark to return to the keelboat. The tense situation that followed arose not only from Indian arrogance, but also probably from the lack of a Sioux interpreter. Nonetheless, the captains were not ready to submit to payments; their military pride and sense of security required a show of strength. They readied their weapons and made plain their intention to fight—fortunately, the Sioux backed off. Afterward the leaders feared that the Tetons planned a surprise attack and they kept a tight guard until well out of the area. To indicate their irritation, the captains called the island where they camped after the episode "Bad Humored Island." Lewis later called the Tetons "the vilest miscreants of the savage race" and the "pirates of the Missouri." A few days later, on October 8, they reached the earth-lodge villages of the Arikaras in northern South Dakota. Their reception by these sedentary farmers was quite hospitable, and the party remained with them for several days.

Lewis and Clark were the first Americans to evaluate the Great Plains, an area so different from the wooded lands of the East to which they were accustomed. Their conclusions were more optimistic than those of some later explorers who labeled the region the "Great American Desert." Between the Kansas and the Platte Rivers they noted a difference in topography, but their impressions did not greatly change. Beyond the Platte, terms like "high and dry" were more frequent than the usual "beautiful and well-watered." Nonetheless, they still considered the plains a virtual paradise. Even on the high plains above the Niobrara River it was the profusion of animal life that caught their attention rather than the terrain, with its absence of trees and unbroken, featureless horizon, and its short grasses and semiarid climate. In fact, they did not use negative terms to describe the plains until they reached its western edge.

The men were fascinated by the region's new and varied animal life. In present northeast Nebraska they spent time hauling barrels of water from the river to a prairie dog hole in order to flush out a live specimen. Such was the work of pioneering naturalists. Besides the prairie dog the captains were the first to scientifically describe coyotes, pronghorns, jackrabbits, mule deer, black-billed magpies, and northern flickers. Moreover, they told of vast numbers of buffalo, the mainstay of plains Indian life. From a vantage point in present central South Dakota, Lewis estimated that one immense herd numbered at least three thousand of the shaggy beasts. It was the captains' return reports of the abundance of beaver that sent eager bands of fur trappers to the farthest reaches of the Missouri's drainage.

As they crossed the Great Plains, Clark was struck by the grandeur of the land and in his own inimitable style declared, "What a field for a Botents [botanist] and a natirless [naturalist]." On another occasion he was moved to write one of his most elegant and descriptive passages:

The Plains of this countrey are covered with a Leek Green Grass, well calculated for the sweetest and most norushing hay—interspersed with Cops [copses] of trees, Spreding ther lofty branchs over Pools Springs or Brooks of fine water. Groops of Shrubs covered with the most delicious froot is to be seen in every direction, and nature appears to have exerted herself to butify the Senery by the variety of flours Delicately and highly flavered raised above the Grass, which Strikes & profumes the Sensation, and amuses the mind throws it into Conjecterng the cause of So magnificent a Senerey in a Country thus Situated far removed from the Sivilised world to be enjoyed by nothing but the Buffalo Elk Deer & Bear in which it abounds & Savage Indians

It is important to remember that the men's evaluation of the plains was developed from a river valley perspective. They never ventured far from the rich bottomland—a fact that prejudiced and narrowed their opinions considerably. Nonetheless, twentieth-century biologists have been impressed with the men's perceptions of plains biota and their acute ecological distinctions.

It had been a good summer for the Corps. Now, as days grew shorter, trees dropped their leaves and plants and shrubs began to fade. The men watched as migrating waterfowl passed overhead on their southward flights. They saw temperatures dip to the freezing point and frost form overnight. In late October they hurried on to their winter encampment—the most distance outpost in the new lands of a young republic.

Knife River Winter

As the party came up the Missouri River in late October they passed abandoned villages of the Mandan Indians. Such deserted settlements attested to the tribe's weakened state and to the ferocity of their enemies, the Sioux. On October 25 the explorers arrived at the outskirts of the lower Mandan village and were ogled by curious Indians who lined the banks and called for them to come ashore. By their estimate the men were now sixteen hundred miles out of Camp Dubois and 164 days into their transcontinental trip. Winter was near and the captains discovered that the Missouri would soon freeze. They decided, therefore, to make their winter quarters among these friendly folk.

The Mandans and their immediate neighbors to the north, the Hidatsas, were established in five villages about the mouth of the Knife River, where they lived in circular earth lodges. Lewis and Clark estimated their population to be about four thousand persons—the largest concentration of Indians on the Missouri River. The captains found the Mandans in the two lower villages, Mitutanka and Ruptáre, now designated as the Deapolis and Black Cat sites. Any trace of the villages is now gone, lost to modern construction or to the Missouri's changing course.

The Mandans were primarily horticulturists, growing corn, beans, and squash, and they gathered native plants to supplement their crops. They also turned out for seasonal buffalo hunts to augment their food sources. A peaceful people, they were generous and fair with the American visitors. Fair-skinned, light-haired persons among them led to stories that they were descendants of Welsh travelers who supposedly had wandered to the deep interior of North America. They had lived on the Missouri

River since they were first known to Europeans, but they may have come from the Mississippi valley in the distant past. They had moved to the Knife River region after experiencing a devastating smallpox epidemic in 1780–81. The disease reduced their population by perhaps two-thirds in their former villages at the mouth of the Heart River near present Bismarck, North Dakota. In this decimated state they were forced to move north because their Sioux enemies threatened further destruction. For protection they joined the Hidatsas to whom they were related culturally and linguistically.

To the north were the Hidatsas, or Minitaris to Lewis and Clark, who lived in three villages. The first village, Mahawha, was occupied by the Awaxawis, a people somewhat distinct from their neighbors but considered a branch of the Hidatsas; it is the present Amahami site, after an alternate name for the band. Lewis and Clark called them by a variety of names, but they are most easily remembered as Hidatsas, with whom they shared much in language and in custom. Above them were the villages Metaharta of the Awatixas, and Menetarra of the Hidatsas Proper, known today as the Sakakawea and Big Hidatsa sites.

The three villages roughly approximated the three divisions of the Hidatsas, but such distinctions were disappearing by Lewis and Clark's time because ravages had so decreased their numbers as to consolidate their cultures. The Mandans were joining this cultural pool and further disintegration of the tribes forced an unexpected homogeneity. The Hidatsas also participated in an agricultural life, and they too pursued buffalo on the plains. More aggressive than their Knife River neighbors, the Hidatsas raided as far as the foothills of the Rocky Mountains in search of martial glory and kinship revenge. As soldiers themselves, Lewis and Clark were impressed with the tribe's warrior societies and military exploits. Moreover, the wide-ranging Hidatsas were excellent informants to the captains' queries about regions to the west.

On November 3, after several days of hunting for the best location, the party began construction of Fort Mandan. By November 20 everyone was inside but work continued for several more days. The fort was located on the east side of the Missouri a few miles below the mouth of the Knife River and nearly opposite the lower Mandan village. The spot is now beneath the river, but a modern reconstruction is not far from its historic location—about fifty miles northwest of Bismarck. Sergeant Gass, a carpenter and perhaps the fort's construction chief, described the structure as roughly triangular, with two rows of huts along each side. The roofs of the huts came off the outer side walls, about eighteen feet high, and descended shedlike toward the center. The picketed front of the triangle served as the fort's main gate, while a small enclosure filled the semicircular point at the rear. That shed was used to house the expedition's supplies and its flat roof served as the sentry's watchtower.

The stockaded log fort would be their home for five months, during a bitter northern plains winter in which temperatures sometimes dropped to lower than forty degrees below zero and venturing outside was likely to result in frostbite. Nevertheless, Clark described the party as being in good spirits. On both Christmas and New Year's Day, the explorers had celebrations with music, dancing, and frolic. Moreover, Indians visited the fort frequently and the chiefs, at least, expected to be entertained by the captains. The winter was by no means a period of idleness—hunting, in spite of the fierce cold, was necessary to provide meat. To augment their food, the men built a forge and blacksmiths like Private John Shields were kept busy making war axes and other metal goods to exchange for village crops. The men visited the villages regularly and some soldiers contracted venereal disease from liaisons with Indian women. York was a particular novelty to these Indians who had never seen a black man. The Hidatsa Indian chief Le Borgne was so incredulous that he rubbed York's dark skin with his moistened finger trying to remove the "paint."

Lewis and Clark arrived among these farmer-hunter-traders with two principal goals based on Jefferson's precepts. One was diplomatic—to apprise the tribes of the new sovereignty of the United States under the Louisiana Purchase and to explain the purposes of their own mission. In this regard they also hoped to shift trade toward American interests at St. Louis and away from the English in Canada. They also wanted to establish intertribal peace; for the Mandans and Hidatsas that meant better relations with the Sioux and Arikaras.

Lewis and Clark's other function was ethnographic—to gather information about the tribes in order to increase knowledge. The men obtained their information in a number of ways: by interviewing natives and traders who lived among them, by collecting cultural objects, by reporting on firsthand observations, and by participating in some Indian activities. The captains did their best work in recounting objective matters: describing villages, weapons, food, clothing, and other external aspects. They were not as good at describing ritualistic behavior or subjective matter and they misunderstood and misinterpreted some activities they observed or participated in. They also missed some important ceremonies and activities because of the time of year they lived with the Indians.

Soon after arriving at the Indian villages, the captains hired René Jusseaume as a temporary interpreter. Jusseaume was a independent trader who had lived with the Mandans for about fifteen years but never seemed competent with the tribe's language. Another Frenchman, Jean Baptiste Lepage, was hired as for the permanent party to replace the discharged Newman. Lepage had previously ventured some distance up the Missouri and may have journeyed into the interior, even to the Black Hills of present South Dakota. Because of this he was valuable as an informant and may have aided Clark in preparing his map of the West at Fort Mandan.

Others also joined as permanent members of the Corps of Discovery. A French-Canadian trader, Toussaint Charbonneau, was brought in as an interpreter of Hidatsa. He had lived among the tribe as an independent trader for several years and he had two wives from the Shoshone tribe of the northern Rockies. The captains decided to hire Charbonneau and one of the women, Sacagawea, to serve as intermediaries with the Shoshones, whom they anticipated meeting in the mountains. Charbonneau spoke French and Hidatsa, the latter with deficiencies it seems, while Sacagawea spoke Shoshone and Hidatsa. Through this language channel the captains hoped to communicate with Rocky Mountain tribes. Charbonneau has typically been portrayed in negative terms, as a bungler and a wife-beater, and Lewis declared him "a man of no particular merit." Clark seems to have thought better of him. At least he fulfilled his obligations to the expedition, however slight.

Sacagawea was born in 1787 or 1788 among the Lemhi band of Shoshones. She had been captured by a Hidatsa war party on one of their raids into Shoshone country about 1800, when she was approximately thirteen years old. Her first child, Jean Baptiste, was born at the fort on February 11, 1805, and the infant became the youngest participant in the expedition—carried by his young mother across the continent and back. Sacagawea experienced some difficulty in childbirth, so Jusseaume recommended a folk medication of ground-up rattlesnake rattles to ease her labor. Lewis prepared the potion and administered it to her, but doubted its effectiveness even though the young woman gave birth soon after taking the mixture.

Sacagawea has probably received more attention than any other member of the expedition, save the captains. Time has not diminished her acclaim and no amount of historical scrutiny has been able to correct distortions about her role in the expedition. Obvious and seemingly trivial items like the spelling of her name and its meaning and pronunciation generate heated debate. The captains' journals clearly give it as Sacagawea or some close approximation of that spelling. They state that it meant Bird Woman and the name most likely comes from the Hidatsa language. Their rendering of the word shows that they pronounced it *Sa-ca-ga-we-a* and probably stressed each syllable equally. Alternate spellings, pronunciations, and translations of the word have had to rely on complicated interpretations that argue against the original records. In fact, most of what we know about her is found in expedition journals and it is very meager material on which to build a legend.

She and her husband, Charbonneau, were not hired as guides but as interpreters. Her services in that capacity among her people and other Shoshonean-speaking Indians in the Rockies were indispensable, while her presence with a baby calmed Indian fears that the party was a war expedition. She did recognize some geographic features when the party reached the region of her girlhood in southwestern Montana. Beyond this, she may have been a pleasant companion, and the baby, called Pomp by Clark, was probably a source of some delight to the travel-weary explorers, but she was by no means the girl guide often depicted in art and fiction.

As spring approached and the ice broke up in the Missouri, the captains prepared to resume their trek westward. They also readied the return party for its departure. Corporal Richard Warfington with a small squad of soldiers, the remaining French boatmen, and the two expelled men, Reed and Newman, were to take the keelboat back to St. Louis. With them, carefully packed and destined for Jefferson, went the captains' journals completed to that date, tables of observations, letters, maps, a large number of natural history specimens, and live animals: four magpies, a sharp-tailed grouse, and a prairie dog. Only the prairie dog and one of the magpies made it all the way to Jefferson's Monticello. Selected items of the material culture of plains Indians were also boxed up for Jefferson's inspection. Also included was an "Estimate of Eastern Indians" (those east of the Rocky Mountains), providing all that the captains had learned about prairie-plains Indians. It was an incredible array of information about the new lands of the Louisiana Purchase.

Into the Unknown

Just five weeks short of a year after leaving Camp Dubois, the party was set to go, with half a continent to cross before they reached the Pacific. On April 3, four days before the actual departure, an eager and impatient Clark wrote, "we Shall . . . Set out tomorrow." A bracing twenty-eight degrees greeted the explorers on the morning of April 7, but by the time of departure the temperature climbed to a balmy sixty-four, and a brisk wind blew in to push against their pirogues. Bidding farewell to the St. Louis–bound keelboat and its occupants, the permanent party set out at four o'clock in the afternoon. The Corps of Discovery now numbered thirty-three persons: the two leaders, three sergeants (John Ordway, Nathaniel Pryor, and Patrick Gass); two interpreters (Drouillard and Charbonneau), twenty-three privates, York, Sacagawea, and the infant Jean Baptiste. The end of the season at Fort Mandan marked an important transition. Difficult and potentially dangerous as the route had been thus far, others had ventured here before them and had already mapped the way. From Fort Mandan on, the Corps entered country for which they had only Indian and speculative information.

Lewis was in a buoyant mood that afternoon and took to the shore for some exercise in a walk to their night's encampment. The uncounted but faithful Newfoundland, Seaman, probably loped along at his master's side. This day Lewis returned to his diary after a long period of infrequent writing; he would keep a steady record until August when his writing fell off once again. Some of Lewis's best observations and most elegant prose fill the pages of this period. Consider his exuberance at the moment of departure:

> Our vessels consisted of six small canoes, and two large perogues. This little fleet altho' not quite so rispectable as those of Columbus or Capt. Cook were still viewed by us with as much pleasure as those deservedly famed adventurers every beheld theirs; and I dare say with quite as much anxiety for their safety and preservation . . . The party are in excellent health and sperits, zealously attatched to the enterprise, and anxious to proceed; not a whisper of murmur or discontent to be heard among them, but all act in unison, and with the most perfect harmony.

As the explorers traveled farther west into today's Montana, the terrain became more arid, treeless, and rugged. They had left the mid-grass prairies of the northern Great Plains and were moving into a region of sagebrush, juniper, and drought-tolerant short grasses. New animals, like bighorn sheep, were also seen, and the famed grizzly bear made its appearance. The men discounted stories they had heard about the ferocity of the animal. Now out on the plains again, the hunters were anxious to meet one. A limited encounter came on April 29 near the Yellowstone River when Lewis and a companion met two grizzlies, both of which the men wounded. One bear pursued the captain but was so badly hurt that Lewis was able to reload and kill him. The confident captain wrote: "the Indians may well fear this anamal . . . but in the hands of skillfull riflemen they are by no means as formidable or dangerous as they have been represented." Lewis would soon be less assured.

A bear killed on May 5 near the Milk River gave some pause. Lewis wrote: "it was . . . extreemly hard to kill notwithstanding he had five balls through his lungs and five others in various parts he swam more than half the distance across the river to a sandbar & it was at least twenty minutes before he died." The next day when the party saw a grizzly, Lewis commented that "the curiossity of our party is pretty well satisfyed with respect to this anamal . . . [and] has staggered the resolution of several of them, others however seem keen for action with the bear."

The chance for the men of action came on May 14 when six hunters went after a single bear. A volley of four balls ripped into the animal, but it simply charged ahead, took two more rounds from a second volley, and kept coming. One of the balls broke the animal's shoulder, slowing it slightly, but even so it was on them faster than they could believe. The terrified men ran pell-mell toward the river. Two made it to a canoe while the others took cover, hastily reloaded, and fired again. When the bear turned on them, they flung aside their rifles and plunged down an embankment, the grizzly tumbling after them into the water. Finally a rifleman on shore put a round through its brain, killing it instantly. They found eight balls in its carcass.

All the while the less exciting work of the mission went forward. Lewis led a small patrol ahead of the main party on April 25 in order to reach the Yellowstone River and take astronomical readings. For the explorers this spot effectively divided the known from the unknown; as far as they knew no one but natives had ventured beyond this point. They would not reenter lands known to the outside world again until they neared the Pacific Ocean. The boat party came in the next day and to celebrate the occasion a dram of whiskey was rationed around, Cruzatte brought out his fiddle, and dancing and singing continued through the evening. Two days later they set out again, passing into the modern state of Montana.

On May 14, a few days short of the Musselshell River, Lewis and Clark were both ashore—an unusual circumstance. Charbonneau temporarily had control of the main pirogue when suddenly a squall of wind struck the boat and turned it. Charbonneau, whom Lewis called the "most timid waterman in the world," swung the boat farther around, bringing the wind's full force against the sail jerking it from the hands of a boatman. The pirogue tilted on its side and began to fill with water, ready to go under. Cruzatte, an expert boatman on board, proved equal to the situation. Threatening to shoot Charbonneau if he did not reclaim the rudder, he also ordered men to bail water and row toward the shore, where they arrived barely above water. All the while Sacagawea, with baby in one hand, calmly bailed water or collected floating items with the other. Lewis, viewing the distressing scene from the shore, shouted orders to Charbonneau but could not be heard. He knew that the endangered boat contained the party's most important articles, including papers, instruments, medicine, and a large share of the Indian trade goods. Realizing the value of the cargo and forgetting himself, Lewis threw down his gun and prepared to jump into the river and swim to the boat, when the folly of the idea struck him. All he could do was stand fretfully by.

In late May the expedition entered the Breaks of the Missouri, a region of broken, dark terrain and impressive geological formations. On the western end of the Breaks lie the spectacular White Cliffs. Lewis's journal passages celebrate the harsh beauty of this rugged land. He was especially struck by white sandstone outcroppings imbedded in black igneous rocks, while erosion created fanciful forms in his mind and enlivened his prose: "with the help of a little immagination and an oblique view at a distance, are made to represent eligant ranges of lofty freestone buildings . . . As we passed on it seemed as if those seens of visionary inchantment would never have and end . . . so perfect indeed are those walls that I should have thought that nature had attempted here to rival the human art of masonry had I not recollected that she had first began her work."

On May 26 Lewis climbed to the top of a hill and saw what he thought were the snow-capped Rockies for the first time. Despite this premature sighting, his elation was real, for now he anticipated reaching the headwaters of the Missouri. But a geographic dilemma and a formidable obstacle stood in the Corps' way. In early June they reached the Marias River, where they encountered the dilemma. The Hidatsas had not told them of the Marias; the captains had to determine which stream was the true Missouri, knowing that a wrong decision might cost them valuable time and strand them in the Rockies in wintertime. Extensive reconnaissance convinced them that the river to the southwest was the Missouri, although most of the party believed otherwise. After nearly a week the captains' belief was confirmed when Lewis discovered the Great Falls of the Missouri. On June 13, as Lewis walked upstream with an advance party, the men heard a roaring noise and saw clouds of spray that could only come from the falls. They had learned of this place during the previous winter; now they had arrived at the threshold of the Rocky Mountains. Despite their joy, the presence of cascades and rapids presented serious problems, for the canoes and supplies must now be portaged around this barrier. This task would consume an entire month of precious time and test the endurance, patience, and ingenuity of the Corps of Discovery as no other episode to this point.

Portaging the Falls

Lewis called the Great Falls the "grandest sight I ever beheld." His description of it showed his romantic inclinations; he wished "I might be enabled to give to the enlightened world some just idea of this truly magnifficent and sublimely grand object, which has from the commencement of time been concealed from the view of civilized man; but this was fruitless and vain . . . I hope still to give to the world some faint idea of an object which at this moment fills me with such pleasure and astonishment, and which of it's kind I will venture to ascert is second to but one in the known world." Displeased with his feeble prose, he lay down his pen and longed for the abilities of some great poet or artist.

Clark's survey showed that a diversion of about eighteen miles would be necessary to skirt the falls. The captains had wagon frames constructed on which they placed the canoes to carry supplies. Meanwhile, the men buried the pirogues and excess items to be left behind at a spot they called the Lower Portage Camp, northeast of the modern city of Great Falls. During the portage the men had to endure backbreaking labor, pulling heavy loads across roughened grounds infested with cactus, tormenting their moccasined feet without relief. The exertion was so great that at every rest stop they fell down exhausted. On one trip some ingenious fellows even hoisted a sail over the wagon in order to take advantage of the wind. "This is really sailing on dry land," Lewis commented. Men exempted from this labor hunted for the party's food, but they had to contend with grizzly bears. Occasional heavy rains drenched everyone, and large hailstones injured several; rattlesnakes and mosquitoes were also constant menaces. Sacagawea became ill during this time and there was great fear that she might die. Fortunately, a nearby sulfur spring provided some relief and she recovered.

Complaining of fatigue, the explorers nevertheless revealed extraordinary stamina under such conditions. They could also display amazing coolness in the face of physical peril. A torrent of rain and hail on June 29 caught Clark and a small party near the river. Taking refuge in a ravine, they were deluged by a wall of water running through the gully and were nearly swept into the Missouri. Quick action by Clark, who was waist deep in water himself, saved Sacagawea and her child. Looking back, he saw the water rise to a depth of fifteen feet, carrying everything before it, including some of his valuable equipment. Meanwhile, south of the falls at the party's Upper Portage Camp, Lewis put together the iron-frame, collapsible boat he had designed at Harpers Ferry and carried across the continent. Unfortunately, the lack of pine trees at the falls made it impossible to obtain the tar necessary for waterproofing and the craft simply would not float. The failure of his invention embarrassed Lewis, but the only solution was to construct two more dugout canoes and proceed on.

Shadows of the Rockies

Upriver from the falls the party entered the Rockies, passing through the spectacular canyon the explorers called the "Gates of the Mountains," near today's Helena, Montana. Beautiful canyon walls did not, however, relieve sore feet and aching muscles. They were now anxiously seeking the Shoshones, but although they saw signs, the Indians were not to be found. Sacagawea began to recognize familiar landmarks; a meeting with her people was now their most urgent concern. On July 25 Clark, leading an overland patrol, reached the Three Forks of the Missouri. Lewis came up with the boat party two days later and found his friend Clark utterly exhausted and quite ill. The explorers remained here for a few days to rest and to tend to blistered feet and sore backs. Since he considered the Three Forks a significant point in western geography, Lewis also needed time to obtain accurate astronomical readings.

The leaders decided to name the three streams the Jefferson, the Madison, and the Gallatin, after the president and his secretaries of state and treasury. The Jefferson, the westernmost stream, seemed most likely to lead them to the Continental Divide, and so they set off up that fork on July 30. Leaving the ailing Clark with the boat party, Lewis pushed ahead with a few men to try to make contact with the Shoshones. On August 12 he finally came to the head of the stream he regarded as the ultimate source of the "heretofore deemed endless Missouri." Atop a ridge at today's Lemhi Pass on the Montana-Idaho border he saw further ranges of snow-capped mountains and realized that the portage to the Columbia would not be so easy as hoped. Despite this discouraging prospect Lewis gave no hint of despair, perhaps because for the first time he tasted waters that touched the Pacific.

Just before crossing the divide Lewis had encountered a lone Shoshone on horseback who fled at his approach, perhaps thinking the men were enemy raiders. On the western side of the ridge the captain entered the valley of the Lemhi River seeking contact with the Indians. The success of the expedition hinged on a friendly meeting, since Lewis needed assistance if a long overland journey proved necessary. Eventually, he was able to meet peacefully with the Shoshones, but they remained apprehensive, fearing treachery. If their misgivings overcame them and they fled, Lewis knew his command might be stranded in the mountains. Consequently, he made every effort to convince them of his good faith, even giving the Shoshone chief his own rifle with which to shoot him if he proved unfaithful.

In the meantime, Clark led the main party up the increasingly narrowing Jefferson. Repeating a mistake made by Lewis, he got diverted on the wrong stream, causing delay and extra effort for the hard-pressed boatmen. In almost comic circumstances, a beaver had chewed down a pole on which Lewis had left a message pointing the correct way along the Beaverhead River. When Clark and party finally reunited with Lewis on August 17, the situation with the Shoshones changed dramatically. The chief, Cameahwait, proved to be the brother or a close relative of Sacagawea, and her services as interpreter helped establish good relations. The captains learned that a long land journey through the mountains would be necessary, for the rivers in the vicinity, although they led to the Columbia, were unnavigable. The Shoshones' description of the route ahead, while dismaying, was informative, and their reports of new tribes to be encountered was important. In spite of discouraging news, the captains anointed the spot Camp Fortunate. It now lies beneath the waters of Clark Canyon Reservoir at the forks of the Beaverhead River. They would stay here until August 24, reconnoitering the area and preparing to surmount the Rockies.

While at Camp Fortunate, Lewis had time to record his impressions of the Shoshones. He found them a poor people despite their riches in horses, an element added to their life after 1700 when they began converting to plains culture. In all, the captain was decidedly complimentary of the Shoshones; he found them "frank, communicative, fair in dealing, generous with the little they possess, extreemly honest, and by no means beggarly." By Lewis and Clark's time they were a people of two traditions, digging camas roots and fishing for salmon in the mountains part of the year, then hunting buffalo on the plains at alternate seasons. East of the Rockies they were much abused by their better-armed enemies the Blackfeet and the Hidatsas—Sacagawea's capture by the latter illustrating the oppression. Therefore, they left their mountain fastnesses only under starving circumstances when their over-Rockies food supply of small game, roots, and fish forced them onto the plains to take up buffalo hunts at great peril. The Shoshones welcomed talk of trade with Americans, since they wanted to obtain guns and challenge their oppressors. The captains made promises in this area, knowing full well that it would be a long time before such merchandise could reach this remote area. By such promises they hoped the Shoshones would be willing to sell them horses and supplies for their trip through the mountains. Without being entirely deceitful, the leaders did bend the truth because of their critical needs.

On August 18, at Camp Fortunate, Lewis celebrated his thirty-first birthday and penned a reflective passage. Disregarding his considerable achievements, he pledged to redouble his efforts at improving himself and in the future to "live for *mankind*, as I have heretofore lived *for myself*." In the days ahead, the mountains facing them would call for redoubled efforts on the part of every member of the Corps of Discovery. Optimistic and eager to be on the way, Lewis wrote on August 24 that he had "the inexpressible satisfaction to find myself once more under way." Yet ahead of him and the Corps loomed one of the most difficult periods of the entire trip. Having scaled the mountains on a relatively easy ascent, the party now faced the greatest physical challenge of the entire trip—crossing the rugged Bitterroot Range. This challenge called for a carefully calculated strategy, since the most direct route was extremely treacherous, if not impossible. It also called for stamina, courage, and ingenuity—qualities the Corps had demonstrated in the past and soon would be called to display again.

Those Tremendous Mountains

Geographical information from the Shoshones about a route to the Columbia River was not encouraging. Clark's reconnaissance of the nearby Salmon confirmed that although the river flowed toward the Columbia,

it was unnavigable because of rapids. Moreover, sheer cliffs and precipices along its banks made land travel equally impractical; the perilous
stream has earned the nickname "River of No Return." Scarce game and
unsuitable timber for canoes were additional deterrents. Evading the direct but dangerous route on the Salmon altogether, the men decided to
follow a path along the Bitterroots and come out of the mountains farther to the north. Fortunately, the captains were able to secure the services of a Shoshone Indian guide, Old Toby, who knew of a route over the
ranges. And after a great deal of dickering with their Shoshone hosts, they
obtained about thirty horses, not all in the best of shape and fewer in
number than needed. Diversion and improvisation at the Missouri's
Great Falls were now replaced by avoidance of a treacherous route and
dependence on Indian assistance in the Bitterroots. Indian aid and advice
were now, and at other times, crucial to the success of the expedition.

The explorers set out northward from the Shoshone encampment on
the Lemhi River on August 30, while the Indians traveled eastward toward the Missouri's Three Forks for their seasonal buffalo hunt. The
Corps followed the Lemhi, a safe portion of the Salmon, and then the
North Fork Salmon through difficult terrain along a ridge of the Bitterroots near the Continental Divide. "Horrid bad going," Joseph Whitehouse called it on one of the worst days. On September 3 Old Toby led
them through a pass at the divide near present Lost Trail Pass and they
crossed from modern Idaho back into Montana. The next day they came
upon a tribe of Indians who, like the Shoshones, may never have seen
white men before. At an area later favored by fur trappers who called it
Ross's Hole, the auspicious meeting occurred—lucky because the tribe
had numerous horses. The party was able to barter for additions to their
herd and increase it to more than forty animals—for mounts, for pack
horses, and eventually, a few for food.

The Flatheads, more properly called Salish, were much like their Shoshone neighbors, splitting their time between mountains and plains—
they too being severely pressed by aggressive plains warriors. In fact, they
were at this very time moving to the plains to join the Shoshones for mutual protection in buffalo hunts. Their tribal name appears to come from
the Indian sign language designation, hands pressed against the sides of
the head. They did not, however, practice skull deformation as did coastal

Indians the explorers would later encounter. Their language, completely unlike Shoshone, made communication in sign language necessary until a Shoshone captive was discovered among them and Sacagawea brought forward as interpreter. Then followed a laborious line of communication from English to French, to Hidatsa, to Shoshone, to Salish, and then back again. On September 6, with horse trading and customary exchanges completed, the Corps headed north along the Bitterroot River while the Flatheads set out for their Missouri rendezvous with the Shoshones. Calling the stream the Flathead River at first, Lewis eventually named it Clark's River to honor his friend.

Knowing that an even more difficult road lay ahead, the leaders decided to take advantage of clear skies and fair weather, and to rest and prepare themselves for the coming trek out of the mountains. On September 9, 1805, they established camp a few miles south of today's Missoula, Montana, on a little stream they christened Travelers' Rest, now Lolo Creek. The camp has likewise been so named. Here they spent two days taking celestial observations, repacking and adjusting loads, hunting game (somewhat unsuccessfully) to replenish their dwindling supply, and resting up for the demanding trip ahead. A passing Indian joined the party briefly and confirmed that a stream to the west was navigable to the ocean and but five days' march ahead. In fact, their trip, marked by incredible hardships, consumed more than twice that optimistic estimate.

Eleven harrowing days in September 1805 were spent on the demanding Lolo Trail. The descent from the Bitterroots via that trail was perhaps the severest physical test of the whole expedition. Winter was already beginning in the high country, and the party struggled through deepening snow. The explorers had to lead their horses along narrow, rocky mountain paths. Some of the horses lost their footing and one fell to its death and precious supplies and equipment were lost. As winter set in game animals became scarce and the party went hungry before they resorted to eating their pack horses. Old Toby misled them at one point, costing precious time and adding miles to their hardships. On September 16, one of the worst days, Clark wrote, "I have been wet and as cold in every part as I ever was in my life," and he feared that his thinly clad feet would freeze.

Reaching near-desperation circumstances, the captains decided to adopt a procedure used previously. Clark would press ahead quickly with a small detachment to find open country and make contact with Indians.

Setting out with six men on September 18, he arrived two days later at Weippe Prairie, an open area southeast of present Orofino, Idaho. On September 21 Clark sent Reubin Field back with some food supplies obtained from natives to guide the main party in; they staggered in the next day. The long and difficult trip from mountain pass to meadows dashed all hope of a short portage across the Rocky Mountains and ended dreams of an easy passage to the Orient. At the moment those larger consequences were probably forgotten in the face of the immediate accomplishment of coming safely out of the mountains, finding helpful natives, and perhaps obtaining adequate food.

At Weippe Prairie Clark became the first white man to meet the Nez Perce Indians. The captain found them living in two seasonal camps near the prairie where they came to collect a basic food source, camas. Camas roots were sometimes eaten after being steamed and sometimes pounded and formed into loaves. Sergeant Gass thought they tasted like pumpkins. Camas and dried salmon formed the staples of the Nez Perce diet and these hospitable people graciously shared their supply with Clark and his men. The famished explorers eagerly ate the food, but it proved a mixed blessing since it caused indigestion and diarrhea among the soldiers, who were more accustomed to wild game. They, and the main party later, suffered mightily for several weeks as their systems adjusted to the new diet.

The day after Lewis's arrival, on September 23, the captains held council with Twisted Hair, the ranking chief, while other leaders were away with a war party. Difficult communications followed, for the explorers had encountered another language group. The Nez Perces spoke a variety of Sahaptian, a tongue unfamiliar to Sacagawea or Old Toby, so conversation reverted to the nearly universal sign language. The usual medals and gifts were passed out and close inquiries were made about the route ahead. The name for the Nez Perces comes from the French for "pierced noses." The captains called them Chopunnish, a phonetic spelling of one self-designation, also related to the term piercing. Lewis and Clark noted the tribe's fine horses. The Nez Perces are renowned for their spotted Appaloosas, but there is some dispute about their development of the breed. Nonetheless, after acquiring horses, they too made periodic trips to buffalo grounds. In fact, the Lolo Trail was their ancient route across the mountains.

In their conversations with the Nez Perces, Lewis and Clark discovered that the Corps could return to water transport for their passage to the sea, so they quickly set about to locate a camp and begin building canoes. By September 26 the whole party had moved to a spot Clark found with Twisted Hair. Canoe Camp, as it has come to be called, was about five miles west of present Orofino, on the south side of the Clearwater River and opposite the mouth of the North Fork Clearwater, called the Kooskooskee and Chopunnish rivers by the captains. The explorers remained here until October 7, resting up after the difficult mountain crossing, recovering from bouts with dysentery and from general ill health, and building dugout canoes for the downriver trip.

Roll On Columbia

On October 7 they were ready, and leaving their horses with the Nez Perces to await their return, they set out in five canoes. The Corps of Discovery was now on the long-sought water route to the Pacific. Following the Clearwater and the Snake Rivers, the latter called Lewis's in the captain's honor, the Corps passed down to the Great Columbian Plain. The party had traveled through a variety of ecosystems previously unknown to Anglo-Americans. From the Great Plains, semiarid and largely treeless yet teeming with game, they had entered the Rocky Mountains, the first whites on record to do so in the region they crossed. In the mountains they found dense forests in many places, where the game necessary for sustenance was scarce and the natives often lived on the edge of starvation. Coming to the Columbian Plain, they again entered a new world, barren of trees like the Great Plains but also barren of game. They shifted from an area inhabited by horseback tribes east of the mountains to tribes who traveled by canoe and subsisted on salmon and roots on the west side.

As they followed these streams they encountered great numbers of villagers living on the river banks, their livelihood dependent on the annual run of fish. Some of these people provided assistance and with some the men traded for food, since game was nearly impossible to find. Tiring of the monotonous diet of fish and roots, the explorers frequently bought dogs to replace the deer, elk, and other game they were unable to obtain. Soon Old Toby abandoned the enterprise, thinking perhaps his usefulness was ended when he could no longer guide or interpret. Twisted Hair and Tetoharsky, another Nez Perce chief, accompanied the party for several days. On October 16 the Corps reached the Columbia, the Great River of the West. They set up camp on a point at the confluence of Snake and Columbia and during the next two days the explorers reconnoitered the area. Here they observed the seasonal end of the great salmon run on the Columbia, the numbers of fish Clark found "incredible to say." Here also they took astronomical observations, met with nearby Yakama and Wanapam Indians (Sahaptian speakers like the Nez Perce chiefs), purchased forty dogs for food, and prepared for the final drive to the sea.

From Indian information the captains expected to find rapids and falls farther down the Columbia, but even the most accurate accounts could not prepare them for the difficulties to come. In one fifty-five-mile stretch, they encountered the most treacherous river conditions of the entire trip. They portaged some of the swirling waters. At other times, eager to reach the Pacific, they plunged directly through the rapids in their ungainly canoes, much to the amazement of Indians who were watching from the shore. On October 23, 1805, the Corps entered this spectacular but dangerous stretch of the river, a few miles east of present The Dalles, Oregon. They found a series of three major barriers created by the stream as it cut through the Cascade Range in its descent to the sea. More than a week of demanding physical effort was required to pass through this part of the river. They made a short, successful portage of their first obstacle, Celilo Falls. Local Indians, on the other hand, maneuvered their own heavily loaded crafts skillfully through the high waters. Expedition boatmen looked on with envy and admiration. In addition to battling the river, the explorers were now set upon by infuriating fleas and irritating body lice, picked up from native huts.

Immediately below the falls were The Dalles, as later travelers named it, comprising two stretches where the river narrowed considerably—the Short and Long Narrows to Lewis and Clark. In spite of the "horrid appearance of this agitated gut Swelling, boiling & whorling," as Clark described it, the party was forced to run the narrow passage since no portage was possible. Under the steady hand of Cruzatte the boats and much of the cargo were guided through the straits to the astonishment of onlooking Indians. Nonswimmers walked on shore carrying what they could of valuable supplies as the boats careened by. That evening the unperturbed Cruzatte played the fiddle as the men danced and entertained locals. The American expedition must have been exceptional amusement for shorelined natives that fall of 1805.

The area's rapids and falls not only hindered Lewis and Clark but also slowed spawning fish going upstream. As such it became a favorite fishing ground for local Indians. Over time The Dalles became a market center as well, controlled by the Wishram and Wasco Indians whose houses lined the banks. Clark called it "the Great Mart of all this Country." The Wishram-Wasco plank-house villages served as the region's entrepôt for river-traffic trade goods. Pacific Northwest goods found their way up the Columbia to meet over-mountain merchandise relayed from the Middle Missouri by Shoshone traders. On the Columbia dried salmon replaced Dakota corn and jerked buffalo as the principal medium of exchange at The Dalles market.

The Dalles was also a dividing line between language families. Upriver were Sahaptian speakers like the Yakamas and Nez Perces, while at The Dalles and below Indians spoke varieties of Chinook. Although similar linguistically, the myriad tongues along the river were not mutually understood. In time a universal language developed, called the Chinook jargon, which served Columbian natives much like sign language on the Great Plains. Lewis and Clark discovered not only a difference in language and a variation in customs at The Dalles, but also a change in attitude near this point. Instances of petty thievery became routine and a source of some irritation to the party. Although the explorers could not understand the cultural backdrop for such activities, the Indians did not consider it dishonorable. The Americans, however, found it troublesome, and possibly dangerous, especially if they lost vital supplies. They were universally scornful of the natives because of this practice. Potentially explosive as the acts of pilfering were, no violence occurred and the expedition moved on.

After a few days' rest and some drying out of supplies at their Fort Rock camp at The Dalles, the party approached the final barrier, the Cascades of the Columbia, which they negotiated on November 1–2. Here the river passed through a series of chutes and falls with such velocity that it was again necessary to portage some men and equipment. Now somewhat familiar with the routine, the boatmen ran the rapids with little damage to the canoes and without injury to personnel. Lewis and Clark were much relieved at their success. After passing the Cascades the river broadened and the party entered tidewater. On November 2 they passed an imposing formation on the north shore and named it Beacon Rock, a name restored in the twentieth century. Near the mouth of the Willamette River and today's Portland, Oregon, they reentered the world of previously known geography, for boats of George Vancouver's British expedition had come this far up the Columbia in 1792. To the north and south they noticed snow-peaked mountains, some named by Vancouver's party, including Mount Hood, Mount St. Helens, and Mount Rainier. Clark could now check the accuracy of Vancouver's maps, copies of which he carried with him, and add firsthand observations to his own maps.

Evidence of European contact became more apparent as the party moved on; they saw pieces of sailor's clothes and heard occasional English words, most of it salty sailor language. They also encountered a new geographic and climatic zone as they approached the coast. From the relatively dry and barren plateau they moved into the rainy coastal region with its thick forests and fogs. The broad Columbia estuary now opened before them, and Clark exclaimed triumphantly, if prematurely, on November 7, "Ocian in View! O! the joy." He was probably looking only at the waters of the estuary, but in a few days more they did indeed see their long-sought goal. As they worked their way along the Washington side, the men took to carving their names on trees to mark their triumphant transcontinental crossing. Later, copying Alexander Mackenzie, who had crossed Canada in 1793 and inscribed a rock at the conclusion, Clark etched these words on a large pine: "William Clark December 3rd 1805. By Land. U States in 1804 & 1805."

Their satisfaction was tempered by the miserable weather, rain, and wind which forced them to huddle, wet and cold, on the Washington side of the high waves. The immediate goal was to find a place for winter quarters. Since there seemed to be no really suitable spot on the north side of the Columbia, they looked to the southern shore. Considering whether to winter on the coast or seek some drier spot back up the Columbia, the captains put the question to a vote. Even York, the slave, and Sacagawea, the Indian woman, had their opinions recorded. The final decision was to cross to the south side of the Columbia to seek a location with adequate

game and proper timber to build a stockade. After a few days of search-
ing, on December 7 they picked a site on the banks of Lewis and Clark
River, a short distance from today's Astoria, Oregon—4,118 miles from
Camp Dubois by their estimate, after 573 days on the trail. Here would be
their home for the next three and one-half months, until March 23, 1806.

Pacific Coast Winter

Fort Clatsop, named after the local Indians, was the party's third and final
wintering outpost. Although the stockade's purposes were similar to
those of Camp Dubois and Fort Mandan—protection from the elements,
security against assault, and separation from neighboring inhabitants—
the temperament of its occupants differed from that of previous winters.
The depressing weather, marked by rain, storms, and gray skies, acted on
the men's spirits and may have influenced their relations with the natives.
Indeed, the journals reflect a dislike, even disgust, with the coastal tribes.
Peaceful relations were maintained, but the party did not warm to these
people, who were sharp traders, as they had to the Mandans, Hidatsas,
Shoshones, and Nez Perces.

Jefferson's original plan included the possibility that the party might
meet a coastal trading vessel and return by sea. The captains apparently
discarded this idea, but they still hoped that such a ship would enable
them to send dispatches and specimens back to guard against accident on
the return trip. No ship appeared, so with spring the party packed up,
faced east, and began the long trip back to St. Louis. If the winter at Camp
Dubois was one of preparation, and at Fort Mandan one of anticipation,
the winter at Fort Clatsop may well be called the period of reflection. Here
Lewis accomplished some of his most important natural history writing,
summarizing his observations and discoveries from the Rocky Mountains westward. Here, too, Clark completed an initial draft of his great
map of the West, incorporating all he had learned from traders, Indians,
and firsthand experience about vast areas only conjectured at before.

After deciding on the location for their fort on December 7, the men
set to felling trees and preparing the land for their winter quarters. Axe
men found excellent timber nearby. Clark called it the "Streight butifull
balsom pine" (probably grand fir) and carpenter Gass declared that it

made "the finest puncheons" he had ever seen. By December 12 they had finished three cabins; two days later all seven huts were up with roofs yet to go. Chinking, daubing, and general sealing of openings to keep out the interminable rain kept builders busy for several more days. On Christmas Eve most of the party moved into their huts but were soon smoked out, so chimneys were added throughout. The fort was completed by December 30 so the party could retreat to relative dryness. The stockade was about fifty feet square with three huts on one side, four on the other, and an open yard between. The enlisted men occupied three rooms along one row, while across the grounds Lewis and Clark shared a room, the Charbonneau family another, with the remaining two rooms left for storage. Palisades at the front and rear joined the two rows of cabins. The main gate opened to a cleared area and a small rear gate provided access to a nearby spring.

The Corps did not starve, but food was neither plentiful nor good that winter. The inability to preserve meat in the damp climate meant that the company lived much of the time on spoiled elk, deer, and small game. The quest for food kept hunting parties out constantly and at ever increasing distances, elk being the chief game animal. After one productive hunt Lewis commented: "This evening we had what I call an excellent supper   it consisted of a marrowbone a piece and a brisket of boiled Elk . . . this for Fort Clatsop is living in high stile." At times the party's provisions were down to only a few days' rations and the captains fretted about their situation. The men, however, seemed wasteful and largely unconcerned about declining food resources. Lewis scolded them for their profligate ways on several occasions. Native plants, dried fish, and dogs were purchased from the Indians, but those seasoned traders demanded high prices and the explorers' store of trade goods dwindled rapidly.

To aid in food preservation the captains set up a camp on the coast where workers boiled seawater to obtain salt. Now called the Saltmaking Camp, it is at Seaside, Oregon, about fifteen miles from Fort Clatsop by way of the party's overland trail. It was initially established by Joseph Field, William Bratton, and George Gibson, but saltmakers varied during its operation, with three men usually present. About four bushels of salt were obtained before shutting it down on February 21. In January Indians brought word of a whale stranded a few miles south of the Saltmaking Camp at today's Cannon Beach. Clark led a detachment of about thirteen men to obtain the meat; Sacagawea insisted on seeing the "monstrous fish" and the ocean, so she joined the excursion, with baby Jean Baptiste. By the time Clark arrived local Indians had stripped the whale and left only the huge skeleton. He was able to purchase a few hundred pounds of meat and a few gallons of oil and returned to the fort four days later.

The men passed their days hunting and dressing animal skins for clothing. Near the end of their stay the men counted over three hundred pairs of moccasins, a seeming abundance of footwear but a number necessary for the return. Routine soldiering duties such as cleaning and caring for equipment also filled their time. It was nonetheless a winter of boredom for the soldiers, but now more disciplined they were not the raucous lot of Camp Dubois. Undoubtedly they danced to the music of Cruzatte's fiddle, and being young men away from home, they had affairs with local women. The captains, fearing venereal disease and complications with Indians, soon advised against such contacts and the men promised to refrain. Minor illnesses flourished in the camp because of the dampness and cold, accidents and injuries occurred, and biting insects annoyed the men without relief.

On Christmas morning the captains wakened to shouts and singing from the men. The leaders divided the last of the tobacco to users and gave a silk handkerchief to each of the others. Some special presents were also exchanged. Clark received woolen clothing from Lewis, moccasins from Whitehouse, an Indian basket from Goodrich, and two dozen white weasel tails from Sacagawea. Ordway commented that they had no liquor for toasting "but all are in good health which we esteem more than all the ardent Spirits in the world." Again on New Year's Day another salute resounded through the woods as the men fired their weapons. Lewis thought ahead to January 1, 1807, when he would find himself "in the bosom of our friends . . . [to] enjoy the repast which the hand of civilization has prepared for us." This day he contented himself with boiled elk, cooked roots, and "pure water."

Coastal natives at the mouth of the Columbia were part of a linguistically related group known as Chinooks. The Chinooks proper occupied the north bank of the Columbia across from the expedition's post. Their territory extended some distance up the river and north along the Washington coast to Willapa Bay. The Chinooks occupied villages along the Columbia during the summer fishing season, then moved north to the bay for the winter. The explorers had little contact with them and most of their information about them came from the Clatsops. The Clatsops (also Chinookans) lived on the south side of the Columbia as far upstream as Tongue Point, and south along the Oregon coast to Seaside. The Clatsops and the Chinooks proper spoke nearly identical dialects of Lower Chinook. Later, the Chinook jargon became a convenient means of communication along the river corridor, even among non-Chinookans.

The trip down the Columbia had perhaps predisposed the party to view their Fort Clatsop neighbors in an negative light. Having experienced petty thefts along the way, the men were weary of the nuisance and were not ready to put up with it at the fort. Indicative of the men's feeling was the password at the post, "No Chinook." Customary civilities were shown to visitors, less frequent here than at Fort Mandan, but a genuine cordiality was never established. Lewis and Clark found the Clatsops to be gracious hosts on their infrequent visits to Indian lodges, but the Indians seemed to view the contacts not as social gatherings but as commercial encounters.

Local trading practices created a hindrance to ideal relations. The Indians were accustomed to hard bargaining with ship traders who had been coming to their shores to barter for sea otter skins for over a decade. The Clatsops expected the explorers to accept and follow time-honored conventions. Instead, Lewis and Clark thought the Clatsops overcharged for goods they desperately needed. What the Clatsops viewed as good business, the Corps saw as gouging transactions directed unfairly at them, especially since they were short of trade goods and in need of basic necessities. Blue beads were the favorite medium of exchange, but the party lacked enough to last a winter of intense haggling. The Corps found little of the milk of human kindness among these inveterate traders.

The captains' diplomatic efforts were either slighted or inconclusive at Fort Clatsop. Although the Chinooks, estimated at four hundred persons, were the most influential tribe at the Columbia's mouth, the leaders never ventured across the river for negotiating, and visits from Chinook chiefs were rare and unproductive. Their brief meetings with Chinooks in

November while on the Washington side had likewise been inconsequential. Diplomatic ventures with the Clatsops were similarly indefinite. Although only half the size in population as their cross-river cultural kinsmen, the Clatsops should have been the focus of the captains' diplomacy due to their accessibility. The leaders knew personally only one chief, Coboway, however, and they never carried out the round of discussions that had been so customary in the past. Perhaps the value of American interests was not as clear at Fort Clatsop as before, and the men's store of Indian presents had dwindled by this time, especially in the face of intense trading.

Many aspects of the local culture aroused negative reactions from the captains, who were not the wholly disinterested ethnographers they had been before. Chinookan sexual practices provoked a censorious tone not apparent when the men wrote of similar customs among plains Indians. Lewis commented, "they do not hold the virtue of their women in high estimation, and will even prostitute their wives and daughters for a fishinghook or stran of beads." The leaders noticed, however, that the Clatsops "do not appear to abhor it as a Crime in the unmarried State." Head deformation, a coastal custom quite new to the captains, did not come in for condemnation, however. In infancy Chinookan children were placed in special cradles equipped with a board that pressed against the forehead. Over time the pressure of the board brought about the desired effect, a nearly straight slope of the forehead from the top of the skull to the nose, yielding a pointed look when viewed from the side and a flattened appearance when seen from the front. Clark drew pictures of the cradle and the result of its work in his journal. The look was considered a mark of status, which slaves and non-Chinookans were not permitted to imitate.

Lewis and Clark discovered that resident Indians made rich use of native plant resources. Roots played important roles in the Indian diet, including edible thistle, western bracken fern, rushes, cat-tail, seashore lupine, and most importantly, wapato. The enlisted men, used to a diet of buffalo, deer, and elk, probably agreed with Lewis when he described one of the plants as "reather insipid." The greatest part of native subsistence, however, was based on the river's rich and ever recurring resource of running fish. The river provided sturgeon, eulachon, trout, and other fish, but most importantly, salmon, in several varieties. The coastal Indians possessed many skills in this livelihood that the newcomers admired. The captains described in great detail the types of canoes utilized by Chinookans and their dexterous handling of the boats on the Columbia's choppy waves. The explorers also noted the Indian methods of fishing and their use of nets, gigs, hooks, and line, all intricately fashioned from native resources.

At Fort Clatsop the captains had time to reflect on the Indian tribes from the Rockies westward. In their journals they gave careful attention to native clothing, houses, utensils, weapons, and implements, and they wrote general descriptions of coastal material culture. They also developed an elaborate document called the "Estimate of Western Indians" (west of the Rocky Mountains), comparable to a similar one completed at Fort Mandan for Eastern Indians. They gave extra space in their writing to tribes in the vicinity of Fort Clatsop. The Wahkiakums and Cathlamets lived on the north and south sides of the Columbia and to the east of the Chinooks and Clatsops. They spoke a dialect known as Kathlamet, a part of the Upper Chinook language, but they differed from upstream Chinookans in several respects and were a transitional group between those above and below them. Such cultural subtleties either confused the captains or were totally lost on them. South of the Clatsops along the Oregon coast lived the Tillamook Indians, who had a village at present Seaside and were neighbors to expedition saltmakers. They belonged to the coastal branch of the Salishan-language family. As noted by Lewis and Clark, the Tillamooks shared a number of outward cultural traits with the neighboring Clatsops, despite language differences.

Dreary as the stay at Fort Clatsop was, the captains did not lack occupation. Lewis, who had neglected his journals for some time, returned to writing at Fort Clatsop. On January 1, 1806, Lewis took up a new journal and continued writing consistently until August 12 when he laid his pen down, ending his record of the expedition. This new journal contains extensive descriptions of flora and fauna and the life of local Indians. Nowhere else did Lewis give more time and journal space to fulfilling the scientific objectives of the mission than in this writing, the product perhaps of enforced leisure in a strange, new environment. Until late March he devoted the greater part of journal entries to detailed records, often accompanied by sketches, of animal and plant species observed in the mountains, across the interior, and on the coast, a large portion of them unknown to science. Perhaps to ensure preservation by keeping a duplicate record, Clark copied most of the scientific matter almost verbatim into his own notebooks.

While Lewis wrote, Clark spent the winter months preparing his maps of the route from Fort Mandan and sorting out geographical information. Clark drew numerous maps in his journals of this territory and augmented them with larger, more detailed sheets. Neatly executed finished versions showing the route over the mountains and down to the coast were probably completed at Fort Clatsop. As the Corps moved into unknown lands, Clark relied heavily on Indian informants for mapping peripheral areas. Indian maps were eagerly sought because they enabled the captains not only to look ahead to country they were to enter, but also to look beyond to lands outside their route of travel. Often the maps were no more than rude charcoal drawings on animal skins or stick scratches in the dirt to show rivers and trails with small mounds of earth to represent hills. Indian cartographic concepts were sometimes difficult to interpret and language differences added an extra burden, but native knowledge was essential to Clark's mapping success.

Clark brought all of this information together and at Fort Clatsop he completed a large map of the country west of the Missouri River. The new map was a vast improvement over the map he had sent to Jefferson from Fort Mandan. With great accuracy Clark delineated the avenue of their traverse and filled in the large blank spaces of previous maps. Areas to the north and south of their line of march were sketchier. Clark based his work on outlying lands on knowledge acquired from Indians and traders and on maps the leaders had examined in the East. Lewis and Clark carried the new map back to St. Louis, then Lewis took it on to Washington DC, where a cartographer hastily prepared a finished version for the waiting president. It was the most accurate map then available of the trans-Missouri West.

Homeward Bound

Boredom, sickness, a monotonous diet, and the dreary weather all enhanced the party's impatience to start for home as soon as receding mountain snows were thought to permit their passage. The captains knew that the Nez Perces, with whom they had left their horses, would cross the Rockies to hunt buffalo as soon as the snows melted. They were anxious to secure their horses, cross the mountains themselves, and explore a more direct route from the mountains to the Missouri. They also wanted to carry out a separate exploration of the Yellowstone River. These separate excursions demanded a division of the Corps, a plan they settled on at Fort Clatsop.

They had planned to leave on April 1, but eagerness to be underway prompted them to move up the date to March 20, then bad weather and the need to secure additional canoes held them another few days. Lewis and Clark feared that the price the Indians wanted for a canoe would severely deplete their small stock of trade goods and cripple their ability to obtain needed supplies on the way home. The captains succumbed to temptation and violated their longstanding and consistently observed rule against stealing Indian property and sent out a party to take an unattended canoe nearby. They rationalized that the Clatsops had once taken elk shot by expedition hunters before the men could return to claim them.

A few days before leaving, Lewis reflected on the Pacific Coast stay. "Alto' we have not fared sumptuously this winter and spring at Fort Clatsop, we have lived quite as comfortably as we have any reason to expect we should; and have accomplished every object which induced our remaining at this place except that of meeting with the traders who visit the entrance of this river." On March 22 he wrote, "we determined to set out tomorrow at all events." The last morning at Fort Clatsop was similar to so many others at the post since December 7—a steady rain fell and strong winds prevailed, making departure uncertain. At one o'clock the weather cleared and Lewis wrote, "we bid a final adieu to Fort Clatsop." Sluggish muscles strained against the river's current in the five canoes and they made only sixteen miles that first day, camping a few miles beyond modern Astoria, barely a start up the Columbia. St. Louis must have seemed much more than half a continent away, and Virginia, the other side of the world. No doubt tired arms and sore backs were evident that evening, attesting to a winter of inactivity. Any complaints went unrecorded, probably out of elation to be headed home.

Clark's geographical inquiries and mapping at Fort Clatsop required the party to make a stop in the area of present Portland, to seek a river that had begun to figure prominently in their conception of Western geography. The natives called it the Multnomah, a name adopted by the captains; it is today's Willamette River. Hidden by a large island, they had missed it on their downriver trip. In fact, they missed it again, but Clark retraced his steps, took a small detachment and an Indian guide, and investigated the stream's lower reaches on April 2 and 3. Indian information became garbled with their geographic theories to the extent that the captains confused the courses of the Willamette and Snake Rivers and gave the former more prominence than it deserves. On Clark's final map he showed the river as coming from much deeper in the continent than it actually does. They were correct, however, in their assessment of the "Columbian valley," the area between the Cascade and Coast Ranges. Lewis declared it "the only desireable situation for a settlement which I have seen on the West side of the Rocky mountains" and capable of supporting fifty thousand persons. On April 6 the party was again on its way.

They were nearly two weeks getting upriver past the Cascades and the Celilo Falls. To the wearisome labor of portaging these obstacles again was added the aggravation of bad relations with Indians in the vicinity. Although hunters were out constantly, an occasional elk or deer could not feed hungry laborers. So the explorers had to supplement their hard-won game with dogs, dried fish, and roots from river tribes as before. Again, the natives demanded high prices, perhaps understandable now since fish were late in coming and the Indians were facing hard times. As before, some of them could not resist stealing the explorers' belongings. It was a repeat of the previous year's frustrations. The captains' patience was at low ebb and they threatened violence if stolen goods were not returned. An exasperated Lewis declared them "poor, dirty, proud, haughty, inhospitable, parsimonious and faithless in every rispect." When some Indians made off with Seaman, the captain sent a party of men to recover his dog, with orders to shoot if necessary. Fortunately, no one was killed and Seaman was returned. Sergeant Gass probably summed up the men's opinion in the blunt, sweeping words of an enlisted man: "All the Indians from the Rocky Mountains to the falls of Columbia, are an honest, ingenious and well disposed people; but from the falls to the seacoast, and along it, they are a rascally, thieving set."

Once past the falls they traded canoes for horses and continued their journey by land, making their way up the north side of the Columbia. On the westward journey the captains had promised to visit Chief Yelleppit of the Walulas (or Walla Wallas) and to remain with him for a few days on the way back. They kept their promise and camped among these neighborly people from April 27 to 29 at the mouth of the Walla Walla River. Yelleppit provided much-needed food and entertained the expedition with festivities. The explorers returned the favor in kind—out came Cruzatte's fiddle and the men danced until late in the evening. Yelleppit also loaned them canoes to cross the Columbia and told them about an overland shortcut to the Nez Perces. Providing such a contrast to Indians at The Dalles, Lewis called the Walulas "the most hospitable, honest, and sincere people that we have met with in our voyage." On the morning of April 30 they set out guided by a Nez Perce they had met several days earlier. They were anxious to reach his people and recover the horses they had left with the tribe on the westbound trip.

This route took the party over new ground. With their guide's aid and the help of twenty-three horses, they covered the distance between the Columbia and Clearwater Rivers in six days, circumventing the Snake River almost entirely. The cross-country trip followed Indian trails, meandered along the Touchet River, and passed the present towns of Waitsburg, Dayton, and Pomeroy, Washington. Reaching the Snake on May 4, the party crossed over and continued up its north side to the Clearwater, then followed it some distance before crossing to its south side for a better road. They now headed southeasterly, looking for a campsite among the Nez Perces, whose lodges they were passing, hoping to find a spot where game might prove plentiful.

On May 14 the party settled in to a camp on the east side of the Clearwater at the modern town of Kamiah, Idaho, where they would remain for nearly a month. The Nez Perces told them that it would be at least that long before the snows in the Bitterroot Mountains melted sufficiently to allow passage over the Lolo Trail. An impatient Lewis looked to the mountains and wrote of "that icy barrier which separates us from my friends and country, from all which makes life esteemable." Their campsite has come to be called Camp Chopunnish after the explorers' name for the Nez Perces. Except for the two wintering posts, it was the longest encampment of the expedition. They passed their time seeking food, counciling and socializing with the Indians, and obtaining more horses for the next stage of the trip.

The captains also assumed a new and demanding role as physicians. On the westward trip some expedition prescriptions had eased Indian ailments and had, Clark said, "given those nativs an exolted oppinion of my skill as a phisician." Back again, Clark became the natives' "favorite phisician," according to Lewis. During this stay the captain was visited by a host of afflicted persons, complaining of a variety of ills, notably rheumatic problems, sore eyes, and abscesses. Lewis was doubtful if any permanent cures could result, but the immediate benefits were good relations with the Nez Perces including payment in much-needed foodstuffs. The captains wished that they could indeed cure these "poor wretches."

The captains also mediated a dispute between the local Nez Perce leaders. The previous fall they had left their horses with Chief Twisted Hair. Some more prominent chiefs, Cut Nose and Broken Arm, who had then been absent were annoyed with him on returning, thinking that he had assumed too much authority. Twisted Hair had apparently overused the mounts, then displeased with the criticism had neglected the horses and finally let them wander over a considerable area. Now Lewis and Clark did their best to reconcile the squabbling chiefs and sent some men to recover their animals. Tribal horses eventually made up for any lost or damaged ones, bringing the count to sixty-five animals. Some rather fractious stallions were castrated in Indian fashion, which the explorers found superior to their own method.

In councils with local chiefs Lewis and Clark promised that American merchants would follow with trade goods, especially guns, so the Nez Perces could defend themselves against the Blackfeet and other enemies. They also promised, if they should meet the Blackfeet on their eastward trip, to try to persuade them to make peace with the Nez Perces. Their hosts may have been a bit skeptical on this point, but the desire to obtain weapons to match those of their enemies inspired hope. The men found much to admire about their hosts' customs, hospitality, and appearance. At leisure times, the fiddle was once more brought out and dancing and singing ensued; friendly footraces and competitive games were also a part of camp activities. Camp Chopunnish was by no means a "summer camp," but it was quite a contrast to the most recent winter camp. The traveling ethnographers recorded much about Nez Perce material culture during the forced stay. Food, clothing, and housing, of course, caught their attention. The horse culture of this equestrian people was also a matter of serious consideration. Finally, the captains tried to explain Nez Perce attitudes, ceremonies, and rituals.

According to the Nez Perces the snow would not be gone from the Lolo Trail until the beginning of July, but the whole party was anxious to start homeward, so they left the valley of the Clearwater "elated," Lewis said, "with the idea of moving on towards their friends and country." On June 10 the Corps of Discovery moved to higher ground on Weippe Prairie. From here they set out on June 15 but soon realized that they could not find their way in the deep snow. Two days later, after caching many of their supplies, they turned back. Lewis lamented, "this is the first time since we have been on this long tour that we have ever been compelled to retreat." They returned to Weippe Prairie and sent to the Nez Perces for guides. Three young men offered to serve for the price of two guns. On June 24 the party set out again; the Indians found the trail easily and they made their way to their old camp at Travelers' Rest. This time they took only six days on the Lolo Trail in contrast to the eleven days of the westbound trip and without a repeat of severe hardships. They spent a few days resting for the next stage of the journey.

Separation and Reunion

At Fort Clatsop the captains had decided to divide the party for an extended time to investigate previously unexplored territory. Each captain would lead a detachment over new ground, eventually reuniting at a predetermined spot, the mouth of the Yellowstone River on the Missouri. On July 3 the two groups went their separate ways. It was the first time during the expedition that they had separated for such a long time and over so great a distance. Lewis admitted, "I could not avoid feeling much concern on this occasion although I hoped this seperation was only momentary." It would be nearly six weeks before these friends were together once again and there would be much to tell. Without doubt Lewis had the more disquieting news.

Lewis and Clark knew that their outbound route, following the Missouri to its headwaters, had been needlessly roundabout, and that there were trails across the mountains which would shorten the journey considerably. This quicker route needed to be examined. Moreover, they wished to discover the northernmost reach of the Marias River, hoping to expand the United States' claims under the Louisiana Purchase. Consequently, Lewis would investigate the shortcut by heading east to the Great Falls of the Missouri, then explore the Marias before returning to the Missouri. Clark's mission was to explore the Yellowstone River. He would travel southeast to the site of Camp Fortunate, then follow the Beaverhead and the Jefferson Rivers to the Three Forks of the Missouri. Part of his group would then take canoes down the Missouri to the Great Falls to meet Lewis's party there, while Clark went overland to the Yellowstone. Thus, Clark's reduced detachment would carry out the investigation of the Yellowstone. The scattered groups would eventually recombine at the Yellowstone's entrance into the Missouri.

On his trip Lewis was accompanied by nine men, volunteers for what was considered the more dangerous assignment, and five Nez Perce guides who left the detachment the next day. With their seventeen horses the party moved north down the Bitterroot River to the vicinity of present Missoula, Montana. From there they headed east across the Continental Divide following the Clark Fork and Big Blackfoot Rivers on a route previously recommended by the mountain Indians. After the Indian name, Lewis called the last stream the "River of the Road to the Buffaloe." Eventually, Lewis and his men crossed the divide over what is now called Lewis and Clark Pass, although Clark never saw it.

By July 13 they were at the old Upper Portage Camp above the Great Falls—one year minus two days since they left this spot. It had taken eleven days of travel to cover the distance; the previous year the Corps had labored nearly two months in linking Upper Portage Camp to Travelers' Rest. The new route was also a savings of nearly 600 miles. The soldiers were delighted after months of meager rations to be eating buffalo again. Lewis was amazed that "there were not less than 10 thousand buffaloe within a circle of 2 miles" about the place. But buffalo country was also bear country and they were not thrilled at the grizzlies that greeted them at the camp. Some gave the men trouble as the soldiers dug up the cache they had hidden the previous year. Hugh McNeal had a close call with one in which he broke his musket over the beast's head and then spent several hours in a tree waiting for the stunned and angry bear to leave. Memories surely stirred of former battles with bears.

Lewis was disheartened to find some of the materials at the Upper Portage Camp cache damaged by water, including the loss of all the botanical items he had so carefully collected and preserved between Fort Mandan and the Great Falls. Losing several horses, perhaps to Indian thieves, Lewis decided to make the journey up the Marias accompanied by only three of his best men, Drouillard and the Field brothers. Sergeant Gass and the others would await the canoe party from Clark's detachment, then all would portage the Great Falls, recover additional supplies buried there, and finally proceed to the mouth of the Marias to meet the returning Lewis and his detachment. Before departing, Lewis instructed Gass that he should meet him at the Marias about August 5, but if he had not arrived by September 1, that the sergeant should leave to join Clark at the Yellowstone. Lewis was quite aware of the potential danger of the mission.

They set out on July 16, heading north to the Marias and then along its banks to the river's upper forks. After several days' travel the captain began to doubt that the Marias extended as far north as he had hoped. On Cut Bank Creek, near the mountains, they camped from July 22 to 26, the most northern camp of the expedition, about twelve miles northeast of today's Browning, Montana. Here Lewis attempted to take astronomical observations but was frustrated by overcast skies. Thus hindered, Lewis named the place Camp Disappointment. He was further disappointed that the potential for additional American territory was lost, since the Marias did not drain from the north. The four men now turned about to rejoin their companions. The night of July 26 they bedded down along the banks of Two Medicine River. Extra hands warmed themselves at the evening's campfire.

That day Lewis and his men had encountered a party of eight Blackfeet Indians of the Piegan tribe. Lewis knew that he was in their territory and that they were the avowed enemies of many of the Indians that the Corps had befriended. It was the one Indian tribe he had hoped to avoid. Having been spotted by the Indians, however, he believed a retreat might be interpreted as weakness and perhaps invite attack. Moreover, at first Lewis was unsure of the Indians' numbers, as the horse herd in sight seemed to indicate many more than eight. Others might be nearby and cut off any hasty retreat, so he advanced and engaged in friendly sign language talk. The two parties camped together beneath three cottonwood trees on Two Medicine River.

The next morning the explorers were awakened by the noise of a struggle; one of the Indians had tried to make off with some of the party's guns. Joseph Field, the early morning guard, quickly awakened his brother, Reubin, who pursued the Piegan and stabbed him to death. Another Indian seized the rifles of Drouillard and Lewis, but Drouillard saw him and wrested back his own gun. His shouts and struggles aroused the soundly sleeping Lewis, who took up his pistol and pursued an Indian fleeing with his rifle. He caught the thief, and with pistol at ready ordered him to lay down the rifle. When the Indian did so, Lewis allowed him to go, denying his men's request to kill the thief.

Failing to obtain the explorers' guns, the Blackfeet rushed to take their horses, hoping perhaps to restore some lost honor. The Indians split into two groups; Lewis pursued one group of two Piegans, while his men went after the rest. One Indian turned to fire on Lewis, who got off the first shot, hitting the man in the stomach. The fatally wounded warrior fired a final shot and Lewis later recalled, "being bearheaded I felt the wind of his bullet very distinctly." Both whites and Indians had had enough. The six surviving Piegans fled north, while Lewis and his men quickly gathered up their belongings and began two days of hard riding back to the Missouri. The fear of avenging Blackfeet warriors spurred them on. At the mouth of the Marias they met the canoes under Sergeant Ordway, who had picked up the men Lewis had left at the Great Falls. Once on the canoes the whole party easily outdistanced any potential pursuit by the Blackfeet.

Clark's trip on the Yellowstone was a good deal less dramatic. He too departed Travelers' Rest on July 3 and took his division by another new route out of the mountains. Going south along the Bitterroot Valley, the group retraced part of the previous year's trek but diverted to cross the Continental Divide at present Gibbons Pass, giving themselves a straighter shot to their destination. They then proceeded into the Big

Hole River valley following buffalo and Indian trails southeasterly to their old Camp Fortunate where they arrived on July 8. During this time Sacagawea was able to point the way—one of only two occasions in which she may be said to have served as a guide. The men quickly dug up the goods and canoes they had cached at the camp the preceding year. Although the items were a little water-soaked, they were for the most part undamaged. Especially gratifying to users was the unharmed tobacco, which they immediately put to use, having been without the substance for several months.

From Camp Fortunate the returning explorers journeyed by horse and canoe down to the Three Forks. The summer before it had taken almost three weeks to cover this distance; now they were able to make the trip in as many days. They arrived on July 13, just as Lewis reached the Upper Portage Camp, some 150 miles to the north. At the Three Forks Clark wasted no time. The same day he divided his party, sending Ordway with nine men down the Missouri in canoes to meet the Gass contingent, while he led a party of twelve persons, including the Charbonneau family, east to the Yellowstone. Clark and his group set out through the valleys of the Gallatin and East Gallatin Rivers. The area was a vast landscape of wildlife, with enormous herds of deer, elk, and antelope to be seen in all directions, and great numbers of beaver in the rivers. Again following well-worn but confusing trails the party moved through Bozeman Pass and crossed to the Yellowstone on July 15. Along this route Sacagawea was again able to point out an accessible route. Thus Clark remarked that Sacagawea had been of great service "as a pilot through this country."

Traveling along the north side of the Yellowstone the party kept watch for trees large enough to serve as canoes. In the vicinity of present Laurel, Montana, they found cottonwood trees of sufficient size to build canoes and continue their journey by water. While the boat-builders were at work, Indian prowlers also kept busy—taking twenty-four of the party's fifty mounts. The horse thieves were probably Crow Indians, since the party was in the tribe's hunting territory. Clark decided to split his unit once more. He sent an advance party under Sergeant Pryor with the remaining horses cross-country to the Mandan villages. The sergeant carried a message to a Canadian trader, asking him to induce some Teton Sioux chiefs to go to Washington with the captains. The groups separated on July 24. Shortly after Pryor and his three companions set out, their horses were stolen, again perhaps by stealthy Crows. Pryor handled the emergency admirably. His party killed some buffalo and used the hides to build bowl-shaped "bull boats" such as they had observed among Missouri River tribes. Then they set off down the Yellowstone in pursuit of Clark's party, whom they overtook on August 8.

Clark's trip down the Yellowstone was uneventful. On July 25, near today's Billings, Montana, he arrived at the landmark he named "Pompy's Tower" after little Jean Baptiste; it is now called Pompeys Pillar. Clark also carved his name and the date on the rock—still visible on this National Historic Landmark. Proceeding on, they arrived at the mouth of the Yellowstone on August 3. There Clark had intended to wait for Lewis, but he found the mosquitoes so intolerable and game in such short supply that he decided to go on down the Missouri, leaving a message for Lewis telling of his move. On August 11 Clark's party met two trappers, the first whites they had seen since April 1805.

Lewis arrived at the Yellowstone on August 7, read Clark's message, and moved on. On August 11 he was the victim of a painful and embarrassing accident. He was out hunting with Cruzatte, an excellent boatman but poor of sight. Seeing a movement which he took to be an elk, Cruzatte fired and hit Lewis in the buttocks. Lewis thought he had been wounded by an Indian, but it proved to be Cruzatte's blunder. The wound, though not terribly serious, was quite painful. In fact, a few days later as Clark was dressing the wound, Lewis fainted. Ever the naturalist, Lewis found energy to discover one last plant, the pin cherry, about which he wrote a lengthy description on August 12, before he lay down his pen. On that same day, a few miles below the Little Knife River in present North Dakota, Lewis and Clark reunited. Clark assumed the remaining writing duties for his ailing comrade.

Hurrying Home

The full party reached the Mandan and Hidatsa villages two days later, where they stayed until August 17. To their dismay the captains discovered that their peace plans for the plains had fallen apart. After they departed, Hidatsa warriors had attacked a Shoshone village near the Rockies, Sioux war parties had attacked and killed some Mandans and Hidatsas, and the Hidatsas had stolen Arikara horses and killed two of the tribe. Hoping to restore their damaged plans, the captains persuaded the Mandan chief Big White to accompany them to Washington to see the president. As they departed they left behind Sacagawea, Charbonneau, and little Pomp. Clark offered to take the boy and treat him as if he were his own son, but father and mother thought him too young; they promised to bring him to Clark in a year or so. Here also John Colter took his discharge in order to join two American trappers bound up the Missouri. On their way out they made a brief stop at Fort Mandan and found it nearly all burned down, perhaps the work of prairie fires. The next day Lewis celebrated his last birthday on the trail, his thirty-second; Clark had turned thirty-six on the first of the month.

At the Arikara villages on August 21 the captains faced an awkward situation, for the chief they had convinced on their way upriver to travel to Washington had not yet returned and the villagers had grown suspicious. No other chiefs would agree to go. In fact, though the captains had no way of knowing it, the chief had died of illness in Washington. They smoothed over the situation as well as they could, but ultimately the resulting hostility of the Arikaras would cause a great deal of trouble. On August 30 they met some Teton Sioux, giving them the cold shoulder because of the troubles of 1804. They held a friendly meeting with the Yankton Sioux near the mouth of the Niobrara on September 1, and on September 4 they revisited Sergeant Floyd's grave.

The rest of the downriver journey was made as fast as possible, by men eager to return home. They were now meeting trading parties bound upriver, who gave them the news of over two years, including the fact that many people in the United States had given them up for lost, although "the President of the U. States had yet hopes of us." The traders also sold them some whiskey which was distributed to the party, the first that had been tasted since the Fourth of July 1805. Lewis was recovering from his wound as they passed the scenes of the toilsome upriver journey, several campsites each day. On September 20, near La Charette, they saw the first cows since leaving the settlements. The next day they reached St. Charles, meeting old friends.

Emerging from the river's mouth on September 23, they briefly visited

the camp at Wood River that they had left some twenty-eight months before, then crossed over and reached St. Louis at noon. The citizens, having received advance word, lined the riverfront and cheered. Two days
later, at Christy's Tavern, they were treated to a lavish dinner, with eighteen toasts, ending with "Captains Lewis and Clark—Their perilous services endear them to every American heart." The next day Clark brought
his journal to an end with the anticlimactic words, "a fine morning we
commenced wrighting &c."

Editorial Principles

The procedures that guided the editorial work of the complete edition of the expedition journals are those generally followed here. Readers may turn to the editorial procedures statement in volume 2 of the *Journals of the Lewis and Clark Expedition* for an extended discussion of those guidelines. The principal goal remains the same: to provide users with a reliable text that is largely uncluttered with editorial interference. By using the text from the full edition, I have retained the enigmatic writing of the journalists that has so captivated, bedeviled, and delighted readers for nearly two hundred years. Comments are provided here on editorial features of this work that differ from those in the larger work.

Under limited circumstances I retain emendations in the notebooks made by Nicholas Biddle as he prepared the first edition of the journals in 1814. Because Biddle's comments occasionally clarify or complete a passage that is otherwise unclear or unfinished, they are important to keep. Such material is designated by placing his initials and comments in italics and within square brackets: [*NB:*]. Otherwise, the remarks are not included or are changed to the editor's insertion. The editor's additions are also placed in square brackets but without italics or identifying initials. In the same way, supplied or corrected words or phrases are inserted and conjectural readings of the text are shown. Words or phrases that were deleted by the writer and restored by the editor are placed in angle brackets. Double punctuation in the entries is removed, for example, if there is a period and a long dash at the end of a line, only the period is retained. The same is true for double words, expressions, and abbreviations, the multiple use of "&c." (et cetera) being a prime example of the latter. The long dash as end-of-line punctuation is retained except at the end of entries where a period is substituted. A period also ends every entry, whether or not punctuation was supplied in the original.

Multiple drafts of a single entry by the same writer presented a selection dilemma. My solution was to keep entries separate and not blend or conflate the material. In most instances I selected the entry I considered superior in content or style and let it stand alone without editorial comment. For instance, Clark's draft entry of July 19, 1804, has an immediacy that is lacking in the finished version, thus I draw only from the draft entry on this occasion without so stating. And only in his draft entry of July 13, 1804, does Clark reveal that his notes for the day were lost in a storm. In some cases two entries for the same day were dissimilar enough or had such unique features that it was important to supply both versions. For example, Clark has two entries for November 24, 1805. In one he lists the votes of party members on the question of where to locate winter quarters, while in the other he discusses the rationale for the final decision. In such circumstances the first entry is the draft while the finished version follows. When there might be confusion, I address the fact in notes, otherwise I am again silent.

Multiple entries for a single day by different writers presented another sort of problem. In this abridgment Lewis's entries (when available) take precedence over those of other writers in the party, then comes Clark, Ordway, Floyd, Gass, and Whitehouse. This order observes not only the relative military rank of the individuals, but also reflects the merits of their writing. However, when one person's writing is clearly superior in either content or style, I abandon the order and choose the best piece. Certainly, Gass's account of "the *fair sex* of the Missouri" on April 5, 1805, is the clear choice and takes priority over the writing of his comrades. Since Gass's entries are drawn from a version edited in 1807 by David McKeehan (the original journal has been lost), they stand in contrast to the rough writing of his fellow soldiers. Ordway was the most consistent journalist, having an entry for each day of the expedition, while Floyd's journal is brief due to his death early in the expedition, and Whitehouse's journal is in two parts, a truncated original and an incomplete contemporary copy. Whitehouse's multiple entries are handled in the same way as Clark's.

The design of the present work is intended to allow readers to negotiate the text without the clutter of unnecessary editorial impediments, while at the same time to supply aids that clarify and enhance the writers' words. In the end, it is the words of Lewis and Clark and their fellow diarists that people have found so compelling for almost two centuries. I hope that I have not cut too much or interfered too often.

MEMBERS OF THE PERMANENT PARTY

Those thirty-three persons who were members of the expedition party who left Fort Mandan in April 1805 and traveled to the Pacific and back:

Meriwether Lewis, captain
William Clark, captain
William E. Bratton, private
Jean Baptiste Charbonneau (the baby, "Pomp")
Toussaint Charbonneau, interpreter
John Collins, private
John Colter, private
Pierre Cruzatte, private
George Drouillard, interpreter
Joseph Field, private
Reubin Field, private
Robert Frazer, private
Patrick Gass, sergeant
George Gibson, private
Silas Goodrich, private
Hugh Hall, private
Thomas Proctor Howard, private
François Labiche, private
John Baptiste Lepage, private
Hugh McNeal, private
John Ordway, sergeant
John Potts, private
Nathaniel Hale Pryor, sergeant
Sacagawea, interpreter
George Shannon, private
John Shields, private
John B. Thompson, private
Peter Weiser, private
William Werner, private
Joseph Whitehouse, private
Alexander Hamilton Willard, private
Richard Windsor, private
York, Clark's slave

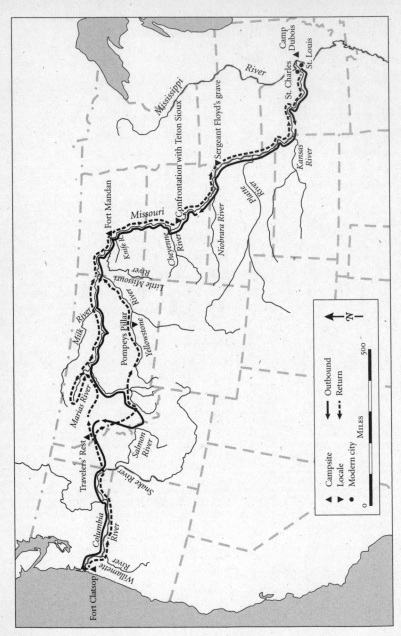

The Expedition's Route, May 14, 1804 – September 23, 1806

The Lewis and Clark Journals

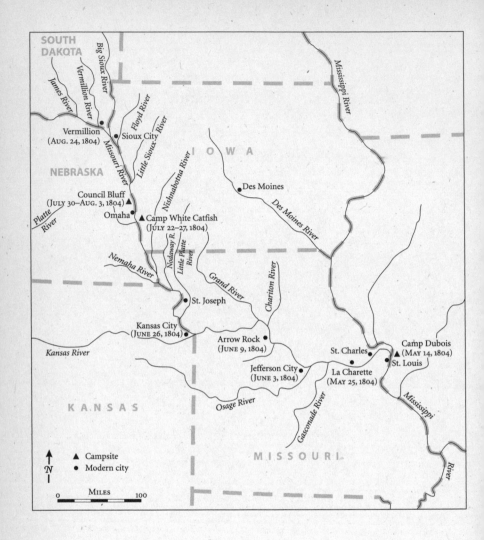

The Expedition's Route, May 14–August 24, 1804

CHAPTER 1

Expedition Underway

May 14 – August 24, 1804

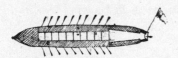

May 14, 1804

[CLARK] I Set out at 4 oClock P. M. in the presence of many of the Neighbouring inhabitents, and proceeded on under a jentle breaze up the Missourie to the upper Point of the 1st Island 4 Miles and Camped on the Island which is Situated Close on the right (or Starboard) Side, and opposit the mouth of a Small Creek called Cold water,[1] a heavy rain this afternoon. [Camped in St. Charles County, Missouri, near and across from Fort Bellefontaine, St. Louis County.]

May 15, 1804

[CLARK] Rained the greater part of the last night, and this morning untile 7 oClock — at 9 oClock Set out and proceeded on 9 miles   passed two Islands & incamped on the Starbd. Side at a Mr. Pipers Landing opposit an Island,[2] the Boat[3] run on Logs three times to day, owing her being too heavyly loaded a Sturn. [Camped below St. Charles, St. Charles County, Missouri.]

May 16, 1804

[CLARK] we arrived at St. Charles at 12 oClock   a number Spectators french & Indians flocked to the bank to See the party . . . I was invited to Dine with a Mr. Ducett this gentleman was once a merchant from Cana-

---

1. Coldwater Creek, St. Louis County, Missouri.

2. James Piper may have owned the landing across from the now lost Charbonnier Island along with his other holdings in the St. Charles district.

3. Meaning the keelboat.

dia, from misfortunes aded to the loss of a Cargo Sold to the late Judge Turner he has become Somewhat reduced.[4] [Camped at St. Charles.]

May 17, 1804
[CLARK] a fine Day   3 men[5] Confined for misconduct, I had a Court martial & punishment   Several Indians, who informed me that the Saukees[6] had lately Crossed to war against the Osage Nation. [Remained at St. Charles.]

[CLARK] George Drewyer arrive.

May 18, 1804
[CLARK] I had the loading in the Boat & perogue[7] examined and changed So as the Bow of each may be heavyer laded than the Stern . . . I Sent George Drewyer with a Letter to Capt Lewis   Two Keel Boats arrive from Kentucky to day loaded with whiskey Hats &c. [Remained at St. Charles.]

[WHITEHOUSE] passed the evening verry agreeable dancing with the french ladies.

May 19, 1804
[CLARK] I heard of my Brothers illness to day which has given me much Concurn.[8] [Remained at St. Charles.]

[CLARK] A Violent Wind last night from the W. S. W. accompanied with rain which lasted about three hours   Cleared away this morn'g at 8 oClock, I took receipt for the pay of the men up to the 1St. of Decr. next . . . I recve an invitation to a Ball, it is not in my power to go. George

4. François Duquette must have mentioned his loss to George Turner at dinner.

5. Collins, Hall, and Werner.

6. Sauk, or Sac, Indians.

7. Pirogues were usually large dugout canoes or open boats; the captains used the terms "pirogue" and "canoe" interchangeably.

8. It is not known which of Clark's brothers was ill.

Drewyer return from St Louis and brought 99 Dollars, he lost a letter from Cap Lewis to me, Seven Ladies visit me to day.

May 20, 1804
[LEWIS] The morning was fair, and the weather pleasent; at 10 oCk A M. agreably to an appointment of the preceeding day, I was joined by Capt. Stoddard, Lieuts. Milford & Worrell together with Messrs. A. Chouteau, C. Gratiot,[9] and many other respectable inhabitants of St. Louis, who had engaged to accompany me to the Vilage of St. Charles; accordingly at 12 Oclk after bidding an affectionate adieu to my Hostis, that excellent woman the spouse of Mr. Peter Chouteau, and some of my fair friends of St. Louis, we set forward to that village in order to join my friend companion and fellow labourer Capt. William Clark who had previously arrived at that place with the party destined for the discovery of the interior of the continent of North America. [Lewis arrived at St. Charles in the evening.]

[CLARK] I gave the party leave to go and hear a Sermon to day. [Remained at St. Charles.]

May 21, 1804
[CLARK] All the forepart of the Day Arranging our party and prcureing the different articles necessary for them at this place—   Dined with Mr. Ducett and *Set* out at half passed three oClock under three Cheers from the gentlemen on the bank and proceeded on. [Camped above St. Charles, on an island that apparently has since disappeared.]

May 22, 1804
[CLARK] Delay one hour for 4 french men who got liberty to return to arrange Some business they had forgotten in Town, at 6 oClock we proceeded on, passed Several Small farms on the bank, and a large creek on the Lbd. Side Called *Bonom*[10]   a Camp of Kickapoos on the St. Side

9. Amos Stoddard, Clarence Mulford, Stephen Worrell, René Auguste Chouteau, and Charles Gratiot.
10. Bonhomme Creek, St. Louis County, Missouri.

Those Indians told me Several days ago that they would Come on & hunt and by the time I got to their Camp they would have Some Provisions for us . . . Soon after we came too the Indians arrived with 4 Deer as a Present, for which we gave them two qts. of whiskey. [Camped near the mouth of Femme Osage River, St. Charles County, Missouri.]

May 23, 1804

[CLARK] ran on a Log and detained one hour, proceeded the Course of Last night 2 Miles to the mouth of a Creek on the Stbd. Side Called Osage Womans R,[11] about 30 yds. wide . . . (on this Creek 30 or 40 famlys are Settled,[)] Crossed to the Settlemt. and took in R & Jo: Fields who had been Sent to purchase Corn & Butter &c. many people Came to See us, we passed a large *Cave* on the Lbd. Side about 120 feet wide 40 feet Deep & 20 feet high many different immages are Painted on the Rock at this place. the Inds & French pay omage. many nams are wrote on the rock, Stoped about one mile above for Capt Lewis who had assended the Clifts which is at the Said Cave 300 fee[t] high, hanging over the Water . . . Capt. Lewis near falling from the Pencelia of rocks 300 feet, he caught at 20 foot.[12] [Camped in either St. Charles or Franklin County, Missouri, above Tavern Creek.]

[WHITEHOUSE] passed some Plantations, which is called Boons settlement lying on the North side of the River. This settlement was made by Colonel Daniel Boone, the person who first discovrer'd Kentucky, & who was residing at this place, with a number of his family and friends.

May 24, 1804

[CLARK] passed a Verry bad part of the River Called the Deavels race ground, this is where the Current Sets against Some projecting rocks for half a mile on the Labd. Side . . . we attempted to pass up under the Lbd. Bank which was falling in So fast that the evident danger obliged us to Cross between the Starbd. Side and a Sand bar in the middle of the river, we *hove* up near the head of the Sand bar, the Sand moveing & banking caused us to run on the Sand. The Swiftness of the Current wheeled the

11. Femme Osage Creek, St. Charles County, Missouri.
12. Lewis had his accident near Tavern Cave, Franklin County, Missouri.

boat, Broke our *Toe* rope, and was nearly over Setting the boat, all hand Jumped out on the upper Side and bore on that Side untill the Sand washed from under the boat and wheeled on the next bank   by the time She wheeled a 3rd Time got a rope fast to her Stern and by the means of Swimmers was Carred to Shore and when her Stern was down whilst in the act of Swinging a third time into Deep water near the Shore, we returned, to the Island where we Set out and assended under the Bank which I have just mentioned . . . all in Spirits. [Camped below Washington, Franklin County, Missouri.]

May 25, 1804

[CLARK] Camped at the mouth of a Creek called <*River a Chauritte*>,[13] above a Small french Village of 7 houses and as many families, Settled at this place to be convt. to hunt, & trade with the Indians, here we met with Mr. Louisell[14] imedeately down from the <*Seeeder*> [Cedar] Isld. Situated in the Countrey of the *Suxex*[15] 400 Leagues up   he gave us a good Deel of information   Some letters   he informed us that he Saw no Indians on the river below the *Poncrars*[16] . . . The people at this Village is pore, houses Small, they Sent us milk & eggs to eat. [Camped at La Charette, Warren County, Missouri.]

May 26, 1804

[LEWIS AND CLARK, DETACHMENT ORDERS] The Commanding Officers direct, that the three Squads under the command of Sergts. Floyd Ordway and Pryor heretofore forming two messes each, shall untill further orders constitute three messes only, the same being altered and organized as follows (viz) —

    1   *Sergt. Charles Floyd.*

    Privates:
    2   Hugh McNeal
    3   Patric Gass

13. Charette Creek
14. Régis Loisel was living at La Charette on Charette Creek.
15. Sioux Indians.
16. Ponca Indians.

	4	Reubin Fields (2)
+	5	John B Thompson
+	6	John Newman
	7	Richard Winsor
+		Francis Rivet &
	8	Joseph Fields (3)

| | 9 | *Sergt. John Ordway.* |

Privates.

	10	William Bratton (4)
	11	John Colter (5)
×	12	Moses B. Reed
	13	Alexander Willard
	14	William Warner
	15	Silas Goodrich
	16	John Potts &
	17	Hugh Hall

| | 18 | *Sergt. Nathaniel Pryor. (6)* |

Privates.

	19	George Gibson (7)
	20	George Shannon (8)
	21	John Shields (9)
	22	John Collins
	23	Joseph Whitehouse
	24	Peter Wiser
F	25	Peter Crusat &
F	26	Francis Labuche

The commanding officers further direct that the remainder of the detachmen shall form two messes; and that the same be constituted as follows. (viz) —

Patroon, Baptist Dechamps

Engages
Etienne Mabbauf

Paul Primaut
Charles Hébert
Baptist La Jeunesse
Peter Pinaut
Peter Roi &
Joseph Collin

1   *Corpl. Richard Warvington.*

Privates.
2   Robert Frasier
3   John Boleye
4   John Dame
5   Ebinezer Tuttle &
6   Isaac White

The Commanding officers further direct that the messes of Sergts. Floyd, Ordway and Pryor shall untill further orders form the crew of the Batteaux;[17] the Mess of the Patroon La Jeunesse will form the permanent crew of the red Perogue; Corpl. Warvington's mess forming that of the white perogue . . .

The posts and duties of the Sergts. shall be as follows (viz) — when the Batteaux is under way, one Sergt. shall be stationed at the helm, one in the center on the rear of the Starboard locker, and one at the bow. *The Sergt. at the helm*, shall steer the boat, and see that the baggage on the quarter-deck is properly arranged and stowed away in the most advantageous manner; to see that no cooking utensels or loos lumber of any kind is left on the deck to obstruct the passage between the burths — he will also attend to the compas when necessary.

The Sergt at the center will command the guard, manage the sails, see that the men at the oars do their duty; that they come on board at a proper season in the morning, and that the boat gets under way in due time; he will keep a good lookout for the mouths of all rivers, creeks, Islands and other remarkable places and shall immediately report the same to the commanding officers; he will attend to the issues of sperituous liquors; he

17. Occasional term for the party's keelboat.

shall regulate the halting of the batteaux through the day to give the men refreshment, and will also regulate the time of her departure taking care that not more time than is necessary shall be expended at each halt — it shall be his duty also to post a centinel on the bank, near the boat whenever we come too and halt in the course of the day, at the same time he will (acompanied by two his guard) reconnoiter the forrest arround the place of landing to the distance of at least one hundred paces.   when we come too for the purpose of encamping at night, the Sergt. of the guard shall post two centinels immediately on our landing; one of whom shal be posted near the boat, and the other at a convenient distance in rear of the encampment; at night the Sergt. must be always present with his guard, and he is positively forbidden to suffer any man of his guard to absent himself on any pretext whatever; he will at each relief through the night, accompanyed by the two men last off their posts, reconnoiter in every direction around the camp to the distance of at least one hundred and fifty paces, and also examine the situation of the boat and perogues, and see that they ly safe and free from the bank.

It shall be the duty of the *sergt. at the bow*, to keep a good look out for all danger which may approach, either of the enimy, or obstructions which may present themselves to passage of the boat; of the first he will notify the Sergt. at the center, who will communicate the information to the commanding officers, and of the second or obstructions to the boat he will notify the Sergt. at the helm; he will also report to the commanding officers through the Sergt. at the center all perogues boats canoes or other craft which he may discover in the river, and all hunting camps or parties of Indians in view of which we may pass.   he will at all times be provided with a seting pole and assist the bowsman in poling and managing the bow of the boat.   it will be his duty also to give and answer all signals, which may hereafter be established for the government of the perogues and parties on shore.

The Sergts. will on each morning before our departure relieve each other in the following manner — (viz) The Sergt. at the helm will parade the new guard, relieve the Sergt. and the old guard, and occupy the middle station in the boat; the Sergt. of the old guard will occupy the station at the bow, and the Sergt. who had been stationed the preceeding day at the bow will place himself at the helm. The sergts. in addition to those duties are directed each to keep a seperate journal from day today of all passing occurences, and such other observations on the country &c. as shall appear to them worthy of notice —

The Sergts. are relieved and exempt from all labour of making fires, pitching tents or cooking, and will direct and make the men of their several messes perform an equal propotion of those duties.

The guard shall hereafter consist of one sergeant and six privates & engages.

Patroon, Dechamp, Copl. Warvington, and *George Drewyer*, are exempt from guad duty; the two former will attend particularly to their perogues at all times, and see that their lading is in good order, and that the same is kept perfectly free from rain or other moisture; the latter will perform certain duties on shore which will be assigned him from time to time: all other soldiers and engaged men of whatever discription must perform their regular tour of guad duty . . .

Sergt. John Ordway will continue to issue the provisions and make the detales for guard or other duty. The day after tomorrow lyed corn and grece will be issued to the party, the next day Poark and flour, and the day following indian meal and poark; and in conformity to that ratiene provisions will continue to be issued to the party untill further orders. should any of the messes prefer indian meal to flour they may recieve it accordingly — no poark is to be issued when we have fresh meat on hand.

Labuche and Crusat will man the larboard bow oar alternately, and the one not engaged at the oar will attend as the Bowsman, and when the attention of both these persons is necessary at the bow, their oar is to be maned by any idle hand on board. [Camped on an island opposite Hermann, Gasconade County, Missouri.]

May 27, 1804
[CLARK] as we were pushing off this Morning two Canoos Loaded with fur &c. Came to from the Mahars[18] nation, which place they had left two months, at about 10 oClock 4 *Cajaux*[19] or rafts loaded with furs and pel-

18. Omaha Indians.
19. *Cajeu* (plural *cajeux*), usually two canoes lashed together.

Monday May 14th 1804

Rained the fore part of the day I determined to go as far as St. Charles a french Village 7 Leags. up the Missourie, and wait at that place untile Capt. Lewis Could finish the business in which he was obliged to attend to at St. Louis and join me by land from that place 24 Miles; by this movement I calculated that, if any alterations in the loading) of the Vestles or other Changes necessary that they) might be made at St. Charles. I Set out at 4 oClock P.M. in the presence of many of the neighbouring inhabitents, and proceeded on under a jentle breeze up the Missourie to the upper Point of the 1st Island 4 Miles

Journal entry of William Clark, May 14, 1804. Courtesy American Philosophical Society, Philadelphia, Pennsylvania

tres came too one from the *Paunees*,[20] the other from Grand Osage, they informed nothing of Consequence. [Camped at Gasconade River, Gasconade County, Missouri.]

May 29, 1804
[ORDWAY] One man Whitehouse lost hunting   Frenchman's pearogue Std. for him.[21] [Camped near the Osage-Gasconade county line, Missouri.]

June 1, 1804
[CLARK] this osages river Verry high, felled all the Trees in the point to Make observations   Sit up untill 12 oClock taken oservation this night. [Camped near the mouth of Osage River, near Osage-Cole county line, Missouri.]

[GASS] The two men[22] who went by land with the horses, came to us here: they represented the land they had passed through as the best they had ever seen, and the timber good, consisting chiefly of oak, ash, hickory, and black walnut.

June 2, 1804
[CLARK] from this pt. which Comds both rivers I had a delightfull prospect of the Missouries up & down, also the Osage R. up. George Drewyer & John Shields who we had Sent with the horses by Land on the N Side joined us this evening much worsted, they being absent Seven Days depending on their gun, the greater part of the time rain, they were obliged to raft or Swim many Creeks, those men gave a flattering account of the Countrey Commencing below the first hill on the N Side and extendg Parrelal with the river for 30 or 40 Ms. [Remained at Osage River.]

June 3, 1804
[CLARK] We made other Observations in the evening after the return of Capt Lewis from a walk of three or four ms. round . . . at the mouth of the

20. Pawnee Indians
21. Whitehouse was left behind while he was exploring a cave.
22. Drouillard and Shields. Clark, unlike Gass, has them returning on June 2.

Murow Creek I Saw much Sign of war parties of Inds. haveing Crossed from the mouth of this Creek. I have a bad Cold with a Sore throat. [Camped at the mouth of Moreau River, Cole County, Missouri.]

June 4, 1804
[CLARK] the Sergt. at the helm run under a bending Tree & broke the mast . . . I got out and walked on the L. Sd. thro a rush bottom for 1 Miles & a Short Distance thro: Nettles as high as my brest   assended a hill of about 170 foot to a place where the french report that Lead ore has been found, I saw no mineral of that description. [Camped in the vicinity of later Sugar Loaf Rock, Cole County, Missouri.]

[WHITEHOUSE] we branded Several trees.

June 5, 1804
[CLARK] at 11 oClock brought too a Small *Caissee* [cajeu] in which was two french men, from 80 Leagues up the Kansias R. where they wintered, and Cought a great quantity of Beaver, the greater part of which they lost by fire from the Praries, those men inform that the Kansas Nation are now out in the plains hunting Buffalow, they hunted last winter on this river   Passed a projecting rock on which was painted a figu[r]e and a Creek at 2 ms. above Called Little Manitou Creek[23] from the Painted rock . . . my Servent York Swam to the Sand bar to geather greens for our Dinner and returnd with a Sufficent quantity wild *Creases* or Teng grass . . . our Scout discovd. the fresh sign of about 10 Inds. I expect that those Indians are on their way to war against the Osages nation   proba- bly they are the Saukees. [Camped in Boone County, Missouri, across from Sandy Hook.]

June 6, 1804
[CLARK] Mended our Mast this morning &, Set out at 7 oClock under a jentle breise from S. E. by S . . . at 8 ms. passed the mouth of a Creek Called *Saline* or Salt R[24] on the L. Sd.   this River is about 30 yds. wide,

23. Moniteau Creek, near the Moniteau-Cole county line, Missouri.
24. Petite Saline Creek, entering the Missouri near the Cooper-Moniteau county line, Missouri.

and has So many Licks & Salt Springs on its banks that the Water of the Creek is Brackish . . . Some buffalow Sign to day   I am Still verry unwell with a Sore throat & head ake. [Camped downstream from Interstate Highway 70 highway, Boone County, Missouri.]

June 7, 1804
[CLARK] brackfast at the Mouth of a large Creek on the S. S. of 30 yds wide Called big Monetou[25] . . . a Short distance above the mouth of this Creek, is Several Courious Paintings and Carveing in the projecting rock of Limestone inlade with white red & blue flint, of a verry good quallity, the Indians have taken of this flint great quantities. We landed at this Inscription and found it a Den of rattle Snakes. [Camped at the mouth of Bonne Femme Creek, Howard County, Missouri, and below Booneville on the opposite side.]

June 8, 1804
[CLARK] passed the *Mine* River[26] at 9 ms.   this river is about 70 yards wide at its mouth and is Said to be navagable for Perogues 80 or 90 ms. . . . The french inform that Lead Ore has been found in defferent parts of this river . . . Capt. Lewis went out above the river & proceeded on one mile, finding the Countrey rich, the wedes & Vines So thick & high he came to the Boat . . . [Camped] about 4 ms. above Mine River   at this place I found Kanteens, Axs, Pumey [pumice] Stone & peltrey [pelts] hid & buried (I suppose by some hunters)   none of them (except the pumey Stone) was teched by one of our party. [Camped on later Arrow Rock Island near the Saline-Cooper county line, Missouri.]

June 9, 1804
[CLARK] we had like to have Stove our boat, in going round a Snag her Stern Struck a log under Water & She Swung round on the Snag, with her broad Side to the Current expd. to the Drifting timber, by the active exertions of our party we got her off in a fiew Mints. [Camped near Bluff Port, Howard County, Missouri.]

25. Moniteau Creek, meeting the Missouri at Rocheport, on the Howard-Boone county line, Missouri.
26. The Lamine River, reaching the Missouri in Cooper County, Missouri.

June 10, 1804

[CLARK] passed the two River of *Charletons* which mouth together,[27] above Some high land which has a great quantity of Stone Calculated for whetstons . . . I walked out three miles, found the prarie composed of good Land and plenty of water . . . they abound with Hasel[28] Grapes & a wild plumb of a Superior quallity, called the Osages Plumb[29] Grows on a bush the hight of a Hasel <and is three times the sise of other Plumbs,> and hang in great quantities on the bushes I Saw great numbers of Deer in the Praries . . . our party in high Spirits. [Camped about five miles above Chariton River, Saline County, Missouri.]

June 12, 1804

[CLARK] at 1 oClock we brought too two *Chaussies* one Loaded with furs & Pelteries, the other with Greece buffalow grease & tallow We purchased 300 lb. of Greese, and finding that old Mr. Durioun[30] was of the party we questioned him untill it was too late to Go further and Concluded to Camp for the night, those people inform nothing of much information Colcluded to take old Durioun back as fur as the Soux nation with a view to get some of their Chiefs to Visit the Presdt. of the United S. (This man being a verry Confidential friend of those people, he having resided with the nation 20 odd years) and to accompany them on. [Camped near the terminal point of Missouri Highway J, Chariton County.]

[WHITEHOUSE] Sent One of Our Men Belonging to the white pierouge back that Belongd. to Captn Stodders Company of Artilery.[31]

27. The Little Chariton River joins the Chariton a short distance above its mouth in Chariton County, Missouri.

28. Hazelnuts.

29. Possibly the wild goose plum.

30. Pierre Dorion Sr., a trader among the Yankton Sioux. The captains hired him for a time as an interpreter and emissary to the Sioux and other tribes.

31. Whitehouse is the only journalist to mention that a member of the party from Captain Amos Stoddard's artillery company, perhaps John Robertson, was sent back.

June 13, 1804

[CLARK] in the bend is a Prarie in which the Missouries Indians once lived and the Spot where 300 of them fell a Sacrifise to the fury of the *Saukees*   This nation (Missouries) once the most noumerous nation in this part of the Continent now reduced to about 80 f[ir]es. and that fiew under the protection of the Otteaus[32] on R Platt who themselves are declineing . . . We came too in the Mouth of Grand River on S. S. and Camped for the night, this River is from 80 to 100 yards wide at its Mouth and navagable for Perogues a great distance . . . Capt Lewis and my Self walked to the hill from the top of which we had a butifull prospect of Serounding Countrey   in the open Prarie we Caught a racoon. [Camped at the mouth of Grand River, Carroll-Chariton county line, Missouri.]

[GASS] This is as handsome a place as I ever saw in an uncultivated state.

June 14, 1804

[CLARK] we met a *Causseu* from the Pania[33] on the River Platt,[34] we detained 2 hours with a view of engageing one of the hands to go to the Pania nation with a View to get those people to meet us on the river . . . George Drewyer, gives the following act. of a Pond . . . he heard in this Pond a Snake makeing Goubleing Noises like a turkey.   he fired his gun & the noise was increased, he has heard the indians Mention This Species of Snake   one Frenchman give a Similar account. [Camped in Carroll County, Missouri, opposite Miami.]

June 15, 1804

[WHITEHOUSE] the party drank a Drachm [dram] of whisky and Roe on. [Camped in the southwestern tip of Saline County, Missouri.]

32. Otoe Indians.
33. Pawnee Indians.
34. The Platte River in Nebraska.

June 16, 1804

[CLARK] we came to on the S. S. in a Prarie at the place where Mr. Mackey lay down a old french fort, I could See no traces of a Settlement of any Kind.[35] in the evening I walked on the S. S. to see if any timber was Convt. to make Oars, which we were much in want of, I found Som indifferent timber . . . Camped in a bad place, the misquitoes and Ticks are noumerous & bad. [Camped in Carroll County, Missouri, opposite nearby Waverly.]

June 17, 1804

[CLARK] Sent out Sjt. Pryor and Some men to get ash timber for ores, and Set Some men to make a Toe Rope out of the Cords of a *Cable* which had been provided by Capt Lewis at Pitts burg for the Cable of the boat— George Drewyer our hunter and one man came in with 2 Deer & a Bear, also a young Horse, they had found in the Prarie, this horse has been in the Prarie a long time and is fat, I suppose he has been left by Some war party against the *Osage*, This is a Crossing place for the war partis against that nation from the *Saukees, Aiaouez*,[36] & Souix. The party is much aflicted with *Boils* and Several have the Decissentary, which I contribute to the water . . . The Ticks & Musquetors are verry troublesom. [Camped about one mile above the previous day's camp, Carroll County, Missouri.]

June 19, 1804

[ORDWAY] we Got Musquetoes bears[37] from Capt Lewis to sleep in. [Camped a few miles below Lexington, Lafayette County, Missouri.]

June 20, 1804

[CLARK] passed Som verry Swift water to day, I saw *Pelicans* to day on a Sand bar, my servant York nearly loseing an eye by a man throwing

35. Fort Orleans, founded by Etienne Véniard, Sieur de Bourgmont, in 1723 in Carroll County, Missouri. James Mackay made a trip up the Missouri in 1795 accompanied by John Thomas Evans. Mackay was at St. Louis during the time Lewis and Clark were at Camp Dubois and provided the captains a great deal of information and perhaps copies of Evans's maps of the Missouri, to which Clark may here refer.

36. Ioway Indians.

37. A mosquito net.

Sand into it . . . the party on Shore we have not Seen Since we passed Tiger R—[38] . . . we took Some Loner [lunar] observations, which detained us untill 1 oClock. [Camped a few miles below Wellington, Lafayette County, Missouri.]

June 21, 1804
[CLARK] after the Bows man Peter Crousat viewed The water on each Side of the Island which presented a most unfavourable prospect of Swift water over roleing Sands which rored like an immence falls, we Concluded to assend on the right Side, and with much dificuilty, with the assistance of a long Cord or Tow rope, & the *anchor* we got the Boat up with out any furthr dang. [damage] than Bracking a Cabbin window & loseing Some *oars* which were Swong under the windows . . . [The country] may be classed as follows.   viz: the low or over flown points or bottom land, of the groth of Cotton & Willow,[39] the 2nd or high bottom of rich furtile Soils of the groth of Cotton, Walnut, Som ash, Hack berry, Mulberry, Lynn & Sycamore.[40]   the third or high Lands risees gradually from the 2nd bottom (cauht whin it Coms to the river then from the river) about 80 or 100 foot roleing back Supplied with water the Small runs of (which losees themselves in the bottom land) and are covered with a variety of timber Such as Oake of different Kinds Blue ash, walnut[41] &c. [Camped in Lafayette County, Missouri, with Camden on the opposite shore.]

June 24, 1804
[CLARK] I joined the boat this morng at 8 oClock (I will only remark that dureing the time I lay on the band [bank] waiting for the boat, a large Snake Swam to the bank imediately under the Deer which was hanging over the water, and no great distance from it, I threw chunks and drove this Snake off Several times. I found that he was So determined on getting to the meet I was Compelld to Kill him, the part of the Deer which attracted this Snake I think was the milk from the bag of the Doe.) [Camped above Missouri City, Jackson County, Missouri.]

38. Crooked River, Ray County, Missouri.
39. Cottonwoods and willows.
40. Cottonwood, walnut, ash, hackberry, mulberry, linden, and sycamore trees.
41. Oak, ash, and walnut trees.

June 25, 1804
[CLARK] at 3 miles passed a Coal-mine, or Bank of Stone Coal,[42] on the South Side, this bank appears to Contain great quantity of fine Coal, the river being high prevented our Seeeing that contained in the Cliffs of the best quallity. [Camped opposite the town of Sugar Creek, Jackson County, Missouri.]

June 26, 1804
[CLARK] I observed a great number of *Parrot queets*[43] this evening. [Camped just above the mouth of the Kansas River, Wyandotte County, Kansas.]

June 27, 1804
[CLARK] we determin to delay at this Place three or four Days to make ob-servations & recruit the party . . . unloaded one Perogue, and turned her up to Dry with a view of repairing her after Completeing a Strong re-doubt or brest work frome one river to the other, of logs & Bushes Six feet high, The Countrey about the mouth of this river is verry fine on each Side . . . Measured The width of the Kansas River by an angle and made it 230 yds ¼ wide, it is wider above the mouth the Missouries at this place is about 500 yards wide. [Remained at the Kansas River.]

[ORDWAY] all the party out eairly this morning cutting the Timber off a cross the point and made a Hadge a cross of the Timber & bushes to an-swer as defence & made Room for Capts to take obser.

June 28, 1804
[CLARK] To Describe the most probable of the various accounts of this great river of the Kansas, would be too lengthy & uncertain to insert here, it heads with the river Del Norid[44] in the black Mountain[45] or ridge which Divides the waters of the Kansas *Del Nord*, & Callarado[46] & opp-

42. Coal banks are known in the eastern part of Jackson County, Missouri.
43. Carolina parakeets, now extinct.
44. Rio Grande.
45. Black Hills.
46. Colorado River.

soitly from those of the Missoureis (and not well assertaind)   This River recves its name from a nation which dwells at this time on its banks & 2 villages one about 20 Leagues & the other 40 Leagues up, those Indians are not verry noumerous at this time, reduced by war with their neigh-bours, &c.   they formerly liveid on the South banks of the Missouries 24 Leagues above this river in a open & butifull plain and were verry noumerous at the time the french first Settled the Illinois, I am told they are a fierce & warlike people, being badly Supplied with fire arms, be-come easily conquered by the Aiauway & Saukees who are better fur-nished with those materials of war, This nation is now out in the plains hunting the Buffalow . . . a butifull place for a fort, good landing place. [Remained at the Kansas River.]

[ORDWAY] I went out hunting 2½ miles & passed a fine Spring Running from under the hills   I drank hearty of the water & found it the best & coolest I have seen in the country.

June 29, 1804
[CLARK] a Court martial will Set this day at 11 oClock, to Consist of five members, for the trial of *John Collins* and *Hugh Hall*, Confined on Charges exhibited against them by Sergeant Floyd, agreeable to the ar-ticles of War.

Detail for the Court

Sergt Nat. Pryor presd.
2 John Colter
3 John Newmon
4 Pat. Gass   } mbs.
1. J. B. Thompson
John Potts to act as Judge advocate.

    The Court Convened agreeable to order and proceeded to the trial of the Prisoners Viz John Collins Charged "with getting drunk on his post this morning out of whiskey put under his Charge as a Sentinal and for Suffering *Hugh Hall* to draw whiskey out of the Said Barrel intended for the party." To this Charge the prisoner plead *not guilty*.

The Court after mature deliveration on the evidence abduced &c. are of oppinion that the prisoner is *Guilty* of the Charge exibited against him, and do therefore Sentence him to recive *one hundred Lashes on his bear Back.*

Hugh Hall was brought with ["]takeing whiskey out of a Keg this morning which whiskey was Stored on the Bank (and under the Charge of the guard) Contrary to all order, rule, or regulation." To this Charge the prisoner "Pleades Guilty."

The Court find the prisoner guilty and Sentence him to receive *fifty* Lashes on his bear Back.

The Commanding Officers approve of the Sentence of the Court and orders that the Punishment take place at half past three this evening, at which time the party will Parrade for inspection. [Camped in the vicinity of Riverside, Platte County, Missouri.]

[FLOYD] armes and amunition enspected   all in Good order.

June 30, 1804

[CLARK] a verry large wolf[47] Came to the bank and looked at us this morning, passd the mouth of a Small river 10 ms. above the *Kanseis* Called by the french Petite River Platte[48] (or Shoal river) from the number of falls in it . . . came to at 12 oClock & rested three hours, the [sun or day?] being hot the men becom verry feeble, Farnsts. Thermometer at 3 oClock Stood at 96° above 0 . . . Broke our mast. [Camped in the vicinity of Walcott, Wyandotte County, Kansas.]

July 1, 1804

[CLARK] last night one of the Sentinals Chang'd [challenged] either a man or Beast, which run off, all prepared for action . . . one of our French hands tels me that the French intended to Settle here once & brought their Cows and put them on those Islands,[49] Mr Mackey Says the first village of the Kanseis was a little above this Island & made use of as fields,

47. Probably a gray wolf.
48. Little Platte River, which joins the Missouri in Platte County, Missouri.
49. Perhaps Leavenworth Island, Leavenworth County, Kansas.

no trace of anything of that Kind remains to be Seen on the Isds. [Camped opposite Leavenworth, Leavenworth County, Kansas.]

July 2, 1804
[CLARK] we Camped after dark on the S. S. opposit the 1st old Village of the Kanzas which was Situated in a Valley between two points of high land . . . The french formerly had a Fort at this place, to protect the trade of this nation,[50] the Situation appears to be a verry elligable one for a Town . . . We made a Mast of Cotton wood. [Camped near Weston, Platte County, Missouri.]

[ORDWAY] Our flanking party did not Join us at night.

July 4, 1804
[CLARK] pass a Creek on the L. S. about 15 yards wide cuming out of an extensive Prarie as this Creek has no name, and this day is the 4th of July, we name this Independance us. Creek[51] . . .

The Plains of this countrey are covered with a Leek Green Grass, well calculated for the sweetest and most norushing hay—interspersed with Cops of trees, Spreding ther lofty branchs over Pools Springs or Brooks of fine water. Groops of Shrubs covered with the most delicious froot is to be seen in every direction, and nature appears to have exerted herself to butify the Senery by the variety of flours Delicately and highly flavered raised above the Grass, which Strikes & profumes the Sensation, and amuses the mind throws it into Conjecterng the cause of So magnificent a Senerey in a Country thus Situated far removed from the Sivilised world to be enjoyed by nothing but the Buffalo Elk Deer & Bear in which it abounds & Savage Indians. [Camped near Doniphan, Doniphan County, Kansas.]

[FLOYD] a Snake Bit Jo. Fieldes on the Side of the foot which Sweled much apply Barks.[52]

---

50. The French Fort de Cavagnial was occupied from 1744 to 1764; it was about three miles north of Fort Leavenworth, Leavenworth County.

51. Independence Creek, on the Atchison-Doniphan county line, Kansas.

52. Joseph Field may have had a poultice of Peruvian bark.

[GASS] We fired a swivel at sunrise in honour of the day . . . and saluted the departing day with another gun.

July 5, 1804

[CLARK] proceeded on near the bank where the old village Stood for two miles . . . The Origan of this old village is uncertain   M. de Bourgmont a French officer who Comdd. a fort near the Town of the Missouris in about the year 1724 and in July of the Same year he visited this Village   at that time the nation was noumerous & well desposed towards the French . . . Those people must have been verry noumerous at that time as Mr. De B: was accompanied by 300 Warriers, 500 young people & 300 Dogs of burthen out of this Village[53]   The Cause of Those Indians movéing over to the Kanzis river I have never lernt . . . I observe great quantities of Summer & fall Grapes, Berries & Wild roases on the banks — Deer is not so plenty as usual, great Deel of Elk Sign. [Camped a few miles northeast of Doniphan, Doniphan County, Kansas.]

July 6, 1804

[CLARK] (worthy of remark that the water of this river or Some other Cause, I think that the most Probable throws out a greater preposn. of Swet than I could Suppose Could pass thro: the humane body   Those men that do not work at all will wet a Shirt in a Few minits & those who work, the Swet will run off in Streams). [Camped near St. Joseph, Buchanan County, Missouri, but it is unclear whether in Kansas or Missouri.]

[ORDWAY] a whiper will perched on the Boat for a short time.

July 7, 1804

[CLARK] those Praries on the river has verry much the appeerence of farms from the river Divided by narrow Strips of wood land, which wood land is Situatd. on the runs leading to the river . . . Saw a large rat on the bank. Killed a Wolf . . . one man verry Sick, Struck with the Sun, Capt.

53. Bourgmont first visited the Missouria Indians in 1714 and lived with the Missourias and Osages for a time; he made numerous trips on the Missouri.

Lewis bled him & gave Niter which has revived him much.[54] [Camped upstream from St. Joseph, Buchanan County, Missouri, but perhaps on the Kansas side in Doniphan County.]

[ORDWAY] I went on Shore with the Horses in the afternoon In the North Side   crossed a Creek 2 miles up in the evening.   as this Creek is without name & my Describeing it to my Capt. He named it Ordway Creek.[55]

[WHITEHOUSE] Six Miles from whare we Started Came to the most beautifull prarie On the E. S. Whare Nature formd Some battryes And Read Outs [redoubts].

July 8, 1804
[LEWIS AND CLARK, DETACHMENT ORDERS] The Commanding Officers Do appoint the following persons to *recieve, cook*, and *take charges of* the provisions which may from time to time be issued to their respective messes, (viz) John B. Thompson to Sergt. Floyd's mess, William Warner to Sergt. Ordway's mess, and John Collins to Sergt. Pryor's Mess. These *Superintendants of Provision*, are held immediately responsible to the commanding Officers for a judicious consumption of the provision which they recieve; they are to cook the same for their several messes in due time, and in such manner as is most wholesome and best calculated to afford the greatest proportion of nutriment; in their mode of cooking they are to exercise their own judgment; they shall allso point out what part, and what proportion of the mess provisions are to be consumed at each stated meal (i. e.) morning, noon and night; nor is any man at any time to take or consume any part of the mess provisions without the privity, knowledge and consent of the Superintendant. The superintendant is also held responsible for all the cooking eutensels of his mess.   in consideration of the duties imposed by this order on Thomp-

54. Bleeding was the standard medical practice of the day; potassium nitrate ("Niter") was administered to increase perspiration and urine and reduce fevers.
55. Perhaps Mace Creek, north of the Andrew-Buchanan county line, Missouri.

son, Warner, and Collins, they will in future be exempt from guard duty, tho' they will still be held on the royster for that duty, and their regular tour—shall be performed by some one of their rispective messes; they are exempted also from pitching the tents of the mess, collecting fire- wood, and forks poles &c. for cooking and drying such fresh meat as may be furnished them; those duties are to be also performed by the other members of the mess. [Camped near the mouth of Nodaway River, An- drew County, Missouri.]

July 9, 1804
[CLARK] Camped at a point on the L. S. opposit the head of the Island, our party was incamped on the Opposit Side, their not answering our Signals Caused us to Suspect the persons Camped opposit to us was a war party of Soux, we fired the Bow piece to alarm the party on Shore, alled prepared to oppose if attacted. [Camped near the present town of Iowa Point, Doniphan County, Kansas.]

July 10, 1804
[CLARK] Crossd the river with a view to See who the party was that Camped on the other Side, we Soon discovered them to be our men . . . The men of the party getting better, but much fatigued. [Camped near the Nebraska-Kansas border, but on the opposite side in Holt County, Missouri.]

July 11, 1804
[CLARK] I joined the party on a large Sand Island imediately opposit the mouth os <*Ne Ma haw* River>,[56] at which place they had Camped, this Island is Sand about half of it Covered with Small Willows of two differ- ent Kinds, one Narrow & the other a Broad Leaf.[57] [Camped in Holt County, Missouri, opposite the mouth of the Big Nemaha River, which enters the Missouri River on the Nebraska side, just above the Nebraska- Kansas state line.]

56. Big Nemaha River.
57. Probably sandbar willow ("narrow") and peach-leaved willow ("broad leaf").

July 12, 1804

[CLARK] Concluded to Delay here to day with a view of takeing equal altitudes & makeing observations[58] as well as refreshing our men who are much fatigued— after an early Brackfast I with five men in a Perogue assended the River *Ne-Ma-haw* about 2 miles to the mouth of a Small Creek[59] on the Lower Side, here I got out of the Perogue, after going to Several Small Mounds in a leavel plain, I assended a hill on the Lower Side, on this hill Several Artificial Mounds[60] were raised, from the top of the highest of those Mounds I had an extensive view of the Serounding Plains, which afforded one of the most pleasing prospects I ever beheld, under me a Butifull River of Clear water of about 80 yards wide Meandering thro: a leavel and extensive Meadow, as far as I could See, the prospect Much enlivened by the fine Trees & Srubs which is bordering the bank of the river, and the Creeks & runs falling into it. The bottom land is covered with Grass[61] of about 4½ feet high, and appears as leavel as a Smoth Surfice, the <2 bottom> is also covered with Grass and rich weeds[62] & flours, interspersed with Copses of the Osage Plumb. on the riseing lands, Small groves of trees are Seen, with a numbers of Grapes and a Wild Cherry resembling the Common Wild Cherry, only larger and grows on a Small bush on the tops of those hills in every derection. I observed artifical mounds (or as I may more Justly term Graves) which to me is a Strong indication of this Country being once Thickly Settled. (The Indians of the Missouris Still Keep up the Custom of Burrying their dead on high ground) . . . on a Sandstone Bluff about ¼ of a mile from its mouth on the Lower Side I observed Some Indian marks, went to the rock which jucted over the water and marked my name & the day of the month & year. [Remained in camp opposite the Big Nemaha River.]

58. Lewis took "equal altitudes" by aiming his sextant at the sun in the morning and locking its position. In the afternoon he would sight west until the sun reached the previously locked position of the instrument. He then averaged the two recorded times (from multiple sightings in each instance) in order to obtain local apparent noon and set his chronometer accordingly.

59. Probably Roys Creek, Richardson County, Nebraska.

60. Part of a late prehistoric Oneota village, the Leary site.

61. May be prairie cordgrass, big bluestem, and other tall grasses.

62. Probably richweed.

[LEWIS AND CLARK] Capt. M. Lewis & W. Clark constituted themselves a Court martial for the trial of Such prisoners as are *Guilty* of *Capatol Crimes*, and under the rules and articles of *War* punishable by *Death*. *Alexander Willard* was brought foward Charged with "*Lying down and Sleeping on his post whilst a Sentinal, on the night* of the 11th. Instant" (by John Ordway Sergeant of the Guard)— To this Charge the prisoner pleads. *Guilty* of *Lying Down*, and *not Guilty, of Going to Sleep*. The Court after Duly Considering the evidence aduced, are of oppinion that the *Prisoner* Alexdn. Willard is guilty of every part of the Charge exhibited against him. it being a breach of the *rules* and articles of *War* (as well as tending to the probable distruction of the party) do *Sentence* him to receive *One hundred lashes on his bear back, at four different times in equal propation*. and order that the punishment Commence this evening at Sunset, and Continue to be inflicted, (by the Guard) every evening untill Completed.

July 13, 1804
[CLARK] My notes of the 13th of July by a Most unfortunate accident blew over Board in a Storm in the morning of the 14th obliges me to refur to the Journals of Serjeants, and my own recollection [of] the accurrences Courses Distance &c. of that day. [Camped in eastern Richardson County, Nebraska.]

July 14, 1804
[CLARK] The Storm which passd over an open Plain from the N. E. Struck the our boat on the Starbd. quarter, and would have thrown her up on the Sand Island dashed to peces in an Instant, had not the party leeped out on the Leward Side and kept her off with the assistance of the .ancker & Cable, untill the *Storm* was over, the waves Dashed over her windward Side and She must have filled with water if the Lockers which is covered with Tarpoling & Threw of[f] the water & prevented any quantity Getting into Bilge of the Boat   In this Situation we continued about 40 Minits. when the Storm Sudenly Seased and the river become Instancetaniously as Smoth as Glass . . . passed a Small Tradeing fort on the S. S. where, Mr. Bennet[63] of St. Louis Traded with the Otteaus & Panies

63. Probably François M. Benoit.

two years . . . on the S. S. a large Creek coms into the river Called by the *Maha's* Indians *Neesh-nah-ba-to-na*[64] . . . Several men unwell with *Boils, Fel[o]ns,* &c. [Camped near the Nemaha-Richardson county line, Nebraska, and near the mouth of the Nishnabotna River coming in from the other side.]

July 15, 1804
[LEWIS] This evening I discovered that my Chronometer had stoped, nor can I assign any cause for this accedent; she had been wound up the preceding noon as usual. This is the third instance in which this instrument has stopt in a similar manner since she has been in my possession, tho' the fi[r]st only since our departure from the River Dubois . . . In consequence of the chronometer's having thus accedentally stoped, I determined to come too at the first convenient place and make such observations as were necessary to ascertain her error, establish the Latitude & Longitude, and determine the variation of the nedle, in order to fix a *second point of departure.* [Camped in Nemaha County, Nebraska, somewhat above the town of Nemaha.]

July 16, 1804
[LEWIS] I now set the Chronometer as near noon as this observation would enable me. [Camped in either Nemaha County, Nebraska, or Atchison County, Missouri, a few miles northeast of Peru, Nebraska.]

[CLARK] This Prarie I call *Ball pated Prarie*,[65] from a range of Ball Hills[66] parrelel to the river & at from 3 to 6 miles distant from it.

July 17, 1804
[CLARK] We Concluded lay by at this place to day to fix the Lattitude & Longitude of this place to Correct the cromometer run down Sunday. [Remained in camp northeast of Peru, Nebraska.]

64. The Nishnabotna River, entering the Missouri near the Atchison-Holt county line, Missouri.
65. Open prairies on the Missouri-Iowa state line and north along the Iowa side of the Missouri River.
66. Loess hills with prairie vegetation.

July 18, 1804
[CLARK] but little timber is to be Seen except in the Low points on Islands
& on Creeks, the Groth of timber is generally cotton Mulberry Elm Syco-
more &c. [Camped a little below Nebraska City, Otoe County, Nebraska.]

[FLOYD] Saw a Dog on the Bank Which we Sepose to be Indians   had ben
Lost   this is the first Sine of Indians we have Saw.

July 19, 1804
[CLARK] afte[r] breakfast which was on a rosted Ribs of a Deer a little and
a little Coffee I walked on Shore . . . Came Suddenly into an open and
bound less Prarie, I Say bound less because I could not See the extent of
the plain in any Derection, the timber appeared to be confined to the
River Creeks & Small branches, this Prarie was Covered with grass about
18 Inches or 2 feat high and contained little of any thing else, except as before mentioned on the River Creeks &c, This prospect was So Sudden &
entertaining that I forgot the object of my prosute [pursuit] and turned
my attention to the Variety which presented themselves to my view.
[Camped apparently in Fremont County, Iowa, two to three miles upstream and opposite Nebraska City, Otoe County, Nebraska.]

[ORDWAY] we gethered a quantity of cherries at noon time & put in to the
Whisky barrel[67]   G. Drewyer Joined us with 2 Deer this evening. Bratton
also.   he found Callimous opposite where we camped & a large quantity.
(Sweet flag we call it).

July 20, 1804
[CLARK] George Drewyer Sick . . . Bratten Swam the river to get his gun
& Clothes left last night . . . passed the mouth of *l'Eau que pleure* the
English of which is *the water which Cry's*[68] . . . I killed an emence large

67. The enlisted men all mention putting the cherries, probably choke cherries, in the
whiskey barrel.
68. Weeping Water Creek, entering the Missouri in Otoe County, Nebraska.

yellow Wolf.[69] [Camped in Cass County, Nebraska, a little above Spring Creek.]

[CLARK] The Soil of Those Praries appears rich but much Parched with the frequent fires.

July 21, 1804
[LEWIS] the particles of [the Platte River's][70] sand being remarkably small and light it is easily boied up and is hurried by this impetuous torrent in large masses from place to place in with irristable forse, collecting and forming sandbars in the course of a few hours which as suddingly disapated to form others and give place perhaps to the deepest channel of the river. where it enters the Missouri it's superior force changes and directs the courant of that river against it's northern bank where it is compressed within a channel less than one third of the width it had just before occupyed. it dose not furnish the missouri with it's colouring matter as has been asserted by some, but it throws into it immence quantities of sand and gives a celerity to it's courant of which it abates but little untill it's junction with the Mississippy. the water of this river is turbid at all seasons of the year but is by no means as much so as that of the Missourie. The sediment it deposits, consists of very fine particles of white sand while that of the Missoury is composed principally of a dark rich loam — in much greater quantity. [Camped in Sarpy County, a little above the mouth of Papillion Creek.]

[CLARK] Capt Lewis and My Self with 6 men in a perogue went up this Great river Plate about 1 miles, found the Current verry rapid roleing over Sands, passing through different Channels none of them more than five or Six feet deep, about 600 yards Wide at the mouth — I am told by one of our Party who wintered two winters on This river that "it is much wider above, and does not rise more than five or Six feet."

69. An extinct subspecies of the gray wolf of a yellow hue.

70. The Platte River, joining the Missouri between Cass and Sarpy Counties, Nebraska.

[GASS] At one we came to the great river Platte, or shallow river, which comes in on the south side, and at the mouth is three quarters of a mile broad. The land is flat about the confluence. Up this river live three nations of Indians, the Otos, Panis, and Loo[p]s, or Wolf Indians.[71]

July 22, 1804
[CLARK] This being a good Situation and much nearer the Otteaus town than the Mouth of the Platt, we concluded to delay at this place a fiew days and Send for Some of the Chiefs of that nation to let them Know of the Change of Government, The wishes of our Government to Cultivate friendship with them, the Objects of our journy and to present them with a flag and Some Small presents. [Camped at the party's Camp White Catfish, near the Mills-Pottawattamie county line, Iowa, and opposite Bellevue, Sarpy County, Nebraska, where the Corps remained until July 27.]

July 23, 1804
[CLARK] at 11 oClock Sent off George Drewyer & *Peter Crousett* with Some tobacco to invite the Otteaus if at their town and Panies if they Saw them to Come and talk with us at our Camp &c. (at this Season the Indians on this river are in the Praries Hunting the Buffalow but from Some Signs of hunters near this place & the Plains being on fire near their towns induce a belief that they this nation have returned to get Some Green Corn or rosting Ears)   raised a flag Staff Sund & Dryed our provisions &c. I commence Coppying a map of the river below to Send to the P[resident] U S . . . one man with a tumer on his breast. [Remained at Camp White Catfish.]

[GASS] Our people were all busily engaged in hunting, making oars, dressing skins, and airing our stores, provisions, and baggage. We killed two deer and caught two beaver. Beaver appear plenty in this part of the country.

71. The Skiri band of Pawnees.

July 24, 1804
[CLARK] I am much engaged drawing off a map, Capt. Lewis also much engaged in prepareing Papers to Send back by a pirogue — Which we intended to Send back from the river Plate — observations at this place makes the *Lattitude* 41° 3′ 19″ North [72] This evening Guthrege [Goodrich] Cought a *white Catfish*. [Remained at Camp White Catfish.]

[FLOYD] Histed ouer Collars in the morning for the Reseptions of Indians who we expected Hear   when the Rain and wind Came So that we wase forst to take it down.

July 25, 1804

[CLARK] at 2 oClock *Drewyer & Peter* [Cruzatte] returned from the *Otteaus* Village; and informs that no Indians were at their towns, They Saw Some fresh Signs of a Small party but Could not find them.   in their rout to the Towns (Which is about 18 miles West) they passed thro a open Prarie Crossed papillion or Butterfly Creek [73] and a Small butifull river which run into the Platt a little below the Town Called *Corne de charf*. [74] [Remained at Camp White Catfish.]

[FLOYD] Continued Hear as the Capts is not Don there Riting.

July 26, 1804
[CLARK] the wind blustering and hard from the South all day which blowed the Clouds of Sand in Such a manner that I could not complete my p[l]an in the tent, the Boat roled in Such a manner that I could do nothing in that, I was Compessed to go to the woods and Combat with the Musqutors, I opened the Tumer of a man on the left breast, which discharged half a point [pint?]. [Remained at Camp White Catfish.]

72. The approximate latitude of Camp White Catfish is 41° 10′ 0″ N.
73. Papillion Creek, reaching the Missouri in Sarpy County, Nebraska.
74. Elkhorn River, entering the Platte in Sarpy County.

July 28, 1804
[CLARK] G Drewyer brought in a *Missourie Indian* which he met with hunting in the Prarie This Indian is one of the fiew remaining of that nation, & lives with the Otteauz, his Camp about 4 miles from the river, he informs that the "great gangue" of the nation were hunting the Buffalow in the Plains. h[i]s party was Small Consisting only of about 20 Lodges. [Camped north of Council Bluffs, Pottawattamie County, Iowa.]

July 29, 1804
[CLARK] Sent a french man *la Liberty* with the Indian to Otteaze Camp to invite the Indians to meet us on the river above. [Camped in Pottawattamie County, Iowa, somewhat above the Washington-Douglas county line, Nebraska, on the opposite side.]

[ORDWAY] Willard Sent back to last nights Camp for his Tommahawk, which he left we Delayed about 2 hours. Willard lost his rifle in a large Creek Called Boyer.[75]

[FLOYD] the Reasen this man Gives of His being with So Small a party is that He Has not Got Horses to Go in the Large praries after the Buflows but Stayes about the Town and River to Hunte the Elke to Seporte thare famileys.

July 30, 1804
[LEWIS] this day Joseph Fields killed a *Braro*[76] as it is called by the French *engáges*. this is a singular anamal not common to any part of the United States. it's weight is sixteen pounds. it is a carniverous anamal. on both sides of the upper jaw is fexed one long and sharp canine tooth. it's eye are small black and piercing. [Camped near Fort Calhoun, Washington County, Nebraska, the party's Council Bluff.]

[CLARK] Capt. Lewis and my Self walked in the Prarie on the top of the Bluff and observed the most butifull prospects imagionable, this Prarie is

75. Boyer River, joining the Missouri in Pottawattamie County, Iowa.
76. A badger.

Covered with grass about 10 or 12 Inch high, (Land rich)   rises about ½ a mile back Something higher and is a Plain as fur as Can be Seen, under those high Lands next the river is butifull Bottom interspersed with Groves of timber, the River may be Seen for a great Distance both above & below meandering thro: the plains between two ranges of High land which appear to be from 4 to 20 ms. apart, each bend of the river forming a point which Contains tall timber, principally Willow Cotton wood some Mulberry elm Sycamore & ash.   the groves Contain walnut coffeenut[77] & Oake in addition & Hickory & Lynn.

[CLARK] everything in prime order.   men in high Spirits.

July 31, 1804
[FLOYD] I am verry Sick and Has ben for Somtime but have Recoverd my helth again. [Remained at the party's Council Bluff.]

August 1, 1804
[CLARK] This being my birth day I order'd a Saddle of fat Vennison, an Elk fleece & a Bevertail to be cooked and a Desert of Cheries, Plumbs, Raspberries Currents and grapes of a Supr. quallity. The Indians not yet arrived.   a Cool fine eveninge   Musquetors verry troublesom, the Praries Contain Cheres, Apple, Grapes, Currents, Rasp burry, Gooseberris Hastlenuts and a great Variety of Plants & flours not Common to the U S. What a field for a Botents [botanist] and a natirless [naturalist]. [Remained at the party's Council Bluff.]

August 2, 1804
[CLARK] at Sunset Mr. *Fairfong* and a pt. of Otteau & Missourie Nation Came to Camp, among those Indians 6 were Chiefs, the principal Chiefs Capt. Lewis & myself met those Indians & informed them we were glad to See them, and would Speak to them tomorrow, Sent them Som rosted meat Pork flour & meal, in return they Sent us Water millions.   [every?]

77. Kentucky coffee tree.

man on his Guard & ready for any thing. [Remained at the party's Council Bluff.]

[FLOYD] the Indianes Came whare we had expected thay fired meney Guns when thay Came in Site of us and we ansered them withe the Cannon.

[WHITEHOUSE] They [Otoes and Missourias] are a handsome stout well made set of Indians & have good open Countenances, and are of a light brown colour, and have long black hair, which they do wear without cutting; and they all use paint in order to compleat their dress.

August 3, 1804
[CLARK] after Brackfast we Collected those Indians under an orning of our Main Sail, in presence of our Party paraded & Delivered a long Speech to them expressive of our journey the wirkes of our Government, Some advice to them and Directions how They were to Conduct themselves, the princapal Chief for the nation being absente we sent him the Speech *flag* Meadel & Some Cloathes. after hering what they had to say Delivered a medal of Second Grade to one for the Ottos & and one for the Missourie present and 4 medals of a third Grade to the inferior Chief two for each tribe. Those two parts of nations, Ottos & Missouries now residing together is about 250 men are the Ottoes Composeing ⅔d and Missourie ⅓ part . . . Those Chiefs all Delivered a Speech acknowledgeing Their approbation to the Speech and promissing to prosue the advice & Derictions given them that they wer happy to find that they had fathers which might be depended on &c. We gave them a Cannister of Powder and a Bottle of whiskey and delivered a few presents to the whole after giveing a *Br: Cth*: [breech cloth] Some Paint guartering[78] & a Meadele to those we *made* Cheifs after Capt Lewis's Shooting the air gun a feiw Shots (which astonished those nativs) we Set out and proceeded on five miles . . . The man *Liberty* whome we Sent for the Ottoes has not Come up. [Camped in either Harrison County, Iowa, or Washington County, Nebraska, some miles south of Blair, Nebraska.]

78. Cloth used for making garters.

[WHITEHOUSE] the Indians Beheavd. well while Incampd. Neer our party.

August 4, 1804
[CLARK] proceeded on . . . the Banks washing away & trees falling in constantly for 1 mile, abov this place is the remains of an old Tradeing establishment L. S. where Petr. Crusett one of our hands Stayed two years & traded with the *Mahars* . . . *Reed* a man who went back to Camp for his knife has not joined us. [Camped in either Washington County, Nebraska, or Harrison County, Iowa, northeast of Blair, Nebraska.]

August 5, 1804
[LEWIS] Killed a serpent[79] on the bank of the river adjoining a large prarie.

	F	Inch
Length from nose to tail	5	2
Circumpherence in largest part —		4½
Number of scuta on belly — 221		
Do. on Tale — 53		

No pison teeth therefore think him perfectly innocent — eyes, center black with a border of pale brown yellow Colour of skin on head yellowish green with black specks on the extremity of the scuta which are pointed or triangular   colour of back, transverse stripes of black and dark brown of an inch in width, succeeded by a yellowish brown of half that width — the end of the tale hard and pointed like a cock's spur — the sides are speckled with yellowish brown and black. two roes of black spots on a lite yellow ground pass throughout his whole length on the upper points of the scuta of the belly and tale ½ Inch apart   this snake is vulgarly called the cow or bull snake from a bellowing nois which it is said sometimes to make resembling that anamal, tho' as to this fact I am unable to attest it never having heard them make that or any other noise myself.

I have frequently observed an acquatic bird[80] in the cours of asscending this river but have never been able to procure one before today . . . they lay their eggs on the sand bars without shelter or nest, and produce

79. A bullsnake.
80. A least tern.

their young from the 15th to the last of June, the young ones of which we caught several are covered with down of a yellowish white colour and on the back some small specks of a dark brown. they bear a great resemblance to the young quale of ten days oald, and apear like them to be able to runabout and peck their food as soon as they are hatched— this bird, lives on small fish, worms and bugs which it takes on the virge of the water it is seldom seen to light on trees an quite as seldom do they lite in the water and swim tho' the foot would indicate that they did it's being webbed . . . this bird is very noysey when flying which is dose exttreemly swift the motion of the wing is much like that of *kildee*[81] it has two notes one like the squaking of a small pig only on reather a high kee, and the other kit'-tee'-kit'-tee'- as near as letters can express the sound. [Camped in Harrison County, Iowa, across from the Burt-Washington county line, Nebraska.]

[CLARK] In every bend the banks are falling in from the Current being thrown against those bends by the Sand points which inlarges and the Soil I believe from unquestionable appearns. of the entire bottom from one hill to the other being the mud or ooze of the River at Some former Period mixed with Sand and Clay easily melts and Slips into the River, and the mud mixes with the water & the Sand is washed down and lodges on the points— Great quantites of Grapes on the banks, I observe three different Kinds[82] at this time ripe, one Of the no. is large & has the flaver of the Purple grape.

August 6, 1804
[CLARK] We have every reason to belive that one man has *Deserted Moses B: Reed* he has been absent three Days and one french man we Sent to the Indian Camps has not joined us, we have reasons to beleve he lost himself in attempting to join us at the *Council Bluff*. [Camped apparently in Harrison County, Iowa, about halfway between the Soldier and Little Sioux Rivers.]

81. Killdeer.
82. The summer grape, river-bank grape, and winter grape.

August 7, 1804

[CLARK] at 1 oClock dispatched George Drewyer, R. Fields, Wm. Bratten & Wm. Labieche back after the Deserter reid with order if he did not give up Peaceibly to put him to Death &c. to go to the Ottoes Village & enquire for La Liberty and bring him to the Mahars Village, also with a Speech on the occasion to the Ottoes & Missouries— and directing a few of their Chiefs to come to the Mahars, & we would make a peace between them & the Mahar and *Souex*, a String of wompom & a Carrot of Tobacco. [Camped a few miles below the mouth of the Little Sioux River, probably on the Iowa side in Harrison County.]

[FLOYD] on the 4th of this month one of ouer men by the name of Moses B. Reed went Back to ouer Camp whare we had Left in the morning, to Git his Knife which he Had Left at the Camp . . . pon examining his nap-Sack we found that he had taken his Cloas and all His powder and Balles, and had hid them out that night and had made that an excuse to Desarte from us with out aney Jest Case.

August 8, 1804

[GASS] In a bag under the bill and neck of the pelican, which Captain Lewis killed, we put five gallons of water. [Camped probably on the Iowa side, in southwest Monona County, not far above the Harrison County line.]

August 9, 1804

[CLARK] Musquetors worse this evening than ever I have Seen them. [Camped a mile or two south of Onawa, Harrison County, Iowa.]

August 11, 1804

[CLARK] a hard wind accompanied with rain from the S. E. after the rain was over Capt. Lewis myself & 10 men assended the Hill on the L. S. under which there was Some fine Springs to the top of a high point where the *Mahars King Black* Bird[83] was burried 4 years ago. a mound of earth

83. Omaha chief Blackbird, who had a reputation for killing his adversaries through sorcery, or more likely, by the use of poison he obtained from traders.

about 12 Diamuter at the base & 6 feet high is raised over him turfed, and a pole 8 feet high in the Center   on this pole we fixed a white flage bound with red Blue & white. [Camped in the vicinity of Badger Lake, Monona County, Iowa.]

[FLOYD] Capt Lewis and Clark . . . histed a flage on [Blackbird's] Grave as noner [honor] for him which will pleas the Indianes.

[GASS] His name was Blackbird, king of the Mahas; an absolute monarch while living, and the Indians suppose can exercise the power of one though dead.

August 12, 1804
[CLARK] a *Prarie Wolf* [84] Come near the bank and Barked at us this evening, we made an attempt but could not git him, this Animale Barkes like a large *feste* [feist] Dog. Beever is verry Plenty on this part of the river. I prepare Some presents for to give the Indians of the *Mahars* nation. Wiser apt. Cook & Supentdt. of the Provisions of Sergt. Floyds Squad. [Camped in either Monona or Woodbury County, Iowa, near the county line.]

August 13, 1804
[CLARK] [passed] the place Mr. Ja: McKey had a tradeing house in 95 & 96 & named it Fort Charles [85] . . . Detached Sergt. Ordeway Peter Crusatt, Geroge Shannon Werner & Carrn. to the Mahar Village [86] with a flag & Some Tobacco to invite the Nation to See & talke with us on tormorrow. [Camped a few miles south of Dakota City, Dakota County, Nebraska, or opposite in Woodbury County, Iowa, the party's Fish Camp.]

[ORDWAY] I and 3 more of the party went out to the [Omaha] Village or to the place where it formely Stood.   we passed through high Grass in the

---

84. Coyote.
85. Mackay's fort was southeast of Homer, Dakota County, Nebraska.
86. Tonwontonga, the main village of the Omaha tribe.

low prarie & came to the Mahar Creek on our way . . . which was verry fatigueing for the high Grass Sunflowers & thistles &C all of which were above 10 feet high, a great quantity of wild peas among those weeds, we broke our way through them till we came to where their had been a village of about 300 Cabbins called the Mahar village.   it was burned about 4 years ago immediately after near half the Nation died with the Small pox, which was as I was informed about 400, we found none of the natives about the place   they were out hunting the Buffelow.

August 14, 1804
[CLARK] Those people haveing no houses no Corn or any thing more than the graves of their ancesters to attach them to the old Village, Continue in pursuite of the Buffalow longer than others who had greater attachments to their native Village —   the ravages of the Small Pox (which Swept off 400 men & women & Children in perpoposion) has reduced this Nation not exceeding 300 men and left them to the insults of their weaker neighbours which before was glad to be on friendly turms with them —   I am told whin this fatal malady was among them they Carried ther franzey to verry extroadinary length, not only of burning their Village, but they put their *wives* & Children to *Dath* with a view of their all going together to Some better Countrey —   They burry their Dead on the tops of high hills and rais mounds on the top of them,   The cause or way those people took the Small Pox is uncertain, the most Probable from Some other Nation by means of a warparty. [Remained at Fish Camp.]

[ORDWAY] we Set out at light, & walked along down the hills past the Graves.   we Saw also a nomber of large holes in the Ground where they used to hide their peltry &C. in, when they went out hunting and when they returned they would dig it out again, I put up a paper on a pole Stuck in a round hill, as a Signal for G. Drewyer &C . . . we walked along the ridge which is high prarie all back as far as my [eye?] could behold.   we expected to have found Some corn or Something growing Some where in the bottom but we could not see any appearence of anythig being planted this year . . . Returned to the Boats about 10 oClock A. M.

August 15, 1804

[CLARK] we mad a Drag and haulted up the Creek, and Cought 318 fish of different kind I'e' Peke,[87] Bass, Salmon,[88] perch, red horse, Small Cat,[89] and a kind of perch Called Silverfish,[90] on the Ohio. I cought a Srimp[91] prosisely of Shape Size & flavour of those about N. Orleans & the lower party of the Mississippi   in this Creek which is only the pass or Streight from Beaver Pond to another, is Crouded with large Mustles[92] Verry fat, Ducks, Pliver of different Kinds are on those Ponds as well as on the river. [Remained at Fish Camp.]

August 17, 1804

[CLARK] at 6 oClock this evening *Labieche* one of the Party Sent to the Ottoes joined, and informed that the Party was behind with one of the Deserters M B. Reed and the 3 principal Chiefs of the Nations — La Liberty they cought but he decived them and got away—   the object of those Chiefs comeing forward is to make a peace with the Mahars thro: us.   as the Mahars are not at home this great object cannot be accomplished at this time   Set the Praries on fire to bring the Mahars & Soues if any were near, this being the usial Signal. [Remained at Fish Camp.]

August 18, 1804

[CLARK] in the after part of the Day the Party with the Indians arrivd. we meet them under a Shade near the Boat and after a Short talk we gave them Provisions to eat & proceeded to the trail of Reed, he Confessed that he "Deserted & Stold a public Rifle[93] Shot-pouch Powder & Bals" and requested we would be as favourable with him as we Could consistantly with our Oathes—which we were and only Sentenced him to run the Gantlet four times through the Party & that each man with 9 Swichies

87. Pike.
88. Mooneye or goldeye.
89. Channel catfish.
90. Freshwater drum.
91. Crayfish.
92. Mussels.
93. Reed's "public Rifle" may have been one of the party's U.S. Model 1803 rifles that Lewis acquired at the federal arsenal at Harpers Ferry in present West Virginia.

Should punish him and for him not to be considered in future as one of the Party— The three principal Chiefs petitioned for Pardin for this man After we explained the injurey Such men could doe them by false representation, & explang. the Customs of our Countrey they were all Satisfied with the propriety of the Sentence & was witness to the punishment. after which we had Some talk with the Chiefs about the orrigan of the war between them & the Mahars &c. it commenced in this way I'e' in two of the Missouries Tribe resideing with the Ottoes went to the Mahars to Steel horses, they Killed them both which was a cause of revenge on the part of the Missouris & Ottoes, they also brought war on themselves Nearly in the Same way with the Panea Loups and they are greatly in fear of a just revenge from the Panies for takeing their Corn from the Pania Towns in their absence hunting this Summer. the evening was Closed with an extra Gill of Whiskey & a Dance untill 11 oClock. [Remained at Fish Camp.]

August 19, 1804
[CLARK] at 10 oClock we assembled the Cheifs & Warriers under an Orning and delivered a Speech, explanitary of the One Sent to this Nation from the *Council Bluff*, &c.

Children When we Sent the 4 men to your towns, we expected to See & Speake with the Mahas by the time you would arrive and to lay the foundation of a peace between you and them

The Speech of Petieit Villeu Little Thief, If you think right and Can waite untill all our Warriers Come from the Buffalows hunt, we Can then tell you who is our men of Consequnce— My fathers always lived with the father of the B together & we always live with the Big hose— all the men here are the Suns of Chief and will be glad to get Something from the hands of their fathers. My father always directed me to be friendly with the white people, I have always done So and went often to the french, give my party pieces of Paper & we will be glad . . .

The Speach of the Big Horse I went to the hunt Buffalow I heard your word and I returned, I and all my men with me will attend to your words— you want to make peace with all, I want to make peace also, the young me[n] when they want to go to war where is the goods you give me to Keep them at home, if you give me Some Whisky to give a Drop to my men at home. I came here naked and must return home naked. if I have Something to give the young men I can prevent their going to war. You want to make peace with all, It is good   we want Something to give my men at home. I am a pore man, and cant quiet without means, a Spoon ful of your milk will qui[e]t all . . .

   Sergt. Floyd was taken violently bad with the Beliose Cholick [bilious colic] and is dangerously ill   we attempt in Vain to releive him, I am much concerned for his Situation —   we could get nothing to Stay on his Stomach a moment   nature appear exosting fast in him   every man is attentive to him <york prlly>. [Remained at Fish Camp.]

August 20, 1804

[CLARK] Serjeant Floyd as bad as he can be   no pulse & nothing will Stay a moment on his Stomach or bowels —   Passed two Islands on the S. S. and at first Bluff on the S S. Serj.' Floyd Died with a great deel of Composure, before his death he Said to me, "I am going away" ["]I want you to write me a letter" —   We buried him on the top of the bluff ½ Miles below a Small river to which we Gave his name, he was buried with the Honors of War much lamented; a Seeder post with the Name Sergt. C. Floyd died here 20th of August 1804 was fixed at the head of his grave —   This Man at all times gave us proofs of his firmness and Deturmined resolution to doe Service to his Countrey and honor to himself   after paying all the honor to our Decesed brother we Camped in the mouth of *floyds* river about 30 yards wide, a butifull evening. [Camped just above the mouth of Floyd River, Sioux City, Woodbury County, Iowa.]

[GASS] Here Sergeant Floyd died, notwithstanding every possible effort was made by the commanding officers, and other persons, to save his life.

August 22, 1804

[CLARK] this Bluff Contained alum, Copperas,[94] Cobalt, Pyrites; a alum rock Soft & Sand Stone. Capt. Lewis in proveing the quality of those min-

94. Melanterite.

erals was near poisoning himself by the fumes & tast of the *Cabalt* which had the appearance of Soft Isonglass— Copperas & alum is verry pure . . . Seven miles above is a Clift of Allom Stone of a Dark Brown Colr. Containing also in crusted in the Crevices & Shelves of the rock great qts. of Cabalt, Semented Shels & a red earth . . . Capt Lewis took a Dost of Salts to work off the effects of the Arsenic[95] . . . ordered a vote for a Serjeant to chuse one of three which may be the highest number   the highest numbers are P. Gass had 19 Votes, Bratten & Gibson.[Camped south of Elk Point, Union County, South Dakota.]

August 23, 1804

[ORDWAY] Jo. Fields came to the Boat   informed us that he had killed a Bull Buffelow.[96] [Camped in either Dixon County, Nebraska, or Clay County, South Dakota, a mile or so southeast of Vermillion, South Dakota.]

August 24, 1804

[LEWIS] the Chronometer stoped again just after being wound up; I know not the cause, but fear it procedes from some defect which it is not in my power to remedy. [Camped near Vermillion, Clay County, South Dakota.]

[CLARK] in an imence Plain a high Hill[97] is Situated, and appears of a Conic form and by the different nations of Indians in this quarter is Suppose to be the residence of Deavels. that they are in human form with remarkable large heads and about 18 Inches high, that they are Very watchfull, and are arm'd with Sharp arrows with which they Can Kill at a great distance; they are Said to Kill all persons who are So hardy as to attempt to approach the hill; they State that tradition informs them that many Indians have Suffered by those little people and among others three *Mahar*

95. Lewis probably took Epsom or Glauber's salts as a purgative to work off the effects of an unknown substance.

96. Joseph Field killed the party's first buffalo.

97. Spirit Mound, about eight miles north of the town of Vermillion.

men fell a Sacrefise to their murceyless fury not many years Since— So much do the Maha, Souis, Ottoes and other neighbouring nations believe this fable that no Consideration is Suffecient to induce them to apporach the hill.

[ORDWAY] we found a great quantity of red berries [98] which grows on a handsome bush about as high as I could reach.   these Berries are a little Sour (& are called Rabbit berries) (English) But pleasant to the taste.

98. Buffaloberry.

CHAPTER 2

The Middle Missouri

August 25–October 26, 1804

August 25, 1804

[CLARK] Capt Lewis & my Self Concluded to go and See the Mound which was viewed with Such turrow [terror] by all the different Nation in this quarter . . . this mound appears of a Conic form . . . our Dog was So Heeted & fatigued we was obliged Send him back to the Creek, at 12 oClock we arrived at the hill Capt Lewis much fatigued from heat the day it being verry hot & he being in a debilitated State from the Precautions he was obliged to take to provent the affects of the Cobalt, & Minl. Substance which had like to have poisoned him two days ago, his want of water, and Several of the men [1] complaining of Great thirst, deturmined us to make for the first water . . . The reagular form of this hill would in Some measure justify a belief that it owed its Orrigin to the hand of man; but as the earth and loos pebbles and other Substances of which it was Composed, bare an exact resemblance to the Steep Ground which border on the Creek in its neighbourhood we Concluded it was most probably the production of nature . . . The Surrounding Plains is open void of Timber and leavel to a great extent: hence the wind from whatever quarter it may blow, drives with unusial force over the naked Plains and against this hill; the insects of various kinds are thus involuntaryly driven to the mound by the force of the wind, or fly to its Leward Side for Shelter; the Small Birds whoes food they are, Consequently resort in great numbers to this place in Surch of them . . .

1. The captains were accompanied by Bratton, E. Cann, Colter, Drouillard, Joseph Field, Frazer, Ordway, Shields, Warfington, York, and perhaps Labiche.

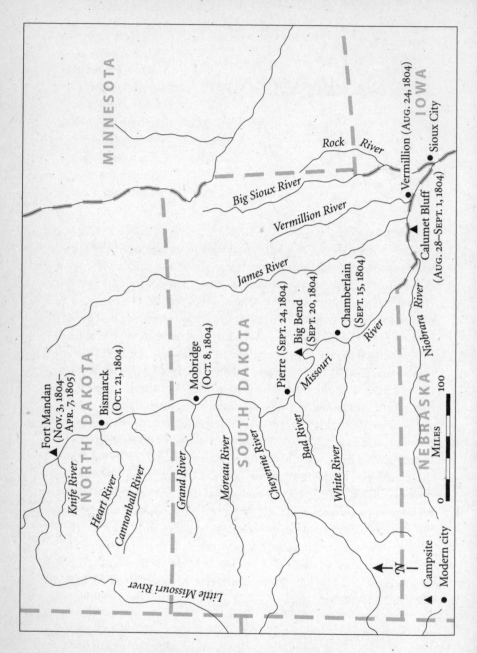

The Expedition's Route, August 25–October 26, 1804

One evidence which the Inds Give for believeing this place to be the residence of Some unusial Spirits is that they frequently discover a large assemblage of Birds about this mound — is in my opinion a Suffient proof to produce in the Savage mind a Confident belief of all the properties which they ascribe it. from the top of this Mound we beheld a most butifull landscape; Numerous herds of buffalow were Seen feeding in various directions, the Plain to North N. W & N E extends without interuption as far as Can be Seen . . . if all the timber which is on the Stone Creek was on 100 a[c]res it would not be thickly timbered, the Soil of those Plains are delightfull. [The main party camped near the Cedar-Dixon county line, Nebraska.]

[WHITEHOUSE] some of our Men caught Nine Cat fish.   5 of them was very large, weighing on an average each 100 lbs.

August 26, 1804
[LEWIS AND CLARK, DETACHMENT ORDERS] The commanding officers have thought it proper to appoint Patric Gass, a Sergeant in *the corps of volunteers for North Western Discovery*, he is therefore to be obeyed and respected accordingly. Sergt. Gass is directed to take charge of the late Sergt. Floyd's mess . . . The Commanding officers have every reason to hope from the previous faithfull services of Sergt. Gass, that this expression of their approbation will be still further confirmed, by his vigilent attention in future to his duties as a Sergeant.   the Commanding officers are still further confirmed in the high opinion they had previously formed of the capacity, deligence and integrety of Sergt. Gass, from the wish expresssed by a large majority of his comrades for his appointment as Sergeant. [Camped in Clay County, South Dakota, opposite the mouth of Bow Creek, Cedar County, Nebraska.]

August 27, 1804
[CLARK] G. Drewyer Came up and informed that he Could neither find Shannon nor horses, we Sent Shields & J Fields, back to hunt Shannon & the horses . . . we had the Prarie Set on fire to let the Souix See that we were on the river, & as a Signal for them to Come to it.   at 2 oClock passed the mouth of *River Jacque*, or Yeankton   one Indian at the mouth of this

river Swam to the Perogue, we landed and two others came to us, those Inds. informed that a large Camp of Soues, were on R. Jacque near the mouth. we Sent Sergt. Pryor & a Frenchman with Mr. Durioin the Souis interpeter to the Camp with derections to invite the Principal Chiefs to councel with us at a Bluff above Called the Calumet. [Camped between the mouth of the James River and the town of Yankton, Yankton County, South Dakota.]

August 28, 1804

[CLARK] Capt Lewis & my Self much indisposed— I think from the Homney w[e] Substitute in place of bread, (or Plumbs). [Camped in Cedar County, Nebraska, just below present Gavins Point Dam, at the party's Calumet Bluff camp.]

[CLARK] one of the Perogues run a Snag thro her and was near Sinking in the opinions of the Crew— we came too below the *Calumet Bluff* and formed a camp in a Butifull Plain near the foot of the high land which rises with a gradual assent . . . The Perogue which was injurd I had un- loaded and the Loading put into the other Perogue which we intended to Send back . . . after examoning her & finding that She was unfit for Ser- vice deturmined to Send her back by the party   Some load which was in the Perogue much inju'd . . . J. Shields & J. Fields who was Sent back to look for Shannon & the Horses joined us & informed that Shannon had the horses a head and that they Could not over take him   This man not being a first rate Hunter, we deturmined to Send one man in pursute of him with Some Provisions.

August 29, 1804

[CLARK] I am much engaged reriteing— at 4 oClock P M. Sergt. Pryor & Mr. Dorion with 5 Chiefs and about 70 men &c. arrived on the oppo- site Side   we Sent over a Perogue & Mr. Dorrion & his Son[2] who was tradeing with the Indians Came over with Serjt Pryer, and informed us that the Chiefs were there   we Sent Serjt. Pryor & yound Mr. Dorion with Som Tobacco, Corn & a few Kittles for them to Cook in, with directions

2. Pierre Dorion Sr. and his son, Pierre Dorion Jr.

to inform the Chiefs that we would Speek to them tomorrow . . . Serjt. Pryor informs me that when Came near the Indian Camp they were met by men with a Buffalow roabe to Carry them, Mr. Dorion informed ["]they were not the Owners of the Boats & did not wish to be Carried" — the Sceouex Camps[3] are handson of a Conic form Covered with Buffalow Roabs Painted different Colours and all Compact & hand Somly arranged, covered all round an orpen part in the Center for the fire, with Buffalow roabs each Lodg has a place for Cooking detached, the lodges contain 10 to 15 persons— a Fat Dog was presented as a mark of their Great respect for the party of which they partook hartily and thought it good & well flavored. [Remained at Calumet Bluff camp.]

[ORDWAY] we have plenty of fine fat Cat fish the most of the Time. Several large ones caught last night. The Misouri river affords us pleanty of fish, & the Country pleanty of all kinds of Game.

August 30, 1804

[CLARK] after Prepareing Some presents for the Chiefs which we intended make by giving Meadals, and finishing a Speech what we intend'd to give them, we Sent Mr. Dorion in a Perogue for the Chiefs & warreirs to a Council under an Oak tree near wher we had a flag flying on a high flag Staff at 12 OClock we met and Cap L. Delivered the Speach & thin made one great Chiff by giving him a meadal & Some Cloathes one 2d Chief & three third Chiefs in the Same way, They recvd. those thing with the goods and tobacco with pleasure To the Grand Chief we gave a Flag and the parole[4] & wampom with a hat & Chiefs Coat, we Smoked out of the pipe of peace, & the Chiefs retired to a Bourey [bowery] made of bushes by their young men to Divide their presents and Smoke eate and Council . . . The Souix is a Stout bold looking people, (the young men hand Som) & well made, the greater part of them make use of Bows & arrows, Some fiew fusees[5] I observe among them . . . the Warriers are Verry

3. Yankton Sioux.
4. Lewis and Clark carried certificates ("parole") to present to Indian dignitaries. The documents declared the recipient to be an ally of the United States and one who should be treated in a friendly manner.
5. Fusils, a type of musket.

much deckerated with Paint Porcupin quils & feathers, large leagins & mockersons, all with buffalow roabs of Different Colours. the Squars wore Peticoats & and a white Buffalow roabes with the black hair turned back over their necks & Sholders. [Remained at Calumet Bluff camp.]

[ORDWAY] after dark we Made a large fire for the Indians to have a war dance, all the young men prepared themselves for the dance. Some of them painted themselves in curious manner   Some of the Boys had their faces & foreheads all painted white &C   a drum was prepared, the Band began to play on their little Instruments, & the drum beat & they Sang. the young men commenced dancing around the fire.   it always began with a houp & hollow & ended with the Same, and in the intervales, one of the warries at a time would rise with his weapen & Speak of what he had done in his day, & what warlike actions he had done &c.   this they call merrit &C   they would confess how many they had killed & of what nation they were off & how many horses they had Stole &C— they Camped along Side of us & behaved honestly.

August 31, 1804
[CLARK] I took a Vocabulary of the Scioux Language—   and the Answer to a fiew quaries Such a[s] refured to ther Situation, Trade, number War, &c. This Nation is Divided into 20 Tribes, possessing Seperate interests— Collectively they are noumerous Say from 2 to 3000 men, their interests are so unconnected that Some bands are at war with Nations which other bands are on the most friendly terms. This Great Nation who the French has given the nickname of Sciouex, Call them selves *Dar co tar*   their language is not peculiarly their own, they Speak a great number of words, which is the Same in every respect with the Maha, Poncaser, Osarge & Kanzies. which Clearly proves that those nation at Some Period not more that a century or two past [were once?] the Same nation—   Those *Dar ca ter's* or Scioux inhabit or rove over the Countrey on the Red river of Lake Winipeck, St. Peter's & the West of the Missippie above Prarie De chain heads of River Demoin, and the Missouri and its waters on the N. Side for a great extent. They are only at peace with 8 Nations, & agreeable to their Calculation at war with twenty odd. Their trade Coms from the British, except this Band and one on Demoin who trade with the Traders of St

Louis— The[y] furnish *Beaver* Martain,[6] <Loues>[7] Pikon,[8] Bear and Deer Skins—and have about 40 Traders among them. The *Dar co tar* or Sceouex rove & follow the Buffalow raise no corn or any thing else the woods & praries affording a Suffcency, the[y] eat Meat, and Substitute the Ground potato[9] which grow in the Plains for bread. [Remained at Calumet Bluff camp.]

September 3, 1804

[CLARK] we Saw Some Signs of the two men Shannon & Colter, Shannon appeared to be a head of Colter. [Camped in Knox County, Nebraska, probably near the western boundary of the Santee Sioux Reservation.]

September 4, 1804

[CLARK] at 4 mes. ½ passed the mouth of the River *Que Courre (rapid R[)]*[10] on the L. S. and Came to a Short distance above, this River is 152 yards wide at the mouth & 4 feet Deep Throwing out Sands like the Platt (only Corser) forming bars in its mouth, I went up this river three miles to a butifull Plain on the upper Side where the Panias[11] once had a Village this river widens above its mouth and is devided by Sand and Islands, the Current verry rapid, not navagable for even Canoos without Great dificulty owing to its Sands; the colour like that of the Plat is light. [Camped at the mouth of the Niobrara River, Knox County, Nebraska.]

September 5, 1804

[CLARK] Sent Shields & Gibson to the Poncas Towns, which is Situated on the Ponca river on the lower side about two miles from its mouth in an open butifull Plain, at this time this nation is out hunting the biffalow they raise no corn or Beens, Gibson killed a Buffalow in the Town, The two men which has been absent several Days is ahead. [Camped on an

6. Marten.
7. Wolf.
8. Fisher or lynx.
9. Indian breadroot.
10. Niobrara River.
11. Here, Poncas rather than Pawnees.

island that lay between southeastern Charles Mix County, South Dakota, and northwestern Knox County, Nebraska.]

September 7, 1804
[CLARK] Capt Lewis & my Self walked up, to the top which forms a Cone and is about 70 feet higher than the high lands around it . . . in decending this Cupola,[12] discovered a Village of Small animals[13] that burrow in the grown (those animals are Called by the french Pitite Chien)   Killed one & Cought one a live by poreing a great quantity of water in his hole   we attempted to dig to the beds of one of thos animals, after diging 6 feet, found by running a pole down that we were not half way to his Lodges, we found 2 frogs in the hole, and killed a Dark rattle Snake near with a Ground rat in him, (those rats are numerous)   the Village of those animals Covs. about 4 acrs of Ground on a Gradual decent of a hill and Contains great numbers of holes on the top of which those little animals Set erect make a Whistleing noise and whin allarmed Slip into their hole — we por'd into one of the holes 5 barrels of water without filling it . . . it is Said that a kind of Lizard also a Snake reside with those animals.   did not find this correct. [Camped in eastern Boyd County, Nebraska, about four miles downriver from the Nebraska-South Dakota border.]

[ORDWAY] Shields killed a prarie dog, which was cooked for the Capts dinner.

September 10, 1804
[CLARK] on a hill on the L. S. we found the back bone of a fish,[14] 45 feet long tapering to the tale, <Some teeth> &c.   those joints were Seperated and all petrefied, opposit this Island 1½ miles from the river on the L. S. is a large Salt Spring of remarkable Salt water. [Camped on an island between Gregory and Charles Mix Counties, South Dakota.]

September 11, 1804
[CLARK] here the man who left us with the horses 22 days ago and has been a head ever Since joined, us nearly Starved to Death,[15] he had been

12. Old Baldy, Boyd County, Nebraska.
13. Prairie dog.
14. Plesiosaur, an aquatic dinosaur of the Mesozoic era.
15. Shannon finally rejoined the party after having been absent since August 27.

12 days without any thing to eate but Grapes & one Rabit, which he Killed
by shooting a piece of hard Stick in place of a ball. This man Supposeing
the boat to be a head pushed on as long as he Could, when he became
weak and fiable deturmined to lay by and waite for a tradeing boat, which
is expected Keeping one horse for the last resorse, thus a man had like to
have Starved to death in a land of Plenty for the want of Bulletes or Something to kill his meat. [Camped just above the mouth of Landing Creek,
Gregory County, South Dakota.]

September 13, 1804
[LEWIS] Killed a . . . Porcupine; found it in a Cottonwood tree near the
river on the Lard. Shore— the leaves of the Cottonwood were much distroyed— as were those of the Cottonwood trees in it's neighbourhood.
I therefore supposed that it fed on the folage of trees at this season, the
flesh of this anamal is a pleasant and whoalsome food— the quills had
not yet obtained their usual length. [Camped in Brule County, South
Dakota.]

September 14, 1804
[CLARK] in my walk I Killed a Buck Goat[16] of this Countrey, about the
hight of the Grown Deer, its body Shorter, the Horns which is not very
hard and forks ⅔ up one prong Short the other round & Sharp arched,
and is imediately above its Eyes the Colour is a light gray with black behind its ears down its neck, and its Jaw white round its neck, its Sides and
its rump round its tail which is Short & white verry actively made, has
only a pair of hoofs to each foot. his brains on the back of his head, his
Norstral large, his eyes like a Sheep— he is more like the Antilope or
Gazella of Africa than any other Species of Goat. [Camped just below the
mouth of Bull Creek, Lyman County, South Dakota.]

[ORDWAY] Capt. Clark joined us had killed a curious annamil resembling
a Goat Willard brought it on board . . . Such an anamil was never yet
known in U. S. States. The Capt had the Skins of the hair & Goat Stuffed
in order to Send back to the city of Washington. the bones and all.

16. Pronghorn.

September 16, 1804

[LEWIS] we concluded to ly by at this place the ballance of this day and the next, in order to dry our baggage which was wet by the heavy showers of rain which had fallen within the last three days, and also to lighten the boat by transfering a part of her lading to the red perogue, which we now determined to take on with us to our winter residence wherever that might be; while some of the men were imployed in this necessary labour others were dressing of skins washing and mending their cloaths &c. . . . on this bottom which had more timber on it than any part of the river we had seen for many days past, consisting of Cottonwood Elm, some indifferent ash and a considerable quanty of a small species of white oak [17] which is loaded with acorns of an excellent flavor . . . almost every species of wild game is fond of the acorn, the Buffaloe Elk, deer, bear, turkies, ducks, pigegians and even the wolves feed on them . . . as usual no timber appeared except such as from the steep declivities of hills, or their moist situations, were sheltered from the effects of the fire. [Camped near Oacoma, Lyman County, South Dakota.]

September 17, 1804

[LEWIS] Having for many days past confined myself to the boat, I determined to devote this day to amuse myself on shore with my gun and view the interior of the country lying between the river and the Corvus Creek—[18] accordingly before sunrise I set out with six of my best hunters . . . the country breakes of[f] as usual into a fine leavel plain extending as far as the eye can reach. from this plane I had an extensive view of the river below, and the irregular hills which border the opposite sides of the river and creek. the surrounding country had been birnt about a month before and young grass had now sprung up to hight of 4 Inches presenting the live green of the spring. to the West a high range of hills, strech across the country from N. to S and appeared distant about 20 miles . . . this senery already rich pleasing and beatiful, was still farther hightened by immence herds of Buffaloe deer Elk and Antelopes which we saw in every direction feeding on the hills and plains . . . we found the

17. Bur oak.
18. American Crow Creek, Lyman County, South Dakota.

Antelope extreemly shye and watchfull insomuch that we had been unable to get a shot at them; when at rest they generally seelect the most elivated point in the neighbourhood, and as they are watchfull and extreemly quick of sight and their sense of smelling very accute it is almost
impossible to approach them within gunshot; in short they will frequently discover and flee from you at the distance of three miles . . . an-
tilopes which had disappeared in a steep revesne now appeared at the distance of about three miles on the side of a ridge which passed obliquely
across me and extended about four miles.   so soon had these antelopes
gained the distance at which they had again appeared to my view I
doubted at ferst that they were the same that I had just surprised, but my
doubts soon vanished when I beheld the rapidity of their flight along the
ridge before me it appeared reather the rappid flight of irds than the motion of quadrupeds. I think I can safely venture the asscertion that the
speed of this anamal is equal if not superior to that of the finest blooded
courser. [Remained near Oacoma.]

[CLARK] Colter Killed . . . a curious kind of deer[19] of a Dark gray Colr.
more so than common, hair long & fine, the ears large & long, a Small re-
septical under the eyes; like an Elk, the Taile about the length of Common
Deer, round (like a Cow) a tuft of black hair about the end, this Speces of
Deer jumps like a goat or Sheep.

September 18, 1804
[CLARK] I Killed a Prarie Wollf, about the Size of a gray fox bushey tail
head & ear like a wolf, Some fur   Burrows in the ground and barks like a
Small Dog. what has been taken heretofore for the Fox was those wolves,
and no Foxes has been Seen; The large wolves are verry numourous, they
are of a light Colr. large & has long hair with Corrs fur. [Camped a few
miles northeast of Oacoma, Lyman County, South Dakota.]

[ORDWAY] the Bones of the woolf was taken apart and Saved as well as the
Skins .`. . in order to Send back to the States next Spring, with the other
curiousities.

19. Mule deer.

September 20, 1804

[GASS] passed a long chain of bluffs on the north side, of a dark colour. From these and others of the same kind the Missouri gets its muddy colour. The earth of which they are composed dissolves like sugar; every rain washes down great quantities of it, and the rapidity of the stream keeps it mixing and afloat in the water, until it reaches the mouth of the Mississippi. [Camped on an island in Hughes County, South Dakota.]

September 21, 1804

[CLARK] at half past one oClock this morning the Sand bar on which we Camped began to under mind and give way which allarmed the Sergeant on Guard, the motion of the boat awakened me; I get up & by the light of the moon observed that the land had given away both above and below our Camp & was falling in fast . . . we had pushed off but a few minets before the bank under which the Boat & perogus lay give way, which would Certainly have Sunk both Perogues, by the time we made the opsd. Shore our Camp fell in . . . at Daylight proceeded on to the Gouge of this Great bend[20] and Brackfast, we Sent a man to measure step off the Distance across the gouge, he made it 2000 yds. The distance arround is 30 mes. [Camped on an island in Hughes County, South Dakota.]

September 22, 1804

[CLARK] passed Cedar Island . . . near the upper part of this Island[21] on its S. Side a Tradeing fort is Situated built of Cedar — by a Mr. Louiselle of St Louis, for the purpose of Tradeing with the Teton Bands of Soues[22] about this Fort I saw numbers of Indians Temporary Lodges, & horse Stables, all of them round and to a point at top. [Camped nearly opposite Loiselle Creek, Hughes County, South Dakota.]

September 23, 1804

[CLARK] passed Elk Island . . . covered with Cotton wood the read [red] Current Called by the French *Gres de Butiff*[23] & grapes &c. . . . three Souex

20. Big Bend of the Missouri, Lyman County, South Dakota.
21. Perhaps Dorion Island No. 2, Lyman County, now under Big Bend Reservoir.
22. Loisel built Fort aux Cedres about 1800 to trade with the Sioux.
23. Buffaloberry, or *graisse de boeuf* ("buffalo grease"), the French term for buffaloberry.

boys Came to us Swam the river and informd that the Band of Soauex called the Teton of 80 Lodges were Camped at the next Creek above, & 60 Lodges more a Short distance above, we gave those boys two Carrots of Tobacco to Carry to their Chiefs, with derections to tell them that we would Speek to them tomorrow. [Camped in Hughes County, South Dakota, just below the mouth of Antelope Creek on the opposite side.]

[LEWIS AND CLARK, WEATHER REMARKS] aire remarkably dry   in 36 hours two Spoonfuls of water aveporated in a sauser.

September 24, 1804
[CLARK] we prepared Some Clothes and a fiew meadels for the Chiefs of the Teton's hand of Seaux which we expect to See to day at the next river . . . [We] prepared all things for action in Case of necessity, our Perogus went to the Island for the meet, Soon after the man on Shore run up the bank and reported that the Indians had Stolen the horse[24] we Soon after met 5 Inds. and ankered out Some distance & Spoke to them   informed them we were friends, & wished to Continue So but were not afraid of any Indians, Some of their young men had taken the horse Sent by their Great father for ther Chief and we would not Speek to them until the horse was returned to us again. The Tribes of the Scouix Called the Teton, is Camped about 2 miles up on the N W Side and we Shall Call the River[25] after that nation, Teton. [Camped above the mouth of the Bad River, Stanley County, South Dakota, opposite Pierre.]

September 25, 1804
[CLARK]a fair morning the wind from the S. E. all well, raised a Flag Staff & made a orning or Shade on a Sand bar in the mouth of Teton River for the purpose of Speeking with the Indians under, the Boat Crew on board at 70 yards Distance from the bar   The 5 Indians which we met last night Continued, about 11 oClock the 1s & 2d Chief Came we gave them Some of our Provsions to eat, they gave us great quantites of meet Some of which was Spoiled   we feel much at a loss for the want of an interpeter the one we have can Speek but little.

24. Colter's horse.
25. Bad River.

Met in council at 12 oClock and after Smokeing, agreeable to the usial Custom, Cap Lewis proceeded to Deliver a Speech which we oblige to Curtail for want of a good interpeter all our Party paraded. gave a medal to the Grand Chief Calld. in Indian *Un ton gar Sar bar* in French *Beefe nure* Black Buffalow[26] Said to be a good man, 2 Chief *Torto hon gar*— or the *Partisan*[27]—or Partizan—*bad* the 3rd is the Beffe De Medison[28] his name is *Tar ton gar wa ker* . . .

Envited those Cheifs on board to Show them our boat and Such Curiossities as was Strange to them, we gave them ¼ a glass of whiskey which they appeared to be verry fond of, Sucked the bottle after it was out & Soon began to be troublesom, one the 2d Cheif assumeing Drunkness, as a Cloake for his rascally intentions I went with those Cheifs (which left the boat with great reluctiance) to Shore with a view of reconseleing those men to us, as Soon as I landed the Perogue three of their young men Seased the Cable of the Perogue the Chiefs Soldr. Huged the mast, and the 2d Chief was verry insolent both in words & justures declareing I Should not go on, Stateing he had not recved presents Suffient from us, his justures were of Such a personal nature I felt my Self Compeled to Draw my Sword, at this motion Capt. Lewis ordered all under arms in the boat, those with me also Showed a Disposition to Defend themselves and me, the grand Chief then took hold of the roop & ordered the young warrers away, I felt my Self warm & Spoke in verry positive terms

Most of the warriers appeared to have ther Bows Strung and took out their arrows from ther quves. as I was not permited to return, I Sent all the men except 2 Inpt. [interpreters] to the boat, the perogu Soon returned with about 12 of our detumind men ready for any event   this movement caused a no: of the Indians to withdraw at a distance, Their treatment to me was verry rough & I think justified roughness on my part, they all left my Perogue and Councild. with themselves the result I could not lern and nearly all went off   after remaining in this Situation Some time I offered my hand to the 1 & 2 Chief who refusd to recve it. I turned off & went with my men on board the perogue, I had not progd.

26. Black Buffalo.
27. The Partisan.
28. Buffalo Medicine.

more the 10 paces before the 1st Cheif 3rd & 2 Brave men waded in after me. I took them in & went on board

we proceeded on about 1 mile & anchored out off a willow Island placed a guard on Shore to protect the Cooks & a guard in the boat, fastened the Perogues to the boat, I call this Island bad humered Island as we were in a bad humer. [Camped on later Marion Island, opposite Pierre, Hughes County, South Dakota.]

[ORDWAY] the large Swivel loaded immediately with 16 Musquet Ball in it the 2 other Swivels loaded well with Buck Shot, Each of them manned. Capt. Clark used moderation with them told them that we must and would go on the chief Sayed he had warriers too and if we were to go on they would follow us and kill [us] then Capt. Clark told them that we were Sent by their great father the presidant of the U. S. and that if they misused us that he or Capt. Lewis could by writing to him have them all distroyed as it were in a moment the chief then let go the Cable, and Sayed that he was Sorry.

September 26, 1804
[CLARK] (they [Tetons] offered us women, which we did not except). [Camped about four miles north of Fort Pierre, Stanley County, South Dakota.]

[CLARK] [The Tetons] appear Spritely, generally ill looking & not well made thier legs & arms Small . . . they Grese & <Black> themselves with coal when they dress, make use of a hawks feather about their heads the men a robe & each a polecats[29] Skins, for to hold ther *Bais roly*[30] for Smokeing fond of Dress & Show badly armed with fuseis [fusils] &. The Squaws are Chearfull fine lookg womin not handson, High Cheeks Dressed in Skins a Peticoat and roab which foldes back over thir Sholder, with long wool. doe all ther laborious work & I may Say perfect Slaves to the men, as all Squars of nations much at war . . . after Comeing too Capt. Lewis & 5 men went on Shore with the Chiefs, who appeared desposed to

29. Colloquial name for a skunk.
30. *Bois roulé*, otherwise kinnikinnick: a mixture of barks with tobacco.

make up & be friendly, after Captain Lewis had been on Shore about 3 hours I became uneasy for fear of Some Deception & sent a Serjeant to See him and know his treatment which he reported was friendly, & thy were prepareing for a Dance this evening

The[y] made frequent Selecitiation for us to remain one night only and let them Show their good disposition towards us, we deturmined to remain, after the return of Capt. Lewis, I went on Shore I saw Several Maha Prisoners and Spoke to the Chiefs   it was necessary to give those prisoners up & become good friends with the Mahars if they wished to follow the advice of their Great father   I was in Several Lodges neetly formed as before mentioned as to the Bauruly Tribe[31] —   I was met by about 10 well Dressd. yound men who took me up in a roabe Highly a decrated and Set me Down by the Side of their Chief on a Dressed robe in a large Council House   this house formed a ¾ Cercle of Skins well Dressed and Sown together   under this Shelter about 70 men Set forming a Circle in front of the Chiefs ‚ a plac of 6 feet Diameter was Clear and the pipe of peace raised on Sticks under which there was Swans down Scattered, on each Side of the Circle two Pipes, The flags of Spain 2 & the Flag we gave them in front of the Grand Chief . . .

Soon after they set me Down, the men went for Capt Lewis brough him in the same way and placed him also by the Chief   in a fiew minits an old man rose & Spoke approveing what we had done & informing us of their Situation requesting us to take pity on them &c which was answered—   The Great Chief then rose with great State to the Same purpote as far as we Could learn & then with Great Solemnity took up the pipe of peace whin the principal Chiefs Spoke with the pipe of Peace he took in one hand Some of the most Delicate parts of the Dog which was prepared for the feist & made a Sacrifise to the flag— & after pointing it to the heavins the 4 quarter of the Globe & the earth, lit it and prosist presented the Stem to us to Smoke, after a Smoke had taken place, & a Short Harange to his people, we were requested to take the meal we Smoked for an hour [until] Dark & all was Cleared away a large fire made in the Center, about 10 misitions playing on tamberins long sticks with Deer & Goats Hoofs tied So as to make a gingling noise and many others of a

31. Clark's mention of Bois Brulé is in error; he meant the Yanktons.

Similer kind, those men began to Sing, & Beet on the Tamboren, the women Came foward highly Deckerated in theire way, with the Scalps and Trofies of war of ther father Husbands Brothers or near Connection & proceeded to Dance the war Dance which they done with Great Chearfullness untill 12 oClock when we informed the Cheifs that they were fatigued &c. they then retired & we Accompd. by 4 Chiefs returned to our boat, they Stayed with us all night. Those people have Some brave men which they make use of as Soldiers those men attend to the police of the Village Correct all errors[32]   I saw one of them to day whip 2 Squars who appeared to have fallen out, when he approachd all about appeared to flee with great turrow   at night thy keep two 3 4 or 5 men at deffinit Distances walking around Camp Singing the accurrunces of the night . . .

I Saw & eat *Pemitigon*[33] the Dog, Grou[n]d potatoe[34] made into a Kind of homney, which I thought but little inferior — I also Saw a Spoon made of a horn of an animile of the Sheep kind[35]   the spoon will hold 2 quarts.

September 27, 1804
[CLARK] (when a[ny] of thos people Die they pierce ther flesh with arrows above & below ther elbows as a testimony of ther grief)   after a delay of half an hour I went with them on Shore, they left the boat with reluctiance (we Suspect they are treacherous and are at all times guarded & on our guard)   They again offered me a young woman and wish me to take her & not Dispise them, I wavered the Subject, at Dark the Dance began as usial and performed as last night. [Remained at camp north of Fort Pierre.]

[CLARK] Capt. Lewis came on Shore and we Continued untill we were Sleepy & returned to our boat, the 2nd Chief & one principal man accompanid us, those two Indians accompanied me on board in the Small Perogue, Capt. Lewis with a guard Still on Shore, the man who Steered not being much acustomed to Steer, passed the bow of the boat & peroge

32. The Teton soldiers were members of a warrior society, *akicita*, who acted as a constabulary.

33. Pemmican is dried, pulverized meat mixed with berries.

34. Indian potato.

35. Bighorn sheep.

Came broad Side against the Cable & broke it which obliged me to order in a loud voice all hands up & at their ores, my preempty order to the men and the bustle of their getting to their ores allarmd the Cheifs, togethr with the appearance of the men on Shore, as the boat turnd. The Cheif hollowered & allarmed the Camp or Town informing them that the Ma-hars was about attacting us. in about 10 minits the bank was lined with men armed the 1st Cheif at their head, about 200 men appeared and after about ½ hour returned all but about 60 men who Continued on the bank all night, the Cheifs Contd. all night with us— This allarm I as well as Captn. Lewis Considered as the Signal of their intentions (which was to Stop our proceeding on our journey and if Possible rob us) we were on our Guard all night, the misfortune of the loss of our Anchor obliged us to Lay under a falling bank much exposd. to the accomplishment of their hostile intentions P. C[ruzatte]—our Bowman who Cd. Speek Mahar informed us in the night that the Maha Prisoners informed him we were to be Stoped— we Shew as little Sighns of a Knowledge of their inten-tions as possible all prepared on board for any thing which might hapen, we kept a Strong guard all night in the boat no sleep.

[GASS] the Indians made preparations for a dance. At dark it com-menced. Captain Lewis, myself and some of our party went up to see them perform. Their band of musick, or orchestra, was composed of about twelve persons beating on a buffaloe hide, and shaking small bags that made a rattling noise. They had a large fire in the centre of their camp; on one side the women, about 80 in number, formed in a solid col-umn round the fire, with sticks in their hands, and the scalps of the Ma-has they had killed, tied on them. They kept moving, or jumping round the fire, rising and falling on both feet at once; keeping a continual noise, singing and yelling. In this manner they continued till 1 o'clock at night.

September 28, 1804
[CLARK] when we was about Setting out the Class Called the Soldiers took possession of the Cable the 1s Chief which was Still on board & in-tended to go a Short distance up with us, I told him the men of his nation Set on the Cable, he went out & told Capt Lewis who was at the bow the men who Set on the Roap was Soldiers and wanted Tobacco Capt.

L. Said would not agree to be forced into any thing, the 2d Chief Demanded a flag & Tobacco which we refusd. to Give Stateing proper reasons to them for it   after much difucelty—which had nearly reduced us
to hostility I threw a Carot of Tobacco to 1s Chief Spoke So as to touch
his pride took the port fire from the gunner the Chief gives the Tobaco
to his Soldiers & he jurked the rope from them and handed it to the bows
man . . . I am Verry unwelle for want of Sleep Deturmined to Sleep to
night if possible, the men Cooked & we rested well. [Camped on a sandbar about three miles above Oahe Dam, Stanley and Hughes Counties,
South Dakota; the area is now inundated by Lake Oahe.]

[GASS] While I was at the Indian camp yesterday they yoked a dog to a
kind of car,[36] which they have to haul their baggage from one camp to another; the nation having no settled place or village, but are always moving about. The dogs are not large, much resemble a wolf, and will haul
about 70 pounds each.

September 29, 1804
[CLARK] at 9 oClock we observed the 2d Chief with 2 men and Squars on
Shore . . . we refused to let one more Come on board Stateing Suffient
reasons, observd they would walk on Shore to the place we intended to
Camp, offered us women   we objected and told them we Should not
Speake to another teton except the one on board with us, who might go
on Shore when ever he pleased, those Indians proceeded on untill later in
the evening when the Chief requested that the Perogue might put him
across the river which we agreed to. [Camped on a sandbar between Stanley and Sully Counties, South Dakota, about three and one-half miles
above Chantier Creek, Stanley County.]

September 30, 1804
[CLARK] the Stern of the boat got fast on a log and the boat turned & was
verry near filling before we got her righted, the waves being verry high,
The Chief on board was So fritined at the motion of the boat which in its
rocking caused Several loose articles to fall on the Deck from the lockers,

36. Indian dog travois.

he ran off and hid himself, we landed   he got his gun and informed us he wished to return, that all things were Cleare for us to go on we would not See *any* more Tetons &c. [Camped on a sandbar in Sully County, South Dakota, just below the mouth of Cheyenne River opposite.]

October 1, 1804
[CLARK] Sand bars are So noumerous, that it is impossible to discribe them, & think it unnecessary to mention them.   we Saw a man opposit to our Camp on the L. S. which we discovd. to be a Frenchman . . . This Mr. *Jon Vallie*[37] informs us that he wintered last winter 300 Leagues up the Chien River under the Black mountains, he informs that this river is verry rapid and dificiult even for Canoos to assend . . . The black Mountains he Says is verry high, and Some parts of it has Snow on it in the Summer   great quantities of Pine Grow on the mountains, a great noise is heard frequently on those mountains, on the mountains great numbers of goat, and a kind of Anamale with large Circuler horns,[38] This animale is nearly the Size of an Argalia Small Elk. White bear[39] is also plenty— The Chien Inds.[40] <are about 300 lodges they> inhabit this river princi- pally, and Steel horses from the Spanish Settlements <to the S W>   This excurtion they make in one month . . . This frenchman gives an account of a white booted turkey[41] an inhabitant of the Cout Noie.[42] [Camped on a sandbar a few miles above the mouth of Cheyenne River, in either Dewey or Sully Counties, South Dakota.]

[LEWIS AND CLARK, WEATHER REMARKS] the leaves of the ash popular & most of the shrubs begin to turn yellow and decline.

October 2, 1804
[WHITEHOUSE] about 2 oClock P M. we discovered a number of Indians, on the hills on the North side of the River, One of those Indians came on the bank of the River, and fired off his Gun, and hallowed to us. We

37. Jean Vallé, a trader from Ste. Genevieve, Missouri.
38. Bighorn sheep.
39. Grizzly bear.
40. Cheyenne Indians.
41. Probably the sharp-tailed grouse.
42. Black Hills.

hardly knew his meaning, but stood in readiness, in case any of these Savages should attackt us, Our Officers being determin'd to proceed on our Voyage, at the risque of their lives, and the Men determin'd to support them in the attempt. [Camped on a sandbar just above later Plum Island (now submerged), with Sully County, South Dakota, on the east and Dewey County on the west.]

October 4, 1804
[CLARK] Capt. Lewis and 3 men walked on Shore & crossed over to an Island[43] Situated on the S. S. . . . in the Center of this Island was an old Village of the rickeries[44] Called *La ho catt*   it was Circular and walled Containing 17 lodges and it appears to have been deserted about five years. [Camped on a sandbar above later Dolphees Island (now submerged), between Dewey and Potter Counties, South Dakota.]

October 6, 1804
[CLARK] passed a village of about 80 neet Lodges covered with earth and picketed around,[45] those loges are Spicious [spacious] of an Octagon form as close together as they can possibly be placed and appear to have been inhabited last Spring, from the Canoes of Skins Mats buckets & found in the lodges, we are of appinion they were the recrereis we found Squashes of 3 Different Kinds growing in the Village. [Camped at the mouth of Swan Creek, Walworth County, South Dakota.]

October 7, 1804
[ORDWAY] we killed . . . a handsome Brarow which Capts. had the Bones & skin Saved in order to Send back to the States.

October 8, 1804
[CLARK] 2 of our men discovered the reckerrei village, about the Center of the Island[46] on the L. Side . . . The Isld. is covered with fields, where

43. Dolphees Island, now submerged.
44. Arikara Indians.
45. Clark described the typical earth lodges of Missouri River Indians (see also Gass's entry, October 10, 1804).
46. Ashley Island, Corson County, South Dakota.

those people raise their Corn Tobacco Beens &c. Great numbers of those People came on   the Island to See us pass, we passed above the head of the Island & Capt. Lewis with 2 interpeters & 2 men went to the Village   I formed a Camp of the french & the guard on Shore, with one Sentinal on board of the boat at anchor, a pleasent evening   all things arranged both for Peace or War . . . Several french men Came up with Capt Lewis in a Perogue, one of which is a Mr. Gravellin[47] a man well versed in the language of this nation and gave us Some information relitive to the Countrey naton &c. [Camped between Oak and Fisher Creeks, Corson County, South Dakota.]

October 9, 1804
[CLARK] all the grand Chiefs visited us to day also Mr Taboe,[48] a trader from St. Louis—   Many Canoes of a Single Buffalow Skin[49] made in the form of a Bowl Carrying generally 3 and Sometimes 5 & 6 men, those Canoes, ride the highest Waves . . . I saw at Several times to day 3 Squars in single Buffalow Skin Canoes loaded with meat Cross the River, at the time the waves were as high as I ever Saw them in the Missouri. [Remained at the camp between Oak and Fisher Creeks.]

[CLARK] the three great Chiefs [of the Arikaras] . . .

> 1st Chiefs name *Kakawissassa* (lighting Crow.)
> 2d   do   do   *Pocasse* (or Hay)
> 3d   do   do   *Piaheto* (or Eagles feather)

October 10, 1804
[CLARK] the Inds. much astonished at my black Servent, who made him Self more turrible in thier view than I wished him to Doe as I am told telling them that before I cought him he was wild & lived upon people, young children was verry good eating   Showed them his Strength &c. [Remained at the camp between Oak and Fisher Creeks.]

---

47. Joseph Gravelines, a trader among the Arikaras for more than twenty years.
48. Pierre-Antoine Tabeau, associated with Gravelines.
49. Possibly bullboats, hemispherical vessels covered with buffalo skins.

[CLARK] we prepare all things ready to Speak to the Indians, Mr. Tabo & Mr. Gravolin Came to brackfast with us   the Chiefs & came from the lower Town, but none from the 2 upper Towns, which is the largest . . . at 12 oClock Dispatchd Gravelin to envite them to Come down, we have every reason to believe that a jellousy exists between the Villages for fear of our makeing the 1st Cheif from the lower Village, at one oClock the Cheifs all assembled & after Some little Cerrimony the Council Commenced, we informd them what we had told the others before i' e' Ottoes & Seaux.   made 3 Cheif 1 for each Village.   gave them presents.   after the Council was Over we Shot the air guns which astonished them much, the[y] then Departed and we rested Secure all night.

[GASS] The following is a description of the form of these lodges and the manner of building them. In a circle of a size suited to the dimensions of the intended lodge, they set up 16 forked posts five or six feet high, and lay poles from one fork to another. Against these poles they lean other poles, slanting from the ground, and extending about four inches above the cross poles: these are to receive the ends of the upper poles, that support the roof. They next set up four large forks, fifteen feet high, and about ten feet apart, in the middle of the area; and poles or beams between these. The roof poles are then laid on extending from the lower poles across the beams which rest on the middle forks, of such a length as to leave a hole at the top for a chimney. The whole is then covered with willow branches, except the chimney and a hole below to pass through. On the willow branches they lay grass and lastly clay. At the hole below they build a pen about four feet wide and projecting ten feet from the hut; and hang a buffaloe skin, at the entrance of the hut for a door. This labour like every other kind is chiefly performed by the squaws.

October 11, 1804
[CLARK] at 11 oClock we met the Grand Chief in Council & and he made a Short Speech thanking us for what we had Given him & his nation promisseing to attend to the Council we had given him & informed us the road was open & no one dare Shut it, & we might Departe at pleasure, at 1 oClock we Set out for the upper villages 3 miles distant . . . after being treated by everry civility by those people who are both pore & Durtey we

returned to our boat at about 10 oClk. P M. informing them before we Departed that we would Speek to them tomorrow at there Seperate Villages. Those people gave us to eate bread made of Corn & Beens, also Corn & Beans boild.   a large Been,[50] which they rob the mice of the Prarie which is rich & verry nurrishing also Squashes &c.   all Tranquil-lity. [Camped a few miles above Fisher Creek, Corson County, South Dakota.]

[ORDWAY] Some of the party down at the village below this last night they informed us that one of the chiefs lost all the good he Recd. from us in the River, Going home.   the Skin cannoe got over Set turned everry thing out of it   he Grieved himself considerable about his loss &C.

October 12, 1804
[CLARK] went to the house of the 2nd Chief *Lassil*[51] where there was many Chief and warriers & about 7 bushels of Corn, a pr Leagins a twist of their Tobacco & Seeds of 2 Kind of Tobacco   we Set Some time before the Councill Commenced   this man Spoke at Some length declareing his dispotion to believe and prosue our Councils, his intention of going to Visit his great father   acknowledged the Satisfaction in receiveing the presents &c. rais'g a Doubt as to the Safty on passing the nations below particularly the Souex.   requested us to take a Chief of their nation and make a good pact with Mandins[52] & nations above.   after answering those parts of the 2d Chiefs Speech which required it, which appeared to give General Satisfaction we went to the Village of the 3rd Chief and as usial Some Serimony took place before he Could Speek to us on the Great Subject . . .
  ' The Nation of the Rickerries is about 600 men able to bear arms   a Great perpotion of them have fusees   they appear to be peacefull, their men tall and perpotiend, womin Small and industerous, raise great quan-tities of Corn Beens Simmins[53] &c. also Tobacco for the men to Smoke they Collect all the wood and do the drugery as Common amongst Sav-

50. Product of the hog peanut, gathered from the stores of the meadow mouse.
51. Perhaps another name for Pocasse, the second chief.
52. Mandan Indians.
53. Probably Clark's version of "simlin," a term for summer squashes.

ages. Thise <nation is> made up of <10> Different Tribes of the Pania, who had formerly been Seperate, but by Commotion and war with their neighbours have Come reduced and compelled to Come together for protection, The Curruption of the language of those different Tribes has So reduced the language that the Different Villages do not understade all the words of the others. Those people are Durtey, Kind, pore, & extravigent pursessing national pride.   not beggarley reive what is given with great pleasure . . .

Those people express an inclination to be at peace with all nations— The Seaux who trade the goods which they get of the British Traders for their corn, and great influence over the Rickeres, poisen their minds and keep them in perpetial dread . . .

a curious Cuistom with the Souix as well as the reckeres is to give handsom Squars to those whome they wish to Show Some acknowledgements to— The Seauix we got Clare of without taking their Squars, they followed us with Squars . . . two days. The Rickores we put off dureing the time we were at the Towns but 2 Handsom young Squars were Sent by a man to follow us, they Came up this evening and peresisted in their Civilities. [Camped about ten miles above the previous camp but on the opposite shore, Campbell County, South Dakota.]

October 13, 1804

[CLARK] a fiew miles from the river on the S. S. 2 Stones resembling humane persons & one resembling a Dog is Situated in the open Prarie, to those Stone the Rickores pay Great reverance make offerings whenever they pass (Infomtn. of the Chief & Intepeter)   those people have a Curious Tredition of those Stones, one was a man in Love, one a Girl whose parents would not let marry, the Dog went to mourn with them   all turned to Stone gradually, Commenceing at the feet. Those people fed on grapes untill they turned, & the woman has a bunch of grapes yet in her hand   on the river near the place those are Said to be Situated, we obsd. a greater quantity of fine grapes than I ever Saw at one place. [Camped about a mile south of the North Dakota state line, Campbell County, South Dakota.]

[LEWIS AND CLARK] A court Martial to Consist of nine members will set to day at 12 oClock for the trial of John Newman now under Confinement

Capt. Clark will attend to the forms & rules of a president without giveing his opinion

Detail for the Court Martial

Sert. John Ordaway
Sergeant Pat. Gass
H. Hall
Jo. Collins
Wm. Werner
Wm. Bratten
Jo. Shannon
<P Wiser>
Silas Goodrich

. . . the Court martial convened this day for the trial of John Newman, charged with "having uttered repeated expressions of a highly criminal and mutinous nature; the same having a tendency not only to distroy every principle of military discipline, but also to alienate the affections of the individuals composing this Detachment to their officers, and disaffect them to the service for which they have been so sacredly and solemnly engaged." The Prisonar plead *not guilty* to the charge exhibited against him. The court . . . are unanimously of opinion that the prisonar John Newman is guilty of every part of the charge exhibited against him, and do sentence him agreeably to the rules and articles of war, to receive seventy five lashes on his bear back, and to be henceforth discarded from the perminent party engaged for North Western discovery; two thirds of the Court concurring in the sum and nature of the punishment awarded. the commanding officers approve and confirm the sentence of the court, and direct the punishment take place tomorrow between the hours of one and two P. M. The commanding officers further direct that John Newman in future be attatched to the mess and crew of the red Perogue as a labouring hand on board the same, and that he be deprived of his arms and accoutrements, and not be permited the honor of mounting guard untill further orders; the commanding officers further direct that in lue of the guard duty from which Newman has been exempted by virtue of this order, that he shall be exposed to such drudgeries as they may think

proper to direct from time to time with a view to the general relief of the
detachment.

October 14, 1804
[CLARK] after Dinner executed the Sentence of the Court Martial So far
a[s] giveing the Corporal punishment, & proceeded on a fiew miles . . .
The punishment of this day allarmd. the Indian Chief verry much, he
Cried aloud (or effected to Cry) I explained the Cause of the punishment
and the necessity He thought examples were also necessary, & he him-
self had made them by Death, [but] his nation never whiped even their
Children, from their burth. [Camped a few miles above the state line in
Emmons County, North Dakota.]

[LEWIS AND CLARK, WEATHER REMARKS] the leaves of all the trees as
ash, elm &c except the cottonwood is now fallen.

October 15, 1804
[CLARK] at Sunset we arrived at a Camp of Ricares of 10 Lodges on the
S. S. . . . Capt Lewis & my Self went with the Chief who accompanis us, to
the Huts of Several of the men all of whome Smoked & gave us Something to eate also Some meat to take away, those people were kind and appeared to be much plsd. at the attentioned paid them. Those people are
much pleased with my black Servent — Their womin verry fond of car-
ressing our men. [Camped in Emmons County, North Dakota, near Fort
Yates, on the opposite side.]

[ORDWAY] the Greatest Curiousity to them was York Capt. Clarks Black
Man . . . the children would follow after him, & if he turned towards them
they would run from him & hollow as if they were terreyfied, & afraid
of him.

October 16, 1804
[LEWIS] This day took a small bird alive of the order of the [blank] or goat
suckers. it appeared to be passing into the dormant state.[54] on the

54. Lewis identified the common poorwill. In the 1940s zoologists acknowledged the
common poorwill's tendency to hibernate.

morning of the 18th the murcury was at 30 a[bove] 0.   the bird could
scarcely move. I run my penknife into it's body under the wing and completely distroyed it's lungs and heart — yet it lived upwards of two hours
this fanominon I could not account for unless it proceeded from the want
of circulation of the blo[o]d.   the recarees call this bird to'-na . . . a noc-
turnal bird, sings only in the night as does the whipperwill.   it's weight —
1 oz 17 Grains Troy. [Camped about two miles above and opposite Big
Beaver Creek, Sioux County, North Dakota.]

October 17, 1804
[CLARK]. This Chief tells me of a number of their Treditions about
Turtles, Snakes, & and the power of a perticiler rock or Cave on the next
river which informs of everr thing   none of those I think worth while
mentioning. [Camped a few miles below the mouth of Cannonball River,
Sioux County, North Dakota.]

October 20, 1804
[CLARK] I walked out to view those remarkable places pointed out by
Evens . . . Saw an old Village of the Mandans below the Chess chi ter R.⁵⁵
appear to have been fortified . . . the Countrey thro which I passed this
day is Delightfull, Timber in the bottoms, Saw great nos. of Buffalow Elk
Goats & Deer   as we were in want of them I Killed 3 Deer, our hunters 10
Deer and wounded a white Bear, I Saw Several fresh tracks of that animal
double the Sise of the largest track I ever Saw, great numbers of wolves,
those animals follow the buffalow and devour, those that die or are Killed,
and those too fat or pore to Keep up with the gangue. [Camped below the
mouth of Heart River, Morton County, North Dakota, and a few miles
south of the town of Mandan.]

October 21, 1804
[CLARK] at Day light it began to *Snow* and Continud all the fore part of
the Day   passed just above our Camp a Small river on the L. S. Called by
the Indians *Chiss-Cho-tar* . . . Some Distance up this River is Situated a

55. Heart River; Clark's "Chess chi ter" is an Arikara word for "fork (of a river)."

Stone which the Indians have great fath in & Say they See painted on the Stone, ["]all the Calemites & good fortune to hapin the nation & partes who visit it"— a tree (an oak[)] which Stands alone near this place about 2 miles off in the open prarie which has with Stood the fire they pay Great respect to, make Holes and tie Strings thro the Skins of their necks and around this tree to make them brave   (all this is the information of Too ne is a whipper will) the Chief of the Ricares who accompanied us to the Mandins.[56] [Camped in or somewhat above Mandan, Morton County, North Dakota.]

October 22, 1804

[CLARK] last night at about 1 oClock I was violently attacked with Rhumetism in my neck, which was so violently I could not move, Cap L. applied a hot Stone raped in flannel which gave temperry ease, we passed a War party of Tetons on their way as we Supposed to the Mandans of 12 men on the L. S.   we gave them nothing and refused to put them across the river, passed . . . the upper of the 6 Villages the Mandans occupied about 25 years ago   this village[57] was entirely cut off by the *Sioux* & one of the óthers nearly, the Small Pox distroyed great Numbers. [Camped in Oliver County, North Dakota, near the Oliver-Morton county line.]

October 24, 1804

[CLARK] Some little Snow in the morning   I am Something better of the Rhumutim in my neck . . . we have Seen no game on the river to day a pro[o]f of the Indians hunting in the neighbourhod . . . we Saw one of the Grand Chiefs of the Mandins . . . this Cheif met the Chief of the *Ricares* who accompanied us with great Cordiallity & Sermony   Smoked the pipe & Capt. Lewis with the Interpeter went with the Chiefs to his Lodges at 1 mile distant, after his return we admited the Grand Chief & his brother for a few minits on our boat. [Camped about two miles below Washburn, McLean County, North Dakota.]

56. "Too ne" and "whipper will" appear to be other names for the Arikara chief Piaheto.

57. Double Ditch site, Burleigh County, North Dakota.

October 25, 1804

[CLARK] Several parties of Mandins rode to the river on the S. S. to view us indeed they are *continuelly* in Sight Satisying their Curiossities as to our apperance &c. we are told that the Seaux has latterly fallen in with & Stole the horses of the *Big belley*,[58] on their way home they fell in with the Ossiniboin[59] who killed them and took the horses . . . Several Indians Come to See us this evening, amongst others the Sun of the late great Cheif of the Mandins, this man has his two little fingers off; on inqureing the Cause, was told it was Customary for this nation to Show their greaf by Some testimony of pain, and that it was not uncommon for them to take off 2 Smaller fingers of the hand and Some times more with ther marks of Savage effection . . . R. Fields with the rhumitim in his neck, P. Crusat with the Same Complaint in his Legs— the party other wise is well, as to my Self I feel but Slight Simptoms of that disorder at this time. [Camped in Oliver County, North Dakota, south of the Mercer-Oliver county line.]

[LEWIS AND CLARK, WEATHER REMARKS] all the leaves of the trees have now fallen— the snow did not lye.

October 26, 1804

[CLARK] we Set the Ricara Chief on Shore with Some Mandans, many on each Side veiwing of us, we took in 2 Chiefs (Coal and Big Man) and halted a feiw minits at their Camps . . . here we Saw a trader from the Ossinniboin River Called McCracken,[60] this man arrived 9 day ago with goods to trade for horses & Roabs . . . we Camped on the L. Side a Short distanc below the 1st mandan village[61] . . . many men women & Children flocked down to See us— Capt Lewis walked to the Village with the Chief and interpeters, my Rheumitism increasing prevented me from go-

58. Hidatsa Indians, also called Minitaris and Gros Ventres.

59. Assiniboine Indians.

60. Hugh McCracken, a trader among the Mandans for many years.

61. Mitutanka, the Deapolis site, near the now defunct town of Deapolis, Mercer County, North Dakota.

ing also, and we had Deturmined that both would not leave the boat at the Same time untill we Knew the Desposition of the Nativs, Some Chieef visited me & I Smoked with them— they appeared delighted with the Steel Mill . . . also with my black Servent, Capt Lewis returned late. [Camped south of Stanton, Mercer County, North Dakota.]

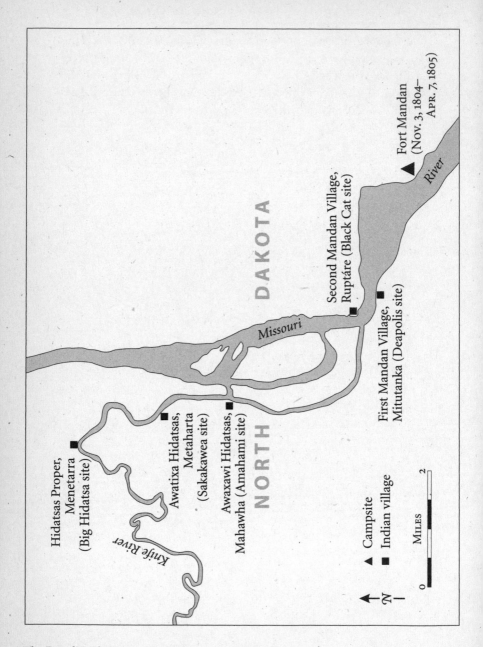

The Expedition's Route, October 27, 1804–April 6, 1805

Fort Mandan
(Nov. 3, 1804–
Apr. 7, 1805)

River

DAKOTA

Second Mandan Village,
Ruptáre (Black Cat site)

Missouri

First Mandan Village,
Mitutanka (Deapolis site)

NORTH

Awatixa Hidatsas,
Metaharta
(Sakakawea site)

Awaxawi Hidatsas,
Mahawha (Amahami site)

Hidatsas Proper,
Menetarra
(Big Hidatsa site)

Knife River

▲ Campsite
■ Indian village

MILES

0   2

N

CHAPTER 3

Knife River Winter

October 27, 1804–April 6, 1805

October 27, 1804

[CLARK] Came too at the village on the L. S. where we delayed a few minits, I walked to a Chiefs Logg & Smoked with them, but Could not eat, which did displease them a little, here I met with a Mr: Jessomme,[1] who lived in this nation 18 [13?] years, I got him to interpet & he proceedd on with us we proceeded on to a Centeral point opposit the Knife River, & formed a Camp on the S. S. above the 2d Mandan village[2] & opsd. the Mah-har-ha village[3] . . . we endeaver to precure Some Knowledge of the principal Chiefs of the Different nations &. well to give my ideas as to the impression thais man[4] makes on me is a Cunin artfull an insoncear— he tels me he was once empld. by my brother in the Illinois & of his description I conceve as a Spye upon the British of Michillinicknac & St Joseph, we think he may be made use full to us & do employ him as an interpeter. [Camped opposite Stanton, Mercer County, North Dakota.]

October 28, 1804

[CLARK] Consulted the Black Cat M[andan] Chief about the Chiefs of the Different Villages, who gave his Oppinion to us. [Remained at the camp opposite Stanton.]

1. René Jusseaume, a free trader with the Mandans for about fifteen years.
2. Ruptáre, McLean County, North Dakota, now lost; known as the Black Cat site, after its chief.
3. Mahawha was an Awaxawi Hidatsa village, known as the Amahami site, on the grounds of the Mercer County Courthouse, Stanton, North Dakota.
4. Jusseaume.

[ORDWAY] the form of these Savvages burrying their dead is after they have disceased they fix a Scaffel on & raised 4 forks abt 8 or 10 feet from the Ground. they lye the dead body on the Sd. Scaffel Raped up in a Buffalow Robe a little distance from their villages.

October 29, 1804

[CLARK] The Chief who recved Medals to Day are as follows viz—   in Council

> 1s Mandan village Ma-too-tonka—
> > 1s Chief *Sha-ha-ka* Big White
> > 2nd *Ka-goh-ha-me* little Crow
> 2 do village *Roop tar-hee*
> > 1s & grand Chief Poss-cop-sa-he   Black Cat—
> > 2d Chief *Car-gar-no-mok-she* raven man Chief—
> *Mah har-ha* village
> > 1s Chief *Ta-tuck-co pin re has*, white Buffalow Skin unfolded
> Little Menetarre village[5]
> > 1s Chief Omp-Se-ha-ra Black mockerson.
> > 2d Chief *Oh-harh* little Fox

The Grand village of Manetarres,[6] The One Eye is the principal Chief and he is out on a hunting party. we Send by the Grape[7] all the articles for this grand Chief and all the Village what goods was intended for that Village—   The Prarie got on fire and went with Such Violenc & Speed as to Catch a man & woman & burn them to Death, Several escapd. among other a Small boy who was Saved by getting under a green Buffalow Skin, this boy was half white, & the Indians Say all white flesh is medisan, they Say the grass was not burnt where the boy Sat &c. [Remained at the camp opposite Stanton.]

[CLARK] after Brackfast we were visited by the old Cheaf of the *Big bellies* or [blank]   this man was old and had transfered his power to his Sun,

5. Metaharta, village of the Awatixa Hidatsas, called the Sakakawea site, Mercer County, North Dakota.

6. Menetarra, village of the Hidatsas Proper, the Big Hidatsa site, Mercer County.

7. The old chief of the Hidatsas, known by many names, such as The Grape.

who was then out at war against the Snake Indians[8] who inhabit the rockey mountains — at 10 oClock the S W. wind rose verry high, we Collected the Chiefs and Commened a Council . . . at the end of the Speech mentioned the *Ricare* who Accompanied us to make a firm peace, they all Smoked with him (I gave this Cheaf a Dollar of the American Coin as a Meadel with which he was much pleased) In Councel we prosented him with a Certificate of his Sincrrity and good Conduct &c.   after the Coun[c]i[l] we gave the presents with much Seremoney, and put the Meadels on the Cheifs we intended to make viz. one for each Town to whome we gave Coats hats & flags, one Grand Cheif to each nation to whome we gave meadels with the presidents likeness.

October 30, 1804
[CLARK] Two Chiefs came to have Some talk   one the princapal of the lower Village the other the one who thought himself the principal mane, & requested to hear Some of the Speech that was Delivered yesterday they were gratified, and we put the medal on the neck of the Big White to whome we had Sent Clothes yesterday & a flag . . . I took 8 men in a Small perogue and went up the river as far as the 1st Island about 7 miles to See if a Situation Could be got on it for our Winter quarters, found the wood on the Isd. as also on the pt. above So Distant from the water that, I did not think that we Could get a good wintering ground there, and as all the white men here informed us that wood was Sceres, as well as game above, we Deturmined to drop down a fiew miles near wood and game. [Remained at the camp opposite Stanton.]

November 1, 1804
[CLARK] Mr. McCrackin a Trader Set out at 7 oClock to the fort on the Ossiniboin by him Send a letter, (incloseing a Copy of the British Ministers protection)[9] to the principal agent of the Company — at about 10 OClock the Cheifs of the Lower Village Cam and after a Short time informed us they wished they would us to call at their village & take Some Corn, that they would make peace with the *Ricares* they never made war

8. Shoshones, Sacagawea's people.
9. Edward Thornton was the British minister who issued Lewis's passport.

against them but after the *rees* Killed their Chiefs they killed them like the birds, and were tired and would Send a Chief and Some brave men to the *Ricares* to Smoke with that people. [The party moved a short distance downriver, north of their later site of Fort Mandan.]

November 2, 1804
[LEWIS] This morning early we fixed on the site for our fortification which we immediately set about. This place we have named Fort Mandan in honour of our Neighbours.[10]

November 3, 1804
[CLARK] Discharged the french hands. [All of the men have apparently relocated to the Fort Mandan site, where they remained until April 7, 1805. Campsite locations will be noted again beginning with that date.]

[CLARK] we commence building our Cabins, Send Down in Perogue 6 men to hunt   Engaged one man[11] . . . Mr. Jessomme with his Squar & Children come Down to live, as Interpter . . . in the evening the *Ka goh ha mi* or little ravin Came & brought us on his Squar about 60 Wt. of Dried Buffalow meat a roabe, & Pot of Meal &.   they Delayed all night— we gave his Squar an ax & a fiew Small articles & himself a piece of Tobacco, the Men were indulged with a Dram, this evening.

[GASS] The following is the manner in which our huts and fort were built; the huts were in two rows, containing four rooms each, and joined at one end forming an angle. When rasied about 7 feet high a floor of puncheons or split plank were laid, and covered with grass and clay; which made a warm loft. The upper part projected a foot over and the roofs were made shed-fashion, rising from the inner side, and making the outer wall about 18 feet high. The part not inclosed by the huts we intended to picket. In the angle formed by the two rows of huts we built two rooms, for holding our provisions and stores.[12]

    10. Clark found the site of Fort Mandan, about fourteen miles west of Washburn, McLean County, North Dakota.
    11. Jean Baptiste Lepage took Newman's place.
    12. Compare Whitehouse's description of Fort Mandan of December 31 to Gass's.

November 4, 1804

[CLARK] a french man by Name Chabonah,[13] who Speaks the Big Belley language visit us, he wished to hire & informed us his 2 Squars were Snake Indians, we engau him to go on with us and take one of his wives[14] to interpet the Snake language.

[ORDWAY] we got one line of our huts raised So that we got the Eve Beames on & all of large Timber So that it took all the men hard lifting to put the 16 foot eve Beames.

November 5, 1804

[CLARK] I have the Rhumitism verry bad, Cap Lewis writeing all Day.

November 6, 1804

[CLARK] last night late we wer awoke by the Sergeant of the Guard to See a nothern light, which was light, not red, and appeared to Darken and Some times nearly obscered, and many times appeared in light Streeks, and at other times a great Space light & containing floating Collomns which appeared opposite each other & retreat leaveing the lighter Space at no time of the Same appearence . . . Mr. Jo Gravilin . . . return to the ricaree nation & the Illinois, Mr. Gravilin has instructions to take on the recarees in the Spring &c. Continue to build the huts, out of Cotton Timber, &c. this being the only timber we have.

November 7, 1804

[ORDWAY] the Capts. Room being hughn down the inside, we layed the loft over with hughn punchien then Stoped the craks with Some old tarpolin & Grass Some morter then a thick coat of earth over all, which will make it verry warm.

November 9, 1804

[CLARK] a verry hard frost this morning we Continue to build our Cabens, under many disadvantages . . . Several Indians pass with flying

13. Toussaint Charbonneau, the Hidatsa interpreter.
14. Sacagawea of the Shoshone ("Snake") Indians.

news . . . we are Situated in a point of the Missouri North Side in a Cotton wood Timber, this Timber is tall and heavy Containing an imence quantity of water Brickle & Soft food for Horses to winter (as is Said by the Indians) The Mandans Graze their horses in the day on Grass, and at night give them a Stick of Cotton wood to eate, Horses Dogs & people all pass the night in the Same Lodge or round House, Covd. with earth with a fire in the middle.

November 11, 1804
[LEWIS] Latitude . . . N. 47° 21′ 32.8″.[15]

November 12, 1804
[CLARK] early this morning the Big White princapal Chief of the lower Village of the Mandans Came Down, he packd about 100 W. of fine meet on his Squar for us . . . The interpeter Says that the Mandan nation as they old men Say Came out of a <Small lake> where they had Gardins, maney years ago. they lived in Several Villages on the Missourie low down, the Smallpox destroyed the greater part of the nation and reduced them to one large Village and Some Small ones . . . after they were reduced the Sioux and other Indians waged war, and killed a great maney, and they moved up the Missourie, those Indians Still continued to wage war, and they moved Still higher, untill they got in the Countrey of the Panias, whith this ntn. they lived in friendship maney years, inhabiting the Same neighbourhood untill that people waged war, They moved up near the *watersoons* & *winataree*[16] where they now live in peace with those nations, the mandans Specke a language peculial to themselves[17]

they can rase about 350 men, the Winatarees about 80 and the Big bellies about 600 or 650 men . . . The Big bellies Winitarees & ravin Indians Speake nearly the Same language and the presumption is they were origionally the Same nation[18] The Ravin Indians "have 400 Lodges & about

15. The approximate latitude of Fort Mandan is 47° 16′ 54″ N (see also January 28, 1805).
16. Expedition names for divisions of the Hidatsas.
17. Although the Mandan language differed from Hidatsa and was distinct, it was part of the common Siouan language family.
18. The "Big bellies" and "Winitarees" (Minitaris) were divisions of the Hidatsas as Lewis and Clark understood them, while the Crow ("ravin") Indians had divided from the Hidatsas some time earlier and spoke nearly the same language.

1200 men, & follow the Buffalow, or hunt for their Subsistance in the plains & on the Court noi & Rock Mountains, & are at war with the Sioux Snake Indians["]

The Big bellies & Watersoons are at war with the Snake Indians & Seaueex, and were at war with the *Ricares* untill we made peace a fiew days passd.

November 13, 1804

[CLARK] at 10 oClock A M the Black Cat the Mandin Chief and *Lagru Che Chark*[19] <Ossiniboin> Chief & 7 men of note visited us at Fort Mandan, I gave him a twist of Tobacco to Smoke with his people & a Gold Cord with a view to Know him again, The nation Consists of about 600 men, hunt in the Plains & winter and trade on the Ossiniboin River, they are Decendants of the Siaux and Speake their language, they Come to the nations to this quarter to trade or (make preasthts) for horses <& robes>.

[LEWIS AND CLARK, WEATHER REMARKS] the river has every appearance of closing for winter.

[ORDWAY] Capt. Lewis returned with his party towards evening much fatigued.   they got fast on a Sand bar & had to be out in the water abto. 2 hours.   the Ice running against their legs.   their close frooze on them.   one of them got 1 of his feet frost bit.   it hapned that they had Some whiskey with them to revive their Spirits.

November 14, 1804

[CLARK] only two Indians visit us to day Owing to a Dance at the Village last night in Concluding a Serimoney of adoption, and interchange of property, between the Ossiniboins, and the nations of this neighbourhood.

November 18, 1804

[CLARK] the Black Cat, Chief of the Mandans Came to See us, he made Great inquiries respecting our fashions.   he also Stated the Situation of

19. La Grue in French, or Che Chark, apparently in Cree, means "The Crane."

their nation, he mentioned that a Council had been held the day before and it was thought advisable to put up with the resent insults of the Ossiniboins & Christonoes[20] untill they were Convinced that what had been told thim by us . . . we advised them to remain at peace & that they might depend upon Getting *Supplies* through the Channel of the Missouri, but it requred time to put the trade in opperation.[21]

November 19, 1804
[CLARK] our Perogue of Hunters arrive with 32 Deer, 12 Elk & a Buffalow, all of this meat we had hung up in a Smoke house, a timeley supply . . . our men move into their huts, Several little Indian aneckdts. told me to day.

November 20, 1804
[CLARK] Capt Lewis & my Self move into our huts . . . three Chiefs from the 2d Mandan Village Stay all Day, they are verry Curious in examining our works. Those Chiefs informs us that the Souix settled on the Missourie above Dog River,[22] threten to attacked them this winter, and have treated 2 Ricares who Carried the pipe of peace to them Verry roughly. whiped & took their horses from them &c. is much displeased with Ricares for makeing a peace with the Mandans through us, we gave them a Sattisfactory answer.

November 22, 1804
[CLARK] I was allarmed about 10 oClock by the Sentinal, who informed that an Indian was about to Kill his wife in the interpeters <hut> fire about 60 yards below the works, I went down and Spoke to the fellow about the rash act which he was like to commit and forbid any act of the kind near the fort— Some missunderstanding took place between this man & his fife about 8 days ago, and She came to this place, & Continued with the Squars of the interpeters, 2 days ago She returned to the Villg. in the evening of the Same day She came to the interpeters fire appearently

20. Cree Indians,
21. Lewis and Clark hoped that Missouri River Indians would be patient as American merchants from St. Louis established consistent trade up to the Mandans and beyond.
22. Cheyenne River.

much beat, & Stabed in 3 places— We Derected that no man of this party have any intercourse with this woman under the penelty of Punishment— he the Husband observed that one of our Serjeants Slept with his wife & if he wanted her he would give her to him, We derected the Serjeant Odway to give the man Some articles, at which time I told the Indian that I believed not one man of the party had touched his wife except the one he had given the use of her for a nite, in his own bed, no man of the party Should touch his Squar, or the wife of any Indian, nor did I believe they touch a woman if they knew her to be the wife of another man, and advised him to take his Squar home and live hapily together in future.

November 25, 1804

[CLARK] a fine day warm & pleasent   Capt. Lewis 2 Interpeters & 6 men Set out to See the Indians in the different Towns & Camps in this neighbour hood, we Continu to Cover & dob our huts, two Chiefs Came to See me to day one named Wau-ke-res-sa-ra, a Big belley and the first of that nation who has visited us Since we have been here, I gave him a Handkerchef Paint & a Saw band, and the other Some fiew articles, and paid a perticular attention which pleased them verry much, the interpeters being all with Capt. Lewis I could not talk to them.   we Compleated our huts— Several men with bad Colds.

November 27, 1804

[CLARK] Capt. Lewis returned from the Villages with two Chiefs Marnoh toh & Man-nes-sur ree & a Considerate man with the party who accompanied him, The Menitares, (or Big bellies) were allarmed at the tales told them by the Mandans Viz: that we intended to join the *Seaux* to Cut off them in the Course of the winter, many Circumstances Combind to give force to those reports i' e' the movements of the interpeters & their families to the *Fort*, the strength of our work &.

all those reports was contridicted by Capt Louis with a Conviction on the minds of the Indians of the falsity of those reports— the Indians in all the towns & Camps treated Capt Lewis & the party with Great respect except one of the principal Cheifs *Mar par pa par ra pas a too* or (Horned Weasel) who did not Chuse to be Seen by the Capt. & left word that he was not at home &.

Seven Traders arrived from the fort on the Ossinaboin from the N W Companey   one of which Lafrances[23] took upon himself to speak unfavourably of our intentions &. the princpal Mr. *La Rock*,[24] (& Mr. McKensey)[25] was informed of the Conduct of their interpeter & the Consiquinces if they did not put a Stop to unfavourable & ill founded assursions.

[ORDWAY] we had a dance this evening. Rivet danced on his head.

November 28, 1804
[CLARK] at 8 oClock the *Poss-cop-so-he* or Black Cat Grand Chief of the Mandans Came to See us, after Showing Those Chiefs many thing which was Curiossities to them, and Giveing a fiew presents of Curioes Hand-kerchiefs arm bans & paint with a twist of Tobaco they departed at 1 oClock much pleased, at parting we had Some little talk on the Subject of the British Trader Mr. Le rock Giveing Meadils & Flags, and told those Chiefs to impress it on the minds of their nations that those Simbells were not to be recved by any from them, without they wished incur the dis-plieasure of their Great American Father.

November 29, 1804
[CLARK] Mr. *La Rock* and one of his men Came to visit us   we informed him what we had herd of his intentions of makeing Chiefs &c. and forbid him to give meadels or flags to the Indians, he Denied haveing any Such intention, we agreeed that one of our interpeters Should Speak for him on Conditions he did not Say any thing more than what tended to trade alone— he gave fair promises &. Sergeant Pryor in takeing down the mast put his Sholder out of Place, we made four trials before we replaced it.

November 30, 1804
[CLARK] [An Indian] informed us as follows. Viz: "five men of the Man-dan Nation out hunting in a S. W. derection about Eight Leagues was

23. Baptiste Lafrance, an interpreter for the North West Company.
24. François-Antoine Larocque.
25. Charles McKenzie.

Suprised by a large party of *Sceoux* & Panies, one man was Killed and two wounded with arrows & 9 Horses taken, 4 of the We ter Soon nation was missing, & they expected to be attacked by the Souix &c.["] . . . I Deturmined to go to the town with Some men, and if the Sceoux were comeing to attact the nation to Collect the worriers from each Village and meet them, thos Ideas were also those of Capt Lewis, I crossed the river in about an hour after the arrival of the Indian express with 23 men including the interpeters . . . I then informed them that if they would assemble their warrers and those of the different Towns I would to meet the Army of Souix & Chastise thim for takeing the blood of our dutifull Children &c.   after a conversation of a fiew minits amongst themselves, one Chief the *Big Man Cien* Said they now Saw that what we hade told them was the trooth . . . ["]my father the Snow is deep and it is cold   our horses Cannot travel thro the the plains,   those people who have Spilt our blood have gorn back?   if you will go with us in the Spring after the Snow goes off we will raise the Warriers of all the Towns & nations around about us, and go with you."

December 2, 1804

[CLARK] at 11 oClock the Chiefs of the Lower village of the Mandans with maney of theire young men and 4 of the *Shar-ha's*[26] who had come to Smoke with the pipe of Peace with the Mandans, we explained to them our intentions our views and advised them to be at peace, Gave them a flag for theire nation, Some Tobacco with a Speech to Deliver to their nation on theire return, also Sent by them a letter to Mrs. [Messrs.] Tabbo & Gravoline, at the Ricares Village, to interseid in proventing Hostilities, and if they Could not effect those measures to Send & informe us of what was going on, Stateing to the Indians the part we intend to take if the Rickores & Seauex did not follow our Derections and be at peace with the nations which we had addopted.

December 3, 1804

[CLARK] The Father of the Mandan who was killed Came and made us a present of Some Dried Simnens & a little pemicon, we made him Some Small preasents for which he was much pleased.

26. Cheyenne Indians.

December 4, 1804
[CLARK] the Black Cat and two young Chiefs Visit us and as usial Stay all Day   finish the main *bastion*, our interpetr.[27] we discover to be assumeing and discontent'd.

December 7, 1804
[CLARK] Big White Grand Chief of the 1s Village, Came and informed us that a large Drove of Buffalow was near and his people was wating for us to join them in a Chase   Capt. Lewis took 15 men & went out joined the Indians, who were at the time he got up, Killing the Buffalows on Horseback with arrows which they done with great dexterity, his party killed 14 Buffalow, *five* of which we got to the fort . . . those we did not get in was taken by the indians under a Custon which is established amongst them 'i 'e. any person Seeing a buffalow lying without an arrow Sticking in him, or Some purticular mark takes possesion, many times (as I am told) a hunter who Kills maney Buffalow in a chase only Gets a part of one, all meat which is left out all night falls to the Wolves which are in great numbers, always in the Buffalows —   The Thermometer Stood this morning at 1 d. below 0 —   three men frost bit badly to day.

[GASS] They shoot them [buffalo] with bows and arrows, and have their horses so trained that they will advance very near and suddenly wheel and fly off in case the wounded buffaloe attempt an attack.

December 8, 1804
[CLARK] I with 15 men turned out   and killed 8 buffalow & one Deer . . . This day being Cold Several men returned a little frost bit; one of men with his feet badly frost bit   my Servents feet also *frosted* & his P—s a little, I feel a little fatigued haveing run after the Buffalow all day in Snow many Places 10 inches Deep.

December 10, 1804
[ORDWAY] Blanket cappoes[28] provided for each man who Stood in need of them &C.

27. Jusseaume.
28. A capote, or blanket coat.

December 12, 1804

[CLARK] the Thormometer at Sun rise Stood at 38° below 0, moderated untill 6 oClock at which time it began to get Colder. I line my Gloves and have a cap made of the Skin of the *Louservia* (*Lynx*) (or wild Cat of the North)   the fur near 3 inches long   a Indian Of the *Shoe* nation[29] Came with the half of a *Cabra*[30] ko kâ[31] or Antilope which he killed near the Fort, Great numbers of those anirmals are near our fort but the weather is So Cold that we do not think it prudent to turn out to hunt in Such Cold weather, or at least untill our Consts. are prepared to under go this Climate.

[ORDWAY] the Sentinel who Stood out in the open weather had to be re-lieved every hour all this day.

December 15, 1804

[ORDWAY] although the day was cold & Stormy we Saw Several of the chiefs and warries were out at a play . . . they had flattish rings made out of clay Stone & two men had Sticks abt. 4 feet long with 2 Short peaces across the fore end of it, and neathing on the other end, in Such a man-ner that they would Slide Some distance   they had a place fixed across their green . . . which was Smothe as a house flour   they had a Battery fixed for the rings to Stop against.   two men would run at a time with Each a Stick & one carried a ring.   they run abt. half way and then Slide their Sticks after the ring.   they had marks made for the Game but I do not understand how they count the game.[32]

December 17, 1804

[CLARK] a verry Cold morning   the Thrmt. Stood a 43° [WC: 45] below 0. We found Mr. Henny[33] a verry intelligent man from whome we

29. One of the many names for the Awaxawi Hidatsas.
30. Pronghorn.
31. Roughly the Mandan designation for pronghorn.
32. The Mandan hoop and pole game.
33. Hugh Henny was another employee of the North West Company with a letter from Charles Chaboillez, North West Company factor on the Assiniboine River.

obtained Some Scetches of the Countrey between the Mississippi & Missouri, and Some Sketches from him, which he had obtained from the Indins. to the *West* of this place   also the names and charecktors of the Sceoux &c   about 8 oClock P M. the thermometer fell to 74° below the freesing pointe.

December 18, 1804
[CLARK] I imploy my Self makeing a Small map of Connection &.   Sent Jessomme to the Main Chief of the mandans to know the Cause of his de-taining or takeing a horse of *Chabonoe* our big belly interpeter, which we found was thro: the rascallity of one Lafrance a trader from the N W. Company, who told this Cheif that Chabonah owd. him a horse to go and take him   he done So agreeable to an indian Custom —   he gave up the horse.

December 20, 1804
[CLARK] a moderate day, the Thermometr 37° [*WC: 24°*] above o, which givs an oppertunity of putting up our pickets next the river, nothing remarkable took place to Day.

December 21, 1804
[CLARK] the Indian whome I stoped from Commiting murder on his wife, thro jellousy of one of our interpeters, Came & brought his two wives and Showed great anxiety to make up with the man with whome his joulassey Sprung—   a womin brought a Child with an abcess on the lower part of the back, and offered as much corn as She Could carry for Some medison, Capt Lewis administered.

December 22, 1804
[CLARK] a number of Squars womn & men Dressed in Squars Clothes Came with Corn to Sell to the men for little things, we precured two horns of the animale the french Call the rock mountain Sheep[34]   those horns are not of the largest kind . . . it is about the Size of a large Deer, or

34. Bighorn sheep.

Small Elk, its Horns Come out and wind around the head like the horn of a Ram and the teckere [texture] not unlike it.

[ORDWAY] a Great nomber of the Savages visited us brought corn & beans to Trade with us   they wanted of us looking Glases Beeds buttens or & other kinds of articles pleasing to the Eye.

December 23, 1804
[CLARK] the *little Crow*, loadd. his wife & Sun with corn for us, Cap. Lewis gave him a few presents as also his wife, She made a Kettle of boild Simnins, beens, Corn & Choke Cherris with the Stones which was paletable   This Dish is Considered, as a treat among those people, The Chiefs of the Mandans are fond of Stayin & Sleeping in the fort.

December 24, 1804
[ORDWAY] we finished Setting pickets & arected a blacksmiths Shop.

December 25, 1804
[CLARK] I was awakened before Day by a discharge of 3 platoons from the Party and the french, the men merrily Disposed, I give them all a little Taffia[35] and permited 3 Cannon fired, at raising Our flag, Some men went out to hunt & the Others to Danceing and Continued untill 9 oClock P, M, when the frolick ended &c.

[ORDWAY] we had the Best to eat that could be had, & continued firing dancing & frolicking dureing the whole day.   the Savages did not Trouble us as we had requested them not to come as it was a Great mediçian day with us.

[GASS] we hoisted the American flag in the garrison, and its first waving in fort Mandan was celebrated with another glass.

December 31, 1804
[CLARK] a Number of indians here every Day   our blck Smitth[36] mending their axes hoes &c. for which the Squars bring Corn for payment.

---

35. Tafia, an inferior grade of rum.
36. Shields and Willard.

[WHITEHOUSE] The Fort[37] which we built here & which we named Fort Mandan, is situated on the North East side of the Mesouri River. It was built in a triangular form, with its base fronting the same, had a platform on the No. Side 12 feet high with Pickets on it, six feet, and a Room of 12 feet square, the under part serving as a Storehouse for provisions &ca. the three sides were 60 feet in length each, & picketted on the front side only, with pickets of 18 feet long & the houses which we resided in lay on the So West side & the Smith & Armourer Workshop was at the South point of the Fort.

January 1, 1805
[CLARK] The Day was ushered in by the Discharge of two Cannon, we Suffered 16 men with their musick to visit the 1st Village for the purpose of Danceing, by as they Said the perticular request of the Chiefs of that village, about 11 oClock I with an inturpeter & two men walked up to the Village (my views were to alay Some little miss understanding which had taken place thro jelloucy and mortificatiion as to our treatment towards them[)]   I found them much pleased at the Danceing of our men, I ordered my black Servent to Dance which amused the Croud verry much, and Some what astonished them, that So large a man Should be active &c. I went into the lodges of all the men of note except two, whome I heard had made Some expressions not favourable towards us, in Compareing us with the trabers from the north.

January 3, 1805
[CLARK] a Gross Ventre came after his wife, who had been much abused, & come here for Protection.

January 4, 1805
[CLARK] I am verry unwell the after part of the Daye.

January 5, 1805
[CLARK] I imploy my Self drawing a Connection of the Countrey from what information I have recved—   a Buffalow Dance (or Medison)[38] for

37. Compare Whitehouse's description of Fort Mandan with Gass's of November 3.
38. Mandans' buffalo-calling ceremony.

3 nights passed in the 1st Village, a curious Custom the old men arrange themselves in a circle & after Smoke a pipe, which is handed them by a young man, Dress up for the purpose, the young men who have their wives back of the circle go to one of the old men with a whining tone and [ask] the old man to take his wife (who presents necked except a robe) and—(or Sleep with him)   the Girl then takes the Old man (who verry often can Scercely walk) and leades him to a Convenient place for the business, after which they return to the lodge, if the Old man (or a white man) returns to the lodge without gratifying the man & his wife, he offers her again and again; it is often the Case that after the 2d time without Kissing the Husband throws a nice robe over the old man & and begs him not to dispise him, & his wife   (we Sent a man to this Medisan <Dance> last night, they gave him 4 Girls)   all this is to cause the buffalow to Come near So that They may kill thim.

January 7, 1805

[CLARK] Big White Chef of the Lower Mandan Village, Dined with us, and gave me a Scetch of the Countrey as far as the high mountains, & on the South Side of the River Rejone,[39] he Says that the river rejone recves 6 Small rivers on the S. Side, & that the Countrey is verry hilley and the greater part Covered with timber, Great numbers of beaver &c. . . . I continue to Draw a connected plote from the information of Traders, Indians & my own observation & idea—   from the best information, the Great falls is about [NB?: 800] miles nearly west.

January 9, 1805

[CLARK] Several Indians Call at the Fort nearly frosed, one man reported that he had Sent his Son a Small boy to the fort about 3 oClock, & was much distressed at not finding him here.

January 10, 1805

[CLARK] last night was excessively Cold   the murkery this morning Stood at 40° below 0 which is 72° below the freesing point, we had one man out last night, who returned about 8 oClock this morning   The Indians of

39. *Rochejaune*, French for the Yellowstone.

the lower Villages turned out to hunt for a man & a boy who had not returnd from the hunt of yesterday, and borrowd a Slay to bring them in expecting to find them frosed to death   about 10 oclock the boy about 13 years of age Came to the fort with his feet frosed and had layen out last night without fire with only a Buffalow Robe to Cover him, the Dress which he wore was a pr of Cabra Legins, which is verry thin and mockersons— we had his feet put in Cold water and they are Comeing too— Soon after the arrival of the Boy, a man Came in who had also Stayed out without fire, and verry thinly Clothed, this man was not the least injured— Customs & the habits of those people has ancered to bare more Cold than I thought it possible for man to indure.

January 13, 1805

[CLARK] those people Kill a number of Buffalow near their Villages and Save a great perpotion of the meat, their Custom of makeing this article of life General[ly available] leaves them more than half of their time without meat   Their Corn & Beans &c they Keep for the Summer, and as a reserve in Case of an attack from the Soues, which they are always in dread, and Sildom go far to hunt except in large parties, about ½ the Mandan nation passed this to day to hunt on the river below, they will Stay out Some Days . . . Chaboneu informs that the Clerk of the Hudsons Bay Co. with the *Me ne tar res* has been Speaking Some fiew expressns. unfavourable towards us, and that it is Said the N W Co. intends building a fort at the *Mene tar re's*— he Saw the Grand Chief of the *Big bellies* who Spoke Slightly of the Americans, Saying if we would give our great flag to him he would Come to See us.

January 14, 1805

[LEWIS] Observed an Eclips of the Moon. I had no other glass to assist me in this observation but a small refracting telescope belonging to my sextant, which however was of considerable service, as it enabled me to define the edge of the moon's immage with much more precision that I could have done with the natural eye. The commencement of the eclips was obscured by clouds, which continued to interrupt me throughout the whole observation; to this cause is also attributable the inacuracy of the observation of the *commencement of total darkness*. I do not put much confidence in the observation of the middle of the Eclips, as it is the wo[r]st point of the eclips to distinguish with accuracy. The two last observations (i. e.) the *end of total darkness*, and the *end of the eclips*, were more satisfactory; they are as accurate as the circumstances under which I laboured would permit me to make them.

[WHITEHOUSE] I got my feet So froze that I could not walk to the fort.

January 16, 1805
[CLARK] one of the 1st War Chiefs[40] of the big belles nation Came to See us to day with one man and his Squar to wate on him [*NB: requested that she might be used for the night*]   we Shot the Air gun, and gave two Shots with the Cannon which pleased them verry much . . . This war Chief gave us a Chart in his way of the Missourie, he informed us of his intentions of going to war in the Spring against the Snake Indians   we advised him to look back at the number of nations who had been distroyed by war, and reflect upon what he was about to do, observing if he wished the hapiness of his nation, he would be at peace with all, by that by being at peace and haveing plenty of goods amongst them & a free intercourse with those defenceless nations, they would get on easy terms a great Number of horses, and that nation would increas, if he went to war against those Defenceless people, he would displease his great father, and he would not receive that pertection & Care from him as other nations who listened to his word—   This Chief who is a young man 26 yr. old replied that if his going to war against the Snake indians would be displeasing to us he would not go, he had horses enough.

[WHITEHOUSE] I Came to the fort & 2 more men with me   my feet got Some easier.

January 20, 1805
[CLARK] a miss understanding took place between the two inturpeters on account of their Squars, one of the Squars of Shabownes Squars being Sick, I ordered my Servent to, give her Some froot Stewed and tee at dift Tims which was the Cause of the misundstd.

40. Perhaps Seeing Snake of the Hidatsas, who came again February 1.

[WHITEHOUSE] Some of them [Mandans] & indeed the most of them have Strange & uncommon Ideas, but verry Ignorant of our forms & customs, but quick & Sensible in their own way & in their own conceit &c.

January 21, 1805
[CLARK] one ban [man] verry bad with the <pox>.[41]

January 24, 1805
[CLARK] our inturpeters appear to understand each others better than a fiew days past.

January 25, 1805
[CLARK] we are informed of the arrival of a Band of Asniboins at the Villages . . . to trade.

January 27, 1805
[CLARK] I Bleed the man with the Plurisy to day & Swet him, Capt Lewis took of the Toes of one foot of the Boy who got frost bit Some time ago.

January 28, 1805
[LEWIS] Longitude of Fort Mandan as deduced from the observation of the end of toal darkness when the eclips of the moon tok place the 14th of January . . . W. from Greenwich . . . 99° 22′ 45.3″ Longitude of Fort Mandan as deduced from the *end* of the same eclips . . . 99° 26′ 45″.[42]

January 29, 1805
[CLARK] we are now burning a large Coal pit, to mend the indians hatchets, & make them war axes, the only means by which we precure Corn from them.

January 30, 1805
[CLARK] Mr. La Rocke paid us a Visit, & we gave him an answer respecting the request he made when last here of accompanying us on our Journey &c. [*NB: refused*].

41. Syphilis, not smallpox.
42. The approximate longitude of Fort Mandan is 101° 16′ 24″ W (see also November 11, 1804).

January 31, 1805
[CLARK] Sawed off the boys toes.

February 1, 1805
[CLARK] a war Chief of the *Me ne tar ras* Came with Some Corn   requested to have a War hatchet made, & requested to be allowed to go to war against the Souis & Ricarres who had Killed a mandan Some time past— we refused, and gave reassons, which he verry readily assented to, and promised to open his ears to all we Said   this man is young and named (*Seeing Snake—Mar-book, She-ah-O-ke-ah*[)].

February 3, 1805
[LEWIS] the situation of our boat and perogues is now allarming, they are firmly inclosed in the Ice and almost covered with snow . . . the instruments we have hitherto used has been the ax only, with which, we have made several attempts that proved unsuccessfull . . . we then determined to attempt freeing them from the ice by means of boiling water which we purposed heating in the vessels by means of hot stones, but this expedient proved also fruitless, as every species of stone which we could procure in the neighbourhood partook so much of the calcarious genus that they burst into small particles on being exposed to the heat of the fire. we now determined as the dernier resort to prepare a parsel of Iron spikes and attatch them to the end of small poles of convenient length and endeavour by means of them to free the vessels from the ice. we have already prepared a large rope of Elk-skin and a windless by means of which we have no doubt of being able to draw the boat on the bank provided we can free from the ice.

[CLARK] our provisions of meat being nearly exorsted I concluded to Decend the River on the Ice & hunt, I Set out with about 16 men[43] 3 horses & 2 Slays Descended nearly 60 miles Killed & loaded the horses back, & made 2 pens which we filed with meat, & returned on the 13th   we Killed 40 Deer, 3 Bulls 19 Elk, maney So meager that they were unfit for use.

43. Gass and Joseph Field were with Clark.

February 4, 1805
[LEWIS] no buffaloe have made their appearance in our neighbourhood for some weeks and I am informed that our Indian neighbours—suffer extreemly at this moment for the article of *flesh*.

February 5, 1805
[LEWIS] visited by many of the natives who brought a considerable quanty of corn in payment for the work which the blacksmith had done for them— they are pecuarly attatched to a *battle ax* formed in a very inconvenient manner in my opinion.   it is fabricated of iron only, the blade is extreemly thin, from 7 to nine inches in length and from 4¾, to 6 Inches on it's edge, from whence the sides proceed nearly in a straight line to the eye where it's width is generally not more than an inch. The eye is round & about one inch in diameter.   the handle seldom more than fourteen inches in length, the whole weighing about one pound— the great length of the blade of this ax, added to the small size of the handle renders a stroke uncertain and easily avoided, while the shortness of the handel must render a blow much less forceable if even well directed, and still more inconvenient as they uniformly use this instrument in action on horseback.

February 6, 1805
[LEWIS] visited by many of the natives among others the Big white, the Coal, big-man, hairy horn and the black man, I smoked with them, after which they retired, a deportment not common, for they usually pester us with their good company the ballance of the day after once being introduced to our apartment . . . the blacksmith's have proved a happy resoce to us in our present situation as I believe it would have been difficult to have devised any other method to have procured corn from the natives. the Indians are extravegantly fond of sheet iron of which they form arrow-points and manufacter into instruments for scraping and dressing their buffaloe robes— I permitted the blacksmith to dispose of a part of a sheet-iron callaboos[44] which had been nearly birnt out on our passage up the river, and for each piece about four inches square he obtained

44. A type of stove or oven.

from seven to eight gallons of corn from the natives who appeared extreemly pleased with the exchange.

February 7, 1805
[LEWIS] The Sergt. of the guard reported that the Indian women (wives
to our interpreters[)] were in the habit of unbaring the fort gate at any
time of night and admitting their Indian visitors, I therefore directed a
lock to be put to the gate and ordered that no Indian but those attatched
to the garrison should be permitted to remain all night within the fort or
admitted during the period which the gate had been previously ordered
to be kept shut which was from sunset untill sunrise.

February 8, 1805
[LEWIS] visited by the *black-Cat* the principal chief of the Roop-tar-he,
or upper mandane vilage.   this man possesses more integrety, firmness,
inteligence and perspicuety of mind than any indian I have met with in
this quarter, and I think with a little management he may be made a usefull agent in furthering the views of our government.

February 9, 1805
[LEWIS] this evening a man by the name of Howard whom I had given
permission to go the Mandane vilage returned after the gate was shut and
rether than call to the guard to have it opened scaled the works   an indian
who was looking on shortly after followed his example. I convinced the
Indian of the impropryety of his conduct, and explained to him the riske
he had run of being severely treated, the fellow appeared much allarmed,
I gave him a small piece of tobacco and sent him away   Howard I had
comitted to the care of the guard with a determineation to have him tryed
by a Courtmartial for this offence.   this man is an old soldier which still
hightens this offince.

February 10, 1805
[ORDWAY] to day at 12 oClock [Howard] was tried by a court martial.   at
Sunset the proceedings of The court martial came out   the prisoner was
Sentenced 50 lashes & laid to the mercy of the commanding officer who
was pleased to forgive him the punishment awarded by the court.

February 11, 1805

[LEWIS] about five oclock this evening one of the wives[45] of Charbono was delivered of a fine boy.[46] it is worthy of remark that this was the first child which this woman had boarn and as is common in such cases her labour was tedious and the pain violent; Mr. Jessome informed me that he had freequently adminstered a small portion of the rattle of the rattle-snake, which he assured me had never failed to produce the desired ef-fect, that of hastening the birth of the child; having the rattle of a snake by me I gave it to him and he administered two rings of it to the woman bro-ken in small pieces with the fingers and added to a small quantity of wa-ter. Whether this medicine was truly the cause or not I shall not under-take to determine, but I was informed that she had not taken it more than ten minutes before she brought forth   perhaps this remedy may be wor-thy of future experiments, but I must confess that I want faith as to it's efficacy.

February 12, 1805

[LEWIS] I directed some meal brands given them [horses] moisened with a little water but to my astonishment found that they would not eat it but prefered the bark of the cotton wood which forms the principall article of food usually given them by their Indian masters in the winter season; for this purpose they cause the trees to be felled by their women and the horses feed on the boughs and bark of their tender branches.   the Indi-ans in our neighbourhood are freequently pilfered of their horses by the Recares, Souixs and Assinniboins and therefore make it an invariable rule to put their horses in their lodges at night.   in this situation the only food of the horse consists of a few sticks of the cottonwood from the size of a man's finger to that of his arm. The Indians are invariably severe riders, and frequently have occasion for many days together through the whole course of the day to employ their horses in pursuing the Buffaloe or transporting meat to their vilages during which time they are seldom suf-fered to tast food; at night the Horse returned to his stall where his food is what seems to me a scanty allowance of wood.   under these circum-

45. Sacawagea.
46. Jean Baptiste Charbonneau.

stances it would seem that their horses could not long exist or at least could not retain their flesh and strength, but the contrary is the fact, this valuable anamall under all those disadvantages is seldom seen meager or unfit for service.

February 15, 1805
[CLARK] Capt. Lewis with a party of men[47] & 4 Indians went in pursute of the Sioux, the Indians returned the next Day & informed me that the Sioux had Burnt all my meat & gorn home.

February 18, 1805
[CLARK] I am much engaged makeing a discriptive List of the Rivers from Information   our Store of Meat is out to day.

February 20, 1805
[CLARK] I am informed of the Death of an old man whome I Saw in the Mandan Village.   this man, informed me that he "was 120 winters old, he requested his grand Children to Dress him after Death & Set him on a Stone on a hill with his face towards his old Village or Down the river, that he might go Streight to his brother at their old village under ground.["]

February 21, 1805
[CLARK] a Delightfull Day   put out our Clothes to Sun —   Visited by the big white & Big man   they informed me that Several men of their nation was gorn to Consult their Medison Stone[48] about 3 day march to the South West to know What was to be the result of the insuing year — They have great confidence in this Stone and Say that it informs them of every thing which is to happen, & visit it every Spring & Sometimes in the Summer . . . The Big Bellies have a Stone to which they ascribe nearly the Same Virtues   Capt Lewis returned with 2 Slays loaded with meat, after finding that he could not overtake the Souis war party.

47. The party included Ordway and Gass.
48. A sandstone outcrop covered with paintings and carvings in Medicine Rock State Historic Park, Grant County, North Dakota.

February 23, 1805

[CLARK] The father of the Boy whose feet were frose near this place, and nearly Cured by us took him home in a Slay.

February 25, 1805

[CLARK] one of the Big Bellies asked leave for himself & his two wives to Stay all night, which was granted, also two Boys Stayed all night, one the Sun of the Black Cat.

February 27, 1805

[CLARK] I commence a Map of the Countrey on the Missouries & its waters &c.

February 28, 1805

[CLARK] a fine morning, two men of the N W Compy arrve with letters and Sacka comah[49] also a Root and top of a plant[50] presented by Mr. Haney, for the Cure of mad Dogs Snakes &c, and to be found & used as follows vz: "this root is found on high lands and asent of hills, the way of useing it is to Scarify the part when bitten to chu or pound an inch or more if the root is Small, and applying it to the bitten part renewing it twice a Day. the bitten person is not to chaw nor Swallow any of the Root for it might have contrary effect." Mr. Gravelin two frenchmen[51] & two Inds. arrive from the Ricara Nation with Letters from Mr. Anty Tabeaux, informing us of the peaceable dispositions of that nation towards the Mandans & Me ne ta res & their avowed intentions of pursueing our Councils & advice, they express a wish to visit the Mandans, & Know if it will be agreeable to them to admit the Ricaras to Settle near them and join them against their common Enimey the *Souis* we mentioned this to the mandans, who observed they had always wished to be at peace and good neighbours with the *Ricaras*, and it is also the Sentiments of all the Big Bellies, & Shoe Nations Mr. Gravilin informs that the *Sisetoons* and the

49. Bearberry, or kinnikinnick.
50. Purple coneflower.
51. Peter Roi was with Gravelines.

3 upper bands of the *Tetons*, with the Yanktons of the North intend to come to war in a Short time against the nations in this quarter, & will Kill everry white man they See.

March 1, 1805
[CLARK] I am ingaged in Copying a map, men building perogus, make-ing Ropes, Burning Coal, Hanging up meat & makeing battle axes for Corn.

[ORDWAY] the perogue men got their axes repaired and drew two days provisions and went up to camp out near their work untill they Git it done or Git the 4 perogues completed.

March 2, 1805
[ORDWAY] the Savages continue to visit us in Order to git their impli-ments of War made.   they bring us in pay [pied?] corn and beans dryed meat & persimblans [persimmons] &C.

[WHITEHOUSE] the Men are all employed in Cutting, wood, and Repair-ing & mending their Cloathes, dressing Deer & Elk Skins & making of mockasins &ca.

March 4, 1805
[CLARK] The Assinniboins who visited the Mandans a fiew Days ago re-turned and attempted to take horses of the Minetarres & were fired on by them.

March 6, 1805
[CLARK] a Cloudy morning & Smokey all Day from the burning of the plains, which was Set on fire by the *Minetarries* for an early crop of Grass as an endusement for the Buffalow to feed on— the horses which was Stolen Some time ago by the Assinniboins from the *minetarries* were re-turned yesterday . . . one man *Shannon* Cut his foot with the ads [adze] in working at a perogue.

March 7, 1805

[CLARK] the *Coal* visited us with a Sick child, to whome I gave Some of rushes Pills.[52]

March 8, 1805

[CLARK] a young Indian same nation & Differnt Village Stole the Doughter of the Black man [*NB: Mandan (Minetarie)*], he went to his Village took his horse & returned & took away his doughter.

March 9, 1805

[CLARK] walked up to See the Party that is makeing Perogues, about 5 miles above this . . . on my way up I met The Main Chief of the Manitar-res[53] with four Indians on Thier way to See us . . . Sent the interpeter back with him and proceeded on my Self to the Canoes   found them nearly finished, the timber verry bad, after visiting all the perogues where I found a number of Indans I wind to the upper mandan Village & Smoked a pipe the greatest mark of friendship and attention with the Chief and returned   on my return found the Manitarree Chief about Setting out on his return to his village, having recieved of Captain M. Lewis a *medel* Gor-get armbans, a *Flag* Shirt, Scarlet &c. for which he was much pleased Those Things were given in place of Sundery articles Sent to him which he Sais he did not receive   2 guns were fired for this Great man.

March 10, 1805

[CLARK] we are visited by the Black mockersons, Chief of the 2d Mane-tarre Village and the Chief[54] of the Shoeman Village or Mah ha hâ V. those Chiefs Stayed all day and the latter all night and gave us man[y] Strang accounts of his nation &c   this Little tribe or band of Menitaraies Call themselves Ah-nah-hâ-way or people whose village is on the hill. nation formerleyed lived about 30 miles below this but beeing oppressed by the Asinniboins & Sous were Compelled to move 5 miles the Mini-

52. The pills, a powerful laxative of calomel and jalap, were a concoction of Benjamin Rush, Lewis's medical advisor in Philadelphia.

53. Le Borgne, or One Eye, who Clark mentioned on October 29.

54. White Buffalo Robe Unfolded, chief of Mahawha.

taries, where, the Assinniboins Killed the most of them   those remaining
built a village verry near to the Minitarries at the mouth of Knife R where
they now live and Can raise about 50 men, they are intermixed with the
Mandans & Minatariers —   the Mandans formerly lived in 6 large villages
at and above the mouth of *Chischeter* or Heart River   five Villages on the
West Side & two on the East   one of those Villages on the East Side of the
Missouri & the larges was intirely Cut off by the Sioux & the greater part
of the others and the Small Pox reduced the others.

March 11, 1805

[CLARK] We have every reason to believe that our Menetarre interpeter,
(whome we intended to take with his wife, as an interpeter through his
wife to the Snake Indians of which nation She is) has been Corupted by
the [blank] Companeys &c.   Some explenation has taken place which
Clearly proves to us the fact, we give him to night to reflect and deturmin
whether or not he intends to go with us under the regulations Stated.

March 12, 1805

[CLARK] our Interpeter Shabonah, detumins on not proceeding with us
as an interpeter under the terms mentioned yesterday   he will not agree
to work let our Situation be what it may not Stand a guard, and if miffed
with any man he wishes to return when he pleases, also have the disposal
of as much provisions as he Chuses to Carrye.   in admissable and we Suffer him to be off the engagement which was only virbal.

March 14, 1805

[ORDWAY] Mr. Sharbono a frenchman who we expected would go with
us has lately too[k] another notion and has pitched a lodge outside of the
Garrison and moved out. Mr Gravelleen has joined in his place.

March 16, 1805

[LEWIS] Mr. Gurrow[55] a Frenchman who has lived many years with the
Ricares & Mandans shewed us the process used by those Indians to make

55. Joseph Garreau, a trader and interpreter among the Arikaras and Mandans for
some forty years.

beads.   the discovery of this art these nations are said to have derived from the Snake Indians who have been taken prisoners by the Ricaras. the art is kept a secret by the Indians among themselves and is yet known to but few of them.

[CLARK] one Indian much displeased with whitehouse for Strikeing his hand when eating with a Spoon for behaveing badly.

March 17, 1805
[CLARK] Mr. Chabonah Sent a french man of our party that he was Sorry for the foolissh part he had acted and if we pleased he would accompany us agreeabley to the terms we had perposed and doe every thing we wished him to doe &c. . . . to excuse his Simplicity and take him into the cirvise, after he had taken his things across the River we called him in and Spoke to him on the Subject, he agreed to our terms and we agreed that he might go on with us &c.

March 20, 1805
[CLARK] I with all the men which could be Speared from the Fort went to <Perogues> Canoes, there I found a number of Indians   the men carried 4 [canoes] to the River about 1½ miles thro the Bottom.

March 24, 1805
[ORDWAY] two men making cages for the Magpyes and the prarie hens[56] which is to be Sent down the River.

March 25, 1805
[CLARK] The ice began to brake away this evening and was near distroy-ing our Canoes as they wer decnding to the fort.

March 28, 1805
[CLARK] but few Indians visit us to day   they are watching to catch the floating Buffalow which brake through the ice in Crossing, those people are fond of those animals ta[i]nted and Catch great numbers every Spring.

56. Sharp-tailed grouse.

March 29, 1805

[CLARK] I observed extrodanary dexterity of the Indians in jumping from one Cake of ice to another, for the purpose of Catching the buffalow as they float down   maney of the Cakes of ice which they pass over are not two feet Square. The Plains are on fire in view of the fort on both Sides of the River, it is Said to be common for the Indians to burn the Plains near their villages every Spring for the benifit of ther horse, and to induce the Buffalow to come near to them.

March 30, 1805

[CLARK] [The party] are helth. except the—vn. [venereal]—which is common with the Indians and have been communicated to many of our party at this place—   those favores bieng easy acquired.

[CLARK] all the party in high Spirits   they pass but fiew nights without amuseing themselves danceing possessing perfect harmony and good understanding towards each other.

April 1, 1805

[CLARK] The fore part of to day haile rain with Thunder & lightning, the rain continued by intimitions all day, it is worthey of remark that this is the 1st rain which has fallen Since we have been here or Since the 15 of October last, except a fiew drops at two or three defferent times—   had the Boat Perogus & Canoes all put into the water.

April 2, 1805

[CLARK] we are writeing and prepareing dispatches all day—   I conclude to Send my journal to the President of the United States in its original State for his own perusual, untill I call for it or Some friend if I should not return . . . wrote untill verry late at night but little time to devote to my friends.

April 3, 1805

[CLARK] we are all day ingaged packing up Sundery articles to be Sent to the President of the U. S.

April 5, 1805
[CLARK] we have our 2 perogues & Six Canoes loaded.

[GASS] we ought . . . to give some account of the *fair sex* of the Missouri; and entertain [readers] with narratives of feats of love as well as of arms. Though we could furnish a sufficient number of entertaining stories and pleasant anecdotes, we do not think it prudent to swell our Journal with them; as our views are directed to more useful information . . . It may be observed generally that chastity is not very highly esteemed by these people, and that the severe and loathsome effects *of certain French principles* are not uncommon among them. The fact is, that the women are generally considered an article of traffic and *indulgencies* are sold at a very moderate price. As a proof of this I will just mention, that for an old tobacco box, one of our men was granted the honour of passing a night with the daughter of the headchief of the Mandan nation. An old bawd with her punks, may also be found in some of the villages on the Missouri, as well as in the large cities of polished nations.

April 6, 1805
[CLARK] we are informed of the arrival of the whole of the *ricarra* nation on the other Side of the river near their old village. we Sent an interpreter to See with orders to return imediately and let us know if their Chiefs ment to go down to See their great father.

[LEWIS AND CLARK, WEATHER REMARKS] all the birds that we believe visit this country have now returned.

CHAPTER 4

Into the Unknown

April 7–June 2, 1805

April 7, 1805

[LEWIS] Having on this day at 4 P. M. completed every arrangement necessary for our departure, we dismissed the barge and crew with orders to return without loss of time to S. Louis, a small canoe with two French hunters accompanyed the barge; these men had assended the missouri with us the last year as engages . . . We gave Richard Warfington, a discharged Corpl., the charge of the Barge and crew, and confided to his care likewise our dispatches to the government, letters to our private friends, and a number of articles to the President of the United States . . .

At same moment that the Barge departed from Fort Mandan, Capt. Clark embaked with our party and proceeded up the river. as I had used no exercise for several weeks, I determined to walk on shore as far as our encampment of this evening . . . Our party now consisted of the following Individuals. Sergts. John Ordway, Nathaniel Prior, & Patric Gass; Privates, William Bratton, John Colter, Reubin, and Joseph Fields, John Shields, George Gibson, George Shannon, John Potts, John Collins, Joseph Whitehouse, Richard Windsor, Alexander Willard, Hugh Hall, Silas Goodrich, Robert Frazier, Peter Crouzatt, John Baptiest la Page, Francis Labiech, Hue McNeal, William Werner, Thomas P. Howard, Peter Wiser, and John B. Thompson. *Interpreters*, George Drewyer and Tauasant Charbono also a Black man by the name of York, servant to Capt. Clark, an Indian Woman [1] wife to Charbono with a young child, and a Mandan man who had promised us to accompany us as far as the Snake Indians with a view to bring about a good understanding and friendly intercourse between that nation and his own, the Minetares and Ahwahharways.

1. Sacagawea.

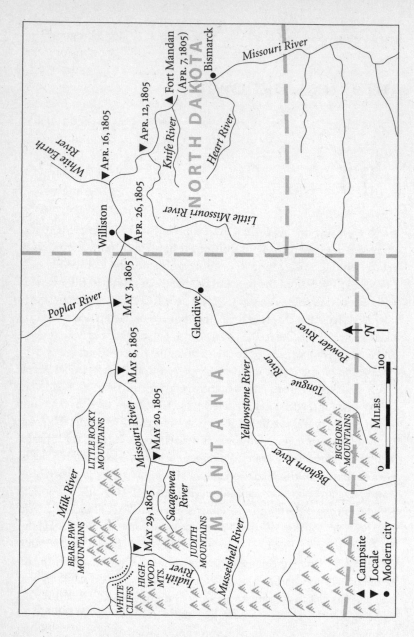

The Expedition's Route, April 7–June 2, 1805

Missouri River

Bismarck

Fort Mandan
(Apr. 7, 1805)

Knife River

Heart River

NORTH DAKOTA

Apr. 12, 1805

Apr. 16, 1805

White Earth River

Little Missouri River

Williston

Apr. 26, 1805

Poplar River

May 3, 1805

Glendive

Powder River

N

Tongue River

May 8, 1805

100

Yellowstone River

Bighorn River

BIGHORN MOUNTAINS

May 20, 1805

Miles

0

Missouri River

Sacagawea River

LITTLE ROCKY MOUNTAINS

MONTANA

May 29, 1805

Milk River

JUDITH MOUNTAINS

Musselshell River

BEARS PAW MOUNTAINS

HIGH-WOOD MTS.

Judith River

WHITE CLIFFS

▲ Campsite
▼ Locale
● Modern city

Our vessels consisted of six small canoes, and two large perogues. This little fleet altho' not quite so rispectable as those of Columbus or Capt. Cook were still viewed by us with as much pleasure as those deservedly famed adventurers ever beheld theirs; and I dare say with quite as much anxiety for their safety and preservation. we were now about to penetrate a country at least two thousand miles in width, on which the foot of civillized man had never trodden; the good or evil it had in store for us was for experiment yet to determine, and these little vessells contained every article by which we were to expect to subsist or defend ourselves . . . entertaing as I do, the most confident hope of succeading in a voyage which had formed a da[r]ling project of mine for the last ten years, I could but esteem this moment of my departure as among the most happy of my life. The party are in excellent health and sperits, zealously attatched to the enterprise, and anxious to proceed; not a whisper of murmur or discontent to be heard among them, but all act in unison, and with the most perfect harmony. [Camped in McLean County, North Dakota, a few miles below Stanton on the opposite shore.]

[WHITEHOUSE] The Natives [Mandans] have large fields, which they cultivate and which produces plentifully, They have likewise Gardens, which they plant & have several kinds of Garden Vegetables in it . . . They are in general peaceable well disposed people — and have less of the Savage nature in them, than any Indians we met with on the Mesouri River. They are of a very light Colour, the Men are very well featur'd and Stout; the Women are in general handsome . . . the Indians here live to a very old age, numbers being 100 Years old.

April 8, 1805
[LEWIS] I walked on shore, and visited the *black Cat*, took leave of him after smoking a pipe as is their custom, and then proceeded on slowly by land about four miles where I wated the arrival of the party, at 12 Oclock they came up and informed me that one of the small canoes was behind in distress. Capt Clark returned fou[n]d she had filled with water and all her loading wet. we lost half a bag of bisquit, and about thirty pounds of powder by this accedent; the powder we regard as a serious loss, but we spread it to dry immediately and hope we shall still be enabled to restore

the greater part of it. this was the only powder we had which was not perfectly secure from geting wet. [Camped in McLean County, North Dakota, a mile or so below Garrison Dam.]

[LEWIS AND CLARK, WEATHER REMARKS] the only birds that I obseved during the winter at Fort Mandan was the Missouri Magpie, a bird of the Corvus genus, the raven in immence numbers, the small woodpecker or *sapsucker*[2] as they are sometimes called, <and> the beautifull eagle, or *calumet bird*,[3] so called from the circumstance of the natives decorating their pipe-stems with it's plumage and the Prairie Hen or grouse.[4]

April 9, 1805

[LEWIS] we saw a great number of *brant*[5] passing up the river, some of them were white, except the large feathers in the first and second joint of the wing which are black. there is no other difference between them and the common gray brant but that of their colour ... Capt Clark walked on shore to-day and informed me on his return, that passing through the prarie he had seen an anamal[6] that precisely resembled the burrowing squrril, accept in point of size, it being only about one third as large as the squirrel, and that it also burrows. I have observed in many parts of the plains and praries the work of an anamal[7] of which I could never obtain a view. their work resembles that of the salamander common to the sand hills of the States of South Carolina and Georgia; and like that anamal also it never appears above the ground ... the Bluffs of the river which we passed today were upwards of a hundred feet high, formed of a mixture of yellow clay and sand— many horizontal stratas of carbonated wood, having every appearance of pitcoal at a distance; were seen in the the face of these bluffs. these stratas are of unequal thicknesses from 1 to 5 feet, and appear at different elivations above the water some of them as much as eighty feet. the hills of the river are very broken and many of them

2. An unknown woodpecker.
3. Golden eagle.
4. Sharp-tailed grouse.
5. White and blue genetic morphs of the snow goose.
6. Probably Richardson's ground squirrel.
7. Maybe the northern pocket gopher.

have the apearance of having been on fire at some former period . . . when we halted for dinner the squaw busied herself in serching for the wild artichokes which the mice collect and deposit in large hoards. this operation she performed by penetrating the earth with a sharp stick about some small collections of drift wood. her labour soon proved successful, and she procurrd a good quantity of these roots. the flavor of this root resembles that of the Jerusalem Artichoke,[8] and the stalk of the weed which produces it is also similar, tho' both the root and stalk are much smaller than the Jarusale Artichoke. the root is white and of an ovate form, from one to three inches in length and usually about the size of a man's finger. one stalk produces from two to four, and somitimes six of these roots . . . Three miles above the mouth of this creek we passed a hunting camp of Minetares[9] who had prepared a park and were wating the return of the Antelope; which usually pass the Missouri at this season of the year from the Black hills on the South side, to the open plains on the north side of the river. [Camped in McLean County, North Dakota, a few miles southwest of Garrison.]

[ORDWAY] the Musquetoes begin to Suck our blood this afternoon.

April 10, 1805
[LEWIS] The country on both sides of the missouri from the tops of the river hills, is one continued level fertile plain as far as the eye can reach, in which there is not even a solitary tree or shrub to be seen except such as from their moist situations or the steep declivities of hills are sheltered from the ravages of the fire . . . at 1 P. M. we overtook three french hunters who had set out a few days before us with a view of traping beaver; they had taken 12 since they left Fort Mandan. these people avail themselves of the protection which our numbers will enable us to give them against the Assinniboins who sometimes hunt on the Missouri and intend ascending with us as far as the mouth of the Yellow stone river and continue there hunt up that river. this is the first essay of a beaver hunter of any

8. Sacagawea's roots may have come from the hog peanut, which Lewis compared to the Jerusalem artichoke.
9. The Hidatsa hunting camp was above Snake Creek, McLean County, North Dakota.

discription on this river.   the beaver these people have already taken is by far the best I have ever seen. [Camped above the later site of Fort Berthold, McLean County, North Dakota.]

April 11, 1805
[LEWIS] the country from fort Mandan to this place is so constantly hunted by the Minetaries that there is but little game   we halted at two P. M. and made a comfortable dinner on a venison stake and beavers tales with the bisquit which got wet on the 8th inst. . . . the powder which got wet by the same accedent, and which we had spread to dry on the baggage of the large perogue, was now examined and put up; it appears to be almost restored. [Camped in McLean County, North Dakota, a few miles below the mouth of the Little Missouri River, coming in on the opposite side.]

April 12, 1805
[LEWIS] the red perogue contrary to my expectation or wish passed under [a] bank by means of her toe line where I expected to have seen her carried under every instant. I did not discover that she was about to make this attempt untill it was too late for the men to reembark, and retreating is more dangerous than proceeding in such cases; they therefore continued their passage up this bank, and much to my satisfaction arrived safe above it. this cost me some moments of uneasiness, her cargo was of much importance to us in our present advanced situation—   We proceeded on six miles and came too on the lower side of the entrance of the little Missouri . . . where we determined to spend the day for the purpose of celestial observation . . . The little Missouri disembogues on the S. side of the Missouri 1693 miles from the confluence of the latter with the Mississippi. [Camped at the mouth of the Little Missouri River, Dunn County, North Dakota.]

[ORDWAY] the Soil back from the River is tollarable Good but barron plains without timber on water &c.

April 13, 1805
[LEWIS] about 2 in the afternoon . . . a suddon squall of wind struck us and turned the [white] perogue so much on the side as to allarm Shar-

bono who was steering at the time, in this state of alarm he threw the perogue with her side to the wind, when the spritsail gibing was as near overseting the perogue as it was possible to have missed. the wind however abating for an instant I ordered Drewyer to the helm and the sails to be taken in, which was instant executed and the perogue being steered before the wind was agin plased in a state of security. this accedent was very near costing us dearly. beleiving this vessell to be the most steady and safe, we had embarked on board of it our instruments, Papers, medicine and the most valuable part of the merchandize which we had still in reserve as presents for the Indians. we had also embarked on board ourselves, with three men who could not swim and the squaw with the young child, all of whom, had the perogue overset, would most probably have perished, as the waves were high, and the perogue upwards of 200 yards from the nearest shore; however we fortunately escaped and pursued our journey . . . we saw also many tracks of the white bear of enormous size, along the river shore and about the carcases of the Buffaloe, on which I presume they feed. we have not as yet seen one of these anamals, tho' their tracks are so abundant and recent. the men as well as ourselves are anxious to meet with some of these bear. the Indians give a very formidable account of the strengh and ferocity of this anamal, which they never dare to attack but in parties of six eight or ten persons; and are even then frequently defeated with the loss of one or more of their party. the savages attack this anamal with their bows and arrows and the indifferent guns with which the traders furnish them, with these they shoot with such uncertainty and at so short a distance, that they frequently mis their aim & fall a sacrefice to the bear. two Minetaries were killed during the last winter in an attack on a white bear. this anamall is said more frequently to attack a man on meeting with him, than to flee from him. When the Indians are about to go in quest of the white bear, previous to their departure, they paint themselves and perform all those supersticious rights commonly observed when they are about to make war uppon a neighbouring nation. [Camped in Mountrail County, North Dakota, in the later Fort Maneury Bend.]

April 14, 1805
[LEWIS] Capt. Clark [found abandoned camps that] . . . must have been the camps of the Assinniboins, as no other nation who visit this part of

the missouri ever indulge themselves with spirituous liquor. of this article the Assinniboins are pationately fond, and we are informed that it forms their principal inducement to furnish the British establishments on the Assinniboin river with the dryed and pounded meat and grease which they do. they also supply those establishments with a small quantity of fur, consisting principally of the large and small wolves and the small fox skins . . . passed an Island, above which two small creeks fall in on Lard side; the upper creek largest, which we called Sharbono's Creek after our interpreter who encamped several weeks on it with a hunting party of Indians. this was the highest point to which any whiteman had ever ascended; except two Frenchmen [10] who having lost their way had straggled a few miles further, tho' to what place precisely I could not learn. [Camped a little above the mouth of Bear Den Creek, but opposite, in Mountrail County, North Dakota.]

April 15, 1805
[LEWIS] I walked on shore, and Capt. Clark continued with the party it being an invariable rule with us not to be both absent from our vessels at the same time. [Camped in McKenzie County, North Dakota, several miles above the mouth of Little Knife River, on the opposite side.]

[CLARK] I saw a large Strong pen made for the purpose of Catching the antelope, with wings projecting from it widining from the pen.

April 16, 1805
[LEWIS] the hills of the river still continue extreemly broken for a few miles back, when it becomes a fine level country of open fertile lands   immediately on the river there are many fine leavel extensive and extreemly fertile high plains and meadows. I think the quantity of timbered land on the river is increasing.   the mineral appearances still continue. [Camped in McKenzie County, North Dakota, above Beaver Creek, on the other side.]

April 17, 1805
[LEWIS] we saw immence quantities of game in every direction around us as we passed up the river; consisting of herds of Buffaloe, Elk, and An-

10. Lepage and another unknown person.

telopes with some deer and woolves. tho' we continue to see many tracks of the bear we have seen but very few of them, and those are at a great distance generally runing from us; I thefore presume that they are extreemly wary and shy; the Indian account of them dose not corrispond with our experience so far. [Camped in McKenzie County, North Dakota.]

April 18, 1805
[LEWIS] one Beaver caught this morning by two traps, having a foot in each; the traps belonged to different individuals [of the party], between whom, a contest ensued, which would have terminated, most probably, in a serious rencounter had not our timely arrival at the place prevented it . . . found a species of pea [11] bearing a yellow flower, and now in blume; it seldom rises more than 6 inches high, the leaf & stalk resembles that of the common gardin pea, the root is pirenial . . . I also saw several parsels of buffaloe's hair hanging on the rose bushes, which had been bleached by exposure to the weather and became perfectly white. it every appearance of the wool of the sheep, tho' much finer and more silkey and soft. I am confident that an excellent cloth may be made of the wool of the Buffaloe. the Buffaloe I killed yesterday had cast his long hare, and the poil which remained was very thick, fine, and about 2 inches in length. I think this anamal would have furnished about five pounds of wool. we were detained today from one to five P. M. in consequence of the wind which blew so violently from N. that it was with difficulty we could keep the canoes from filling with water altho' they were along shore. [Camped in Williams County, North Dakota.]

April 20, 1805
[LEWIS] in the course of my walk I . . . [saw] a small scaffold of about 7 feet high on which were deposited two doog slays with their harnis. underneath this scaffold a human body was lying, well rolled in several dressed buffaloe skins and near it a bag of the same materials containg sundry articles belonging to the disceased; consisting of a pare of mockersons, some red and blue earth, beaver's nails, instruments for dressing the Buffalo skin, some dryed roots, several platts of the sweet grass, and a small quantity of Mandan tobacco. I presume that the body, as well as the

11. Golden pea.

bag containing these articles . . . had fallen down by accedent.   near the scaffold I saw the carcase of a large dog not yet decayed, which I supposed had been killed at the time the human body was left on the scaffold; this was no doubt the reward, which the poor doog had met with for per-forming the [blank] — friendly office to his mistres of transporting her corps to the place of deposit.   it is customary with the Assinniboins, Mandans, Minetares &c who scaffold their dead, to sacrefice the favorite horses and doggs of their disceased relations, with a view of their being servicable to them in the land of sperits. I have never heard of any in-stances of human sacrefices on those occasions among them. [Camped in Williams County, North Dakota.]

April 22, 1805
[LEWIS] the broken hills of the Missouri about this place exhibit large ir-regular and broken masses of rocks and stones; some of which tho' 200 feet above the level of the water seem at some former period to have felt it's influence, fo[r] they appear smoth as if woarn by the agetation of the water . . . I asscended to the top of the cutt bluff this morning, from whence I had a most delightfull view of the country, the whole of which except the vally formed by the Missouri is void of timber or underbrush, exposing to the first glance of the spectator immence herds of Buffaloe, Elk, deer, & Antelopes feeding in one common and boundless pasture . . . walking on shore this evening I met with a buffaloe calf which attatched itself to me and continued to follow close at my heels untill I embarked and left it.   it appeared allarmed at my dog which was probably the cause of it's so readily attatching itself to me. [Camped a few miles from Willis-ton, and opposite in McKenzie County, North Dakota.]

[CLARK] I observed a large drove of buffalow prosued by wolves   the wolves cought one of their Calves in my view, those animals defend their young as long as they Can keep up with the drove.

April 24, 1805
[LEWIS] The wind blew so hard during the whole of this day, that we were unable to move . . . Soar eyes is a common complaint among the party. I

believe it origenates from the immence quantities of sand which is driven by the wind from the sandbars of the river in such clouds that you are unable to discover the opposite bank of the river in many instances. the particles of this sand are so fine and light that they are easily supported by the air, and are carried by the wind for many miles, and at a distance exhibiting every appearance of a collumn of thick smoke. so penitrating is this sand that we cannot keep any article free from it; in short we are compelled to eat, drink, and breath it very freely. my pocket watch, is out of order, she will run only a few minutes without stoping. I can discover no radical defect in her works, and must therefore attribute it to the sand, with which, she seems plentifully charged, notwithstanding her cases are double and tight. [Remained at the camp of April 23 in Williams County, North Dakota.]

April 25, 1805

[LEWIS] I determined . . . to proceed by land with a few men [12] to the entrance of that river [Yellowstone] . . . our rout lay along the foot of the river hills. when we had proceeded about four miles, I ascended the hills from whence I had a most pleasing view of the country, perticularly of the wide and fertile vallies formed by the missouri and the yellowstone rivers, which occasionally unmasked by the wood on their borders disclose their meanderings for many miles in their passage through these delightfull tracts of country . . . the whol face of the country was covered with herds of Buffaloe, Elk & Antelopes; deer are also abundant, but keep themselves more concealed in the woodland. the buffaloe Elk and Antelope are so gentle that we pass near them while feeding, without apearing to excite any alarm among them, and when we attract their attention, they frequently approach us more nearly to discover what we are, and in some instances pursue us a considerable distance apparenly with that view. [Lewis camped at the mouth of the Yellowstone River, McKenzie County, North Dakota; Clark and the main party camped in Williams County, North Dakota, in the vicinity of Glass Bluffs.]

[ORDWAY] Capt. Lewis Shot a goose on hir nest   we got 6 eggs out of it.

12. Lewis had Ordway, Drouillard, Joseph Field, and one other man with him.

[GASS] I remarked, as a singular circumstance, that there is no dew in this Country, and very little rain. Can it be owing to the want of timber?

April 26, 1805
[LEWIS] there is more timber in the neighbourhood of the junction of these rivers, and on the Missouri as far below as the White earth river, than there is on any part of the Missouri above the entrance of the Chyenne river to this place.   the timber consists principally of Cottonwood, with some small elm, ash and boxalder.   the under growth on the sandbars and verge of the river is the small leafed willow; the low bottoms, rose bushes which rise to three or four fe[e]t high, the redburry,[13] servicebury, and the redwood;[14] the high bottoms are of two discriptions either timbered or open; the first lies next to the river and it's under brush is the same with that of the low timbered bottoms with the addition of the broad leafed willow, Goosbury, choke cherry, purple currant; and honeysuckle bushis; the open bottoms border on the hills, and are covered in many parts by the wild hyssop[15] which rises to the hight of two feet. I observe that the Antelope, Buffaloe Elk and deer feed on this herb; the willow of the sandbars also furnish a favorite winter food to these anamals as well as the growse, the porcupine, hare, and rabbit . . . after I had completed my observations in the evening I walked down and joined the party at their encampment on the point of land fromed by the junction of the rivers; found them all in good health, and much pleased at having arrived at this long wished for spot, and in order to add in some measure to the general pleasure which seemed to pervade our little community, we ordered a dram to be issued to each person; this soon produced the fiddle, and they spent the evening with much hilarity, singing & dancing, and seemed as perfectly to forget their past toils, as they appeared regardless of those to come. [Camped at the mouth of the Yellowstone River, McKenzie County, North Dakota.]

April 27, 1805
[LEWIS] the most eligible site for an establishment . . . this site recommended is about 400 yards distant from the Missouri and about double

13. Probably the buffaloberry.
14. Red osier dogwood.
15. Possibly big sagebrush.

that distance from the river yellowstone . . . and is one of the ha[n]dsomest plains I ever beheld . . . altho' game is very abundant and gentle, we only kill as much as is necessary for food. I believe that two good hunters could conveniently supply a regiment with provisions. for several days past we have observed a great number of buffaloe lying dead on the shore, some of them entire and others partly devoured by the wolves and bear. those anamals either drownded during the winter in attempting to pass the river on the ice during the winter or by swiming acrss at present to bluff banks which they are unable to ascend, and feeling themselves too weak to return remain and perish for the want of food . . . The Eagles, Magpies, and gees have their nests in trees adjacent to each other; the magpye particularly appears fond of building near the Eagle, as we scarcely see an Eagle's nest unaccompanyed with two or three Magpies nests within a short distance. The bald Eagle are more abundant here than I ever observed them in any part of the country. [Remained at the mouth of the Yellowstone River.]

April 29, 1805
[LEWIS] I walked on shore with one man. about 8 A. M. we fell in with two brown or <yellow> bear; both of which we wounded; one of them made his escape, the other after my firing on him pursued me seventy or eighty yards, but fortunately had been so badly wounded that he was unable to pursue so closely as to prevent my charging my gun; we again repeated our fir and killed him.[16] it was a male not fully grown, we estimated his weight at 300 lbs. not having the means of ascertaining it precisely. The legs of this bear are somewhat longer than those of the black, as are it's tallons and tusks incomparably larger and longer. the testicles, which in the black bear are placed pretty well back between the thyes and contained in one pouch like those of the dog and most quadrupeds, are in the yellow or brown bear placed much further forward, and are suspended in seperate pouches from two to four inches asunder; it's colour is yellowish brown, the eyes small, black, and piercing; the front of the fore legs near the feet is usually black; the fur is finer thicker and deeper than that of the black bear. these are all the particulars in which this anamal appeared to me to differ from the black bear; it

16. Today the hunters took their first specimen of grizzly.

is a much more furious and formidable anamal, and will frequently pursue the hunter when wounded.   it is asstonishing to see the wounds they will bear before they can be put to death.   the Indians may well fear this anamal equiped as they generally are with their bows and arrows or indifferent fuzees, but in the hands of skillfull riflemen they are by no means as formidable or dangerous as they have been represented.   game is still very abundant we can scarcely cast our eyes in any direction without percieving deer Elk Buffaloe or Antelopes. The quantity of wolves appear to increase in the same proportion; they generally hunt in parties of six eight or ten; they kill a great number of the Antelopes at this season; the Antelopes are yet meagre and the femals are big with young; the wolves take them most generally in attempting to swim the river; in this manner my dog caught one drowned it and brought it on shore; they are but clumsey swimers, tho' on land when in good order, they are extreemly fleet and dureable.   we have frequently seen the wolves in pursuit of the Antelope in the plains; they appear to decoy a single one from a flock, and then pursue it, alturnately relieving each other untill they take it. [Camped at the mouth of Big Muddy Creek, Roosevelt County, Montana.]

[CLARK] we Saw a female & her faun of the Bighorn animal on the top of a Bluff lying, the noise we made allarmed them and they came down on the Side of the bluff which had but little Slope being nearly purpindicular, I directed two men to kill those anamals, one went on the top and the other man near the water   they had two Shots at the doe while in motion without effect, Those animals run & Skiped about with great ease on this declivity & appeared to prefur it to the leavel bottom or plain.

April 30, 1805

[CLARK] I walked on Shore to day   our interpreter & his Squar followed, in my walk the Squar found & brought me a bush Something like the Current,[17] which She Said bore a delicious froot and that great quantites grew on the Rocky Mountains, this Srub was in bloom has a yellow flower with a deep Cup, the froot when ripe is yellow and hangs in bunches like

17. Buffalo currant.

Cheries, Some of those berries yet remained on the bushes. [Camped in Richland County, Montana, across from and near Brockton, Roosevelt County.]

May 1, 1805
[LEWIS] the country appears much more pleasant and fertile than that we have passed for several days; the hills are lower, the bottoms wider, and better stocked with timber, which consists principally of cottonwood, not however of large size; the under-growth willow on the verge of the river and sandbars, rose bushes, red willow and the broad leafed willow in the bottom lands; the high country on either side of the river is one vast plain, intirely destitute of timber, but is apparently fertile, consisting of a dark rich mellow looking lome . . . Shannon killed a bird of the plover kind. weight one pound. . . . their note resembles that of the grey plover, tho' is reather louder and more varied, their habits appear also to be the same, with this difference; that it sometimes rests on the water and swims which I do not recollect having seen the plover do. this bird [18] which I shall henceforth stile the *Missouri plover*, generally feeds about the shallow bars of the river; to collect it's food which consists of [blank], it immerces it's beak in the water and throws it's head and beak from side to side at every step it takes. [Camped in the vicinity of later Elkhorn Point, Roosevelt County, Montana.]

[WHITEHOUSE] I and one more was in the cannoe and ware obledged to lay out all night without any blanket. it being verry cold I Suffered verry much.

May 2, 1805
[LEWIS] on our way this evening we also shot three beaver along the shore; these anamals in consequence of not being hunted are extreemly gentle, where they are hunted they never leave their lodges in the day, the flesh of the beaver is esteemed a delecacy among us; I think the tale a most delicious morsal, when boiled it resembles in flavor the fresh tongues and sounds of the codfish, and is usually sufficiently large to afford a plenti-

18. American avocet.

full meal for two men. Joseph Fields one of the hunters who was out to-day found several yards of scarlet cloth which had been suspended on the bough of a tree near an old indian hunting cam[p], where it had been left as a sacrefice to the deity by the indians, probably of the Assinniboin nation, it being a custom with them as well as all the nations inhabiting the waters of the Missouri so far as they are known to us, to offer or sacrefice in this manner to the deity watever they may be possessed off which they think most acceptable to him . . . the article which they most prize themselves . . . this morning one of the men shot the indian dog that had followed us for several days, he would steal their cooked provision. [Camped in the vicinity of the crossing of Montana Highway 251, Richland County, Montana.]

May 3, 1805
[LEWIS] traces of the ancient beds of the river are visible in many places through the whole extent of this valley. since the hills have become lower the appearance of the stratas of coal burnt hills and pumice stone have in a great measure ceased; I saw none today . . . we saw an unusual number of Porcupines from which we determined to call the river after that ana-mal, and accordingly denominated it *Porcupine river*[19] . . . this anamal is exceedingly clumsy and not very watchfull   I approached so near one of them before it percieved me that I touched it with my espontoon.[20] [Camped a few miles above the town of Poplar, Roosevelt County, Montana, but on the opposite side in McCone County.]

May 5, 1805
[LEWIS] Capt. Clark and Drewyer killed the largest brown bear this evening which we have yet seen. it was a most tremendious looking anamal, and extreemly hard to kill notwithstanding he had five balls through his lungs and five others in various parts he swam more than half the distance acoss the river to a sandbar & it was at least twenty minutes before he died; he did not attempt to attact, but fled and made the most tremendous roaring from the moment he was shot. We had no means of weigh-

19. Poplar River, Roosevelt County, Montana.
20. A spear-like implement with a wooden shaft and metal blade which Lewis used as a weapon, walking stick, or rifle support.

ing this monster; Capt. Clark thought he would weigh 500 lbs. for my own part I think the estimate too small by 100 lbs. he measured 8 Feet 7½ Inches from the nose to the extremety of the hind feet, 5 F. 10½ Inch arround the breast, 1 F. 11 I. arround the middle of the arm, & 3 F. 11 I. arround the neck; his tallons which were five in number on each foot were 4⅜ Inches in length. he was in good order, we therefore divided him among the party and made them boil the oil and put it in a cask for future uce; the oil is as hard as hogs lard when cool, much more so than that of the black bear. this bear differs from the common black bear in several respects; it's tallons are much longer and more blont, it's tale shorter, it's hair which is of a redish or bey brown, is longer thicker and finer than that of the black bear; his liver lungs and heart are much larger even in proportion with his size; the heart particularly was as large as that of a large Ox. his maw was also ten times the size of black bear, and was filled with flesh and fish. his testicles were pendant from the belly and placed four inches assunder in seperate bags or pouches. this animal also feeds on roots and almost every species of wild fruit. [Camped in McCone County, Montana, southest of Wolf Point, Roosevelt County.]

[ORDWAY] Capt. Clark and Several more of the party killed a verry large bair which the natives and the french tradors call white but all of the kind that we have seen is of a light brown only owing to the climate as we suppose.

May 6, 1805
[LEWIS] I find that the curiossity of our party is pretty well satisfyed with rispect to this anamal [grizzly], the formidable appearance of the male bear killed on the 5th added to the difficulty with which they die when even shot through the vital parts, has staggered the resolution several of them, others however seem keen for action with the bear; I expect these gentlemen will give us some amusement shotly as they soon begin now to coppolate. [Camped in McCone County, Montana, a few miles southwest of Oswego, Valley County.]

May 8, 1805
[LEWIS] we nooned it just above the entrance of a large river which disimbogues on the Lard. side . . . from the quantity of water furnised by this

river it must water a large extent of country; perhaps this river also might furnish a practicable and advantageous communication with the Saskashiwan river; it is sufficiently large to justify a belief that it might reach to that river if it's direction be such. the water of this river possesses a peculiar whiteness, being about the colour of a cup of tea with the admixture of a tablespoonfull of milk. from the colour of it's water we called it Milk river.[21] (we think it possible that this may be the river called by the Minitares *the river which scoalds at all others*[)] . . . The white apple[22] is found in great abundance in this neighbourhood; it is confined to the highlands principally . . . This root forms a considerable article of food with the Indians of the Missouri, who for this purpose prepare them in several ways. they are esteemed good at all seasons of the year, but are best from the middle of July to the latter end of Autumn when they are sought and gathered by the provident part of the natives for their winter store. when collected they are striped of their rhind and strung on small throngs or chords and exposed to the sun or placed in the smoke of their fires to dry; when well dryed they will keep for several years, provided they are not permitted to become moist or damp; in this situation they usually pound them between two stones placed on a piece of parchment, untill they reduce it to a fine powder   thus prepared they thicken their soope with it; sometimes they also boil these dryed roots with their meat without breaking them; when green they are generally boiled with their meat, sometimes mashing them or otherwise as they think proper.   they also prepare an agreeable dish with them by boiling and mashing them and adding the marrow grease of he buffaloe and some buries, until the whole be of the consistency of a haisty pudding.   they also eat this root roasted and frequently make hearty meals of it raw without sustaining any inconvenience or injury therefrom. The White or brown bear feed very much on this root, which their tallons assist them to procure very readily.   the white apple appears to me to be a tastless insippid food of itself tho' I have no doubt but it is a very healthy and moderately nutricious food. I have no doubt but our epicures would admire this root very much, it would serve them in their ragouts and gravies in stead of the

21. The Milk River, entering the Missouri River in Valley County, Montana.
22. Indian breadroot.

truffles morella . . . we saw where an Indian had recently grained, or taken the hair off of a goatskin; we do not wish to see those gentlemen just now as we presume they would most probably be the Assinniboins and might be troublesome to us. [Camped a short distance above Fort Peck Dam, Valley County, Montana.]

May 9, 1805
[LEWIS] today we passed the bed of the most extraordinary river that I ever beheld. it is as wide as the Missouri is at this place or ½ a mile wide and not containing a single drop of runing water; some small standing pools being all the water that could be perceived . . . This stream (if such it can properly be termed) we called Big dry river [23] . . . from the cow I killed we saved the necessary materials for making what our wrighthand cook Charbono calls the *boudin blanc*, and immediately set him about preparing them for supper; this white pudding we all esteem one of the greatest delacies of the forrest, it may not be amiss therefore to give it a place. About 6 feet of the lower extremity of the large gut of the Buffaloe is the first mosel that the cook makes love to, this he holds fast at one end with the right hand, while with the forefinger and thumb of the left he gently compresses it, and discharges what he says *is not good to eat*, but of which in the squel we get a moderate portion; the mustle lying under-neath the shoulder blade next to the back, and fillets are next saught, these are needed up very fine with a good portion of kidney suit [suet]; to this composition is then added a just proportion of pepper and salt and a small quantity of flour; thus far advanced, our skilfull opporater C—o seizes his recepticle, which has never once touched the water, for that would intirely distroy the regular order of the whole procedure . . . the operator sceizes the recepticle I say, and tying it fast at one end turns it inwards and begins now with repeated evolutions of the hand and arm, and a brisk motion of the finger and thumb to put in what he says is *bon pour manger*; thus by stuffing and compressing he soon distends the re-cepticle to the utmost limmits of it's power of expansion, and in the course of it's longtudinal progress it drives from the other end of the re-cepticle a mch larger portion of the [blank] . . . all is compleatly filled with

23. Big Dry Creek, McCone and Garfield Counties, Montana.

something good to eat, it is tyed at the other end, but not any cut off, for that would make the pattern too scant; it is then baptised in the missouri with two dips and a flirt, and bobbed into the kettle; from whence after it be well boiled it is taken and fryed with bears oil untill it becomes brown, when it is ready to esswage the pangs of a keen appetite or such as travelers in the wilderness are seldom at a loss for. [Camped a few miles above the town of Fort Peck, Valley County, Montana.]

[ORDWAY] the Game is gitting So pleanty and tame in this country that Some of the party clubbed them out of their way.

May 10, 1805
[LEWIS] we still beleive ourselves in the country usually hunted by the Assinniboins, and as they are a vicious illy disposed nation we think it best to be on our guard, accordingly we inspected the arms and accoutrements the party and found them all in good order . . . from the appearance of the Mule deer and the bighorned anamals we beleive ourselves fast approaching a hilly or mountainous country; we have rarely found the mule deer in any except a rough country . . . ther are several esscential differences between the Mule and common deer as well in form as in habits.   they are fully a third larger in general, and the male is particularly large . . . the ears are peculiarly large; I measured those of a large buck which I found to be eleven inches long and 3½ in width at the widest part . . . the most striking difference of all, is the white rump and tale . . . from this black hair of the tail they have obtained among the French engages the appelation of the black taled deer, but this I conceive by no means characteristic of the anamal as much the larger portion of the tail is white . . . we have by way of distinction adapted the appelation of the mule deer which I think much more appropriate . . .

Boils and imposthumes[24] have been very common with the party Bratton is now unable to work with one on his hand; soar eyes continue also to be common to all of us in a greater or less degree.   for the imposthume I use emmolient poltices, and for soar eyes a solution of white

24. Dietary deficiencies may have led to the boils and abscesses ("imposthumes").

vitriol and the sugar of lead in the proportion of 2 grs. of the former and one of the latter to each ounce of water. [Camped in either Garfield or Valley County, Montana.]

May 11, 1805

[LEWIS] Set out this morning at an early hour, the courant strong; and river very crooked; the banks are falling in very fast; I sometimes wonder that some of our canoes or perogues are not swallowed up by means of these immence masses of earth which are eternally precipitating themselves into the river; we have had many hair breadth escapes from them but providence seems so to have ordered it that we have as yet sustained no loss in consequence of them . . . About 5 P. M. my attention was struck by one of the Party runing at a distance towards us and making signs and hollowing as if in distress, I ordered the perogues to put too, and waited untill he arrived; I now found that it was Bratton the man with the soar hand whom I had permitted to walk on shore, he arrived so much out of breath that it was several minutes before he could tell what had happened; at length he informed me that . . . he had shot a brown bear which immediately turned on him and pursued him a considerable distance but he had wounded it so badly that it could not overtake him; I immediately turned out with seven of the party in quest of this monster, we at length found his trale and persued him about a mile by the blood through very thick brush of rosbushes and the large leafed willow; we finally found him concealed in some very thick brush and shot him through the skull with two balls . . . it was a monstrous beast, not quite so large as that we killed a few days past but in all other rispects much the same   the hair is remarkably long fine and rich tho' he appears parshally to have discharged his winter coat; we now found that Bratton had shot him through the center of the lungs, notwithstanding which he had pursued him near half a mile and had returned more than double that distance and with his tallons had prepared himself a bed in the earth of about 2 feet deep and five long and was perfectly alive when we found him which could not have been less than 2 hours after he reeived the wound; these bear being so hard to die reather intimedates us all; I must confess that I do not like the gentlemen and had reather fight two Indians than one bear; there is no other chance to conquer them by a single shot but by shooting them through the brains, and this becomes difficult in consequence of two large muscles which cover the sides of the forehead and the sharp projection of the center of the frontal bone, which is also of a pretty good thickness. [Camped in Garfield County, Montana.]

May 12, 1805
[LEWIS] I walked on shore this morning for the benifit of exersize which I much wanted, and also to examine the country and it's productions, in these excurtions I most generally went alone armed with my rifle and espontoon; thus equiped I feel myself more than an equal match for a brown bear provided I get him in open woods or near the water, but feel myself a little diffident with respect to an attack in the open plains, I have therefore come to a resolution to act on the defencive only, should I meet these gentlemen in the open country . . . the choke cherry also grows here in the hollows and at the heads of the gullies; the choke Cherry has been in blume since the ninth inst.   this growth has freequently made it's appearance on the Missouri from the neighbourhood of the *Baldpated Prarie*, to this place . . . and of course of the Class and order Pentandria Monogynia . . . The Indians of the Missouri make great uce of this cherry which they prepare for food in various ways, sometimes eating when first plucked from the trees or in that state pounding them <and> mashing the seed boiling them with roots or meat, or with the prarie beans [25] and white-apple; again for their winter store they geather them and lay them on skins to dry in the sun, and frequently pound them and make them up in small roles or cakes and dry them in the sun; when thus dryed they fold them in skins or put them in bags of parchment and keep them through the winter either eating them in this state or boiling them as before mentioned. [Camped in Garfield County, Montana.]

May 14, 1805
[LEWIS] In the evening the men in two of the rear canoes discovered a large brown bear lying in the open grounds about 300 paces from the river, and six of them went out to attack him, all good hunters; they took

25. Hog peanut.

the advantage of a small eminence which concealed them and got within 40 paces of him unperceived, two of them reserved their fires as had been previously conscerted, the four others fired nearly at the same time and put each his bullet through him, two of the balls passed through the bulk of both lobes of his lungs, in an instant this monster ran at them with open mouth, the two who had reserved their fires discharged their pieces at him as he came towards them, boath of them struck him, one only slightly and the other fortunately broke his shoulder, this however only retarded his motion for a moment only, the men unable to reload their guns took to flight, the bear pursued and had very nearly overtaken them before they reached the river; two of the party betook themselves to a canoe and the others seperated an concealed. themselves among the willows, reloaded their pieces, each discharged his piece at him as they had an opportunity they struck him several times again but the guns served only to direct the bear to them, in this manner he pursued two of them seperately so close that they were obliged to throw aside their guns and pouches and throw themselves into the river altho' the bank was nearly twenty feet perpendicular; so enraged was this anamal that he plunged into the river only a few feet behind the second man he had compelled take refuge in the water, when one of those who still remained on shore shot him through the head and finally killed him; they then took him on shore and butched him when they found eight balls had passed through him in different directions . . . it was after the sun had set before these men come up with us, where we had been halted by an occurrence, which I have now to recappitulate, and which altho' happily passed without ruious injury, I cannot recollect but with the utmost trepidation and horror; this is the upseting and narrow escape of the white perogue It happened unfortunately for us this evening that Charbono was at the helm of this Perogue, in stead of Drewyer, who had previously steered her; Charbono cannot swim and is perhaps the most timid waterman in the world; perhaps it was equally unluckey that Capt. C. and myself were both on shore at that moment, a circumstance which rarely happened; and tho' we were on the shore opposite to the perogue, were too far distant to be heard or to do more than remain spectators of her fate; in this perogue [blank] were embarked, our papers, Instruments, books medicine, a great part of our merchandize and in short almost every article indispensibly necessary to further the views, or insure the success of the enterprize in which we are now launched to the distance of 2200 miles. surfice it to say, that the Perogue was under sail when a sudon squawl of wind struck her obliquely, and turned her considerably, the steersman allarmed, in stead of puting her before the wind, lufted her up into it, the wind was so violent that it drew the brace of the squarsail out of the hand of the man who was attending it, and instantly upset the perogue and would have turned her completely topsaturva, had it not have been from the resistance mad by the oarning against the water; in this situation Capt. C and myself both fired our guns to attract the attention if possible of the crew and ordered the halyards to be cut and the sail hawled in, but they did not hear us; such was their confusion and consternation at this moment, that they suffered the perogue to lye on her side for half a minute before they took the sail in, the perogue then wrighted but had filled within an inch of the gunwals; Charbono still crying to his god for mercy, had not yet recollected the rudder, nor could the repeated orders of the Bowsman, Cruzat, bring him to his recollection untill he threatend to shoot him istantly if he did not take hold of the rudder and do his duty, the waves by this time were runing very high, but the fortitude resolution and good conduct of Cruzat saved her . . . she arrived scarcely above the water; we now took every article out of her and lay them to drane as well as we could for the evening, baled out the canoe and secured her; there were two other men beside Charbono on board who could not swim, and who of course must also have perished had the perogue gone to the bottom. while the perogue lay on her side, finding I could not be heard, I for a moment forgot my own situation, and involluntarily droped my gun, threw aside my shot pouch and was in the act of unbuttoning my coat, before I recollected the folly of the attempt I was about to make, which was to throw myself into the river and indevour to swim to the perogue; the perogue was three hundred yards distant the waves so high that a perogue could scarcely live in any situation, the water excessively could, and the stream rappid; had I undertaken this project therefore, there was a hundred to one but what I should have paid the forfit of my life for the madness of my project, but this had the perogue been lost, I should have valued but little. After having all matters arranged for the evening as well as the nature of circumstances would permit, we thought it a proper occa-

sion to console ourselves and cheer the sperits of our men and accordingly took a drink of grog and gave each man a gill of sperits. [Camped a
few miles below Snow Creek, Garfield County, Montana, but on the opposite side in Valley County.]

May 16, 1805

[LEWIS] by 4 oClock in the evening our Instruments, Medicine, merchandize provision &c, were perfectly dryed, repacked and put on board
the perogue . . . our medicine sustained the greatest injury, several articles
of which were intirely spoiled, and many others considerably injured; the
ballance of our losses consisted of some gardin seeds, a small quantity of
gunpowder, and a few culinary articles which fell overboard and sunk,
the Indian woman to whom I ascribe equal fortitude and resolution, with
any person onboard at the time of the accedent, caught and preserved
most of the light articles which were washed overboard. [Camped in
Garfield County, Montana.]

May 17, 1805

[LEWIS] Capt. Clark narrowly escaped being bitten by a rattlesnake[26] in
the course of his walk, the party killed one this evening at our encampment, which he informed me was similar to that he had seen; this snake
is smaller than those common to the middle Atlantic States, being about
2 feet 6 inches long; it is of a yellowish brown colour on the back and
sides, variagated with one row of oval spots of a dark brown colour lying
transversely over the back from the neck to the tail, and two other rows
of small circular spots of the same colour which garnis the sides along the
edge of the scuta.   it's bely contains 176 scuta on the belly and 17 on the
tale . . . we were roused late at night by the Sergt. of the guard, and warned
of the danger we were in from a large tree that had taken fire and which
leant immediately over our lodge.   we had the loge removed, and a few
minutes after a large proportion of the top of the tree fell on the place the
lodge had stood; had we been a few minutes later we should have been
crushed to attoms. [Camped a little upstream of Seven Blackfoot Creek,
Garfield County, Montana.]

26. Prairie rattlesnake.

[LEWIS AND CLARK, WEATHER REMARKS] the Gees have their young; the Elk begin to produce their young, the Antelope and deer as yet have not. the small species of Goatsucker or whiperwill[27] begin to cry— the black-birds both small[28] and large[29] have appeared.

May 19, 1805

[LEWIS] one of the party wounded a beaver, and my dog as usual swam in to catch it; the beaver bit him through the hind leg and cut the artery; it was with great difficulty that I could stop the blood; I fear it will yet prove fatal to him.[30] [Camped near later Long Point, in either Phillips or Garfield County, Montana.]

May 20, 1805

[LEWIS] At the distance of 2¼ miles passed the entrance of a large Creek, affording but little water; this stream we named *Blowing Fly Creek*,[31] from the immence quantities of those insects[32] found in this neighbourhood, they infest our meat while roasting or boiling, and we are obliged to brush them off our provision as we eat . . . about five miles ab[ov]e the mouth of shell river[33] a handsome river of about fifty yards in width discharged itself into the shell river on the Stard. or upper side; this stream we called Sâh-câ-gar me-âh [*NB: Sah ca gah we a*] or bird woman's River,[34] after our interpreter the Snake woman. [Camped in either Garfield or Petroleum County, Montana, on the upstream side of Musselshell River, which here forms the boundary between those counties.]

May 22, 1805

[LEWIS] I do not believe that the Black bear common to the lower part of this river and the Atlantic States, exists in this quarter; we have neither

27. Common poorwill.
28. Maybe the rusty blackbird or Brewer's blackbird.
29. Probably the grackle.
30. Lewis's dog, Seaman, survived the bite.
31. Squaw Creek, Garfield County, Montana.
32. Not specifically identified, but may be from either the Calliphoridae or Sacrophagidae families.
33. Musselshell River.
34. Sacagawea River, Petroleum County, Montana, called Crooked Creek for many years.

seen one of them nor their tracks which would be easily distinguished by it's shortness of tallons when compared with the brown grizly or white bear. I believe that it is the same species or family of bears which assumes all those colours at different ages and seasons of the year.[35] [Camped below CK, or Kannuck, Creek, Phillips County, Montana.]

May 23, 1805
[LEWIS] just above the entrance of Teapot Creek[36] on the stard. there is a large assemblage of the burrows of the Burrowing Squirrel[37]   they generally seelect a south or a south Easterly exposure for their residence, and never visit the brooks or river for water; I am astonished how this anamal exists as it dose without water,[38] particularly in a country like this where there is scarcely any rain during ¾ of the year and more rarely any due [dew]; yet we have sometimes found their villages at the distance of five or six miles from any water, and they are never found out of the limits of the ground which their burrows occupy; in the Autumn when the hard frosts commence they close their burrows and do not venture out again untill spring, indeed some of them appear to be yet in winter quarters. [Camped a little below Rock Creek, Fergus County, Montana.]

[WHITEHOUSE] about 2 oC. P. M. we halted and made fire to dine at a timbred bottom on N. S.   one of the hunters took his rifle & bullitt pouch on Shore   the fire broke out into the woods, and burned up his shot pouch powder horn & the stalk of his rifle.

May 24, 1805
[LEWIS] The country high and broken, a considerable portion of black rock and brown sandy rock appear in the faces of the hills; the tops of the hills covered with scattering pine spruce and dwarf cedar;[39] the soil poor

35. The party is not out of the range of the black bear, and the "brown grizly or white bear" is indeed all one species, the grizzly, but its color variations are not due to age or seasonal changes.

36. CK, or Kannuck, Creek.

37. Prairie dog.

38. The prairie dog obtains water through its food and is well adapted to an arid environment.

39. Probably ponderosa pine, Engelmann spruce, and creeping juniper.

and sterile, sandy near the tops of the hills, the whole producing but little grass; the narrow bottoms of the Missouri producing little else but Hysop or southern wood [40] and the pulpy leafed thorn. [41] [Camped about three miles above the crossing of Highway 191, in either Fergus or Phillips County, Montana.]

May 25, 1805

[CLARK] In my walk of this day I saw mountts. on either side of the river at no great distance, those mountains appeared to be detached, and not ranges as laid down by the *Minetarrees*, I also think I saw a range of high mounts. at a great distance to the S S W. but am not certain as the horozon was not clear enough to view it with Certainty. [42] [Camped about five or six miles below Cow Island Landing Recreation Area, Fergus County, Montana.]

[WHITEHOUSE] Gibson one of the hunters putt one of his Shoulders out of place to day but got it in again.

May 26, 1805

[LEWIS] In the after part of the day I also walked out and ascended the river hills which I found sufficiently fortiegueing. on arriving to the summit one of the highest points in the neighbourhood I thought myself well repaid for any labour; as from this point I beheld the Rocky Mountains for the first time, [43] I could only discover a few of the most elivated points above the horizon, the most remarkable of which by my pocket compass I found bore N. 65° W. . . . while I viewed these mountains I felt a secret pleasure in finding myself so near the head of the heretofore conceived boundless Missouri; but when I reflected on the difficulties which

40. Probably big sagebrush.

41. Greasewood.

42. These are not a continuation of the Black Hills of South Dakota as described by the Hidatsas, who led the captains to a larger conception of those hills. To the north are the Little Rocky and Bears Paw Mountains and to the south, the Judith Range. In the distance Clark may have seen the Highwood Mountains near the Great Falls.

43. Lewis is not seeing the Rocky Mountains from this vantage point, but the Highwood Mountains that Clark had viewed the previous day.

this snowey barrier would most probably throw in my way to the Pacific, and the sufferings and hardships of myself and party in them, it in some measure counterballanced the joy I had felt in the first moments in which I gazed on them; but as I have always held it a crime to anticipate evils I will believe it a good comfortable road untill I am compelled to beleive differently. [Camped about two miles below and opposite Windsor Creek, in Fergus County, Montana.]

[CLARK] this Countrey may with propriety I think be termed the Deserts of America, as I do not Conceive any part can ever be Settled, as it is deficent in water, Timber & too Steep to be tilled.

May 27, 1805
[GASS] We have now got into a country which presents little to our view, but scenes of barrenness and desolation; and see no encouraging prospects that it will terminate. Having proceeded (by the course of this river) about two thousand three hundred miles, it may therefore not be improper to make two or three general observations respecting the country we have passed . . . From the confluence of the river Platte with the Missouri to the Sterile desert we lately entered a distance of upwards of fifteen hundred miles the soil is less rich, and except in the bottoms, the land of an inferior quality; but may in general be called good second rate land . . . This kind of country and soil which has fallen under our observation in our progress up the Missouri, extends it is understood, to a great distance on both sides of the river. Along the Missouri and the waters which flow into it, cotton wood and willows are frequent in the bottoms and islands; but the upland is almost entirely without timber, and consists of large prairies or plains the boundaries of which the eye cannot reach. The grass is generally short on these immense natural pastures, which in the proper seasons are decorated with blossoms and flowers of various colours. The views from the hills are interesting and grand. Wide extended plains with their hills and vales, stretching away in lessening wavy ridges, until by their distance they fade from the sight; large rivers and streams in their rapid course, winding in various meanders; groves of cotton wood and willow along the waters intersecting the landscapes in different directions, dividing them into various forms, at length appearing like dark

clouds and sinking in the horizon; these enlivened with the buffaloe, elk, deer, and other animals which in vast numbers feed upon the plains or pursue their prey, are the prominent objects, which compose the extensive prospects presented to the view and strike the attention of the beholder. [Camped near later McGarry Bar, Fergus County, Montana.]

May 28, 1805
[LEWIS] the riffles and rocky points . . . are as numerous and many of them much worse than those we passed yesterday; arround those points the water drives with great force, and we are obliged in many instaces to steer our vessels through the appertures formed by the points of large sharp rocks which reach a few inches above the surface of the water, here sould our chord give way the bough is instantly drivin outwards by the stream and the vessel thrown with her side on the rocks where she must inevitably overset or perhaps be dashed to peices . . . found a new indian lodge pole today which had been brought down by the stream, it was woarn at one end as if draged by dogs or horses; a football [44] also, and several other articles were found, which have been recently brought down by the courant; these are strong evedences of Indians being on the river above us, and probably at no great distance; the football is such as I have seen among the Minetaries and therefore think it most probable that they are a band of the Minetaries of Fort de Prarie. [45] [Camped near Judith Landing Recreation Area, Chouteau County, Montana.]

[LEWIS AND CLARK, WEATHER REMARKS] the air was turbid in the forenoon and appeared to be filled with smoke; we supposed it to proceed from the burning of the plains, which we are informed are frequently set on fire by the Snake Indians to compell the antelopes to resort to the woody and mountanous country which they inhabit.

May 29, 1805
[LEWIS] Last night we were all allarmed by a large buffaloe Bull, which swam over from the opposite shore and coming along side of the white

44. Probably a buckskin ball used in Plains Indian games.
45. The Atsinas, distinct from the Minitaris at the Knife River, who were Hidatsas.

perogue, climbed over it to land, he then alarmed ran up the bank in full speed directly towards the fires, and was within 18 inches of the heads of some of the men who lay sleeping before the centinel could allarm him or make him change his course, still more alarmed, he now took his direction immediately towards our lodge, passing between 4 fires and within a few inches of the heads of one range of the men as they yet lay sleeping, when he came near the tent, my dog saved us by causing him to change his course a second time, which he did by turning a little to the right, and was quickly out of sight, leaving us by this time all in an uproar with our guns in or hands, enquiring of each other the case of the alarm, which after a few moments was explained by the centinel; we were happy to find no one hirt. The next morning we found that the buffaloe in passing the perogue had trodden on a rifle, which belonged to Capt. Clark's black man, who had negligently left her in the perogue, the rifle was much bent, he had also broken the spindle, pivit, and shattered the stock of one of the bluntderbushes on board, with this damage I felt well content, happey indeed, that we had sustaned no further injury.   it appears that the white perogue, which contains our most valuable stores, is attended by some evil gennii. This morning we set out at an early hour and proceded as usual by the Chord.   at the distance of 2½ miles passed a handsome river which discharged itself on the Lard. side . . . Cap. C who assended this R. much higher than I did has <thought proper to> call it *Judieths River*[46] . . . today we passed on the Stard. side the remains of a vast many mangled carcases of Buffalow which had been driven over a precipice of 120 feet by the Indians . . . they created a most horid stench.   in this manner the Indians of the Missouri distroy vast herds of buffaloe at a stroke; for this purpose one of the most active and fleet young men is scelected and disguised in a robe of buffaloe skin, having also the skin of the buffaloe's head with the years and horns fastened on his head in form of a cap, thus caparisoned he places himself at a convenient distance between a herd of buffaloe and a precipice proper for the purpose, which happens in many places on this river for miles together; the other indians now surround the herd on the back and flanks and at a signal agreed on all shew them-

46. Judith River, Fergus County, Montana, was named for Clark's future wife, Julia Hancock.

selves at the same time moving forward towards the buffaloe; the disguised indian or decoy has taken care to place himself sufficiently nigh the buffaloe to be noticed by them when they take to flight and runing before them they follow him in full speede to the precepice, the cattle behind driving those in front over and seeing them go do not look or hesitate about following untill the whole are precipitated down the precepice forming one common mass of dead an mangled carcases; the decoy in the mean time has taken care to secure himself in some cranney or crivice of the clift which he had previously prepared for that purpose.   the part of the decoy I am informed is extreamly dangerous, if they are not very fleet runers the buffaloe tread them under foot and crush them to death, and sometimes drive them over the precepice also, where they perish in common with the buffaloe.[47] [Camped at or near Slaughter River Landing Recreation Area, Chouteau County, Montana.]

May 30, 1805
[LEWIS] the air of the open country is asstonishingly dry as well as pure. I found by several experiments that a table spoon full of water exposed to the air in a saucer would avaporate in 36 hours when the murcury did not stand higher than the temperate point at the greatest heat of the day; my inkstand so frequently becoming dry put me on this experiment. I also observed the well seasoned case of my sextant shrunk considerably and the joints opened. [Camped opposite Sheep Shed Coulee, Chouteau County, Montana.]

May 31, 1805
[LEWIS] The obstructions of rocky points and riffles still continue as yesterday; at those places the men are compelled to be in the water even to their armpits, and the water is yet very could, and so frequent are those point that they are one fourth of their time in the water, added to this the banks and bluffs along which they are obliged to pass are so slippery and the mud so tenacious that they are unable to wear their mockersons, and

47. Lewis accurately described the Plains Indian buffalo jump, but at this place the dead buffalo were more likely the result of winter-killed float bison that had stacked up here.

in that situation draging the heavy burthen of a canoe and walking ocasionally for several hundred yards over the sharp fragments of rocks
which tumble from the clifts and garnish the borders of the river; in short
their labour is incredibly painfull and great, yet those faithfull fellows
bear it without a murmur. The toe rope of the white perogue, the only
one indeed of hemp, and that on which we most depended, gave way today at a bad point, the perogue swung and but slightly touched a rock, yet
was very near overseting; I fear her evil gennii will play so many pranks
with her that she will go to the bottomm some of those days[48] . . .

The hills and river Clifts[49] which we passed today exhibit a most romantic appearance. The bluffs of the river rise to the hight of from 2 to
300 feet and in most places nearly perpendicular; they are formed of remarkable white sandstone which is sufficiently soft to give way readily to
the impression of water; two or thre thin horizontal stratas of white freestone, on which the rains or water make no impression, lie imbeded in
these clifts of soft stone near the upper part of them; the earth on the top
of these Clifts is a dark rich loam, which forming a graduly ascending
plain extends back from ½ a mile to a mile where the hills commence and
rise abruptly to a hight of about 300 feet more. The water in the course
of time in decending from those hills and plains on either side of the
river has trickled down the soft sand clifts and woarn it into a thousand
grotesque figures, which with the help of a little immagination and an
oblique view at a distance, are made to represent eligant ranges of lofty
freestone buildings, having their parapets well stocked with statuary; collumns of various sculpture both grooved and plain, are also seen supporting long galleries in front of those buildings; in other places on a
much nearer approach and with the help of less immagination we see
the remains or ruins of eligant buildings; some collumns standing and
almost entire with their pedestals and capitals; others retaining their
pedestals but deprived by time or accident of their capitals, some lying
prostrate an broken   othe[r]s in the form of vast pyramids of connic
structure bearing a sereis of other pyramids on their tops becoming less

48. The white pirogue, despite its numerous mishaps, was the only vessel to survive the
entire trip and return with the party to St. Louis in September 1806.

49. The White Cliffs area of the Missouri River Breaks, Chouteau County, Montana.

as they ascend and finally terminating in a sharp point. nitches and al-
coves of various forms and sizes are seen at different hights as we pass . . .
As we passed on it seemed as if those seens of visionary inchantment
would never have and end; for here it is too that nature presents to the
view of the traveler vast ranges ofwalls of tolerable workmanship, so perfect indeed are those walls that I should have thought that nature had attempted here to rival the human art of masonry had I not recollected that
she had first began her work . . . I saw near those bluffs the most beautifull fox that I ever beheld, the colours appeared to me to be a fine orrange
yellow, white and black, I endevoured to kill this anamal but it discovered
me at a considerable distance, and finding that I could get no nearer, I
fired on him as he ran, and missed him; he concealed himself under the
rocks of the clift; it appeared to me to be about the size of the common
red fox of the Atlantic states, or reather smaller than the large fox common to this country; convinced I am that it is a distinct species.[50]
[Camped just above Eagle Creek, Chouteau County, Montana.]

[LEWIS AND CLARK, WEATHER REMARKS] The Antelope now bring forth
their young. from the size of the young of the bighorned Antelope I suppose they bring forth their young as early at least as the Elk.

[WHITEHOUSE] the hunters came in at dark had hilled 1 black taild. Deer
2 Ibex or mountain Sheep (rams) which had handsome large horns. we
took care of the horns in order to take them back to the U. States.

June 2, 1805
[LEWIS] Game becomeing more abundant this morning and I thought it
best now to loose no time or suffer an opportunity to escape in providing the necessary quantity of Elk's skins to cover my leather boat[51] which
I now expect I shall be obliged to use shortly. Accordingly I walked on
shore most of the day with some of the hunters for that purpose and
killed 6 Elk 2 buffalo 2 Mule deer and a bear . . . the bear was very near

50. Not a distinct species, but a cross fox, a color phase of the red fox.
51. An unassembled, iron-framed boat that Lewis brought from the East to use in the
shallow waters of the upper Missouri.

catching Drewyer; it also pursued Charbono who fired his gun in the air as he ran but fortunately eluded the vigilence of the bear by secreting himself very securely in the bushes untill Drewyer finally killed it by a shot in the head; the [only] shot indeed that will conquer the farocity of those tremendious anamals. [Camped on the south side of the Missouri River, Chouteau County, Montana, opposite the mouth of the Marias River.]

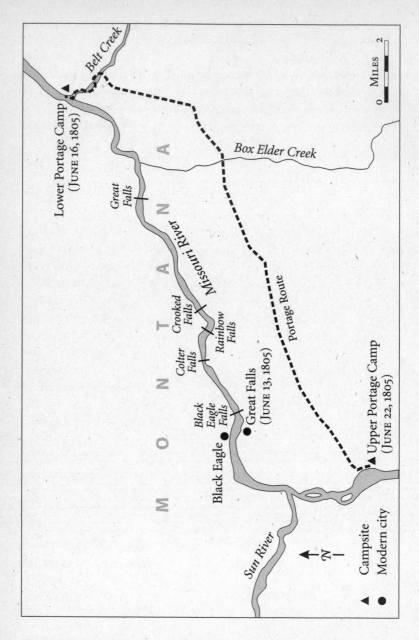

The Expedition's Route, June 3–July 14, 1805

CHAPTER 5

Portaging the Falls

June 3, 1805

[LEWIS] An interesting question was now to be determined; which of these rivers was the Missouri, or that river which the Minnetares call *Amahte Arz zha*[1] or Missouri, and which they had discribed to us as approaching very near to the Columbia river. to mistake the stream at this period of the season, two months of the traveling season having now elapsed, and to ascend such stream to the rocky Mountain or perhaps much further before we could inform ourselves whether it did approach the Columbia or not, and then be obliged to return and take the other stream would not only loose us the whole of this season but would probably so dishearten the party that it might defeat the expedition altogether. convinced we were that the utmost circumspection and caution was necessary in deciding on the stream to be taken. to this end an investigation of both streams was the first thing to be done; to learn their widths, debths, comparitive rappidity of their courants and thence the comparitive bodies of water furnished by each; accordingly we dispatched two light canoes with three men in each up those streams;[2] we also sent out several small parties by land with instructions to penetrate the country as far as they conveniently can permiting themselves time to return this evening and indeavour if possible to discover the distant bearing of those rivers by ascending the rising grounds . . . we took the width of the two rivers, found the left hand or S. fork 372 yards and the N. fork 200. The noth fork is deeper than the other but it's courant not so swift; it's waters

1. The Hidatsa word for the Missouri River.
2. Sergeant Pryor with two unnamed men went up the Marias, while Sergeant Gass with Whitehouse and another man went up the Missouri.

run in the same boiling and roling manner which has uniformly charac-
terized the Missouri throughout it's whole course so far; it's waters are of
a whitish brown colour very thick and terbid, also characteristic of the
Missouri; while the South fork is perfectly transparent runds very rappid
but with a smoth unriffled surface it's bottom composed of round and
flat smooth stones like most rivers issuin from a mountainous country.
the bed of the N. fork composed of some gravel but principally mud; in
short the air & character of this river is so precisely that of the missouri
below that the party with very few exceptions have already pronounced
the N. fork to be the Missouri; myself and Capt. C. not quite so precipi-
tate have not yet decided but if we were to give our opinions I believe we
should be in the minority, certain it is that the North fork gives the
colouring matter and character which is retained from hence to the gulph
of Mexico. I am confident that this river rises in and passes a great distance through an open plain country   I expect that it has some of it's
souces on the Eastern side of the rocky mountain South of the Saskashawan, but that it dose not penetrate the first range of these Mountains and that much the greater part of it's sources are in a northwardly
direction towards the lower and middle parts of the Saskashawan in the
open plains.   convinced I am that if it penetrated the Rocky Mountains
to any great distance it's waters would be clearer unless it should run an
immence distance indeed after leaving those mountains through these
level plains in order to acquire it's turbid hue. what astonishes us a little
is that the Indians who appeared to be so well acquainted with the geography of this country should not have mentioned this river on wright
hand if it be not the Missouri; *the river that scolds at all others*, as they call
it if there is in reallity such an one, ought agreeably to their account, to
have fallen in a considerable distance below, and on the other hand if this
righthand or N. fork be the Missouri I am equally astonished at their not
mentioning the S. fork which they must have passed in order to get to
those large falls which they mention on the Missouri.   thus have our cog-
itating faculties been busily employed all day . . . In the evening the parties whom we had sent out returned agreeably to instructions . . . Thos accounts being by no means satisfactory as to the fundamental point; Capt.
C. and myself concluded to set out early the next morning with a small
party each, and ascend these rivers untill we could perfectly satisfy our-

selves of the one, which it would be most expedient for us to take on our main journey to the Pacific.   accordingly it was agreed that I should ascend the right hand fork[3] and he the left.[4] I gave orders to Sergt. Pryor Drewyer, Shields, Windsor, Cruzatte and La Page to hold themselves in readiness to accompany me in the morning. Capt. Clark also selected Reubin & Joseph Fields, Sergt. Gass, Shannon and his black man York, to accompany him.[5]   we agreed to go up those rivers one day and a halfs march or further if it should appear necessary to satisfy us more fully of the point in question . . . we took a drink of grog this evening and gave the men a dram, and made all matters ready for an early departure in the morning. I had now my sack and blanket happerst in readiness to swing on my back, which is the first time in my life that I had ever prepared a burthen of this kind, and I am fully convinced that it will not be the last.[6] I take my Octant with me also, this I confide La Page. [Camped across from their previous camp, on the west side of the Missouri and south side of the Marias, at the point where the two rivers meet, southeast of Loma, Chouteau County, Montana.]

June 4, 1805

[LEWIS] [I observed] also a small bird[7] which in action resembles the lark, it is about the size of a large sparrow of a dark brown colour with some white fathers in the tail; this bird or that which I take to be the male rises into the air about 60 feet and supporting itself in the air with a brisk motion of the wings sings very sweetly, has several shrill soft notes reather of the plaintive order which it frequently repeats and varies, after remaining stationary about a minute in his aireal station he descends obliquely occasionly pausing and accomnying his decension with a note something like *twit twit twit*; on the ground he is silent.   thirty or forty of these birds will be stationed in the air at a time in view, these larks as I shall call them add much to the gayety and cheerfullness of the scene.

3. Marias River.

4. Missouri River.

5. Lewis with his detachment will ascend the Marias, while Clark will lead a party up the Missouri.

6. Lewis is unaccustomed to carrying his own haversack.

7. McCown's longspur.

[Lewis's party camped some distance above Sheep Coulee, on the opposide side in Chouteau County, Montana; Clark's party camped somewhat
over a mile above present Carter Ferry, Chouteau County; the rest of the
party remained at the mouth of the Marias.]

June 5, 1805
[CLARK] From the ridge at which place I Struck the river last, I could discover that the river run west of South a long distance, and has a Strong
rapid Current . . . as this river Continued its width debth & rapidity and
the Course west of South, going up further would be useless, I deturmined to return. [Lewis's party camped a short distance below the crossing of Montana Highway 223, Chouteau County, Montana; Clark's party
camped on the Teton River, west of Fort Benton, Chouteau County. The
main party waited at the mouth of the Marias.]

[ORDWAY] the men engaged Dressing Skins for to make themselves moccasons leggins &C.   one man by the name of Goodrich has caught a considerable quantity of fish. Some of which are Shell fish, but the most part
are Small cat fish.   we have caught none as large this Season as we did last
as yet, as we have a great pleanty of meat we do not trouble ourselves for
to catch fish.

[LEWIS AND CLARK, WEATHER REMARKS] great numbers of the sparrows
larks, Curloos and other small birds common to praries are now laying
their eggs and seting, their nests are in great abundance.[8]   the large batt,[9]
or night hawk appears.   the Turkey buzzard[10] appears.   first saw the
mountain cock[11] near the entrance of Maria's river.

June 6, 1805
[LEWIS] I now became well convinced that this branch of the Missouri
had it's direction too much to the North for our rout to the Pacific, and

8. The sparrows, larks, and curlews cannot be specifically identified.
9. Not a bat, but the common nighthawk, a bird.
10. Turkey vulture.
11. Sage grouse.

therefore determined to return the next day after taking an observation of the ☉'s Meridian Altitude in order to fix the latitude of the place. [Lewis's party camped near the mouth of Black Coulee Creek, Chouteau County, Montana; Clark's party rejoined the main group at the mouth of the Marias.]

[ORDWAY] Jos. Fields was attacted by an old hea bear & his gun missed fire and he was in danger of being killed by that venimous animel had the rest of the party not been in hearing, who fired at him and he turned his course and left the man.

June 7, 1805
[LEWIS] It continued to rain almost without intermission last night and as I expected we had a most disagreable and wrestless night. our camp possessing no allurements, we left our watery beads at an early hour and continued our rout down the river . . . In passing along the face of one of these bluffs today I sliped at a narrow pass of about 30 yards in length and but for a quick and fortunate recovery by means of my espontoon I should been precipitated into the river down a craggy pricipice of about ninety feet. I had scarcely reached a place on which I could stand with tolerable safety even with the assistance of my espontoon before I heard a voice behind me cry out god god Capt. what shall I do on turning about I found it was Windsor who had sliped and fallen abut the center of this narrow pass and was lying prostrate on his belley, with his wright hand arm and leg over the precipice while he was holding on with the left arm and foot as well as he could which appeared to be with much difficulty. I discovered his danger and the trepedation which he was in gave me still further concern for I expected every instant to see him loose his strength and slip off; altho' much allarmed at his situation I disguised my feelings and spoke very calmly to him and assured him that he was in no kind of danger, to take the knife out of his belt behind him with his wright hand and dig a hole with it in the face of the bank to receive his wright foot which he did and then raised himself to his knees; I then directed him to take off his mockersons and to come forward on his hands and knees holding the knife in one hand and the gun in the other this he happily effected and escaped . . . we roasted and eat

a hearty supper of our venison not having taisted a mosel before during the day; I now laid myself down on some willow boughs to a comfortable nights rest, and felt indeed as if I was fully repaid for the toil and pain of the day, so much will a good shelter, a dry bed, an comfortable supper revive the sperits of the waryed, wet and hungry traveler. [Lewis's detachment camped some distance below Sheep Coulee, on the opposide side in Chouteau County, Montana; the main party continued at the mouth of the Marias.]

June 8, 1805
[LEWIS] The whole of my party to a man except myself were fully peswaided that this river was the Missouri, but being fully of opinion that it was neither the main stream or that which it would be advisable for us to take, I determined to give it a name and in honour of Miss Maria W—d.[12] called it Maria's River. it is true that the hue of the waters of this turbulent and troubled stream but illy comport with the pure celestial virtues and amiable qualifications of that lovely fair one; but on the other hand it is a noble river; one destined to become in my opinion an object of contention between the two great powers of America and Great Britin with rispect to the adjustment of the North westwardly boundary of the former; and that it will become one of the most interesting brances of the Missouri in a commercial point of view . . . Capt. Clark ploted the courses of the two rivers as far as we had ascended them. I now began more than ever to suspect the varacity of Mr. Fidler[13] or the correctness of his instruments. for I see that Arrasmith in his late map of N. America has laid down a remarkable mountain in the chain of the Rocky mountains called the tooth nearly as far South as Latitude 45°, and this is said to be from the discoveries of Mr. Fidler. we are now within a hundred miles of the Rocky Mountains, and I find from my observation of the 3rd Inst that the latitude of this place is 47° 24′ 12.8″. the river must therefore turn much

12. Maria Wood was Lewis's cousin.

13. Aaron Arrowsmith's map of 1802, with which Lewis was familiar, incorporated information from Peter Fidler, a surveyor for Hudson's Bay Company. Fidler himself had not traveled this far south but gained his information from Ackomokki, a Blackfeet chief.

to the South, between this and the rocky Mountain to have permitted
Mr. Fidler to have passed along the Eastern border of these mountains
as far S. as nearly 45° without even seeing it.   but from hence as far as
Capt. C. had ascended the S. fork or Missouri being the distance of 55
miles   it's course is S. 29° W. and it still appeared to bear considerably to
the W. of South as far as he could see it. I think therefore that we shall find
that the Missouri enters the rocky mountains to the North of 45°. [Lewis
rejoined the main party at the mouth of the Marias.]

June 9, 1805
[LEWIS] We determined to deposite at this place the large red perogue all
the heavy baggage which we could possibly do without and some provision, salt, tools powder and Lead &c with a view to lighten our vessels and
at the same time to strengthen their crews by means of the seven hands
who have been heretofore employd. in navigating the red perogue; accordingly we set some hands to diging a hole or cellar for the reception of
our stores.   these holes in the ground or deposits are called by the engages
cashes; on enquiry I found that Cruzatte was well acquainted this business
and therefore left the management of it intirely to him.   today we examined our maps, and compared the information derived as well from them
as from the Indians and fully settled in our minds the propryety of ad-
dopting the South fork for the Missouri . . . The Indian information also
argued strongly in favour of the South fork.   they informed us that the
water of the Missouri was nearly transparent at the great falls, this is the
case with the water of the South fork; that the falls lay a little to the South
of sunset from them; this is also brobable as we are only a few minutes
North of Fort Mandan and the South fork bears considerably South from
hence to the Mountains . . . Those ideas as they occurred to me I inde-
voured to impress on the minds of the party all of whom except Capt. C.
being still firm in the beleif that the N. Fork was the Missouri and that
which we ought to take; they said very cheerfully that they were ready to
follow us any wher we thought proper to direct but that they still thought
that the other was the river . . . Cruzatte who had been an old Missouri
navigator and who from his integrity knowledge and skill as a waterman
had acquired the confidence of every individual of the party declared it as
his opinion that the N. fork was the true genuine Missouri and could be

no other. finding them so determined in this beleif, and wishing that if we were in an error to be able to detect it and rectify it as soon as possible it was agreed between Capt. C. and myself that one of us should set out with a small party by land up the South fork and continue our rout up it untill we found the falls or reached the snowy Mountains by which means we should be enabled to determine this question pretty accurately. this expedition I prefered undertaking as Capt. C best waterman &c. and determined to set out the day after tomorrow; I wished to make some further observations at this place, and as we had determined to leave our blacksmith's bellows and tools here it was necessary to repare some of our arms, and particularly my Airgun the main spring of which was broken, before we left this place. these and some other preperations will necessarily detain us two perhaps three days. I felt myself very unwell this morning and took a portion of salts from which I feel much releif this evening . . . In the evening Cruzatte gave us some music on the violin and the men passed the evening in dancing singing &c and were extreemly cheerfull. [Remained at the mouth of the Marias.]

June 10, 1805
[LEWIS] Shields renewed the main Spring of my air gun   we have been much indebted to the ingenuity of this man on many occasions; without having served any regular apprenticeship to any trade, he makes his own tools principally and works extreemly well in either wood or metal, and in this way has been extreenely servicable to us, as well as being a good hunter and an excellent waterman . . . we now scelected the articles to be deposited in this cash which consisted of 2 best falling axes, one auger, a set of plains, some files, blacksmiths bellowses and hammers Stake tongs &c. 1 Keg of flour, 2 Kegs of parched meal, 2 Kegs of Pork, 1 Keg of salt, some chissels, a cooper's Howel,[14] some tin cups, 2 Musquets, 3 brown bear skins, beaver skins, horns of the bighorned anamal, a part of the men's robes clothing and all their superfluous baggage of every discription, and beaver traps. we drew up the red perogue into the middle of a small Island at the entrance of Maria's river, and secured and made her

14. A type of plane.

fast to the trees to prevent the high floods from carrying her off   put my brand[15] on several trees standing near her, and covered her with brush to shelter her from the effects of the sun . . . *Sâh-câh-gâh, we â*, our Indian woman is very sick this evening; Capt. C. blead her . . . Mean Latitude of the Entrance of Maria's river . . . 47° 25′ 17.2″ North.[16] [Remained at the mouth of the Marias.]

June 11, 1805
[LEWIS] This morning I felt much better, but somewhat w[e]akened by my disorder. at 8 A. M. I swung my pack, and set forward with my little party[17] . . . [before dinner] I was taken with such violent pain in the intesteris that I was unable to partake of the feast of marrowbones. my pain still increased and towards evening was attended with a high fever; finding myself unable to march, I determined to prepare a camp of some willow boughs and remain all night.   having brought no medecine with me I resolved to try an experiment with some simples; and the Choke cherry which grew abundanly in the bottom first struck my attention; I directed a parsel of the small twigs to be geathered striped of their leaves, cut into pieces of about 2 Inches in length and boiled in water untill a strong black decoction of an astringent bitter tast was produced; at sunset I took a point [pint] of this decoction and abut an hour after repeated the dze by 10 in the evening I was entirely releived from pain and in fact every symptom of the disorder forsook me; my fever abated, a gentle perspiration was produced and I had a comfortable and refreshing nights rest. [Lewis's party camped a few miles northeast of Fort Benton, Chouteau County, Montana.]

[CLARK] the Indian woman verry Sick, I blead her which appeared to be of great Service to her. [Clark remained at the Marias with the main party.]

15. Lewis's branding iron was inscribed "U. S. Capt. M. Lewis," and is now at the Oregon Historical Society, Portland.
16. The approximate latitude of the mouth of the Marias is 47° 55′ 45″ N.
17. Lewis had Drouillard, Joseph Field, Gibson, and Goodrich with him.

June 12, 1805
[LEWIS] This morning I felt myself quite revived, took another portion of
my decoction and set out at sunrise . . . we had a most beatifull and pic-
turesk view of the Rocky mountains which wer perfectly covered with
Snow and reaching from S. E. to the N. of N. W.   they appear to be
formed of several ranges each succeeding range rising higher than the
preceding one untill the most distant appear to loose their snowey tops
in the clouds; this was an august spectacle and still rendered more formidable by the recollection that we had them to pass [18] . . . This evening I ate
very heartily and after pening the transactions of the day amused myself
catching those white fish [19] mentioned yesterday; they are here in great
abundance I caught upwards of a douzen in a few minutes; they bit most
freely at the melt of a deer [20] which goodrich had brought with him for the
purpose of fishing. [Lewis camped a short distance upstream of Black
Coulee, Chouteau County, Montana.]

[CLARK] The interpreters wife verry Sick   So much So that I move her
into the back part of our Covered part of the Perogue which is Cool, her
own situation being a verry hot one in the bottom of the Perogue exposed
to the Sun. [Clark camped about five miles downstream from Fort Benton, Chouteau County, Montana.]

[WHITEHOUSE] Our interpreters wife got very Sick, and great care was
taken of her, knowing, what a great loss she would be, if she died, she being our only Interpreter, for the Snake Indians, who reside in those
Mountains lying West of us, and from whom we expect assistance, in
prosecuting our Voyage.

June 13, 1805
[LEWIS] I had proceded on . . . about two miles . . . whin my ears were
saluted with the agreeable sound of a fall of water . . . a roaring too

18. Lewis was probably seeing the Highwood, Little Belt, and Big Belt Mountains with
the main Rockies beyond to the west.
19. Saugers.
20. Deer spleen.

tremendious to be mistaken for any cause short of the great falls of the Missouri.   here I arrived about 12 OClock having traveled by estimate about 15 Miles. I hurryed down the hill which was about 200 feet high and difficult of access, to gaze on this sublimely grand specticle. I took my position on the top of some rocks about 20 feet high opposite the center of the falls.   this chain of rocks appear once to have formed a part of those over which the waters tumbled, but in the course of time has been seperated from it to the distance of 150 yards lying prarrallel to it and forming a butment against which the water after falling over the precipice beats with great fury . . . immediately at the cascade the river is about 300 yds. wide; about ninty or a hundred yards of this next the Lard. bluff is a smoth even sheet of water falling over a precipice of at least eighty feet, the remaining part of about 200 yards on my right formes the grandest sight I ever beheld, the hight of the fall is the same of the other but the irregular and somewhat projecting rocks below receives the water in it's passage down and brakes it into a perfect white foam which assumes a thousand forms in a moment sometimes flying up in jets of sparkling foam to the hight of fifteen or twenty feet and are scarcely formed before large roling bodies of the same beaten and foaming water is thrown over and conceals them.   in short the rocks seem to be most happily fixed to present a sheet of the whitest beaten froath for 200 yards in length and about 80 feet perpendicular.   the water after decending strikes against the butment before mentioned or that on which I stand and seems to reverberate and being met by the more impetuous courant they role and swell into half formed billows of great hight which rise and again isappear in an instant . . . from the reflection of the sun on the spray or mist which arrises from these falls there is a beatifull rainbow produced which adds not a little to the beauty of this majestically grand senery. after wrighting this imperfect discription I again viewed the falls and was so much disgusted with the imperfect idea which it conveyed of the scene that I determined to draw my pen across it and begin agin, but then reflected that I could not perhaps succeed better than pening the first impressions of the mind; I wished for the pencil of Salvator Rosa [21] or the pen of Thompson,[22] that

21. A seventeenth-century Italian landscape painter.
22. James Thomson, an eighteenth-century Scottish poet.

I might be enabled to give to the enlightened world some just idea of this truly magnifficent and sublimely grand object, which has from the commencement of time been concealed from the view of civilized man; but this was fruitless and vain. I most sincerely regreted that I had not brought a crimee obscura[23] with me by the assistance of which even I could have hoped to have done better but alas this was also out of my reach; I therefore with the assistance of my pen only indeavoured to trace some of the stronger features of this seen by the assistance of which and my recollection aided by some able pencil I hope still to give to the world some faint idea of an object which at this moment fills me with such pleasure and astonishment, and which of it's kind I will venture to ascert is second to but one in the known world. I retired to the shade of a tree where I determined to fix my camp for the present and dispatch a man in the morning to inform Capt. C. and the party of my success in finding the falls and settle in their minds all further doubts as to the Missouri . . . on my return I found the party at camp; they had butchered the buffaloe and brought in some more meat as I had directed. Goodrich had caught half a douzen very fine trout[24] and a number of both species of the white fish. these trout are from sixteen to twenty three inches in length, precisely resemble our mountain or speckled trout in form and the position of their fins, but the specks on these are of a deep black instead of the red or goald colour of those common to the U.' States. these are furnished long sharp teeth on the pallet and tongue and have generally a small dash of red on each side behind the front ventral fins; the flesh is of a pale yellowish red, or when in good order, of a rose red.

I am induced to believe that the Brown, the white and the Grizly bear of this country are the same species only differing in colour from age or more probably from the same natural cause that many other anamals of the same family differ in colour. one of those which we killed yesterday was of a creemcoloured white while the other in company with it was of the common bey or rdish brown, which seems to be the most usual colour of them . . . the young cubs which we have killed have always been

23. A camera obscura allowed an image of the thing observed to be projected on a part of its box so the user could trace its features.

24. Cutthroat trout, named scientifically for Clark (*Oncorhynchus clarki*).

of a brownish white, but none of them as white as that we killed yesterday . . . the grizly bear we have never yet seen. I have seen their tallons in
possession of the Indians and from their form I am perswaded if there is
any difference between this species and the brown or white bear it is very
inconsiderable . . . my fare is really sumptuous this evening; buffaloe's
humps, tongues and marrowbones, fine trout parched meal pepper and
salt, and a good appetite; the last is not considered the least of the luxuries. [Lewis camped near the Great Falls, the first in a series of five falls in
the area, on the north side of the river in Cascade County, Montana. The
main party camped in the vicinity of Bird Coulee, Chouteau County,
Montana.]

June 14, 1805
[LEWIS] This morning at sunrise I dispatched Joseph Fields with a letter
to Capt. Clark and ordered him to keep sufficiently near the river to observe it's situation in order that he might be enabled to give Capt. Clark
an idea of the point at which it would be best to halt to make our portage . . . about ten OClock this morning while the men were engaged with
the meat I took my Gun and espontoon and thought I would walk a few
miles and see where the rappids termineated above, and return to dinner.
accordingly I set out and proceeded up the river about S. W. after passing
one continued rappid and three small cascades of abut for or five feet
each at the distance of about five miles I arrived at a fall of about 19 feet;
the river is here about 400 yds. wide.   this pitch which I called the
crooked falls[25] occupys about three fourths of the width of the river . . . I
should have returned from hence but hearing a tremendious roaring
above me I continued my rout across the point of a hill a few hundred
yards further and was again presented by one of the most beatifull objects
in nature, a cascade[26] of about fifty feet perpendicular streching at righ-
tangles across the river from side to side to the distance of at least a quarter of a mile . . . I now thought that if a skillfull painter had been asked to
make a beautifull cascade that he would most probably have pesented the

25. Crooked Falls, the second in the series of five falls from northeast to southwest, all
in Cascade County, Montana.
26. Rainbow Falls, Lewis and Clark's "Handsom Falls."

precise immage of this one; nor could I for some time determine on which of those two great cataracts to bestoe the palm, on this or that which I had discovered yesterday; at length I determined between these two great rivals for glory that this was *pleasingly beautifull*, while the other was *sublimely grand*. I had scarcely infixed my eyes from this pleasing object before I discovered another fall[27] above at the distance of half a mile; thus invited I did not once think of returning but hurried thither to amuse myself with this newly discoered object . . . still pursuing the river with it's course about S. W. passing a continued sene of rappids and small cascades, at the distance of 2½ miles I arrived at another cataract[28] of 26 feet . . . below this fall at a little distance a beatifull little Island well timbered is situated about the middle of the river. in this Island on a Cottonwood tree an Eagle has placed her nest; a more inaccessable spot I beleive she could not have found; for neither man nor beast dare pass those gulphs which seperate her little domain from the shores. the water is also broken in such manner as it decends over this pitch that the mist or sprey rises to a considerable hight. this fall is certainly much the greatest I ever behald except those two which I have mentioned below . . . from hence I overlooked a most beatifull and extensive plain reaching from the river to the base of the Snowclad mountains to the S. and S. West; I also observed the missoury streching it's meandering course to the South through this plain to a great distance filled to it's even and grassey brim; another large river flowed in on it's Western side about four miles above me and extended itself though a level and fertile valley of 3 miles in width a great distance to the N. W. rendered more conspicuous by the timber which garnished it's borders. in these plains and more particularly in the valley just below me immence herds of buffaloe are feeding. the missouri just above this hill makes a bend to the South where it lies a smoth even and unruffled sheet of water of nearly a mile in width bearing on it's watry bosome vast flocks of geese which feed at pleasure in the delightfull pasture on either border. the young geese are now completely feathered except the wings which both in the young and old are yet deficient. after feasting my eyes on this ravishing prospect and resting

27. Colter Falls, now submerged.
28. Black Eagle Falls, named for the eagle on the island below the falls.

myself a few minutes I determined to procede as ar as the river which I
saw discharge itself on the West side of the Missouri convinced that it was
the river which the Indians call *medicine river*[29] and which they informed
us fell into the Missouri just above the falls   I decended the hills and directed my course to the bend of the Missouri near which there was a herd
of at least a thousand buffaloe; here I thought it would be well to kill a
buffaloe . . . I scelected a fat buffaloe and shot him very well, through the
lungs; while I was gazeing attentively on the poor anamal discharging
blood in streams from his mouth and nostrils, expecting him to fall every
instant, and having entirely forgotton to reload my rifle, a large white, or
reather brown bear, had perceived and crept on me within 20 steps before
I discovered him; in the first moment I drew up my gun to shoot, but at
the same instant recolected that she was not loaded and that he was too
near for me to hope to perform this opperation before he reached me, as
he was then briskly advancing on me; it was an open level plain, not a
bush within miles nor a tree within less than three hundred yards of me;
the river bank was sloping and not more than three feet above the level of
the water; in short there was no place by means of which I could conceal
myself from this monster untill I could charge my rifle; in this situation I
thought of retreating in a brisk walk as fast as he was advancing untill I
could reach a tree about 300 yards below me, but I had no sooner terned
myself about but he pitched at me, open mouthed and full speed, I ran
about 80 yards and found he gained on me fast, I then run into the water
the idea struk me to get into the water to such debth that I could stand
and he would be obliged to swim, and that I could in that situation defend
myself with my espontoon; accordingly I ran haistily into the water about
waist deep, and faced about and presented the point of my espontoon, at
this instant he arrived at the edge of the water within about 0 feet of me;
the moment I put myself in this attitude of defence he sudonly wheeled
about as if frightened, declined the combat on such unequal grounds, and
retreated with quite as great precipitation as he had just before pursued
me. as soon as I saw him run of[f] in that manner I returned to the shore
and charged my gun, which I had still retained in my hand throughout

29. Sun River, meeting the Missouri at the city of Great Falls, Cascade County,
Montana.

this curious adventure. I saw him run through the level open plain about three miles, till he disappeared in the woods on medecine river; during the whole of this distance he ran at full speed, sometimes appearing to look behind him as if he expected pursuit. I now began to reflect on this novil occurrence and indeavoured to account for this sudden retreat of the bear. I at first thought that perhaps he had not smelt me before he arrived at the waters edge so near me, but I then reflected that he had pursued me for about 80 or 90 yards before I took the water and on examination saw the grownd toarn with his tallons immediately on the impression of my steps; and the cause of his allarm still remains with me misterious and unaccountable.   so it was and I feelt myself not a little gratifyed that he had declined the combat. My gun reloaded I felt confidence once more in my strength; and determined not to be thwarted in my design of visiting medicine river, but determined never again to suffer my peice to be longer empty than the time she necessarily required to charge her . . .

  in returning through the level bottom of Medecine river and about 200 yards distant from the Missouri, my direction led me directly to an anamal that I at first supposed was a wolf;[30] but on nearer approach or about sixty paces distant I discovered that it was not, it's colour was a brownish yellow; it was standing near it's burrow, and when I approached it thus nearly, it couched itself down like a cat looking immediately at me as if it designed to spring on me . . . It now seemed to me that all the beasts of the neighbourhood had made a league to distroy me, or that some fortune was disposed to amuse herself at my expence . . . I then continued my rout homewards passed the buffaloe which I had killed, but did not think it prudent to remain all night at this place which really from the succession of curious adventures wore the impression on my mind of inchantment; at sometimes for a moment I thought it might be a dream, but the prickley pears which pierced my feet very severely once in a while, particularly after it grew dark, convinced me that I was really awake, and that it was necessary to make the best of my way to camp.   it was sometime after dark before I returned to the party; I found them extremely uneasy for my safety; they had formed a thousand conjectures, all of which

30. Perhaps a wolverine.

equally forboding my death, which they had so far settled among them, that they had already agreed on the rout which each should take in the morning to surch for me. I felt myself much fortiegued, but eat a hearty supper and took a good night's rest. [Lewis apparently camped in the same spot as the previous night.]

[CLARK] the Indian woman complaining all night & excessively bad this morning— her case is Somewhat dangerous. [Clark's camp was near the entrance of Black Coulee, Chouteau County, Montana.]

June 15, 1805
[LEWIS] This evening after dark Joseph Fields returned and informed me that Capt Clark had arrived with the party at the foot of a rappid about 5 miles below which he did not think proper to ascend and would wait my arrival there. I had discovered from my journey yesterday that a portage on this side of the river will be attended by much difficulty in consequence of several deep ravines which intersect the plains nearly at right angles with the river to a considerable distance, while the South side appears to be a delighfull smoth unbroken plain; the bearings of the river also make it pobable that the portage will be shorter on that side than on this.[31] [Lewis remained at the camp of June 13.]

[CLARK] the curt. excessively rapid and dificuelt to assend   great numbers of dangerous places, and the fatigue which we have to encounter is incretiatable   the men in the water from morning untill night hauling the Cord & boats walking on Sharp rocks and round Sliperery Stones which alternately cut their feet & throw them down, not with Standing all this dificuelty they go with great chearfulness, aded to those dificuelties the rattle Snakes inumerable & require great caution to prevent being bitten . . . the Indian woman much wors this evening, She will not take any medison, her husband petetions to return &c. [Clark's camp was a little below and opposite the mouth of Belt Creek, Chouteau County, Montana.]

31. Lewis's south side of the Missouri is the east side from a larger perspective, and the side from which the party would make their way around the falls.

[LEWIS AND CLARK, WEATHER REMARKS] The deer now begin to bring forth their young the young Magpies begin to fly. The Brown or grizzly bear begin to coppolate.

June 16, 1805

[LEWIS] about 2 P. M. I reached the [main party's] camp found the Indian woman extreemly ill and much reduced by her indisposition. this gave me some concern as well for the poor object herself, then with a young child in her arms, as from the consideration of her being our only dependence for a friendly negociation with the Snake Indians on whom we depend for horses to assist us in our portage from the Missouri to the columbia River . . . Capt. C. had already sent two men this morning to examine the country on the S. side of the river; he now passed over with the party to that side and fixed a camp about a mile blow the entrance of a Creek³² where there was a sufficient quantity of wood for fuel, an article which can be obtained but in few places in this neighbourhood . . . one of the small canoes was left below this rappid in order to pass and repass the river for the purpose of hunting as well as to procure the water of the Sulpher spring,³³ the virtues of which I now resolved to try on the Indian woman. this spring is situated about 200 yards from the Missouri on the N. E. side nearly opposite to the entrance of a large creek . . . Capt. Clark determined to set out in the morning to examine and survey the portage, and discover the best rout. as the distance was too great to think of transporting the canoes and baggage on the men's shoulders, we scelected six men, and ordered them to look out some timber this evening, and early in the morning to set about making a parsel of truck wheels in order to convey our canoes and baggage over the portage. we determined to leave the white perogue at this place, and substitute the Iron boat, and also to make a further deposit of a part of our stores. in the evening the men who had been sent out to examine the country and made a very unfavourable report. they informed us that the creek just above us and two deep ravenes still higher up cut the plain between the rivr and mountain

32. Clark moved the party across the Missouri below Belt Creek to Lower Portage Camp, the starting point for the portaging the falls.

33. Sulphur, or Sacagawea, Springs, opposite the mouth of Belt Creek.

in such a manner, that in their opinions a portage for the canoes on this side was impracticable.   g[o]od or bad we must make the portage. notwithstanding this report I am still convinced from the view I had of the country the day before yesterday that a good portage may be had on this side at least much better than on the other, and much nearer also. I found that two dozes of barks and opium which I had given her [Sacagawea] since my arrival had produced an alteration in her pulse for the better; they were now much fuller and more regular. I caused her to drink the mineral water altogether.   wen I first came down I found that her pulse were scarcely perceptible, very quick frequently irregular and attended with strong nervous symptoms, that of the twitching of the fingers and leaders of the arm; now the pulse had become regular much fuller and a gentle perspiration had taken place; the nervous symptoms have also in a great measure abated, and she feels herself much freeer from pain.   she complains principally of the lower region of the abdomen, I therefore continued the cataplasms of barks and laudnumn which had been previously used by my friend Capt Clark. I beleive her disorder originated principally from an obstruction of the mensis in consequence of taking could.[34] [Camped below Belt Creek, Cascade County, Montana, at the site that became Lower Portage Camp.]

[CLARK] the Indian woman verry bad, & will take no medisin what ever, untill her husband finding her out of her Senses, easyly provailed on her to take medison, if She dies it will be the fault of her husband as I am now convinced.

June 17, 1805
[LEWIS] I employed [the men] in taking five of the small canoes up the creek which we now call portage creek about 1¾ miles . . . from this place ther is a gradual ascent to the top of the high plain to which we can now take them with ease . . . we were fortunate enough to find one cottonwood

34. The springs' waters, as well as Peruvian bark and laudanum (opium mixed with alcohol), were used as medicine for Sacagawea's illness, which may have been chronic pelvic inflammatory disease due to gonorrheal infection, aggravated by weakness from being bled.

tree just below the entrance of portage creek that was large enough to make our carrage wheels about 22 Inches in diameter; fortunate I say because I do not beleive that we could find another of the same size perfectly sound within 20 miles of us. the cottonwood which we are obliged to employ in the other parts of the work is extreemly illy calculated for it being soft and brittle. we have made two axeltrees of the mast of the white peroge, which I hope will answer tolerably well tho' it is reather small. The Indian woman much better today, I have still continued the same course of medecine; she is free from pain clear of fever, her pulse regular, and eats as heartily as I am willing to permit her of broiled buffaloe well seasoned with pepper and salt and rich soope of the same meat; I think therefore that there is every rational hope of her recovery. saw a vast number of buffaloe feeding in every direction arround us in the plains, others coming down in large herds to water at the river; the fragments of many carcases of these poor anamals daily pass down the river, thus mangled I pesume in decending those immence cataracts above us. as the buffaloe generally go in large herds to water and the passages to the river about the falls are narrow and steep the hi[n]der part of the herd press those in front out of their debth and the water instatly takes them over the cataracts where they are instantly crushed to death without the possibility of escaping. in this manner I have seen ten or a douzen disappear in a few minutes. their mangled carcases ly along the shores below the falls in considerable quantities and afford fine amusment for the bear wolves and birds of prey; this may be one reason and I think not a bad one either that the bear are so tenatious of their right of soil in this neighbourhood. [Remained at Lower Portage Camp.]

[CLARK] I Set out with 5 men[35] at 8 oClock, and proceeded on up the Creek Some distance to examine that & if possable assend that Suffcently high, that a Streight Cours to the mouth of Medison river would head the 2 reveins . . . I in assendending the Clifts to take the hith of the fall[36] was near Slipping into the water, at which place I must have been Sucked under in an instant, and with deficuelty and great risque I assended again, and decended the Clift lower down (but few places Can be descended to

---

35. Clark's party included Colter, Willard, and perhaps Joseph Field.
36. Great Falls.

the river) and took the hight with as much accuricy as possible with a Spirit Leavels[37] &c. dined at a fine Spring 200 yards below the pitch near which place 4 Cotton willow trees grew. on one of them I marked my name the date, and hight of the falls. [Clark's party camped below Crooked Falls, Cascade County, Montana.]

June 18, 1805
[LEWIS] This morning I employed all hands in drawing the perogue on shore in a thick bunch of willow bushes some little distance below our camp; fastened her securely, drove out the plugs of the gage holes of her bottom and covered her with bushes and driftwood to shelter her from the sun[38] . . . The waggons are completed this evening, and appear as if they would answer the purpose very well if the axetrees prove sufficiently strong . . . The Indian woman is recovering fast she set up the greater part of the day and walked out for the fist time since she arrived here; she eats hartily and is free from fever or pain. I continue same course of medecine and regimen except that I added one doze of 15 drops of the oil of vitriol[39] today about noon. There is a species of goosberry[40] which grows very common about here in open situations among the rocks on the sides of the clifts. they are now ripe of a pale red colour, about the size of a common goosberry . . . immence quantities of small grasshoppers of a brown colour in the plains, they no doubt contribute much to keep the grass as low as we find it which is not generally more than three inches, the grass is a narrow leaf, soft, and affords a fine pasture for the Buffaloe. [Remained at Lower Portage Camp.]

[CLARK] we proceeded on up the river a little more than a mile to the largest fountain or Spring[41] I ever Saw, and doubt if it is not the largest in

37. A spirit level is similar to a bubble level but was filled with alcohol (hence spirit) to prevent freezing. It was one of the expedition's scientific instruments and was used for measuring altitudes and heights.

38. The white pirogue was left at the Lower Portage Camp and retrieved on the return.

39. Sulfuric acid, here used as a tonic.

40. Western red currant.

41. Giant Springs, northeast of the city of Great Falls, now part of a city park.

America Known, this water boils up from under th rocks near the edge of the river and falls imediately into the river 8 feet and keeps its Colour for ½ a mile which is emencely Clear and of a bluish Cast. [Clark camped at the party's Upper Portage Camp and "White Bear Islands," Cascade County, Montana, at the southern edge of the city of Great Falls on the east side of the Missouri.]

June 19, 1805
[LEWIS] the Indian woman was much better this morning   she walked out and gathered a considerable quantity of the white apples[42] of which she eat so heartily in their raw state, together with a considerable quantity of dryed fish without my knowledge that she complained very much and her fever again returned. I rebuked Sharbono severely for suffering her to indulge herself with such food he being privy to it and having been previously told what she must only eat. I now gave her broken dozes of diluted nitre[43] untill it produced perspiration and at 10 P. M. 30 drops of laudnum which gave her a tolerable nights rest. [Remained at Lower Portage Camp.]

[CLARK] in my last rout I lost a part of my notes which could not be found as the wind must have blown them to a great distance. [Remained at White Bear Islands.]

June 20, 1805
[LEWIS] The Indian woman is qute free from pain and fever this morning and appears to be in a fair way for recovery, she has been walking about and fishing . . . At our camp below the entrance of portage creek observed . . . Latitude . . . 47°7′10.3″.[44] [Remained at Lower Portage Camp, where Clark and his group rejoined the main party.]

June 21, 1805
[LEWIS] having determined to go to the upper part of the portage tomorrow . . . I caused the Iron frame of the boat and the necessary tools my private baggage and Instruments to be taken as a part of this load, also the baggage of Joseph Fields, Sergt. Gass and John sheilds, whom I had

42. Indian breadroot.
43. Potassium nitrate, or saltpeter, here used for fever.
44. The approximate latitude of Lower Portage Camp is 47°36′38″ N.

scele̜cted to assist me in constructing the leather boat . . . I readily preceive several difficulties in preparing the leather boat which are the want of convenient and proper timber; bark, skins, and above all that of pitch to pay her seams, a deficiency that I really know not how to surmount un- less it be by means of tallow and pounded charcoal which mixture has an- swered a very good purpose on our wooden canoes heretofore. I have seen for the first time on the Missouri at these falls, a species of fishing ducks[45] with white wings, brown and white body and the head and part of the neck adjoining of a brick red, and the beak narrow; which I take to be the same common to James river, the Potomac and Susquehanna . . . The growth of the neighbourhood what little there is consists of the broad and narrow leafed cottonwood, box alder, the large or sweet willow, the narrow and broad leafed willow.[46]   the sweet willow has not been com- mon to the Missouri below this or the entrance of Maria's river; here at- tains to the same size and in appearance much the same as in the Atlan- tic States.   the undergrowth consists of rosebushes, goosberry and current bushes, honeysuckle small, and the red wood, the inner bark of which the engages are fond of smoking mixed with tobacco. [Remained at the Lower Portage Camp.]

June 22, 1805
[LEWIS] This morning early Capt Clark and myself with all the party ex- cept Sergt. Ordway Sharbono, Goodrich, york and the Indian woman, set out to pass the portage with the canoe and baggage to the Whitebear Is- lands, where we intend that this portage shall end. Capt. Clarke piloted us through the plains.   about noon we reached a little stream about 8 miles on the portage where we halted and dined;[47] we were obliged here to re- new both axeltrees and the tongues and howns of one set of wheels which took us no more than 2 hours.[48]   these parts of our carriage had been made of cottonwood and one axetree of an old mast, all of which proved deficient and had broken down several times before we reached this place

45. Female red-breasted merganser or the female common merganser.

46. Cottonwood, narrowleaf cottonwood, boxelder, peach-leaved willow, sandbar wil- low, and yellow willow.

47. The party dined at Box Elder Creek, "Willow Run" to expedition members, Cas- cade County, Montana, and the only source of water on the portage.

48. Axeltrees, tongues, and hounds are all parts of the party's improvised wagon.

we have now renewed them with the sweet willow and hope that they will answer better.   after dark we had reached within half a mile of our intended camp when the tongues gave way and we were obliged to leave the canoe, each man took as much of the baggage as he could carry on his back and proceeded to the river where we formed our encampment much fortiegued.   the prickly pears were extreemly troublesome to us sticking our feet through our mockersons. [Camped at the Upper Portage Camp, while a few remained at the Lower Portage Camp.]

[ORDWAY] we are a little South of the Mandans but have had cold weather as yet.   it must of course be a healthy country.   we all enjoy good health as yet.

June 23, 1805
[CLARK] the men mended their mockersons with double Soles to Save their feet from the prickley pear, (which abounds in the Praries,) and the hard ground which in Some & maney places So hard as to hurt the feet verry much, the emence number of Buffalow after the last rain has trod the flat places in Such a manner as to leave it uneaven, and that has tried [dried] and is wors than frozen ground, added to those obstructions, the men has to haul with all their Strength wate & art, maney times every man all catching the grass & knobes & Stones with their hands to give them more force in drawing on the Canoes & Loads, and notwithstanding the Coolness of the air in high presperation and every halt, those not employed in reparing the Cou[r]se; are asleep in a moment, maney limping from the Soreness of their feet Some become fant for a fiew moments, but no man Complains   all go Chearfully on—   to State the fatigues of this party would take up more of the journal than other notes which I find Scercely time to Set down. I had the best rout Staked out and measured which is 17 miles ¾ to the river & ½ a mile up i.'e 18¼ miles portage. [Lewis remained at the Upper Portage Camp with three men, while Clark and the rest of the party were at the Lower Portage Camp.]

June 25, 1805
[LEWIS] such as were able to shake a foot amused themselves in dancing on the green to the music of the violin which Cruzatte plays extreemly well. [Lewis remained at Upper Portage Camp.]

[CLARK] I feel my Self a little unwell with a looseness &c.   put out the Stores to dry & Set Chabonah &c to Cook for the party against their re-turn—he being the only man left on this Side with me   I had a little Cof-fee for brackfast which was to me a riarity as I had not tasted any Since last winter . . . the plains are inferior in point of Soil to those below, more Stone on the sides of the hill, grass but a few inches high and but few flow-ers in the Plains, great quantites of Choke Cheries, Goose burres, red & yellow berries, & red & Purple Currents on the edges of water Courses in bottoms & damp places, about my Camp the Cliffs or bluffs are a hard red or redish brown earth Containing Iron.   we Catch great quantities of Trout, and a kind of mustel, flat backs & a Soft fish resembling a Shad and a few Cat . . . the Sales were hoised in the Canoes as the men were draw-ing them and the wind was great relief to them being Sufficently Strong to move the Canoes on the Trucks, this is Saleing on Dry land in every Sence of the word, Serjeant N Pryor Sick. [Clark and the majority of the party worked out of Lower Portage Camp.]

June 26, 1805
[LEWIS] to myself I assign the duty of cook as well for those present as for the party which I expect again to arrive this evening from the lower camp. I collected my wood and water, boiled a large quantity of excellent dryed buffaloe meat and made each man a large suet dumpling by way of a treat . . . late in the evening the party arrived with two more canoes and an-other portion of the baggage. Whitehouse one of them much heated and fortiegued on his arrivall dank a very hearty draught of water and was taken almost instanly extreemly ill. his pulse were very full and I therefore bled him plentifully from which he felt great relief. I had no other instru-ment with which to perform this opperation but my pen knife, however it answered very well. [Lewis at Upper Portage Camp, Clark at Lower.]

June 27, 1805
[CLARK] I proceed to finish a rough draugh of the river & Distances to leve at this place. [Lewis at Upper Portage Camp, Clark at Lower.]

[ORDWAY] I came to the Spring[49] which was the finest tasted water I ever Saw and the largest fountain which up through a ledge of rocks near the

49. Giant Springs again.

River and forces its way up about 10 feet for Some distance around then forms a fall in to the River. it is clear as a cristal I could have Seen to the bottom of the fountain to pick up a pin. the water cold and pure.

June 28, 1805

[LEWIS] The White bear have become so troublesome to us that I do not think it prudent to send one man alone on an errand of any kind, particularly where he has to pass through the brush. we have seen two of them on the large Island opposite to us today but are so much engaged that we could not spare the time to hunt them but will make a frolick of it when the party return and drive them from these islands. they come close arround our camp every night but have never yet ventured to attack us and our dog gives us timely notice of their visits, he keeps constantly padroling all night. I have made the men sleep with their arms by them as usual for fear of accedents. [Lewis at Upper Portage Camp, Clark at Lower.]

June 29, 1805

[LEWIS] I have scarcely experienced a day since my first arrival in this quarter without experiencing some novel occurrence among the party or witnessing the appearance of some uncommon object. [Lewis at Upper Portage Camp.]

[CLARK] Soon after I arrived at the falls, I perceived a Cloud which appeared black and threaten imediate rain, I looked out for a Shelter but Could See no place without being in great danger of being blown into the river if the wind Should prove as turbelant as it is at Some times about ¼ of a mile above the falls I obsd a Deep rivein in which was Shelveing rocks under which we took Shelter . . . in a place which was verry Secure from rain . . . Soon after a torrent of rain and hail fell more violent than ever I Saw before, the rain fell like one voley of water falling from the heavens and gave us time only to get out of the way of a torrent of water which was Poreing down the hill in the rivin with emence force tareing every thing before it takeing with it large rocks & mud, I took my gun & Shot pouch in my left hand, and with the right Scrambled up the hill pushing the Interpreters wife (who had her Child in her arms) before me, the Interpreter himself makeing attempts to pull up his wife by the hand much Scared and nearly without motion— we at length retched the top of the hill Safe where I found my Servent in Serch of us greatly agitated, for our wellfar. before I got out of the bottom of the revein which was a flat dry rock when I entered it, the water was up to my waste & wet my watch, I Scrcely got out before it raised 10 feet deep with a torrent which turrouble to behold, and by the time I reached the top of the hill, at least 15 feet water, I directed the party to return to the Camp at the run as fast as possible to get to our lode where Clothes Could be got to Cover the Child whose Clothes were all lost, and the woman who was but just recovering from a Severe indispostion, and was wet and Cold, I was fearfull of a relaps I caused her as also the others of the party to take a little Spirits, which my Servent had in a Canteen, which revived verry much. on arrival at the Camp on the willow run—met the pary who had returned in great Confusion to the run leaveing their loads in the Plain, the hail & wind being So large and violent in the plains, and them naked, they were much brused, and Some nearly killed one knocked down three times, and others without hats or any thing on their heads bloodey & Complained verry much; I refreshed them with a little grog— Soon after the run began to rise and rose 6 feet in a few minits. I lost at the river in the torrent the large *Compas*, an eligant fusee, Tomahawk *Humbrallo*, Shot pouh, & horn wih powder & Ball, mockersons, & the woman lost her Childs Bear[50] & Clothes bedding &c. The Compass is a Serious loss; as we have no other large one. [Clark at Lower Portage Camp.]

June 30, 1805
[LEWIS] I begin to be extremely impatient to be off as the season is now waisting a pace   nearly three months have now elapsed since we left Fort Mandan and not yet reached the Rocky Mountains   I am therefore fully preswaded that we shall not reach Fort Mandan again this season if we even return from the ocean to the Snake Indians. [Lewis at Upper Portage Camp.]

[CLARK] The two men dispatched in Serch of the articls lost yesterday returned and brought the Compass which they found in the mud & Stones

---

50. Sacagawea's "Childs Bear" was not a toy for Jean Baptiste but mosquito netting.

near the mouth of the revein, no other articles found, the place I Sheltered under filled up with hugh Rocks . . . Great numbers of Buffalow in every direction, I think 10,000 may be Seen in a view. [Clark at Lower Portage Camp.]

July 1, 1805
[LEWIS] all matters were now in readiness to commence the opperation of puting the parts of the boat together in the morning . . . the difficulty in obtaining the necessary materials has retarded my operations in forming this boat extreemly tedious and troublesome; and as it was a novel peice of machinism to all who were employed my constant attention was necessary to every part of the work; this together with the duties of cheif cook has kept me pretty well employed . . . the bear were about our camp all last night, we have therefore determined to beat up their quarters tomorrow, and kill them or drive them from their haunts about this place. [The entire party reunited at Upper Portage Camp.]

July 2, 1805
[LEWIS] in moving some of the baggage we caught a large rat.[51]   it was somewhat larger than the common European rat, of lighter colour; the body and outer part of the legs and head of a light lead colour, the belly and inner side of the legs white as were also the feet and years.   the toes were longer and the ears much larger than the common rat; the ears uncovered with hair.   the eyes were black and prominent the whiskers very long and full.   the tail was reather longer than the body and covered with fine fur or poil of the same length and colour of the back.   the fur was very silkey close and short. I have frequently seen the nests of these rats in clifts of rocks and hollow trees but never before saw one of them.   they feed very much on the fruit and seed of the prickly pear; or at least I have seen large quantities of the hulls of that fruit lying about their holes and in their nests. [Remained at Upper Portage Camp.]

[GASS] In the evening, the most of the corps crossed over to an island, to attack and rout its monarch, a large brown bear, that held possession and

51. Bushy-tailed woodrat.

seemed to defy all that would attempt to besiege him there. Our troops, however, stormed the place, gave no quarter, and its commander fell. Our army returned the same evening to camp without having suffered any loss on their side.

July 3, 1805

[LEWIS] the Indians have informed us that we should shortly leave the buffaloe country after passing the falls; this I much regret for I know when we leave the buffaloe that we shal sometimes be under the necessity of fasting occasionally.   and at all events the white puddings will be irretreivably lost and Sharbono out of imployment. [Remained at Upper Portage Camp.]

[ORDWAY] the men not other ways directed are dressing Skins to make themselves mockinsons as they have wore them all out in the plains   one pair of good mockins will not last more than 2 days.   will ware holes in them the first day and patch them for the next.

[WHITEHOUSE] We fixed the leather on the Iron boat, & then took the boat apart, she had 8 Sections of 4 feet each.

July 4, 1805

[LEWIS] not having seen the Snake Indians or knowing in fact whether to calculate on their friendship or hostility or friendship we have conceived our party sufficiently small and therefore have concluded not to dispatch a canoe with a part of our men to St. Louis as we had intended early in the spring.   we fear also that such a measure might possibly discourage those who would in such case remain, and might possibly hazzard the fate of the expedition.   we have never once hinted to any one of the party that we had such a scheme in contemplation, and all appear perfectly to have made up their minds to suceed in the expedition or purish in the attempt. we all beleive that we are now about to enter on the most perilous and difficult part of our voyage, yet I see no one repining; all appear ready to met those difficulties which wait us with resolution and becoming fortitude . . . since our arrival at the falls we have repeatedly witnessed a nois which proceeds from a direction a little to the N. of West as loud and resembling precisely the discharge of a piece of ordinance of 6 pounds at the distance of three miles . . . I have thout it probable that it might be caused by runing water in some of the caverns of those immence mountains, on the principal of the blowing caverns;[52] but in such case the sounds would be periodical & regular, which is not the case with this, being sometimes heard once only and at other times, six or seven discharges in quick succession. it is heard also at different seasons of the day and night. I am at a loss to account for this phenomenon. our work being at an end this evening, we gave the men a drink of sperits, it being the last of our stock, and some of them appeared a little sensible of it's effects the fiddle was plyed and they danced very merrily untill 9 in the evening when a heavy shower of rain put an end to that part of the amusement tho' they continued their mirth with songs and festive jokes nd were extreemly merry untill late at night. we had a very comfortable dinner, of bacon, beans, suit dumplings & buffaloe beaf &c. in short we had no just cause to covet the sumptuous feasts of our countrymen on this day. [Remained at Upper Portage Camp.]

July 5, 1805

[LEWIS] I then set a couple of men to pounding of charcoal to form a composition with some beeswax which we have and buffaloe tallow now my only hope and resource for paying my boat; I sincerely hope it may answer yet I fear it will not. the boat in every other rispect completely answers my most sanguine expectation; she is not yet dry and eight men can carry her with the greatest ease; she is strong and will carry at least 8,000 lbs. with her suit of hands; her form is as complete as I could wish it. the stitches begin to gape very much since she has began to dry. [Remained at Upper Portage Camp.]

[ORDWAY] the 3 men returned fr[om] the falls & had killed Several buffalow   might have killed hundreds if they had wished where they were pened under high clifts of rocks at the falls.   they went So close among them as to reach them with the muzzle of their guns, &.C.

---

52. Lewis is referring to the Blowing Cave of Bath County, Virginia, which emitted a strong current of air.

July 6, 1805
[LEWIS AND CLARK, WEATHER REMARKS] about day had a violent thunderstorm attended with Hail and rain. the Hail Covered the ground and was about the Size of Musquet balls. I have Seen only one black bird killed with the hail, and am astonished that more have not Suffered in a similar manner as they are abundant. [Remained at Upper Portage Camp.]

July 7, 1805
[LEWIS] Capt. Clarks black man York is very unwell today and he gave him a doze of tartar emettic[53] which operated very well and he was much better in the evening. this is a discription of medecine that I nevr have recourse to in my practice except in cases of the intermittent fever. [Remained at Upper Portage Camp.]

July 8, 1805
[LEWIS] the men also brought me a living ground squirrel[54] which is something larger than those of the U' States or those of that kind which are also common here . . . it's principal colour is a redish brown but is marked longitudinally with a much greater number of black or dark bron stripes; the spaces between which is marked by ranges of pure white circular spots . . . this is an inhabitant of the open plain altogether, wher it burrows and resides; nor is it like the other found among clifts of rocks or in the woodlands. their burrows sometimes like those of the mole run horizontally near the surface of the ground for a considerable distance, but those in which they reside or take refuge strike much deeper in the earth. [Remained at Upper Portage Camp.]

[GASS] We finished the boat this evening, having covered her with tallow and coal-dust. We called her the Experiment, and expect she will answer our purpose.

July 9, 1805
[LEWIS] we corked the canoes and put them in the water and also launched the boat, she lay like a perfect cork on the water . . . late in the

53. A white salt compound used to induce vomiting.
54. Thirteen-lined ground squirrel.

evening . . . we discovered that a greater part of the composition had seperated from the skins and left the seams of the boat exposed to the water and she leaked in such manner that she would not answer. I need not add that this circumstance mortifyed me not a little; and to prevent her leaking without pich was impossible with us, and to obtain this article was equally impossible, therefore the evil was irraparable   I now found that the section formed of the buffaloe hides on which some hair had been left, answered much the best purpose; this leaked but little and the parts which were well covered with hair about ⅛th of an inch in length retained the composition perfectly and remained sound and dry.   from these circumstances I am preswaided, that had I formed her with buffaloe skins singed not quite as close as I had done those I employed, that she would have answered even with this composition.   but to make any further experiments in our present situation seemed to me madness . . . I therefore relinquished all further hope of my favorite boat and ordered . . . to take her in peices tomorrow and deposite the iron fraim at this place as it could probably be of no further service to us.   had I only singed my Elk skins in stead of shaving them I beleive the composition would have remained and the boat have answered; at least untill we could have reached the pine country which must be in advance of us . . . and which is probably at no great distance where we might have supplyed ourselves with the necessary pich or gum.   but it was now too late to introduce a remidy and I bid a dieu to my boat, and her expected services.[55] [Remained at Upper Portage Camp.]

July 10, 1805
[CLARK] I Set out with Sergt. Pryor four Choppers two Involids & one man to hunt, Crossed to the Std. Side and proceeded on up the river 8 miles by land (distance by water 23¼ ms.) and found two Trees which I thought would make Canoes, had them fallen, one of them proved to be hollow & Split at one End & verry much win[d] Shaken at the other, the other much win[d] Shaken . . . I deturmined to make Canoes out of the two first trees we had fallen, to Contract thir length so as to clear the hollow & winshakes, & ad to the width as much as the tree would allow.

55. There is no record of the iron-frame boat's recovery on the return trip in 1806.

The Musquitors emencely noumerous & troublesom . . . we ar much at a lo'ss for wood to make ax hilthes,[56] 13 hath been made & broken in this piece of a day by the four Choppers, no other wood but Cotton Box elder Choke Cherry and red arrow wood.   we Substitute the Cherry in place of Hickory for ax hilthes ram rods, &c. [Lewis with the main party remained at Upper Portage Camp. Clark and his group camped a few miles northeast of Ulm, Cascade County, Montana, at the canoe-making camp. Ordway and eight men in canoes camped somewhere between the two locations.]

July 11, 1805
[LEWIS] this evening a little before the sun set I heared two other discharges of this unaccounable artillery of the Rocky Mountains proceeding from the same quarter that I had before heard it. I now recollected the Minnetares making mention of the nois which they had frequently heard in the Rocky Mountains like thunder; and which they said the mountains made; but I paid no attention to the information supposing it either false or the fantom of a supersticious immagination. [Lewis remained at Upper Portage Camp; Clark stayed at the canoe-making camp.]

[WHITEHOUSE] I walked a Short distance in the plains to day when we were waiting for the wind to abate, and trod on a verry large rattle Snake. it bit my leggin on my legg I shot it. it was 4 feet 2 Inches long, & 5 Inches & a half round.

July 13, 1805
[LEWIS] This morning being calm and Clear I had the remainder of our baggage embarked in the six small canoes and maned them with two men each. I now bid a cheerfull adue to my camp and passed over to the opposite shore . . . I passed a very extraordinary Indian lodge,[57] or at least the fraim of one; it was formed of sixteen large cottonwood poles each about fifty feet long and at their larger end which rested on the ground as thick as a man's body; these were arranged in a circular manner at bottom

56. Helves, or axe handles.
57. Perhaps a Blackfeet medicine lodge, where an annual sun dance was performed.

and equally distributed except the omission of one on the East side which
I suppose was the entrance to the lodge; the upper part of the poles are
united in a common point above and secured with large wyths of willow
brush.   in the center of this fabric there was the remains of a large fire;
and about the place the marks of about 80 leather lodges. I know not what
was the intention or design of such a lodge but certain I am that it was not
designed for a dwelling of any one family.   it was 216 feet in circumpherence at the base.   it was most probably designed for some great feast, or
a council house on some great national concern. I never saw a similar one
nor do the nations lower down the Missouri construct such . . . The
hunters killed three buffaloe today . . . we eat an emensity of meat; it requires 4 deer, an Elk and a deer, or one buffaloe, to supply us plentifully
24 hours.   meat now forms our food prinsipally as we reserve our flour
parched meal and corn as much as possible for the rocky mountains
which we are shortly to enter, and where from the indian account game
is not very abundant. [All have relocated, or are in the process of relocat-
ing, to Clark's canoe-making camp.]

July 14, 1805
[LEWIS] The country in most parts very level and in others swelling
with gentle rises and decents, or in other wirds what I have heretofore
designated a wavy country destitute of timber except along the water-
courses . . . the grass and weeds in this bottom are about 2 feet high; which
is a much greater hight than we have seen them elsewhere this season.
here I found the sand rush and nittles in small quantities. the grass in the
plains is not more than 3 inches high.   grasshoppers innumerable in the
plains and the small birds before noticed together with the brown Cur-
looe still continue nomerous in every part of the plains. [Remained at the
canoe-making camp.]

CHAPTER 6

Shadows of the Rockies

July 15–August 9, 1805

July 15, 1805

[LEWIS] We arrose very early this morning, assigned the canoes their loads and had it put on board. we now found our vessels eight in number all heavily laden, notwithstanding our several deposits; tho' it is true we have now a considerable stock of dryed meat and grease. we find it extreemly difficult to keep the baggage of many of our men within reasonable bounds; they will be adding bulky articles of but little use or value to them. At 10 A. M. we once more saw ourselves fairly under way much to my joy and I beleive that of every individual who compose the party . . . we have now passed Fort Mountain[1] on our right it appears to be about ten miles distant. this mountain has a singular appearance it is situated in a level plain, it's sides stand nearly at right angles with each other and are each about a mile in extent . . . the prickly pear is now in full blume and forms one of the beauties as well as the greatest pests of the plains. the sunflower is also in blume and is abundant. this plant is common to every part of the Missouri from it's entrance to this place. the lambs-quarter, wild coucumber,[2] sand rush[3] and narrow dock[4] are also common here. [Camped a few miles southwest of Ulm, Cascade County, Montana.]

1. Square Butte, south of the town of Fort Shaw, Cascade County, Montana.
2. Mock-cucumber.
3. Scouring-rush.
4. Mexican dock.

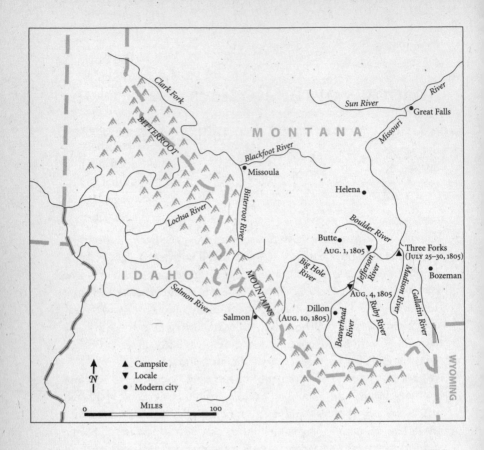

The Expedition's Route, July 15–August 9, 1805

July 16, 1805
[LEWIS] sen one man back this morning for an ax that he had carelessly left last evening some miles below, and set out at an early hour . . . Drewyer killed a buffaloe this morning near the river and we halted and breakfasted on it. here for the first time I ate of the small guts of the buffaloe cooked over a blazing fire in the Indian stile without any preperation of washing or other clensing and found them very good . . . the Musquetoes are extreemly troublesome this evening and I had left my bier, of course suffered considerably, and promised in my wrath that I never will be guily of a similar peice of negligence while on this voyage. [Lewis's campsite is uncertain; Clark and the main party camped near Tintinger Slough, Cascade County, Montana.]

July 17, 1805
[LEWIS] The sunflower is in bloom and abundant in the river bottoms. The Indians of the Missouri particularly those who do not cultivate maze make great uce of the seed of this plant for bread, or use it in thickening their soope. they most commonly first parch the seed and then pound them between two smooth stones untill they reduce it to a fine meal. to this they sometimes mearly add a portion of water and drink it in that state, or add a sufficient quantity of marrow grease to reduce it to the consistency of common dough and eate it in that manner. the last composition I think much best and have eat it in that state heartily and think it a pallateable dish. there is but little of the broad leafed cottonwood above the falls, much the greater portion being of the narrow leafed kind. there are a great abundance of red yellow perple & black currants,[5] and service berries now ripe and in great perfection. I find these fruits very pleasent particularly the yellow currant which I think vastly preferable to those of our gardens . . . The survice berry differs somewhat from that of the U' States   the bushes are small sometimes not more than 2 feet high and scarcely ever exceed 8 and are proportionably small in their stems, growing very thickly ascosiated in clumps. the fruit is the same form but for the most part larger more lucious and of so deep a perple that on first sight you would think them black. there are two species of goosbirris[6]

5. Golden currant.
6. Bristly gooseberry and swamp currant.

here allso but neither of them yet ripe. the choke cherries also abundant and not yet ripe. [Camped as a recombined party a few miles downstream from the Dearborn River, Lewis and Clark County, Montana.]

[ORDWAY] we left Some articles and doubled maned the canoes and [got] them all over [the rapid][7] Safe which was about half a mile long, & roled white over the rocks, but by the assistance of the towing lines we got up all the canoes without Injury.

[GASS] We proceeded on through the mountains, a very desert looking part of the country.

July 18, 1805
[LEWIS] previous to our departure saw a large herd of the Bighorned ana-mals on the immencely high and nearly perpendicular clift[8] opposite to us; on the fase of this clift they walked about and bounded from rock to rock with apparent unconcern where it appared to me that no quadruped could have stood, and from which had they made one false step the[y] must have been precipitated at least à 500 feet. this anamal appears to frequent such precepices and clifts where in fact they are perfectly secure from the pursuit of the wolf, bear, or even man himself . . . in the evening we passed a large creek about 30 yds. wide which disembogues on the Stard. side; it discharges a bold current of water it's banks low and bed frormed of stones altogether; this stream we called Ordway's creek[9] after Sergt. John Ordway. I have observed for several days a species of flax[10] growing in the river bottoms the leaf stem and pericarp of which re-sembles the common flax cultivated in the U' States . . . the bark of the stem is thick strong and appears as if it would make excellent flax.   the seed are not yet ripe but I hope to have an opportunity of collecting some of them after they are so   if it should on experiment prove to yeald good flax and at the same time admit of being cut without injuring the peren-

7. In Cascade County, Montana.

8. Eagle Rock, Lewis and Clark County, Montana.

9. Little Prickly Pear Creek, meeting the Missouri in Lewis and Clark County, Montana.

10. Blue flax, named scientifically in honor of Lewis based on his collected specimen (*Linum lewisii*).

nial root it will be a most valuable plant, and I think there is the greatest
probability that it will do so. [Lewis and the main party camped above
Holter Dam, Lewis and Clark County, Montana.]

[CLARK] passed a Considerable river which falls in on the Stard Side and
nearly as wide as the Missouri   we call Dearbournes riaver[11] after the
Sety. of war.   we thought it prudent for a partey to go a head for fear our
fireing Should allarm the Indians and cause them to leave the river and
take to the mountains for Safty from their enemes who visit them thro
this rout. I deturmined to go a head with a Small partey a few days and
find the Snake Indians if possible   after brackfast I took J. Fields Potts &
my Servent proceeded on. [Clark's detachment camped a few miles west
of Beartooth Mountain, Lewis and Clark County, Montana.]

July 19, 1805
[LEWIS] this evening we entered much the most remarkable clifts that we
have yet seen.   these clifts rise from the waters edge on either side perpendicularly to the hight of 1200 feet.   every object here wears a dark and
gloomy aspect.   the tow[er]ing and projecting rocks in many places seem
ready to tumble on us.   the river appears to have forced it's way through
this immence body of solid rock for the distance of 5¾ miles and where
it makes it's exit below has thown on either side vast collumns of rocks
mountains high.   the river appears to have woarn a passage just the width
of it's channel or 150 yds.   it is deep from side to side nor is ther in the 1st
3 miles of this distance a spot except one of a few yards in extent on which
a man could rest the soal of his foot.   several fine springs burst out at the
waters edge from the interstices of the rocks.   it happens fortunately that
altho' the current is strong it is not so much so but what it may be overcome with the oars for there is hear no possibility of using either the cord
or Setting pole . . . from the singular appearance of this place I called it
the *gates of the rocky mountains*.[12] [Lewis's camp was at the upper end of
the Gates of the Mountains and a short distance downstream from Up-

11. The Dearborn River, named after Secretary of War Henry Dearborn, forms the
boundary between Cascade and Lewis and Clark Counties.
12. The Gates of the Mountains formation, about halfway between Holter and Hauser
Dams, Lewis and Clark County, Montana.

per Holter Lake, Lewis and Clark County, Montana; Clark's camp is difficult to ascertain but was probably below the mouth of Spokane Creek, Lewis and Clark County.]

July 20, 1805

[CLARK] the feet of the men with me So Stuck with Prickley pear & cut with the Stones that they were Scerseley able to march at a Slow gate this after noon. [Lewis camped between Soup and Trout Creeks, Lewis and Clark County, Montana; Clark was above Beaver Creek, Broadwater County.]

July 22, 1805

[LEWIS] We set out early as usual. The river being divided into such a number of channels by both large and small Island that I found it impossible to lay it down correctly following one channel only in a canoe and therefore walked on shore took the general courses of the river and from the rising grounds took a view of the Islands and it's different channels which I laid don in conformity thereto on my chart. there being but little timber to obstruct my view I could see it's various meanders very satisfactorily. I passed through a large Island which I found a beautifull level and fertile plain about 10 feet above the surface of the water and never overflown. on this Island I met with great quantities of a smal onion [13] about the size of a musquit ball and some even larger; they were white crisp and well flavored I geathered about half a bushel of them before the canoes arrived. I halted the party for breakfast and the men also geathered considerable quantities of those onions. it's seed had just arrived to maturity and I gathered a good quantity of it. This appears to be a valuable plant inasmuch as it produces a large quantity to the squar foot and bears with ease the rigor of this climate, and withall I think it as pleasantly flavored as any species of that root I ever tasted. I called this beatifull and fertile island after this plant Onion Island [14] . . . The Indian woman recognizes the country and assures us that this is the river on which her relations live, and that the three forks are at no great distance. this peice of

13. Either nodding onion or Geyer's onion.
14. Since disappeared under Canyon Ferry Lake.

information has cheered the sperits of the party who now begin to console themselves with the anticipation of shortly seeing the head of the
missouri yet unknown to the civilized world . . . altho' Capt C. was much
fatiegued his feet yet blistered and soar he insisted on pursuing his rout
in the morning nor weould he consent willingly to my releiving him at
that time by taking a tour of the same kind.   finding him anxious I readily consented to remain with the canoes; he ordered Frazier and Jo. &
Reubin Filds to hold themselves in readiness to accompany him in the
morning. Sharbono was anxious to accompany him and was accordingly
permitted. [Clark rejoined Lewis and the party camped on an island,
since submerged, a few miles upstream from Beaver Creek, Broadwater
County, Montana.]

[ORDWAY] Capt. Lewis forgot his Thurmometer where we dined   I went
back for it.   it Stood in the heat of the day at 80 degrees abo. o, which has
only been up to that point but once before this Season as yet.

July 23, 1805
[LEWIS] I halted rearther early for dinner today than usual in order to dry
some articles which had gotten wet in several of the canoes. I ordered the
canoes to hoist their small flags in order that should the indians see us
they might discover that we were not Indians, nor their enemies.   we
made great uce of our seting poles and cords the uce of both which the
river and banks favored.   most of our small sockets were lost, and the
stones were so smooth that the points of their poles sliped in such manner that it increased the labour of navigating the canoes very considerably, I recollected a parsel of giggs which I had brought on, and made the
men each atatch one of these to the lower ends of their poles with strong
wire, which answered the desired purpose . . . I saw a black snake [15] today
about two feet long the Belly of which was as black as any other part or as
jet itself.   it had 128 scuta on the belley 63 on the tail. [Lewis camped near
the south end of Canyon Ferry Lake and near Townsend, Broadwater
County, Montana, while Clark was about four miles downstream from
Toston, Broadwater County.]

15. Western hog-nosed snake.

July 24, 1805

[LEWIS] we observed a great number of snakes about the water of a brown uniform colour, some black, and others speckled on the abdomen and striped with black and brownish yellow on the back and sides.   the first of these is the largest being about 4 feet long, the second is of that kind mentioned yesterday, and the last is much like the garter snake of our country and about it's size.[16]   none of these species are poisonous   I examined their teeth and fund them innosent.   they all appear to be fond of the water, to which they fly for shelter immediately on being pursued . . . from the appearance of bones and excrement of old date the buffaloe sometimes straggle into this valley; but there is no fresh sighn of them and I begin think that our harrvest of white puddings is at an end, at least untill our return to the buffaloe country.   our trio of pests still invade and obstruct us on all occasions, these are the Musquetoes eye knats and prickley pears, equal to any three curses that ever poor Egypt laiboured under, except the *Mahometant yoke.*   the men complain of being much fortiegued, their labour is excessively great. I occasionly encourage them by assisting in the labour of navigating the canoes, and have learned to *push a tolerable good pole* in their fraize. [Lewis camped about seven miles north of Toston, Broadwater County, Montana, while Clark camped north of Trident, Broadwater County.]

[GASS] The morning was fine, and we early prosecuted our voyage; passed a bank of very red earth, which our squaw told us the natives use for paint.

July 25, 1805

[LEWIS] we saw some antelopes of which we killed one.   these anamals appear now to have collected again is small herds several females with their young and one or two males compose the herd usually.   some males are yet soletary or two perhaps together scattered over the plains which they seen invariably to prefer to the woodlands.   if they happen accedentaly in the woodlands and are allarmed they run immediately to the

16. The snakes may be identified as: bullsnake, western hog-nosed, and wandering garter snake.

plains, seeming to plaise a just confidence in their superior fleetness and bottom.   we killed a couple of young gees which are very abundant and fine; but as they are but small game to subsist a party on of our strength I have forbid the men shooting at them as it waists a considerable quantity of amunition and delays our progress. [Lewis camped above Toston Dam, Broadwater County, Montana.]

[CLARK] we proceeded on a fiew miles to the three forks of the Missouri those three forks are nearly of a Size, the North fork [17] appears to have the most water and must be Considered as the one best calculated for us to assend . . . I wrote a note informing Capt Lewis the rout I intended to take, and proeeded on up the main North fork thro' a vallie. [18] [Clark camped on the north side of Jefferson River above Willow Creek, Jefferson County, Montana.]

[WHITEHOUSE] we found Several bad rockey rapids which we had to pass through and So Shallow the rocks Show themselves across the River and appear Shallow all the way across.   we double manned and got up Safe. I cut my foot with the Stone a towing along the Shore.

July 26, 1805
[LEWIS] the high lands are thin meagre soil covered with dry low sedge and a species of grass also dry the seeds of which are armed with a . . . barbed seed [19] [that] penetrate our mockersons and leather legings and give us great pain untill they are removed.   my poor dog suffers with them excessively, he is constantly binting and scratching himself as if in a rack of pain.   the prickly pear also grow here as abundantly as usual. [Lewis camped at the formation Eagle Rock, Gallatin County, Montana.]

17. Jefferson River.

18. Clark arrived at the Three Forks of the Missouri at the Broadwater-Gallatin county line, Montana; Lewis will join him in two days and the party will remain here until July 30. Clark followed the Jefferson River and found Willow Creek, Gallatin County, which the party named Philosophy River.

19. Needle and thread grass.

Journal entry of William Clark, [July 4, 1804]. Courtesy Beinecke Rare Book and Manuscript Library, Yale University, New Haven, Connecticut

Interpreters, George Drewyer and Tausaant Charbono also a Black Man by the name of York, servant to Capt. Clark, an Indian Woman Wife to Charbono with a young child, and a Mandan Man who had promised us to accompany us as far as the Snake Indians with a view to bring about a good understanding and friendly intercourse between that nation and his own, the Minetares and Ahwahharways.

Our vessels consisted of six small canoes, and two large peroagues. This little fleet altho' not quite so respectable as those of Columbus or Capt. Cook, were still viewed by us with as much pleasure as those deservedly famed adventurers ever beheld theirs; and I dare say with quite as much anxiety for their safety and preservation. we were now about to penetrate a country at least two thousand miles in width, on which the foot of civillized man had never trodden; the good or evil it had in store for us was for experiment yet to determine, and these little vessells contained every article by which we were to expect to subsist or defend ourselves. however as the the state of mind in which we are, generally gives the colouring to events, when the immagination is suffered to wander into futurity, the picture which now presented itself to me was a most pleasing one. entertaing as I do the most confident hope of succeeding

Capt C. walked on shore this morning but found it so
excessively bad that he shortly returned. at 12 OCk ove came
too for refreshment and gave the men a dram which
they received with much cheerfullness, and well deserved.—

The hills and river clifts which we passed today exhi-
-bit a most romantic appearance. The bluffs of the river
rise to the hight of from 2 to 300 feet and in most places
nearly perpendicular; they are formed of remarkable
white sandstone which is sufficiently soft to give way
readily to the impression of water; two or three thin
horizontal stratas of white free-stone, on which the rains or
water make no impression, lie imbeded in these clifts
of soft stone near the upper part of them. the earth
on the top of these blifts is a dark rich loam, which
forming a gradualy ascending plain extend back from ½
a mile to a mile where the hills commence and rise ab-
-ruptly to a hight of about 300feet more. The water in
the course of time in decending from these hills and plains
on either side of the river has trickled down the soft sand
clifts and woarn it into a thousand grotesque figures,
which with the help of a little immagination and an
oblique view at a distance, are made to represent eligant ranges
of lofty freestone buildings, having their parapets well
stocked with statuary; collumns of various sculpture both grooved and plain
are also seen supporting long galleries in front of these
buildings; in other places on a much nearer approach
and with the help of less immagination we see the
remains or ruins of eligant buildings; some collumns stand-
-ing and almost entire with their pedestals and capitals,
others retaining their pedestals but deprived by time or
accident of their capitals, some lying prostrate an broken
others in the form of vast pyramids of connic structure
bearing a series of other pyramids on their tops becoming less as they
ascend and finally terminating in a sharp point. nitches

Journal entry of Meriwether Lewis, May 31, 1805. Courtesy
American Philosophical Society, Philadelphia, Pennsylvania

329
1805

Journal &c

We saluted our officers, by each of our party firing off
his gun at day break in honor to the day (Christmass
Our Officers in return presented to each of the party
that used Tobacco *a part of* what Tobacco they had remain
=ing; and to those who did not make use of it. they
gave a handkerchief or some other article, in remem
-brance of Christmass. We had no *ardent* spirit of any
kind among us; but are mostly in good health A
blessing, which we esteem more, than all the luxuries
this life can afford. and the party are all thankful
to the Supreme Being, for his goodness towards us.
hoping he will preserve us in the same, & enable us to
return to the United States again in safety., We
have at present nothing to eat but lean Elk meat
& that without Salt. but the whole of our party are
content with this fare.—

Thursday 2 We had Stormy weather the whole of this

Journal entry of Joseph Whitehouse, December 25, 1805.
Courtesy Newberry Library, Chicago, Illinois

[CLARK] I deturmined to leave Shabono & one man who had Sore feet to rest & proceed on with the other two[20] to the top of a mountain 12 miles distant west and from thence view the river & vallies a head, we with great dificuelty & much fatigue reached the top at 11 oClock   from the top of this mountain I could see the Course of the North fork about 10 miles meandering through a Vallie but Could discover no Indians or Sign which was fresh. I could also See Some distance up the Small River below, and also the middle fork   after Satisfying my Self returned to the two me[n] by an old Indian parth . . . I felt my Self verry unwell & took up Camp on the little river[21] 3 miles above its mouth. [Clark camped on Willow Creek, above the town of Willow Creek, Gallatin County, Montana.]

July 27, 1805
[LEWIS] we arrived at 9 A. M. at the junction of the S. E. fork[22] of the Missouri and the country opens suddonly to extensive and beatifull plains and meadows which appear to be surrounded in every direction with distant and lofty mountains; supposing this to be the three forks of the Missouri I halted the party on the Lard. shore for breakfast and walked up the S. E. fork about ½ a mile and ascended the point of a high limestone clift from whence I commanded a most perfect view of the neighbouring country . . . beleiving this to be an essential point in the geography of this western part of the Continent I determined to remain at all events untill I obtained the necessary data for fixing it's latitude Longitude &c. . . . at 3 P. M. Capt Clark arrived very sick with a high fever on him and much fatiegued and exhausted.   he informed me that he was very sick all last night had a high fever and frequent chills & constant aking pains in all his mustles.   this morning notwithstanding his indisposition he pursued his intended rout to the middle fork[23] about 8 miles and finding no recent sign of Indians rested about an hour and came down the middle fork to this place. Capt. C. thought himself somewhat bilious and had not had a

20. Clark left Charbonneau and Joseph Field and made the trip with Frazer and Reubin Field.
21. Willow Creek, the party's Philosophy River.
22. Gallatin River, for Albert Gallatin, Jefferson's secretary of the treasury.
23. Madison River, for James Madison, Jefferson's secretary of state.

passage for several days; I prevailed on him to take a doze of Rushes pills, which I have always found sovereign in such cases and to bath his feet in warm water and rest himself. Capt. C's indisposition was a further inducement for my remaining here a couple of days; I therefore informed the men of my intention, and they put their deer skins in the water in order to prepare them for dressing tomorrow. we begin to feel considerable anxiety with rispect to the Snake Indians. if we do not find them or some other nation who have horses I fear the successfull issue of our voyage will be very doubtfull or at all events much more difficult in it's accomplishment. we are now several undred miles within the bosom of this wild and mountanous country, where game may rationally be expected shortly to become scarce and subsistence precarious without any information with rispect to the country not knowing how far these mountains continue, or wher to direct our course to pass them to advantage or intersept a navigable branch of the Columbia, or even were we on such an one the probability is that we should not find any timber within these mountains large enough for canoes if we judge from the portion of them through which we have passed. however I still hope for the best, and intend taking a tramp myself in a few days to find these yellow gentlemen if possible. my two principal consolations are that from our present position it is impossible that the S. W. fork[24] can head with the waters of any other river but the Columbia, and that if any Indians can subsist in the form of a nation in these mountains with the means they have of acquiring food we can also subsist. [Camped at Three Forks between two branches of the Jefferson River, northeast of the town of Three Forks, Gallatin County, Montana.]

July 28, 1805
[LEWIS] Both Capt. C. and myself corrisponded in opinon with rispect to the impropriety of calling either of these streams the Missouri and accordingly agreed to name them after the President of the United States and the Secretaries of the Treasury and state[25] . . . I had all our baggage spread out to dry this morning; and the day proving warm, I had a small

24. Jefferson River.
25. Lewis and Clark's names for the three forks have survived.

bower or booth erected for the comfort of Capt. C.   our leather lodge when exposed to the sun is excessively hot. I observe large quantities of the sand rush in these bottoms which grow in many places as high as a man's breast and stand as thick as the stalks of wheat usually do.   this affords one of the best winter pastures on earth for horses or cows, and of course will be much in favour of an establishment should it ever be thought necessary to fix one at this place.   the grass is also luxouriant and would afford a fine swarth of hay at this time in parsels of ma[n]y acres together . . . Our present camp is precisely on the spot that the Snake Indians were encamped at the time the Minnetares of the Knife R. first came in sight of them five years since.   from hence they retreated about three miles up Jeffersons river and concealed themselves in the woods, the Minnetares pursued, attacked them, killed 4 men 4 women a number of boys, and mad prisoners of all the females and four boys, *Sah-cah-gar-we-ah* or Indian woman was one of the female prisoners taken at that time; tho' I cannot discover that she shews any immotion of sorrow in recollecting this event, or of joy in being again restored to her native country; if she has enough to eat and a few trinkets to wear I beleive she would be perfectly content anywhere . . . near the junction of the three forks of the Missouri . . . Latitude . . . 45° 24' 54".[26] [Remained at the Three Forks camp.]

[WHITEHOUSE] I am employed makeing the chief part of the cloathing for the party.

July 29, 1805
[LEWIS] we see a great abundance of fish in the stream some of which we take to be trout[27] but they will not bite at any bate we can offer them.   the King fisher[28] is common on the river since we have left the falls of the Missouri.   we have not seen the summer duck[29] since we left that place,

---

26. Lewis has several variations for the latitude of Three Forks; Clark gives it as 45° 22' 34" (similar to Ordway, Gass, and Whitehouse). The approximate latitude of Three Forks is 45° 55' 27" N.

27. Probably cutthroat trout.

28. Belted kingfisher.

29. Wood duck.

nor do I beleive that it is an inhabitant of the Rocky mountains.   the Duckanmallard [30] were first seen with their young on the 20th inst. and I forgot to note it; they are now abundant with their young but do not breed in the missouri below the mountains.   the grasshopers and crickets are abundant in the plains as are also the small birds frequently mentioned.   there is also in these plains a large ant [31] with a redish brown body and legs, and a black head and abdomen; they construct little perimids of small gravel in a conic shape, about 10 or 12 inches high without a mixture of sticks and with but little earth. Capt. Clark is much better today, is perfectly clear of fever but still very languid and complains of a general soarness in all his limbs. I prevailed on him to take the barks which he has done and eate tolerably freely of our good venison. [Remained at the Three Forks camp.]

July 31, 1805

[LEWIS] nothing killed today and our fresh meat is out.   when we have a plenty of fresh meat I find it impossible to make the men take any care of it, or use it with the least frugallity.   tho' I expect that necessity will shortly teach them this art . . . we have a lame crew just now, two with tumers or bad boils on various parts of them, one with a bad stone bruise, one with his arm accedently dislocated but fortunately well replaced, and a fifth has streigned his back by sliping and falling backwards on the gunwall of the canoe.   the latter is Sergt. Gass. [32]   it gives him great pain to work in the canoe in his present situation, but he thinks he can walk with convenience, I therefore scelected him as one of the party to accompany me tomorrow, being determined to go in quest of the Snake Indians. I also directed Drewyer and Charbono to hold themselves in readiness. Charbono thinks that his ankle is sufficiently recovered to stand the march but I entertain my doubts of the fact; he is very anxious to accompany me and I therefore indulge him. [Camped near the mouth of Antelope Creek in either Gallatin or Madison County, Montana.]

30. Mallard.

31. Western harvester ant.

32. Sergeant Pryor may have been the one with the dislocated arm. Gass did not mention his accident in the canoe.

August 1, 1805

[LEWIS] at ½ after 8 A. M. as had been previously concerted betwen Capt. Clark and myself I set out with three men in surch of the Snake Indians or Sosonees . . . our rout lay through the steep and narrow hollows of the mountains exposed to the intese heat of the midday sun without shade or scarcely a breath of air: to add to my fatiegue in this walk of about 11 miles, I had taken a doze of glauber salts in the morning in consequence of a slight disentary with which I had been afflicted for several days. being weakened by the disorder and the operation of the medicine I found myself almost exhausted before we reached the river. I felt my sperits much revived on our near approach to the river at the sight of a herd of Elk, of which Drewyer and myself soon killed a couple. we then hurryed to the river and allayed our thirst. I ordered two of the men to skin the Elk and bring the meat to the river, while myself and the other prepared a fire and cooked some of the meat for our dinner. we made a comfortable meal on the Elk, and left the ballance of the meat and skins on the bank of the river for Capt. Clark and party. this supply will no doubt be acceptable to them, as they had had no fresh meat when I left them for almost 2 days except one beaver; game being very scarce and shy above the forks . . . I also saw near the top of the mountain among some scattering pine a blue bird [33] about the size of the common robbin. it's action and form is somewhat that of the jay bird and never rests long in any one position but constantly flying or hoping from sprey to sprey. I shot at one of them but missed it. their note is loud and frequently repeated both flying and when at rest and is char âh´, char´âh, char âh´, as nearly as letters can express it. after dinner we resumed our march and my pack felt mch lighter than it had done about 2 hours before. [Lewis camped above Cardwell, Jefferson County, Montana, while Clark and the main party camped opposite Boulder River in Madison County.]

[WHITEHOUSE] it being Capt. Clarks birth day he ordered Some flour gave out to the party. [34]

33. Pinyon jay.

34. Whitehouse is the only diarist to mention Clark's birthday. Although Clark did not mention his thirty-fifth birthday, the next day the captains named present Whitetail Creek "Birth Creek" to recognize the occasion.

August 2, 1805

[LEWIS] soon after passing the river this morning Sergt. Gass lost my tommahawk in the thick brush and we were unable to find it, I regret the loss of this usefull implement, however accedents will happen in the best families, and I consoled myself with the recollection that it was not the only one we had with us. [Lewis camped in the vicinity of Waterloo, Madison County, Montana; Clark camped below Big Pipestone Creek, Madison County.]

August 4, 1805

[LEWIS] the middle fork[35] is gentle and possesses about ⅔ds as much water as this rappid stream,[36] it's cours so far as I can observe it is about S. W. and it appears to be navigable; its water is much warmer than that of the rappid fork and somewhat turbid, from which I concluded that it had it's source at a greater distance in the mountains and passed through an opener country than the other.   under this impression I wrote a note to Capt. Clark recommending his taking the middle fork provided he should arrive at this place before my return which I expect will be the day after tomorrow.   the note I left on a pole at the forks of the river[37] and having refreshed ourselves and eat heartily of some venison we killed this morning I continued my rout. [Lewis camped on the Big Hole River above Nez Perce Creek near the Madison-Beaverhead county line, Montana.]

[CLARK] the method we are compelled to take to get on is fatigueing & laborious in the extreen, haul the Canoes over the rapids, which Suckceed each other every two or three hundred yards and between the water rapid oblige to towe & walke on Stones the whole day except when we have poleing   men wet all day Sore feet &c. [Clark camped in the vicinity of Silver Star, Madison County, Montana.]

35. Beaverhead River.
36. Big Hole River.
37. Lewis arrived at the so-called forks of the Jefferson, where the Big Hole River (the party's Wisdom River), coming from the west, joins the Jefferson River. The latter forms a few miles upstream where the Ruby River (the party's Philanthropy River) comes in from the east to the Beaverhead River (Jefferson River to the party).

August 5, 1805

[LEWIS] from this eminance I had a pleasing view of the valley through which I had passed many miles below and the continuation of the middle fork through the valley equally wide above me to the distance of about 20 miles when that also appeared to enter the mountains and disappeared to my view; however the mountains which termineate the valley in this direction appeared much lower than those up either of the other forks . . . the middle fork as I suspected dose bear considerably to the West of South and the gap formed by it in the mountains after the valley terminates is in the same direction. under these circumstances I did not hesitate in beleiving the middle fork the most proper for us to ascend.[38] [Lewis camped on the Beaverhead River, Madison County, Montana, a few miles above the mouth of the Ruby River. Clark camped a mile or so up the Big Hole from its mouth, in Madison County.]

[ORDWAY] we was not certian whether Capt. Lewis was up the left fork or right So Capt Clark left a note for him on the point which is level prarie, & proceeded on up the right hand fork, which is amazeing rapid Some of which falls nearly 3 feet in the length of a canoe, but with hard labour we draged them over. we passed thro a channel which was filled with willows and young cotton wood & brush, Some of which was fell across by the beaver. the currents So rapid we were oblidged to hall by the bushes, and Some places be out in the water where we could Scarsely kick our feet for the rapidity of the current . . . the party much fatigued and wish to go by land.[39]

August 6, 1805

[LEWIS] one of their [Clark's] canoes had just overset and all the baggage wet, the medecine box among other articles and several articles lost a shot pouch and horn with all the implements for one rifle lost and never recovered. I walked down to the point where I waited their return. on their

38. Lewis climbed a high point for a view of the route of the rivers. He found that the course of the Beaverhead ("middle fork") followed the route he preferred and that the Big Hole ("rapid fork") disappeared in successive mountain ranges.

39. Clark's party, as Ordway indicates, followed the Big Hole River under very difficult circumstances.

· arrival found that two other canoes had filled with water and wet their cargoes completely. Whitehouse had been thrown out of one of the canoes as she swing in a rapid current and the canoe had rubed him and pressed him to the bottom as she passed over him and had the water been 2 inches shallower must inevitably have crushed him to death. our parched meal, corn, Indian preasents, and a great part of our most valuable stores were wet and much damaged on this ocasion. to examine, dry and arrange our stores was the first object . . . a part of the load of each canoe consisted of the leaden canestirs of powder which were not in least injured, tho' some of them had remained upwards of an hour under water. about 20 lbs. of powder which we had in a tight Keg or at l[e]ast one which we thought sufficiently so got wet and intirely spoiled. this would have been the case with the other had it not have been for the expedient which I had fallen on of securing the powder by means of the lead having the latter formed into canesters which were filled with the necessary proportion of po[w]der to discharge the lead when used, and those canesters well secured with corks and wax . . . Shannon had been dispatched up the rapid fork this morning to hunt, by Capt Clark before he met with Drewyer or learnt his mistake in the rivers. when he returned he sent Drewyer in surch of him, but he rejoined us this evening and reported that he had been several miles up the river and could find nothing of him. we had the trumpet sounded and fired several guns but he did not join us this evening. I am fearful he is lost again. this is the same man who ws seperated from us 15 days as we came up the Missouri and subsisted 9 days of that time on grapes only . . . we therefore determined that the middle fork was that which ought of right to bear the name we had given to the lower portion or *River Jefferson* and called the bold rapid an clear stream *Wisdom*, and the more mild and placid one which flows in from the S. E. *Philanthrophy*, in commemoration of two of those cardinal virtues, which have so eminently marked that deservedly selibrated character through life. [The recombined party camped on the Jefferson River, opposite the mouth of the Big Hole, just north of Twin Bridges, Madison County, Montana.]

[CLARK] we proceeded on with much dificuelty and fatigue over rapids & Stones . . . Drewyer Came to me from Capt. Lewis and informed me that they had explored both forks for 30 or 40 miles & that the one we were ascending was impractiabl much further up & turned imediately to the north, The middle fork he reported was jintle and after a Short distanc turned to the S. W. and that all the Indian roades leades up the middle fork. this report deturmind me to take the middle fork, accordingly Droped down to the forks where I met with Capt Lewis & party, Capt Lewis had left a Letter on a pole in the forks informing me what he had discovered & the course of the rivers &c. this lettr was Cut down by the [beaver] as it was on a green pole & Carried off.

[WHITEHOUSE] in going through a difficult place which we went up thro last evening, one canoe got up Set and everry perticle of the loading got wet . . . I was in the Stern when She Swang & jumped out to prevent hir from turning over but the current took hir round So rapid that caught my leg under hir and lamed me & was near breaking my leg. lost my Shot pouch powder horn full of powder a bunch of thred and Some mockisons &c.

August 7, 1805
[LEWIS] Dispatched Reubin Fields in surch of Shannon . . . we have not heard any thing from Shannon yet, we expect that he has pursued Wisdom river upwards for som distance probably killed some heavy animal and is waiting our arrival. the large biteing fly or hare fly as they sometimes called are very troublesome to us. I observe two kinds of them a large black species and a small brown species with a green head.[40] the musquetoes are not as troublesome as they were below, but are still in considerable quantities. the eye knats[41] have disappeared. the green or blowing flies[42] are still in swarms. [Camped just above Twin Bridges, Madison County, Montana.]

August 8, 1805
[LEWIS] at Noon Reubin Fields arrived and reported that he had been up Wisdom river some miles above where it entered the mountain and could

40. Horse fly and deer fly.
41. Buffalo gnats.
42. Unidentified flies.

find nothing of Shannon . . . t[h]e tumor on Capt. Clarks ankle has discharged a considerable quantity of matter but is still much swolen and
inflamed and gives him considerable pain . . . the Indian woman recognized the point of a high plain to our right which she informed us was not
very distant from the summer retreat of her nation on a river beyond the
mountains which runs to the west.   this hill she says her nation calls the
beaver's head [43] from a conceived remblance of it's figure to the head of
that animal.   she assures us that we shall either find her people on this
river or on the river immediately west of it's source; which from it's present size cannot be very distant.   as it is now all important with us to meet
with those people as soon as possible, I determined to proceed tomorrow
with a small party to the source of the principal stream of this river and
pass the mountains to the Columbia; and down that river untill I found
the Indians; in short it is my resolusion to find them or some others, who
have horses if it should cause me a trip of one month.   for without horses
we shall be obliged to leave a great part of our stores, of which, it appears
to me that we have a stock already sufficiently small for the length of the
voyage before us. [Camped between the mouth of Ruby River and
Beaverhead Rock, Madison County, Montana.]

[ORDWAY] the beaver abounds on these Rivers.   they have dams and
ponds &C. in different places.   the Soil of these praries is much better
than it has been below for a long distance.

August 9, 1805
[LEWIS] while we halted here Shannon arrived, and informed us that having missed the party the day on which he set out he had returned the next
morning to the place from whence he had set out or furst left them and
not finding that he had supposed that they wer above him; that he then
set out and marched one day up wisdom river, by which time he was convinced that they were not above him as the river could not be navigated;
he then returned to the forks and had pursued us up this river . . . he had
lived very plentifully this trip but looked a good deel worried with his
march.   he informed us that Wisdom river still kept it's course obliquely

43. Beaverhead Rock on the Beaverhead River, in Madison County, Montana, near the
Beaverhead county line to the south.

down the Jefferson's river as far as he was up it.   immediately after break-fast I slung my pack and set out accompanyed by Drewyer Shields and McNeal. [Lewis camped northeast of Dillon, Beaverhead County, Montana.]

[CLARK] Capt Lewis and 3 men Set out after brackft. . . . I Should have taken this trip had I have been able to march, from the rageing fury of a tumer on my anckle musle. [Clark camped below the Beaverhead County line and short of Beaverhead Rock in Madison County, Montana.]

CHAPTER 7

Those Tremendous Mountains

August 10 – October 10, 1805

August 10, 1805

[LEWIS] we arrived in a hadsome open and leavel vally where the river divided itself nearly into two equal branches;[1] here I halted and examined those streams and readily discovered from their size that it would be vain to attempt the navigation of either any further. here also the road forked one leading up the vally of each of these streams. I therefore sent Drewer on one and Shields on the other to examine these roads for a short distance and to return and compare their information with respect to the size and apparent plainness of the roads as I was now determined to pursue that which appeared to have been the most traveled this spring.   in the mean time I wrote a note to Capt. Clark informing him of the occurrences which had taken place, recommending it to him to halt at this place untill my return and informing him of the rout I had taken which from the information of the men on their return seemed to be in favour of the S W or Left hand fork which is reather the smallest.   accordingly I put up my note on a dry willow pole at the forks,[2] and set out up the S. E. fork, after proceeding about 1½ miles I discovered that the road became so blind that it could not be that which we had followed to the forks of Jefferson's river, neither could I find the tracks of the horses which had passed early in the spring along the other; I therefore determined to return and examine the other myself, which I did, and found that the same

1. Lewis's "two equal branches" are Red Rock River from the east and Horse Prairie Creek from the west, coming together to form the Beaverhead River in Beaverhead County, Montana.

2. The place would become the party's Camp Fortunate.

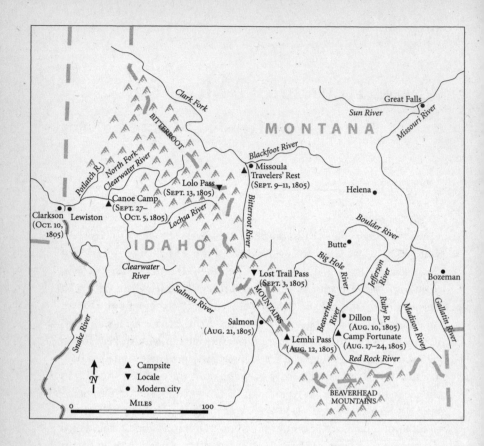

The Expedition's Route, August 10–October 10, 1805

horses had passed up the West fork[3] which was reather largest, and more in the direction that I wished to pursue; I therefore did not hesitate about changing my rout but determined to take the western road. I now wrote a second note to Capt C. informing him of this change and sent Drewyer to put it with the other at the forks and waited untill he returned . . . I do not beleive that the world can furnish an example of a river runing to the extent which the Missouri and Jefferson's rivers do through such a mounainous country and at the same time so navigable as they are. if the Columbia furnishes us such another example, a communication across the continent by water will be practicable and safe. but this I can scarcely hope from a knowledge of its having in it comparitively short course to the ocean the same number of feet to decend which the Missouri and Mississippi have from this point to the Gulph of Mexico. The valley of the west fork . . . is surrounded on all sides by a country of roling or high wavy plains through which several little rivulets extend their wide vallies quite to the Mountains which surround the whole in an apparent Circular manner; forming one of the handsomest coves[4] I ever saw, of about 16 or 18 miles in diameter. [Lewis camped in Shoshone Cove about six miles east of Grant, Beaverhead County, Montana. Clark camped near the Madison-Beaverhead county line and above Beaverhead Rock.]

[ORDWAY] we have now to live on poor venison & goat or antelopes which goes hard with us as the fatigues is hard.[5]

August 11, 1805
[LEWIS] I now sent Drewyer to keep near the creek to my right and Shields to my left, with orders to surch for the road which if they found they were to notify me by placing a hat in the muzzle of their gun. I kept McNeal with me; after having marched in this order for about five miles I discovered an Indian on horse back about two miles distant coming down the plain toward us. with my glass I discovered from his dress that he was of a different nation from any that we had yet seen, and was satis-

3. Horse Prairie Creek.
4. Shoshone Cove.
5. Ordway remained with Clark and the main party.

fyed of his being a Sosone ... I was overjoyed at the sight of this stranger
and had no doubt of obtaining a friendly introduction to his nation provided I could get near enough to him to convince him of our being whitemen. I therefore proceeded towards him at my usual pace.   when I had
arrived within about a mile he mad a halt which I did also and unloosing
my blanket from my pack, I mad him the signal of friendship known to
the Indians of the Rocky mountains and those of the Missouri, which is
by holding the mantle or robe in your hands at two corners and then
throwing up in the air higher than the head bringing it to the earth as if
in the act of spreading it, thus repeating three times ... this signal had not
the desired effect, he still kept his position and seemed to view Drewyer
an Shields who were now comiming in sight on either hand with an air of
suspicion, I wold willingly have made them halt but they were too far distant to hear me and I feared to make any signal to them least it should increase the suspicion in the mind of the Indian of our having some un-
friendly design upon him. I therefore haistened to take out of my sack
some b[e]ads a looking glas and a few trinkets which I had brought with
me for this purpose and leaving my gun and pouch with McNeal advanced unarmed towards him.   he remained in the same stedfast pois-
ture untill I arrived in about 200 paces of him when he turn his ho[r]se
about and began to move off slowly from me; I now called to himin as
loud a voice as I could command repeating the word *tab-ba-bone*, which
in their language signifyes *white man*.   but loking over his sholder he still
kept his eye on Drewyer and Sheilds who wer still advancing neither of
them haveing segacity enough to recollect the impropriety of advancing
when they saw me thus in parley with the Indian. I now made a signal to
these men to halt, Drewyer obeyed but Shields who afterwards told me
that he did not obseve the signal still kept on   the Indian halted again and
turned his hor[s]e about as if to wait for me, and I beleive he would have
remained untill I came up whith him had it not been for Shields who still
pressed forward.   whe I arrived within about 150 paces I again repepeated
the word tab-ba-bone and held up the trinkits in my hands and striped
up my shirt sleve to give him an opportunity of seeing the colour of my
skin and advanced leasure towards him but he did not remain untill I got
nearer than about 100 paces when he suddonly turned his ho[r]se about,
gave him the whip leaped the creek and disapeared in the willow brush in

an instant and with him vanished all my hopes of obtaining horses for the preasent. I now felt quite as much mortification and disappointment as I had pleasure and expectation at the first sight of this indian. I fet soarly chargrined at the conduct of the men particularly Sheilds to whom I principally attributed this failure in obtaining an introduction to the natives. I now called the men to me and could not forbare abraiding them a little for their want of attention and imprudence on this occasion . . . we now set out on the track of the horse hoping by that means to be lead to an indian camp. [Lewis camped near the northwest end of Shoshone Cove, Beaverhead County, Montana. Clark camped about halfway between Beaverhead Rock and Dillon, Beaverhead County.]

August 12, 1805

[LEWIS] the road took us to the most distant fountain of the waters of the mighty Missouri in surch of which we have spent so many toilsome days and wristless nights. thus far I had accomplished one of those great objects on which my mind has been unalterably fixed for many years, judge then of the pleasure I felt in allying my thirst with this pure and ice cold water which issues from the base of a low mountain or hill of a gentle ascent for ½ a mile. the mountains are high on either hand leave this gap at the head of this rivulet through which the road passes. here I halted a few minutes and rested myself. two miles below McNeal had exultingly stood with a foot on each side of this little rivulet[6] and thanked his god that he had lived to bestride the mighty & heretofore deemed endless Missouri. after refreshing ourselves we proceeded on to the top of the dividing ridge from which I discovered immence ranges of high mountains still to the West of us with their tops partially covered with snow. I now decended the mountain about ¾ of a mile which I found much steeper than on the opposite side, to a handsome bold running Creek[7] of cold Clear water. here I first tasted the water of the great Columbia river . . . as we had killed nothing during the day we now boiled and eat the remainder of our pork, having yet a little flour and parched meal. at the creek on this side of the mountain I observed a species of deep perple

6. Trail Creek on the Montana side of Lemhi Pass.
7. Probably Agency Creek, Lemhi County, Idaho.

currant[8] lower in its growth, the stem more branched and leaf doubly as large as that of the Missouri. the leaf is covered on it's under disk with a hairy pubersence. the fruit is of the ordinary size and shape of the currant and is supported in the usual manner, but is ascid & very inferior in point of flavor. [Lewis camped between Agency and Pattee Creeks, a few miles from their confluences with the Lemhi River, Lemhi County, Idaho.]

[CLARK] the river much more Sholey than below which obliges us to haul the Canoes over those Sholes which Suckceed each other at Short intervales emencely laborious men much fatigued and weakened by being continualy in the water drawing the Canoes over the Sholes encamped on the Lard Side men complain verry much of the emence labour they are obliged to undergo & wish much to leave the river. I passify them. [Clark camped north of Dillon, Beaverhead County, Montana.]

August 13, 1805
[LEWIS] we had proceeded about four miles through a wavy plain parallel to the valley or river bottom when at the distance of about a mile we saw two women, a man and some dogs on an eminence immediately before us. they appeared to vew us with attention and two of them after a few minutes set down as if to wait our arrival we continued our usual pace towards them. when we had arrived within half a mile of them I directed the party to halt and leaving my pack and rifle I took the flag which I unfurled and avanced singly towards them the women soon disappeared behind the hill, the man continued untill I arrived within a hundred yards of him and then likewise absconded. tho' I frequently repeated the word *tab-ba-bone* sufficiently loud for him to have heard it. I now haistened to the top of the hill where they had stood but could see nothing of them. the dogs were less shye than their masters they came about me pretty close I therefore thought of tying a handkerchief about one of their necks with some beads and other trinkets and then let them loose to surch their fugitive owners thinking by this means to convince them of our pacific disposition towards them but the dogs would not suf-

8. Hudson gooseberry.

fer me to take hold of them; they also soon disappeared . . . we had not continued our rout more than a mile when we were so fortunate as to meet with three female savages.   the short and steep ravines which we passed concealed us from each other untill we arrived within 30 paces.   a young woman immediately took to flight, an Elderly woman and a girl of about 12 years old remained. I instantly laid by my gun and advanced towards them.   they appeared much allarmed but saw that we were to near for them to escape by flight they therefore seated themselves on the ground, holding down their heads as if reconciled to die which the expected no doubt would be their fate; I took the elderly woman by the hand and raised her up repeated the word *tab-ba-bone* and strip up my shirt sleve to sew her my skin; to prove to her the truth of the ascertion that I was a white man for my face and hads which have been constantly exposed to the sun were quite as dark as their own.   they appeared instantly reconciled, and the men coming up I gave these women some beads a few mockerson awls some pewter looking-glasses and a little paint . . . I now painted their tawny cheeks with some vermillion which with this nation is emblematic of peace.   after they had become composed I informed them by signs that I wished them to conduct us to their camp that we wer anxious to become acquainted with the chiefs and warriors of their nation.   they readily obeyed and we set out, still pursuing the road down the river.   we had marched about 2 miles when we met a party of about 60 warriors mounted on excellent horses who came in nearly full speed, when they arrived I advanced towards them with the flag leaving my gun with the party about 50 paces behind me.   the chief and two others who were a little in advance of the main body spoke to the women, and they informed them who we were and exultingly shewed the presents which had been given them   these men then advanced and embraced me very affectionately in their way which is by puting their left arm over you wright sholder clasping your back, while they apply their left cheek to yours and frequently vociforate the word *âh-hi'-e, âh-hi'-e* that is, I am much pleased, I am much rejoiced.   bothe parties now advanced and we wer all carressed and besmeared with their grease and paint till I was heartily tired of the national hug. I now had the pipe lit and gave them smoke; they seated themselves in a circle around us and pulled of their mockersons before they would receive or smoke the pipe.   this is a

custom among them as I afterwards learned indicative of a sacred obliga-
tion of sincerity in their profession offriendship given by the act of receiving and smoking the pipe of a stranger. or which is as much as to say
that they wish they may always go bearfoot if they are not sincere; a pretty
heavy penalty if they are to march through the plains of their country. after smoking a few pipes with them I distributed some trifles among them,
with which they seemed much pleased particularly with the blue beads
and vermillion. I now informed the chief that the object of our visit was
a friendly one, that after we should reach his camp I would undertake to
explain to him fully those objects, who we wer, from whence we had
come and wither we were going; that in the mean time I did not care how
soon we were in motion, as the sun was very warm and no water at hand.
they now put on their mockersons, and the principal chief Ca-me-âh-
wait made a short speach to the warriors. I gave him the flag which I informed him was an emblem of peace among whitemen and now that it
had been received by him it was to be respected as the bond of union between us . . . on our arrival at their encampmen on the river in a handsome level and fertile bottom at the distance of 4 Ms. from where we had
first met them they introduced us to a londge made of willow brush and
an old leather lodge which had been prepared for our reception by the
young men which the chief had dispatched for that purpose. Here we
were seated on green boughs and the skins of Antelopes. one of the warriors then pulled up the grass in the center of the lodge forming a smal
circle of about 2 feet in diameter   the chief next produced his pipe and
native tobacco and began a long cerimony of the pipe when we were requested to take of our mockersons, the Chief having previously taken off
his as well as all the warriors present.   this we complyed with; the Chief
then lit his pipe at the fire kindled in this little magic circle, and standing
on the oposite side of the circle uttered a speach of several minutes in
length atthe conclusion of which he pointed the stem to the four cardinal
points of the heavens first begining at the East and ending with the North.
he now presented the pipe to me as if desirous that I should smoke, but
when I reached my hand to receive it, he drew it back and repeated the
same cremony three times, after which he pointed the stem first to the
heavens then to the center of the magic circle smoked himself with three
whifs and held the pipe untill I took as many as I thought proper; he then

held it to each of the white persons and then gave it to be consumed by
his warriors. this pipe was made of a dense simitransparent green stone[9]
very highly polished about 2½ inches long and of an oval figure, the bowl
being in the same direction with the stem. a small piece of birned clay is
placed in the bottom of the bowl to seperate the tobacco from the end of
the stem and is of an irregularly rounded figure not fitting the tube pur-
fectly close in order that the smoke may pass . . . I now explained to them
the objects of our journey &c. all the women and children of the camp
were shortly collected about the lodge to indulge themselves with looking at us, we being the first white persons they had ever seen. after the
cerimony of the pipe was over I distributed the remainder of the small articles I had brought with me among the women and children.   by this
time it was late in the evening and we had not taisted any food since the
evening before. the Chief informed us that they had nothing but berries
to eat and gave us some cakes of serviceberries and Choke cherries which
had been dryed in the sun; of these I made a hearty meal, and then walked
to the river, which I found about 40 yards wide very rapid clear and about
3 feet deep.   the banks low and abrupt as those of the upper part of the
Missouri, and the bed formed of loose stones and gravel. Cameahwait informed me that this stream discharged itself into another oubly as large
at the distance of half a days march which came from the S. W. but he
added on further enquiry that there was but little more timber below the
junction of those rivers than I saw here, and that the river was confined
between inacessable mountains, was very rapid and rocky insomuch that
it was impossible for us to pass either by land or water down this river to
the great lake where the white men lived as he had been informed.   this
was unwelcome information but I still hoped that this account had been
exagerated with a view to detain us among them.   as to timber I could
discover not any that would answer the purpose of constructing canoes
or in short more than was bearly necessary for fuel consisting of the narrow leafed cottonwood and willow, also the red willow Choke Cherry service berry and a few currant bushes such as were common on the Missouri . . . I still observe a great number of horses feeding in every direction
around their camp and therefore entertain but little doubt but we shall be

9. Either pale green talc or darker green massive serpentine.

enable to furnish ourselves with an adiquate number to transport our stores even if we are compelled to travel by land over these mountains. on my return to my lodge an indian called me in to his bower and gave me a small morsel of the flesh of an antelope boiled, and a peice of a fresh salmon roasted; both which I eat with a very good relish. this was the first salmon I had seen and perfectly convinced me that we were on the waters of the Pacific Ocean. the course of this river is a little to the North of west as far as I can discover it; and is bounded on each side by a range of high Mountains. tho' those on the E. side are lowest and more distant from the river.

This evening the Indians entertained us with their dancing nearly all night. at 12 O'Ck. I grew sleepy and retired to rest leaving the men to amuse themselves with the Indians. I observe no essential difference between the music and manner of dancing among this nation and those of the Missouri. I was several times awoke in the course of the night by their yells but was too much fortiegued to be deprived of a tolerable sound night's repose. [Lewis camped with the Shoshones on the Lemhi River about seven miles north of Tendoy, Lemhi County, Idaho. Clark camped a few miles southwest of Dillon, Beaverhead County, Montana.]

August 14, 1805
[LEWIS] the game which they [Shoshones] principally hunt is the Antelope which they pursue on horseback and shoot with their arrows. this animal is so extreemly fleet and dureable that a single horse has no possible chance to overtake them or run them down. the Indians are therefore obliged to have recorce to strategem when they discover a herd of the Antelope they seperate and scatter themselves to the distance of five or six miles in different directions arround them generally scelecting some commanding eminence for a stand; some one or two now pursue the herd at full speed over the hills vallies gullies and the sides of precipices that are tremendious to view. thus after runing them from five to six or seven miles the fresh horses that were in waiting head them and drive them back persuing them as far or perhaps further quite to the other extreem of the hunters who now in turn pursue on their fresh horses thus worrying the poor animal down and finally killing them with their arrows. forty or fifty hunters will be engaged for half a day in this

manner and perhaps not kill more than two or three Antelopes.   they
have but few Elk or black tailed deer, and the common red deer they cannot take as they secrete themselves in the brush when pursued . . .

The means I had of communicating with these people was by way of
Drewyer who understood perfectly the common language of jesticulation
or signs which seems to be universally understood by all the Nations we
have yet seen.   it is true that this language is imperfect and liable to error
but is much less so than would be expected.   the strong parts of the ideas
are seldom mistaken.

I now prevailed on the Chief to instruct me with rispect to the geography of his country.   this he undertook very cheerfully, by delienating the
rivers on the ground.   but I soon found that his information fell far short
of my expectation or wishes.   he drew the river on which we now are to
which he placed two branches just above us, which he shewed me from
the openings of the mountains were in view; he next made it discharge itself into a large river which flowed from the S. W. about ten miles below
us, then continued this joint stream in the same direction of this valley or
N. W. for one days march and then enclined it to the West for 2 more days
march, here he placed a number of heeps of sand on each side which he
informed me represented the vast mountains of rock eternally covered
with snow through which the river passed.   that the perpendicular and
even juting rocks so closely hemned in the river that there was no possi-
bilyte of passing along the shore; that the bed of the river was obstructed
by sharp pointed rocks and the rapidity of the stream such that the whole
surface of the river was beat into perfect foam as far as the eye could
reach.   that the mountains were also inaccessible to man or horse.[10]   he
said that this being the state of the country in that direction that himself
nor none of his nation had ever been further down the river than these
mountains. I then enquired the state of the country on either side of the

10. In explaining the geography of the country, Cameahwait first sketched out the
course of the Lemhi River on which the Shoshones were camped. His "two branches" to
the southeast may in fact have been the Lemhi itself and Hayden Creek, joining near the
town of Lemhi, Lemhi County, Idaho. To the northwest the Lemhi joins the Salmon
River, near the town of Salmon, and the chief's pessimistic views of the party's chance of
passing out of the mountains by way of the Salmon River will soon be confirmed by
Clark's reconnaissance of the so-called "River of No Return."

river but he could not inform me.   he said there was an old man of his
nation a days march below who could probably give me some information of the country to the N. W. and refered me to an old man then present for that to the S. W.   the Chief further informed me that he had understood from the persed nosed Indians [11] who inhabit this river below
the rocky mountains that it ran a great way toward the seting sun and
finally lost itself in a great lake of water which was illy taisted, and where
the white men lived.   I next commenced my enquiries of the old man to
whom I had been refered for information relative the country S W. of us.
this he depicted with horrors and obstructions scarcely inferior to that
just mentioned . . . I thanked him for his information and advise and gave
him a knife with which he appeared to be much gratified.   from this nar-
ative I was convinced that the streams of which he had spoken as runing
through the plains and that on which his relations lived were southern
branches of the Columbia, heading with the rivers Apostles [12] and Collo-
rado, and that the rout he had pointed out was to the Vermillion Sea or
gulph of Callifornia. I therefore told him that this rout was more to the
South than I wished to travel . . . I now asked Cameahwait by what rout
the Pierced nosed indians, who he informed me inhabited this river below the mountains, came over to the Missouri; this he informed me was
to the north, but added that the road was a very bad one as he had been
informed by them and that they had suffered excessively with hunger on
the rout being obliged to subsist for many days on berries alone as there
was no game in that part of the mountains which were broken rockey and
so thickly covered with timber that they could scarcely pass.   however
knowing that Indians had passed, and did pass, at this season on that side
of this river to the same below the mountains, my rout was instantly
settled in my own mind, povided the account of this river should prove
true on an investigation of it, which I was determined should be made before we would undertake the rout by land in any direction. I felt perfectly
satisfyed, that if the Indians could pass these mountains with their
women and Children, that we could also pass them; and that if the nations on this river below the mountains were as numerous as they were
stated to be that they must have some means of subsistence which it

11. Nez Perce Indians.
12. The Rio de los Apostolos was a mythical river of the Southwest.

would be equally in our power to procure in the same country.[13] they informed me that tere was no buffaloe on the West side of these mountains; that the game consisted of a few Elk deer and Antelopes, and that the natives subsisted on fish and roots principally. in this manner I spent the day smoking with them and acquiring what information I could with respect to their country . . . they told me that to avoid their enemies who were eternally harrassing them that they were obliged to remain in the interior of these mountains at least two thirds of the year where the suffered as we then saw great heardships for the want of food sometimes living for weeks without meat and only a little fish roots and berries. but this added Cameahwait, with his ferce eyes and lank jaws grown meager for the want of food, would not be the case if we had guns, we could then live in the country of buffaloe and eat as our enimies do and not be compelled to hide ourselves in these mountains and live on roots and berries as the bear do. we do not fear our enimies when placed on an equal footing with them. I told them that the Minnetares Mandans & Recares of the Missouri had promised us to desist from making war on them & that we would indevour to find the means of making the Minnetares of fort d Prarie or as they call them Pahkees[14] desist from waging war against them also. that after our finally returning to our homes towards the rising sun whitemen would come to them with an abundance of guns and every other article necessary to their defence and comfort, and that they would be enabled to supply themselves with these articles on reasonable terms in exchange for the skins of the beaver Otter and Ermin[15] so abundant in their country. they expressed great pleasure at this information and said they had been long anxious to see the whitemen that traded guns; and that we might rest assured of their friendship and that they would do whatever we wished them.

I now told Cameahwait that I wished him to speak to his people and engage them to go with me tomorrow to the forks of Jeffersons river where our baggage was by this time arrived with another Chief and a large

13. Lewis immediately decided that if the Nez Perces could make their way along the Lolo Trail and the Bitterroot Valley then the Corps could accomplish the same. In the days to follow, all information and reasoning will point toward this early determination.

14. Atsinas, as distinguished from the Minitaris of the Missouri, who are Hidatsas.

15. Long-tailed weasel.

party of whitemen who would wait my return at that place. that I wish them to take with them about 30 spare horses to transport our baggage to this place where we would then remain sometime among them and trade with them for horses, and finally concert our future plans for geting on to the ocean and of the traid which would be extended to them after our return to our homes. he complyed with my request and made a lengthey harrangue to his village. he returned in about an hour and a half and informed me that they would be ready to accompany me in the morning. I promised to reward them for their trouble. [Lewis remained at the Shoshone village on Lemhi River. Clark camped about ten miles southwest of Dillon, Beaverhead County, Montana, near Barretts Siding.]

[ORDWAY] the [water?] is verry cold. We have to waid in it which makes our feet and legs ake with cold. we expect it is made of Springs and near the head of the most of them which causes the River water to be as cold as Spring water.

August 15, 1805
[LEWIS] I hurried the departure of the Indians. the Chief addressed them several times before they would move they seemed very reluctant to accompany me. I at length asked the reason and he told me that some foolish persons among them had suggested the idea that we were in league with the Pahkees and had come on in order to decoy them into an ambuscade where their enimies were waiting to receive them. but that for his part he did not believe it . . . I told Cameahwait that I was sorry to find that they had put so little confidence in us, that I knew they were not acquainted with whitemen and therefore could forgive them. that among whitemen it was considered disgracefull to lye or entrap an enimy by falsehood. I told him if they continued to think thus meanly of us that they might rely on it that no whitemen would ever come to trade with them or bring them arms and amunition and that if the bulk of his nation still entertained this opinion I still hoped that there were some among them that were not affraid to die, that were men and would go with me and convince themselves of the truth of what I had asscerted. that there was a party of whitemen waiting my return either at the forks of Jefferson's river or a little below coming on to that place in canoes loaded with

provisions and merchandize.   he told me for his own part he was determined to go, that he was not affraid to die.   I soon found that I had
touched him on the right string; to doubt the bravery of a savage is at once
to put him on his metal.   he now mounted his horse and haranged his
village a third time . . . shortly after this harange he was joined by six or
eight only and with these I smoked a pipe and directed the men to put on
their packs being determined to set out with them while I had them in the
humour   at half after 12 we set out, several of the old women were crying
and imploring the great sperit to protect their warriors as if they were going to inevitable distructon.   we had not proceeded far before our party
was augmented by ten or twelve more, and before we reached the Creek [16]
which we had passed in the morning of the 13th it appeared to me that we
had all the men of the village and a number of women with us.   this may
serve in some measure to ilustrate the capricious disposition of those
people who never act but from the impulse of the moment.   they were
now very cheerfull and gay, and two hours ago they looked as sirly as so
many imps of satturn . . . about sunset we reached the upper part of the
level valley of the Cove which now called Shoshone Cove. [Lewis camped
with the Shoshones a few miles west of Grant, Beaverhead County, Montana. Clark apparently camped just below the mouth of Gallagher's
Creek, Beaverhead County.]

August 16, 1805
[LEWIS] I sent Drewyer and Shields before this morning in order to kill
some meat as neither the Indians nor ourselves had any thing to eat. I informed the Ceif of my view in this measure, and requested that he would
keep his young men with us lest by their hooping and noise they should
allarm the game and we should get nothing to eat, but so strongly were
there suspicions exited by this measure that two parties of discovery immediately set out one on ech side of the valley to watch the hunters as I
beleive to see whether they had not been sent to give information of their
approach to an enemy that they still preswaided themselves were lying in
wait for them. I saw that any further effort to prevent their going would
only add strength to their suspicions and therefore said no more.   after

16. Pattee Creek, Lemhi County, Idaho.

the hunters had been gone about an hour we set out. we had just passed through the narrows when we saw one of the spies comeing up the level plain under whip, the chief pawsed a little and seemed somewhat concerned. I felt a good deel so myself and began to suspect that by some unfortunate accedent that perhaps some of there enimies had straggled hither at this unlucky moment; but we were all agreeably disappointed on the arrival of the young man to learn that he had come to inform us that one of the whitemen had killed a deer. in an instant they all gave their horses the whip and I was taken nearly a mile before I could learn what were the tidings; as I was without tirrups and an Indian behind me the jostling was disagreeable I therefore reigned up my horse and forbid the indian to whip him who had given him the lash at every jum for a mile fearing he should loose a part of the feast. the fellow was so uneasy that he left me the horse dismounted and ran on foot at full speed, I am confident a mile. when they arrived where the deer was which was in view of me they dismounted and ran in tumbling over each other like a parcel of famished dogs each seizing and tearing away a part of the inestens which had been previously thrown out by Drewyer who killed it; the seen was such when I arrived that had I not have had a pretty keen appetite myself I am confident I should not have taisted any part of the venison shortly. each one had a peice of some discription and all eating most ravenously. some were eating the kidnies the melt and liver and the blood runing from the corners of their mouths, others were in a similar situation with the paunch and guts but the exuding substance in this case from their lips was of a different discription. one of the last who attacted my attention particularly had been fortunate in his allotment or reather active in the division, he had provided himself with about nine feet of the small guts one end of which he was chewing on while with his hands he was squezzing the contents out at the other. I really did not untill now think that human nature ever presented itself in a shape so nearly allyed to the brute creation. I viewed these poor starved divils with pity and compassion . . . being now informed of the place at which I expected to meat Capt C. and the party they insisted on making a halt, which was complyed with. we now dismounted and the Chief with much cerimony put tippets about our necks such as they temselves woar I redily perceived that this was to disguise us and owed it's origine to the same cause already mentioned. to give them further confidence I put my cocked hat with feather on the chief and my over shirt being of the Indian form my hair deshivled and skin well browned with the sun I wanted no further addition to make me a complete Indian in appearance the men followed my example and we were son completely metamorphosed . . . when we arrived in sight [of the forks] at the distance of about 2 miles I discovered to my mortification that the party had not arrived, and the Indians slackened their pace. I now scarcely new what to do and feared every moment when they would halt altogether, I now determined to restore their confidence cost what it might and therefore gave the Chief my gun and told him that if his enimies were in those bushes before him that he could defend himself with that gun, that for my own part I was not affraid to die and if I deceived him he might make what uce of the gun he thought proper or in other words that he might shoot me. the men also gave their guns to other indians which seemed to inspire them with more confidence; they sent their spies before them at some distance and when I drew near the place I thought of the notes which I had left and directed Drewyer to go with an Indian man and bring them to me which he did. the indian seeing him take the notes from the stake on which they had been plased I now had recource to a stratagem in which I thought myself justifyed by the occasion, but which I must confess set a little awkward. it had it's desired effect.   after reading the notes which were the same I had left I told the Chief that when I had left my brother Chief with the party below where the river entered the mountain that we both agreed not to bring the canoes higher up than the next forks of the river above us wherever this might happen, that there he was to wait my return, should he arrive first, and that in the event of his not being able to travel as fast as usual from the difficulty of the water, that he was to send up to the first forks above him and leave a note informing me where he was, that this note was left here today and that he informed me that he was just below the mountains and was coming on slowly up, and added that I should wait here for him, but if they did not beleive me that I should send a man at any rate to the Chief and they might also send one of their young men with him, that myself and two others would remain with them at this place.   this plan was readily adopted and one of the young men offered his services; I promised him a knife and some beads as a reward for his confidence in us. most of them seemed satisfyed but there were several that complained of the Chief's exposing them to danger unnecessarily and said that we told different stories, in short a few were much dissatisfyed. I wrote a note to Capt. Clark by the light of some willow brush and directed Drewyer to set out early being confident that there was not a moment to spare. the chief and five or six others slept about my fire and the others hid themselves in various parts of the willow brush to avoid the enimy whom they were fearfull would attack them in the course of the night. I now entertained various conjectures myself with rispect to the cause of Capt. Clarks detention and was even fearfull that he had found the river so difficult that he had halted below the Rattlesnake bluffs. I knew that if these people left me that they would immediately disperse and secrete themselves in the mountains where it would be impossible to find them or at least in vain to pursue them and that they would spread the allarm to all other bands within our reach & of course we should be disappointed in obtaining horses, which would vastly retard and increase the labour of our voyage and I feared might so discourage the men as to defeat the expedition altogether. my mind was in reallity quite as gloomy all this evening as the most affrighted indian but I affected cheerfullness to keep the Indians so who were about me. we finally laid down and the Chief placed himself by the side of my musquetoe bier. I slept but little as might be well expected, my mind dwelling on the state of the expedition which I have ever held in equal estimation with my own existence, and the fait of which appeared at this moment to depend in a great measure upon the caprice of a few savages who are ever as fickle as the wind. I had mentioned to the chief several times that we had with us a woman of his nation who had been taken prisoner by the Minnetares, and that by means of her I hoped to explain myself more fully tha I could do by signs. some of the party had also told the Indians that we had a man with us who was black and had short curling hair, this had excited their curiossity very much. and they seemed quite as anxious to see this monster as they wer the merchandize which we had to barter for their horses. [Lewis and the Shoshones camped at the junction of Horse Prairie Creek and Red Rock River which form Beaverhead River, Beaverhead County, Montana, in the area of the party's Camp Fortunate. Clark camped just a few miles north of Lewis, also in Beaverhead County.]

August 17, 1805

[LEWIS] This morning I arrose very early and dispatched Drewyer and the Indian down the river ... Drewyer had been gone about 2 hours when an Indian who had straggled some little distance down the river returned and reported that the whitemen were coming, that he had seen them just below.   they all appeared transported with joy, & the chef repeated his fraturnal hug. I felt quite as much gratifyed at this information as the Indians appeared to be. Shortly after Capt. Clark arrived with the Interpreter Charbono, and the Indian woman, who proved to be a sister of the Chif Cameahwait.   the meeting of those people was really affecting, particularly between Sah cah-gar-we-ah and an Indian woman, who had been taken prisoner at the same time with her, and who had afterwards escaped from the Minnetares and rejoined her nation. At noon the Canoes arrived, and we had the satisfaction once more to find ourselves all together, with a flattering prospect of being able to obtain as many horses shortly as would enable us to prosicute our voyage by land should that by water be deemed unadvisable.

We now formed our camp just below the junction of the forks on the Lard. side in a level smooth bottom covered with a fine terf of greenswoard.   here we unloaded our canoes and arranged our baggage on shore; formed a canopy of one of our large sails and planted some willow brush in the ground to form a shade for the Indians to set under while we spoke to them, which we thought it best to do this evening.   acordingly about 4 P. M. we called them together and through the medium of Labuish, Charbono and Sah-cah-gar-weah, we communicated to them [17] fully the objects which had brought us into this distant part of the country ... we made them sensible of their dependance on the will of our government for every species of merchandize as well for their defence & comfort; and apprized them of the strength of our government and it's friendly dispositions towards them.   we also gave them as a reason why we wished to petrate the country as far as the ocean to the west of them was to examine and find out a more direct way to bring merchandize to

17. The conversations would go from the captains in English to Labiche and from him in French to Charbonneau and then in Hidatsa to Sacagawea who would translate the words to Shoshone and then reverse the process.

them. that as no trade could be carryed on with them before our return to our homes that it was mutually advantageous to them as well as to ourselves that they should render us such aids as they had it in their power to furnish in order to haisten our voyage and of course our return home. that such were their horses to transport our baggage without which we could not subsist, and that a pilot to conduct us through the mountains was also necessary if we could not decend the river by water. but that we did not ask either their horses or their services without giving a satisfactory compensation in return.   that at present we wished them to collect as many horses as were necessary to transport our baggage to their village on the Columbia where we would then trade with them at our leasure for such horses as they could spare us. They appeared well pleased with what had been said . . . [Cameahwait] said they had not horses enough with them at present to remove our baggage to their village over the mountain, but that he would return tomorrow and encourage his people to come over with their horses and that he would bring his own and assist us. this was complying with all we wished at present. we next enquired who were chiefs among them. Cameahwait pointed out two others whom he said were Chiefs we gave him a medal of the small size with the likeness of Mr. Jefferson the President of the U' States in releif on one side and clasp hands with a pipe and tomahawk on the other, to the other Chiefs we gave each a small medal which were struck in the Presidency of George Washing[ton] Esqr. . . . every article about us appeared to excite astonishment in ther minds; the appearance of the men, their arms, the canoes, our manner of working them, the b[l]ack man york and the segacity of my dog were equally objects of admiration. I also shot my air-gun which was so perfectly incomprehensible that they immediately denominated it the great medicine.   the idea which the indians mean to convey by this appellation is something that eminates from or acts immediately by the influence or power of the great sperit; or that in which the power of god is manifest by it's incomprehensible power of action. our hunters killed 4 deer and an Antelope this evening of which we also gave the Indians a good proportion. the cerimony of our council and smoking the pipe was in conformity of the custom of this nation perfomed bearfoot. on those occasions points of etiquet are quite as much attended to by the Indians as among scivilized nations. To keep indians in a good humour you must

not fatiegue them with too much business at one time.   therefore after
the council we gave them to eat and amused them a while by shewing
them such articles as we thought would be entertaining to them, and then
renewed our enquiries with rispect to the country.   the information we
derived was only a repetition of that thy had given me before and in
which they appeared to be so candid that I could not avoid yealing
confidence to what they had said. Capt. Clark and myself now concerted
measures for our future operations, and it was mutually agreed that he
should set out tomorrow morning with eleven men furnished with axes
and other necessary tools for making canoes, their arms accoutrements
and as much of their baggage as they could carry.   also to take the indians Carbono and the indian woman with him; that on his arrival at the
Shoshone camp he was to leave Charbono and the Indian woman to haisten the return of the Indians with their horses to this place, and to proceede himself with the eleven men down the Columbia in order to examine the river and if he found it navigable and could obtain timber to
set about making canoes immediately. In the mean time I was to bring on
the party and baggage to the Shoshone Camp, calculating that by the time
I should reach that place that he would have sufficiently informed himself
with rispect to the state of the river &c, as to determine us whether to
prosicute our journey from thence by land or water.   in the former case
we should want all the horses which we could perchase, the latter only to
hire the Indians to transport our baggage to the place at which we made
the canoes . . . this plan being settled we gave orders accordingly and the
men prepared for an early march. [The recombined party camped just
below the forks of the Beaverhead River, Beaverhead County, Montana,
which was designated Camp Fortunate. Some members of the party
would remain here until August 24. The site is now beneath the waters of
Clark Canyon Reservoir.]

[CLARK] I deturmined to go in advance and examine the Countrey, See if
those dificueltes presented themselves in the gloomey picture in which
they painted them, and if the river was practiable and I could find timber
to build Canoes, those Ideas & plan appeard to be agreeable to Capt
Lewis's Ideas on this point, and I selected 11 men, directed them to pack
up their baggage Complete themselves with amunition, take each an ax

and Such tools as will be Soutable to build Canoes, and be ready to Set
out at 10 oClock tomorrow morning.[18]

August 18, 1805
[LEWIS] This day I completed my thirty first year, and conceived that I
had in all human probability now existed about half the period which I
am to remain in this Sublunary world. I reflected that I had as yet done
but little, very little indeed, to further the hapiness of the human race, or
to advance the information of the succeeding generation. I viewed with
regret the many hours I have spent in indolence, and now soarly feel the
want of that information which those hours would have given me had
they been judiciously expended. but since they are past and cannot be
recalled, I dash from me the gloomy thought and resolved in future, to
redouble my exertions and at least indeavour to promote those two primary objects of human existence, by giving them the aid of that portion
of talents which nature and fortune have bestoed on me; or in future, to
live for *mankind*, as I have heretofore lived *for myself*. [Lewis remained at
Camp Fortunate with the main party.]

[CLARK] Purchased of the Indians three horses for which we gave a Chiefs
Coat Some Handkerchiefs a Shirt Legins & a fiew arrow points &c. I gave
two of my coats to two of the under Chiefs who appeared not well
Satisfied that the first Chief was dressed so much finer than themselves.
at 10 oClock I Set out. [Clark camped about eight miles west of Grant,
Beaverhead County, Montana.]

[WHITEHOUSE] these Indian are verry poor and vallue a little worth a
great deal, as they never had Scarsely any kind of a kinife or Tommahawk
or any weapons of war or to use.

August 19, 1805
[LEWIS] from what has been said of the Shoshones it will be readily perceived that they live in a wretched stait of poverty.   yet notwithstanding

18. Clark took Gass, Pryor, Collins, Colter, Cruzatte, Shannon, Windsor, and four
other unidentified men with him. Charbonneau, Sacagawea, and the baby accompanied
him as far as the Shoshone village on the Lemhi River.

their extreem poverty they are not only cheerfull but even gay, fond of gaudy dress and amusements; like most other Indians they are great ego- tists and frequently boast of heroic acts which they never performed. they are also fond of games of wrisk. they are frank, communicative, fair in dealing, generous with the little they possess, extreemly honest, and by no means beggarly. each individual is his own sovereign master, and acts from the dictates of his own mind; the authority of the Cheif being noth- ing more than mere admonition supported by the influence which the propiety of his own examplery conduct may have acquired him in the minds of the individuals who compose the band. the title of cheif is not hereditary, nor can I learn that there is any cerimony of instalment, or other epo[c]h in the life of a Cheif from which his title as such can be dated. in fact every man is a chief, but all have not an equal influence on the minds of the other members of the community, and he who happens to enjoy the greatest share of confidence is the principal Chief. The Shoshonees may be estimated at about 100 warriors, and about three times that number of woomen and children. they have more children among them than I expected to have seen among a people who procure subsistence with such difficulty. there are but few very old persons, nor did they appear to treat those with much tenderness or rispect. The man is the sole propryetor of his wives and daughters, and can barter or dis- pose of either as he thinks proper. a plurality of wives is common among them, but these are not generally sisters as with the Minnetares & Man- dans but are purchased of different fathers. The father frequently disposes of his infant daughters in marriage to men who are grown or to men who have sons for whom they think proper to providewives. the compensa- tion given in such cases usually consists of horses or mules which the fa- ther receives at the time of contract and converts to his own uce. the girl remains with her parents untill she is conceived to have obtained the age of puberty which with them is considered to be about the age of 13 or 14 years. the female at this age is surrendered to her sovereign lord and hus- band agreeably to contract, and with her is frequently restored by the fa- ther quite as much as he received in the first instance in payment for his daughter; but this is discretionary with the father. Sah-car-gar-we-ah had been thus disposed of before she was taken by the Minnetares, or had ar- rived to the years of puberty. the husband was yet living and with this band. he was more than double her age and had two other wives. he claimed her as his wife but said that as she had had a child by another man, who was Charbono, that he did not want her. They seldom correct their children particularly the boys who soon become masters of their own acts. they give as a reason that it cows and breaks the Sperit of the boy to whip him, and that he never recovers his independence of mind after he is grown. They treat their women but with little rispect, and compel them to perform every species of drudgery. they collect the wild fruits and roots, attend to the horses or assist in that duty cook dreess the skins and make all their apparal, collect wood and make their fires, arrange and form their lodges, and when they travel pack the horses and take charge of all the baggage; in short the man dose little else except attend his horses hunt and fish. the man considers himself degraded if he is compelled to walk any distance, and if he is so unfortunately poor as only to possess two horses he rides the best himself and leavs the woman or women if he has more than one, to transport their baggage and children on the other, and to walk if the horse is unable to carry the additional weightof their persons — the chastity of their women is not held in high estimation, and the husband will for a trifle barter the companion of his bead for a night or longer if he conceives the reward adiquate; tho' they are not so importunate that we should caress their women as the siouxs were and some of their women appear to be held more sacred than in any nation we have seen   I have requested the men to give them no cause of jealousy by having connection with their women without their knowledge, which with them strange as it may seem is considered as disgracefull to the husband as clandestine connections of a similar kind are among civilized nations.   to prevent this mutual exchange of good officies altogether I know it impossible to effect, particularly on the part of our young men whom some months abstanence have made very polite to those tawney damsels. no evil has yet resulted and I hope will not from these connections . . . these people are deminutive in stature, thick ankles, crooked legs, thick flat feet and in short but illy formed, at least much more so in general than any nation of Indians I ever saw. their complexion is much that of the Siouxs or darker than the Minnetares mandands or Shawnees . . . I was anxious to learn whether these people had the venerial, and made the enquiry through the intrepreter and his wife; the information was that they sometimes had it but I could not learn their remedy; they most usually die with it's effects. this seems a strong proof that these disorders bothe gonaroehah and Louis venerae are native disorders of America. tho' these people have suffered much by the small pox which is known to be imported and perhaps those other disorders might have been contracted from other indian tribes who by a round of communication might have obtained from the Europeans since it was introduced into that quarter of the globe.   but so much detatched on the other ha[n]d fro all communication with the whites that I think it most probable that those disorders are original with them. from the middle of May to the firt of September these people reside on the waters of the Columbia where they consider themselves in perfect security from their enimies as they have not as yet ever found their way to this retreat; during this season the salmon furnish the principal part of their subsistence and as this firsh either perishes or returns about the 1st of September they are compelled at this season in surch of subsistence to resort to the Missouri, in the vallies of which, there is more game even within the mountains. here they move slowly down the river in order to collect and join other bands either of their own nation or the Flatheads, and having become sufficiently strong as they conceive venture on the Eastern side of the Rockey mountains into the plains, where the buffaloe abound.   but they never leave the interior of the mountains while they can obtain a scanty subsistence, and always return as soon as they have acquired a good stock of dryed meat in the plains; when this stock is consumed they venture again into the plains; thus alternately obtaining their food at the risk of their lives and retiring to the mountains, while they consume it. These people are now on the eve of their departure for the Missouri, and inform us that they expect to be joined at or about the three forks by several bands of their own nation, and a band of the Flatheads. [Lewis remained at Camp Fortunate.]

[GASS] At 1 o'clock we dined at the head spring of the Missouri and Jefferson river . . . It is not more than a mile from the head spring of the Missouri to the head of one of the branches of the Columbia. [Clark's party, including Gass, may have camped on Pattee Creek, Lemhi County, Idaho.]

August 20, 1805

[LEWIS] I walked down the river about ¾ of a mile and scelected a place near the river bank unperceived by the Indians for a cash, which I set three men to make, and directed the centinel to discharge his gun if he pereceived any of the Indians going down in that direction which was to be the signal for the men at work on the cash to desist and seperate, least these people should discover our deposit and rob us of the baggage we intend leaving here. by evening the cash was completed unperceived by the Indians, and all our packages made up . . . I made up a small assortment of medicines, together with the specemines of plants, minerals, seeds &c. which, I have collected betwen this place and the falls of the Missouri which I shall deposit here . . . The tippet of the Snake Indians is the most eligant peice of Indian dress I ever saw, the neck or collar of this is formed of a strip of dressed Otter skin with the fur. it is about four or five inches wide and is cut out of the back of the skin the nose and eyes forming one extremity and the tail the other.   begining a little behind the ear of the animal at one edge of this collar and proceeding towards the tail, they attatch from one to two hundred and fifty little roles of Ermin skin . . . covers the solders and body nearly to the waist and has the appearance of a short cloak and is really handsome.   these they esteem very highly, and give or dispose of only on important occasions.[19] [Lewis remained at Camp Fortunate.]

[CLARK] Set out at half past 6 oClock and proceeded on (met maney parties of Indians) thro' a hilley Countrey to the Camp of the Indians on a branch of the Columbia River, before we entered this Camp a Serimonious hault was requested by the Chief and I Smoked with all that Came around for Several pipes, we then proceeded on to the Camp & I was introduced into the only Lodge they had which was pitched in the Center for my party all the other Lodges made of bushes, after a fiew Indian Seremonies I . . . requested them all to take over their horses & assist Capt Leiwis across &c. also informing them the oject of my journey down the river and requested a guide to accompany me, all of which was repeited

19. Lewis received such a tippet from Cameahwait and was portrayed wearing it after the expedition by the artist Charles B. J. F. de Saint-Mémin.

by the Chief to the whole village . . . at 3 oClock after giveing a fiew Small articles as presents I set out accompanied by an old man as a Guide[20] (I endevered to procure as much information from thos people as possible without much Suckcess they being but little acquainted or effecting to be So — [)] . . . I left our interpreter & his woman to accompany the Indians to Capt Lewis tomorrow the Day they informed me they would Set out. [Clark camped on the west side of the Lemhi River in the vicinity of Baker, Lemhi County, Idaho.]

August 21, 1805
[LEWIS] Mean Latitude of the Forks of Jefferson's river . . . on the 20th Instant   N. 44° 35' 28.1".[21] [Lewis remained at Camp Fortunate.]

[CLARK] The men who passed by the forks informed me that the S W. fork[22] was double the Size of the one I came down,[23] and I observed that it was a handsom river at my camp   I shall in justice to Capt Lewis who was the first white man ever on this fork of the Columbia Call this Louis's river.[24] [Clark camped a few miles north of Carmen, Lemhi County, Idaho, on the east side of Salmon River.]

[LEWIS AND CLARK, WEATHER REMARKS] Most astonishing difference between the hight of the Murcury at ☉ rise and at 4 P. M. today   there was 59° and this in the Space of 8 hours, yet we experience this wonderfull transicion without feeling it near so Sensibly as I should have expected.[25]

August 22, 1805
[LEWIS] late last night Drewyer returned with a fawn he had killed and a considerable quantity of Indian plunder.   the anecdote with rispect to the

20. The captains later nicknamed the Shoshone guide "Old Toby."
21. The latitude of the approximate site of Camp Fortunate is 44° 59' 25" N.
22. Salmon River, called by Clark the "West Fork of Lewis's River."
23. Lemhi River, named by Clark the "East Fork of Lewis's River."
24. The Snake River eventually became the main "Lewis's River."
25. On this day the captains recorded the temperature at sunrise as 19° and at 4:00 P.M. as 78°.

latter is perhaps worthy of relation. he informed me that while hunting in the Cove yesterday about 12 OCk. he came suddonly upon an Indian Camp, at which there were a young man an Old man a boy and three women, that they seemed but little supprised at seeing him and he rode up to them and dismounted turning horse out to graize. these people had just finished their repast on some roots, he entered into conversation with them by signs, and after about 20 minutes one of the women spoke to the others of the party and they all went immediately and collected their horses brought them to camp and saddled them at this moment he thought he would also set out and continue his hunt, and accorgingly walked to catch his horse at some little distance and neglected to take up his gun which, he left at camp. the Indians perceiving him at the distance of fifty paces immediately mounted their horses, the young man took the gun and the whole of them left their baggage and laid whip to their horses directing their course to the pass of the mountains. finding himself deprived of his gun he immediately mounted his horse and pursued; after runing them about 10 miles the horses of two of the women nearly gave out and the young fellow with the gun from their frequent crys slackened his pace and being on a very fleet horse road around the women at a little distance at length Drewer overtook the women and by signs convinced them that he did not wish to hirt them they then halted and the young fellow approached still nearer, he asked him for his gun but the only part of the answer which he could understand was pah kee which he knew to be the name by which they called their enimies. watching his opportunity when the fellow was off his guard he suddonly rode along side of him seized his gun and wrest her out of his hands. the fellow finding Drewyer too strong for him and discovering that he must yeald the gun had pesents of mind to open the pan and cast the priming before he let the gun escape from his hands; now finding himself devested of the gun he turned his horse about and laid whip leaving the women to follow him as well as they could. Drewyer now returned to the place they had left their baggage and brought it with him to my camp. it consisted of . . . about a bushel of roots of three different kinds dryed and prepared for uce . . . another speceis[26] was much mutilated but appeared to be fibrous; the parts were

---

26. Bitterroot, named scientifically in Lewis's honor after the expedition (*Lewisia rediviva*).

brittle, hard of the size of a small quill, cilindric and as white as snow throughout, except some small parts of the hard black rind which they had not seperated in the preperation. this the Indians with me informed were always boiled for use. I made the exprement, found that they became perfectly soft by boiling, but had a very bitter taste, which was naucious to my pallate, and I transfered them to the Indians who had eat them heartily. [Lewis remained at Camp Fortunate.]

[CLARK] I Saw to day Bird of the wood pecker kind²⁷ which fed on Pine burs its Bill and tale white the wings black every other part of a light brown, and about the Size of a robin. [Clark camped a few miles southwest of North Fork, Lemhi County, Idaho, after following the Salmon River to this point.]

[GASS] The people of these three lodges have gathered a quantity of sunflower seed, and also of the lambs-quarter, which they pound and mix with service berries, and make of the composition a kind of bread; which appears capable of sustaining life for some time. On this bread and the fish they take out of the river, these people, who appear to be the most wretched of the human species, chiefly subsist.

[WHITEHOUSE] the men at Camp employed dressing their deer Skins & makeing their mockasons &c. I am employed makeing up their leather Shirts & overalls²⁸ . . . [The Shoshones] appear to live in fear of other nations who are at war with them, but Capt. Lewis tells them that these other nations promise to let them alone and if they do not, their Great father will Send them arms and amunition to defend themselves with, but rather that they would live in peace &c.

August 23, 1805
[CLARK] The River²⁹ from the place I left my party to this Creek is almost one continued rapid, five verry Considerable rapids the passage of either with Canoes is entirely impossable, as the water is Confined betwen hugh

27. Clark's nutcracker.
28. Heavy trousers worn over regular pants.
29. Salmon River.

Rocks & the Current beeting from one against another for Some distance below &c. at one of those rapids the mountains Close So Clost as to prevent a possibility of a portage with great labour in Cutting down the Side of the hill removeing large rocks &c. all the others may be passed by takeing every thing over Slipery rocks, and the Smaller ones Passed by letting down the Canoes empty with Cords, as running them would certainly be productive of the loss of Some Canoes, those dificuelties and necessary precautions would delay us an emince time in which provisions would be necessary. (we have but little and nothing to be precured in this quarter except Choke Cheres & red haws not an animal of any kind to be seen and only the track of a Bear) . . . below my guide and maney other Indians tell me that the Mountains Close and is a perpendicular Clift on each Side, and Continues for a great distance and that the water runs with great violence from one rock to the other on each Side foaming & roreing thro rocks in every direction, So as to render the passage of any thing impossible. those rapids which I had Seen he said was Small & trifleing in comparrison to the rocks & rapids below, at no great distance & The Hills or mountains were not like those I had Seen but like the Side of a tree Streight up . . . my guide Shewed me a road from the N Which Came into the one I was in which he Said went to a large river which run to the north on which was a Nation he called Tushapass, he made a map of it.[30] [Lewis remained at Camp Fortunate. Clark with Old Toby and three men camped on Squaw Creek, Lemhi County, Idaho, northeast of Shoup, while the remainder of his party stayed somewhere between North Fork and Shoup, Lemhi County.]

August 24, 1805

[LEWIS] I had now nine horses and a mule, and two which I had hired made twelve these I had loaded and the Indian women took the ballance of the baggage. I had given the Interpreter some articles with which to purchase a horse for the woman which he had obtained. at twelve Oclock

30. Clark followed the Salmon River to perhaps three miles above Shoup before returning a distance to his camp for the night. Old Toby showed the captain a road that connected to the North Fork Salmon River and then with the Bitterroot River, a route the party would follow to link up to Lolo Trail and take out of the mountains.

we set out and passed the river below the forks, directing our rout towards the cove along the track formerly mentioned.   most of the horses
were heavily laden, and it appears to me that it will require at least 25
horses to convey our baggage along such roads as I expect we shall be
obliged to pass in the mountains. I had now the inexpressible satisfaction
to find myself once more under way with all my baggage and party . . .
Cameahwait literally translated is *one who never walks*.   he told me that
his nation had also given him another name by which he was signalized
as a warrior which was Too-et'-te-con'-e or *black gun*.   these people have
many names in the course of their lives, particularly if they become distinguished characters.   for it seems that every important event by which
they happen to distinguish themselves intitles them to claim another
name which is generally scelected by themselves and confirmed by the
nation.   those distinguishing acts are the killing and scalping an enemy,
the killing a white bear, leading a party to war who happen to be successfull either in destroying their enemies or robing them of their horses, or
individually stealing the horses of an enemy.   these are considered acts of
equal heroism among them, and that of killing an enemy without scalping him is considered of no importance; in fact the whole honour seems
to be founded in the act of scalping, for if a man happens to slay a dozen
of his enemies in action and others get the scalps or first lay their hand on
the dead person the honor is lost to him who killed them and devolves on
those who scalp or fist touch them. Among the Shoshones, as well as all
the Indians of America, bravery is esteemed the primary virtue; nor can
any one become eminent among them who has not at some period of his
life given proofs of his possessing this virtue.   with them there can be no
preferment without some warelike achievement, and so completely interwoven is this principle with the earliest Elements of thought that it will
in my opinion prove a serious obstruction to the restoration of a general
peace among the nations of the Missouri.   while at Fort Mandan I was
one day addressing some cheifs of the Minetares wo visited us and pointing out to them the advantages of a state of peace with their neighbours
over that of war in which they were engaged.   the Chiefs who had already
geathered their havest of larals, and having forceably felt in many instances some of those inconveniences attending a state of war which I
pointed out, readily agreed with me in opinon.   a young fellow under the

full impression of the Idea I have just suggested asked me if they were in a state of peace with all their neighbours what the nation would do for Cheifs?, and added that the cheifs were now oald and must shortly die and that the nation could not exist without cheifs. taking as granted that there could be no other mode devised for making Cheifs but that which custom had established through the medium of warlike acievements. [Lewis camped a few miles east of Grant, Beaverhead County, Montana.]

[CLARK] I wrote a letter to Capt Lewis informing him of the prospects before us and information recved of my guide which I thought favourable & Stating two plans one of which for us to pursue &c. and despatched one man & horse . . . The plan I stated to Capt Lewis if he agrees with me we shall adopt is to procure as many horses (one for each man) if possible and to hire my present guide who I sent on to him to interegate thro' the Intprtr. and proceed on by land to Some navagable part of the *Columbia* River, or to the *Ocean*, depending on what provisions we can procure by the gun aded to the Small Stock we have on hand depending on our horses as the last resort. a second plan to divide the party one part to attempt this deficuet river with what provisions we had, and the remaindr to pass by Land on hose back Depending on our gun &c for Provisions &c. and come together occasionally on the river. the 1s of which I would be most pleased with &c.[31] [Clark camped with his recombined party on the Salmon River, a few miles southwest of North Fork, Lemhi County, Idaho.]

August 25, 1805
[LEWIS] Charbono mentioned to me with apparent unconcern that he expected to meet all the Indians from the camp on the Columbia tomorrow on their way to the Missouri. allarmed at this information I asked why he expected to meet them. he then informed me that the 1st Cheif had dispatched some of his young men this morning to this camp requesting the Indians to meet them tomorrow and that himself and those with him would go on with them down the Missouri, and consequently leave me and my baggage on the mountain or thereabouts. I was out of

31. Clark set down on paper his conclusions at this point and demonstrated his grasp of the difficulties of using the Salmon River route, wisely opting for the North Fork Salmon–Bitterroot–Lolo passage to the Columbia River and the Pacific Ocean.

patience with the folly of Charbono who had not sufficient sagacity to see the consequencies which would inevitably flow from such a movement of the indians, and altho' he had been in possession of this information since early in the morning when it had been communicated to him by his Indian woman yet he never mentioned it untill the after noon. I could not forbear speaking to him with some degree of asperity on this occasion. I saw that there was no time to be lost in having those orders counter-manded, or that we should not in all probability obtain any more horses or even get my baggage to the waters of the Columbia. I therefore Called the three Cheifs together and having smoked a pipe with them, I asked them if they were men of their words, and whether I could depent on the promises they had made me; they readily answered in the affermative; I then asked them if they had not promised to assist me with my baggage to their camp on the other side of the mountains, or to the place at which Capt. Clark might build the canoes, should I wish it. they acknowledged that they had. I then asked them why they had requested their people on the other side of the mountain to meet them tomorrow on the mountain where there would be no possibility of our remaining together for the purpose of trading for their horses as they had also promised . . . that if they wished the white men to be their friends and to assist them against their enemies by furnihing them with arms and keeping their enemies from attacking them that they must never promis us anything which they did not mean to perform . . . Cameahwait remained silent for some time, at length he told me that he knew he had done wrong but that he had been induced to that measure from seeing all his people hungary, but as he had promised to give me his assistance he would not in future be worse than his word. I then desired him to send immediately and countermand his orders; acordingly a young man was sent for this purpose and I gave him a handkerchief to engage him in my interest. [Lewis camped west of the fork of Horse Prairie Creek and Trail Creek, Beaverhead County, Montana. Clark camped a few miles north of Carmen, Lemhi County, Idaho, on the east side of Salmon River, his campsite of August 21.]

August 26, 1805
[LEWIS] one of the women who had been assisting in the transportation of the baggage halted at a little run about a mile behind us, and sent on the two pack horses which she had been conducting by one of her female

friends. I enquired of Cameahwait the cause of her detention, and was informed by him in an unconcerned manner that she had halted to bring fourth a child and would soon overtake us; in about an hour the woman arrived with her newborn babe and passed us on her way to the camp apparently as well as she ever was. It appears to me that the facility and ease with which the women of the aborigines of North America bring fourth their children is reather a gift of nature than depending as some have supposed on the habitude of carrying heavy burthens on their backs while in a state of pregnancy.   if a pure and dry air, an elivated and cold country is unfavourable to childbirth, we might expect every difficult incident to that operation of nature in this part of the continent; again as the snake Indians possess an abundance of horses, their women are seldom compelled like those in other parts of the continent to carry burthens on their backs, yet they have their children with equal convenience, and it is a rare occurrence for any of them to experience difficulty in childbirth. I have been several times informed by those who were conversant with the fact, that the indian women who are pregnant by whitemen experience more difficulty in childbirth than when pregnant by an Indian.   if this be true it would go far in suport of the opinion I have advanced . . . I found Colter here who had just arrived with a letter from Capt. Clark in which Capt. C. had given me an account of his perigrination and the description of the river and country as before detailed from this view of the subject I found it a folly to think of attemping to decend this river in canoes and therefore <determined> to commence the purchase of horses in the morning from the indians in order to carry nto execution the design [of] passing the rocky Mountains. I now informed Cameahwait of my intended expedition overland to the great river which lay in the plains beyond the mountains and told him that I wished to purchase 20 horses of himself and his people to convey our baggage. he observed that the Minnetares had stolen a great number of their horses this spring but hoped his people would spear me the number I wished. I also asked a guide, he observed that he had no doubt but the old man who was with Capt. C. would accompany us if we wished him and that he was better informed of the country than any of them. matters being thus far arranged I directed the fiddle to be played and the party danced very merily much to the amusement and gratification of the natives, though I must confess that the state of my own mind at this moment did not well accord with the prevailing mirth as I somewhat feared that the caprice of the indians might suddenly induce them to withhold their horses from us without which my hopes of prosicuting my voyage to advantage was lost; however I determined to keep the indians in a good humour if possible, and to loose no time in obtaining the necessary number of horses.[32] [Lewis camped about four miles north of Tendoy, Lemhi County, Idaho, where the Shoshones had relocated on August 20. Clark camped about five miles southeast of Salmon, Lemhi County, where he would remain until August 29.]

[ORDWAY] we Set out at Sunrise and proceeded on with our big coats on and our fingers ackd with the Cold.

August 27, 1805
[CLARK] my party hourly Complaining of their retched Situation and [contemplating?] doubts of Starveing in a Countrey where no game of any kind except a fiew fish can be found. [Lewis remained with the Shoshones, while Clark stayed at his camp near Salmon.]

[ORDWAY] Capt. Lewis bought 8 or 9 horses this day. the natives do not wish to part with any more of their horses without gitting a higher price for them. the most of those he has bought as yet was for about 3 or 4 dollars worth of marchandize at the first cost, but we will have to give a little more to git a fiew more horses. in the evening the natives had a war dance and danced with their guns those that had any but they had only three or 4 among them. they were verry merry but did not dance So regular as the Indians on the Missourie. their women Sang with them, but did not dance any they tell us that Some of their horses will dance but they have not brought them out yet. they have different kinds of plays and games they have a game[33] which they play most like playing butten only they kick singing and do all by motions they risk all the property

32. This entry ends Lewis's consistent daily journal-keeping until January 1, 1806, when he begins writing regularly again. There is no explanation for the gaps, leading some persons to speculate that there are missing journals.

33. Clark discusses this game more fully on December 9, 1805.

they git for their horses or Some of them but it does not trouble them they appear to be easy & well contented let the world go as it may.

August 28, 1805

[CLARK] Those Sammon which I live on at present are pleasent eateing, not with standing they weaken me verry fast and my flesh I find is de-clineing. [Lewis remained with the Shoshones, while Clark stayed at his camp near Salmon.]

[ORDWAY] these Savages are fond of Salt.   the first we have Seen that would taste it.

August 29, 1805

[CLARK] I left our baggage in possession of 2 men and proceeded on up to join Capt Lewis at the upper Village of Snake Indians where I arrived at 1 oClock found him much engaged in Counceling and attempting to purchase a fiew more horses. I Spoke to the Indians on various Subjects endeavoring to impress on theire minds the advantaje it would be to them for to Sell us horses and expedite the our journey the nearest and best way possibly that we might return as Soon as possible and winter with them at Some place where there was plenty of buffalow, our wish is to get a horse for each man to Carry our baggage and for Some of the men to ride occasionally, The horses are handsom and much acustomed to be changed as to their Parsture; we cannot Calculate on their carrying large loads & feed on the Grass which we may Calculate on finding in the Mountain. [Clark joined Lewis at the Shoshone campsite.]

[ORDWAY] about 8 oClock A. M. a nomber of Indians arived here who had been gone along time from the nation   one of them got Sculped by some Indians in the prarie or plain   he did not know what nation they be-longed to. Some of their relations cryed when they came in the village.

[GASS] While I lay here to day, one of the natives shewed me their method of producing fire, which is somewhat curious. They have two sticks ready for the operation, one about 9 and the other 18 inches long: the short stick they lay down flat and rub the end of the other upon it in a perpendicular direction for a few minutes; and the friction raises a kind of dust, which in a short time takes fire. These people make willow basket so close and to such perfection as to hold water, for which purpose they make use of them.

August 30, 1805
[CLARK] finding that we Could purchase no more horse than we had for our goods &c. (and those not a Sufficint number for each of our Party to have one which is our wish) I Gave my Fuzee to one of the men & Sold his musket for a horse which Completed us to 29 total horses, we Purchased pack Cords Made Saddles & Set out on our rout down the river by land guided by my old guide one other who joined him, the old gude's 3 Sons followed him [34] . . . Those horses are indifferent, maney Sore backs and others not acustomed to pack, and as we Cannot put large loads on them are Compelled to purchase as maney as we Can to take our Small propotion of baggage of the Parties. (& Eate if necessary). [Camped on the Lemhi River, below Baker, Lemhi County, Idaho.]

September 2, 1805
[CLARK] proceded on thro' thickets in which we were obliged to Cut a road, over rockey hill Sides where our horses were in pitial danger of Slipping to Ther certain distruction & up & Down Steep hills, where Several horses fell, Some turned over, and others Sliped down Steep hill Sides, one horse Crippeled & 2 gave out. with the greatest dificuelty risque &c. we made five miles. [Camped on the North Fork Salmon River northwest of Gibbonsville, Lemhi County, Idaho.]

[ORDWAY] we call this place dismal Swamp . . . this is a verry lonesome place.[35]

[WHITEHOUSE] horrid bad going.

34. Old Toby's sons and the other Shoshones left the party on September 1.
35. Dismal Swamp is an area of southeast Virginia and northeast North Carolina; here Ordway is in the vicinity of Gibbonsville, Lemhi County, Idaho.

September 3, 1805

[CLARK] we met with a great misfortune, in haveing our last Thmometer broken by accident, This day we passed over emence hils and Some of the worst roade that ever horses passed   our horses frequently fell   Snow about 2 inches deep when it began to rain which termonated in a Sleet. [Camped probably to the west of Lost Trail Pass in either Ravalli County, Montana, or Lemhi County, Idaho.]

[ORDWAY] we dined at a branch   eat the last of our pork &.C.   Some of the men threaten to kill a colt to eat they being hungry, but puts if off untill tomorrow noon hopeing the hunters will kill Some game.

[WHITEHOUSE] Set in to raining hard at dark So we lay down and Slept, wet hungry and cold.

September 4, 1805

[CLARK] prosued our Course down the Creek to the forks about 5 miles where we met a part of the <*Flat head*> nation [36] of 33 Lodges about 80 men 400 Total and at least 500 horses, those people recved us friendly, threw white robes over our Sholders & Smoked in the pipes of peace, we Encamped with them & found them friendly but nothing but berries to eate a part of which they gave us, those Indians are well dressed with Skin Shirts & robes, they Stout & light complected more So than Common for Indians, The Chiefs harangued untill late at night, Smoked our pipe and appeared Satisfied. I was the first white man who ever wer on the waters of this river.[37] [Camped in the valley called Ross's Hole, east of Sula, Ravalli County, Montana.]

[ORDWAY] we had nothing but a little pearched corn to eat   the air on the mountains verry chilley and cold.   our fingers aked with the cold . . . our hunter killed a deer on which we dined.   our guide and the young Indian who accompanied him eat the verry guts of the deer.

36. The Flatheads are now more generally called Salish Indians.

37. In 1806 in order to honor Clark being "the first white man" on the Bitterroot River (or its affluents), the captains called it "Clark's River" and enlarged its scope to include the Clark Fork and Pend Oreille Rivers in that designation (see Lewis's entry of May 6, 1806).

September 5, 1805
[CLARK] we assembled the Chiefs & warriers and Spoke to them (with much dificuely as what we Said had to pass through Several languajes before it got in to theirs, which is a gugling kind of languaje Spoken much thro the Throught)[38] we informed them who we were, where we Came from, where bound and for what purpose &c. and requsted to purchase & exchange a fiew horses with them, in the Course of the day I purchased 11 horses & exchanged 7 for which we gave a fiew articles of merchendize. those people possess ellegant horses . . . They Call themselves Eoote-lash-Schute[39] and consist of 450 Lodges in all and divided into Several bands on the heads of Columbia river & Missouri, Some low down the Columbia River. [Remained at Ross's Hole.]

[ORDWAY] the Indian dogs are so ravinous that they eat Several pair of the mens Moccasons . . . these natives have the Stranges language of any we have ever yet Seen. they appear to us as though they had an Impedement in their Speech or brogue on their tongue. we think perhaps that they are the welch Indians,[40] &C. they are the likelyest and honestest we have seen and are verry friendly to us. they Swaped to us Some of their good horses and took our worn out horses, and appeared to wish to help us as much as lay in their power.

September 6, 1805
[CLARK] rained this evening   nothing to eate but berries, our flour out, and but little Corn, the hunters killed 2 pheasents only. [Camped a few miles northwest of Sula, Ravalli County, Montana, along the East Fork Bitterroot River.]

[WHITEHOUSE] Capt. Lewis took down the Names of everry thing in their Language, in order that it may be found out whether they are or whether they Sprang or origenated first from the welch or not.

38. The transfer of information was aided by a Shoshone speaker found among the Salish who could translate to Sacagawea, she to her husband, he to one of the French-speaking party members, and then to the captains.

39. Perhaps another area tribe besides the Salish.

40. Ordway touched on the myth that some interior Indians may have descended from Welsh travelers.

September 7, 1805

[GASS] We halted at 12 o'clock, and one of the hunters killed 2 deer; which was a subject of much joy and congratulation. [Camped southwest of Grantsdale, Ravalli County, Montana, on the east side of the Bitterroot River.]

[WHITEHOUSE] Our party seemed revived at the success that the hunters had met with, however in all the hardship that they had yet undergone they never once complained, trusting to Providence & the Conduct of our Officers in all our difficulties.

September 9, 1805

[LEWIS] our guide could not inform us where this river discharged itself into the columbia river, he informed us that it continues it's course along the mountains to the N. as far as he knew it and that not very distant from where we then were it formed a junction with a stream nearly as large as itself which took it's rise in the mountains near the Missouri to the East of us and passed through an extensive valley generally open prarie which forms an excellent pass to the Missouri   the point of the Missouri where this Indian pass intersects it, is about 30 miles above the *gates of the rocky mountain*, or the place where the valley of the Missouri first widens into an extensive plain after entering the rockey mountains.   the guide informed us that a man might pass to the missouri from hence by that rout in four days.   we continued our rout down the W. side of the river about 5 miles further and encamped on a large creek which falls in on the West as our guide informes that we should leave the river at this place and the weather appearing settled and fair I determined to halt the next day rest our horses and take some scelestial Observations.[41]   we called this Creek *Travellers rest*.[42] [Camped on Lolo Creek, in the vicinity of Lolo, Missoula County, Montana, where they would remain until September 11.]

41. Old Toby knew that the Bitterroot River joined the Clark Fork just west of Missoula, Montana, but did not know the course of the Clark Fork. The captains now confirmed that a shorter route from the Great Falls connected to this point which would cut considerable time off the large dip to the south the party took while seeking the headwaters of the Missouri River.

42. Lolo Creek, Missoula County, Montana.

September 10, 1805

[LEWIS] this evening one of our hunters[43] returned accompanyed by three men of the Flathead nation[44] whom he had met in his excurtion up *travellers rest* Creek. on first meeting him the Indians were allarmed and prepared for battle with their bows and arrows, but he soon relieved their fears by laying down his gun and advancing towards them . . . our guide could not speake the language of these people but soon engaged them in conversation by signs or jesticulation, the common language of all the Aborigines of North America . . . in this manner we learnt from these people that two men which they suppoșed to be of the Snake nation had stolen 23 horses from them and that they were in pursuit of the theaves. they told us they were in great hast, we gave them some boiled venison, of which the eat sparingly. the sun was now set, two of them departed after receiving a few small articles which we gave them, and the third remained, having agreed to continue with us as a guide, and to introduce us to his relations whom he informed us were numerous and resided in the plain below the mountains on the columbia river, from whence he said the water was good and capable of being navigated to the sea; that some of his relation were at the sea last fall and saw an old whiteman who resided there by himself and who had given them some handkerchiefs such as he saw in our possession. he said it would require five sleeps wich is six days travel, to reach his relations.[45] [Remained at Travelers' Rest.]

[CLARK] The day proved fair and we took equal altitudes & Some luner observations. The Latd. *46° 48′ 28″*.[46]

September 11, 1805

[WHITEHOUSE] passed a tree on which was a nomber of Shapes drawn on it with paint by the natives. a white bear Skin hung on the Same tree. we Suppose this to be a place of worship among them . . . [We saw] pine trees

43. Colter.

44. Probably Nez Perces.

45. The Nez Perce Indian who remained was gone by the next day.

46. Other journalists added .8″ to Clark's latitude reading; the approximate latitude of the Travelers' Rest site is 46° 45′ 02″ N.

pealed as far up as a man could reach. we Suppose that the natives done it to git the enside beark to mix with their dryed fruit to Eat. [Camped about one-half mile east of Woodman Creek, Missoula County, Montana.]

September 12, 1805
[ORDWAY] we found no water nor place to Camp untill 10 oClock at night . . . we could not find a level place to Sleep, and Scarcely any feed for our horses. [Camped about two miles east of Lolo Hot Springs, Missoula County, Montana.]

September 13, 1805
[CLARK] at 2 miles passed Several Springs which I observed the Deer Elk &c. had made roads to, and below one of the Indians had made a whole to bathe, I tasted this water and found it hot & not bad tasted . . . in further examonation I found this water nearly boiling hot at the places it Spouted from the rocks (which a hard Corse Grit, and of great size the rocks on the Side of the Mountain of the Same texture[)] I put my finger in the water, at first could not bare it in a Second—[47] as Several roads led from these Springs in different derections, my Guide took a wrong road and took us out of our rout 3 miles through intolerable rout, after falling into the right road I proceeded on thro tolerabl rout for abt. 4 or 5 miles and halted to let our horses graze as well as waite for Capt Lewis who has not yet Come up.[48] [Camped on Pack Creek on the lower end of Packer Meadows, Idaho County, Idaho.]

September 14, 1805
[CLARK] here we wer compelled to kill a Colt for our men & Selves to eat for the want of meat & we named the South fork Colt killed Creek,[49] and this river we Call *Flathead* River—[50] The Mountains which we passed to

47. The waters of Lolo Hot Springs, Missoula County, Montana, have been measured at 111°F.
48. The party crossed from Montana into Idaho east of Lolo Pass, and went down to Pack Creek to set up camp for the night.
49. Colt Killed Creek in Idaho County has been restored to the expedition name.
50. Lochsa River, Idaho County, Idaho.

day much worst than yesterday the last excessively bad & Thickly Strowed with falling timber & Pine Spruc fur Hackmatak & Tamerack,[51] Steep & Stoney   our men and horses much fatigued. [Camped on the Lochsa River, Idaho County, Idaho, near Powell Ranger Station.]

[GASS] Capt. Lewis gave out some portable soup,[52] which he had along, to be used in cases of necessity. Some of the men did not relish this soup, and agreed to kill a colt; which they immediately did, and set about roasting it; and which appeared to me to be good eating.

September 15, 1805
[CLARK] proceeded on Down the right Side of River[53] over Steep points rockey & buschey as usial for 4 miles to an old Indian fishing place, here the road leaves the river to the left and assends a *mountain* winding in every direction to get up the Steep assents & to pass the emence quantity of falling timber[54] . . . 4 miles up the mountain I found a Spring and halted for the rear to come up and to let our horses rest & feed, about 2 hours the rear of the party came up much fatigued & horses more So, Several horses Sliped and roled down Steep hills which hurt them verry much   The one which Carried my desk & Small trunk Turned over & roled down a mountain for 40 yards & lodged against a tree, broke the Desk the horse escaped and appeared but little hurt   Some others verry much hurt, from this point I observed a range of high mountains[55] Covered with Snow from S E. to S W with Their top bald or void of timber. after two hours delay we proceeded on up the mountain Steep & ruged as usial, more timber near the top, when we arrived at the top As we Conceved we could find no water and Concluded to Camp and make use of the Snow we found on the top to cook the remnt. of our Colt & make our Supe, evening verry Cold and Cloudy. Two of our horses gave out, pore

51. Lodgepole pine, Engelmann spruce, subalpine fir, and a larch with multiple common names, including hackmatack and tamarack.

52. Lewis's portable soup was a mixture of dry powder or thick liquid that he purchased in Philadelphia as emergency field rations.

53. Lochsa River, Idaho County, Idaho, paralleling modern U.S. Highway 12.

54. Bitterroot Range of the Rockies, along the Montana-Idaho border.

55. The party climbed north up Wendover Ridge to return to Lolo Trail.

and too much hurt to proceed on and left in the rear — nothing killed to day except 2 Phests. [Camped where Wendover Ridge rejoins the Lolo Trail near Forest Road 500, Idaho County, Idaho.]

September 16, 1805
[CLARK] began to Snow about 3 hours before Day and Continud all day the Snow in The morning 4 Inches deep on The old Snow, and by night we found it from 6 to 8 Inches deep   I walked in front to keep the road and found great dificuelty in keeping it as in maney places the Snow had entirely filled up the track, and obliged me to hunt Several minits for the track   at 12 oClock we halted on the top of the mountain to worm & dry our Selves a little as well as to let our horses rest and graze a little on Some long grass . . . a thickly timbered Countrey of 8 different kinds of pine,[56] which are So covered with Snow, that in passing thro them we are continually covered with Snow, I have been wet and as cold in every part as I ever was in my life, indeed I was at one time fearfull my feet would freeze in the thin mockersons which I wore, after a Short delay in the middle of the Day, I took one man and proceeded on as fast as I could about 6 miles to a Small branch passing to the right, halted and built fires for the party agains their arrival which was at Dusk   verry cold and much fatigued we Encamped at this Branch in a thickly timbered bottom which was Scercely large enough for us to lie leavil, men all wet cold and hungary. Killed a Second Colt which we all Suped hartily on and thought it fine meat . . . to describe the road of this day would be a repitition of yesterday excpt the Snow which made it much wors to proseed as we had in maney places to derect our Selves by the appearence of the rubbings of the Packs against the trees which have limbs quiet low and bending downwards. [Camped near a spot on Lolo Trail called Indian Post Office (a term not used by the party), Idaho County, Idaho.]

[GASS] proceeded over the most terrible mountains I ever beheld . . . The snow fell so thick, and the day was so dark, that a person could not see to

56. Clark used the term "pine" for many types of evergreens in the area which include lodgepole pine, Douglas fir, subalpine fir, Engelmann spruce, whitebark pine, grand fir, mountain hemlock, and western larch.

a distance of 200 yards. In the night and during the day the snow fell about 10 inches deep.

[WHITEHOUSE] we mended up our mockasons. Some of the men without Socks raped rags on their feet, and loaded up our horses and Set out without any thing to eat, and proceeded on.

September 17, 1805

[CLARK] road excessively bad   Snow on the Knobs, no Snow in the vallies   Killed a fiew Pheasents which was not Sufficient for our Supper which compelled us to kill Something.   a coalt being the most useless part of our Stock he fell a Prey to our appetites. The after part of the day fare, we made only 10 miles to day   two horses fell & hurt themselves very much. [Camped east of Indian Grave Peak, Idaho County, Idaho.]

[WHITEHOUSE] the mare which owned the colt, which we killed, went back & led 4 more horses back to where we took dinner yesterday.

September 18, 1805

[LEWIS] Cap Clark set out this morning to go a head with six hunters.[57] there being no game in these mountains we concluded it would be better for one of us to take the hunters and hurry on to the leavel country a head and there hunt and provide some provision while the other remained with and brought on the party . . . accordingly I directed the horses to be gotten up early being determined to force my march as much as the abilities of our horses would permit.   the negligence of one of the party Willard who had a spare horse not attending to him and bringing him up last evening was the cause of our detention this morning untill ½ after 8 A M when we set out . . . we suffered for water this day passing one rivulet only; we wer fortunate in finding water in a steep raviene about ½ maile from our camp.   this morning we finished the remainder of our last coult.   we dined & suped on a skant proportion of portable soupe, a few canesters of which, a little bears oil and about 20 lbs. of candles form our stock of provision, the only recources being our guns & packhorses.   the

57. The hunting party included Reubin Field and Shields.

first is but a poor dependance in our present situation where there is nothing upon earth exept ourselves and a few small pheasants,[58] small grey Squirrels,[59] and a blue bird of the vulter kind[60] about the size of a turtle dove or jay bird. [Lewis camped about three miles west of Bald Mountain, Idaho County, Idaho.]

[CLARK] Encamped on a bold running Creek passing to the left which I call *Hungery Creek* as at that place we had nothing to eate. I halted only one hour to day to let our horses feed on Grass and rest. [Clark camped on Hungery Creek, formerly called Obia Creek, Idaho County, Idaho.]

September 19, 1805
[LEWIS] Set out this morning a little after sun rise and continued our rout about the same course of yesterday or S. 20 W. for 6 miles when the ridge terminated and we to our inexpressable joy discovered a large tract of Prairie country lying to the S. W. and widening as it appeared to extend to the W.[61]   through that plain the Indian informed us that the Columbia river, in which we were in surch run. this plain appeared to be about 60 Miles distant, but our guide assured us that we should reach it's borders tomorrow the appearance of this country, our only hope for subsistance greately revived the sperits of the party already reduced and much weakened for the want of food . . . the road was excessively dangerous along this creek being a narrow rockey path generally on the side of steep precipice, from which in many places if ether man or horse were precipitated they would inevitably be dashed in pieces. Fraziers horse fell from this road in the evening, and roled with his load near a hundred yards into the Creek.[62]   we all expected that the horse was killed but to our astonishment when the load was taken off him he arose to his feet & appeared to be but little injured, in 20 minutes he proceeded with his

58. Grouse of various kinds.
59. Probably Richardson's red squirrel.
60. Probably the pinyon jay or Steller's jay.
61. Lewis viewed the prairies in Lewis and Idaho Counties, Idaho, from Sherman Peak, including Camas and Nez Perce Prairies northwest of Grangeville, which Clark had observed the previous day from the same vantage point.
62. Hungery Creek, Idaho County.

load. this was the most wonderfull escape I ever witnessed, the hill down which he roled was almost perpendicular and broken by large irregular and broken rocks . . . several of the men are unwell of the disentary. brakings out, or irruptions of the Skin, have also been common with us for some time. [Lewis camped on Hungery Creek, Idaho County, Idaho. Clark camped on Cedar Creek, near Lewis and Clark Grove, Idaho County.]

[GASS] We have, however, some hopes of getting soon out of this horrible mountainous desert, as we have discovered the appearance of a valley or level part of the country about 40 miles ahead. When this discovery was made there was as much joy and rejoicing among the corps, as happens among passengers at sea, who have experienced a dangerous and protracted voyage, when they first discover land on the long looked for coast.

September 20, 1805
[LEWIS] This morning my attention was called to a species of bird[63] which I had never seen before. It was reather larger than a robbin, tho' much it's form and action. the colours were a blueish brown on the back the wings and tale black, as wass a stripe above the croop ¾ of an inch wide in front of the neck, and two others of the same colour passed from it's eyes back along the sides of the head. the top of the head, neck brest and belley and butts of the wing were of a fine yellowish brick reed. it was feeding on the buries of a species of shoemake or ash[64] which grows common in country & which I first observed on 2d of this month. I have also observed two birds of a blue colour both of which I believe to be of the haulk or vulter kind. the one[65] of a blue shining colour with a very high tuft of feathers on the head a long tale, it feeds on flesh the beak and feet black. it's note is chă-ăh, chă-ăh. it is about the size of a pigeon; and in shape and action resembles the jay bird. another bird[66] of very similar genus, the note resembling the mewing of the cat, with a white head

63. Varied thrush.
64. Mountain ash.
65. Steller's jay.
66. Perhaps the gray jay.

and a light blue colour is also common, as are a black species of wood-pecker[67] about the size of the lark woodpecker   Three species of Pheasants, a large black species,[68] with some white feathers irregularly scattered on the brest neck and belley   a smaller kind[69] of a dark uniform colour with a red stripe above the eye, and a brown and yellow species[70] that a good deel resembles the phesant common to the Atlantic States.   we were detained this morning untill ten oclock in consequence of not being enabled to collect our horses.   we had proceeded about 2 miles when we found the greater part of a horse which Capt Clark had met with and killed for us.   he informed me by note that he should proceed as fast as possible to the leavel country whch lay to the S. W. of us, which we discovered from the hights of the mountains on the 19th   there he intended to hunt untill our arrival.   at one oclock we halted and made a hearty meal on our horse beef much to the comfort of our hungry stomachs. here I larnt that one of the Packhorses with his load was missing and immediately dispatched Baptiest Lapage who had charge of him, to surch for him.   he returned at 3 OC. without the horse. The load of the horse was of considerable value consisting of merchandize and all my stock of winter cloathing. I therefore dispatched two of my best woodsmen in surch of him, and proceeded with the party . . . saw the hucklebury,[71] honeysuckle,[72] and alder[73] common to the Atlantic states, also a kind of honeysuckle[74] which bears a white bury and rises about 4 feet high not common but to the western side of the rockey mountains.   a growth which resembles the choke cherry[75] bears a black bury with a single stone of a sweetish taste, it rises to the hight of 8 or 10 feet and grows in thick clumps.   the Arborvita[76] is also common and grows to an immence size,

67. Lewis's woodpecker.
68. Blue grouse.
69. Spruce grouse.
70. Oregon ruffed grouse.
71. Mountain huckleberry.
72. Western trumpet honeysuckle.
73. Sitka alder.
74. Common snowberry.
75. Choke cherry.
76. Western redcedar.

being from 2 to 6 feet in diameter. [Lewis camped between Dollar and Sixbit Creeks, Idaho County, Idaho.]

[CLARK] at 12 miles decended the mountain to a leavel pine Countrey proceeded on through a butifull Countrey for three miles to a Small Plain in which I found maney Indian lodges, at the distance of 1 mile from the lodges I met 3 boys, when they Saw me ran and *hid* themselves [*WC: in the grass   I dismounted gave my gun & horse to one of the men,*] searched [*WC: in the grass and*] found [*WC: 2 of the boys*]   gave them Small pieces of ribin & Sent them forward to the village   a man Came out to meet me with great Caution & Conducted us to a large Spacious Lodge which he told me (by Signs) was the Lodge of his great Chief who had Set out 3 days previous with all the Warriers of the nation to war on a South West derection & would return in 15 or 18 days.   the fiew men that were left in the Village aged, great numbers of women geathered around me with much apparent Signs of fear, and apr. pleased   they gave us a Small piece of Buffalow meat, Some dried Salmon beries & roots in different States, Some round and much like an onion which they call quamash[77] the Bread or Cake is called Pas-she-co[78] Sweet, of this they make bread & Supe   they also gave us the bread made of this root all of which we eate hartily, I gave them a fiew Small articles as preasents, and proceeded on with a Chief to his Village 2 miles in the Same Plain, where we were treated kindly in their way and continued with them all night   Those two Villages consist of about 30 double lodges, but fiew men a number of women & children; They call themselves *Cho pun-nish*[79] or *Pierced Noses*; their dialect appears verry different from the Tushapaws altho origneally the Same people[80]   They are darker than the Tushapaws   Their dress Similar, with more beads white & blue principally, brass & Copper in different forms, Shells and ware their haire in the Same way.   they are large Portley men Small women & handsom fetued [featured]   Emence quantity of the

77. The Nez Perce term for camas.

78. The Shoshone designation for camas.

79. The party's common name for the Nez Perces.

80. The Salish ("Tushapaws") are not connected with the Nez Perces, who speak a form from the Sahaptian language family unrelated to the Salishan family.

quawmash or *Pas-shi-co* root gathered & in piles about the plains, those roots grow much an onion in marshey places the seed are in triangular Shell on the Stalk.   they Sweat them in the following manner i. e. dig a large hole 3 feet deep Cover the bottom with Split wood on the top of which they lay Small Stones of about 3 or 4 Inches thick, a Second layer of Splited wood & Set the whole on fire which heats the Stones, after the fire is extinguished they lay grass & mud mixed on the Stones, on that dry grass which Supports the Pash-Shi-co root a thin Coat of the Same grass is laid on the top, a Small fire is kept when necessary in the Center of the kile &c.   I find myself verry unwell all the evening from eateing the fish & roots too freely. Sent out the hunters   they killed nothing. [Clark camped at a village of Nez Perce Indians on Weippe Prairie, near the town of Weippe, Clearwater County, Idaho.]

[ORDWAY] we found a handful or 2 of Indian peas [81] and a little bears oil which we brought with us   we finished the last morcil of it and proceeded on half Starved and very weak.

[WHITEHOUSE] our horses got Stung by the yellow wasps. [82]

September 21, 1805

[LEWIS] encamped in a small open bottom where there was tolerable food for our horses. I directed the horses to be hubbled to prevent delay in the morning being determined to make a forced march tomorrow in order to reach if possible the open country.   we killed a few Pheasants, and I killd a prarie woolf which together with the ballance of our horse beef and some crawfish which we obtained in the creek enabled us to make one more hearty meal, not knowing where the next was to be found.   the Arborvita increases in quantity and size. I saw several sticks today large enough to form eligant perogues of at least 45 feet in length. I find myself growing weak for the want of food and most of the men complain of a similar deficiency and have fallen off very much. [Lewis camped on Lolo Creek, Clearwater County, Idaho.]

81. Possibly hog peanuts, which the party could have carried from the Missouri River in North Dakota.

82. Perhaps the western yellow jacket.

[CLARK] Sent out all the hunters in different directions to hunt deer, I myself delayd with the Chief to prevent Suspission and to Collect by Signs as much information as possible about the river and Countrey in advance. The Cheif drew me a kind of chart of the river, and informed me that a greater Cheif than himself was fishing at the river half a days march from his village called the twisted hare[83] . . . The hunters all return without any thing, I purchased as much Provisions as I could with what fiew things I chaned to have in my Pockets, Such a Salmon Bread roots & berries, & Sent one man R. Fields with an Indian to meet Capt. Lewis, and at 4 oClock P M. Set out to the river, met a man at dark on his way from the river to the village, whome I hired and gave the neck handkerchief of one of the men, to polit me to the Camp of the twisted hare, we did not arrive at the Camp of the Twisted hare but oppost, untill half past 11 oClock P M. found at this Camp five Squars & 3 Children. my guide called to the Chief who was Encamped with 2 others on a Small Island in the river, he Soon joind me, I found him a Chearfull man with apparant Siencerity, I gave him a medal &c. and Smoked untill 1 oClock a. m. and went to Sleep . . . I am verry Sick to day and puke which relive me. [Clark camped on the Clearwater River about a mile from Orofino, Clearwater County, Idaho.]

September 22, 1805
[LEWIS] Notwithstanding my positive directions to hubble the horses last evening one of the men neglected to comply. he plead ignorance of the order. this neglect however detained us untill ½ after eleven OCk at which time we renewed our march, our course being about west. we had proceeded about two and a half miles when we met Reubin Fields . . . with some dryed fish and roots that he had procured from a band of Indians, whose lodges were about eight miles in advance. I ordered the party to halt for the purpose of taking some refreshment. I divided the fish roots and buries, and was happy to find a sufficiency to satisfy compleatly all our appetites . . . the pleasure I now felt in having tryumphed over the rocky Mountains and decending once more to a level and fertile country

83. The captains knew him as Twisted Hair, but his name may have been Walamottinin, meaning "hair bunched and tied."

where there was every rational hope of finding a comfortable subsistence for myself and party can be more readily conceived than expressed, nor was the flattering prospect of the final success of the expedition less pleasing. [Lewis camped on Weippe Prairie.]

[CLARK] the hunters Shild killed 3 Deer this morning. I left them on the Island and Set out with the Chief & his Son . . . I found Capt Lewis & the party Encamped, much fatigued, & hungery, much rejoiced to find something to eate of which They appeared to partake plentifully. I cautioned them of the Consequences of eateing too much &c. . . . Those Indians Stole out of R. F. Shot pouch his knife wipers[84] Compas & Steel, which we Could not precure from them, we attempted to have Some talk with those people but Could not for the want of an Interpreter thro' which we Could Speake, we were Compelled to converse alltogether by Signs— I got the Twisted hare to draw the river[85] from his Camp down which he did with great cherfullness on a white Elk Skin, from the 1s fork[86] which is a few seven miles below, to the large fork[87] on which the *So So ne* or Snake Indians fish, is South 2 Sleeps; to a large river[88] which falls in on the N W. Side and into which The *Clarks river*[89] empties itself is 5 Sleeps from the mouth of that river to the *falls*[90] is 5 Sleeps   at the falls he places Establishments of white people &c. and informs that great numbers of Indians reside on all those foks as well as the main river . . . I precured maps of the Country & river with the Situation of Indians, To come from Several men of note Seperately which varied verey little. [Clark joined Lewis at Weippe Prairie.]

[ORDWAY] these natives have a large quantity of this root bread which they call Commass.   the roots grow in these plains.   they have kills en-

84. "Wipers" may have been a cloth or leather piece used for cleaning weapons.
85. Clearwater River.
86. North Fork Clearwater.
87. Snake River.
88. Columbia River.
89. Combined Clark Fork–Pend Oreille River.
90. Celilo Falls, a great meeting place of Indians.

geaniously made where they Sweet these roots and make them Sweet and good to the taste.[91]

September 23, 1805
[CLARK] We assembled the principal Men as well as the Chiefs and by Signs informed them where we came from where bound our wish to inculcate peace and good understanding between all the red people &c. which appeared to Satisfy them much, we then gave 2 other Medals to other Chefs of bands, a flag to the *twisted hare*, left a flag & Handkerchief to the grand Chief gave, a Shirt to the *Twisted hare* & a knife & Handkerchif with a Small pece of Tobacco to each . . . Capt. Lewis & 2 men verry Sick this evening, my hip verry Painfull, the men trade a few old tin Canisters for dressed Elk Skin to make themselves Shirts, at dark a hard wind from The S W accompaned with rain which lasted half an hour. The *twisted hare* envited Capt Lewis & myself to his lodge which was nothin more than Pine bushes & bark, and gave us Some broiled dried *Salmon* to eate. [Camped at another Nez Perce village nearby, about one mile southwest of Weippe, Clearwater County, Idaho.]

September 24, 1805
[CLARK] Capt Lewis Scercely able to ride on a jentle horse which was furnishd by the Chief, Several men So unwell that they were Compelled to lie on the Side of the road for Some time   others obliged to be put on horses. I gave rushes Pills to the Sick this evening. [Camped on an island in Clearwater River, about one mile above Orofino, Clearwater County, Idaho.]

September 26, 1805
[CLARK] proceeded on down the river to a bottom opposit the forks of the river on the South Side and formed a Camp.[92] Soon after our arrival a raft Came down the N. fork on which was two men, they came too, I had the axes distributed and handled and men apotned. ready to commence build-

91. Ordway described how the Nez Perces baked ("Sweet" or sweat) the camas roots in kilns.
92. The party would call this spot "Canoe Camp" and remain here until October 7.

ing canoes on tomorrow, our axes are Small & badly Calculated to build Canoes of the large Pine, Capt Lewis Still very unwell, Several men taken Sick on the way down, I administered *Salts* Pils Galip, Tarter emetic &c.[93] I feel unwell this evening. [Camped on the south bank of the Clearwater River opposite the mouth of the North Fork Clearwater about five miles west of Orofino, Clearwater County, Idaho, the party's Canoe Camp.]

[GASS] There appears to be a kind of sheep[94] in this country, besides the Ibex or mountain sheep,[95] and which have wool on. I saw some of the skins, which the natives had, with wool four inches long, and as fine, white and soft as any I had ever seen.

September 28, 1805
[CLARK] Our men nearly all Complaining of ther bowels, a heaviness at the Stomach & Lax, Some of those taken first getting better . . . nothing killed men complaining of their diat of fish & roots. all that is able working at the Canoes. [Remained at Canoe Camp.]

September 29, 1805
[LEWIS AND CLARK, WEATHER REMARKS] ¾ of the party Sick. [Remained at Canoe Camp.]

October 2, 1805
[CLARK] Despatched 2 men Frasure & S. Guterich back to the village with 1 Indian & 6 horses to purchase dried fish, roots &c. we have nothing to eate but roots, which give the men violent pains in their bowels after eating much of them . . . Hunters killed nothing excep a Small Prarie wolf. Provisions all out, which Compells us to kill one of our horses to eate and make Suep for the Sick men. [Remained at Canoe Camp.]

[ORDWAY] the party are so weak and unwell living without meat that our officers thought proper with the oppinion of the party to kill a good horse

93. Clark's medications included salts, Rush's pills, jalap, and tartar emetic, all serving as purgatives.
94. Mountain goat.
95. Bighorn sheep.

which was done and we eat the meat as earnest as though it had been the best meat in the world.

October 3, 1805
[CLARK] all our men getting better in helth, and at work at the Canoes. [Remained at Canoe Camp.]

October 5, 1805
[CLARK] had all our horses 38 in number Collected and branded   Cut off their fore top and delivered them to the 2 brothers and one Son of one of the Chiefs who intends to accompany us down the river   to each of those men I gave a Knife & Some Small articles &c.   they promised to be attentive to our horses untill we Should return . . . Nothing to eate except dried fish & roots. Capt Lewis & myself eate a Supper of roots boiled, which Swelled us in Such a manner that we were Scercely able to breath for Several hours— finished and lanced [launched] 2 of our Canoes this evening which proved to be verry good   our hunters with every diligence Could kill nothing . . . Several Squars Came with Fish and roots which we purchased of them for Beeds, which they were fond of— Capt Lewis not So well to day as yesterday. [Remained at Canoe Camp.]

[WHITEHOUSE] the distance over the mountn. is estimated to be 160 odd miles from where we left Flatt head River, to this place.[96]

October 6, 1805
[CLARK] had all our Saddles Collected a whole dug and in the night buried them, also a Canister of powder and a bag of Balls at the place the Canoe which Shields made was cut from the body of the tree— The Saddles were buried on the Side of a bend about ½ a mile below— all the Canoes finished this evening ready to be put into the water. I am taken verry unwell with a paine in the bowels & Stomach, which is certainly the effects of my diet—which last all night . . . The river below this

96. Whitehouse's estimate of the distance is quite close to the modern length of the Lolo Trail.

forks is Called *Kos kos kee*[97] it is Clear rapid with Shoals or Swift places. [Remained at Canoe Camp.]

October 7, 1805
[CLARK] I continu verry unwell but obliged to attend every thing   all the Canoes put into the water and loaded, fixed our Canoes as well as possible and Set out   as we were about to Set out we missd. both of the Chiefs who promised to accompany us;[98] I also missed my Pipe Tomahawk which Could not be found. [Camped near Lenore, Nez Perce County, Idaho.]

October 8, 1805
[CLARK] Set out at 9 oClock   passed 15 rapids four Islands and a Creek[99] on the Stard Side   at 16 miles just below which one canoe in which Serjt. Gass was Stearing and was nearle turning over, She Sprung a leak or Split open on one Side and Bottom filled with water & Sunk on the rapid, the men, Several of which Could not Swim hung on to the Canoe, I had one of the other Canoes unloaded & with the assistance of our Small Canoe and one Indian Canoe took out every thing & toed the empty Canoe on Shore, one man Tompson a little hurt, every thing wet perticularly the greater part of our Small Stock of merchindize, had every thing opened, and two Sentinals put over them to keep off the Indians, who are enclined to theave haveing Stole Several Small articles   those people appeared disposed to give us every assistance in their power dureing our distress. [Camped below the mouth of Potlatch River, a few miles from Spalding, Nez Perce County, Idaho, where the party remained until October 10.]

October 9, 1805
[CLARK] at Dark we were informed that our old guide & his Son had left us and had been Seen running up the river Several miles above, we Could not account for the Cause of his leaveing us at this time, without receiving his pay for the Services he had rendered us, or letting us know anything of

97. Clearwater River.
98. Twisted Hair and Tetoharsky joined the party on October 8.
99. Potlatch River.

his intention.[100] we requested the Chief to Send a horseman after our old guide to come back and recive his pay &c. which he advised us not to do as his nation would take his things from him before he passed their camps . . . Capt Lewis recovring fast. [Remained at the Potlatch River.]

[ORDWAY] in the evening Some of our party fiddled and danced, which pleased the natives verry much. one of their women was taken with fit by one of our fires. She began Singing Indian and to giving all around hir Some commass roots, and brasslets which hung about hir one of our party refused to take them from hir. She then appeared angry threw them in the fire. took a Sharp flint from hir husband and cut both of hir arms in Sundry places So that the blood gushed out. She Scraped the blood in hir hand and Eat it, and So continued in this way about half an hour then fainted or went in to a fit Some time then came too by their puting water on hir and Seemed to take great care of hir &C.

October 10, 1805
[CLARK] arived at a large Southerly fork which is the one we were on with the *Snake* or *So-So-nee* nation . . . This South fork or *Lewis's River*[101] which has two forks[102] which fall into it on the South the 1st Small the upper large . . . I think Lewis's River is about 250 yards wide, the *Koos koos ke*[103] River about 150 yards wide and the river below the forks about 300 yards wide. a miss understanding took place between Shabono one of our interpreters, and Jo. & R Fields which appears to have originated in just —[104] our diet extremely bad haveing nothing but roots and dried fish to eate, all the Party have greatly the advantage of me, in as much as they all relish the flesh of the dogs, Several of which we purchased of the nativs for to add to our Store of fish and roots &c.

The *Cho-pun-nish* or Pierced nose Indians are Stout likeley men,

100. Old Toby departed, not to be seen again.
101. Snake River.
102. Perhaps the Grande Ronde and Salmon Rivers.
103. Clearwater River.
104. The Field brothers and Charbonneau probably argued over a point that began in jest.

handsom women, and verry dressey in their way, the dress of the men are a white Buffalow robe or Elk Skin dressed with Beeds which are generally white, Sea Shells—i e the Mother of Pirl hung to ther hair & on a pice of otter Skin about their necks hair Cewed in two parsels hanging forward over their Sholders, feathers, and different Coloured Paints which they find in their Countrey Generally white, Green & light Blue. Some fiew were a Shirt of Dressed Skins and long legins, & Mockersons Painted, which appears to be their winters dress, with a plat of twisted grass about their necks. The women dress in a Shirt of Ibex, or <Goat> Skins which reach quite down to their anckles with a girdle, their heads are not orne-mented, their Shirts are ornemented with quilled Brass, Small peces of Brass Cut into different forms, Beeds, Shells & curios bones &c. The men expose those parts which are generally kept from few [view] by other na-tions but the women are more perticular than any other nation which I have passed in Screting the parts   Their amusements appear but fiew as their Situation requires the utmost exertion to prcure food they are gen-erally employed in that pursute, all the Summer & fall fishing for the Salmon, the winter hunting the deer on Snow Shoes in the plains and takeing care of ther emence numbers of horses, & in the Spring cross the mountains to the Missouri to get Buffalow robes and meet &c. at which time they frequent meet with their enemies & lose their horses & maney of ther people   Ther disorders are but fiew and those fiew of a Scofelous nature.[105]   they make great use of Swetting. The hot and cold baethes, They are verry Selfish and Stingey of what they have to eate or ware, and they expect in return Something for everything give as presents or the Survices which they doe let it be however Small, and fail to make those returns on their part. [Camped opposite Clarkston, Whitman County, Washington.]

105. Scrofulous disorders indicate a number of skin diseases.

CHAPTER 8

Roll On Columbia

October 11–November 14, 1805

October 11, 1805

[CLARK] Came to and encamped at 2 Indian Lodges at a great place of fishing here we met an Indian of a nation near the mouth of this river.[1] we purchased three dogs and a fiew fish of those Indians, we Passed today nine rapids all of them great fishing places, at different places on the river saw Indian houses and Slabs & Spilt timber raised from the ground being the different parts of the houses of the natives when they reside on this river for the purpose of fishing at this time they are out in the Plain on each side of the river hunting the antilope as we are informed by our Chiefs, near each of those houses we observe Grave yards picketed, or pieces of wood stuck in permicuesly over the grave or body which is Covered with earth, The Country on either Side is an open plain leavel & fertile after assending a Steep assent of about 200 feet not a tree of any kind to be Seen on the river. [Camped in the vicinity of Almota, Whitman County, Washington.]

[ORDWAY] these Savages have among them pleanty of beeds and copper trinkets, copper kittles &C which must have come from white people.

[GASS] Most of our people having been accustomed to meat, do not relish the fish, but prefer dog meat; which, when well cooked, tastes very well.

---

1. The party met several bands of Nez Perces or possibly Palouses in this area.

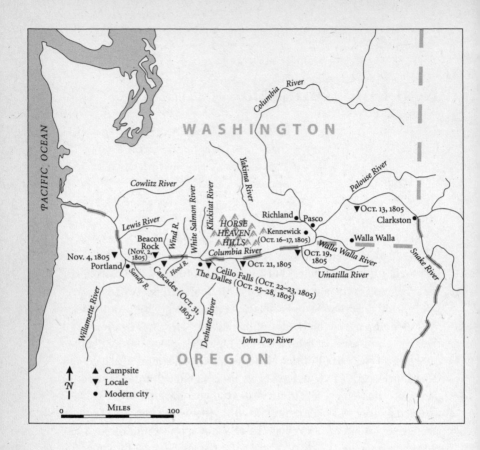

The Expedition's Route, October 11–November 14, 1805

October 13, 1805

[CLARK] The wife of Shabono our interpetr we find reconsiles all the Indians, as to our friendly intentions a woman with a party of men is a token of peace. [Camped in Franklin County, Washington, nearly opposite Ayer, Walla Walla County.]

[WHITEHOUSE] We took 2 of our Canoes at a time down the Rapids.[2] The Men that were among us, that could not swim, went by land, to go below these Rapids. They carried with them some Rifle Guns & Mathematical Instruments &ca. We were fortunate in getting all our Canoes safe over these Rapids.

October 14, 1805

[CLARK] after dinner we Set out and had not proceded on two miles before our Stern Canoe in passing thro a Short rapid opposit the head of an Island, run on a Smoth rock and turned broad Side, the men got out on the [rock] all except one of our Indian Chiefs who Swam on Shore, The Canoe filed and Sunk a number of articles floated out, Such as the mens bedding clothes & Skins, the Lodge &c. the greater part of which were cought by 2 of the Canoes, whilst a 3rd was unloading & Steming the Swift Current to the relief of the men on the rock who could with much dificuelty hold the Canoe. however in about an hour we got the men an Canoe to Shore with the Loss of Some bedding Tomahaws Shot pouches Skins Clothes &c. all wet we had every articles exposed to the Sun to dry on the Island, our loss in provisions is verry Considerable all our roots was in the Canoe that Sunk, and Cannot be dried Sufficint to Save, our loose powder was also in the Canoe and is all wett This I think, we Shall saved. In this Island we found some Spilt timber the parts of a house which the Indians had verry Securely covered with Stone, we also observed a place where the Indians had buried there fish, we have made it a point at all times not to take any thing belonging to the Indians even their wood. but at this time we are Compelled to violate that rule and take a part of the Split timber we find here bured for fire wood, as no other is to

2. Near the mouth of Tucannon River, Columbia County, Washington.

be found in any direction. [Camped in Franklin County, Washington, in the area of former Burr Canyon, now covered by Lake Sacajawea.]

October 15, 1805
[GASS] This river in general is very handsome, except at the rapids, where it is risking both life and property to pass; and even these rapids, when the bare view or prospect is considered distinct from the advantages of navigation, may add to its beauty, by interposing variety and scenes of romantick grandeur where there is so much uniformity in the appearance of the country. [Camped below Fishhook Rapids, Franklin County, Washington.]

October 16, 1805
[CLARK] five Indians[3] came up the river in great haste, we Smoked with them and gave them a piece of tobacco to Smoke with their people and Sent them back, they Set out in a run . . . proceeded on Seven miles to the junction of this river and the Columbia which joins from the N. W. . . . after we had our camp fixed and fires made, a Chief came from their Camp which was about ¼ of a mile up the Columbia river at the head of about 200 men Singing and beeting on their drums Stick and keeping time to the musik, they formed a half circle around us and Sung for Some time, we gave them all Smoke, and Spoke to their Chiefs as well as we could by Signs informing them of our friendly disposition to all nations,[4] and our joy in Seeing those of our Children around us, Gave the principal chief a large Medal Shirt and Handkf. [Camped at the point between the Snake and Columbia Rivers, in Franklin County, Washington, southeast of Pasco.]

October 17, 1805
[CLARK] The number of dead Salmon on the Shores & floating in the river is incrediable to Say and at this Season they have only to collect the fish Split them open and dry them on their Scaffolds on which they have great numbers, how far they have to raft their timber they make their Scaffolds of I could not lern; but there is no timber of any Sort except

---

3. Probably Yakamas.
4. Besides Yakamas, Wanapams also lived in the vicinity, while Walula, Umatilla, and Palouse Indians visited the area.

Small willow bushes in Sight in any direction— from this Island the natives showed me the enterance of a large Westerly fork which they Call
Tâpetêtt[5] at about 8 miles distant . . . The Dress of those natives differ but
little from those on the Koskoskia[6] and Lewis's rivers,[7] except the women
who dress verry different in as much as those above ware long leather
Shirts which highly orniminted with beeds Shells &c. and those on the
main Columbia river only ware a truss or pece of leather tied around
them at their hips and drawn tite between ther legs and fastened before
So as barly to hide those parts which are So Sacredly hid & Scured by our
women. Those women are more inclined to Copulency than any we have
yet Seen, with low Stature broad faces, heads flatened and the foward
compressed so as to form a Streight line from the nose to the Crown of
the head,[8] their eyes are of a Duskey black, their hair of a corse black without orniments of any kind braded as above,

The orniments of each Sects are Similar, Such as large blue & white
beeds, either pendant from their ears or encircling their necks, or wrists
& arms. they also ware bracelets of Brass, Copper & horn, and trinkets
of Shells, fish bones and curious feathers. Their garments Consists of a
short Shirt of leather and a roabe of the Skins of Deer or the Antilope but
fiew of them ware Shirts all have Short robes. Those people appears to live
in a State of comparitive happiness: they take a greater Share labor of
the woman, than is common among Savage tribes, and as I am informd.
Content with one wife (as also those on the Ki moo e nim river)[9] Those
people respect the aged with veneration, I observed an old woman in one
of the Lodges which I entered   She was entirely blind as I was informed
by Signs, had lived more than 100 winters, She occupied the best position
in the house, and when She Spoke great attention was paid to what She
Said. Those people as also those of the *flat heads* which we had passed on
the Koskoske and Lewis's rivers are Subject to Sore eyes, and maney are
blind of one and Some of both eyes. this misfortune must be owing to

5. Yakima River, meeting the Columbia at Richand, Benton County, Washington.

6. Another variant for the Clearwater River.

7. Snake River.

8. Clark was probably describing regional dress and culture rather than specific tribal
traits, among which was the custom of skull deformation.

9. Another variant for the Snake River.

the reflections of the Sun &c. on the waters in which they are continually fishing during the Spring Summer & fall, & the Snows dureing the, winter Seasons, in this open countrey where the eye has no rest. I have observed amongst those, as well in all other tribes which I have passed on these waters who live on fish maney of different Sectes who have lost their teeth about middle age, Some have their teeth worn to the gums, perticelar those of the upper jaws, and the tribes generally have bad teeth   the cause of it I cannot account   sand attachd. to the roots &c   the method they have of useing the dri'd Salmon, which is mearly worming it and eating the rine & Scales with the flesh of the fish, no doubt contributes to it

The Houses or Lodges of the tribes of the main Columbia river is of large mats made of rushes, Those houses are from 15 to 60 feet in length generally of an Oblong Squar form, Suported by poles on forks in the iner Side, Six feet high, the top is covered also with mats leaveing a Seperation in the whole length of about 12 or 15 inches wide, left for the purpose of admitting light and for the Smok of the fire to pass which is made in the middle of the house. The roughfs are nearly flat, which proves to me that rains are not common in this open Countrey

Those people appeare of a mild disposition and friendly disposed — They have in their huts independant of their nets gigs & fishing tackling each bows & large quivers of arrows on which they use flint Spikes. Theire ammusements are Similar to those of the Missouri.   they are not beggerley and receive what is given them with much joy.

I saw but fiew horses   they appeared make but little use of those animals principally useing Canoes for their uses of procureing food &c. [Remained at point of confluence of the Snake and Columbia Rivers.]

October 18, 1805
[CLARK] Lattitudes . . . is 46° 15′ 13⁹⁄₁₀″ North.[10]

[CLARK] The Great Chief[11] and one of the *Chim-nâ pum* nation[12] drew me a Sketch of the Columbia above and the tribes of his nation, living on

10. Clark's latitude reading is from his draft entry; the approximate latitude of the confluence of the Columbia and Snake Rivers is 46° 12′ 12″ N.
11. Unknown; it is not Yelleppit of the next day.
12. Probably Yakama Indians.

the bank, and its waters, and the *Tâpe têtt* river which falls in 18 miles above on the westerly side. [Camped south of the mouth of the Walla Walla River, Walla Walla County, Washington.]

October 19, 1805
[CLARK] The great chief *Yel-lep-pit*[13] two other chiefs, and a Chief of Band below presented themselves to us verry early this morning.   we Smoked with them, enformed them as we had all others above as well as we Could by Signs of our friendly intentions towards our red children Perticular those who opened their ears to our Councils.   we gave a Medal, a Handkercheif & a String of Wompom to *Yelleppit* and a String of wompom to each of the others.   *Yelleppit* is a bold handsom Indian, with a dignified countenance about 35 years of age, about 5 feet 8 inches high and well perpotiond.   he requested us to delay untill the Middle of the day, that his people might Come down and See us, we excused our Selves and promised to Stay with him one or 2 days on our return which appeared to Satisfy him . . . I deturmined to walk down on the Lard Side, with the 2 Chiefs the interpreter & his woman, and derected the Small canoe to prcede down on the Lard Side to the foot of the rapid which was about 2 miles in length   I Sent on the Indian Chiefs &c. down and I assended a high clift about 200 feet above the water . . . from this place I descovered a high mountain of emence hight covered with Snow, this must be one of the mountains laid down by Vancouver, as Seen from the mouth of the Columbia River, from the Course which it bears which is *West* I take it to be Mt. St. Helens, destant 156 miles[14] . . . I landed in front of five Lodges which was at no great distance from each other . . . entered the third 4h & fifth Lodge which I found Somewhat passified . . . as Soon as they Saw the Squar wife of the interperters they pointed to her and informed those who continued yet in the Same position I first found them, they imediately all came out and appeared to assume new life, the sight of This Indian woman, wife to one of our interprs. confirmed those people of our friendly intentions, as no womn ever accompanies a war party of

13. Chief of the Walula (or Walla Walla) Indians.
14. Clark probably saw Mount Adams, not Mount St. Helens, which may not have been visible from his vantage point.

Indians in this quarter . . . Soon after we landed which was at a fiew willow trees about 100 Indians Came from the different Lodges, and a number of them brought wood which they gave us, we Smoked with all of them, and two of our Party Peter Crusat & Gibson played on the *violin* which delighted them greatly, we gave to the principal man a String of wompon treated them kindly for which they appeared greatfull, This Tribe can raise about 350 men   their Dress are Similar to those at the fork except their robes are Smaller and do not reach lower than the waste and ¾ of them have Scercely any robes at all, the women have only a Small pece of a robe which Covers their Sholders neck and reaching down behind to their wastes, with a tite piece of leather about the waste, the brests are large and hang down verry low illy Shaped, high Cheeks flattened heads, & have but fiew orniments, they are all employed in fishing and drying fish of which they have great quantites on their Scaffolds, their habits customs &c. I could not lern. [Camped apparently between Irrigon and Boardman, Morrow County, Oregon, in the vicinity of Blalock Island.]

[WHITEHOUSE] We now begin to find the Indians very numerous, and their Camps lay near each other along the Shores on both sides of the River.

October 20, 1805
[CLARK] our curiosity induced us to examine the methot those nativs practicd in diposeing the dead, the Vau[l]t was made by broad poads and pieces of Canoes leaning on a ridge pole which was Suported by 2 forks Set in the ground Six feet in hight in an easterly and westerly direction and about 60 feet in length, and 12 feet wide, in it I observed great numbers of humane bones of every description perticularly in a pile near the Center of the vault, on the East End 21 Scul bomes forming a circle on Mats; in the Westerley part of the *Vault* appeared to be appropriated for those of more resent death, as many of the bodies of the deceased *raped* up in leather robes lay on board covered with mats, &c   we observed, independant of the canoes which Served as a Covering, fishing nets of various kinds, Baskets of different Sizes, wooden boles, robes Skins, trenchers, and various Kind of trinkets, in and Suspended on the ends of the pieces

forming the vault; we also Saw the Skeletons of Several Horses at the vault & great number of bones about it, which Convinced me that those animals were Sacrefised as well as the above articles to the Deceased. [Camped in the vicinity of Roosevelt, Klickitat County, Washington.]

October 21, 1805

[CLARK] Those people recived us with great kindness, and examined us with much attention, their employments custom Dress and appearance Similar to those above; Speak the Same language, here we Saw two Scarlet and a blue cloth blanket, also a Salors Jacket[15] . . . we halted a fiew minits to examine the rapid before we entered it which was our constant Custom, and at all that was verry dangerous put out all who could not Swim to walk around, after passing this rapid we proceeded on . . . after Passing this dificult rapid to the mouth of a Small river[16] on the Larboard Side 40 yards wide descharges but little water at this time, and appears to take its Sourse in the Open plains to the S. E. . . . imediately above & below this little river comences a rapid which is crouded with large rocks in every direction . . . from this rapid the Conocil mountain is *S. W.* which the Indians inform me is not far to the left of the great falls; this I call the *Timm* or falls mountain[17] it is high and the top is covered with Snow) . . . one of our party J. Collins presented us with Some verry good *beer* made of the *Pa-shi-co-quar-mash* bread, which bread is the remains of what was laid in as Stores of Provisions, at the first flat heads or Cho-pun-nish Nation at the head of the *Kosskoske* river which by being frequently wet molded & Sowered &c.[18] [Camped in the vicinity of John Day Dam, Klickitat County, Washington.]

15. Clark saw the Euro-American clothing at a Methow Indian village, between Roosevelt and Blalock, Klickitat County. The Methows are a Salishan-speaking people, unlike the Sahaptian speakers upstream.

16. The John Day River, serving as the boundary between Gilliam and Sherman Counties, Oregon, was named by the captains for party member Lepage.

17. Mount Hood, Hood River County, Oregon, first viewed on October 18.

18. Collins made beer from moldy camas roots, which the party probably obtained from the Nez Perces.

October 22, 1805

[CLARK] we discovered the enterence of a large river on the Lard. Side which appeared to Come from the S. E.—[19] we landed at Some distance above the mouth of this river and Capt. Lewis and my Self Set out to view this river above its mouth, as our rout was intersepted by a deep narrow Chanel which runs out of this river into the Columbia a little below the place we landed, leaving a high dry rich Island[20] of about 400 yards wide and 800 yards long   here we Seperated, I proceeded on to the river and Struck it at the foot of a verry Considerable rapid, here I beheld an emence body of water Compressd in a narrow Chanel of about 200 yds in width, fomeing over rocks maney of which presented their tops above the water, when at this place Capt. Lewis joined me haveing delayed on the way to examine a root[21] of which the nativs[22] had been digging great quantities in the bottoms of this River . . . we landed and walked down accompanied by an old man to view the falls,[23] and the best rout for to make a portage which we Soon discovered was much nearest on the Stard. Side . . . at the lower part of those rapids we arrived at 5 Large Lodges of nativs drying and prepareing fish for market, they gave us Philburts, and berries to eate, we returned droped down to the head of the rapids and took every article except the Canoes across the portag where I had formed a camp on ellegable Situation for the protection of our Stores from Thieft, which we were more fearfull of, than their arrows. we despatched two men to examine the river on the opposit Side, and reported that the Canoes could be taken down a narrow Chanel on the opposit Side after a Short portage at the head of the falls, at which place the Indians take over their Canoes. Indians assisted us over the portage with our heavy articles on their horses . . . at and about their Lodges I observe great numbers of Stacks of pounded Salmon neetly preserved in the fol-

19. Deschutes River, the boundary between Wasco and Sherman Counties, Oregon. The captains settled on the name "Towanahiooks," a Chinookan term for the Deschutes, on the return trip.

20. Miller Island.

21. Wapato, a staple of Columbia River natives.

22. Probably the Tenino Indians.

23. Celilo Falls, at Wishram, Klickitat County, Washington, and Celilo, Wasco County, Oregon.

lowing maner, i e after Suffiently Dried it is pounded between two Stones fine, and put into a speces of basket neetly made of grass and rushes of better than two feet long and one foot Diamiter, which basket is lined with the Skin of Salmon Stretched and dried for the purpose, in theis it is pressed down as hard as is possible, when full they Secure the open part with the fish Skins across which they fasten tho' the loops of the basket that part very Securely, and then on a Dry Situation they Set those baskets the Corded part up, their common Custom is to Set 7 as close as they can Stand and 5 on the top of them, and secure them with mats which is raped around them and made fast with cords and Covered also with mats, those 12 baskets of from 90 to 100 w. each form a Stack.   thus preserved those fish may be kept Sound and Sweet Several years, as those people inform me, Great quantities as they inform us are Sold to the whites people who visit the mouth of this river as well as to the nativs below. [Camped near Wishram, Klickitat County, Washington, where the party remained until October 24.]

October 23, 1805
[CLARK] I with the greater part of the men Crossed in the Canoes to opposit Side above the falls and hauled them across the portage of 457 yards which is on the Lard. Side and certainly the best side to pass the canoes   I then decended through a narrow chanel of about 150 yards wide forming a kind of half circle in it course of a mile to a pitch of 8 feet in which the chanel is divided by 2 large rocks   at this place we were obliged to let the Canoes down by Strong ropes of Elk Skin which we had for the purpose, one Canoe in passing this place got loose by the Cords breaking, and was cought by the Indians below. I accomplished this necessary business and landed Safe with all the Canoes at our Camp below the falls by 3 oClock P. M. nearly covered with flees which were So thick amongst the Straw and fish Skins at the upper part of the portage at which place the nativs had been Camped not long Since; that every man of the party was obliged to Strip naked dureing the time of takeing over the canoes, that they might have an oppertunity of brushing the flees of[f] their legs and bodies— Great numbers of *Sea Otters*[24] in the river below the falls, I Shot

24. Sea otters never leave salt water, so Clark probably saw harbor seals.

one in the narrow chanel to day which I could not get. Great numbers of
Indians visit us both from above and below — one of the old Chiefs who
had accompanied us from the head of the river, informed us that he herd
the Indians Say that the nation below intended to kill us, we examined all
the arms &c. complete the amunition to 100 rounds. The nativs leave us
earlyer this evening than usial, which gives a Shadow of Confirmation to
the information of our Old Chief, as we are at all times & places on our
guard, are under no greater apprehention than is common.   we purchased 8 Small fat dogs for the party to eate   the nativs not being fond of
Selling their good fish, compells us to make use of Dog meat for food, the
flesh of which the most of the party have become fond of fromthe habits
of useing it for Some time past . . . I observed on the beach near the Indian Lodges two Canoes butifull of different Shape & Size to what we had
Seen above wide in the midde and tapering to each end, on the bow
curious figures were Cut in the wood &c.   Capt. Lewis went up to the
Lodges to See those Canoes and exchanged our Smallest Canoe for one of
them by giveing a Hatchet & few trinkets to the owner who informed that
he purchased it of a white man below for a horse, these Canoes are neeter
made than any I have ever Seen and Calculated to ride the waves, and
carry emence burthens, they are dug thin and are suported by cross pieces
of about 1 inch diamuter tied with Strong bark thro' holes in the Sides.
our two old Chiefs appeared verry uneasy this evening. [Remained near
Wishram.]

October 24, 1805
[CLARK] our two old chiefs expressed a desire to return to their band
from this place, Saying "that they Could be of no further Service to us, as
their nation extended no further down the river than those falls, and as
the nation below had expressed hostile intentions against us, would Certainly kill them; perticularly as They had been at war with each other;" we
requested them to Stay with us *two* nights longer, and we would See the
nation below and make a peace between them, they replied they "were
anxious to return and See our horses"   we insisted on their Staying with
us two nights longer to which they agreed; our views were to detain those
Chiefs with us untill we Should pass the next falls, which we were told was
verry bad, and at no great distance below, that they might inform us of
any designs of the nativs, and if possible to bring about a peace between

them and the tribes below . . . at this place the water of this great river is
compressed into a Chanel between two rocks not exceeding *forty five*
yards wide and continues for a ¼ of a mile when it again widens to 200
yards and continues this width for about 2 miles when it is again intersepted by rocks. This obstruction in the river accounts for the water in
high floods riseing to Such a hite at the last falls. The whole of the Current of this great river must at all Stages pass thro' this narrow chanel of
45 yards wide.   as the portage of our canoes over this high rock would be
impossible with our Strength, and the only danger in passing thro those
narrows was the whorls and Swills arriseing from the Compression of the
water, and which I thought (as also our principal watermen Peter Crusat)
by good Stearing we could pass down Safe, accordingly I deturmined to
pass through this place notwithstanding the horrid appearance of this agitated gut Swelling, boiling & whorling in every direction (which from
the top of the rock did not appear as bad as when I was in it;[)] however
we passed Saf to the astonishment of all the Inds: of the last Lodges who
viewed us from the top of the rock . . . The principal Chief from the nation below with Several of his men visited us, and afforded a favourable
oppertunity of bringing about a Piece and good understanding between
this chief and his people and the two Chiefs who accompanied us which
we have the Satisfaction to Say we have accomplished, as we have every
reason to believe and that those two bands or nations are and will be on
the most friendly terms with each other.   gave this Great Chief a Medal
and Some other articles, of which he was much pleased, Peter Crusat
played on the *violin* and the men danced which delighted the nativs, who
Shew every civility towards us.   we Smoked with those people untill late
at night, when every one retired to rest.[25] [Camped in the vicinity of
Horsethief Lake State Park, Klickitat County, Washington.]

[ORDWAY] we camped little above at an Indian village which was made
half under the surface of the ground and the upper part well formed and

25. The party arrived at the Short, or Little, Narrows of the Columbia, which with the
Long Narrows make up The Dalles of the Columbia River, at the town of The Dalles,
Wasco County, Oregon. Wishram-Wasco Chinookans resided at The Dalles, but the area
was a great meeting and marketplace for and dividing line between Sahaptian speakers to
the east and the Chinookan speakers to the west.

covred with white ceeder bark.   they are verry comfortable houses.
we bought a number of fat dogs, crambries and white cakes of root
bread.

[WHITEHOUSE] We saw also a Child among them, which was a mix'd
breed, between a White Man & Indian Women. The fairness of its Skin,
& rosey colour, convinced us that it must have been the case, and we have
no doubt, but that white Men trade among them.

October 25, 1805

[CLARK] Capt Lewis and my Self walked down to See the place the Indians pointed out as the worst place in passing through the gut,[26] which we
found difficuelt of passing without great danger, but as the portage was
impractiable with our large Canoes, we Concluded to Make a portage of
our most valuable articles and run the canoes thro   accordingly on our
return divided the party Some to take over the Canoes, and others to take
our Stores across a portage of a mile to a place on the Chanel below this
bad whorl & Suck, with Some others I had fixed on the Chanel with
roapes to throw out to any who Should unfortunately meet with diffi-
cuelty in passing through; great number of Indians viewing us from the
high rocks under which we had to pass, the 3 firt Canoes passed thro very
well, the 4th nearly filled with water, the last passed through by takeing in
a little water, thus Safely below what I conceved to be the worst part of this
Chanel, felt my Self extreamly gratified and pleased. [Camped at the
mouth of Mill Creek, The Dalles, Wasco County, Oregon, at a spot the
captains named "Fort Camp" or "Fort Rock Camp" and where they remained until October 28.]

October 26, 1805

[WHITEHOUSE] Capt. Lewis compared the languages of these with those
which he had taken down all the way this Side of the mountains and find
them to be all one nation but differ a little in their languages, caused by
the different tribes of them Scatered Such a long distance from each

26. Long Narrows of the Columbia at The Dalles.

other.[27]   all the way thick along the kimoo-e-nem[28] & Columbia Rivers
and to the head of all the Rivers runing in to it. we think the flat head nation[29] to be ten Thousand Strong in all. [Remained at The Dalles.]

October 27, 1805
[CLARK] Some words with Shabono our interpreter about his duty. Sent
out Several hunters who brought in *four Deer*, one *Grouse* & a *Squirel*.
The two Chiefs & party was joined by Seven others from below in two canoes, we gave them to eate & Smoke   Several of those from below returned down the river in a bad humer, haveing got into this pet by being
prevented doeing as they wished with our articles which was then exposed to dry— we took a Vocabelary of the Languages of those two
chiefs which are verry different notwithstanding they are Situated within
Six miles of each other, Those at the *great falls*[30] Call themselves *E-nee-
shur*[31] and are understood on the river above: Those at the Great Narrows[32] Call themselves *E-che-lute*[33] and is understood below, maney
words of those people are the Same, and Common to all the *flat head*
Bands which we have passed on the river, all have the *clucking* tone
anexed which is prodomonate above.   all the Bands flatten the heads of
the female Children, and maney of the male children also. [Remained at
The Dalles.]

[GASS] We suppose them to be a band of the Flathead nation,[34] as all their
heads are compressed into the same form . . . This singular and deform-
ing operation is performed in infancy in the following manner. A piece of
board is placed against the back of the head extending from the shoulders

27. See Clark's entry for the next day for language explanations.

28. Snake River.

29. All the natives west of the Rockies.

30. Celilo Falls.

31. Probably Teninos, whom the party encountered on October 22. The Teninos spoke
a Sahaptian language like most tribes from the Rocky Mountains to The Dalles.

32. The Dalles.

33. Wishram-Wascos, who were Chinookan speakers like those toward the coast.

34. By "Flathead" Clark and Gass here meant all those tribes who practiced skull deformation, rather than specifically the Flathead, or Salish, Indians.

some distance above it; another shorter piece extends from the eye brows to the top of the first, and they are then bound together with thongs or cords made of skins, so as to press back the forehead, make the head rise at the top, and force it out above the ears.

October 28, 1805

[CLARK] The wind which is the cause of our delay, does not retard the motions of those people at all, as their canoes are calculated to ride the highest waves, they are built of white cedar or Pine verry light wide in the middle and tapers at each end, with aperns [aprons], and heads of animals carved on the bow, which is generally raised. Those people make great use of Canoes, both for transpotation and fishing, they also use of bowls & baskets made of Grass & Splits to hold water and boil their fish & meat. Maney of the nativs of the last Village Came down Set and Smoke with us, wind blew hard accompanied with rain all the evening, our Situation not a verry good one for an encampment, but Such as it is we are obliged to put up with, the harbor is a Safe one, we encamped on the Sand wet and disagreeable. [Camped in the vicinity of Crates Point, above Rowena, Wasco County, Oregon.]

October 29, 1805

[CLARK] The Chief then directed his wife to hand him his medison bag which he opened and Showed us 14 fingers which he Said was the fingers of his enemies which he had taken in war, and pointed to S. E. from which direction I concluded they were Snake Indians;[35] this is the first Instance I ever knew of the Indians takeing any other trofea of their exploits off the dead bodies of their Enimies except the Scalp— The Chief painted those fingers with Several other articles which was in his bag red and Securely put them back, haveing first mad a Short harrang which I Suppose was bragging of what he had done in war. [Camped a short distance above the mouth of Little White Salmon River, Skamania County, Washington.]

35. These "Snake Indians" were probably Northern Paiute Indians, as are other references to Snake Indians to the south.

October 30, 1805
[CLARK] this day we Saw Some fiew of the large Buzzard[36]   Capt. Lewis
Shot at one, those Buzzards are much larger than any other of ther Spece
or the largest Eagle white under part of their wings &c.   The bottoms
above the mouth of this little river is rich covered with grass & firn & is
about ¾ of a mile wide rich and rises gradually, below the river (which is
60 yards wide above its mouth) the Countery rises with Steep assent.   we
call this little river New Timbered river[37] from a Speces of Ash[38] which
grows on its banks of a verry large and different from any we had before
Seen, and a timber resembling the beech[39] in bark but different in its leaf
which is Smaller and the tree smaller. [Camped in Skamania County,
Washington, nearly opposite Cascade Locks, Hood River County, Oregon, and remained here until November 1.]

October 31, 1805
[CLARK] Those vaults are all nearly the Same Sise and form 8 feet Square,
5 feet high, Sloped a little So as to convey off the rain made of Pine or Cedar boards Closely Connected & Scurely Covered with wide boards, with
a Dore left in The East Side which is partially Stoped with wide boards curiously engraved. In Several of those vaults the dead bodies wre raped up
verry Securely in Skins tied around with cords of grass & bark, laid on a
mat, all east & west and Some of those vaults had as maney as 4 bodies
laying on the Side of each other.   the other Vaults Containing bones only,
Some contained bones for the debth of 4 feet.   on the tops and on poles
attached to those vaults hung Brass kittles & frying pans pearced thro
their bottoms, baskets, bowls of wood, Sea Shels, Skins, bits of Cloth,
Hair, bags of Trinkets & Small peices of bone &c and independant of the
curious ingraveing and Paintings on the boards which formed the vaults
I observed Several wooden Images, cut in the figure of men and Set up on
the Sides of the vaults all round. Some of those So old and worn by time,
that they were nearly out of Shape, I also observed the remains of Vaults

36. California condor.
37. Wind River, Skamania County, Washington.
38. Oregon ash.
39. Red alder.

rotted entirely into the ground and covered with moss. This must bee the burrying place for maney ages for the inhabitants of those rapids, the vaults are of the most lasting timber Pine & Cedar— I cannot Say certainly that those nativs worship those wooden idols as I have every reason to believe they do not; as they are Set up in the most conspicious parts of their houses, and treated more like orniments than objects of aderation [40] . . . a remarkable high detached rock Stands in a bottom on the Stard Side near the lower point of this Island on the Stard. Side about 800 feet high and 400 paces around, we call the *Beaten rock*.[41] a Brook [42] falls into the narrow Chanel which forms the Strawberry Island,[43] which at this time has no running water, but has every appearance of dischargein emence torrents . . .

This Great Shute [44] or falls is about ½ a mile with the water of this great river Compressed within the Space of 150 paces in which there is great numbers of both large and Small rocks, water passing with great velocity forming & boiling in a most horriable manner, with a fall of about 20 feet, below it widens to about 200 paces and current gentle for a Short distance.   a Short distance above is three Small rockey Islands, and at the head of those falls, three Small rockey Islands are Situated Crosswise the river, Several rocks above in the river & 4 large rocks in the head of the Shute; those obstructions together with the high Stones which are continually brakeing loose from the mountain on the Stard Side and roleing down into the Shute aded to those which brake loose from those Islands above and lodge in the Shute, must be the Cause of the rivers daming up to Such a distance above, where it Shows Such evidant marks of the Common current of the river being much lower than at the present day. [Remained at the camp of October 30.]

40. Clark observed the vaults in Skamania County, between Bridge of the Gods and Bradford Island.
41. Beacon Rock, Skamania County.
42. Probably Hamilton Creek, Skamania County.
43. Hamilton Island, Skamania County.
44. The Cascades of the Columbia River, now lost beneath the waters impounded by Bonneville Dam.

[GASS] We unloaded our canoes and took them past the rapids, some part of the way by water, and some over rocks 8 or 10 feet high. It was the most fatiguing business we have been engaged in for a long time, and we got but two over all day, the distance about a mile, and the fall of the water about 25 feet in that distance.

November 1, 1805
[CLARK] The Indians who arrived last evining took their Canoes on ther Sholders and Carried them below the Great Shute, we Set about takeing our Small Canoe and all the baggage by land 940 yards of bad Slippery and rockey way   The Indians we discoverd took ther loading the whole length of the portage 2½ miles, to avoid a Second Shute which appears verry bad to pass, and thro' which they passed with their empty canoes . . .

we got all our baggage over the Portage of 940 yards, after which we got the 4 large Canoes over by Slipping them over the rocks on poles placed across from one rock to another, and at Some places along partial Streams of the river.   in passing those canoes over the rocks &c. three of them re-cived injuries which obliged us to delay to have them repared . . . I cannot lern certainly as to the traffick those Inds. carry on below, if white people or the indians who trade with the Whites who are either Settled or visit the mouth of this river. I believe mostly with the latter as their knowledge of the white people appears to be verry imperfect, and the articles which they appear to trade mostly i e' Pounded fish, Beargrass, and roots; can-not be an object of comerce with furin merchants — however they git in return for those articles Blue and white *beeds* copper Tea Kittles, brass arm bands, some Scarlet and blue robes and a fiew articles of old clothes, they prefer beeds to any thing and will part with the last mouthfull or ar-ticles of clothing they have for a fiew of those beeds, those beeds the trafick with Indians Still higher up this river for roabs, Skins, cha-pel-el bread,[45] beargrass &c. who in their turn trafick with those under the rockey mountains for Beargrass, *Pashico* roots & robes &c.

The nativs of the waters of the Columbia appear helthy, Some have tumers on different parts of their bodies, and Sore and weak Eyes are

45. Chinookan word for cous, an essential foodstuff of Columbia River Indians.

common, maney have lost their Sight entirely great numbers with one eye out and frequently the other verry weak; This misfortune I must again asscribe to the water &c. They have bad teeth, which is not common with indians, maney have worn their teeth down and Some quite into their gums, this I cannot Satisfactorily account for it, do ascribe it in some measure to their method of eateing, their food, roots pertiularly, which they make use of as they are taken out of the earth frequently nearly covered with Sand, I have not Seen any of their long roots offered for Sale clear of Sand. They are rether below the Common Size high cheeks womin Small and homely, and have Swelled legs and thighs, and their knees remarkably large which I ascribe to the method in which they Sit on their hams—go nearly necked wareing only a piece of leather tied about their breast which falls down nearly as low as the waste, a Small roabe about 3 feet Square, and a piece of leather tied about their breach, They have all flat heads in this quarter <both men and women,>   They are tirty [dirty] in the extream, both in their person and cooking, ware their hare loose hanging in every direction. They asc high prices for what they Sell and Say that the white people below give great prices for every thing &c. The noses are all pierced and when they are dressed they have a long tapered piece of white shell or wampum put through the nose, Those Shells are about 2 inches in length. I observed in maney of the villeages which I have passed, the heads of the female children in the press for the purpose of compressing their heads in their infancy into a certain form, between two boards. [Camped near Fort Rains and North Bonneville, Skamania County, Washington.]

November 3, 1805

[CLARK] I arrived at the enterance of a river[46] which appeared to Scatter over a Sand bar, the bottom of which I could See quite across and did not appear to be 4 Inches deep in any part; I attempted to wade this Stream and to my astonishment found the bottom a quick Sand, and impassable—   I called to the Canoes to put to Shore, I got into the Canoe and landed below the mouth, & Capt Lewis and my Self walked up this river

46. Sandy River, joining the Columbia in Multnomah County, Oregon, approximately 120 miles from the ocean.

about 1½ miles to examine this river which we found to be a verry Considerable Stream Dischargeing its waters through 2 Chanels which forms an Island of about 3 miles in length on the river and 1½ miles wide, composed of Corse Sand which is thrown out of this quick Sand river Compressing the waters of the Columbia and throwing the whole Current of its waters against its Northern banks, within a Chanel of ½ a mile wide, Several Small Islands 1 mile up this river, This Stream has much the appearance of the *River Platt* . . . below quick Sand River the Countrey is low rich and thickly timbered on each Side of the river, the Islands open & Some ponds river wide and emence numbers of fowls flying in every direction Such as Swan,[47] geese, Brants, Cranes,[48] Stalks[49] white guls, comerants[50] & plevers[51] &c.   also great numbers of Sea Otter[52] in the river. [Camped on either Government or McGuire Island, the party's "Diamond Island," opposite Portland, Multnomah County, Oregon.]

[WHITEHOUSE] agreeable to all calculations it cannot be more than two hundred miles from this to the ocean.

November 4, 1805
[CLARK] This village contains about 200 men of the *Skil-loot*[53] nation   I counted 52 canoes on the bank in front of this village maney of them verry large and raised in bow.   we recognised the man who over took us last night, he invited us to a lodge in which he had Some part and gave us a roundish roots about the Size of a Small Irish potato which they roasted in the embers until they became Soft, This root they call *Wap-pa-to* which the *Bulb* of the *Chinese* cultivate in great quantities called the *Sa-git ti folia* or common arrow head — it has an agreeable taste and answers verry

47. Either trumpeter or tundra swans.
48. Sandhill cranes.
49. Wood storks.
50. Double-crested cormorants.
51. Plovers.
52. Actually, harbor seals.
53. Probably a Chinookan phrase rather than a tribal name. The natives of this area, modern Portland, Multnomah County, Oregon, were Upper Chinookan Watlalas.

well in place of bread. we purchased about 4 bushels of this root and divided it to our party,

at 7 miles below this village passed the upper point of a large Island [54] nearest the Lard Side, a Small Prarie in which there is a pond opposit on the Stard. here I landed and walked on Shore, about 3 miles a fine open Prarie for about 1 mile, back of which the countrey rises gradually and wood land comencies Such as white oake, pine of different kinds, wild crabs with the taste and flavour of the common crab and Several Species of undergroth of which I am not acquainted, a few Cottonwood trees & the Ash [55] of this countrey grow Scattered on the river bank, Saw Some Elk and Deer Sign and joined Capt. Lewis at a place he had landed with the party for Diner. Soon after Several Canoes of Indians from the village above came down dressed for the purpose as I Supposed of Paying us a friendly visit, they had Scarlet & blue blankets Salors jackets, overalls, Shirts and Hats independant of their Usial dress; the most of them had either war axes Spears or Bows Sprung with quivers of arrows, Muskets or pistols, and tin flasks to hold their powder; Those fellows we found assumeing and disagreeable, however we Smoked with them and treated them with every attention & friendship.

dureing the time we were at dinner those fellows Stold my pipe Tomahawk which They were Smoking with, I imediately Serched every man and the canoes, but Could find nothing of my Tomahawk, while Serching for the Tomahawk one of those Scoundals Stole a Cappoe [56] of one of our interpreters, which was found Stufed under the root of a treer, near the place they Sat, we became much displeased with those fellows, which they discovered and moved off on their return home to their village, except 2 canoes which had passed on down . . . we proceeded on untill one hour after dark with a view to get clear of the nativs who was constantly about us, and troublesom, finding that we could not get Shut of those people for one night, we landed and Encamped on the Stard. Side   Soon after 2 canoes Came to us loaded with Indians, we purchased a fiew roots of them. [Camped apparently near the entrance of Salmon Creek, Clark County, Washington.]

54. Either Hayden or Tomahawk Island.
55. Bigleaf maple.
56. Capote, a hooded blanket coat.

[ORDWAY] towards evening we met several Indians in a handsom canoe which had an Immage on the bow. one of the Indians could talk & Speak Some words English Such as curseing and blackguard.

November 5, 1805
[CLARK] Rained all the after part of last night, rain continues this morning, I [s]lept but verry little last night for the noise Kept dureing the whole of the night by the Swans, Geese, white & Grey Brant Ducks &c. . . . This is the first night which we have been entirely clear of Indians Since our arrival on the waters of the Columbia River. [Camped perhaps near Prescott, Columbia County, Oregon.]

November 7, 1805
[CLARK] Those people call themselves *War-ci-â-cum*[57] and Speake a language different from the nativs above with whome they trade for the *Wapato* roots of which they make great use of as food. their houses differently built, raised entirely above ground eaves about 5 feet from the ground Supported and covered in the same way of those above, dores about the Same size but in the Side of the house in one Corner, one fire place and that near the opposit end; around which they have their beads raised about 4 feet from the flore which is of earth, under their beads they Store away baskets of dried fish Berries & *wappato*, over the fire they hang the flesh as they take them and which they do not make immediate use. Their Canoes are of the Same form of those above. The Dress of the men differ verry little from those above, The womin altogether different, their robes are Smaller only Covering their Sholders & falling down to near the hip— and Sometimes when it is Cold a piec of fur curiously plated and connected So as to meet around the body from the arms to the hips . . .
    Great joy in camp we are in *View* of the *Ocian*, this great Pacific Octean which we been So long anxious to See. and the roreing or noise made by the waves brakeing on the rockey Shores (as I Suppose) may be

57. A Chinookan group who lived in the area of Wahkiakum County. Although the Wahkiakums spoke a Chinookan language, it is considered a distinctive type between Upper Chinook above and Lower Chinook toward the coast. The Wahkiakums, along with neighboring Cathlamets, also differed from their Chinookan affiliates in house styles, canoe types, and dress.

heard distictly.[58] [Camped opposite Pillar Rock between Bookfield and Dahlia, Wahkikum County, Washington.]

[CLARK] *Ocian in view*! O! the joy.[59]

November 8, 1805
[CLARK] we are all wet and disagreeable, as we have been for Several days past, and our present Situation a verry disagreeable one in as much; as we have not leavel land Sufficient for an encampment and for our baggage to lie Cleare of the tide, the High hills jutting in So Close and Steep that we cannot retreat back, and the water of the river too Salt to be used, added to this the waves are increasing to Such a hight that we cannot move from this place, in this Situation we are compelled to form our Camp between the hite of the Ebb and flood tides, and rase our baggage on logs — We are not certain as yet if the whites people who trade with those people or from whome they precure ther goods are Stationary at the mouth, or visit this quarter at Stated times for the purpose of trafick &c. I believe the latter to be the most probable conjucture — The Seas roled and tossed the Canoes in Such a manner this evening that Several of our party were Sea Sick.[60] [Camped near the Wahkiakum-Pacific county line, Washington, where the party remained until November 10.]

November 9, 1805
[CLARK] our camp entirely under water dureing the hight of the *tide*, every man as wet as water could make them all the last night and to day all day as the rain Continued all day . . . notwithstanding the disagreeable Situation of our party all wet and Cold (and one which they have experienced for Several days past) they are chearfull and anxious to See further into the Ocian, The water of the river being too Salt to use we are obliged to make use of rain water — Some of the party not accustomed to Salt

58. Clark was premature — the party was actually looking at the Columbia estuary, not the ocean.

59. The captain's famous phrase is found in a separate list of the party's courses and distances on the Columbia River.

60. In a separate entry Clark named Reubin Field, Weiser, McNeal, and Sacagawea among the seasick.

water has made too free a use of it on them it acts as a pergitive. at this dismal point we must Spend another night as the wind & waves are too high to proceed. [Remained at the camp of November 8.]

November 11, 1805

[CLARK] we are all wet as usial and our Situation is truly a disagreeable one; the great quantites of rain which has loosened the Stones on the hill Sides, and the Small Stones fall down upon us, our canoes at one place at the mercy of the waves, our baggage in another and our Selves and party Scattered on floating logs and Such dry Spots as can be found on the hill Sides, and Crivices of the rocks. we purchased of the Indians 13 red charr[61] which we found to be an excellent fish we have Seen those Indians above and are of a nation who reside above and on the opposit Side who call themselves <*Calt-har-ma*>[62]   they are badly clad & illy made, Small and Speak a language much resembling the last nation, one of those men had on a Salors Jacket and Pantiloons and made Signs that he got those Clothes from the white people who lived below the point &c. those people left us and Crossed the river (which is about 5 miles wide at this place) through the highest waves I ever Saw a Small vestles ride. Those Indians are Certainly the best Canoe navigaters I ever Saw. rained all day. [Camped at the spot the party had moved to on November 10 near Meglar, Pacific County, Washington, where the Corps remained until November 12.]

[GASS] The morning was wet and the wind still blowing, so that we could not proceed; we therefore built large fires and made our situation as comfortable as possible, but still bad enough, as we have no tents, or covering to defend us, except our blankets and some mats we got from the Indians, which we put on poles to keep off the rain.

November 12, 1805

[CLARK] It would be distressing to See our Situation, all wet and Colde our bedding also wet, (and the robes of the party which Compose half the

61. Sockeye salmon.
62. The Cathlamets lived in the area of Clatsop County, Oregon, opposite the closely related Wahkiakums.

bedding is rotten and we are not in a Situation to supply their places) in a wet bottom Scercely large enough to contain us, our baggage half a mile from us and Canoes at the mercy of the waves, altho Secured as well as possible, Sunk with emence parcels of Stone to wate them down to prevent their dashing to pieces against the rocks; one got loose last night and was left on a rock a Short distance below, without rciving more dammage than a Split in her bottom— Fortunately for us our men are healthy. [Moved camp a short distance downriver from the previous camp.]

November 14, 1805
[CLARK] Capt Lewis concluded to proceed on by land & find if possible the white people the Indians Say is below and examine if a Bay is Situated near the mouth of this river as laid down by Vancouver in which we expect, if there is white traders to find them &c.[63] at 3 oClock he Set out with 4 men Drewyer Jos. & Reu. Fields & R. Frasure, in one of our large canoes and 5 men to Set them around the point on the Sand beech. this canoe returned nearly filled with water at Dark which it receved by the waves dashing into it on its return, haveing landed Capt. Lewis & his party Safe on the Sand beech. The rain Continues all day all wet. The rain &c. which has continued without a longer intermition than 2 hours at a time for ten days past has distroyd. the robes and rotted nearly one half of the fiew Clothes the party has, perticularley the leather Clothes, fortunately for us we have no very Cold weather as yet and if we have Cold weather before we Can kill & Dress Skins for Clothing the bulk of the party will Suffer verry much. [Lewis's camp is unknown. Clark and the main party remained at the camp of November 12.]

63. Lewis was apparently seeking Baker Bay as noted on his copies of maps from George Vancouver's voyage of 1792.

CHAPTER 9

Pacific Coast Winter

November 15, 1805 – March 22, 1806

November 15, 1805

[CLARK] About 3 oClock the wind luled, and the river became calm, I had the canoes loaded in great haste and Set Out, from this dismal nitich where we have been confined for 6 days passed, without the possibility of proceeding on, returning to a better Situation, or get out to hunt, Scerce of Provisions, and torents of rain poreing on us all the time. [Camped west of McGown, Pacific County, Washington, on the east side of Baker Bay. The party remained here until November 25 and gave it the name "Station Camp."]

November 16, 1805

[GASS] We are now at the end of our voyage, which has been completely accomplished according to the intention of the expedition, the object of which was to discover a passage by the way of the Missouri and Columbia rivers to the Pacific ocean; notwithstanding the difficulties, privations and dangers, which we had to encounter, endure and surmount.[1] [Apparently remained at Station Camp, although Clark indicates a short move.]

[WHITEHOUSE] We are now in plain view of the *Pacific Ocean*. the waves rolling, & the surf roaring very loud . . . We are now of opinion that we cannot go any further with our Canoes, & think that we are at an end of our Voyage to the Pacific Ocean, and as soon as discoveries necessary are

---

1. The passage from Gass's published journal may have been written by his editor, David McKeehan, as a transition from one chapter to the next. It may have been Gass's sentiments as well, as it seems to be those of Whitehouse.

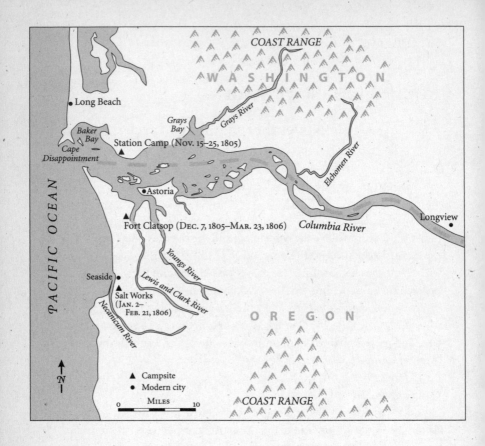

The Expedition's Route, November 15–March 22, 1806

made, that we shall return a short distance up the River & provide our Selves with Winter Quarters.

November 17, 1805

[CLARK] At half past 1 oClock Capt Lewis returned haveing travesed Haleys Bay[2] to Cape Disapointment and the *Sea* Coast to the North for Some distance. Several *Chinnook* Indians followed Capt L—   and a Canoe came up with roots mats &c. to Sell. those Chinnooks made us a present of a rute[3] boiled much resembling the common liquorice in taste and Size: [*ML?: th[e]y call cul-wha-mo*]   in return for this root we gave more than double the value to Satisfy their craveing dispostn. It is a bad practice to receive a present from those Indians as they are never Satisfied for what they re[ce]ive in return if ten time the value of the articles they gave. This *Chin nook* Nation is about 400 Souls inhabid the Countrey on the Small rivrs which run into the bay below us and on the Ponds to the N W of us, live principally on fish and roots, they are well armed with fusees and Sometimes kill Elk Deer and fowl . . . I directed all the men who wished to See more of the main *Ocian* to prepare themselves to Set out with me early on tomorrow morning.[4] The principal Chief[5] of the Chinnooks & his familey came up to See us this evening. [Remained at Station Camp.]

November 19, 1805

[CLARK] The Deer[6] of this Coast differ materially from our Common deer in a much as they are much darker deeper bodied Shorter ledged horns equally branched from the beem the top of the tail black from the rute to the end   Eyes larger and do not lope but jump. [Clark camped in the area of Long Beach, Pacific County, Washington. Lewis and the main party remained at Station Camp.]

2. Baker Bay, Pacific County, Washington.

3. Seashore lupine.

4. The following persons accompanied Clark: Pryor, Ordway, Joseph and Reubin Field, Shannon, Colter, Bratton, Weiser, Charbonneau, Labiche, and York.

5. Evidently the Chinook Chief Comcomly.

6. Columbian black-tailed deer.

November 20, 1805

[CLARK] found maney of the *Chin nooks* with Capt. Lewis of whome there was 2 Cheifs *Com com mo ly* & *Chil-lar-la-wil*[7] to whome we gave Medals and to one a flag. one of the Indians had on a roab made of 2 Sea Otter Skins the fur of them were more butifull than any fur I had ever Seen both Capt. Lewis & my Self endeavored to purchase the *roab* with differant articles   at length we precured it for a belt of blue beeds which the Squar—wife of our interpreter Shabono wore around her waste. [Clark returned to the main party at Station Camp.]

November 21, 1805

[CLARK] Lattitude of this place is *46° 19′ 11¹/₁₀″* North.[8]

[CLARK] An old woman[9] & wife to a Cheif of the *Chinnooks* came and made a Camp near ours   She brought with her 6 young Squars I believe for the purpose of gratifying the passions of the men of our party and receving for those indulgiences Such Small as She (the old woman) thought proper to accept of, Those people appear to view Sensuality as a Necessary evel, and do not appear to abhor it as a Crime in the unmarried State— The young females are fond of the attention of our men and appear to meet the sincere approbation of their friends and connections, for thus obtaining their favours; the womin of the Chinnook Nation have handsom faces low and badly made with large legs & thighs which are generally Swelled from a Stopage of the circulation in the feet (which are Small) by maney Strands of Beeds or curious Strings which are drawn tight around the leg above the anckle, their legs are also picked with different figures, I Saw on the left arm of a Squar the following letters *J. Bowmon*, all those are Considered by the natives of this quarter as handsom deckerations, and a woman without those deckorations is Considered as among the lower Class. [Remained at Station Camp.]

7. Apparently Shelathwell.

8. Clark gave Station Camp's latitude in a draft entry; the approximate latitude is 46° 15′ 42″ N.

9. Perhaps the wife of Delashelwilt.

November 22, 1805

[CLARK] O! how horriable is the day   waves brakeing with great violence against the Shore throwing the Water into our Camp &c.   all wet and Confind to our Shelters. [Remained at Station Camp.]

November 23, 1805

[CLARK] Capt Lewis Branded a tree with his name Date &c.   I marked my name the Day & year on a Alder tree, the party all Cut the first letters of their names on different trees in the bottom.   in the evening Seven indians of the *Clot Sop* Nation Came over in a Canoe, they brought with them 2 Sea otter Skins for which they asked blue beads &c. and Such high pricies that we were unable to purchase them without reducing our Small Stock of merchendize . . . mearly to try the Indian who had one of those Skins, I offered him my Watch, handkerchief a bunch of red beads and a dollar of the American Coin, all of which he refused and demanded "*ti-â, co-mo-shack*["] which is *Chief beads* and the most common blue beads, but fiew of which we have at this time. [Remained at Station Camp.]

November 24, 1805
[CLARK]¹⁰

Sergt J. Ordway	Cross & examine	S
Serjt. N. Pryor	do do	S
Sgt. P. Gass	do do	S
Jo. Shields	proceed to Sandy R	
Go. Shannon	Examn. Cross	falls
T. P. Howard	do do	falls
P. Wiser	do do	S. R
J. Collins	do do	S. R

10. The excerpt is from Clark's draft version for this day. This and Clark's finished version that follows it record the vote for where the party should spend the winter. Depending on how one adds the vote, at least six persons were in favor of returning to Celilo Falls, about ten wanted to return to Sandy River, Multnomah County, Oregon, and the remainder thought the party should examine the opposite shore or move upriver.

Jo Fields	do	do	up
Al. Willard	do	do	up
R Willard [11]	do	do	up
J. Potts	do	do	falls
R. Frasure	do	do	up
Wm. Bratten	do	do	up
R. Fields	do	do	falls
J: B: Thompson	do	do	up
J. Colter	do	do	up
H. Hall	do	do	S. R.
Labeech	do	do	S R
Peter Crusatte	do	do	S R
J. B. Depage	do	do	up
Shabono	—	—	—
S. Guterich	do	do	falls
W. Werner	do	do	up
Go: Gibson	do	do	up
Jos. Whitehouse	do	do	up
Geo Drewyer	Examn other side		falls
McNeal	do	do	up
York	"	"	lookout
	falls	Sandy River	lookout up
	6	10	12

Janey [12] in favour of a place where there is plenty of Potas.

Cp L Proceed on to morrow & examine The other side if good hunting to winter there, as Salt is an objt.   if not to proceed on to Sandy   it is probable that a vestle will come in this winter, & that by proceeding on at any distance would not inhance our journey in passing the Rockey mountains, &c.

W C.   In favour of proceding on without delay to the opposit Shore & there examine, and find out both the disposition of the Indians, & probibilaty of precureing Subsistance, and also enquire if the Tradeing vestles will arrive before the time we Should depart in the Spring, and if the

11. A mistake for Richard Windsor.
12. Nickname for Sacagawea.

Traders, Comonly arive in a Seasonable time, and we Can Subsist without a depends. on our Stores of goods, to Continue as the Climent would
be more favourable on the Sea Coast for our naked men than higher up
the Countrey where the Climate must be more Severe. [Remained at Station Camp.]

[CLARK] being now determined to go into Winter quarters as Soon as
possible, as a convenient Situation to precure the Wild animals of the forest which must be our dependance for Subsisting this Winter, we have
every reason to believe that the nativs have not provisions Suffient for our
Consumption, and if they had, their price's are So high that it would take
ten times as much to purchase their *roots* & *Dried fish* as we have in our
possesion, encluding our Small remains of merchindz and Clothes &c.
This Certinly enduces every individual of the party to make diligient enquiries of the nativs the part of the Countrey in which the wild Animals
are most plenty. They generaly agree that the most *Elk* is on the opposit
Shore, and that the greatest numbers of *Deer* is up the river at Some distance above— The Elk being an animal much larger than Deer, easier
to kiled better meat (in the winter when pore) and Skins better for the
Clothes of our party: added to, a convenient Situation to the Sea coast
where we Could make Salt, and a probibility of vessels Comeing into the
mouth of Columbia ("which the Indians inform us would return to trade
with them in 3 months["]) from whome we might precure a fresh Supply
of Indian trinkets to purchase provisions on our return home: together
with the Solicitations of every individual, except one of our party induced
us Conclude to Cross the river and examine the opposit Side, and if a
Suffcent quantity of Elk could probebly be precured to fix on a Situation
as convenient to the Elk & Sea Coast as we Could find— added to the
above advantagies in being near the Sea Coast one most Strikeing one
occurs to me i' e, the Climate which must be from every appearance
much milder than that above the 1st range of Mountains, The Indians are
Slightly Clothed and give an account of but little Snow, and the weather
which we have experiened Since we arrived in the neighbourhood of the
Sea Coast has been verry arm, and maney of the fiew days past disagree-
ably So.   if this Should be the Case it will most Certainly be the best Situation of our naked party dressed as they are altogether in leather.

November 26, 1805
[CLARK] we Set out out early and crossed a Short distance above the rock
out in the river, & between Some low marshey Islands to the South Side
of the Columbia at a low bottom about 3 miles below Point *Samuel*[13] and
proceeded near the South Side. [Camped near Svenson, Clatsop County,
Oregon.]

November 28, 1805
[CLARK] rained all the last night   we are all wet our bedding and Stores
are also wet, we haveing nothing which is Sufficient to keep ourselves
bedding or Stores dry   Several men in the point hunting deer without
Suckcess . . . we have nothing to eate except pounded fish which we
brought from the Great falls, this is our present Situation; truly disagreeable. about 12 oClock the wind Shifted around to the N W. and blew with
Such violence that I expected every moment to See trees taken up by the
roots, maney were blown down. This wind and rain Continued with
Short intervales all the latter part of the night. O! how disagreeable is our
Situation dureing this dreadfull weather. [Remained at the camp of November 27 on the west side of the neck of Tongue Point and east of Astoria, Clatsop County, Oregon.]

November 29, 1805
[LEWIS][14] the wind being so high the party were unable to proceed with
the perogues. I determined therefore to proceed down the river on it's E.
side in surch of an eligible place for our winters residence and accordingly set out early this morning in the small canoe accompanyed by
5 men.   drewyer R. Fields, Shannon, Colter & labiesh. [Lewis camped
along the shore of Youngs Bay, Clatsop County, Oregon, probably within
the limits of Astoria. Clark remained at the camp of November 27.]

November 30, 1805
[CLARK] The Squar, gave me a piece of Bread to day made of Some flower
She had Cearfully kept for her child, and had unfortunately got wet.

13. Cathlamet Point, Clatsop County, Oregon.
14. Lewis began keeping his journal again this day but apparently laid it aside after the
December 1 entry. He returned to the main party's camp on December 5.

[Lewis camped again within the limits of Astoria, Clatsop County, Oregon, along the shore of Youngs Bay. Clark remained at the camp of November 27.]

[GASS] some hunters went round the cape and killed two or three ducks. This is all the supply of fresh provisions, that we have had since we have been at this camp. We live almost altogether on pounded salmon.

December 1, 1805
[LEWIS] [the hunters] had seen the track of one deer only and a few small grey squirrels.[15] these suirrels are about the size of the red squirrel of the lakes and eastern Atlantic States, their bellies are of a redish yellow, or tanners ooze colour the tale flat and as long as the body eyes black and moderately large back and sides of a greyish brown   the brier[16] with a brown bark and three laves which put forth at the extremety of the twigs like the leaves of the blackbury brier, tho' is a kind of shrub and rises sometimes to the hight of 10 fe[et]   the green brier[17] yet in leaf; the ash[18] with a remarkable large leaf; the large black alder.[19]   the large elder[20] with skey blue buries. the broad leave shrub[21] which grows something like the quill wood but has no joints, the leaf broad and deeply indented the bark p[e]als hangs on the stem and is of a yelowish brown colour. the seven bark[22] is also found here as is the common low cramburry— there is a wild crab apple[23] which the natives eat this growth differs but little in appearance from that of the wild crab of the Atlantic States. but the fruit consists of little oval burries which grow in clusters at the extremities of the twigs like the black haws. the fruit is of a brown colour, oval form and about double as large as the black haw; the rind is smoth and tough somewhat hard; the seed is like that of the wild crab and nearly as large;

15. Probably Richardson's red squirrel.
16. Salmonberry.
17. Pacific blackberry.
18. Probably bigleaf maple.
19. Red alder.
20. Perhaps red elderberry.
21. Ninebark.
22. This is ninebark also.
23. Oregon crabapple.

the pulp is soft of a pale yellow coulour; and when the fruit has been touched by the frost is not unpleasant, being an agreeable assed. the tree which bears a red burry[24] in clusters of a round form and size of a red haw. the leaf like that of the small magnolia, and brark smoth and of a brickdust red coulour it appears to be of the evergreen kind. half after one oclock Drewyer not yet arrived. heard him shoot 5 times just above us and am in hopes he has fallen in with agang of elk. [Lewis remained in his camp of the previous day.]

[CLARK] The emence Seas and waves which breake on the rocks & Coasts to the S W. & N W roars like an emence fall at a distance, and this roaring has continued ever Since our arrival in the neighbourhood of the Sea Coast which has been 24 days Since we arrived in Sight of the Great Western; (for I cannot Say Pacific) Ocian as I have not Seen one pacific day Since my arrival in its vicinity . . . I have no account of Capt. Lewis Since he left me. [Clark remained at the camp of November 27.]

December 2, 1805
[CLARK] I feel verry unwell, and have entirely lost my appetite for the Dried pounded fish which is in fact the cause of my disorder at present — The men are generally Complaining of a lax and gripeing. [Lewis's camp is unknown; Clark remained at the camp of November 27.]

December 3, 1805
[CLARK] the men Sent after an Elk yesterday returnd. with an Elk which revived the Sperits of my men verry much, I am unwell and cannot Eate, the flesh O! how disagreeable my Situation, a plenty of meat and incaple of eateing any . . . I marked my name & the day of the month and year on a large Pine tree on this Peninsella & by land "Capt William Clark December 3rd 1805. By Land. U States in 1804 & 1805" —   The Squar Broke the two Shank bones of the Elk after the marrow was taken out, boiled them & extracted a Pint of Greese or tallow from them. [Lewis's camp is unknown; Clark remained at the camp of November 27.]

24. Pacific madrone.

December 5, 1805

[CLARK] Capt Lewis's long delay below has been the cause of no little un-easiness on my part for him, a 1000 conjectures has crouded into my mind respecting his probable Situation & Safty . . . Capt Lewis returned haveing found a good Situation and Elk Suffient to winter on. [Camped as a recombined party at the camp of November 27.]

[GASS] There is more wet weather on this coast, than I ever knew in any other place; during a month, we have had three fair days; and there is no prospect of a change.

December 7, 1805

[CLARK] Set out to the place Capt Lewis had viewed and thought well Sit-uated for winter quarters . . . I delayed about half an hour before York Came up, and then proceeded around this Bay which I have taken the lib-erty of calling Meriwethers Bay[25] the Cristian name of Capt. Lewis who no doubt was the 1st white man who ever Surveyed this Bay, we assended a river[26] which falls in on the South Side of this Bay . . . this situation is on a rise about 30 feet higher than the high tides leavel and thickly Cov-ered with lofty pine. this is certainly the most eligable Situation for our purposes of any in its neighbourhood. [Camped at the site of Fort Clat-sop, Clatsop County, Oregon, about five miles southwest of Astoria, where the party remained until March 23, 1806. Campsite locations are indicated during this time only when someone is away from the fort.]

December 8, 1805

[CLARK] We haveing fixed on this Situation as the one best Calculated for our Winter quarters I deturmin'd to go as direct a Course as I could to the Sea Coast which we Could here roar and appeared to be at no great dis-tance from us, my principal object is to look out a place to make Salt, blaze the road or rout that they men out hunting might find the direction to the fort if they Should get lost in cloudy weather — and See the pro-

25. Youngs Bay, Clatsop County, Oregon, named by George Vancouver's party in 1792.
26. Lewis and Clark River (the party's "Netul River").

bibillity of game in that direction, for the Support of the Men, we Shall Send to make Salt, I took with me five men and Set out on a Course S 60 W.[27] [Clark camped north of Seaside, Clatsop County, Oregon, a short distance from the coast.]

December 9, 1805

[CLARK] proceeded on to the mouth of the Creek which makes a great bend above the mouth of this Creek or to the S. is 3 houses and about 12 families of the Clat Sop Nation, we cross to those houses, which were built on the S. exposur of the hill, Sunk into the ground about 4 feet the walls roof & gable ends are of Split pine boards, the dores Small with a ladder to decend to the iner part of the house, the fires are 2 in the middle of the house their beads ar all around raised about 2½ feet from the bottom flore all covered with mats and under those beads was Stored their bags baskets and useless mats, those people treated me with extrodeanary friendship, one man attached himself to me as Soon as I entered the hut, Spred down new mats for me to Set on, gave me fish berries rutes &c. on Small neet platteers of rushes to eate which was repeated, all the Men of the other houses Came and Smoked with me   Those people appeared much neeter in their diat than Indians are Comonly, and frequently wash theer faces and hands— in the eveng an old woman presented a bowl made of a light Coloured horn a kind of Surup made of Dried berries which is common to this Countrey which the natives Call *Shele wele*[28] this Surup I though was pleasent, they Gave me Cockle Shells to eate a kind of Seuip made of bread of the *Shele well* berries mixed with roots in which they presented in neet trenchers made of wood . . . those people have a Singular game[29] which they are verry fond of and is performed with Something about the Size of a large been which they pass from, one hand into the other with great dexterity dureing which time they Sing, and ocasionally, hold out their hands for those who Chuse to risque their property to guess which hand the been is in; the individual who has the

27. Clark had Drouillard, Shannon, and three unidentified persons with him.

28. Salal, a plant used extensively by the natives.

29. Ordway also mentions this widespread Indian hand game on August 27, 1805. The second game Clark describes here appears to have been unique to the Clatsops.

been is a banker & opposed to all in the room. on this game they risque their beeds & other parts of their most valuable effects— this ausement has occupied about 3 hours of this evening, Several of the lodge in which I am in have lost all the beeds which they had about them— they have one other game which a man attempted to Show me, I do not properly understand it, they make use of maney peces about the Shape and size of Backgammon Pices which they role through between two pins Stuck up at certain distancies &. when I was Disposed to go to Sleep the man who' had been most attentive named *Cus-ka-lah* producd 2 new mats and Spred them near the fire, and derected his wife to go to his bead which was the Signal for all to retire which they did emediately. I had not been long on my mats before I was attacked most violently by the flees and they kept up a close Siege dureing the night. [Clark camped at the mouth of Necanicum River at Seaside, Clatsop County, Oregon. Lewis remained at the campsite which became Fort Clatsop.]

December 10, 1805
[CLARK] proceeded on through a heavy rain to the Camp at our intended fort . . . The Sea Coast is about 7 miles distant Nearly West about 5 miles of the distance through a thick wood with reveens hills and Swamps the land, rich black moald 2 miles in a open wavering Sandy prarie, ridge runing parrelal to the river, Covered with Green Grass. [Clark returned to the site of Fort Clatsop.]

December 11, 1805
[CLARK] we are all employed putting up huts or Cabins for our winters quarters. Sergeant Pryor unwell from a dislocation of his Sholder, Gibson with the disentary, Jo. Fields with biles on his legs, & Werner with a Strained Knee.

December 12, 1805
[CLARK] in the evening two Canoes of *Clât Sops* Visit us they brought with them *Wap pa to*, a black Sweet root they Call *Sha-na toe qua*,[30] and

30. Edible thistle.

a Small Sea Otter Skin, all of which we purchased for a fiew fishing hooks and a Small Sack of Indian tobacco which was given by the Snake Inds. Those Indians appear well disposed   we gave a Medal to the principal Chief named *Con-ny-au* or *Com mo-wol*[31] and treated those with him with as much attention as we could —   I can readily discover that they are Close deelers, & Stickle for a verry little, never close a bargin except they think they have the advantage   Value Blue beeds highly, white they also prise but no other Colour do they Value in the least —   the *Wap pa to* they Sell high, this root the purchase at a high price from the nativs above.

December 13, 1805

[CLARK] we Continue to put up the Streight butifull balsom pine[32] on our houses — and we are much pleased to find that the timber Splits most butifully and to the width of 2 feet or more.

[ORDWAY] we raised another line of our huts and began the last line of our huts forming three [sides of a] Square and 7 rooms 16 by 18 feet large. the other Square we intend to picket and have gates at the 2 corners, So as to have it a defensive fort.

December 14, 1805

[GASS] We completed the building of our huts, 7 in number, all but the covering, which I now find will not be so difficult as I expected; as we have found a kind of timber in plenty, which splits freely, and makes the finest puncheons I have ever seen. They can be split 10 feet long and two broad, not more than an inch and an half thick.

December 15, 1805

[ORDWAY] Capt. Clark and the most of the party set out with three canoes to go after the 17 Elk . . . [We] got Scattered   night over took Some of us and I Whitehouse Collins and Hugh Mcneal got lost and Stayed out all night with out fire.

31. Coboway, a local leader.
32. Probably grand fir.

December 16, 1805
[CLARK] The winds violent Trees falling in every derection, whorl winds, with gusts of rain Hail & Thunder, this kind of weather lasted all day, Certainly one of the worst days that ever was!

December 17, 1805
[CLARK] all the men at work about the houses, Some Chinking, Dobbing Cutting out dores &c.

December 20, 1805
[CLARK] Men all employd in Carrying punchens or boards & Covering the houses, 4 of which were Covered to day, the after part of the day Cloudy with Several Showers of rain— 3 Indians arrive in a Canoe. they brought with them mats, roots & Sackacome berries[33] to Sell for which they asked Such high prices that we did not purchase any of them. Those people ask generally double and tribble the value of what they have to Sell, and never take less than the real value of the article in Such things as is calculated to do them Service. Such as Blue & white beeds, with which they trade with the nativs above; files which they make use of to Sharpen their tools, fish hooks of different Sises and tobacco— Tobacco and blue beeds they do prefur to every thing.

December 22, 1805
[CLARK] we finish dobbig 4 huts which is all we have Covered, the Punchin floor & Bunks finished . . . Sjt. J. Ordway, Gibson & my Servent Sick Several with Biles on them & bruses of different kinds.

December 23, 1805
[CLARK] Capt Lewis and my Self move into our hut to day unfinished . . . Sent a little pounded fish to *Cus-ca-lah* who was Sick.

December 24, 1805
[CLARK] Cuscalah the Indian who had treated me So politely when I was at the Clâtsops village, come up in a Canoe with his young brother & 2

33. Saccacommis, another term for bearberry, which members of the party mixed with tobacco and smoked.

Squars   he laid before Capt Lewis and my Self each a mat and a parcel
of roots— Some time in the evening two files was demanded for the
presents of mats and roots, as we had no files to part with, we each returned the present which we had received, which displeased Cuscalah a
little. he then offered a woman to each of us which we also declined ax-
cepting of, which displeased the whole party verry much— the female
part appeared to be highly disgusted at our refuseing to axcept of their
favours &c.

December 25, 1805
[CLARK] at day light this morning we we[re] awoke by the discharge of
the fire arm of all our party & a Selute, Shoute and a Song which the
whole party joined in under our windows, after which they retired to
their rooms were Chearfull all the morning— after brackfast we divided
our Tobacco which amounted to 12 carrots one half of which we gave to
the men of the party who used tobacco, and to those who doe not use it
we make a present of a handkerchief, The Indians leave us in the evening
all the party Snugly fixed in their huts— I recved a presnt of Capt L. of
a fleece hosrie Shirt Draws and Socks, a pr. mockersons of Whitehouse a
Small Indian basket of Gutherich, two Dozen white weazils tails of the
Indian woman, & Some black root of the Indians before their departure . . . we would have Spent this day the nativity of Christ in feasting,
had we any thing either to raise our Sperits or even gratify our appetites,
our Diner concisted of pore Elk, So much Spoiled that we eate it thro'
mear necessity, Some Spoiled pounded fish and a fiew roots.

[WHITEHOUSE] We had no ardent spirit of any kind among us; but are
mostly in good health, A blessing, which we esteem more, than all the
luxuries this life can afford, and the party are all thankful to the Supreme
Being, for his goodness towards us. hoping he will preserve us in the
same, & enable us to return to the United States again in safety.

December 26, 1805
[CLARK] Joseph Fields finish a Table & 2 Seats for us.

December 27, 1805
[CLARK] the men Complete Chimneys & Bunks to day.

December 28, 1805
[CLARK] Derected Drewyer, Shannon, Labeash, Reuben Field, and Collins to hunt; Jos. Fields, Bratten, Gibson to proceed to the Ocean at Some Convenient place form a Camp and Commence makeing Salt with 5 of the largest Kittles, and Willard and Wiser to assist them in Carrying the Kittles to the Sea Coast—[34]   all the other men to be employed about putting up pickets & makeing the gates of the *fort*. my man Y[ork] verry unwell from a violent Coald and Strain by Carrying meet from the woods and lifting the heavy logs on the works &c.

December 29, 1805
[CLARK] I can plainly discover that a considerable exchange of property is Continually Carried on between the Tribes and villages of those people they all dress litely ware nothing below the waste, a pice of fur abt. around the body, and a Short robe which Composes the total of their dress, except a few Split hats, and beeds around ther necks wrists and anckles, and a few in their ears. They are small and <homely> not handsom generally Speaking women perticularly. The *Chin nook* womin are lude and Carry on Sport publickly. the Clotsop and others appear deffidend, and reserved The flees are So noumerous in this Countrey and difficult to get Cleare of that the Indians have difft. houses & villages to which they remove frequently to get rid of them, and not withstanding all their precautions, they never Step into our hut without leaveing Sworms of those troublesom insects. Indeed I Scercely get to Sleep half the night Clear of the torments of those flees, with the precaution of haveing my blankets Serched and the flees killed every day.

December 30, 1805
[CLARK] our fortification is Completed this evening—and at Sun Set we let the nativs know that our Custom will be in future, to Shut the gates at Sun Set at which time all Indians must go out of the fort and not return into it untill next morning after Sunrise at which time the gates will be opened.

34. Joseph Field, Bratton, and Gibson established a saltmaking camp at Seaside, Clatsop County, Oregon, which operated under various members of the party until February 21, 1806, producing about four bushels of salt.

[ORDWAY] a fair morning and a little Sun shine which is verry uncommon at this place.

December 31, 1805

[CLARK] two other Canoes arrived, one from the *War ci â cum* Village with 3 indians and the other of 3 men & a Squar from higher up the river and are of the *Skil-lute* nation, those people brought with them Some *Wappato* roots, mats made of flags and rushes dried fish, and a fiew *Shawna tâh-que* and Dressed Elk Skins, all of which they asked enormous prices for, perticularly the dressed Elk Skins, I purchased of those people Some *Wap pa to* two mats and about 3 pipes of their tobacco in a neet little bag made of rushes . . . for those articles I gave a large fishing hook and Several other Small articles, the fishinghooks they were verry fond of . . . we had Sinks dug & a Sentinal box made — a *Skil lute* brought a gun which he requested me to have repared, it only wanted a Screw flattened So as to Catch, I put a flint into his gun & he presented me in return a peck of *Wappato* for payment, I gave him piece of a Sheap Skin and a Small piece of blue Cloth to Cover his lock for which he was much pleased and gave me in return Some roots &c.

Undated, December 1805

[CLARK] A List of the Tribes near the mouth of the Columbia river as given by the Indians, the Places they reside, the names of the Tribes and principal Chiefs of each all of which speak the same language

1st *Clot-sop*[35] Tribe in Several Small villages on the Sea Cost to the S. E. of the Mouth & on the S. E. bank of the Columbia river — not noumerous

1st Chief *Con-ni a*   Co-mo-wool
2   do   *Sha-no-ma*
3   do   *War-ho-lote*

2nd *Chin-nook*[36] Tribe reside opposit on the N. W. Side & in Small villages & Single houses made of Split boards on a Creek of Haleys bay, and

35. Clatsops.
36. Chinooks.

on Small lakes or ponds, at no great distance from the river or bay. Tolerably noumerous—so said

☞ Chinnook

1st	Chief is	*Stock-home*
2d	do	*Com-com-mo-ley*
3	do	*Shil-lar-la-wit*
4	do	*Nor-car-te*
5	do	*Chin-ni-ni*

3rd Chiltch [37] *Tribe reside near the Sea Coast & north of the* Chinnooks *live in houses and is said to be noumerous   Speak same Language*

1st	Chief	*Mar-lock-ke*
2d	do	*Col-chote*
3rd	do	*Ci-in-twar*

4th *Ca-la-mox*[38] Tribe reside on the Sea coast to the S. E of the Columbia River and on a Small river, and as I am informed by the *Clot-sops* inhabit 10 Villages 6 of them on the ocian & 4 on the Little river, those Ca-la-mox are said not to be noumerous   Speake the Clotsop language

1st Chief *O-co-no*

5th *Calt-har-mar*[39] Tribe reside in one village of large Houses built of Split boards and neetly made, on the S. E. Side of the Columbia River, behind a Island in a Deep bend of the River to the S. E.   they are not noumerous, and live as the others do on fish, black roots Lickuerish berries, and *Wap-pe-to* roots, and is as low as those Wapeto roots grow, which is about 15 miles on a Direct line from the Sea.

1st	Chief	*Clax-ter* at war against the
		Snake Inds. to the S of the falls
2d	do	*Cul-te-ell*
3	do	[blank] at war Do.

37. Chehalis.
38. Tillamooks.
39. Cathlamets.

6th *Clax-ter*[40] Nation   This nation reside on [blank] Side of the Columbia River in [blank] villages above about [blank] and are noumerous
they latterly floged the Chinnooks, and are a Dasterly Set

1st and Great Chief Qui oo

7th *War-ci-a-cum*[41] Tribe reside on the N W. Side of the Columbia in
the great bend behind Some Islands   this tribe is not noumerous   reside
in 2 village of Houses

The Chief Scum ar-qua-up

January 1, 1806

[LEWIS] This morning I was awoke at an early hour by the discharge of a
volley of small arms, which were fired by our party in front of our quarters to usher in the new year; this was the only mark of rispect which we
had it in our power to pay this celebrated day. our repast of this day tho'
better than that of Christmass, consisted principally in the anticipation of
the 1st day of January 1807, when in the bosom of our friends we hope to
participate in the mirth and hilarity of the day, and when with the zest
given by the recollection of the present, we shall completely, both men-
tally and corporally, enjoy the repast which the hand of civilization has
prepared for us. at present we were content with eating our boiled Elk
and wappetoe, and solacing our thirst with our only beverage *pure water*.
two of our hunters who set out this morning reterned in the evening having killed two bucks elk; they presented Capt. Clark and myself each a
marrow-bone and tonge, on which we suped. visited today by a few of
the Clotsops who brought some roots and burries for the purpose of
trading with us. we were uneasy with rispect to two of our men, Willard
and Wiser, who were dispatched on the 28th ulto. with the saltmakers,
and were directed to return immediately; their not having returned induces us to believe it probable that they have missed their way.

[LEWIS AND CLARK, DETACHMENT ORDERS][42] The fort being now completed, the Commanding officers think proper to direct: that the guard

40. Perhaps Clatskanies.
41. Wahkiakums.
42. The last detachment order.

shall as usual consist of one Sergeant and three privates, and that the same be regularly relieved each morning at sunrise ... It shall be the duty of the centinel also to announce the arrival of all parties of Indians to the Sergeant of the Guard, who shall immediately report the same to the Commanding officers. The Commanding Officers require and charge the Garrison to treat the natives in a friendly manner; nor will they be permitted at any time, to abuse, assault or strike them; unless such abuse assault or stroke be first given by the natives. nevertheless it shall be right for any individual, in a peaceable manner, to refuse admittance to, or put out of his room, any native who may become troublesome to him; and should such native refuse to go when requested, or attempt to enter their rooms after being forbidden to do so; it shall be the duty of the Sergeant of the guard on information of the same, to put such native out of the fort and see that he is not again admitted during that day unless specially permitted; and the Sergeant of the guard may for this purpose imploy such coercive measures (not extending to the taking of life) as shall at his discretion be deemed necessary to effect the same. When any native shall be detected in theft, the Sergt. of the guard shall immediately inform the Commanding offercers of the same, to the end that such measures may be pursued with rispect to the culprit as they shall think most expedient. At sunset on each day, the Sergt. attended by the interpreter Charbono and two of his guard, will collect and put out of the fort, all Indians except such as may specially be permitted to remain by the Commanding offercers, nor shall they be again admitted untill the main gate be opened the ensuing morning. At Sunset, or immediately after the Indians have been dismissed, both gates shall be shut, ad secured, and the main gate locked and continue so untill sunrise the next morning . . . Any individual selling or disposing of any tool or iron or steel instrument, arms, accoutrements or ammunicion, shall be deemed guilty of a breach of this order, and shall be tryed and punished accordingly. the tools loaned to John Shields are excepted from the restrictions of this order.

January 2, 1806
[LEWIS] The large, and small or whistling swan, sand hill Crane, large and small gees, brown and white brant, Cormorant, duckan mallard, Canvisback duck, and several other species of ducks, still remain with us;

tho' I do not think that they are as plenty as on our first arrival in the neighbourhood.[43]

January 3, 1806
[LEWIS] our party from necessaty having been obliged to subsist some lenth of time on dogs have now become extreemly fond of their flesh; it is worthy of remark that while we lived principally on the flesh of this anamal we were much more healthy strong and more fleshey than we had been since we left the Buffaloe country. for my own part I have become so perfectly reconciled to the dog that I think it an agreeable food and would prefer it vastly to lean Venison or Elk. a small Crow, the blue crested Corvus and the smaller corvus with a white brest, the little brown ren, a large brown sparrow, the bald Eagle and the beatifull Buzzard of the columbia still continue with us.[44]

[CLARK] as for my own part I have not become reconsiled to the taste of this animal as yet.

[LEWIS AND CLARK, WEATHER REMARKS] the loss of my Thermometer I most sincerely regret. I am confident that the climate here is much warmer than in the same parallel of Latitude on the Atlantic Ocean tho' how many degrees is now out of my power to determine. Since our arrival in this neighbourhood on the 7th of November, we have experienced one slight white frost only which happened on the morning of the 16th of that month. we have yet seen no ice, and the weather so warm that we are obliged cure our meat with smoke and fire to save it.

January 4, 1806
[LEWIS] These people the Chinnooks and others residing in this neighbourhood and speaking the same language have been very friendly to us;

43. Birds identified by Lewis are the trumpeter swan ("large"), tundra swan ("small or whistling"), sandhill crane, Canada goose ("large"), an unknown goose ("small"), brant ("brown"), snow goose ("white brant"), mallard, and canvasback.

44. Lewis identified probably the northwestern crow, Steller's jay ("blue crested Corvus"), gray jay ("smaller corvus"), perhaps the winter wren ("little brown ren"), possibly the golden-crowned sparrow ("large brown sparrow"), bald eagle, and California condor ("Buzzard").

they appear to be a mild inoffensive people but will pilfer if they have an opportuny to do so where they conceive themselves not liable to detection.   they are great higlers in trade and if they conceive you anxious to purchase will be a whole day bargaining for a handfull of roots; this I should have thought proceeded from their want of knowledge of the comparitive value of articles of merchandize and the fear of being cheated, did I not find that they invariably refuse the price first offered them and afterwards very frequently accept a smaller quantity of the same article; in order to satisfy myself on this subject I once offered a Chinnook my watch two knives and a considerable quantity of beads for a small inferior sea Otter's skin which I did not much want, he immediately conceived it of great value, and refused to barter except I would double the quantity of beads; the next day with a great deal of importunity on his part I received the skin in exchange for a few strans of the same beads he had refused the day before. I therefore believe this trait in their character proceeds from an avaricious all grasping disposition. in this rispect they differ from all Indians I ever became acquainted with, for their dispositions invariably lead them to give whatever they are possessed off no matter how usefull or valuable, for a bauble which pleases their fancy, without consulting it's usefullness or value.   nothing interesting occurred today, or more so, than our wappetoe being all exhausted.

January 5, 1806
[LEWIS] At 5 P. M. Willard and Wiser returned, they had not been lost as we apprehended.   they informed us that it was not untill the fifth day after leaving the Fort that they could find a convenient place for making salt; that they had at length established themselves on the coast about 15 Miles S. W. from this, near the lodge of some Killamuck[45] families; that the Indians were very friendly and had given them a considerable quantity of the blubber of a whale which perished on the coast some distance S. E. of them; part of this blubber they brought with them, it was white & not unlike the fat of Poark, tho' the texture was more spongey and somewhat coarser. I had a part of it cooked and found it very pallitable and tender, it resembled the beaver or the dog in flavour.   it may appear

45. Tillamook.

somewhat extraordinary tho' it is a fact that the flesh of the beaver and dog possess a very great affinity in point of flavour. These lads also informed us that J. Fields, Bratton and Gibson (the Salt makers) had with their assistance erected a comfortable camp killed an Elk and several deer and secured a good stock of meat; they commenced the making of salt and found that they could obtain from 3 quarts to a gallon a day; they brought with them a specemine of the salt of about a gallon, we found it excellent, fine, strong, & white; this was a great treat to myself and most of the party, having not had any since the 20th ultmo.; I say most of the party, for my friend Capt. Clark declares it to be a mear matter of indifference with him whether he uses it or not; for myself I must confess I felt a considerable inconvenience from the want of it; the want of bread I consider as trivial provided, I get fat meat, for as to the species of meat I am not very particular, the flesh of the dog the horse and the wolf, having from habit become equally formiliar with any other, and I have learned to think that if the chord be sufficiently strong, which binds the soul and boddy together, it dose not so much matter about the materials which compose it.

[CLARK] I determine to Set out early tomorrow with two canoes & 12 men in quest of the whale, or at all events to purchase from the indians a parcel of the blubber, for this purpose I made up a Small assortment of merchindize, and directed the men to hold themselves in readiness &c.

January 6, 1806
[LEWIS] The Clatsops, Chinnooks, Killamucks &c. are very loquacious and inquisitive; they possess good memories and have repeated to us the names capasities of the vessels &c of many traders and others who have visited the mouth of this river; they are generally low in stature, proportionably small, reather lighter complected and much more illy formed than the Indians of the Missouri and those of our frontier; they are generally cheerfull but never gay. with us their conversation generally turns upon the subjects of trade, smoking, eating or their women; about the latter they speak without reserve in their presents, of their every part, and of the most formiliar connection. they do not hold the virtue of their women in high estimation, and will even prostitute their wives and

daughters for a fishinghook or a stran of beads. in common with other savage nations they make their women perform every species of domestic drudgery. but in almost every species of this drudgery the men also participate. their women are also compelled to geather roots, and assist them in taking fish, which articles form much the greatest part of their subsistance; notwithstanding the survile manner in which they treat their women they pay much more rispect to their judgment and oppinions in many rispects than most indian nations; their women are permitted to speak freely before them, and sometimes appear to command with a tone of authority; they generally consult them in their traffic and act in conformity to their opinions. I think it may be established as a general maxim that those nations treat their old people and women with most differrence [deference] and rispect where they subsist principally on such articles that these can participate with the men in obtaining them; and that, that part of the community are treated with least attention, when the act of procuring subsistence devolves intirely on the men in the vigor of life. It appears to me that nature has been much more deficientin her filial tie than in any other of the strong affections of the human heart, and therefore think, our old men equally with our women indebted to civilization for their ease and comfort. Among the Siouxs, Assinniboins and others on the Missouri who subsist by hunting it is a custom when a person of either sex becomes so old and infurm that they are unable to travel on foot from camp to camp as they rome in surch of subsistance, for the children or near relations of such person to leave them without compunction or remose; on those occasions they usually place within their reach a small peace of meat and a platter of water, telling the poor old superannuated wretch for his consolation, that he or she had lived long enough, that it was time they should dye and go to their relations who can afford to take care of them much better than they could. I am informed that this custom prevails even among the Minetares Arwerharmays[46] and Recares when attended by their old people on their hunting excurtions; but in justice to these people I must observe that it appeared to me at their vilages, that they provided tolerably well for their aged persons, and sev-

46. Lewis's rendition of one of the divisions of the Hidatsas.

eral of their feasts appear to have principally for their object a contribution for their aged and infirm persons.

[CLARK] The last evening Shabono and his Indian woman was very impatient to be permitted to go with me, and was therefore indulged; She observed that She had traveled a long way with us to See the great waters, and that now that monstrous fish was also to be Seen, She thought it verry hard that She Could not be permitted to See either (She had never yet been to the Ocian).[47] [Clark camped on either Neawanna Creek or Neacoxie Creek, Clatsop County, Oregon.]

January 7, 1806
[CLARK] I proceeded on about 2 miles to near the base of high Mountain where I found our Salt makers, and with them Sergt. Gass, Geo. Shannon was out in the woods assisting Jo Field and gibson to kill Some meat, the Salt makers had made a neet Close Camp, Convenient to wood Salt water and the fresh water of the Clât Sop river which at this place was within 100 paces of the Ocian   they wer also Situated near 4 houses of Clatsops & Killamox, who they informed me had been verry kind and attentive to them. I hired a young Indian to pilot me to the whale for which Service I gave him a file in hand and promised Several other Small articles on my return, left Sergt. Gass and one man of my party Werner to make Salt & permited Bratten to accompany me, we proceeded on the round Slipery Stones under a high hill which projected into the ocian about 4 miles further than the direction of the Coast.   after walking for 2½ miles on the Stones my guide made a Sudin halt, pointed to the top of the mountain and uttered the word *Pe Shack* which means bad, and made Signs that we could not proceed any further on the rocks, but must pass over that mountain, I hesitated a moment & view this emence mountain the top of which was obscured in the clouds, and the assent appeard. to be almost perpindecular; as the Small Indian parth allong which they had brought emence loads but a fiew hours before, led up this mountain and appeared

47. The following were with Clark: Charbonneau, Sacagawea, Jean Baptiste Charbonneau (the baby), Frazer, McNeal, Pryor, and Werner. Others may have included: Colter, Cruzatte or Weiser, Reubin Field, Labiche, Lepage, Potts, Shields, and Windsor.

to assend in a Sideling direction, I thought more than probable that the assent might be torerably easy and therefore proceeded on, I soon found that the [blank] become much worst as I assended, and at one place we were obliged to Support and draw our Selves up by the bushes & roots for near 100 feet, and after about 2 hours labour and fatigue we reached the top of this high mountain,[48] from the top of which I looked down with estonishment to behold the hight which we had assended, which appeared to be 10 or 12 hundred feet up a mountain which appeared o be almost perpindicular, here we met 14 Indians men and women loaded with the oil & Blubber of the whale. In the face of this tremendeous precipic imediately below us, there is a Strater of white earth[49] (which my guide informed me) the neighbouring indians use to paint themselves, and which appears to me to resemble the earth of which the French Porcelain is made; I am confident that this earth Contains argill, but whether it also Contains Silex[50] or magnesia, or either of those earths in a proper perpotion I am unable to deturmine. [Clark camped on Tillamook Head perhaps on Canyon Creek, Clatsop County, Oregon.]

January 8, 1806
[LEWIS] The Clatsops Chinnooks and others inhabiting the coast and country in this neighbourhood, are excessively fond of smoking tobacco. in the act of smoking they appear to swallow it as they dran it from the pipe, and for many draughts together you will not perceive the smoke which they take from the pipe; in the same manner also they inhale it in their lungs untill they become surcharged with this vapour when they puff it out to a great distance through their nostils and mouth; I have no doubt the smoke of the tobacco in this manner becomes much more intoxicating and that they do possess themselves of all it's virtues in their fullest extent; they freequently give us sounding proofs of it's creating a dismorallity of order in the abdomen, nor are those light matters thought indelicate in either sex, but all take the liberty of obeying the dictates of

48. Clark climbed Tilla-mook Head, and it, or a point on it, became "Clark's Point of View" to the party.
49. May be clay.
50. Either quartz or basalt silica.

nature without reserve. these people do not appear to know the uce of sperituous liquors, they never having once asked us for it; I presume therefore that the traders who visit them have never indulged them with the uce of it; from what ever cause this may proceede, it is a very fortunate occurrence, as well for the natives themselves, as for the quiet and safety of thos whites who visit them.

[CLARK] proceeded to the top of the mountain next to the which is much the highest part and that part faceing the Sea is open, from this point I beheld the grandest and most pleasing prospects which my eyes ever surveyed, in my frount a boundless Ocean; to the N. and N. E. the coast as as far as my sight Could be extended, the Seas rageing with emence wave and brakeing with great force from the rocks of Cape Disapointment as far as I could See to the N. W. . . . The Columbia River for a Some distance up, with its Bays and Small rivers and on the other Side I have a view of the Coast for an emence distance to the S. E. by S. the nitches and points of high land which forms this Corse for a long ways aded to the inoumerable rocks of emence Sise out at a great distance from the Shore and against which the Seas brak with great force gives this Coast a most romantic appearance. from this point of View my guide pointed to a village at the mouth of a Small river near which place he Said the whale was, he also pointed to 4 other places where the princpal Villages of the *Kil la mox* were Situated,[51] I could plainly See the houses of 2 of those Villeges & the Smoke of a 3rd which was two far of for me to disern with my naked eye — after taking the Courses and computed the Distances in my own mind, I proceeded on . . . to the place the whale[52] had perished, found only the Skelleton of this monster on the Sand between 2 of the villages of the *Kil a mox* nation; the Whale was already pillaged of every valuable part by the Kil a mox Inds. in the vecinity of whose village's it lay on the Strand where the waves and tide had driven up & left it. this Skeleton measured 105 feet. I returned to the village of 5 Cabins on the Creek which I shall call *E co-la* or whale Creek, found the nativs busily engaged boiling the blubber, which they performed in a large Squar wooden trought by

51. At Cannon Beach, Clatsop County, Oregon.
52. Probably a blue whale.

means of hot Stones; the oil when extracted was Secure in bladders and the Guts of the whale; the blubber from which the oil was only partially extracted by this process, was laid by in their Cabins in large flickes[53] for use; those flickes they usially expose to the fire on a wooden Spit untill it is prutty well wormed through and then eate it either alone or with roots of the rush, *Shaw na tâk we*[54] or diped in the oil. The *Kil a mox* although they possessed large quantities of this blubber and oil were so prenurious that they disposed of it with great reluctiance and in Small quantities only; insomuch that my utmost exertion aided by the party with the Small Stock of merchindize I had taken with me were not able to precure more blubber than about 300 wt. and a fiew gallons of oil; Small as this Stock is I prise it highly; and thank providence for directing the whale to us; and think him much more kind to us than he was to jonah, having Sent this monster to be *Swallowed by us* in Sted of *Swallowing of us* as jonah's did. [Clark camped on the north side of Ecola Creek, in northern Cannon Beach, Clatsop County, Oregon.]

January 9, 1806
[LEWIS] The Clatsops Chinnooks &c. bury their dead in their canoes . . . a small canoe is placed [in the ground] in which the body is laid after being carefully roled in a robe of some dressed skins; a paddle is also deposited with them; a larger canoe is now reversed, overlaying and imbracing the small one, and resting with it's gunwals on the cross bars; one or more large mats of rushes or flags are then roled around the canoes and the whole securely lashed with a long cord, usually made of the bark of the *Arbor vita* or white cedar.   on the cross bars which support the canoes is frequently hung or laid various articles of cloathing culinary eutensels &c.   I cannot understand them sufficiently to make any enquiries relitive to their releegous opinions, but presume from their depositing various articles with their dead, that they believe in a state of future existence.

The persons who usually visit the entrance of this river for the purpose of traffic or hunting I believe are either English or Americans; the Indians

53. Flitch, a side of meat.
54. Edible thistle.

inform us that they speak the same language with ourselves, and give us
proofs of their varacity by repeating many words of English, as musquit,
powder, shot, nife, file, damned rascal, sun of a bitch &c. whether these
traders are from Nootka sound, from some other late establishment on
this coast, or immediately from the U' States or Great Brittain, I am at a
loss to determine, nor can the Indians inform us. the Indians whom I
have asked in what direction the traders go when they depart from hence,
or arrive here, always point to the S. W. from which it is presumeable that
Nootka cannot be their destination; and as from Indian information a
majority of these traders annually visit them about the beginning of April
and remain with them six or seven Months, they cannot come immediately from Great Britain or the U' States, the distance being too great for
them to go and return in the ballance of the year. from this circumstance
I am sometimes induced to believe that there is some other establishment
on the coast of America south West of this place of which little is but yet
known to the world, or it may be perhaps on some Island in the pacific
ocean between the Continents of Asia and America to the South West of
us. This traffic on the part of the whites consists in vending, guns, (principally old british or American musquits) powder, balls and Shot, Copper and brass kettles, brass teakettles and coffee pots, blankets from two
to three point, scarlet and blue Cloth (coarse), plates and strips of sheet
copper and brass, large brass wire, knives, beads and tobacco with
fishinghooks buttons and some other small articles; also a considerable
quantity of Sailor's cloaths, as hats coats, trowsers and shirts. for these
they receive in return from the natives, dressed and undressed Elkskins,
skins of the sea Otter, common tter, beaver, common fox, spuck,[55] and
tiger cat;[56] also dryed and pounded sammon in baskets, and a kind of
buisquit, which the natives make of roots called by them shappelell.[57] The
natives are extravegantly fond of the most common cheap blue and white
beads, of moderate size, or such that from 50 to 70 will weigh one pen-
neyweight. the blue is usually pefered to the white; these beads constitute the principal circulating medium with all the indian tribes on this
river; for these beads they will dispose any article they possess.

55. A Chinookan word, interpreted by the captains to mean an infant otter.
56. The men's name for the Oregon bobcat.
57. Cous (compare "cha-pel-el bread" at November 1, 1805).

[CLARK] last night about 10 oClock while Smokeing with the nativ's I was
alarmed by a loud Srile voice from the Cabins on the opposite Side, the
Indians all run immediately across to the village, my guide who Continued with me made Signs that Some one's throat was Cut, by enquiry I
found that one man McNeal was absent, I imediately Sent off Sergt. N.
Pryor & 4 men in quest of McNeal who' they met comeing across the
Creak in great hast, and informed me that the people were alarmed on the
opposit Side at Something but what he could not tell, a man had verry
friendly envited him to go and eate in his lodge, that the Indian had
locked armes with him and went to a lodge in which a woman gave him
Some blubber, that the man envited him to another lodge to get Something better, and the woman held him by the blanket which he had
around him another ran out and hollow'd and his pretended friend disappeared— I emediately ordered every man to hold themselves in a State
of rediness and Sent Sergt. Pryor & 4 men to know the cause of the alarm
which was found to be a premeditated plan of the pretended friend of
McNeal to assanate [him] for his Blanket and what fiew articles he had
about him, which was found out by a Chin nook woman who allarmed
the men of the village who were with me in time to prevent the horred
act. this man was of another band at Some distance and ran off as Soon
as he was discovered. we have now to look back and Shudder at the
dreadfull road on which we have to return of 45 miles S E of Point adams
& 35 miles from Fort *Clatsop*. I had the blubber & oil divided among' the
party and Set out about Sunrise and returned by the Same rout we had
went out, met Several parties of men & womin of the Chinnook and Clatsops nations, on their way to trade with the *Kil a mox* for blubber and oil;
on the Steep decent of the Mountain I overtook five men and Six womin
with emence loads of the Oil and blubber of the Whale, those Indians had
passed by Some rout by which e missed them as we went out yesterday;
one of the women in the act of getting down a Steep part of the mountain
her load by Some means had Sliped off her back, and She was holding the
load by a Strap which was fastened to the mat bag in which it was in, in
one hand and holding a bush by the other, as I was in front of my party,
I endeavored to relieve this woman by takeing her load untill She Could
get to a better place a little below, & to my estonishment found the load
as much as I Could lift and must exceed 100 wt. the husband of this
woman who was below Soon came to her releif, those people proceeded

on with us to the Salt works . . . as I was excessively fatigued and my party
appeared verry much so, I deturmined to Stay untill the morning and rest
our Selves a little. The Clatsops proceeded on with their lodes. [Clark
camped at the Salt Works, Seaside, Clatsop County, Oregon.]

January 10, 1806

[LEWIS] About 10 A. M. I was visited by Tia *Shâh-hâr-wâr-cap*[58] and
eleven of his nation in one large canoe; these are the Cuth'-lah-mah nation who reside first above us on the South side of the Columbia river;
this is the first time that I have seen the Chief, he was hunting when we
past his vilage on our way to this place. I gave him a medal of the smallest size; he presented me with some indian tobacco and a basquit of wappetoe, in return for which I gave him some thread for making a skiming
net and a small piece of tobacco. these people speak the same language
with the Chinnooks and Catsops whom they also resemble in their dress
customs manners &c. they brought some dryed salmon, wappetoe, dogs,
and mats made of rushes and flags, to barter; their dogs and a part of their
wappetoe they disposed off, an remained all night near the fort.[59]

[ORDWAY] this Creek was named by Capt. Clark Mcneals folley.[60]

January 12, 1806

[LEWIS] This morning sent out Drewyer and one man to hunt, they returned in the evening, Drewyer having killed seven Elk; I scarcely know
how we should subsist were it not for the exertions of this excellet
hunter . . . We have heretofore usually divided the meat when first killed
among the four messes into which we have divided our party leaving to
each the care of preserving and the discretion of using it, but we find that
they make such prodigal use of it when they hapen to have a tolerable
stock on hand that we have determined to adapt a different system with

58. A chief ("Tia") of the Cathlamets.

59. Clark and his party returned to Fort Clatsop this evening.

60. Contrary to Ordway, Clark called it Ecola Creek in his entries, a name since restored to the stream in Clatsop County, Oregon. Perhaps "McNeal's Folly" was a joke
among the party for the incidents of January 8 and 9.

our present stock of seven Elk; this is to jerk it & issue it to them in small quantities.

January 14, 1806
[LEWIS AND CLARK, WEATHER REMARKS] I never experienced a winter so warm as the present has been.

January 16, 1806
[LEWIS] we have plenty of Elk beef for the present and a little salt, our houses dry and comfortable, and having made up our minds to remain until the 1st of April, every one appears content with his situation and his fare.   it is true that we could even travel now on our return as far as the timbered country reaches, or to the falls of the river; but further it would be madness for us to attempt to proceede untill April, as the indians inform us that the snows lye knee deep in the plains of Columbia during the winter, and in these plains we could scarcely get as much fuel of any kind as would cook our provision as we descended the river; and even were we happyly over these plains and again in the woody country at the foot of the Rocky Mountains we could not possibly pass that immence barrier of mountains on which the snows ly in winter to the debth in many places of 20 feet; in short the Indians inform us that they are impracticable untill about the 1st of June, at which time even there is an abundance of snow but a scanty subsistence may be obtained for the horses.   we should not therefore forward ourselves on our homeward journey by reaching the rocky mountains early than the 1st of June, which we can easily effect by seting out from hence on the 1st of April.

January 17, 1806
[LEWIS] The Culinary articles of the Indians in our neighbourhood consist of wooden bowls or throughs, baskets, wooden spoons and woden scures or spits . . . their baskets are formed of cedar bark and beargrass so closely interwoven with the fingers that they are watertight without the aid of gum or rosin; some of these are highly ornamented with strans of beargrass which they dye of several colours and interweave in a great variety of figures; this serves them the double perpose of holding their water or wearing on their heads; and are of different capacites from that

of the smallest cup to five or six gallons; they are generally of a conic form or reather the segment of a cone of which the smaller end forms the base or bottom of the basket. these they make very expediciously and dispose off for a mear trifle. it is for the construction of these baskets that the beargrass becomes an article of traffic among the natives this grass grows only on their high mountains near the snowey region; the blade is about ⅜ of an inch wide and 2 feet long smoth pliant and strong; the young blades which are white from not being exposed to the sun or air, are those most commonly employed, particularly in their neatest work.

January 18, 1806
[LEWIS] The Clatsops Chinnooks &c construct their houses of timber altogether. they are from 14 to 20 feet wide and from 20 to 60 feet in length, and acommodate one or more families sometimes three or four families reside in the same room. thes houses a[re] also divided by a partition of boards, but this happens only in the largest houses as the rooms are always large compared with the number of inhabitants . . . in the center of each room a space of six by eight feet square is sunk about twelve inches lower than the floor having it's sides secured with four sticks of squar timber, in this space they make their fire, their fuel being generally pine bark. mats are spread arround the fire on all sides, on these they set in the day and frequently sleep at night.

January 19, 1806
[LEWIS] Several families of these people usually reside together in the same room; they appear to be the father & mother and their sons with their son's wives and children; their provision seems to be in common and the greatest harmoney appears to exist among them. The old man is not always rispected as the head of the family, that duty most commonly devolves on one of the young men. They have seldom more than one wife, yet the plurality of wives is not denied them by their customs. These families when ascociated form nations or bands of nations each acknoledging the authority of it's own chieftain who dose not appear to be heriditary, nor his power to extend further than a mear repremand for any improper act of an individual; the creation of a chief depends upon the upright de-

portment of the individual & his ability and disposition to render service
to the community; and his authority or the deference paid him is in exact equilibrio with the popularity or voluntary esteem he has acquired
among the individuals of his band or nation. Their laws like those of all
uncivilized Indians consist of a set of customs which have grown out of
their local situations.   not being able to speak their language we have not
been able to inform ourselves of the existence of any peculiar customs
among them.

January 20, 1806

[LEWIS] on the morning of the eighteenth we issued 6 lbs. of jirked Elk
pr. man, this evening the Sergt. repoted that it was all exhausted; the
six lbs. have therefore lasted two days and a half only.   at this rate our
seven Elk will last us only 3 days longer, yet no one seems much concerned about the state of the stores; so much for habit.   we have latterly
so frequently had our stock of provisions reduced to a minimum and
sometimes taken a small touch of fasting that three days full allowance
excites no concern. In those cases our skill as hunters afford us some
consolation.

January 21, 1806

[LEWIS] The root of the thistle, called by the natives *shan-ne-tâh-que* is a
perpendicular fusiform and possesses from two to four radicles; is from
9 to 15 Inces in length and about the size a mans thumb; the rhind somewhat rough and of a brown colour; the consistence when first taken from
the earth is white and nearly as crisp as a carrot; when prepared for uce
by the same process before discribed of the white bulb or *pashshequo
quawmash*,[61] it becomes black, and is more shugary than any fuit or root
that I have met with in uce among the natives; the sweet is precisely that
of the sugar in flavor; this root is sometimes eaten also when first taken
from the ground without any preperation; but in this way is vastly inferior.   it delights most in a deep rich dry lome which has a good mixture
of sand.

61. Camas.

January 22, 1806

[LEWIS] There are three species of fern in this neighbourhood the root[62] one of which the natves eat; this grows very abundant in the open uplands and praries where the latter are not sandy and consist of deep loose rich black lome . . . there is a white substance which when the root is roasted in the embers is much like wheat dough and not very unlike it in flavour, though it has also a pungency which becomes more visible after you have chewed it some little time; this pungency was disagreeable to me, but the natives eat it very voraciously and I have no doubt but it is a very nutricious food.

January 23, 1806

[LEWIS] The men of the garison are still busily employed in dressing Elk's skins for cloathing, they find great difficulty for the want of branes;[63] we have not soap to supply the deficiency, nor can we procure ashes to make the lye; none of the pines which we use for fuel affords any ashes; extrawdinary as it may seem, the greene wood is consoomed without leaving the residium of a particle of ashes.

January 24, 1806

[LEWIS] the most valuable of all their [the natives'] roots is foreign to this neighbourhood   I mean the *Wappetoe*, or the bulb of the Sagitifolia or common arrow head, which grows in great abundance in the marshey grounds of that beatifull and firtile valley on the Columbia commencing just above the entrance of Quicksand River, and extending downwards for about 70 Miles.   this bulb forms a principal article of traffic between the inhabitants of the valley and those of this neighbourhood or sea coast.

January 25, 1806

[LEWIS] The native fruits and buries in uce among the Indians of this neighbourhood are a deep purple burry about the size of a small cherry

62. The root of the bracken fern.
63. "Brains," which are used in tanning leather.

called by them *Shal-lun*,[64] a small pale red bury called *Sol'-me*;[65] the vine-ing or low Crambury,[66] a light brown bury[67] reather larger and much the shape of the black haw; and a scarlet bury about the size of a small cherry the plant called by the Canadin Engages of the N. W. *sac a commis*[68] pro-duces this bury; this plant is so called from the circumstance of the Clerks of those trading companies carrying the leaves of this plant in a small bag for the purpose of smokeing of which they are excessively fond.   the In-dians call this bury [blank].[69]

January 26, 1806

[LEWIS] Werner and Howard who were sent for salt on the 23rd have not yet returned, we are apprehensive that they have missed their way; neither of them are very good woodsmen, and this thick heavy timbered pine country added to the constant cloudy weather makes it difficult for even a good woodsman to steer for any considerable distance the course he wishes.

[LEWIS AND CLARK, WEATHER REMARKS] it now appears like winter for the first time this season.

[ORDWAY] considerable of Snow fell in the course of last night and con-tinues this morning, and cold freezing weather   the Snow is this evening about 5 Inches deep on a level.

January 27, 1806

[LEWIS] Goodrich has recovered from the Louis veneri which he con-tracted from an amorous contact with a Chinnook damsel. I cured him as I did Gibson last winter by the uce of murcury.[70] I cannot learn that the

64. Salal.
65. Bunchberry.
66. Wild cranberry.
67. Oregon crabapple.
68. Bearberry.
69. Lewis's etymology for the term *saccacommis* is not correct; the word comes from a Chippewa designation.
70. Lewis would not have cured Goodrich or Gibson of syphilis or *lues venerea* ("Louis veneri") by using mercury.

Indians have any simples which are sovereign specifics in the cure of this disease; and indeed I doubt very much wheter any of them have any means of effecting a perfect cure. when once this disorder is contracted by them it continues with them during life; but always ends in decipitude, death, or premature old age; tho' from the uce of certain simples together with their diet, they support this disorder with but little inconvenience for many years, and even enjoy a tolerable share of health . . . notwithstanding that this disorder dose exist among the Indians on the Columbia yet it is witnessed in but few individuals, at least the males who are always sufficiently exposed to the observations or inspection of the phisician. in my whole rout down this river I did not see more than two or three with the gonnaerea and about double that number with the pox.[71]

January 28, 1806

[LEWIS] about noon Howard and Werner returned with a supply of salt; the badness of the weather and the difficulty of the road had caused their delay. they inform us that the salt makers are still much straitened for provision, having killed two deer only in the last six days; and that there are no Elk in their neighbourhood . . . The light brown berry,[72] is the fruit of a tree about the size shape and appearance in every rispect with that in the U. States called the wild crab apple; the leaf is also precisely the same as is also the bark in texture and colour. the berrys grow in clumps at the end of the small branches; each berry supported by a seperate stem, and as many as from 3 to 18 or 20 in a clump. the berry is ovate with one of it's extremities attatched to the peduncle, where it is in a small degre concave like the insertion of the stem of the crab apple . . . The wood of this tree is excessively hard when seasoned. the natives make great uce of it to form their wedges with which they split their boards of pine for the purpose of building houses. these wedges they also employ in splitting their fire-wood and in hollowing out their canoes. I have seen the natives drive the wedges of this wood into solid dry pine which it cleft without fracturing or injuring the wedg in the smallest degree. we have also found this wood usefull to us for ax handles as well as glutts or wedges.

71. Another name for syphilis.
72. Oregon crabapple.

the native also have wedges made of the beams of the Elk's horns which appear to answer extremely well.   this fruit is exceedingly assid, and resembles the flavor of the wild crab.

[WHITEHOUSE] I got during this day my feet severly frost bit.

January 29, 1806
[LEWIS] Nothing worthy of notice occurred today.   our fare is the flesh of lean elk boiled with pure water, and a little salt.   the whale blubber which we have used very sparingly is now exhausted.   on this food I do not feel strong, but enjoy the most perfect health; a keen appetite supplys in a great degree the want of more luxurious sauses or dishes, and still render my ordinary meals not uninteresting to me, for I find myself sometimes enquiring of the cook whether dinner or breakfast is ready.

January 30, 1806
[LEWIS] The dress of the Clatsops and others in this neighbourhood differs but little from that discribed of the skillutes; they never wear leggins or mockersons which the mildness of this climate I presume has rendered in a great measure unnecessary; and their being obliged to be frequently in the water also renders those articles of dress inconvenient.   they wear a hat of a conic figure without a brim confined on the head by means of a stri[n]g which passes under the chin and is attatched to the two opsite sides of a secondary rim within the hat.   the hat at top terminates in a pointed knob of a connic form also . . . these hats are made of the bark of cedar and beargrass wrought with the fingers so closely that it casts the rain most effectually in the shape which they give them for their own uce or that just discribed.   on these hats they work various figures of different colours, but most commonly only black and white are employed. these figures are faint representations of whales the canoes and the harpoonneers striking them.   sometimes squares dimonds triangles &c.

February 1, 1806
[LEWIS] the natives inhabiting the lower portion of the Columbia River make their canoes remarkably neat light and well addapted for riding high waves. I have seen the natives near the coast riding waves in these ca-

noes with safety and apparently without concern where I should have thought it impossible for any vessel of the same size to lived a minute. they are built of whitecedar or Arborvita generally, but sometimes of the firr . . . some of the large canoes are upwards of 50 feet long and will carry from 8 to 10 thousand lbs. or from 20 to thirty persons and some of them particularly on the sea coast are waxed painted and orniminted with curious images at bough and Stern; those images sometimes rise to the hight of five feet; the pedestals on which these immages are fixed are sometimes cut out of the solid stick with the canoe, and the imagary is formed of seperate small peices of timber firmly united with tenants and motices[73] without the assistance of a single spike of any kind.   when the natives are engaged in navigating their canoes one sets in the stern and steers with a paddle the others set by pears and paddle over the gunwall next them, they all kneel in the bottom of the canoe and set on their feet.   their paddles are of a uniform shape . . . I have observed four forms of canoe only in uce among the nations below the grand chatarac of this river . . . They have but few axes among them, and the only too[l] usually imployed in felling the trees or forming the canoe, carving &c is a chissel formed of an old file about an Inch or an Inch and a half broad.   this chissel has sometimes a large block of wood for a handle . . . a person would suppose that the forming of a large canoe with an instrument like this was the work of several years; but these people make them in a few weeks.   they prize their canoes very highly; we have been anxious to obtain some of them, for our journey up the river but hav not been able to obtain one as yet from the natives in this neighbourhood.   today we opened and examined all our ammunition, which had been secured in leaden canesters . . . perfectly as dry as when first put in the canesters, altho' the whole of it from various accedents has been for hours under the water.   these cannesters contain four lbs. of powder each and 8 of lead.   had it not have been for that happy expedient which I devised of securing the powder by means of the lead, we should not have had a single charge of powder at this time . . . we have an abundant stock to last us back; and we always take care to put a proportion of it in each canoe, to the end that should one canoe or more be lost we should still not be entirely bereft of ammunition, which is now

73. Tenons and mortises.

our only hope for subsistence and defence in a rout of 4000 miles through a country exclusively inhabited by savages.

February 2, 1806
[LEWIS] Not any occurrence today worthy of notice; but all are pleased, that one month of the time which binds us to Fort Clatsop and which seperates us from our friends has now elapsed.   one of the games of amusement and wrisk of the Indians of this neighbourhood like that of the Sosones consists in hiding in the hand some small article about the size of a bean; this they throw from one hand to the other with great dexterity accompanying their opperations with a particular song which seems to have been addapted to the game; when the individul who holds the peice has amused himself sufficiently by exchanging it from one hand to the other, he hold out his hands for his compettitors to guess which hand contains the peice; if they hit on the ha[n]d which contains the peice they win the wager otherwise loose . . . these people are excessively fond of their games of risk and bet freely every species of property of which they are possessed.

February 4, 1806
[LEWIS] There are sveral species of fir in this neighbourhood which I shall discribe as well as my slender botanicall skil will enable me and for the convenience of comparison with each other shal number them. (No 1.)[74] a species which grows to immence size; very commonly 27 feet in the girth six feet above the surface of the earth, and in several instances we have found them as much as 36 feet in the girth or 12 feet diameter perfectly solid and entire.   they frequently rise to the hight of 230 feet, and one hundred and twenty or 30 of that hight without a limb.

[LEWIS] Latitude . . . N. 46° 10′ 16.3″.[75]

74. Sitka spruce.
75. The captain's second entry for the day is found at the end of the previous day's entry. The approximate latitude of Fort Clatsop is 46° 8′ 5″ N.

February 5, 1806

[LEWIS] Fir No. 2[76] is next in dignity in point of size. it is much the most common species, it may be sad to constitute at least one half of the timber in this neighbourhood. it appears to be of the spruse kind. it rises to the hight of 160 to 180 feet very commonly and is from 4 to 6 feet in diameter, very streight round and regularly tapering.

February 6, 1806

[LEWIS] No. 3[77]   A species of fir which one of my men informs me is precisely the same with that called the balsam fir of Canada. it grows here to considerable size, being from 2½ to 4 feet in diameter and rises to the hight of eighty or an hundred feet . . . (No. 4)[78] is a species of fir which in point of size is much that of No. 2. the stem simple branching ascending and proliferous; the bark of a redish dark brown and thicker than that of No. 3. it is divided with small longitudinal interstices, but these are not so much ramifyed as in species No. 2 . . . No 5.[79] is a species of fir which arrives to the size of Nos. 2 and 4, the stem simple branching, diffuse and proliferous. the bark thin, dark brown, much divided with small longitudinal interstices and sometimes scaleing off in thin rolling flakes . . . No. 6[80] the white pine; or what is usually so called in Virginia. I see no difference between this and that of the mountains in Virginia; unless it be the uncommon length of cone of this found here, which are sometimes 16 or 18 inches in length and about 4 inches in circumpherence. I do not recollect those of virginia perfectly but it strikes me that they are not so long. this species is not common I have only seen it but in one instance since I have been in this neighbourhood.

February 7, 1806

[LEWIS] This evening we had what I call an excellent supper it consisted of a marrowbone a piece and a brisket of boiled Elk that had the appear-

76. Neither fir nor spruce, but the western hemlock.
77. Grand fir.
78. May be a form of grand fir or perhaps the Pacific silver fir.
79. Douglas fir.
80. Western white pine.

ance of a little fat on it. this for Fort Clatsop is living in high stile . . . The small pox has distroyed a great number of the natives in this quarter. it prevailed about 4 years since among the Clatsops and distroy several hundred of them, four of their chiefs fell victyms to it's ravages. those Clatsops are deposited in their canoes on the bay a few miles below us. I think the late ravages of the small pox may well account for the number of remains of vilages which we find deserted on the river and Sea coast in this quarter.

February 10, 1806
[LEWIS] Willard arrived late in the evening from the Saltworks, had cut his knee very badly with his tommahawk. he had killed four Elk not far from the Salt works the day before yesterday, which he had butched and took a part of the meat to camp, but having cut his knee was unable to be longer ucefull at the works and had returned. he informed us that Bratton was very unwell, and that Gibson was so sick that he could not set up or walk alone and had desired him to ask us to have him brought to the Fort.

February 11, 1806
[LEWIS] sent Sergt Pryor with a party of four men to bring Gibson to the fort. also sent Colter and Wiser to the Salt works to carry on the business with Joseph Fields; as Bratton had been sick we desired him to return to the Fort also if he thought proper; however in the event of his not coming Wiser was directed to return.

February 12, 1806
[LEWIS] There are two species of ever green shrubs which I first met with at the grand rappids of the Columbia and which I have since found in this neighbourhood also; they grow in rich dry ground not far usually from some watercourse. the roots of both species are creeping and celindric. the stem of the 1st[81] is from a foot to 18 inches high and as large as a goosqull; it is simple unbranced and erect. it's leaves are cauline, com-

81. Oregon grape.

pound and spreading . . . The stem of the 2nd[82] is procumbent abot the size of the former, jointed and unbranched.   it's leaves are cauline, compound and oppositely pinnate . . . I do not know the fruit or flower of either.   the 1st resembles the plant common to many parts of the U' States called the mountain holley.

February 14, 1806

[LEWIS] We are very uneasy with rispect to our sick men at the salt works. Sergt. Pryor and party have not yet returned nor can we conceive what causes their delay.

[CLARK] I compleated a *map* of the Countrey through which we have been passing from the Mississippi at the Mouth of Missouri to this place. In the Map the Missouri Jefferson's river the S. E. branch of the Columbia or Lewis's river, Koos-koos-ke and Columbia from the enterance of the S. E fork to the pacific Ocian, as well as a part of Clark's river and our track across the Rocky Mountains are laid down by celestial observations and Survey.   the rivers are also conected at their Sources with other rivers agreeably to the information of the nativs and the most probable conjecture arrising from their capacities and the relative positions of their respective enterances which last have with but fiew exceptions been established by celestial observations. We now discover that we have found the most practicable and· navigable passage across the Continent of North America; it is that which we have traveled with the exception of that part of our rout from the foot of the *Falls* of the Missouri, or in neighbourhood of the enterance of the Rocky Mountains untill we arive on Clarks river at the enterence of Travelers-rest Creek; the distance between those two points would be traveled more advantagiously by land as the navigation of the Missouri above the *Falls* is crooked laborious and 521 miles distant by which no advantage is gained as the rout which we are compelled to travel by land from the Source of Jeffersons River to the enterance of *Travellers* rest Creek is 220 miles being further by abt. 600 miles than that from the Falls of the Missourie to the last mentioned point (Travellers rest Creek) and a much worse rout if indian information is to

82. Dull Oregon grape.

be relied on which is from the So so nee or Snake Indians, and the Flatheads of the Columbia west of the rocky mountains . . . the best and most
practicable rout across the Continent is by way of the Missouri to the
Great *Falls*; thence to *Clarks* river at the enterance of Travellers rest Creek,
from thence u travillers rest Creek to the forks, from whence you prosue
a range of mountains which divides the waters of the two forks of this
Creek, and which still Continues it's westwardly Course on the mountains which divides the waters of the two forks of the Kooskooske river to
their junction; from thence to decend this river to the S. E. branch of the
Columbia, thence down that river to the Columbia, and down the Latter
to the *Pacific Ocian*— There is a large river which falls into the Columbia on its South Side at what point we could not lern;[83] which passes thro
those extencive Columbian Plains from the South East, and as the Indians inform us head in the mountains South of the head of Jeffersons River
and at no great distance from the Spanish Settlements, and that that fork
which heads with the River Rajhone and waters of the Missouri passes
through those extensive plains in which there is no wood, and the river
Crowded with rapids & falls many of which are impassable. the other or
westerly fork passes near a range of mountains and is the fork which great
numbers of Indian Bands of the *So sone* or Snake Indians, this fork most
probably heads with North River or the waters of Callifornia. This River
may afford a practicable land Communication with New Mexico by
means of its western fork. This river cannot be navagable as an unpracti-
cable rapid is within one mile of its enterance into the Columbia, and we
are fully purswaded that a rout by this river if practicable at all, would
lengthen the distance greatly and incounter the Same dificuelties in passing the Rocky Mountains with the rout by way of Travellers rest Creek &
Clarks river.

February 15, 1806
[LEWIS] after dark Sergt. Pryor arrived with Gibson. we are much pleased
in finding him by no means as ill as we had expected. we do no conceive

83. Clark here combined Indian information and geographic inference to formu-
late the existence of the Willamette River (joining the Columbia from the south). The
party missed its entrance on the way out but examined it on the return and named it
"Multnomah."

him in danger by any means, tho' he has yet a fever and is much reduced. we beleive his disorder to have orriginated in a violent cold which he contracted in hunting and pursuing Elk and other game through the swams and marshes about the salt works. he is nearly free from pain tho' a good deel reduced and very languid. we gave him broken dozes of diluted nitre and made him drink plentifully of sage tea, had his feet bathed in warm water and at 9 P. M. gave him 35 drops of laudanum.

The quadrupeds of this country from the Rocky Mountains to the pacific Ocean are 1st the *domestic animals*, consisting of the horse and the dog only; 2cdly the *native wild animals*, consisting of the Brown white or grizly bear, (which I beleive to be the same family with a mearly accedental difference in point of colour) the black bear, the common red deer, the black tailed fallow deer, the Mule deer, Elk, the large brown wolf, the small woolf of the plains, the large wolf of the plains, the tiger cat, the common red fox, black fox or fisher, silver fox, large red fox of the plains, small fox of the plains or kit fox, Antelope, sheep, beaver, common otter, sea Otter, mink, spuck, seal, racoon, large grey squirrel, small brown squirrel, small grey squirrel, ground squirrel, sewelel,[84] Braro,[85] rat, mouse, mole, Panther, hare, rabbit, and polecat or skunk. all of which shall be severally noticed in the order in which they occur as well as shuch others as I learn do exist and which not been here recapitulated. The horse is confined principally to the nations inhabiting the great plains of Columbia extending from Latitude 40° to 50° N. and occuping the tract of country lying between the rocky mountains and a range of Mountains which pass the columbia river about the great falls or from Longitude 116° to 121° West. in this extesive tract of principally untimbered country so far as we have leant the following nations reside (viz) the Sosone or snake Indians, the Chopunnish, sokulks, Cutssahnims, Chymnapums, Ehelutes, Eneshuh & Chilluckkittequaws.[86] all of whom enjoy

84. A Lower Chinookan term for the mountain beaver, which is a rodent, not a beaver.
85. Badger.
86. These tribal groups may be identified as Northern Paiutes ("Sosone or Snake Indians"), Nez Perces ("Chopunnish"), Wanapams ("sokulks"), Yakamas ("Cutssahnims" and "Chymnapums"), Wishram-Wascos ("Ehelutes"), Teninos ("Enes-huh"), and Wishram-Wascos ("Chilluckkittequaws"). "Chilluckkittequaws" is a Chinookan phrase rather than a tribal designation, but the captains associated it with Wishram-Wasco Indians.

the bennefit of that docile, generous and valuable anamal the horse, and all of them except the three last have immence numbers of them. Their horses appear to be of an excellent race; they are lofty eligantly formed active and durable; in short many of them look like he fine English coarsers and would make a figure in any country.   some of those horses[87] are pided [pied] with large spots of white irregularly scattered and intermixed with the black brown bey or some other dark colour, but much the larger portion are of an uniform colour with stars snips and white feet, or in this rispect marked much like our best blooded horses in virginia, which they resemble as well in fleetness and bottom as in form and colours.

February 16, 1806
[LEWIS] no tidings yet of Sergt. Gass and party.[88] Bratton is still very weak and complains of a pain in the lower part of the back when he moves which I suppose procedes from dability. I gave him barks. Gibson's fever still continues obstenate tho' not very high; I gave him a doze of Dr. Rush's which in many instances I have found extreemly efficatious in fevers which are in any measure caused by the presence of boil [bile?]. the nitre has produced a profuse perspiration this evening and the pills operated late at night his fever after which abated almost entirely and he had a good night's rest.

[GASS] During one of the most disagreeable nights, myself and another lay out in our shirts and overalls, with only one elk-skin to defend us from a violent night's rain. We had started a gang of elk, and in order to be light in the pursuit left our clothes where the first was killed, and could not get back before dark. Our shirts and overalls being all of leather made it the more disagreeable.

February 17, 1806
[LEWIS] Shannon brought me one of the large carrion Crow or Buzzads[89] of the Columbia which they had wounded and taken alive. I bleive this to be the largest bird of North America.   it was not in good order and yet it

87. Perhaps Appaloosas, favored by the Nez Perces and other regional natives.
88. Reubin Field and Thompson were with Gass; they returned the next day.
89. California condor.

weighed 25 lbs. had it have been so it might very well have weighed 10 lbs mor or 35 lbs. between the extremities of the wings it measured 9 feet 2 inches . . . we did not met with this bird untill we had decended the Columbia below the great falls, and have found them more abundant below tide-water than above. I beleive that this bird is reather of the Vulture genus than any other, tho' it wants some of their charactaristics particularly the hair on the neck and feathers on the legs. this is a handsome bird at a little distance.

February 20, 1806

[LEWIS] Collins . . . unsuccessfull as to the chase but brought with him some cranberries for the sick. Gibson is on the recovery fast; Bratton has an obstenate cough and pain in his back and still appears to be geting weaker. McNeal from his inattention to his disorder has become worse.

This forenoon we were visited by *Tâh-cum* a principal Chief of the Chinnooks and 25 men of his nation. we had never seen this cheif before he is a good looking man of about 50 years of age reather larger in statue than most of his nation; as he came on a friendly visit we gave himself and party some thing to eat and plyed them plentifully with smoke. we gave this cheif a small medal with which he seemed much gratifyed. in the evening at sunset we desired them to depart as is our custom and closed our gates. we never suffer parties of such number to remain within the fort all night; for notwithstanding their apparent friendly disposition, their great averice and hope of plunder might induce them to be treacherous. at all events we determined allways to be on our guard as much as the nature of our situation will permit us, and never place our selves at the mercy of any savages. we well know, that the treachery of the aborigenes of America and the too great confidence of our countrymen in their sincerity and friendship, has caused the distruction of many hundreds of us. so long have our men been accustomed to a friendly intercourse with the natives, that we find it difficult to impress on their minds the necessity of always being on their guard with rispect to them. this confidence on our part, we know to be the effect of a series of uninterupted friendly intercouse, but the well known treachery of the natives by no means entitle them to such confidence, and we must check it's growth in our own minds, as well as those of our men, by recollecting ourselves, and repeating to our men, that our preservation depends on never loosing sight of this trait in their character, and being always prepared to meet it in whatever shape it may present itself.

February 21, 1806
[LEWIS] Sergt. Ordway returned with the party from the salt camp which we have now evacuated.   they brought with them the salt and eutensils. our stock of salt is now about 20 Gallons . . . gave Willard and bratton each a doze of Scotts pills;[90] on the former they operated and on the latter they did not. Gibson still continues the barks three times a day and is on the recovery fast.

[ORDWAY] much fatigued and I am at this time verry Sick, and wet to my Skins waiding the Slashes and marshes.

February 22, 1806
[LEWIS] the woodwork and sculpture of these people as well as these hats and their waterproof baskets evince an ingenuity by no means common among the Aborigenes of America. in the evening they returned to their village and Drewyer accompanied them in their canoe in order to get the dogs which the Clatsops have agreed to give us in payment for the Elk they stole from us some weeks since.[91] these women informed us that the small fish began to run which we suppose to be herring[92] from their discription . . . our sick consisting of Gibson, Bratton, Sergt. Ordway, Willard and McNeal are all on the recovery.   we have not had as ma[n]y sick at any one time since we left Wood River.   the general complaint seams to be bad colds and fevers, something I beleive of the influenza.

February 25, 1806
[LEWIS] I am mortified at not having it in my power to make more celestial observations since we have been at Fort Clatsop, but such has been the state of the weather that I have found it utterly impracticable.

90. Probably similar to Rush's pills, a strong laxative.
91. On February 6.
92. Probably eulachon.

February 27, 1806
[LEWIS] Willard still continues very unwell the other sick men have nearly recovered. Gutridge and McNeal who have the pox are recovering fast, the former nearly well.

February 28, 1806
[LEWIS] Kuskelar a Clatsop man and his wife visited us today.   they brought some Anchovies,[93] Sturgeon, a beaver robe, and some roots for sail tho' they asked so high a price for every article that we purchased nothing but a part of a Sturgeon for which we gave a few fishing hooks. we suffered them to remain all night.

March 2 , 1806
[LEWIS] The diet of the sick is so inferior that they recover their strength but slowly.   none of them are now sick but all in a state of convalessence with keen appetites and nothing to eat except lean Elk meat . . .

The *Cock of the Plains*[94] is found in the plains of Columbia and are in Great abundance from the entrance of the S. E. fork of the Columbia to that of Clark's river.   this bird is about ⅔rds the size of a turkey.   the beak is large short curved and convex.   the upper exceeding the lower chap. the nostrils are large and the b[e]ak black.   the colour is an uniform mixture of dark brown reather bordeing on a dove colour, redish and yellowish brown with some small black specks.   in this mixture the dark brown prevails and has a slight cast of the dove colour at a little distance. the wider side of the large feathers of the wings are of a dark brown only. the tail is composed of 19 feathers of which that in the center is the longest, and the remaining 9 on each side deminish by pairs as they receede from the center; that is any one feather is equal in length to one equa distant from the center of the tail on the oposite side.   the tail when foalded comes to a very sharp point and appears long in proportion to the body.   in the act of flying the tail resembles that of a wild pigeon.   tho' the motion of the wings is much that of the pheasant and Grouse . . . the wings are also proportionably short, reather more so than those of the

93. Eulachon.
94. Sage grouse.

pheasant or grouse. the habits of this bird are much the same as those of the grouse. only that the food of this fowl is almost entirely that of the leaf and buds of the pulpy leafed thorn;[95] nor do I ever recollect seeing this bird but in the neighbourhood of that shrub.[96] they sometimes feed on the prickley pear . . . the flesh of the cock of the Plains is dark, and only tolerable in point of flavor. I do not think it as good as either the Pheasant or Grouse.

March 3, 1806

[LEWIS] our convalessents are slowly on the recovery. Lapage is taken sick, gave him a doze of Scots pills which did not operate . . . every thing moves on in the old way and we are counting the days which seperate us from the 1st of April and which bind us to fort Clatsop.

March 4, 1806

[LEWIS] Not any occurrence today worthy of notice. we live sumptuously on our wappetoe and Sturgeon. the Anchovey is so delicate that they soon become tainted unless pickled or smoked. the natives run a small stick through their gills and hang them in the smoke of their lodges, or kindle a small fire under them for the purpose of drying them. they need no previous preperation of guting &c and will cure in 24 hours. the natives do not appear to be very scrupelous about eating them when a little feated [fetid?]. the fresh sturgeon they keep for many days by immersing it in water. they coock their sturgeon by means of vapor or steam.

March 5, 1806

[LEWIS] late in the evening the hunters returned from the *kil-haw-â-nack-kle*[97] River which discharges itself into the head of the bay. They had neither killed nor seen any Elk. they informed us that the Elk had all gone off to the mountains a considerable distance from us. this is unwelcome information and reather allarming we have only 2 days provi-

95 Greasewood.

96. The sage grouse is not as dependent on greasewood as Lewis indicated.

97. Youngs River, Clatsop County, Oregon.

sion on hand, and that nearly spoiled. we made up a small assortment of articles to trade with the Indians and directed Sergt. Pryor to set out early in the morning in a canoe with 2 men, to ascend the Columbia to the resort of the Indian fishermen and purchase some fish; we also directed two parties of hunters to renew the Chase tomorrow early. the one up the Netul and the other towards Point Adams. if we find that the Elk have left us, we have determined to ascend the river slowly and indeavour to procure subsistence on the way, consuming the Month of March in the woody country. earlyer than April we conceive it a folly to attempt the open plains where we know there is no fuel except a few small dry shrubs. we shall not leave our quarters at fort Clatsop untill the first of April, as we intended unless the want of subsistence compels us to that measure.

March 6, 1806

[LEWIS] at 11 A. M. we were visited by Comowoll and two of his children. he presented us with some Anchovies which had been well cured in their manner. we foud them excellent. they were very acceptable particularly at this moment. we gave the old man some small articles in return. this we have found much the most friendly and decent savage that we have met with in this neighbourhood. Hall had his foot and ankle much injured yesterday by the fall of a large stick of timber; the bones were fortunately not broken and I expect he will be able to walk again shortly. Bratton is now weaker than any of the convalessants, all of whom recover slowly in consequence of the want of proper diet, which we have it not in our power to procure.

The Aquatic birds of this country, or such as obtain their subsistence from the water, are the large blue[98] and brown heron,[99] fishing hawk,[100] blue crested fisher, gulls of several species of the Coast, the large grey gull[101] of the Columbia, Cormorant, loons of two species, white, and the brown brant, small and large geese, small and large Swan, the Duckin-

---

98. Great blue heron.
99. Perhaps American bittern.
100. Osprey.
101. Western gull.

mallard, canvis back duck, red headed fishing duck,[102] black and white duck,[103] little brown duck,[104] black duck,[105] two speceis of divers, blue winged teal, and some other speceis of ducks.

March 7, 1806

[LEWIS] Bratton is much wose today, he complains of a violent pain in the small of his back and is unable in consequence to set up. we gave him one of our flanel shirts, applyed a bandage of flannel to the part and bathed and rubed it well with some vollatile linniment which I prepared with sperits of wine, camphor, castile soap and a little laudinum. he felt himself better in the evening.

[GASS] Among our other difficulties we now experience the want of to-bacco and out of 33 persons composing our party, there are but 7 who do not make use of it; we use crab-tree bark as a substitute.

March 9, 1806

[LEWIS] the small swan differs only from the larger one in size and it's note. it is about one fourth less and it's note entirely different. the latter cannot be justly immetated by the sound of letters nor do I know any sounds with which a comparison would be pertinent. it begins with a kind of whistleing sound and terminates in a round full note which is reather louder than the whistleing, or former part; this note is as loud as that of the large swan. from the peculiar whistleing of the note of this bird I have called it the *whistleing swan*[106] it's habits colour and contour ap-pear to be precisely those of the large Swan.[107] we first saw them below the great narrows of the Columbia near the Chilluckkittequaw nation. They are very abundant in this neighbourhood and have remained with us all winter. in number they are fully five for one of the large speceis.

102. Either the female red-breasted merganser or the female common merganser.
103. Bufflehead.
104. Unknown teal.
105. American coot.
106. Now the tundra swan.
107. Trumpeter swan.

March 10, 1806

[LEWIS] The hunters[108] who were over the Netull the other day informed us that they measured a pine tree,[109] (or fir No 1) which at the hight of a man's breast was 42 feet in the girth about three feet higher, or as high as a tall man could reach, it was 40 feet in the girth which was about the circumpherence for at least 200 feet without a limb, and that it was very lofty above the commencement of the limbs.   from the appearance of other trees of this speceis of fir and their account of this tree, I think it may be safely estimated at 300 feet.   it had every appearance of being perfectly sound.

March 11, 1806

[LEWIS] we once more live in *clover*; Anchovies fresh Sturgeon and Wappetoe.

March 12, 1806

[LEWIS] Beside the fish of this coast and river already mentioned we have met with the following speceis viz. the Whale, Porpus, Skaite, flounder, Salmon, red charr, two speceis of Salmon trout, mountain or speckled trout, and a speceis similar to one of those noticed on the Missouri within the mountains, called in the Eastern states, bottle-nose.[110] I have no doubt but there are many other speceis of fish, which also exist in this quarter at different seasons of the year, which we have not had an oportunity of seeing.   the shell fish are the Clam, perrewinkle, common mussle, cockle, and a speceis[111] with a circular flat shell.

March 13, 1806

[GASS] I this day took an account of the number of pairs of mockasons each man in the party had; and found the whole to be 338 pair. This stock

---

108. Shields, Reubin Field, and Frazer.

109. Sitka spruce.

110. Lewis identified an unspecified whale, harbor porpoise, big skate, starry flounder, an unspecified salmon, sockeye salmon ("red charr"), coho salmon and steelhead trout ("two species of Salmon trout"), cutthroat trout ("mountain or speckled trout"), and mountain sucker ("bottle-nose").

111. Some species of bivalve.

was not provided without great labour, as the most of them are made of the skins of elk. Each man has also a sufficient quantity of patch-leather.

March 14, 1806
[LEWIS] The Indians tell us that the Salmon begin to run early in the next month; it will be unfortunate for us if they do not, for they must form our principal dependence for food in ascending the Columbia, above the falls and it's S. E. branch [112] to the mountains.

March 15, 1806
[LEWIS] we were visited this afternoon by Delashshelwilt a Chinnook Chief his wife and six women of his nation which the old baud his wife had brought for market. this was the same party that had communicated the venerial to so many of our party in November last, and of which they have finally recovered. I therefore gave the men a particular charge with rispect to them which they promised me to observe . . . Bratton still sick.

March 16, 1806
[LEWIS] two handkercheifs would now contain all the small articles of merchandize which we possess; the ballance of the stock consists of 6 blue robes one scarlet do. one uniform artillerist's coat and hat, five robes made of our large flag, and a few old cloaths trimed with ribbon. on this stock we have wholy to depend for the purchase of horses and such portion of our subsistence from the Indians as it will be in our powers to obtain. a scant dependence indeed, for a tour of the distance of that before us. The *white Salmon Trout* which we had previously seen only at the great falls of the Columbia has now made it's appearance in the creeks near this place.

March 17, 1806
[LEWIS] Old Delashelwilt and his women still remain   they have formed a ca[m]p near the fort and seem to be determined to lay close sege to us but I beleive notwithstanding every effort of their wining graces, the men have preserved their constancy to the vow of celibacy which they made on

112. Snake River.

this occasion to Capt C. and myself. we have had our perogues prepared
for our departer, and shal set out as soon as the weather will permit . . .
Drewyer returned late this evening from the Cathlahmahs with our canoe
which Sergt. Pryor had left some days since, and also a canoe which he
had purchased from those people. for this canoe he gave my uniform
laced coat and nearly half a carrot of tobacco. it seems that nothing excep this coat would induce them to dispose of a canoe which in their
mode of traffic is an article of the greatest val[u]e except a wife, with
whom it is equal, and is generally given in exchange to the father for his
daughter. I think the U' States are indebted to me another Uniform coat,
for that of which I have disposed on this occasion was but little woarn.
we yet want another canoe, and as the Clatsops will not sell us one at a
price which we can afford to give we will take one from them in lue of the
six Elk which they stole from us in the winter.[113]

March 18, 1806

[LEWIS] Comowooll and two Cathlahmahs visited us today; we suffered
them to remain all night. this morning we gave Delashelwilt a certificate
of his good deportment &c. and also a list of our names, after which we
dispatched him to his village with his female band. These lists of our
names we have given to several of the natives and also paisted up a copy
in our room. the object of these lists we stated in the preamble of the
same as follows (viz) "The object of this list is, that through the medium
of some civilized person who may see the same, it may be made known to
the informed world, that the party consisting of the persons whose names
are hereunto annexed, and who were sent out by the government of the
U' States in May 1804 to explore the interior of the Continent of North
America, did penetrate the same by way of the Missouri and Columbia
Rivers, to the discharge of the latter into the Pacific Ocean, where they arrived on the 14th November 1805, and from whence they departed the
[blank] day of March 1806 on their return to the United States by the
same rout they had come out." on the back of some of these lists we
added a sketch of the connection of the upper branches of the Missouri
with those of the Columbia, particularly of it's main S. E. branch, on

113. In his entry for March 18 Ordway mentioned taking the Clatsop canoe.

which we also delienated the track we had come and that we meant to pursue on our return where the same happened to vary. There seemed so many chances against our government ever obtaining a regular report, though the medium of the savages and the traders of this coast that we declined making any. our party are also too small to think of leaving any of them to return to the U' States by sea, particularly as we shall be necessarily divided into three or four parties on our return in order to accomplish the objects we have in view; and at any rate we shall reach the United States in all human probability much earlier than a man could who must in the event of his being left here depend for his passageto the United States on the traders of the coast who may not return immediately to the U' States.

[ORDWAY] 4 men went over to the prarie near the coast to take a canoe which belongd to the Clotsop Indians, as we are in want of it. in the evening they returned 2 of them by land and killd. an Elk. the others took the canoe near the fort and concealed it,[114] as the chief of the Clotsops is now here.

March 19, 1806
[LEWIS] The Killamucks, Clatsops, Chinnooks, Cathlahmahs and Wâc'-ki-a-cums resemble each other as well in their persons and dress as in their habits and manners. their complexion is not remarkable, being the usual copper brown of most of the tribes of North America. they are low in statue reather diminutive, and illy shapen; possessing thick broad flat feet, thick ankles, crooked legs wide mouths thick lips, nose moderately large, fleshey, wide at the extremity with large nostrils, black eyes and black coarse hair. their eyes are sometimes of a dark yellowish brown the puple black. I have observed some high acqualine noses among them but they are extreemly rare. the nose is generally low between the eyes. the most remarkable trait in their physiognomy is the peculiar flatness and width of forehead which they artificially obtain by compressing the head between two boards while in a state of infancy and from which it never afterwards perfectly recovers. this is a custom among all the nations we

114. Joseph Field may have been one of the men taking the Clatsop canoe.

have met with West of the Rocky mountains. I have observed the heads of many infants, after this singular bandage had been dismissed, or about the age of 10 or eleven months, that were not more than two inches thick about the upper edge of the forehead and reather thiner still higher. from the top of the head to the extremity of the nose is one streight line. this is done in order to give a greater width to the forehead, which they much admire. this process seems to be continued longer with their female than their mail children, and neither appear to suffer any pain from the operation. it is from this peculiar form of the head that the nations East of the Rocky mountains, call all the nations on this side, except the Aliahtans or snake Indians, by the generic name of Flat heads. I think myself that the prevalence of this custom is a strong proof that those nations having originally proceeded from the same stock.

March 20, 1806

[LEWIS] Altho' we have not fared sumptuously this winter and spring at Fort Clatsop, we have lived quite as comfortably as we had any reason to expect we should; and have accomplished every object which induced our remaining at this place except that of meeting with the traders who visit the entrance of this river . . . many of our men are still complaining of being unwell; Willard and Bratton remain weak, principally I beleive for the want of proper food. I expect when we get under way we shall be much more healthy. it has always had that effect on us heretofore. The guns of Drewyer and Sergt. Pryor were both out of order. the first was repared with a new lock, the old one having become unfit for uce; the second had the cock screw broken which was replaced by a duplicate which had been prepared for the lock at Harpers ferry where she was manufactured. but for the precaution taken in bringing on those extra locks, and parts of locks, in addition to the ingenuity of John Shields, most of our guns would at this moment been untirely unfit for use; but fortunately for us I have it in my power here to record that they are all in good order.

[GASS] I made a calculation of the number of elk and deer killed by the party from the 1st of Dec. 1805 to the 20th March 1806, which gave 131 elk, and 20 deer.

March 21, 1806

[GASS] The women are much inclined to venery, and like those on the Missouri are sold to prostitution at an easy rate. An old Chin-ook squaw frequently visited our quarters, with nine girls which she kept as prostitutes. To the honour of the Flatheads,[115] who live on the west side of the Rocky Mountains, and extend some distance down the Columbia, we must mention them as an exception; as they do not exhibit those loose feelings of carnal desire, nor appear addicted to the common customs of prostitution: and they are the only nation on the whole route where any thing like chastity is regarded.

March 22, 1806

[LEWIS] at 12 OCk. we were visited by Comowooll and 3 of the Clatsops. to this Cheif we left our houses and funiture.   he has been much more kind an hospitable to us than any other indian in this neighbourhood . . . we determined to set out tomorrow at all events, and to stop the canoes temperarily with Mud and halt the first fair day and pay them.[116]   the leafing of the hucklebury riminds us of spring.

115. Here, probably Nez Perces.
116. To cover with a waterproof substance, such as pitch.

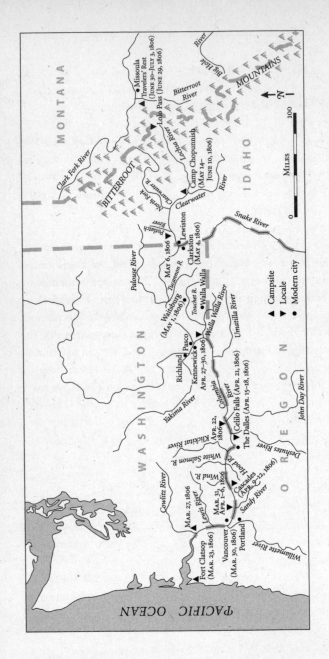

The Expedition's Route, March 23–July 1, 1806

CHAPTER 10

Homeward Bound

March 23–July 2, 1806

March 23, 1806

[CLARK] This morning proved So raney and uncertain that we were un-deturmined for Some time whether we had best Set out & risque the [river?] which appeared to be riseing or not . . . the rained Seased and it became fair about Meridean, at which time we loaded our Canoes & at 1 P. M. left Fort Clatsop on our homeward bound journey. at this place we had wintered and remained from the 7th of Decr. 1805 to this day and have lived as well as we had any right to expect, and we can Say that we were never one day without 3 meals of Some kind a day either pore Elk meat or roots, not withstanding the repeeted fall of rain which has fallen almost Constantly Since we passed the long narrows on the [blank] of Novr. last[1]   indeed w[e] have had only [blank] days fair weather since that time. [Camped just below the mouth of John Day River, Clatsop County, Oregon.]

March 24, 1806

[LEWIS] at half after 3 P. M. we set out and continued our rout among the seal Islands;[2] not paying much attention we mistook our rout which an Indian perceiving pursued overtook us and put us in the wright channel. this Cathlahmah claimed the small canoe which we had taken from the Clatsops. however he consented very willingly to take an Elk's skin for it which I directed should be given him and he immediately returned. [Camped northeast of Brownsmead, Clatsop County, Oregon.]

1. The corps passed the "long narrows" (The Dalles) on October 25, 1805.
2. Karlson, Marsh, and other islands in Cathlamet Bay, Clatsop County, Oregon.

[CLARK] proceeded to the Cath lah mah Village . . . at this village we purchased a fiew wappato and a Dog for our Sick men Willard and Bratten
who are yet in a weak State.   at this Village I saw two very large elegant
Canoes inlaid with Shills, those Shills I took to be teeth at first View, and
the nativs informed Several of the men that they the teeth of their enemies
which they had killed in War.   in examineing of them Closely haveing
taken out Several pices, we found that were Sea Shells which yet contained a part of the iner [blank] they also deckerate their Smaller wooden
vessles with those Shells which have much the appearance of humane
teeth, Capt Cook may have mistaken those Shills verry well for humane
teeth without a Close examination. The Village of these people is the dirt-
iest and Stinkingest place I ever Saw in any Shape whatever, and the inhabitants partake of the carrestick [characteristic] of the Village.

March 26, 1806

[LEWIS] soon after we halted for dinner the two Wackiacums who have
been pursuing us since yesterday morning with two dogs for sale, arrived.
they wish tobacco in exchange for their dogs which we are not disposed
to give as our stock is now reduced to a very few carrots.   our men who
have been accustomed to the use of this article Tobaco and to whom we
are now obliged to deny the uce of this article appear to suffer much for
the want of it.   they substitute the bark of the wild crab which they chew;
it is very bitter, and they assure me they find it a good substitute for tobacco.   the smokers substitute the inner bark of the red willow and the
sacacommis.[3] [Camped on one of the small islands below Longview,
Cowlitz County, Washington, but closer to the opposite side in Columbia County, Oregon.]

March 27, 1806

[LEWIS] the principal village of these Skillutes[4] reside on the lower side
of the Cow-e-lis'-kee[5] river a few miles from it's entrance into the co-

3. A mixture of the inner bark of red osier dogwood ("red willow") and the dried leaves
of bearberry ("sacacommis") or kinnikinnick were common substitutes for tobacco
among the French boatmen.
    4. A Chinookan-speaking people not identifiable in modern tribal designations. "Skil-
lutes" is a phrase rather than a tribal name.
    5. Cowlitz River.

lumbia.   these people are said to be numerous.   in their dress, habits, manners and language they differ but little from the Clatsops Chinnooks &c.   they have latterly been at war with Chinnooks but peace is said now to be restored between them, but their intercourse is not yet resumed. no Chinnooks come above the marshey islands nor do the Skillutes visit the mouth of the Columbia.   the Clatsops, Cathlahmahs and Wack-kiacums are the carriers between these nations being in alliance with both. [Camped somewhat south and in the vicinity of Goble, Columbia County, Oregon.]

March 29, 1806
[LEWIS] their women[6] wear their ornaments robes and hair as those do below tho' here their hair is more frequently braded in two tresses and hang over each ear in front of the body.   in stead of the tissue of bark woarn by the women below, they wear a kind of leather breech clout about the width of a common pocket handkerchief and reather longer. the two corners of this at one of the narrow ends are confined in front just above the hips; the other end is then brought between the legs, com-pressed into a narrow foalding bundel is drawn tight and the corners a little spread in front and tucked at the groin over and arround the part first confind about the waist.   the small robe which dose not reach the waist is their usual and only garment commonly woarn be side that just mentioned.   when the weather is a litte warm this robe is thrown aside and the leather truss or breech-clout constitutes the whole of their ap-parel.   this is a much more indecent article than the tissue of bark, and bearly covers the mons venes,[7] to which it is drawn so close that the whole shape is plainly perceived. [Camped in the vicinity of Ridgefield, Clark County, Washington.]

March 30, 1806
[LEWIS] I took a walk of a few miles through the prarie and an open grove of oak timber which borders the prarie on the back part . . . The timber and apearance of the country is much as before discribed.   the up lands are covered almost entirely with a heavy growth of fir of several speceis

6. Upper Chinookan women.
7. The Latin *mons veneris*, referring to the female pubic area.

like those discribed in the neighbourhood of Fort Clatsop; the white cedar is also found here of large size; no white pine nor pine of any other
kind.   we had a view of mount St. helines and Mount Hood.   the 1st is
the most noble looking object of it's kind in nature . . . the highlands in
this valley are rolling tho' by no means too steep for cultivation   they are
generally fertile of a dark rich loam and tolerably free of stones.   this valley is . . . about 70 miles wide on a direct line and it's length I beleive to be
very extensive tho' how far I cannot determine.   this valley would be
copetent to the mantainance of 40 or 50 thousand souls if properly cultivated and is indeed the only desireable situation for a settlement which I
have seen on the West side of the Rocky mountains. [Camped at Vancouver, Clark County, Washington.]

[ORDWAY] I must give these Savages as well as those on the coast the
praise of makeing the neatest and handsomest lightest best formed canoes I ever Saw & are the best hands to work them.

March 31, 1806
[LEWIS] these people speak a different language from those below tho' in
their dress habits manners &c   they differ but little from the quathlah-
pohtles . . . have a few words the same with those below but the air of the
language is intirely different, insomuch, that it may be justly deemed a
different language [8] . . . we determined to remain at our present encampment a day or two for the several purposes of examining quicksand river [9]
making some Celestial observations, and procuring some meat to serve
us as far as the falls or through the Western mountains where we found
the game scarce as we decended. [10] [Camped above the mouth of
Washougal River, Washougal, Clark County, Washington; the party
stayed here until April 6.]

8. Here Lewis was meeting Upper Chinookan speakers as distinguished from Lower
Chinookan speakers on the coast, but dialectal and cultural differences were found within
these large divisions as indicated by the captain's reference to the Upper Chinookan Cathlapotles.
   9. Sandy River, Multnomah County, Oregon.
   10. The captains supposed the Sandy River was a principal southern drainage of the
Columbia. In a few days they realized that the Willamette was the river they sought and
that they had missed it on the outbound trip.

April 1, 1806

[LEWIS] we were now convinced that there must be some other considerable river which flowed into the columbia on it's south side below us
which we have not yet seen, as the extensive valley on that side of the river
lying between the mountainous country of the Coast and the Western
mountains must be watered by some stream which we had heretofore
supposed was the quicksand river . . . we indeavoured to ascertain by what
stream the southern portion of the Columbian valley was watered but
could obtain no satisfactory information of the natives on this head. they
[Indians] informed us that the quicksand river is navigable a short distance only in consequence of falls and rapids; and that no nation inhabits it . . . they complained much of the scarcity of food among them. they
informed us that the nations above them were in the same situation &
that they did not expect the Salmon to arrive untill the full of the next
moon which happens on the 2d of May . . . This information gave us
much uneasiness with rispect to our future means of subsistence. above
falls or through the plains from thence to the Chopunnish [11] there are no
deer Antelope nor Elk on which we can depend for subsistence; their
horses are very poor most probably at this season, and if they have no fish
their dogs must be in the same situation.   under these circumstances
there seems to be but a gloomy prospect for subsistence on any terms; we
therefore took it into serious consideration what measures we were to
pursue on this occasion; it was at once deemed inexpedient to wait the arrival of the salmon as that would detain us so large a portion of the season that it is probable we should not reach the United States before the
ice would close the Missouri; or at all events would hazard our horses
which we lelft in charge of the Chopunnish who informed us that they intended passing the rocky mountains to the Missouri as early as the season would permit them wich is as we believe bout the begining of May.
should these people leave their situation near kooskooske [12] before our
arrival we may probably find much difficulty in recovering our horses;
without which there will be but little possibility of repassing the mountains; we are therefore determined to loose as little time as possible in geting to the Chopunnish Village. [Remained at Washougal.]

11. Nez Perces.
12. Clearwater River.

April 2, 1806

[LEWIS] This morning we came to a resolution to remain at our present encampment or some where in this neighbourhood untill we had obtained as much dryed meat as would be necessary for our voyage as far as the Chopunnish.   to exchange our perogues for canoes with the natives on our way to the great falls of the columbia or purchase such canoes from them for Elkskins and Merchandize as would answer our purposes. these canoes we intend exchanging with the natives of the plains for horses as we proceed untill we obtain as many as will enable us to travel altogether by land . . . for we now view the horses as our only certain resource for food, nor do we look forward to it with any detestation or horrow, so soon is the mind which is occupyed with any interesting object reconciled to it's situation . . . we now enformed the party of our intention of laying in a store of meat at this place . . . about this time several canoes of the natives arrived at our camp and [informed us] of a large river which discharges itself into the Columbia on it's South side some miles below us.   we readily prevailed on them to give us a sketch of this river which they drew on a mat with a coal.   it appeared that this river which they called Mult-no-mah discharged itself behind the Island which we called the image canoe Island [13] and as we had left this island to the S. both in ascending and decending the river we had never seen it.   they informed us that it was a large river and run a considerable distance to the South between the mountains. Capt. Clark determined to return and examine this river. [Lewis remained at Washougal.]

[CLARK] at half past 11 A. M. I Set out,[14] and had not proceeded far eer I saw 4 large Canoes at Some distance above decending and bending their Course towards our Camp which at this time is very weak Capt. Lewis haveing only 10 men with him. I hisitated for a moment whether it would not be advisable for me to return and delay untill a part of our hunters Should return to add more Strength to our Camp.   but on a Second

13. Today a combination of Hayden and Tomahawk Islands at the mouth of the Willamette River, Multnomah County, Oregon.

14. Clark had the following men with him: Cruzatte, Howard, Potts, Thompson, Whitehouse, Weiser, and York.

reflection and reverting to the precautions always taken by my friend Capt Lewis on those occasions banished all apprehensions and I proceeded on down . . . I entered one of the rooms of this [Indian] house and offered Several articles to the nativs in exchange for Wappato. they were Sulkey and they positively refused to Sell any. I had a Small pece of port fire match in my pocket, off of which I cut a pece one inch in length & put it into the fire and took out my pocket Compas and Set myself doun on a mat on one Side of the fire, and a magnet which was in the top of my ink Stand   the port fire cought and burned vehemently, which changed the Colour of the fire; with the Magnit I turned the Needle of the Compas about very briskly; which astonished and alarmed these nativs and they laid Several parsles of Wappato at my feet, & begged of me to take out the bad fire; to this I consented; at this moment the match being exhausted was of course extinguished and I put up the magnet &c.   this measure alarmed them So much that the womin and children took Shelter in their beads and behind the men, all this time a very old blind man was Speaking with great vehemunce, appearently imploreing his gode. I lit my pipe and gave them Smoke & gave the womin the full amount of the roots which they had put at my feet.   they appeared Somewhat passified and I left them and proceeded on . . . I entered this river which the nativs had informed us of, Called *Multnomah* river so called by the nativs from a Nation who rside on Wappato Island a little below the enterance of this river. Multnomah discharges itself in the Columbia on the S. E. and may be justly Said to be ¼ the Size of that noble river. Multnomah had fallen 18 inches from it's greatest annual height.   three Small Islands are situated in it's mouth which hides the river from view from the Columbia.   from the enterance of this river, I can plainly See Mt. Jefferson which is high and Covered with snow S. E.   Mt. Hood East, Mt St. Helians a high humped Mountain to the East of Mt St. Helians.[15]   I also Saw the Mt. Raneer Nearly North.   Soon after I arived at this river an old man passed down of the *Clark a' mos* Nation[16] who are noumerous and reside on a branch

15. Clark's second reference to Mount St. Helens may have been a mistake for Mount Adams.

16. An alternate spelling for the Clackamas Indians who resided on the Clackamas River, Oregon.

of this river which receives it's waters from Mt. Jefferson which is emensely high and discharges itself into this river one day and a half up, this distance I State at 40 Miles. This nation inhabits 11 Villages their Dress and language is very Similar to the *Quath-lah-poh-tle*[17] and other tribes on Wappato Island.[18] The Current of the Multnomar is as jentle as that of the Columbia glides Smoothly with an eavin surface, and appears to be Sufficiently deep for the largest Ship. I attempted fathom it with a Cord of 5 fathom which was the only Cord I had, could not find bottom ⅓ of the distance across. I proceeded up this river 10 miles from it's enterance into the Columbia to a large house on the N E. Side and Encamped near the house, the flees being So noumerous in the house that we could not Sleep in it. [Clark camped in the northwest part of Portland, Multnomah County, Oregon.]

[WHITEHOUSE] I am of opinion, that if any Welch nation of Indians are in existence, it must be those Indians [Clackamas], & not the flatt head Nation, as before mentioned; this I believe, from their Colour, numbers of Towns, & fire arms among them, which I flatter myself will be confirmed, whenever the River Mult-no-mack is fully explored.[19]

April 3, 1806
[CLARK] being perfectly Satisfyed of the Size and magnitude of this great river which must Water that vast tract of Country betwen the Western range of mountains and those on the Sea coast and as far S. as the Waters of Callifornia about Latd. 37° North I deturmined to return. [Clark rejoined the main party at Washougal.]

April 5, 1806
[LEWIS] Saw the Log cock,[20] the hummingbird, gees ducks &c today. the tick has made it's appearance   it is the same with those of the Atlantic

---

17. Cathlapotles.

18. Sauvie Island, Multnomah County, Oregon.

19. This is the last entry in Whitehouse's known journal; he ended with a final reference to the fabled Welsh Indians.

20. Pileated woodpecker.

States.   the Musquetoes have also appeared but are not yet troublesome . . . The dogwood[21] grows abundantly on the uplands in this neighbourhood.   it differs from that of the United States in the appearance of
it's bark which is much smoother, it also arrives here to much greater size
than I ever observed it elsewhere   sometimes the stem is nearly 2 feet in
diameter.   we measured a fallen tree of fir No.1[22] which was 318 feet including the stump which was about 6 feet high.   this tree was only about
3½ feet in diameter.   we saw the martin,[23] small gees, the small speckled
woodpecker[24] with a white back, the Blue crested Corvus,[25] ravens,
crows, eagles Vultures and hawks.   the mellow bug[26] and long leged spi-
der have appeared, as have also the butterfly blowing fly and many other
insects. I observe not any among them which appear to differ from those
of our country or which deserve particular notice. [Remained at
Washougal.]

[ORDWAY] great numbers of Savages visited the Camp continually Since
we have lay [in?] at this Camp, who were passing down with their famillys
from the country above into the vally of Columbia in Search of food.
they inform us that the natives above the great falls have no provisions
and many are dieing with hunger.   this information has been so repeatedly given by different parties of Indians that it does not admit of any
doubt and is the cause of our delay in this neighbourhood for the purpose
of procureing as much dryed Elk meat as will last us through the Columbia plains in which we do not expect to find any thing to kill &C.

April 6, 1806
[LEWIS] about this place [Willamette River] in different directions Capt.
C. Saw a great number of small canoes lying scattered on the bank.   these
small canoes are employed by the women in collecting wappetoe; with

21. Nuttall's dogwood.
22. Sitka spruce.
23. Perhaps purple martin.
24. Either the hairy woodpecker or downy woodpecker.
25. Steller's jay.
26. A beetle, the "melon bug."

one of these a woman enters a pond where the Sagitaria Sagittifolia grows frequently to her breast in water and by means of her toes and feet breakes the bulb of this plant loos from the parent radicle and disincumbering it from the mud it immediately rises to the surface of the water when she seizes it and throws it into her canoe which she always keeps convenient to her.   they will remain in the water for hours together in surch of this bulb in middle of winter.   those canoes are from 10 to 14 feet in length, from 18 to 23 inches in width near the middle tapering or becoming nar-rower towards either extremity and 9 inches deep . . . they are so light that a woman can draw them over land or take them with ease through the swamps in any direction, and are sufficient to carry a single person and several bushells of roots. [Camped above Latourell Falls and Rooster Rock State Park in the area of Sheppards Dell, Multnomah County, Ore-gon, where the party remained until April 9.]

April 7, 1806
[LEWIS] last evening Reubin Fields killed a bird of the quail kind[27] it is reather larger than the quail, or partridge as they are called in Virginia. it's form is precisely that of our patridge tho' it's plumage differs in every part.   the upper part of the head, sides and back of the neck, including the croop and about ⅓ of the under part of the body is of a bright dove coloured blue, underneath the under beak, as high as the lower edge of the eyes, and back as far as the hinder part of the eyes and thence com-ing down to a point in front of the neck about two thirds of it's length downwards, is of a fine dark brick red.   between this brick red and the dove colour there runs a narrow stripe of pure white. [Remained at Shep-pards Dell.]

[CLARK] I provaled on an old indian to mark the Multnomah R down on the Sand which hid and perfectly Corisponded with the Sketch given me by sundary others, with the addition of a circular mountain which passes this river at the falls and connects with the mountains of the Seacoast.   he also lais down the Clark a' mos passing a high Conical Mountain near it's mouth on the lower Side and heads in Mount Jefferson which he lais

27. Mountain quail.

down by raiseing the Sand as a very high mountain and Covered with eternal Snow.   the high mountain which this Indian lais down near the enterance of Clark a' mos river, we have not Seen as the hills in it's diretion from this vally is high and obscures the Sight of it from us.

April 8, 1806

[CLARK] John Shields Cut out my Small rifle & brought hir to Shoot very well.   the party ows much to the injenuity of this man, by whome their guns are repared when they get out of order which is very often. I observed an Indian Woman who visited us yesterday blind of an eye, and a man who was nearly blind of both eyes.   the loss of Sight I have observed to be more Common among all the nations inhabiting this river than among any people I ever observed.   they have almost invariably Sore eyes at all Stages of life.   the loss of an eye is very Common among them; blindness in persons of middle age is by no means uncommon, and it is almost invariably a concammitant of old age. I Know not to what cause to attribute this prevalent deficientcy of the eye except it be their exposure to the reflection of the Sun on the water to which they are constantly exposed in the Occupation of fishing. [Remained at Sheppards Dell.]

[LEWIS AND CLARK, WEATHER REMARKS] the male flowers of the cottonwood are falling.   the goosburry has cast the petals of it's flowers, and it's leaves obtained their full size.   the Elder which is remarkably large has began to blume.   some of it's flowerets have expanded their corollas.

[GASS] Some of the men are complaining of rheumatick pains; which are to be expected from the wet and cold we suffered last winter.

April 9, 1806

[LEWIS] we passed several beautifull cascades[28] which fell from a great hight over the stupendious rocks which cloles [closes?] the river on both sides nearly, except a small bottom on the South side in which our hunters were encamped.   the most remarkable of these casscades falls about 300 feet perpendicularly over a solid rock into a narrow bottom of

28. Multnomah Falls or similar falls in the vicinity, Multnomah County, Oregon.

the river on the south side. it is a large creek, situated about 5 miles above our encampment of the last evening.   several small streams fall from a much greater hight, and in their decent become a perfect mist which collecting on the rocks below again become visible and decend a second time in the same manner before they reach the base of the rocks . . . during our halt at this village the grand Cheif and two inferior Cheifs of the Chil-luck-kit-te-quaw nation [29] arrived with several men and women of their nation in two large canoes.   these people were on their return up the river, having been on a trading voyage to the Columbean vally, and were loaded with wappetoe dryed anchovies, with some beads &c which they had received in exchange for dryed and pounded salmon shappelell beargrass &c. These people had been very kind to us as we decended the river we therefore smoked with them and treated them with every attention. [Camped near present Bonneville, Multnomah County, Oregon.]

April 10, 1806
[LEWIS] the small canoe [30] got loose from the hunters and went a drift with a tin vessel and tommahawk in her; the Indians caught her at the last village and brought her up to us this evening for which service we gave them a couple of knives. [Camped in the vicinity of North Bonneville, Skamania County, Washington.]

April 11, 1806
[LEWIS] as it continued still raining this morning we concluded to take our canoes first to the head of the rapids, hoping that by evening the rain would cease and afford us a fair afternoon to take our baggage over the portage.   this portage is two thousand eight hundred yards along a narrow rough and slipery road.   the duty of getting the canoes above the rapid was by mutual consent confided to my friend Capt. C. who took with him for that purpose all the party except Bratton who is yet so weak he is unable to work, three others who were lamed by various accedents and one other to cook for the party.   a few men were absolutely necessary

29. A branch of the Wishram-Wascos, but "Chil-luck-kit-te-quaw" is a phrase rather than a tribal name.

30. Canoe of Drouillard and the Field brothers.

at any rate to guard our baggage from the War-clel-lars who crouded about our camp in considerable numbers.   these are the greates theives and scoundrels we have met with.   by the evening Capt. C. took 4 of our canoes above the rapids tho' with much difficulty and labour.   the canoes were much damaged by being driven against the rocks in dispite of every precaution which could be taken to prevent it.   the men complained of being so much fatiegued in the evening that we posponed taking up our 5th canoe untill tomorrow.   these rapids are much worse than they were fall when we passed them, at that time there were only three difficult points within seven miles, at present the whole distance is extreemly difficult of ascent, and it would be impracticable to decend except by leting down the empty vessels by a cord and then even the wrisk would be greater than in taking them up by the same means.   the water appears to be upwards of 20 feet higher than when we decended the river.   the distance by way of the river between the points of the portage is 3 Ms   many of the natives crouded about the bank of the river where the men were engaged in taking up the canoes; one of them had the insolence to cast stones down the bank at two of the men who happened to be a little detatched from the party at the time.   on he return of the party in the evening from the head of the rapids they met with many of the natives on the road, who seemed but illy disposed; two of these fellows met with John Sheilds who had delayed some time in purchasing a dog and was a considerable distance behind the party on their return with Capt. C.   they attempted to take the dog from him and pushed him out of the road.   he had nothing to defend himself with except a large knife which he drew with an intention of puting one or both of them to death before they could get themselves in readiness to use their arrows, but discovering his design they declined the combat and instantly fled through the woods. three of this same tribe of villains the Wah-clel-lars, stole my dog this evening, and took him towards their village; I was shortly afterwards informed of this transaction by an indian who spoke the Clatsop language, [NB: *some of which we had learnt from them during the winter*] and sent three men in pursuit of the theives with orders if they made the least resistence or difficulty in surrendering the dog to fire on them; they overtook these fellows or reather came within sight of them at the distance of about 2 miles; the indians discovering the party in pursuit of them left the dog and fled. they also stole an ax from us, but scarcely had it in their possession before Thompson detected them and wrest it from them. we ordered the centinel to keep them out of camp, and informed them by signs that if they made any further attempts to steal our property or insulted our men we should put them to instant death. a cheif of the Clah-clel-lah tribe informed us that there were two very bad men among the Wah-clel-lahs who had been the principal actors in these seenes of outradge[31] . . . I am convinced that no other consideration but our number at this moment protects us . . . I hope that the friendly interposition of this chief may prevent our being compelled to use some violence with thee people; our men seem well disposed to kill a few of them. we keep ourselves perfectly on our guard. [Remained at the North Bonneville camp.]

April 12, 1806

[LEWIS] a small distance above our camp there is one of the most difficult parts of the rapid. at this place the current sets with great violence against a projecting rock. in hawling the perogue arround this point the bow unfortunately took the current at too great a distance from the rock, she turned her side to the stream and the utmost exertions of all the party were unable to resist the forse with which she was driven by the current, they were compelled to let loose the cord and of course both perogue and cord went a drift with the stream. the loss of this perogue will I fear compell us to purchase one or more canoes of the indians at an extravegant price . . . near the river we find the Cottonwood, sweet willow, broad leafed ash, a species of maple,[32] the purple haw,[33] a small speceis of cherry; purple currant,[34] goosberry, red willow, vining and white burry honeysuckle,[35] huckkle burry, sacacommis, two speceis of mountain holley,[36] & common ash. [Camped at the camp of October 30-31, 1805, in

31. The "Clah-clel-lah tribe" and "War-clel-lars" are Upper Chinookan Watlalas, sometimes grouped with the other natives of the area and called Cascades Indians.
32. Vine maple.
33. Black hawthorn.
34. Red flowering currant.
35. Snowberry.
36. Oregon and dull Oregon grape.

Skamania County, Washington, nearly opposite Cascade Locks, Hood River County, Oregon.]

April 13, 1806
[LEWIS] the dog now constitutes a considerable part of our subsistence and with most of the party has become a favorite food; certain I am that it is a healthy strong diet, and from habit it has become by no means disagreeable to me, I prefer it to lean venison or Elk, and is very far superior to the horse in any state. [Lewis with one contingent camped a few miles above Wind River, Skamania County, Washington, but on the south side of the Columbia in Hood River County, Oregon, while Clark with another group camped on the other side, apparently between Collins Creek and Dog Creek, Skamania County.]

April 15, 1806
[LEWIS] at three in the evening we arrived at the entrance of Quinnette creek which we ascended a short distance and encamped at the place we have called rockfort camp.   here we were visited by some of the people from the villages at the great narrows and falls.   we informed them of our wish to purchase horses, & agreed to meet them on the opposite or North side of the river tomorrow for the purpose of bartering with them. [Camped at Mill ("Quinnette") Creek, the "Fort Rock" camp of October 25-28, 1805, at The Dalles, Wasco County, Oregon, where the party remained until April 18.]

April 16, 1806
[LEWIS] amused myself in making a collection of the esculent plants in the neighbourhood such as the Indians use, a specemine of which I preserved. I also met with sundry other plants which were strangers to me which I also preserved, among others there is a currant [37] which is now in blume and has yellow blossom something like the yellow currant of the Missouri but is a different speceis. Reubin Feilds returned in the evening and brought with him a large grey squrrel [38] and two others of a kind [39] I

37. Golden currant.
38. Western gray squirrel.
39. Perhaps a California ground squirrel.

had never before seen.   they are a size less than the grey squirrel common
to the middle atlantic states and of a pided grey and yellowish brown
colour, in form it resembles our grey squrrel precisely. I had them skined
leaving the head feet and tail to them and placed in the sun to dry. [Lewis
with the main party remained at The Dalles, while Clark with eleven men
moved to the opposite side in order to trade for horses; Clark camped
above Dallesport, Klickitat County, Washington.]

April 17, 1806
[LEWIS] the plain is covered with a rich virdure of grass and herbs from
four to nine inches high and exhibits a beautifull seen particularly pleasing after having been so long imprisoned in mountains and those almost
impenetrably thick forrests of the seacoast . . . This evening Willard
and Cruzatte returned from Capt. Clark and brought me a note in which
Capt. C. informed me that he had sill been unsuccessfull having not obtained a single horse as yet from the natives and the state of our stores are
so low that I begin to fear we shall not be enabled to obtain as many
horses at this place as will convey our baggage and unless we do obtain a
sufficient number for that purpose we shall not hasten our progress as a
part of our baggage must still be conveyed by water . . . I dispatched Shannon with a note to Capt. Clark in which I requested him to double the
price we have heretofore offered for horses and if possible obtain as many
as five, by this means we shall be enabled to proceed immediately with
our small canoes and those horses to the villages in the neighbourhood of
the mussel shell rapid[40] where horses are more abundant and cheaper;
with the remainder of our merchandize in addition to the canoes we can
no doubt obtain as many horses there as will answer our purposes.   delay in the villages at the narrows and falls will be expensive to us inasmuch
as we will be compelled to purchase both fuel and food of the indians, and
might the better enable them to execute any hostile desighn should they
meditate any against us. [Lewis remained at The Dalles.]

[CLARK] I rose early after bad nights rest, and took my merchindize to a
rock which afforded an elegable Situation for my purpose, and at a Short

40. In the area of Plymouth, Benton County, Washington. The party passed this point
on October 19, 1805, on the outbound journey.

distance from the houses, and divided the articles of merchindize into parsels of Such articles as I thought best Calculated to pleas the Indians, and in each parcel I put as many articles as we could afford to give, and thus exposed them to view, informing the Indians that each parcel was intended for a horse. they tanterlised me the greater part of the day, Saying that they had Sent out for their horses and would trade as Soon as they Came. Several parcels of merchindize was laid by for which they told me they would bring horses. I made a bargin with the Chief for 2 horses, about an hour after he canseled the bargin and we again bargained for 3 horses which were brought foward, only one of the 3 could be possibly used the other two had Such intolerable backs as to render them entirely unfit for Service. I refused to take two of them which displeased him and he refused to part with the 3rd. I then packed up the articles and was about Setting out for the Village above when a man Came and Sold me two horses, and another man Sold me one horse, and Several others informed me that they would trade with me if I would Continue untill their horses could be drove up. this induced me to Continue at this Village another day . . . the Chief of the Enesher's [41] and 15 or 20 of his people visited me and appeared to be anxious to See the articles I offered for the horses. Several of them agreeed to let me have horses if I would add Sundery articles to those I offered which I agreeed to, and they lay'd those bundles by and informed me they would deliver me the horses in the morning. I proposed going with them to their Town. the Chief informed me that their horses were all in the plains with their womin gathering roots. they would Send out and bring the horses to this place tomorrow. this entiligence was flattering, tho' I dobted the Sincerity of those people who had Several times disapointed me in a Similar way.   however I determined to Continue untill tomorrow. [Clark remained at Dallesport.]

[ORDWAY] a beautiful warm morning . . . the Small birds of different kinds are Singing around us.

April 18, 1806
[CLARK] about 10 A. M. the Indians Came down from the Eneesher Villages and I expected would take the articles which they had laid by yes-

41. Tenino Indians.

terday. but to my estonishment not one would make the exchange to day.
two other parcels of good were laid by and the horses promised at 2 P. M.
I payed but little attention to this bargain however Suffered the bundles
to lye. I dressed the Sores of the principal Chief gave Some Small things
to his children and promised the Chief Some Medicine for to Cure his
Sores.   his wife who I found to be a Sulky Bitch and was Somewhat
efflicted with pains in her back. this I thought a good oppertunity to get
her on my Side giveing here Something for her back. I rubed a little Cam-
phere on her temples and back, and applyed worm flannel to her back
which She thought had nearly restored her to her former feelings.   this I
thought a favourable time to trade with the Chief who had more horses
than all the nation besides. I accordingly made him an offer which he excepted and Sold me two horses. Great numbers of Indians from defferent
derections visited me at this place to day, none of them appeared willing
to part with their horses. [The party was mostly recombined and camped
near Spearfish Lake, Klickitat County, Washington.]

April 19, 1806

[LEWIS] there was great joy with the natives last night in consequence of
the arrival of the salmon; one of those fish was caught; this was the har-
binger of good news to them.   they informed us that these fish would arrive in great quantities in the course of about 5 days. this fish was dressed
and being divided into small peices was given to each child in the village.
this custom is founded in a supersticious opinon that it will hasten the arrival of the salmon. with much difficulty we obtained four other horses
from the Indians today, we wer obliged to dispence with two of our
kettles in order to acquire those.   we have now only one small kettle to a
mess of 8 men.   in the evening Capt. Clark set out with four men to the
Enesher village at the grand falls in order to make a further attempt to
procure horses. these people are very faithless in their contracts. they
frequently receive the merchandize in exchange for their horses and after
some hours insist on some additional article being given them or revoke
the exchange. they have pilfered several small articles from us this evening. I directed the horses to be hubbled & suffered to graize at a little distance from our camp under the immediate eye of the men who had them
in charge.   one of the men Willard was negligent in his attention to his
horse and suffered it to ramble off; it was not to be found when I ordered

the others to be brought up and confined to the picquits. this in addition to the other difficulties under which I laboured was truly provoking.
I repremanded him more severely for this peice of negligence than had
been usual with me. [Camped above the Long Narrows of The Dalles,
Klickitat County, Washington, where the party remained until April 21.]

April 20, 1806
[LEWIS] [The Teninos] are poor, dirty, proud, haughty, inhospitable,
parsimonious and faithless in every rispect, nothing but our numbers I
beleive prevents their attempting to murder us at this moment. This
morning I was informed that the natives had pilfered six tommahawks
and a knife from the party in the course of the last night. I spoke to the
cheif on this subject. he appeared angry with his people and addressed
them but the property was not restored.   one horse which I had purchased and paid for yesterday and which could not be found when I ordered the horses into close confinement yesterday I was now informed
had been gambled away by the rascal who had sold it to me and had been
taken away by a man of another nation. I therefore took the goods back
from this fellow ... I ordered the indians from our camp this evening and
informed them that if I caught them attempting to perloin any article
from us I would beat them severely.   they went off in reather a bad humour and I directed the party to examine their arms and be on their
guard.   they stole two spoons from us in the course of the day. [Lewis
with the main party remained above the Long Narrows.]

[CLARK] I could not precure a Single horse of those people, dureing
this day at any price, they offered me 2 for 2 kittles of which we Could
not spear. I used every artifice decent & even false Statements to enduce
those pore devils to Sell me horses. [Clark, Pryor, Cruzatte, Labiche,
and Shannon were on a trading mission and camped for the night at a
Tenino ("Eneshur") village in the vicinity of Wishram, Klickitat County,
Washington.]

April 21, 1806
[LEWIS] Notwithstanding all the precautions I had taken with rispect to
the horses one of them had broken his cord of 5 strands of Elkskin and
had gone off spanseled. I sent several men in surch of the horse with

orders to return at 10 A. M. with or without the horse being determined
to remain no longer with these villains.   they stole another tomahawk
from us this morning I surched many of them but could not find it. I ordered all the spare poles, paddles and the ballance of our canoe put on the
fire as the morning was cold and also that not a particle should be left for
the benefit of the indians. I detected a fellow in stealing an iron socket of
a canoe pole and gave him several severe blows and mad the men kick
him out of camp. I now informed the indians that I would shoot the first
of them that attempted to steal an article from us.   that we were not affraid to fight them, that I had it in my power at that moment to kill them
all and set fire to their houses, but it was not my wish to treat them with
severity provided they would let my property alone.   that I would take
their horses if I could find out the persons who had stolen the tommahawks, but that I had reather loose the property altogether than take the
hose of an inosent person.   the chiefs were present hung their heads and
said nothing. [Camped below the mouth of the Deschutes River, Klickitat County, Washington.]

[GASS] While we were making preparations to start, an Indian stole some
iron articles from among the men's hands; which so irritated Captain
Lewis, that he struck him; which was the first act of the kind, that had
happened during the expedition.

April 22, 1806
[LEWIS] we had not arrived at the top of a hill over which the road leads
opposite the village before Charbono's horse threw his load, and taking
fright at the saddle and robe which still adhered, ran at full speed down
the hill, near the village he disengaged himself from the saddle and robe,
an indian hid the robe in his lodge . . . being now confident that the indians had taken it [the robe] I sent the Indian woman on to request Capt.
C. to halt the party and send back some of the men to my assistance being determined either to make the indians deliver the robe or birn their
houses.   they have vexed me in such a manner by such repeated acts of
villany that I am quite disposed to treat them with every severyty, their
defenseless state pleads forgivness so far as rispects their lives.   with this
resolution I returned to their village which I had just reached as Labuish

met me with the robe which he informed me he found in an Indian lodg hid behind their baggage . . . we now made the following regulations as to our future order of march (viz) that Capt. C. & myself should devide the men who were disencumbered by horses and march alternately each day the one in front and the other in rear. [Camped in the vicinity of John Day Dam, Klickitat County, Washington.]

April 23, 1806
[LEWIS] after we had arranged our camp we caused all the old and brave men to set arround and smoke with us. we had the violin played and some of the men danced; after which the natives entertained us with a dance after their method. this dance differed from any I have yet seen. they formed a circle and all sung as well the spectators as the dancers who performed within the circle. these placed their sholders together with their robes tightly drawn about them and danced in a line from side to side, several parties of from 4 to seven will be performing within the circle at the same time. the whole concluded with a premiscuous dance in which most of them sung and danced. these people speak a language very similar to the Chopunnish whome they also resemble in their dress.⁴² [Camped above Rock Creek, Klickitat County, Washington.]

April 24, 1806
[LEWIS] the natives had tantalized us with an exchange of horses for our canoes in the first instance, but when they found that we had made our arrangements to travel by land they would give us nothing for them I determined to cut them in peices sooner than leave them on those terms, Drewyer struck one of the canoes and split of a small peice with his tommahawk, they discovered us determined on this subject and offered us several strands of beads for each which were accepted. we proceeded up the river between the hills and it's Northen shore . . . most of the party complain of the soarness of their feet and legs this evening; it is no doubt caused by walking over the rough stones and deep sands after bing for

42. The party crossed the line at The Dalles between the Chinookan speakers below and the Sahaptian speakers above. Lewis noticed the similarity of the Nez Perce ("Chopunnish") language and those of the Teninos, who were also Sahaptian speakers.

some months passed been accustomed to a soft soil.   my left ankle gives me much pain. I baithed my feet in cold water from which I experienced considerable releif. [Camped in Klickitat County, Washington, opposite Blalock, Gilliam County, Oregon.]

April 25, 1806
[GASS] The men in general complain of their feet being sore; and the officers have to go on foot to permit some of them to ride. [Camped either near Alderdale, Klickitat County, or at Glade Creek, Benton County, both in Washington.]

April 27, 1806
[LEWIS] the principal Cheif of the Wallahwallahs joined us with six men of his nation.   this Cheif by name *Yel-lept* had visited us on the morning of the 19 of October at our encampment a little below this place; we gave him at that time a small medal, and promised him a larger one on our return.   he appeared much gratifyed at seeng us return, invited us to remain at his village three or four days and assured us that we should be furnished with a plenty of such food as they had themselves; and some horses to assist us on our journey . . . Yellept harangued his village in our favour intreated them to furnish us with fuel and provision and set the example himself by bringing us an armfull of wood and a platter of 3 roasted mullets.   the others soon followed his example with rispect to fuel and we soon found ourselves in possession of an ample stock . . . we purchased four dogs of these people on which the party suped heartily having been on short allowance for near two days.   the indians retired when we requested them this evening and behaved themselves in every rispect extreemly well.   the indians informed us that there was a good road which passed from the columbia opposite to this village to the entrance of the Kooskooske on the S. side of Lewis's river; they also informed us, that there were a plenty of deer and Antelopes on the road, with good water and grass.   we knew that a road in that direction if the country would permit would shorten our rout at least 80 miles . . . under these circumstances we did not hesitate in pursuing the rout recommended by our guide whos information was corroberated by Yellept & others. [Camped in Benton County, Washington, opposite and below the mouth of the Walla Walla River.]

April 28, 1806

[LEWIS] This morning early Yellept brought a very eligant white horse to our camp and presented him to Capt. C. signifying his wish to get a kettle but on being informed that we had already disposed of every kettle we could possibly spear he said he was content with whatever he thought proper to give him. Capt. C. gave him his swoard a hundred balls and powder and some s[m]all articles with which he appeared perfectly satisfyed. it was necessary before we entered on our rout through the plains where we were to meet with no lodges or resident indians that we should lay in a stock of provision and not depend altogether on the gun. we directed Frazier to whom we have intrusted the duty of makeing those purchases to lay in as many fat dogs as he could procure; he soon obtained ten. being anxious to depart we requested the Cheif to furnish us with canoes to pass the river, but he insisted on our remaining with him this day at least, that he would be much pleased if we would conset to remain two or three, but he would not let us have canoes to leave him today . . . we found a Shoshone woman, prisoner among these people by means of whome and Sahcahgarweah we found the means of conversing with the Wollahwollahs. we conversed with them for several hours and fully satisfyed all their enquiries with rispect to ourselves and the objects of our pursuit. they were much pleased. they brought several diseased persons to us for whom they requested some medical aid. one had his knee contracted by the rheumatism, another with a broken arm &c to all of which we administered much to the gratification of those poor wretches. we gave them some eye-water which I beleive will render them more essential service than any other article in the medical way which we had it in our power to bestoe on them . . . a little before sunset the Chymnahpos[43] arrived; they were about 100 men and a few women; they joined the Wallahwollahs who were about the same number andformed a half circle arround our camp where they waited very patiently to see our party dance. the fiddle was played and the men amused themselves with dancing about an hour. we then requested the Indians to dance which they very cheerfully complyed with; they continued their dance untill 10 at night. the whole assemblage of indians about 550 men women and children sung and danced at the same time. most of them stood in the same place

43. Yakama Indians.

and merely jumped up to the time of their music.   some of the men who
were esteemed most brave entered the space arrond which the main body
were formed in solid column, and danced in a circular manner sidewise.
[Remained opposite the Walla Walla River.]

April 29, 1806
[LEWIS] by 11 A. M. we had passed the river with our party and baggage
but were detained several hours in consequence of not being able to collect our horses.   our guide now informed us that it was too late in the evening to reach an eligible place to encamp; that we could not reach any water before night.   we therefore thought it best to remain on the
Wallahwollah river. [Camped on the north side of the Walla Walla River,
Walla Walla County, Washington.]

May 1, 1806
[LEWIS] I see very little difference between the apparent face of the country here and that of the plains of the Missouri only that these are not enlivened by the vast herds of buffaloe Elk &c which ornament the other . . .
some time after we had encamped three young men arrived from the
Wallahwollah village bringing with them a steel trap belonging to one
of our party which had been neglegently left behind; this is an act of
integrity rarely witnessed among indians.   during our stay with them
they several times found the knives of the men which had been carelessly
lossed by them and returned them. I think we can justly affirm to the
honor of these people that they are the most hospitable, honest, and sincere people that we have met with in our voyage. [Camped in the vicinity
of Waitsburg, Walla Walla County, Washington.]

May 2, 1806
[LEWIS] the three young men of the Wollahwollah nation continued with
us.   in the course of the day I observed them eat the inner part of the
young and succulent stem of a large coarse plant [44] with a ternate leaf, the
leafets of which are three loabed and covered with a woolly pubersence.
the flower and fructification resembles that of the parsnip   this plant is
very common in the rich lands on the Ohio and it's branches the Missis-

44. Cow parsnip.

sippi &c.   I tasted of this plant found it agreeable and eat heartily of it without feeling any inconvenience. [Camped several miles south of Marengo, Columbia County, Washington.]

May 3, 1806

[LEWIS] we met with We-ark-koomt[45] whom we have usually distinguished by the name of the bighorn Cheif from the circumstance of his always wearing a horn of that animal suspended by a cord to he left arm. he is the 1st Cheif of a large band of the Chopunnish nation.   he had 10 of his young men with him.   this man went down Lewis's river by land as we decended it by water last fall quite to the Columbia and I beleive was very instrumental in procuring us a hospitable and friendly reception among the natives. [Camped on Pataha Creek, east of Pataha City, Garfield County, Washington.]

May 4, 1806

[LEWIS] we met with *Te-toh, ar sky*, the youngest of the two cheifs who accompanied us last fall[46] [to] the great falls of the Columbia   here we also met with our pilot[47] who decended the river with us as far as the Columbia.   these indians recommended our passing the river at this place and ascending the Kooskooske on the N. E. side.   they said it was nearer and a better rout to the forkes of that river where the twisted hair resided in whose charge we had left our horses; thither they promised to conduct us.   we determined to take the advice of the indians.[48] [Camped on the Snake River about three miles below Clarkston, Whitman County, Washington.]

[GASS] we halted at an Indian lodge, and could get nothing to eat, except some bread made of a kind of roots I was unacquainted with. We had, however, a dog, which we bought from the Indians . . . scanty allowance for thirty odd hungry men.

45. Nez Perce chief We-ark-koomt's real name was Apash Wyakaikt, meaning "flint necklace."

46. In October 1805.

47. One of the unnamed Nez Perce guides in October 1805.

48. The party crossed the Snake River to the north side and continued toward the Clearwater ("Kooskooske").

May 5, 1806

[LEWIS] while at dinner an indian fellow verry impertinently threw a poor half starved puppy nearly into my plait by way of derision for our eating dogs and laughed very heartily at his own impertinence; I was so provoked at his insolence that I caught the puppy and thew it with great violence at him and struk him in the breast and face, siezed my tomahawk and shewed him by signs if he repeated his insolence I would tommahawk him, the fellow withdrew apparently much mortifyed and I continued my repast *on dog* without further molestation. [Camped in the vicinity of Arrow, Nez Perce County, Idaho.]

[CLARK] While we were encamped last fall at the enterance of Chopunnish river, I gave an Indian man some volitile leniment to rub his knee and thye for a pain of which he Complained. the fellow Soon after recovered and have never Seased to extol the virtue of our medicines. near the enterance of the Kooskooske, as we decended last fall I met with a man, who Could not walk with a tumure on his thye. this had been very bad and recovering fast. I gave this man a jentle pirge cleaned & dressed his Sore and left him Some Casteel Soap to wash the Sore which Soon got well. this man also assigned the restoration of his leg to me. those two cures has raised my reputation and given those nativs an exolted oppinion of my Skill as a phician. I have already received maney applications. in our present Situation I think it pardonable to continue this deception for they will not give us any provisions without Compensation in merchendize, and our Stock is now reduced to a mear handfull. we take Care to give them no article which Can possibly injure them.   and in maney Cases can administer & give Such Medicine & Sergical aid as will effectually restore in Simple Cases &c.

May 6, 1806

[LEWIS] The river here called Clark's river [49] is that which we have heretofore called the Flathead river, I have thus named it in honour of my worthy friend and fellow traveller Capt. Clark.   for this stream we know no

49. A combination of the Bitterroot, Clark Fork, and Pend Oreille Rivers, first encountered on September 4, 1805.

indian name and no whiteman but ourselves was ever on it's principal branches . . . the stream which I have heretofore called Clark's river[50] has it's three principal sources in mountains Hood, Jefferson & the Northern side of the S. W. Mountains and is of course a short river. this river I shall in future call the To-wannahiooks river it being the name by which it is called by the Eneshur nation. [Camped on the Clearwater River near the mouth of Pine Creek, Nez Perce County, Idaho.]

May 7, 1806
[LEWIS] the Indians inform us that the snow is yet so deep on the [Rocky] mountains that we shall not be able to pass them untill the next full moon or about the first of June; others set the time at still a more distant period. this unwelcom inteligence to men confined to a diet of horsebeef and roots, and who are as anxious as we are to return to the fat plains of the Missouri and thence to our native homes. [Camped probably south of Peck, Nez Perce County, Idaho.]

[GASS] All the Indians from the Rocky mountains to the falls of Columbia, are an honest, ingenuous and well disposed people; but from the falls to the sea-coast, and along it, they are a rascally, thieving set.

May 9, 1806
[LEWIS] The country along the rocky mountains for several hundred miles in length and about 50 in width is level extreemly fertile . . . this country would form an extensive settlement; the climate appears quite as mild as that of similar latitude on the Atlantic coast if not more so and it cannot be otherwise than healthy; it possesses a fine dry pure air. the grass and many plants are now upwards of knee high. I have no doubt but this tract of country if cultivated would produce in great abundance every article essentially necessary to the comfort and subsistence of civillized man. to it's present inhabitants nature seems to have dealt with a liberal hand, for she has distributed a great variety of esculent plants over the face of the country which furnish them a plentifull store of provision; these are acquired with but little toil, and when prepared after the

50. The Deschutes River of Oregon.

method of the natives afford not only a nutricious but an agreeable food. among other roots those called by them the Quawmash[51] and Cows[52] are esteemed the most agreeable and valuable as they are also the most abundant. [Camped on the Clearwater River southwest of Orofino, Clearwater County, Idaho.]

[GASS] Between the great falls of the Columbia and this place, we saw more horses, than I ever before saw in the same space of country.

May 10, 1806
[LEWIS] we proposed exchangeing a good horse in reather low order for a young horse in tolerable order with a view to kill. the hospitality of the [Nez Perce] chief [Broken Arm] revolted at the aydea of an exchange, he told us that his young men had a great abundance of young horses and if we wished to eat them we should by furnished with as many as we wanted. accordingly they soon produced us two fat young horses one of which we killed, the other we informed them we would pospone killing untill we had consumed the one already killed. This is a much greater act of hospitality than we have witnessed from any nation or tribe since we have passed the Rocky mountains. in short be it spoken to their immortal honor it is the only act which deserves the appellation of hospitallity which we have witnessed in this quarter. [Camped on Lawyer Creek, southwest of Kamiah, Lewis County, Idaho, where the party remained until May 13.]

[ORDWAY] Some of the women pitched a leather lodge and brought wood & made a fire in it and chiefs invited our officers to Stay in it . . . in the evening we played the fiddle and danced a while   a number of Indians came from other villages to See us.

May 11, 1806
[LEWIS] we now pretty fully informed ourselves that Tunnachemootoolt, Neeshneparkkeeoook, Yoomparkkartim and Hohastillpilp were the principal Cheif of the Chopunnish nation and ranked in the order here men-

51. Camas.
52. Cous.

tioned; as all those cheifs were present in our lodge we thought it a favourable time to repeat what had been said yesterday and to enter more minutely into the views of our government with rispect to the inhabitants of this western part of the continent, their intention of establishing trading houses for their releif, their wish to restore peace and harmony among the natives, the strength power and wealth of our nation &c. to this end we drew a map of the country with a coal on a mat in their way and by the assistance of the snake boy and our interpretters were enabled to make ourselves understood by them altho' it had to pass through the French, Minnetare, Shoshone and Chopunnish languages. the interpretation being tedious it ocupyed nearly half the day before we had communicated to them what we wished. they appeared highly pleased. after this council was over we amused ourselves with shewing them the power of magnetism, the spye glass, compass, watch, air-gun and sundry other articles equally novel and incomprehensible to them.   they informed us that after we had left the Minnetares[53] last spring that three of their people had visited that nation and that they had informed them of us and had told them that we had such things in our possession but that they could not place confidence in the information untill they had now witnessed it themselves. [Remained on Lawyer Creek.]

May 12, 1806
[LEWIS] The Indians held a council among themselves this morning with rispect to the subjects on which we had spoken to them yesterday. the result as we learnt was favourable. they placed confidence in the information they had received and resolved to pusue our advise. after this council was over the principal Cheif or the *broken Arm*, took the flour of the roots of cows and thickened the soope in the kettles and baskets of all his people, this being ended he made a harangue the purport of which was making known the deliberations of their council and impressing the necessity of unanimity among them and a strict attention to the resolutions which had been agreed on in councill; he concluded by inviting all such men as had resolved to abide by the decrees of the council to come and eat and requested such as would not be so bound to shew themselves by not partaking of the feast. I was told by one of our men who was pres-

53. The familiar Hidatsas.

ent, that there was not a dissenting voice on this great national question, but all swallowed their objections if any they had, very cheerfully with their mush. during the time of this loud and animated harangue of the Cheif the women cryed wrung their hands, toar their hair and appeared to be in the utmost distress . . . [The chiefs] now informed us that they wished to give an answer to what we had said to them the preceeding day, but also informed us that there were many of their people waiting in great pain at that moment for the aid of our medecine. it was agreed between Capt. C. and myself that he should attend the sick as he was their favorite phisician while I would here and answer the Cheifs. The father of Ho-hastillpilp . . . said they were fully sensible of the advantages of peace and that the ardent desire which they had to cultivate peace with their neighbours had induced his nation early last summer to send a pipe by 3 of their brave men to the Shoshonees on the S. side of Lewis's river in the Plains of Columbia, thatthese people had murdered these men, which had given rise to the war expedition against that nation last fall; that their warriors had fallen in with the shoshonees at that time and had killed 42 of them with the loss of 3 only on their part; that this had satisfyed the blood of their disceased friends and that they would never again make war against the Shoshonees, but were willing to receive them as friends. that they valued the lives of their young men too much to wish them to be engaged in war. That as we had not yet seen the black foot Indians and the Minnetares of Fort de Prarie they did not think it safe to venture over to the Plains of the Missouri, where they would fondly go provided those nations would not kill them. [Remained on Lawyer Creek.]

May 13, 1806
[LEWIS] these people have immence numbers of them [horses] 50, 60 or a hundred hed is not unusual for an individual to possess. The Chopunnish are in general stout well formed active men. they have high noses and many of them on the acqueline order with cheerfull and agreeable countenances; their complexions are not remarkable. in common with other savage nations of America they extract their beards but the men do not uniformly extract the hair below, this is more particularly confined to the females. I observed several men among them whom I am convinced if they had shaved their beards instead of extracting it would have

been as well supplyed in this particular as any of my countrymen.   they appear to be cheerfull but not gay; they are fond of gambling and of their amusements which consist principally in shooting their arrows at a bowling target made of willow bark, and in riding and exercising themselves on horseback, racing &c.   they are expert marksmen and good riders. they do not appear to be so much devoted to baubles as most of the nations we have met with, but seem anxious always to obtain articles of utility, such as knives, axes, tommahawks, kettles blankets and mockerson alls.   blue beads however may form an exception to this remark; this article among all the nations of this country may be justly compared to goald or silver among civilized nations. They are generally well cloathed in their stile.   their dress consists of a long shirt which reaches to the middle of thye, long legings which reach as high as the waist, mockersons, and robes.   these are formed of various skins and are in all rispects like those particularly discribed of the Shoshones.   their women also dress like the Shoshones . . . but the article of dress on which they appear to bstow most pains and ornaments is a kind of collar or brestplate; this is most commonly a strip of otterskin of about six inches wide taken out of the center of the skin it's whole length including he head.   this is dressed with the hair on; a hole is cut lengthwise through the skin near the head of the animal sufficiently large to admit the head of the person to pass. thus it is placed about the neck and hangs in front of the body the tail frequently reaching below their knees; on this skin in front is attatched peices of pirl, beads, wampum peices of red cloth and in short whatever they conceive most valuable or ornamental. I observed a tippit woarn by Hohastillpilp, which was formed of human scalps and ornamented with the thumbs and fingers of several men which he had slain in battle. [Camped at Kamiah, Lewis County, Idaho, while the party waited for canoes to pass over the Clearwater River.]

May 14, 1806
[LEWIS] this was a very eligible spot for defence[54]   it had been an ancient habitation of the indians; was sunk about 4 feet in the ground and raised

54. The spot has come to be called Camp Chopunnish, although the party never used the term.

arround it's outer edge about three ½ feet with a good wall of eath ... here we are in the vicinity of the best hunting grounds from indian information, are convenient to the salmon which we expect daily and have an excellent pasture for our horses ... in short as we are compelled to reside a while in this neighbourhood I feel perfectly satisfyed with our position. [Camped at Camp Chopunnish, located on the east bank of the Clearwater River about two miles below the mouth of Lawyer Creek at Kamiah, Idaho County, Idaho. The party remained here until June 10.]

[ORDWAY] we eat Several of our Stud horses as they have been troublesome to us.

May 15, 1806
[LEWIS] These bear[55] gave me a stronger evidence of the various coloured bear of this country being one speceis only, than any I have heretofore had. The female was black with a considerable proportion of white hairs intermixed and a white spot on the breast, one of the young bear was jut black and the other of a light redish brown or bey colour. the poil of these bear were infinitely longer finer and thicker than the black bear their tallons also longer and more blont as if woarn by diging roots. the white and redish brown or bey coloured bear I saw together on the Missouri; the bey and grizly have been seen and killed together here for these were the colours of those which Collins killed yesterday. in short it is not common to find two bear here of this speceis precisely of the same colour, and if we were to attempt to distinguish them by their collours and to denominate each colour a distinct speceis we should soon find at least twenty. some bear nearly white have also been seen by our hunters at this place. the most striking differences between this speceis of bear and the common black bear are that the former are larger, have longer tallons and tusks, prey more on other animals, do not lie so long nor so closely in winter quarters, and will not climb a tree tho' eversoheardly pressed. the variagated bear I beleive to be the same here with those on the missouri but these are not as ferocious as those perhaps from the circumstance of their being compelled from the scarcity of game in this quarter to live

55. Grizzly bear (see also May 31, 1806).

more on roots and of course not so much in the habit of seizing and devouring living animals. [Remained at Camp Chopunnish.]

May 16, 1806
[LEWIS] Sahcargarmeah geathered a quantity of the roots of a speceis of fennel[56] which we found very agreeable food, the flavor of this root is not unlike annis seed, and they dispell the wind which the roots called Cows and quawmash are apt to create particularly the latter. [Remained at Camp Chopunnish.]

May 17, 1806
[LEWIS] It rained the greater part of the last night and this morning untill 8 OCk.   the water passed through flimzy covering and wet our bed most perfectly   in sho[r]t we lay in the water all the latter part of the night.   unfortunately my chronometer which for greater security I have woarn in my fob for ten days past, got wet last night; it seemed a little extraordinary that every part of my breechies which were under my head, should have escaped the moisture except the fob where the time peice was. I opened it and founded it nearly filled with water which I carefully drained out exposed it to the air and wiped the works as well as I could with dry feathers after which I touched them with a little bears oil.   several parts of the iron and steel works were rusted a little which I wiped with all the care in my power. I set her to going and from her apparent motion hope she has sustained no material injury . . . I am pleased at finding the river rise so rapidly, it now doubt is attributeable to the meting snows of the mountains; that icy barier which seperates me from my friends and Country, from all which makes life esteemable.   patience, patience. [Remained at Camp Chopunnish.]

May 19, 1806
[CLARK] the Women had a Variety of Complaints tho' the most general Complaint was the Rhumitism, pains in the back and the Sore eyes . . . I administered eye water to all, two of the women I gave a carthartic, one

56. Western sweet-cicely.

whose Spirets were very low and much hiped[57] I gave 30 drops of Lodomem.[58] [Remained at Camp Chopunnish.]

May 21, 1806
[LEWIS] today we divided the remnant of our store of merchandize among our party with a view that each should purchase therewith a parsel of roots and bread from the natives as his stores for the rocky mountains for there seems but little probability that we shall be enabled to make any dryed meat for that purpose and we cannot as yet form any just idea what resource the fish will furnish us.   each man's stock in trade amounts to no more than one awl, one Kniting pin, a half an ounce of vermillion, two nedles, a few scanes of thead and about a yard of ribbon; a slender stock indeed with which to lay in a store of provision for that dreary wilderness. we would make the men collect these roots themselves but there are several speceis of hemlock which are so much like the cows that it is difficult to discriminate them from the cows and we are affraid that they might poison themselves.   the indians have given us another horse to kill for provision which we keep as a reserved store.   our dependence for subsistence is on our guns, the fish we may perhaps take, the roots we can purchase from the natives and as the last alternative our horses.   we eat the last morsel of meat which we had for dinner this evening, yet nobody seems much conserned about the state of provision. [Remained at Camp Chopunnish.]

[ORDWAY] I and one more[59] of the party went up to a village about 5 miles on South Side on the Side of a hill & Spring run . . . Some of the women in the village were crying aloud at different times in the course of the day. I Signed the reason of their lamenting & they gave me to understand that they had lost Some of their Sons in battle and that was the custom among them when their relation died   they mourn and lement a long time after the aged women only make a loud noise.

57. Afflicted with hypochondria.
58. Lewis had diagnosed the woman as being hysterical. Laudanum, a mixture of alcohol and opium, was given to Sacagawea during her illness in June 1805.
59. Goodrich.

May 22, 1806
[LEWIS] Charbono's Child is very ill this evening; he is cuting teeth, and
for several days past has had a violent lax, which having suddonly stoped
he was attacked with a high fever and his neck and throat are much
swolen this evening. we gave him a doze of creem of tartar[60] and flour of
sulpher and applyed a poltice of boiled onions to his neck as warm as he
could well bear it.[61] [Remained at Camp Chopunnish.]

[GASS] These Indians are the most active horsemen I ever saw: they will
gallop their horses over precipices, that I should not think of riding over
at all. The frames of their saddles are made of wood nicely jointed, and
then covered with raw skins, which when they become dry, bind every
part tight, and keep the joints in their places. The saddles rise very high
before and behind, in the manner of the saddles of the Spaniards, from
whom they no doubt received the form; and also obtained their breed of
horses.

May 23, 1806
[LEWIS] The Creem of tartar and sulpher operated several times on the
child in the course of the last night, he is considerably better this morning, tho' the swelling of the neck has abated but little; we still apply po-
lices of onions which we renew frequently in the course of the day and
night. at noon we were visited by 4 indians who informed us they had
come from their village on Lewis's river at the distance of two days ride in
order to see us and obtain a little eyewater, Capt. C. washed their eyes and
they set out on their return to their village. our skill as phisicans and the
virture of our medecines have been spread it seems to a great distance. I
sincerely wish it was in our power to give releif to these poor afficted
wretches. [Remained at Camp Chopunnish.]

May 24, 1806
[CLARK] the Child was very restless last night its jaw and back of its neck
is much more Swelled than it was yesterday. I gave it a dost of Creme of

60. Potassium bitartrate.
61. Jean Baptiste's illness has been inconclusively diagnosed. Cream of tartar would act
as a diuretic and cathartic, while sulfur would serve as a fungicide and insecticide.

Tarter and a fresh Poltice of Onions . . . W. Brattin is yet very low   he eats hartily but he is So weak in the Small of his back that he Can't walk.   we have made use of every remidy to restore him without it's haveing the desired effect.   one of our party, John Shields observed that he had Seen men in Similar Situations restored by Violent Swets.   and bratten requested that he might be Swetted in the way Sheilds purposed which we agreed to. Shields dug a round hole 4 feet deep & 3 feet Diamuter in which he made a large fire So as to heet the hole after which the fire was taken out a Seet placed in the hole.   the patent was then Set on the Seat with a board under his feet and a can of water handed him to throw on the bottom & Sides of the hole So as to create as greate a heat as he Could bear. and the hole covered with blankets supported by hoops.   after about 20 minits the patient was taken out and put in Cold water a few minits, & returned to the hole in which he was kept about 1 hour.   then taken out and Covered with Several blankets, which was taken off by degrees untill he became Cool.   this remedy took place yesterday and bratten is walking about to day and is much better than he has been. [Remained at Camp Chopunnish.]

May 25, 1806
[LEWIS] we gave it [Jean Baptiste] a doze of creem of tartar which did not operate, we therefore gave it a clyster in the evening.   we caused a sweat to be prepared for the indian Cheif in the same manner in which Bratton had been sweated, this we attempted but were unable to succeed, as he was unable to set up or be supported in the place.   we informed the indians that we knew of no releif for him except sweating him in their sweat houses and giving him a plenty of the tea of the horsemint which we shewed them.   and that this would probably nos succeed as he had been so long in his present situation. I am confident that this would be an excellent subject for electricity and much regret that I have it not in my power to supply it. [Remained at Camp Chopunnish.]

May 26, 1806
[LEWIS] The Clyster given the Child last evening operated very well.   it is clear of fever this evening and is much better, the swelling is considerably abated and appears as if it would pass off without coming to a head.   we

still continue fresh poltices of onions to the swolen part. [Remained at Camp Chopunnish.]

May 27, 1806

[LEWIS] Hohastillpilp told us that most of the horses we saw runing at large in this neighbourhood belonged to himself and his people, and whenever we were in want of meat he requested that we would kill any of them we wished; this is a peice of liberallity which would do honour to such as bost of civilization; indeed I doubt whether there are not a great number of our countrymen who would see us fast many days before their compassion would excite them to a similar act of liberallity . . . Charbono's son is much better today, tho' the swelling on the side of his neck I beleive will terminate in an ugly imposthume a little below the ear. the indians were so anxious that the sick Cheif should be sweated under our inspection that they requested we would make a second attept today; accordingly the hole was somewhat enlarged and his father a very good looking old man, went into the hole with him and sustained him in a proper position during the operation; we could not make him sweat as copiously as we wished. after the operation he complained of considerable pain, we gave him 30 drops of laudanum which soon composed him and he rested very well. this is at least a strong mark of parental affection. they all appear extreemly attentive to this sick man nor do they appear to relax in their asceduity towards him notwithstand he has been sick and helpless upwards of three years. the Chopunnish appear to be very attentive and kind to their aged people and treat their women with more rispect than the nations of the Missouri . . . The Black woodpecker [62] which I have frequently mentioned and which is found in most parts of the roky Mountains as well as the Western and S. W. mountains. I had never an opportunity of examining untill a few days since when we killed and preserved several of them. this bird is about the size of the lark woodpecker [63] of the turtle dove, [64] tho' it's wings are longer than either of those birds. the beak is black, ne inch long, reather wide at the base,

62. Lewis's woodpecker.
63. Northern flicker.
64. Mourning dove.

somewhat curved, and sharply pointed; the chaps are of equal length. ar-round the base of the beak including the eye and a small part of the throat is of a fine crimson red. the neck and as low as the croop in front is of an iron grey. the belly and breast is a curious mixture of white and blood reed which has much the appearance of having been artifically painted or stained of that colour. the red reather predominates. the top of the head back, sides, upper surface of the wings and tail are black, with a gossey tint of green in a certain exposure to the light. the under side of the wings and tail are of a sooty black. it has ten feathers in the tail, sharply pointed, and those in the center reather longest, being 2½ inches in length. the tongue is barbed, pointed, and of an elastic cartelaginous substance. the eye is moderately large, puple black and iris of a dark yellowish brown. this bird in it's actions when flying resembles the small redheaded wood-pecke common to the Atlantic states; it's note also somewhat resembles that bird . . . it feeds on bugs worms and a variety of insects. [Remained at Camp Chopunnish.]

[LEWIS AND CLARK, WEATHER REMARKS] the dove is cooing which is the signal as the indians inform us of the approach of the salmon.

May 28, 1806
[LEWIS] The sick Cheif was much better this morning he can use his hands and arms and seems much pleased with the prospect of recovering, he says he feels much better than he has for a great number of months. I sincerely wish these sweats may restore him . . . The Child is also better, he is free of fever, the imposthume is not so large but seems to be ad-vancing to maturity. [Remained at Camp Chopunnish.]

May 30, 1806
[LEWIS] all our invalides are on the recovery . . . The reptiles which I have observed in this quarter are the Rattlesnake[65] of the speceis discribed on the Missouri, they are abundant in every part of the country and are the only poisonous snake which we have yet met with since we left St. Louis. the 2 speceis[66] of snakes of an inosent kind already discribed. the com-

---

65. Northern Pacific rattlesnake.
66. Perhaps the Great Basin gopher snake and Pacific red-sided garter snake.

mon black lizzard,[67] the horned lizzard, a smal green tree frog,[68] the smal
frog [69] which is common to our country which sings in the spring of the
year, a large speceis of frog [70] which resorts the water considerably larger
than our bull frog, it's shape seems to be a medium between the delicate
and lengthy form of our bull frog and that of our land frog or toad as they
are sometimes called in the U' States. like the latter their bodies are covered with little pustles or lumps, elivated above the ordinary surface of
the body; I never heard them make any sound or nois.   the mockerson
snake or coperhead, a number of vipers a variety of lizzards, the toad
bullfrog &c common to the U' States are not to be found in this country.
most of the insects common to the U' States are found here.   the but-
terflies, common house and blowing flies, the horse flies, except the goald
coloured ear fly, tho' in stead of this fly we have a brown coloured fly
about the same size which attatches itself to that part of the horse and is
equally as troublesome.   the silkworm is also found here.   a great variety
of beatles common to the Atlantic states are found here likewise.   except
from this order the large cow beatle and the black beatle usually [c]alled
the tumble bug[71] which are not found here.   the hornet, the wasp and
yellow wasp or yellow jacket as they are frequently called are not met with
in this quarter. [Remained at Camp Chopunnish.]

May 31, 1806
[LEWIS] Goodrich and Willard visited the indian Villages this morning
and returned in the evening. Willard brought with him the dressed skin
of a bear which he had purchased for Capt. C.   this skin was an uniform
pale redish brown colour, the indians informed us that it was not the
Hoh-host or white bear, that it was the Yâck-kâh.   this distinction of the
indians induced us to make further enquiry relative to their opinons of
the several speceis of bear in this country.   we produced the several skins
of the bear which we had killed at this place and one very nearly white
which I had purchased. The white, the deep and plale red grizzle, the dark

67. Western fence lizard.
68. Pacific tree frog.
69. Chorus frog.
70. Western toad.
71. Dung beetle.

bron grizzle, and all those which had the extremities of the hair of a white or frosty colour without regard to the colour of the ground of the poil, they designated Hoh-host and assured us that they were the same with the white bear, that they ascosiated together, were very vicisious, never climbed the trees, and had much longer nails than the others.   the black skins, those which were black with a number of intire white hairs inter-mixed, the black with a white breast, the uniform bey, brown and light re-dish brown, they designated the Yâck-kâh;—said that they climbed the trees, had short nails and were not vicious, that they could pursue them and kill them with safety, they also affirmed that they were much smaller than the white bear. I am disposed to adopt the Indian distinction with rispect to these bear and consider them two distinct speceis.   the white and the grizzly of this neighbourhood are the same of those found on the upper portion of the Missouri where the other speceis are not, and that the uniform redish brown black &c of this neighbourhood are a speceis distinct from our black bear and from the black bear of the Pacific coast which I believe to be the same with those of the Atlantic coast, and that the common black bear do not exist here. I had previously observed that the claws of some of the bear which we had killed here had much shorter tallons than the variagated or white bear usually have but supposed that they had woarn them out by scratching up roots, and these were those which the indians called Yâk-kâh.   on enquiry I found also that a cub of an uniform redish brown colour, pup to a female black bear intermixed with entire white hairs had climbed a tree. I think this a distinct speceis from the common black bear, because we never find the latter of any other colour than an uniform black, and also that the poil of this bear is much finer thicker and longer with a greater proportion of fur mixed with the hair, in other ispects they are much the same. [Remained at Camp Chopunnish.]

June 1, 1806
[LEWIS] I met with a singular plant today in blume of which I preserved a specemine;[72] it grows on the steep sides of the fertile hills near this place. [Remained at Camp Chopunnish.]

72. The ragged robin (*Clarkia pulchella*) was named scientifically for Clark after the ex-pedition.

June 2, 1806

[LEWIS] having exhausted all our merchandize we are obliged to have recourse to every subterfuge in order to prepare in the most ample manner
in our power to meet that wretched portion of our journy, the Rocky
Mountain, where hungar and cold in their most rigorous forms assail the
waried traveller; not any of us have yet forgotten our sufferings in those
mountains in September last, and I think it probable we never shall. Our
traders McNeal and York were furnished with the buttons which Capt. C.
and myself cut off our coats, some eye water and Basilicon which we
made for that purpose and some Phials and small tin boxes which I had
brought out with Phosphorus. in the evening they returned with about
3 bushels of roots and some bread having made a successfull voyage, not
much less pleasing to us than the return of a good cargo to an East India
Merchant . . . Drewyer arrived this evening with Neeshneparkkeeook and
Hohastillpilp who had accompanyed him to the lodges of the persons
who had our tomahawks. he obtained both the tomahawks principally
by the influence of the former of these Cheifs. the one which had been
stolen we prized most as it was the private property of the late Sergt. Floyd
and Capt. C. was desireous of returning it to his friends. [Remained at
Camp Chopunnish.]

[GASS] About noon three men,[73] who had gone over to Lewis's river,
about two and half days' journey distant, to get some fish, returned . . .
One of these men[74] got two Spanish dollars from an Indian for an old ra-
zor. They said they got the dollars from about a Snake Indian's neck, they
had killed some time ago. There are several dollars among these people
which they get in some way. We suppose the Snake Indians, some of
whom do not live very far from New Mexico, got them from the Spaniards in that quarter.

June 3, 1806

[LEWIS] Our invalids are all on the recovery; Bratton is much stronger
and can walk about with considerable ease. the Indian Cheif appears to

73. Ordway, Frazer, and Weiser.
74. Frazer.

be gradually recovering the uce of his limbs, and the child is nearly well; the imposthume on his neck has in a great measure subsided and left a hard lump underneath his left ear; we still continue the application of the onion poltice . . . today the Indians dispatched an express over the mountains to travellers rest . . . the mountains being practicable for this express we thought it probable that we could also pass, but the indians informed us that several of the creeks would yet swim our horses, that there was no grass and that the roads were extreemly deep and slipery; they inform us that we may pass conveniently in twelve or fourteen days. we have come to a resolution to remove from hence to the quawmash grounds beyond Collins's creek on the 10th to hunt in that neighbourhood a few days, if possible lay in a stock of meat and then attempt the mountains about the middle of this month. I begin to lose all hope of any dependance on the Salmon as this river will not fall sufficiently to take them before we shall leave it, and as yet I see no appearance of their runing near the shores as the indians informed us they would in the course of a few days. [Remained at Camp Chopunnish.]

[ORDWAY] my horse that I wrode over to the kimooenim river[75] nearly failed and his back verry sore and poor & in low Spirits and as luck would have it an Indian brought me a large good strong horse and Swaped with me as he knew my horse to be good when in order to run the buffaloe which is their main object to git horses that will run and Swap their best horses for Servis, for them that will run if they are not half as good as otherways.

June 4, 1806
[LEWIS] [The Nez Perce chiefs] gave us no positive answer to a request which we made, that two or three of their young men should accompany me to the falls of the Missouri and there wait my return from the upper part of Maria's river where it was probable I should meet with some of the bands of the Minnetares from Fort de Prarie;[76] that in such case I should indeavor to bring about a good understanding between those indians and

75. Snake River.
76. Here, Blackfeet and Atsinas.

themselves, which when effected they would be informed of it though the young men thus sent with me, and that on the contrary should I not be fortunate enough to meet with these people nor to prevail on them to be at peace they would equally be informed through those young men, and they might still remain on their guard with rispect to them untill the whites had it in their power to give them more effectual releif. [Remained at Camp Chopunnish.]

June 6, 1806
[CLARK] The Broken arm told me that the nation would not pass the mountains untill the latter part of the Summer, and with respect to the young men who we had requested to accompany us to the falls of Missouri, were not yet Selected for that purpose nor could they be So untill they had a Meeting of the Nation in Council.   that this would happen in the Course of ten or 12 days.[77] [Remained at Camp Chopunnish.]

June 7, 1806
[GASS] Some of the natives again came to visit us, one of whom gave a horse to one of our men, who is very fond of conversing with them and of learning their language.[78] [Remained at Camp Chopunnish.]

June 8, 1806
[LEWIS] several foot rarces were run this evening between the indians and our men.   the indians are very active; one of them proved as fleet as Drewer and R. Fields, our swiftest runners.   when the racing was over the men divided themselves into two parties and played prison base, by way of exercise which we wish the men to take previously to entering the mountain; in short those who are not hunters have had so little to do that they are geting reather lazy and slouthfull.   after dark we had the violin played and danced for the amusement of ourselves and the indians.   one of the indians informed us that we could not pass the mountains untill

77. The Nez Perces would be moving to the head of Lawyer Creek, Lewis County, Idaho.

78. Hohots Ilppilp gave Frazer a horse; the soldier had earlier given the chief a pair of special moccasins.

the full of the next moon or about the first of July, that if we attempted it sooner our horses would be at least three days travel without food on the top of the mountain; this information is disagreable inasmuch as it causes some doubt as to the time at which it will be most proper for us to set out. however as we have no time to loose we will wrisk the chanches and set out as early as the indians generally think it practicable or the middle of this month. [Remained at Camp Chopunnish.]

June 9, 1806
[LEWIS] our party seem much elated with the idea of moving on towards their friends and country, they all seem allirt in their movements today; they have every thing in readiness for a move, and notwithstanding the want of provision have been amusing themselves very merrily today in runing footraces pitching quites,[79] prison basse &c. [Remained at Camp Chopunnish.]

[ORDWAY] a chief we call cut nose went Some distance after young Eagles. got Several by climbing a tree by a rope.   the feathers of these eagles the Indians make head dresses war like & paint them & is a great thing among them.

June 10, 1806
[LEWIS] at 11 A. M. we set out with the party each man being well mounted and a light load on a second horse, beside which we have several supenemary [supernumerary] horses in case of accedent or the want of provision, we therefore feel ourselves perfectly equiped for the mountains. we ascended the river hills which are very high and about three miles in extent our sourse being N. 22° E. thence N. 15 W. 2 m to Collins's creek.[80] thence due North 5 m. to the Eastern border of the quawmash flatts[81] where we encamped near the place we first met with the Chopunnish last fall. [Camped on Weippe Prairie about two miles southeast of Weippe, Clearwater County, Idaho, where the party remained until June 15.]

79. Pitching quoits, or flattened rings, at a pin.
80. Lolo Creek, Clearwater County, on which the main party camped on September 20, 1805.
81. Weippe Prairie, Clearwater County, Idaho.

June 11, 1806

[LEWIS] As I have had frequent occasion to mention the plant which the Chopunnish call quawmash I shall here give a more particular discription of that plant and the mode of preparing it for food as practiced by the Chopunnish and others in the vicinity of the Rocky Mountains with whom it forms much the greatest portion of their subsistence.[82] [Remained at Weippe Prairie.]

June 12, 1806

[LEWIS] the days are now very warm and the Musquetoes our old companions have become very troublesome . . . the quawmash is now in blume and from the colour of its bloom at a short distance it resembles lakes of fine clear water, so complete is this deseption that on first sight I could have swoarn it was water. [Remained at Weippe Prairie.]

June 13, 1806

[LEWIS] we made a digest of the Indian Nations West of the Rocky Mountains which we have seen and of whom we have been repeated informed by those with whom we were conversant.   they amount by our estimate to 69,000 Souls. [Remained at Weippe Prairie.]

June 14, 1806

[LEWIS] we have now been detained near five weeks in consequence of the snows; a serious loss of time at this delightfull season for traveling. I am still apprehensive that the snow and the want of food for our horses will prove a serious imbarrassment to us as at least four days journey of our rout in these mountains lies over hights and along a ledge of mountains never intirely destitute of snow.   every body seems anxious to be in motion, convinced that we have not now any time to delay if the calculation is to reach the United States this season; this I am detirmined to accomplish if within the compass of human power. [Remained at Weippe Prairie.]

82. Lewis here provided an extensive description of camas ("quawmash") and its ethnobotanical uses in a lengthy essay.

June 16, 1806

[LEWIS] vegetation is proportionably backward; the dogtooth violet is just in blume, the honeysuckle,[83] huckburry[84] and a small speceis of white maple[85] are begining to put fourth their leaves; these appearances in this comparatively low region augers but unfavourably with rispect to the practibility of passing the mountains, however we determined to proceed, accordingly after taking a haisty meal we set out and continued our rout though a thick wood much obstructed with fallen timber, and intersepted by many steep ravines and high hills. the snow has increased in quantity so much that the greater part of our rout this evening was over the snow which has become sufficiently firm to bear our horshes, otherwise it would have been impossible for us to proceed as it lay in immence masses in some places 8 or ten feet deep. we found much difficulty in pursuing the road as it was so frequently covered with snow . . . in the fore part of the day I observed the Cullumbine[86] the blue bells[87] and the yelow flowering pea[88] in blume. there is an abundance of a speceis of anjelico[89] in these mountains, much stonger to the taist and more highly scented than that speceis common to the U' States. [Camped at Horsesteak Meadow, on Hungery Creek, Idaho County, Idaho.]

June 17, 1806

[LEWIS] we found ourselves invelloped in snow from 12 to 15 feet deep even on the south sides of the hills with the fairest exposure to the sun; here was winter with all it's rigors; the air was cold, my hands and feet were benumbed. we knew that it would require five days to reach the fish wears at the entrance of Colt Creek,[90] provided we were so fortunate as to be enabled to follow the proper ridges of the mountains to lead us to that place;

83. Orange honeysuckle.
84. Mountain huckleberry.
85. Rocky Mountain maple.
86. Red columbine.
87. Tall bluebells.
88. Mountain thermopsis.
89. Licorice-root.
90. Colt Creek is present Colt Killed Creek from the expedition name. The party reached it on September 14, 1805.

<of this Drewyer our principal dependance as a woodsman and guide was entirely doubtfull;> short of that point we could not hope for any food for our horses not even underwood itself as the whole was covered many feet deep in snow. if we proceeded and should get bewildered in these mountains the certainty was that we should loose all our horses and consequently our baggage instruments perhaps our papers and thus eminently wrisk the loss of the discoveries which we had already made if we should be so fortunate as to escape with life. the snow boar our horses very well and the travelling was therefore infinitely better that the obstruction of rocks and fallen timber which we met with in our passage over last fall when the snow lay on this part of the ridge in detached spots only. under these circumstances we conceived it madnes in this stage of the expedition to proceed without a guide who could certainly conduct us to the fish wears on the Kooskooske,[91] as our horses could not possibly sustain a journey of more than five days without food. we therefore came to the resolution to return with our horses while they were yet strong and in good order and indevour to keep them so untill we could procure an indian to conduct us over the snowey mountains, and again to proceed as soon as we could procure such a guide . . . having come to this resolution, we ordered the party to make a deposit for all the baggage[92] which we had not immediate use for, and also all the roots and bread of cows whic they had except an allowance for a few days to enable them to return to some place at which we could subsist by hunting untill we procured a guide. we left our instruments papers &c beleiving them safer here than to wrisk them on horseback over the roads and creeks which we had passed. our baggage being laid on scaffoalds and well covered we began our retrograde march at 1 P. M. having remained about 3 hours on this snowey mountain . . . the party were a good deel dejected tho' not so as I had apprehended they would have been. this is the first time since we have been on this long tour that we have ever been compelled to retreat or make a retrograde march. it rained on us most of this evening. [Camped on the south side of Hungery Creek, Idaho County, Idaho.]

91. Lewis may mean those at Colt Killed Creek or perhaps some at the fishing camp of Twisted Hair of September 21, 1805, on the Clearwater ("Kooskooske") River.

92. Deposited at Willow Ridge, Idaho County.

June 18, 1806

[LEWIS] we had not proceeded far this morning before Potts cut his leg very badly with one of the large knives; he cut one of the large veigns on the inner side of the leg; I found much difficulty in stoping the blood which I could not effect untill I applyed a tight bandage with a little cushon of wood and tow on the veign below the wound. Colter's horse fel with him in passing hungry creek and himself and horse were driven down the creek a considerable distance rolling over each other among the rocks.   he fortunately escaped without injury or the loss of his gun. [Camped on Eldorado Creek, Idaho County, Idaho.]

June 20, 1806

[LEWIS] we determined to return in the morning as far as the quawmash flatts and indeavour to lay in another stock of meat for the mountains, our former stock being now nearly exhausted as well as what we have killed on our return. by returning to the quawmash flatts we shall sooner be informed whether or not we can procure a guide to conduct us through the mountains; should we fail in procuring one, we have determined to wrisk a passage on the following plan immediately, because should we wait much longer or untill the snow desolves in such manner as to enable us to follow the road we cannot hope to reach the United States this winter; this is that Capt. C. or myself shall take four of our most expert woodsmen with three or four of our best horses and proceed two days in advance taking a plentifull supply of provision. for this party to follow the road by the marks which the baggage of the indians has made in many places on the sides of the trees by rubing against them, and to blaize the trees with a tomahawk as they proceeded . . . should it so happen that the advance could not find the road by the marks on the trees after attempting it for two days, the whole of [them] then would return to the main party. in which case we wold bring back our baggage and attempt a passage over these mountains through the country of the Shoshones further to the South by way of the main S. Westerly fork of Lewis's river and Madison or Gallatin's rivers, where from the information of the Chopunnish there is a passage which at this season of the year is not obstructed by snow, though the round is very distant and would require at least a month in it's performance.[93] The Shoshones informed us when we first met with them that there was a passage across the mountains in that quarter but represented the difficulties arrising from steep high and rugged mountains and also an extensive and barren plain which was to be passed without game, as infinitely more difficult thn the rout by which we came . . . the travelling in the mountains on the snow at present is very good, the snow bears the horses perfictly; it is a firm coase snow without a crust, and the horses have good foot hold without sliping much; the only dificulty is finding the road, and I think the plan we have devised will succeed even should we not be enabled to obtain a guide. [Remained on Eldorado Creek.]

June 21, 1806

[LEWIS] at the pass of Collin's Creek we met two indians who were on their way over the mountain . . . we pressed these indians to remain with us and to conduct us over the mountain on the return of Drewyer and Shannon.   they consented to remain two nights for us. [Camped on Weippe Prairie, Clearwater County, Idaho, where the party had camped June 10-15. The Indians waited at Crane Meadows, north of Lolo Creek, Clearwater County.]

June 23, 1806

[LEWIS] Apprehensive from Drewyer's delay that he had met with some difficulty in procuring a guide, and also that the two indians who had promised to wait two nights for us would set out today, we thought it most advisable to dispatch Frazier and Wiser to them this morning with a vew if possible to detain them a day or two longer; and directed that in the event of their not being able to detain the indians, that Sergt. Gass, R & J. Feilds and Wiser should accompany the indians by whatever rout they might take to travellers rest and blaize the trees well as they proceeded and wait at that place untill our arrivall with the party . . . at

---

93. The captains' alternative route would be by way of the Snake River through southern Idaho and into southwestern Montana, a long, circuitous route to reach their destination at the Three Forks of the Missouri.

[4?] P. M. Drewyer Shannon and Whitehouse returned. Drewyer brought with him three indians who had consented to accompany us to the falls of the Missouri for the compensation of two guns.   one of those men is the brother of the cutnose and the other two are the same who presented Capt. Clark and myself each with a horse on a former occasion at the Lodge of the broken arm.   these are all young men of good character and much respected by their nation. [Remained at Weippe Prairie.]

June 24, 1806
[LEWIS] We collected our horses early this morning and set out accompanyed by our three guides. [Camped on Eldorado Creek, Idaho County, Idaho, where the party had camped June 18-21.]

June 25, 1806
[LEWIS] last evening the indians entertained us with seting the fir trees on fire.   they have a great number of dry lims near their bodies which when set on fire creates a very suddon and immence blaze from bottom to top of those tall trees.   they are a beatifull object in this situation at night.   this exhibition reminded me of a display of fireworks.   the natives told us that their object in seting those trees on fire was to bring fair weather for our journey. We collected our horses readily and set out at an early hour this morning.   one of our guides complained of being unwell, a symptom which I did not much like as such complaints with an indian is generally the prelude to his abandoning any enterprize with which he is not well pleased.   we left them at our encampment and they promised to pursue us in a few hours.   at 11 A. M. we arrived at the branch of hungary creek where we found R. & J. Feilds.   they had not killed anything.   here we halted and dined and our guides overtook us.   at this place I met with a plant the root of which the shoshones eat.[94]   it is a small knob root a good deel in flavor an consistency like the Jerusalem Artichoke ... the indians continued with us and I beleive are disposed to be faithfull to their engagement. I gave the sik indian a buffaloe robe he having no other covering except his mockersons and a dressed Elkskin without the hair.

94. Clark wrote that Sacagawea collected the plant species western spring beauty for Lewis to describe.

[Camped on an unnamed creek running into Hungery Creek, Idaho County, Idaho, near the main party's camp of September 19, 1805.]

June 26, 1806
[LEWIS] about the border of the snowey region we killed 2 of the small black pheasant[95] and a female of the large dommanicker or speckled pheasant,[96] the former have 16 fathers in their tail and the latter 20 while the common pheasant[97] have only 18. the indians informed us that neither of these speceis drumed; they appear to be very silent birds for I never heared either of them make a noise in any situation.[98] [Camped on Bald Mountain, Idaho County, Idaho.]

June 27, 1806
[LEWIS] on an elivated point we halted by the request of the Indians a few minutes and smoked the pipe. on this eminence the natives have raised a conic mound of stones of 6 or eight feet high and on it's summit erected a pine pole of 15 feet long . . . from this place we had an extensive view of these stupendous mountains principally covered with snow like that on which we stood; we were entirely surrounded by those mountains from which to one unacquainted with them it would have seemed impossible ever to have escaped; in short without the assistance of our guides I doubt much whether we who had once passed them could find our way to Travellers rest in their present situation for the marked trees on which we had placed considerable reliance are much fewer and more difficult to find than we had apprehended. these fellows are most admireable pilots . . . after smoking the pipe and contemplating this seene sufficient to have damp the sperits of any except such hardy travellers as we have become, we continued our march. [Camped on Spring Mountain, a little south of the Clearwater-Idaho county line, Idaho.]

[ORDWAY] we came further to day than we went in 2 when we came over.

95. Blue grouse.
96. Spruce grouse.
97. Ruffed grouse.
98. These birds do not drum.

June 29, 1806

[LEWIS] when we decended from this ridge we bid adieu to the snow ...
after dinner we continued our march seven miles further to the warm
springs ... both the men and indians amused themselves with the use of
a bath this evening. I observed that the indians after remaining in the hot
bath as long as they could bear it ran and plunged themselves into the
creek the water of which is now as cold as ice can make it; after remaining here a few minutes they returned again to the warm bath, repeating
this transision several times but always ending with the warm bath.
[Camped at Lolo Hot Springs, Missoula County, Montana.]

June 30, 1806

[LEWIS] in descending the creek this morning on the steep side of a high
hill my horse sliped with both his hinder feet out of the road and fell, I
also fell off backwards and slid near 40 feet down the hill before I could
stop myself such was the steepness of the declivity; the horse was near
falling on me in the first instance but fortunately recovers and we both escaped unhirt. [Camped at Travelers' Rest on the south side of Lolo Creek,
south of Lolo, Missoula County, Montana, where the party had camped
September 9–11, 1805.]

[CLARK] Descended the mountain to Travellers rest leaveing those
tremendious mountanes behind us — in passing of which we have expe-
riensed Cold and hunger of which I shall ever remember.

July 1, 1806

[LEWIS] Capt. Clark & my self consurted the following plan viz.   from
this place I determined to go with a small party by the most direct rout to
the falls of the Missouri, there to leave Thompson McNeal and goodrich
to prepare carriages and geer for the purpose of transporting the canoes
and baggage over the portage, and myself and six volunteers to ascend
Maria's river with a view to explore the country and ascertain whether
any branch of that river lies as far north as Latd. 50 and again return and
join the party who are to decend the Missouri, at the entrance of Maria's
river. I now called for the volunteers to accompany me on this rout, many
turned out, from whom I scelected Drewyer the two Feildses, Werner,

Frazier and Sergt Gass accompanied me   the other part of the men are to proceed with Capt Clark to the head of Jefferson's river where we deposited sundry articles and left our canoes.   from hence Sergt Ordway with a party of 9 men are to decend the river with the canoes; Capt C. with the remaining ten including Charbono and York will proceed to the Yellowstone river at it's nearest approach to the three forks of the missouri, here he will build a canoe and decend the Yellowstone river with Charbono the indian woman, his servant York and five others to the missouri where should he arrive first he will wait my arrival. Sergt Pryor with two other men are to proceed with the horses by land to the Mandans and thence to the British posts on the Assinniboin with a letter to Mr. Heney whom we wish to engage to prevail on the Sioux Chefs to join us on the Missouri, and accompany them with us to the seat of the general government.   these arrangements being made the party were informed of our design and prepared themselves accordingly.[99] [Remained at Travelers' Rest.]

99. The captains' plan has Lewis's party return to the Great Falls, then while he and a small contingent explore the Marias River, the remainder descend the Missouri where all regroup at the mouth of the Marias and descend the Missouri to meet Clark. Clark's party would return to Camp Fortunate and to the Three Forks of the Missouri, then while Ordway's party descended the Missouri to join Lewis at the Marias, Clark would go overland from Three Forks for a trip down the Yellowstone River. Pryor's party was to seek Hugh Heney. All were to reunite at the mouth of the Yellowstone.

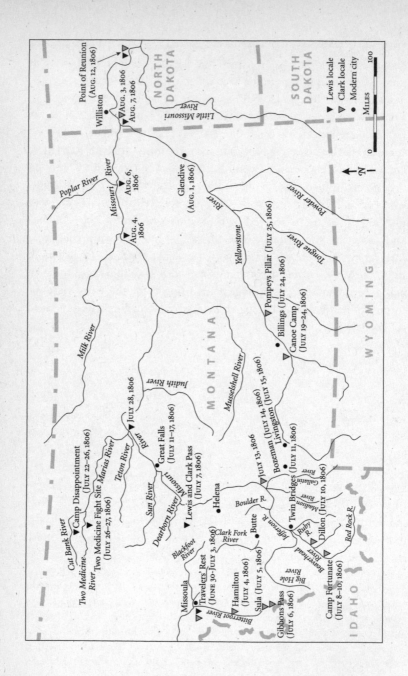

The Expedition's Route, July 3–August 12, 1806

CHAPTER 11

Separation and Reunion

Wm Clark
July 25, 1806

July 3–August 12, 1806

[From this point until the parties reunite on August 12, the captains' journal entries are presented separately, as Lewis heads for the Marias River while Clark seeks the Yellowstone River. The enlisted men's journals are linked with the party to which they were assigned.]

LEWIS ON THE MARIAS

July 3, 1806
[LEWIS] All arrangements being now compleated for carrying into effect the several scheemes we had planed for execution on our return, we saddled our horses and set out I took leave of my worthy friend and companion Capt. Clark and the party that accompanyed him. I could not avoid feeling much concern on this occasion although I hoped this seperation was only momentary. I proceeded down Clark's river seven miles with my party of nine men[1] and five indians . . . These people [the Nez Perce guides] now informed me that the road which they shewed me at no great distance from our Camp would lead us up the East branch of Clark's river and a river they called Cokahlarishkit[2] or the *river of the road to buffaloe* and thence to medicine river[3] and the falls of the Missouri[4] where we wished to go.[5]   they alledged that as the road

1. Lewis's party included Gass, Drouillard, the Field brothers, Frazer, Goodrich, McNeal, Thompson, and Werner.
2. Blackfoot River.
3. Sun River.
4. Great Falls.
5. Lewis proceeded north down the west side of the Bitterroot River to its junction with the Clark Fork, then crossed the latter.

was a well beaten track we could not now miss our way and as they were affraid of meeting with their enimies the Minnetares[6] they could not think of continuing with us any longer. [Camped on Grant Creek near its junction with the Clark Fork, northwest of Missoula, Missoula County, Montana.]

July 4, 1806

[LEWIS] these affectionate people our guides betrayed every emmotion of unfeigned regret at seperating from us; they said that they were confidint that the Pahkees, (the appellation they give the Minnetares) would cut us off. [Camped and on the north side of the Blackfoot River about eight miles from its junction with the Clark Fork, in Missoula County, Montana.]

[GASS] it is but justice to say, that the whole nation [Nez Perce] to which they belong, are the most friendly, honest and ingenuous people that we have seen in the course of our voyage and travels. After taking our farewell of these good hearted, hospitable and obliging sons of the west, we proceeded on.

July 6, 1806

[LEWIS] we expect to meet with the Minnetares and are therefore much on our guard both day and night.   the bois rague[7] in blume.   saw the common small blue flag[8] and peppergrass.[9]   the southern wood[10] and two other speceis of shrub[11] are common in the prarie of knobs.[12]   preserved specemines of them. [Camped on Beaver Creek, Lewis and Clark County, Montana, about two miles west of Lincoln.]

6. Here, the Blackfeet.
7. Red osier dogwood.
8. Western blue flag.
9. Some species from the mustard family, perhaps tall peppergrass.
10. Big sagebrush.
11. Silverberry and antelope-brush.
12. Nevada Valley, Powell County, Montana.

July 7, 1806

[LEWIS] passing the dividing ridge betwen the waters of the Columbia and Missouri rivers at ¼ of a mile. from this gap¹³ which is low and an easy ascent on the W. side the fort mountain¹⁴ bears North Eaast, and appears to be distant about 20 Miles . . . after we encamped Drewyer killed two beaver and shot third which bit his knee very badly and escaped. [Camped about three miles east of Table Mountain, Lewis and Clark County, Montana.]

July 9, 1806

[LEWIS] Joseph fields killed a very fat buffaloe bull and we halted to dine. we took the best of the meat as much as we could possibly carry on our horses. the day continuing rainy and cold I concluded to remain all day. we feasted on the buffaloe.¹⁵ [Camped on the south side of Sun River, near the mouth of Simms Creek, Cascade County, Montana.]

July 11, 1806

[LEWIS] it is now the season at which the buffaloe begin to coppelate and the bulls keep a tremendious roaring we could hear them for many miles and there are such numbers of them that there is one continual roar. our horses had not been acquainted with the buffaloe they appeared much allarmed at their appearance and bellowing. when I arrived in sight of the whitebear Islands the missouri bottoms on both sides of the river were crouded with buffaloe I sincerely belief that there were not less than 10 thousand buffaloe within a circle of 2 miles arround that place. [Camped on the west side of the Missouri, in Cascade County, Montana, and opposite White Bear Islands, the party's Upper Portage Camp of June 1805.]

July 13, 1806

[LEWIS] removed above to my old station opposite the upper point of the white bear island. formed our camp and set Thompson &c at work to complete the geer for the horses. had the cash opened   found my

13. The misnamed Lewis and Clark Pass, Lewis and Clark County, Montana.

14. Square Butte, Cascade County, Montana.

15. This is the first fresh buffalo meat the party had eaten since July 16, 1805.

bearskins entirly destroyed by the water, the river having risen so high that the water had penitrated. all my specimens of plants also lost. the Chart of the Missouri fortunately escaped. opened my trunks and boxes and exposed the articles to dry. found my papers damp and several articles damp. the stoper had come out of a phial of laudinum and the contents had run into the drawer and distroyed a gret part of my medicine in such manner that it was past recovery . . . Musquetoes excessively troublesome insomuch that without the protection of my musquetoe bier I should have found it impossible to wright a moment. the buffaloe are leaving us fast and passing on to the S. East. [Camped at the party's Upper Portage Camp of June 18, 1805, at White Bear Islands on the east side of the Missouri in Cascade County, Montana.]

July 14, 1806
[LEWIS] Had the carriage wheels dug up found them in good order. the iron frame of the boat had not suffered materially. had the meat cut thiner and exposed to dry in the sun. and some roots of cows of which I have yet a small stock pounded into meal for my journey. I find the fat buffaloe meat a great improvement to the mush of these roots. [Remained at White Bear Islands.]

July 15, 1806
[LEWIS] at 1 P. M. Drewyer returned without the horses . . . his safe return has releived me from great anxiety. I had already settled it in my mind that a whitebear had killed him and should have set out tomorrow in surch of him, and if I could not find him to continue my rout to Maria's river. I knew that if he met with a bear in the plains even he would attack him. and that if any accedent should happen to seperate him from his horse in that situation the chances in favour of his being killed would be as 9 to 10. I felt so perfectly satisfyed that he had returned in safety that I thought but little of the horses although they were seven of the best I had. this loss great as it is, is not intirely irreparable, or at least dose not defeat my design of exploring Maria's river. I have yet 10 horses remaining, two of the best and two of the worst of which I leave to assist the party in taking the canoes and baggage over the portage and take the remaining 6

with me; these are but indifferent horses most of them but I hope they may answer our purposes. I shall leave three of my intended party, (viz) Gass, Frazier and Werner, and take the two Feildses and Drewyer.   by having two spare horses we can releive those we ride.   having made this arrangement I gave orders for an early departure in the morning, indeed I should have set out instantly but McNeal road one of the horses which I intend to take and has not yet returned.   a little before dark McNeal returned with his musquet broken off at the breech, and informed me that on his arrival at willow run[16] he had approached a white bear within ten feet without discover him the bear being in the thick brush, the horse took the allarm and turning short threw him immediately under the bear; this animal raised himself on his hinder feet for battle, and gave him time to recover from his fall which he did in an instant and with his clubbed musquet he struck the bear over the head and cut him with the guard of the gn and broke off the breech, the bear stunned with the stroke fell to the ground and began to scratch his head with his feet; this gave McNeal time to climb a willow tree which was near at hand and thus fortunately made his escape.   the bear waited at the foot of the tree untill late in the evening before he left him, when McNeal ventured down and caught his horse which had by this time strayed off to the distance of 2 ms. and returned to camp.   these bear are a most tremenduous animal; it seems that the hand of providence has been most wonderfully in our favor with rispect to them, or some of us would long since have fallen a sacrifice to their farosity.   there seems to be a sertain fatality attatched to the neighbourhood of these falls, for there is always a chapter of accedents prepared for us during our residence at them.   the musquetoes continue to infest us in such manner that we can scarcely exist; for my own part I am confined by them to my bier at least ¾ths of my time.   my dog[17] even howls with the torture he experiences from them, they are almost insupportable, they are so numerous that we frequently get them in our thrats as we breath. [Remained at White Bear Islands.]

16. Box Elder Creek, Cascade County, Montana, crossed on the portage around the Great Falls in June 1805.

17. This is the final mention of Lewis's dog, Seaman.

July 16, 1806

[LEWIS] sent Drewyer and R. Fields with the horses to the lower side of Medecine river, and proceeded myself with all our baggage and J. Fields down the missouri to the mouth of Medecine river in our canoe of buffaloe skins. we were compelled to swim the horses above the whitebear island and again across medicine river as the Missouri is of great width below the mouth of that river. having arrived safely below Medicine river we immediatly sadled our horses and proceeded down the river to the handsom fall of 47 feet where I halted about 2 hours and took a haisty sketch of these falls;[18] in the mean time we had some meat cooked and took dinner after which we proceeded to the grand falls where we arrived at sunset. [Camped at the Great Falls on the north side of the Missouri, Cascade County, Montana.]

[GASS] When Capt. Lewis left us, he gave orders that we should wait at the mouth of Maria's river to the 1st of Sept., at which time, should he not arrive, we were to proceed on and join Capt. Clarke at the mouth of the Yellow-stone river, and then to return home: but informed us, that should his life and health be preserved, he would meet us at the mouth of Maria's river on the 5th of August.[19] [Remained at White Bear Islands.]

July 17, 1806

[LEWIS] at 5 P. M. we arrived at *rose river*[20] where I purposed remaining all night as I could not reach maria's river this evening[21] . . . the Minnetares of Fort de prarie[22] and the blackfoot indians rove through this quarter of the country and as they are a vicious lawless and reather an abandoned set of wretches I wish to avoid an interview with them if pos-

18. Lewis sketched Rainbow Falls, Cascade County. No drawing of the falls by Lewis is known to exist.

19. Gass, with Frazer, Goodrich, McNeal, Thompson, and Werner, prepared to portage the Great Falls and await the arrival of Ordway's party who came up on July 19.

20. Teton River, called "Tansy" in 1805.

21. Lewis, Drouillard, and the Field brothers set out overland for a reconnaissance of the Marias River, while the remainder of the men followed the Missouri in canoes to the mouth of the Marias.

22. The Blackfeet in this instance.

sible. I have no doubt but they would steel our horses if they have it in their power and finding us weak should they happen to be numerous wil most probably attempt to rob us of our arms and baggage; at all events I am determined to take every possible precaution to avoid them if possible. [Camped on Teton River, Chouteau County, Montana, about ten miles northwest of Carter.]

July 18, 1806

[LEWIS] I keep a strict lookout every night, I take my tour of watch with the men. [Camped on the Marias River, Liberty County, Montana, a few miles above the mouth of Dugout Coulee.]

July 19, 1806

[ORDWAY] about 3 P. M. we arived at the white bear Camp at the head of the portage. Sergt. Gass and five more of the party were Camped here.[23]

July 20, 1806

[LEWIS] the plains are more broken than they were yesterday and have become more inferior in point of soil; a great quanty of small gravel is every where distributed over the surface of the earth which renders travling extreemly painfull to our bearfoot horses.   the soil is generally a white or whiteish blue clay, this where it has been trodden by the buffaloe when wet has now become as firm as a brickbat and stands in an inumerable little points quite as formidable to our horses feet as the gravel. the mineral salts common to the plains of the missouri has been more abundant today than usual.   the bluffs of the river are about 200 feet high, steep irregular and formed of earth which readily desolves with water, slips and precipitates itself into the river.[24] [Camped on the north side of the Marias River, Toole County, Montana, about fives miles southwest of Shelby.]

23. Ordway's party (see Clark's entry for July 13) caught up with Gass's party at the White Bear Islands.

24. Late Pleistocene glacial events produced a more rugged topography here than farther to the east. In this area the glacial till is composed of silt- and clay-sized particles and is highly impregnated with salts. The bluffs are also composed of glacial till and easily erodes in contact with running water and slides into the river.

July 21, 1806

[LEWIS] at 2 P. M. we struck a northern branch[25] of Marias river . . . being convinced that this stream came from the mountains I determined to pursue it as it will lead me to the most nothern point to which the waters of Maria's river extend which I now fear will not be as far north as I wished and expected. [Camped on the west side of Cut Bank Creek, Glacier County, Montana, about one mile southwest of the town of Cut Bank.]

July 22, 1806

[LEWIS] we arrived at a clump of large cottonwood trees in a beautifull and extensive bottom of the river about 10 miles below the foot of the rocky mountains where this river enters them; as I could see from hence very distinctly where the river entered the mountains and the bearing of this point being S of West I thought it unnecessary to proceed further and therefore encamped resolving to rest ourselves and horses a couple of days at this place and take the necessary observations . . . I now have lost all hope of the waters of this river ever extending to N Latitude 50° though I still hope and think it more than probable that both *white earth* river[26] and milk river extend as far north as latd. 50°.[27] [Camped on the south side of Cut Bank Creek, Glacier County, Montana, about twelve miles northeast of Browning. The party remained here until July 26 and Lewis named the spot Camp Disappointment.]

July 23, 1806

[LEWIS] Drewyer informed us that there was an indian camp of eleven leather lodges which appeared to have been abandoned about 10 days, the poles only of the lodges remained.   we are confident that these are the Minnetares of fort de prarie and suspect that they are probably at this time somewhere on the main branch of Maria's river on the borders of the buffaloe. [Remained at Camp Disappointment.]

25. Cut Bank Creek.

26. Little Muddy River, Williams County, North Dakota.

27. Lewis hoped that either the Little Muddy River or the Milk River would extend to 50° North and gain more territory for the United States. The Little Muddy does not reach that latitude, but the Milk extends into Canada north of that line.

[ORDWAY] the truck wheels which bore the large canoe broke down often and troubled us much. Wiser cut his leg with a knife So that he is unable to walk & is a bad wound. [Camped at an undetermined spot on the portage around the Great Falls, Cascade County, Montana.]

July 25, 1806
[LEWIS] I determined that if tomorrow continued cloudy to set out as I now begin to be apprehensive that I shall not reach the United States within this season unless I make every exertion in my power which I shall certainly not omit when once I leave this place which I shall do with much reluctance without having obtained the necessary data to establish it's longitude—as if the fates were against me my chronometer from some unknown cause stoped today, when I set her to going she went as usual. [Remained at Camp Disappointment.]

July 26, 1806
[LEWIS] The moring was cloudy and continued to rain as usual, tho' the cloud seemed somewhat thiner. I therefore posponed seting out untill 9 A. M. in the hope that it would clear off but finding the contrary result I had the horses caught and we set out biding a lasting adieu to this place which I now call camp disappointment . . . here[28] it is that we find the three species of cottonwood which I have remarked in my voyage assembled together   that speceis common to the Columbia[29] I have never before seen on the waters of the Missouri, also the narrow[30] and broad leafed speceis[31] . . . after dinner I continued my rout down the river to the North of Ea[s]t about 3 ms. when the hills putting in close on the S side I determined to ascend them to the high plain which I did accordingly, keeping the Fields with me; Drewyer passed the river and kept down the vally of the river . . . I had scarcely ascended the hills before I discovered to my left at the distance of a mile an assembleage of about 30 horses, I halted and used my spye glass by the help of which I discovered several

28. The party stopped for lunch on Two Medicine River, Pondera County, Montana.
29. Black cottonwood.
30. Narrowleaf cottonwood.
31. Plains cottonwood.

indians[32] on the top of an eminence just above them who appeared to be looking down towards the river I presumed at Drewyer. about half the horses were saddled. this was a very unpleasant sight, however I resolved to make the best of our situation and to approach them in a friendly manner. I directed J. Fields to display the flag which I had brought for that purpose and advanced slowly toward them. about this time they discovered us and appeared to run about in a very confused manner as if much allarmed, their attention had been previously so fixed on Drewyer that they did not discover us untill we had began to advance upon them, some of them decended the hill on which they were and drove their horses within shot of it's summit and again returned to the hight as if to wate our arrival or to defend themselves. I calculated on their number being nearly or quite equal to that of their horses, that our runing would invite pursuit as it would convince them that we were their enimies and our horses were so indifferent that we could not hope to make our escape by flight; added to this Drewyer was seperated from us and I feared that his not being apprized of the indians in the event of our attempting to escape he would most probably fall a sacrefice. under these considerations I still advanced towards them; when we had arrived within a quarter of a mile of them, one of them mounted his horse and rode full speed towards us, which when I discovered I halted and alighted from my horse; he came within a hundred paces halted looked at us and turned his horse about and returned as briskly to his party as he had advanced; while he halted near us I held out my hand and becconed to him to approach but he paid no attention to my overtures. on his return to his party they all decended the hill and mounted their horses and advanced towards us leaving their horses behind them, we also advanced to meet them. I counted eight of them but still supposed that there were others concealed as there were several other horses saddled. I told the two men with me that I apprehended that these were the Minnetares of Fort de Prarie and from their known character I expected that we were to have some difficulty with them; that if they thought themselves sufficiently strong I was convinced they would attempt to rob us in which case be their numbers what they would I should resist to the last extremity prefering death to that of being

32. Members of the Piegan division of the Blackfeet.

deprived of my papers instruments and gun and desired that they would
form the same resolution and be allert and on their guard. when we arrived within a hundred yards of each other the indians except one halted
I directed the two men with me to do the same and advanced singly to
meet the indian with whom I shook hands and passed on to those in his
rear, as he did also to the two men in my rear; we now all assembed and
alighted from our horses; the Indians soon asked to smoke with us, but I
told them that the man whom they had seen pass down the river had my
pipe and we could not smoke untill he joined us. I requested as they had
seen which way he went that they would one of them go with one of my
men in surch of him, this they readily concented to and a young man set
out with R. Fields in surch of Drewyer. I now asked them by sighns if they
were the Minnetares of the North which they answered in the affermative; I asked if there was any cheif among them and they pointed out 3   I
did not believe them however I thought it best to please them and gave to
one a medal to a second a flag and to the third a handkercheif, with which
they appeared well satisfyed. they appeared much agitated with our first
interview from which they had scarcely yet recovered, in fact I beleive
they were more allarmed at this accedental interview than we were. from
no more of them appearing I now concluded they were only eight in
number and became much better satisfyed with our situation as I was
convinced that we could mannage that number should they attempt any
hostile measures. as it was growing late in the evening I proposed that
we should remove to the nearest part of the river and encamp together, I
told them that I was glad to see them and had a great deel to say to them.
we mounted our horses and rode towards the river which was at but a
short distance, on our way we were joined by Drewyer Fields and the indian. we decended a very steep bluff about 250 feet high to the river
where there was a small bottom of nearly ½ a mile in length and about
250 yards wide in the widest part . . . in this bottom there stand tree solitary trees near one of which the indians formed a large simicircular camp
of dressed buffaloe skins and invited us to partake of their shelter which
Drewyer and myself accepted and the Fieldses lay near the fire in front of
the sheter. with the asistance of Drewyer I had much conversation with
these people in the course of the evening. I learned from them that they
were a part of a large band which lay encamped at present near the foot

of the rocky mountains on the main branch of Maria's river one ½ days march from our present encampment; that there was a whiteman with their band; that there was another large band of their nation hunting buffaloe near the broken mountains and were on there way to the mouth of Maria's river where they would probably be in the course of a few days. they also informed us that from hence to the establishment where they trade on the Suskasawan river is only 6 days easy march or such as they usually travel with their women and childred which may be estimated at about 150 ms. that from these traders they obtain arm amunition sperituous liquor blankets &c in exchange for wolves and some beaver skins. I told these people that I had come a great way from the East up the large river which runs towards the rising sun, that I had been to the great waters where the sun sets and had seen a great many nations all of whom I had invited to come and trade with me on the rivers on this side of the mountains, that I had found most of them at war with their neighbours and had succeeded in restoring peace among them, that I was now on my way home and had left my party at the falls of the missouri with orders to decend that river to the entrance of Maria's river and there wait my arrival and that I had come in surch of them in order to prevail on them to be at peace with their neighbours particularly those on the West side of the mountains and to engage them to come and trade with me when the establishment is made at the entrance of this river to all which they readily gave their assent and declared it to be their wish to be at peace with the Tushepahs whom they said had killed a number of their relations lately and pointed to several of those present who had cut their hair as an evidince of the truth of what they ha asserted. I found them extreemly fond of smoking and plyed them with the pipe untill late at night. I told them that if they intended to do as I wished them they would send some of their young men to their band with an invitation to their chiefs and warriors to bring the whiteman with them and come down and council with me at the entrance of Maria's river and that the ballance of them would accompany me to that place, where I was anxious now to meet my men as I had been absent from them some time and knew that they would be uneasy untill they saw me. that if they would go with me I would give them 10 horses and some tobacco. to this proposition they made no reply, I took the first watch tonight and set up untill half after eleven; the indians by this time were all asleep, I roused up R. Fields and laid down myself; I directed Fields to watch the movements of the indians and if any of them left the camp to awake us all as I apprehended they would attampt to s[t]eal our horses.   this being done I fell into a profound sleep and did not wake untill the noise of the men and indians awoke me a little after light in the morning. [Camped on the south side of Two Medicine River, about one and one-half miles south of the Glacier-Pondera county line, Montana, at a spot that has come to be called the Two Medicine Fight Site.]

[ORDWAY] returned to willow Creek[33] . . . and halted to asist the horses as the truck wheels Sank in the mud nearly to the hub . . . returned with much hard fatigue to portage River[34] and got the canoes and all the baggage down to the white perogue.[35] [Camped at Belt Creek, the party's Portage Creek and Lower Portage Camp, Cascade and Chouteau Counties, Montana.]

July 27, 1806
[LEWIS] This morning at day light the indians got up and crouded around the fire, J. Fields who was on post had carelessly laid his gun down behid him near where his brother was sleeping, one of the indians the fellow to whom I had given the medal last evening sliped behind him and took his gun and that of his brothers unperceived by him, at the same instant two others advanced and seized the guns of Drewyer and myself, J. Fields seing this turned about to look for his gun and saw the fellow just runing off with her and his brothers he called to his brother who instantly jumped up and pursued the indian with him whom they overtook at the distance of 50 or 60 paces from the camp sized their guns and rested them from him and R Fields as he seized his gun stabed the indian to the heart with his knife   the fellow ran about 15 steps and fell dead; of this I did not know untill afterwards, having recovered their guns they ran back in-

33. Box Elder Creek.
34. Belt Creek.
35. On Belt Creek near where the party had cached the white pirogue on June 18, 1805, at the Lower Portage Camp.

stantly to the camp; Drewyer who was awake saw the indian take hold of his gun and instantly jumped up and s[e]ized her and rested her from him but the indian still retained his pouch, his jumping up and crying damn you let go my gun awakened me I jumped up and asked what was the matter which I quickly learned when I saw drewyer in a scuffle with the indian for his gun. I reached to seize my gun but found her gone, I then drew a pistol from my holster and terning myself about saw the indian making off with my gun I ran at him with my pistol and bid him lay down my gun which he was in the act of doing when the Fieldses returned and drew up their guns to shoot him which I forbid as he did not appear to be about to make any resistance or commit any offensive act, he droped the gun and walked slowly off, I picked her up instantly, Drewyer having about this time recovered his gun and pouch asked me if he might not kill the fellow which I also forbid as the indian did not appear to wish to kill us, as soon as they found us all in possession of our arms they ran an indeavored to drive off all the horses I now hollowed to the men and told them to fire on them if they attempted to drive off our horses, they accordingly pursued the main party who were drving the horses up the river and I pursued the man who had taken my gun who with another was driving off a part of the horses which were to the left of the camp, I pursued them so closely that they could not take twelve of their own horses but continued to drive one of mine with some others; at the distance of three hundred paces they entered one of those steep nitches in the bluff with the horses before them   being nearly out of breath I could pursue no further, I called to them as I had done several times before that I would shoot them if they did not give me my horse and raised my gun, one of them jumped behind a rock and spoke to the other who turned arround and stoped at the distance of 30 steps from me and I shot him through the belly, he fell to his knees and on his wright elbow from which position he partly raised himself up and fired at me, and turning himself about crawled in behind a rock which was a few feet from him. he overshot me, being bearheaded I felt the wind of his bullet very distinctly. not having my shotpouch I could not reload my peice and as there were two of them behind good shelters from me I did not think it prudent to rush on them with my pistol which had I discharged I had not the means of reloading untill I reached camp; I therefore returned leasurely towards camp, on my way I met with Drewyer who having heared the report of the guns had returned in surch of me and left the Fieldes to pursue the indians, I desired him to haisten to the camp with me and assist in catching as many of the indian horses as were necessary and to call to the Fieldes if he could make them hear to come back that we still had a sufficient number of horses, this he did but they were too far to hear him. we reached the camp and began to catch the horses and saddle them and put on the pcks. the reason I had not my pouch with me was that I had not time to return about 50 yards to camp after geting my gun before I was obliged to pursue the indians or suffer them to collect and drive off all the horses. we had caught and saddled the horses and began to arrange the packs when the Fieldses returned with four of our horses; we left one of our horses and took four of the best of those of the indian's; while the men were preparing the horses I put four sheilds and two bows and quivers of arrows which had been left on the fire, with sundry other articles; they left all their baggage at our mercy. they had but 2 guns and one of them they left the others were armed with bows and arrows and eyedaggs.[36] the gun we took with us. I also retook the flagg but left the medal about the neck of the dead man that they might be informed who we were. we took some of their buffaloe meat and set out ascending the bluffs by the same rout we had decended last evening leaving the ballance of nine of their horses which we did not want. the Feildses told me that three of the indians whom they pursued swam the river one of them on my horse. and that two others ascended the hill and escaped from them with a part of their horses, two I had pursued into the nitch one lay dead near the camp and the eighth we could not account for but suppose that he ran off early in the contest. having ascended the hill we took our course through a beatiful level plain a little to the S of East. my design was to hasten to the entrance of Maria's river as quick as possible in the hope of meeting with the canoes and party at that place having no doubt but that they would pursue us with a large party and as there was a band near the broken mountains or probably between them and the mouth of that river we might expect them to receive inteligence from us and arrive at that place nearly as soon as we could, no time was there-

36. A type of dagger with a hole in the handle.

fore to be lost and we pushed our horses as hard as they would bear . . . at
3 P. M. we arrived at rose river about 5 miles above where we had passed
it as we went out, having traveled by my estimate compared with our former distances and couses about 63 ms.   here we halted an hour and a half
took some refreshment and suffered our horses to graize . . . by dark we
had traveled about 17 miles further, we now halted to rest ourselves and
horses about 2 hours, we killed a buffaloe cow and took a small quantity
of the meat.   after refreshing ourselves we again set out by moon light and
traveled leasurely, heavy thunderclouds lowered arround us on every
quarter but that from which the moon gave us light.   we continued to
pass immence herds of buffaloe all night as we had done in the latter part
of the day.   we traveled untill 2 OCk in the morning having come by my
estimate after dark about 20 ms.   we now turned out our horses and laid
ourselves down to rest in the plain very much fatiegued as may be readily conceived.   my indian horse carried me very well   in short much better than my own would have done and leaves me with but little reason to
complain of the robery. [Camped at an undetermined spot some miles
west of Fort Benton, Chouteau County, Montana.]

July 28, 1806

[LEWIS] I slept sound but fortunately awoke as day appeared, I awaked
the men and directed the horses to be saddled, I was so soar from my ride
yesterday that I could scarcely stand, and the men complained of being in
a similar situation however I encourged them by telling them that our
own lives as well as those of our friends and fellow travellers depended on
our exertions at this moment; they were allert soon prepared the horses
and we again resumed our march; the men proposed to pass the missouri
at the grog spring[37] where rose river approaches it so nearly and pass
down on the S. W. side, to this I objected as it would delay us almost all
day to reach the point by this circuetous rout and would give the enemy
time to surprise and cut off the party at the point if they had arrived there,
I told them that we owed much to the safety of our friends and that we
must wrisk our lives on this occasion, that I should proceed immediately

37. The spring was located a few miles northeast of Fort Benton, Chouteau County,
Montana. Clark's party noticed it on June 12, 1805.

to the point and if the party had not arrived that I would raft the missouri a small distance above, hide our baggage and march on foot up the river through the timber untill I met the canoes or joined them at the falls; I now told them that it was my determination that if we were attacked in the plains on our way to the point that the bridles of the horses should be tied together and we would stand and defend them, or sell our lives as dear as we could. we had proceeded about 12 miles on an East course when we found ourselves near the missouri; we heared a report which we took to be that of a gun but were not certain; still continuing down the N. E. bank of the missouri about 8 miles further, being then within five miles of the grog spring we heared the report of several rifles very distinctly on the river to our right, we quickly repared to this joyfull sound and on arriving at the bank of the river had the unspeakable satisfaction to see our canoes coming down. we hurried down from the bluff on which we were and joined them striped our hores and gave them a final discharge imbrarking without loss of time with our baggage. I now learned that they had brought all things safe having sustaned no loss nor met with any accident of importance. Wiser had cut his leg badly with a knife and was unable in consequence to work. we decended the river opposite to our principal cash [38] which we proceeded to open after reconnoitering the adjacent country. we found that the cash had caved in and most of the articles burried therin were injured; I sustained the loss of two very large bear skins which I much regret; most of the fur and baggage belonging to the men were injured. the gunpowder corn flour poark and salt had sustained but little injury the parched meal was spoiled or nearly so. having no time to air these things which they much wanted we droped down to the point to take in the several articles which had been buried at that place in several small cashes; these we found in good order, and recovered every article except 3 traps belonging to Drewyer which could not be found. here as good fortune would have it Sergt. Gass and Willard who brought the horses from the falls joined us at 1 P. M. I had ordered them to bring down the horses to this place in order to assist them in collecting meat which I had directed them to kill and

38. The cache was in Chouteau County, Montana, between the Marias and Missouri Rivers and about a mile upriver from the camp of June 3–12, 1805.

dry here for our voyage, presuming that they would have arrived with the perogue and canoes at this place several days before my return.   having now nothing to detain us we passed over immediately to the island in the entrance of Maria's river to launch the red perogue, but found her so much decayed that it was impossible with the means we had to repare her and therefore mearly took the nails and other ironwork's about her which might be of service to us and left her.   we now reimbarked on board the white peroge and five small canoes and decended the river about 15 ms. and encamped on the S. W. side. [Camped on the south side of the Missouri, Chouteau County, Montana, a little below the mouth of Crow Coulee.]

[ORDWAY] about 9 A. M. we discovred on a high bank a head Capt. Lewis & the three men who went with him on horse back comming towards us on N. Side   we came too Shore and fired the Swivell to Salute him & party we Saluted them also with Small arms and were rejoiced to See them &c. Capt. Lewis took us all by the hand.

July 29, 1806
[LEWIS] Shortly after dark last evening a violent storm came on from N. W. attended with rain hail Thunder and lightning which continued the greater part of the night.   no having the means of making a shelter I lay in the water all night. [Camped on the north side of the Missouri, Chouteau County, Montana, about a mile above the mouth of Arrow Creek and the site of the camp of May 29, 1805.]

[ORDWAY] the 2 Fields killed two large Rams[39] which had large horns. Capt. Lewis had them Scallintinized [skeletonized] and all the bones & horns as well as the Skin to take to the Seat of government.

August 1, 1806
[LEWIS] I determined to halt at this place at least for this evening and in-deavour to dry my skins of the bighorn which had every appearance of spoiling, an event which I would not should happen on any consideration

39. Bighorn sheep.

as we have now passed the country in which they are found and I therefore could not supply the deficiency were I to loose these I have. [Camped
in either Petroleum or Phillips County, Montana, a few miles below the
camp of May 19, 1805.]

August 3, 1806
[LEWIS] in future the party should cook as much meat in the evening after encamping as would be sufficient to serve them the next day; by this
means we forward our journey at least 12 or 15 miles Pr. day.   we saw but
few buffaloe in the course of this day, tho' a great number of Elk, deer,
wolves, some bear, beaver, geese a few ducks, the party coloured covus,[40]
one Callamet Eagle,[41] a number of bald Eagles, red headed woodpeckers
&c. [Camped in Valley County, Montana, about two miles above the
camp of May 12, 1805.]

August 4, 1806
[ORDWAY] I and willard went on eairly with a Small canoe to hunt . . .
about 11 oClock at night we found ourselves in a thick place of Sawyer[42]
as the corrent drawed us in and we had no chance to git out of them So
we run about half way through and the Stern run under a limb of a tree
and caught willard who was in the Stern and drew him out as the current
was verry rapid.   he held by the limb   I being in the bow of the canoe
took my oar and halled the bow first one way and the other So as to clear
the Sawyers and run through Safe and paddled the canoe to Shore and
ran up the Shore opposite willard & he called to me if everry thing was
Safe   I told him yes but he could not hear me as the water roared past the
Sawyers.   he told me he had made a little raft of 2 Small Sticks he caught
floating and tyed them together, and tyed his cloathes on them and would
Swim down through this difficult place and I run down and took out the
canoe and took him in as he Swam through Safe. [Camped with Lewis in
either Valley or McCone County, Montana, about two miles above the
camp of May 7, 1805.]

40. Black-billed magpie.
41. Golden eagle.
42. Partially submerged trees, whose exposed part "saws" the water in a bobbing motion and creates a hazard to boats.

August 6, 1806

[LEWIS] game is so abundant and gentle that we kill it when we please. [Camped about ten miles east of Poplar, in Richland County, Montana.]

August 7, 1806

[LEWIS] at 8 A. M. we passed the entrance of Marthy's river which has changed it's entrance since we passed it last year, falling in at preasent about a quarter of a mile lower down. at or just below the entrance of this river we meet with the first appearance of Coal birnt hills and pumicestone,[43] these appearances seem to be coextensive. here it is also that we find the first Elm and dwarf cedar on the bluffs, the ash first appears in the instance of one solletary tree . . . at 4 P. M. we arrived at the entrance of the Yellowstone river. I landed at the point and found that Capt. Clark had been encamped at this place and from appearances had left it about 7 or 8 days. I found a paper on a pole at the point which mearly contained my name in the hand wrighting of Capt. C. we also found the remnant of a note which had been attatched to a peace of Elk's horns in the camp; from this fragment I learned that game was scarce at the point and musquetoes troublesome which were the reasons given for his going on; I also learnt that he intended halting a few miles below where he intended waiting my arrival. I now wrote a note directed to Colter and Collins provided they were behind, ordering them to come on without loss of time; this note I wraped in leather and attatced onto the same pole which Capt. C. had planted at the point; this being done I instantly reimbarked and decended the river in the hope of reaching Capt. C's camp before night. about 7 miles below the point on the S. W. shore I saw some meat that had been lately fleased and hung on a pole; I directed Sergt. Ordway to go on shore examine the place; on his return he reported that he saw the tracks of two men which appeared so resent that he beleived they had been there today, the fire he found at the plce was blaizing and appeared to have been mended up afresh or within the course of an hour past. he found at this place a part of a Chinnook hat

43. Clinker produced by the burning of the coal beds near Big Muddy Creek, Roosevelt County, Montana, the party's "Marthy's River," passed on April 29, 1805.

which my men recognized as the hat of Gibson; from these circumstances we included that Capt. C's camp could not be distant and pursued our rout untill dark with the hope of reaching his camp   in this however we were disappointed and night coming on compelled us to encamp on the N. E. shore in the next bottom above our encampment of the 23rd and 24th of April 1805. [Camped a few miles south of Trenton, in Williams County, North Dakota.]

August 8, 1806
[LEWIS] not finding Capt. Clark I knew not what calculation to make with rispect to his halting and therefore determined to proceed as tho' he was not before me and leave the rest to the chapter of accedents.   at this place I found a good beach for the purpose of drawing out the perogue and one of the canoes which wanted corking and reparing.   the men with me have not had leasure since we left the West side of the Rocky mountains to dress any skins or make themselves cloaths and most of them are therefore extreemly bare . . . we found the Musquetoes extreemly troublesome but in this rispect there is but little choise of camps from hence down to St. Louis.   from this place to the little Missouri there is an abundance of game   I shall therefore when I leave this place travel at my leasure and avail myself of every opportunity to collect and dry meat untill I provide a sufficient quantity for our voyage not knowing what provision Capt C. has made in this rispect. [Camped several miles southwest of Williston, Williams County, North Dakota.]

August 9, 1806
[LEWIS] Colter and Collins have not yet overtaken us   I fear some missfortune has happened them for their previous fidelity and orderly deportment induces me to beleive that they would not thus intentionally delay. [Remained at the camp of August 8.]

August 11, 1806
[LEWIS] jus opposite to the birnt hills there happened to be a herd of Elk on a thick willow bar and finding that my observation was lost for the present I determined to land and kill some of them   accordingly we put too and I went out with Cruzatte only.   we fired on the Elk I killed one

and he wounded another, we reloaded our guns and took different routs through the thick willows in pursuit of the Elk; I was in the act of firing on the Elk a second time when a ball struck my left thye about an inch below my hip joint, missing the bone it passed through the left thye and cut the thickness of the bullet across the hinder part of the right thye; the stroke was very severe; I instantly supposed that Cruzatte had shot me in mistake for an Elk as I was dressed in brown leather and he cannot see very well; under this impression I called out to him damn you, you have shot me, and looked towards the place from whence the ball had come, seeing nothing I called Cruzatte several times as loud as I could but received no answer; I was now preswaded that it was an indian that had shot me as the report of the gun did not appear to be more than 40 paces from me and Cruzatte appeared to be out of hearing of me; in this situation not knowing how many indians there might be concealed in the bushes I thought best to make good my retreat to the perogue, calling out as I ran for the first hundred paces as loud as I could to Cruzatte to retreat that there were indians hoping to allarm him in time to make his escape also; I still retained the charge in my gun which I was about to discharge at the moment the ball struck me.   when I arrived in sight of the perogue I called the men to their arms to which they flew in an instant, I told them that I was wounded but I hoped not mortally, by an indian I beleived and directed them to follow me that I would return & give them battle and releive Cruzatte if possible who I feared had fallen into their hands; the men followed me as they were bid and Ireturned about a hundred paces when my wounds became so painfull and my thye so stiff that I could scarcely get on; in short I was compelled to halt and ordered the men to proceed and if they found themselves overpowered by numbers to retreat in order keeping up a fire. I now got back to the perogue as well as I could and prepared my self with a pistol my rifle and air-gun being determined as a retreat was impracticable to sell my life as deerly as possible.   in this state of anxiety and suspense remained about 20 minutes when the party returned with Cruzatte and reported that there were no indians nor the appearance of any; Cruzatte seemed much allarmed and declared if he had shot me it was not his intention, that he had shot an Elk in the willows after he left or seperated from me. I asked him whether he did not hear me when I called to him so frequently which he absolutely denied. I do not beleive that the fellow did it intentionally but after finding that he had shot me was anxious to conceal his knowledge of having done so. the ball had lodged in my breeches which I knew to be the ball of the short rifles such as that he had, and there being no person out with me but him and no indians that we could discover I have no doubt in my own mind of his having shot me.   with the assistance of Sergt. Gass I took off my cloaths and dressed my wounds myself as well as I could, introducing tents of patent lint into the ball holes, the wounds blead considerably but I was hapy to find that it had touched neither bone nor artery . . . as it was painfull to me to be removed I slept on board the perogue; the pain I experienced excited a high fever and I had a very uncomfortable night. [Camped a little above the mouth of White Earth River, in southwestern Mountrail County, North Dakota.]

August 12, 1806

[LEWIS] at 8 A. M. the bowsman informed me that there was a canoe and a camp he beleived of whitemen on the N. E. shore. I directed the perogue and canoes to come too at this place and found it to be the camp of two hunters from the Illinois by name Joseph Dickson and Forest Hancock. these men informed me that Capt. C. had passed them about noon the day before.   they also informed me that they had left the Illinois in the summer 1804 since which time they had been ascended the Missouri, hunting and traping beaver; that they had been robed by the indians and the former wounded last winter by the Tetons of the birnt woods; that they had hitherto been unsuccessfull in their voyage having as yet caught but little beaver, but were still determined to proceed. I gave them a short discription of the Missouri, a list of distances to the most conspicuous streams and remarkable places on the river above and pointed out to them the places where the beaver most abounded. I also gave them a file and a couple of pounds of powder with some lead.   these were articles which they assured me they were in great want of. I remained with these men an hour and a half when I took leave of them and proceeded.   while I halted with these men Colter and Collins who seperated from us on the 3rd ist. rejoined us.   they were well no accedent having happened.   they informed me that after proceeding the first day and not overtaking us that they had concluded that we were behind and had delayed several days in waiting for us and had thus been unable to join us untill the present momet. my wounds felt very stiff and soar this morning but gave me no considerable pain. there was much less inflamation than I had reason to apprehend there would be. I had last evening applyed a poltice of peruvian barks. at 1 P. M. I overtook Capt. Clark and party and had the pleasure of finding them all well.[44] as wrighting in my present situation is extreemly painfull to me I hall desist untill I recover and leave to my frind Capt. C. the continuation of our journal.[45] however I must notice a singular Cherry[46] which is found on the Missouri in the bottom lands about the beaverbends and some little distance below the white earth river.[47] [Camped near the McKenzie-Mountrail county line, North Dakota.]

CLARK ON THE YELLOWSTONE

July 3, 1806

[CLARK] we colected our horses and after brackfast I took My leave of Capt Lewis and the indians and at 8 A M Set out with [blank] men interpreter Shabono & his wife & child (as an interpreter & interpretess for the Crow Inds and the latter for the Shoshoni) with 50 horses.[48] [Camped on Blodgett Creek about three miles north of Hamilton, Ravalli County, Montana.]

July 4, 1806

[CLARK] This being the day of the decleration of Independence of the United States and a Day commonly Scelebrated by my Country I had

44. Lewis and Clark reunited about six miles south of Sanish, Mountrail County, North Dakota.

45. Lewis's last entry.

46. Pin cherry.

47. This is Lewis's final botanical description.

48. Clark's party set out to the south up Bitterroot River, crossing from Missoula County to Ravalli County. The captain had with him Ordway and Pryor, Bratton, Collins, Colter, Cruzatte, Gibson, Hall, Howard, Labiche, Lepage, Potts, Shannon, Shields, Weiser, Whitehouse, Willard, Windsor, York, Sacagawea, and Toussaint and Jean Baptiste Charbonneau. Since the Crow language is similar to Hidatsa, Sacagawea and Charbonneau could serve as interpreters.

every disposition to Selebrate this day and therefore halted early and partook of a Sumptious Dinner of a fat Saddle of Venison and Mush of Cows
(roots). [Camped on the north side of West Fork Bitterroot River, near
its junction with the Bitterroot, Ravalli County, Montana.]

July 6, 1806
[CLARK] the Indian woman wife to Shabono informed me that she had
been in this plain frequently and knew it well that the Creek[49] which we
decended was a branch of Wisdom river[50] and when we assended the
higher part of the plain we would discover a gap in the mountains[51] in
our direction to the Canoes,[52] and when we arived at that gap we would
See a high point of a mountain covered with snow in our direction to the
canoes.[53] [Camped apparently on Moose Creek about seven miles southwest of Wisdom, Beaverhead County, Montana.]

[CLARK, WEATHER REMARKS] cold night with frost.   I slept cold under 2
blankets.

July 7, 1806
[CLARK] at the distance of 16 miles we arived at a Boiling Spring[54] Situated about 100 paces from a large Easterly fork of the Small river in a
leavel open vally plain and nearly opposit & E. of the 3 forks of this little
river which heads in the Snowey Mountains to the S E. & S W of the
Springs.   this Spring contains a very considerable quantity of water, and
actually blubbers with heat for 20 paces below where it rises.   it has every
appearance of boiling, too hot for a man to endure his hand in it 3 sec-
onds. I directt Sergt. Pryor and John Shields to put each a peice of meat
in the water of different Sises.   the one about the Size of my 3 fingers
Cooked dun in 25 minits the other much thicker was 32 minits before it

49. Trail Creek.
50. Big Hole River.
51. Big Hole Pass.
52. Cached at Camp Fortunate.
53. Clark crossed the Continental Divide at Gibbons Pass, then followed Trail Creek
toward Wisdom, Beaverhead County, Montana.
54. On Warm Spring Creek, Jackson, Beaverhead County, Montana.

became Sufficiently dun.   this water boils up through some loose hard gritty Stone.   a little sulferish. [Camped near the head of Divide Creek, east of Big Hole Pass, Beaverhead County, Montana.]

July 8, 1806

[CLARK] after dinner we proceeded on . . . to our encampment of 17 Augt. [1805] at which place we Sunk our Canoes & buried Some articles, as before mentioned the most of the Party with me being Chewers of Tobacco become So impatient to be chewing it that they Scercely gave themselves time to take their Saddles off their horses before they were off to the deposit. I found every article Safe, except a little damp. I gave to each man who used tobacco about two feet off a part of a role   took one third of the ballance myself and put up ⅔ in a box to Send down with the most of the articles which had been left at this place, by the Canoes to Capt. Lewis. [Camped at Camped Fortunate.]

[ORDWAY] nothing to eat this evening but the head of a goat or antelope which the party had droped on the road.⁵⁵ [Camped on a tributary of Grasshopper Creek, west and a little south of Bannack, Beaverhead County, Montana.]

July 10, 1806

[CLARK] I had all the Canoes put into the water and every article which was intended to be Sent down put on board, and the horses collected and packed with what fiew articles I intend takeing with me to the River Rochejhone,⁵⁶ and after brackfast we all Set out at the Same time & proceeded on Down Jeffersons river.⁵⁷ [Camped about ten miles northeast of Dillon, Beaverhead County, Montana, on the east side of Beaverhead River.]

55. Ordway, with Collins, Gibson, Labiche, and Shannon, had separated from Clark's party to hunt stray horses; they reunited on July 9.

56. *Rochejaune*, in French, for Yellowstone.

57. Clark set out down the Beaverhead River. For the first part of the trip, Ordway was in charge of the canoe party, while Clark led the group with horses by land. After lunch Clark joined the canoes and Pryor took charge of the horse party.

July 11, 1806

[CLARK] at 7 P M I arrived at the Enterance of Wisdom River[58] and Encampd. in the Spot we had encamped the [6th][59] of August last. here we found a Bayonet which had been left & the Canoe quite safe.[60] I directed that all the nails be taken out of this Canoe and paddles to be made of her Sides. [Camped on the east side of Jefferson River, opposite the mouth of the Big Hole River, in Beaverhead County, Montana.]

July 13, 1806

[CLARK] Set out early this morning and proceded on very well to the enterance of Madicines river at our old Encampment of the 27th July last at 12 where I found Sergt. Pryor and party with the horses, they had arived at this place one hour before us. his party had killed 6 deer & a white bear I had all the horses driven across Madicine & gallitines rivers and halted to dine and let the horses feed imediately below the enterance of Gallitine. had all the baggage of the land party taken out of the Canoes and after dinner the 6 Canoes and the party of 10 men under the direction of Sergt. Ordway Set out.[61]   previous to their departur I gave instructions how they were to proceed &c. I also wrote to Capt Lewis by Sergt. Ordway . . . at 5 P. M I Set out from the head of Missouri at the 3 forks . . . I observe Several leading roads which appear to pass to a gap of the mountain in a E. N E. direction about 18 or 20 miles distant. The indian woman who has been of great Service to me as a pilot through this Country recommends a gap in the mountain more South which I shall cross.[62] [Camped on the north side of the Gallatin River about one mile east of Logan, Gallatin County, Montana.]

58. Big Hole River.

59. Biddle filled in Clark's blank space with the 1805 date.

60. The canoe was deposited on August 7, 1805.

61. Ordway followed the Missouri to link up with Lewis at the Marias; with him were Collins, Colter, Cruzatte, Howard, Lepage, Potts, Weiser, Whitehouse, and Willard.

62. Sacagawea recommended Bozeman Pass, through which Clark and party passed on July 15.

July 14, 1806

[CLARK] The Indian woman informs me that a fiew years ago Buffalow was very plenty in those plains & Vallies quit as high as the head of Jeffersons river, but fiew of them ever come into those Vallys of late years owing to the Shoshones who are fearfull of passing into the plains West of the mountains and Subsist on what game they Can Catch in the Mountains principally and the fish which they take in the E. fork of Lewis's river. Small parties of the Shoshones do pass over to the plains for a few days at a time and kill buffalow for their Skins and dried meat, and return imediately into the Mountains. [Camped on Kelly Creek, about four miles east of Bozeman, Gallatin County, Montana.]

[CLARK, WEATHER REMARKS] Saw a Tobacco worm shown me by *York*.

July 17, 1806

[CLARK] I Saw in one of those Small bottoms which I passed this evening an Indian fort which appears to have been built last Summer. this fort was built of logs and bark. the logs was put up very Closely capping on each other about 5 feet and Closely chinked . . . the Squaw informs me that when the war parties find themselves pursued they make those forts to defend themselves in from the pursuers whose Superior numbers might other wise over power them and cut them off. [Camped on the north side of the Yellowstone, in Sweet Grass County, and west of the Stillwater county line, Montana.]

July 18, 1806

[CLARK] at 11 A. M. I observed a Smoke rise to the S. S. E in the plains towards the termonation of the rocky mountains in that direction (which is Covered with Snow) this Smoke must be raisd. by the Crow Indians in that direction as a Signal for us, or other bands. I think it most probable that they have discovered our trail and takeing us to be Shoshone &c. in Serch of them the Crow Indians to trade as is their Custom, have made this Smoke to Shew where they are — or otherwise takeing us to be their Enemy made this Signal for other bands to be on their guard . . . Gibson in attempting to mount his horse after Shooting a deer this evening fell and on a Snag and sent it nearly [*NB: two*] inches into the Muskeler part of his thy.   he informs me this Snag was about 1 inch in diamuter burnt at the end.   this is a very bad wound and pains him exceedingly. I dressed the wound. [Camped about three miles west of Columbus, Stillwater County, Montana.]

July 19, 1806

[CLARK] I rose early and dressed Gibsons wound.   he Slept but very little last night and complains of great pain in his Knee and hip as well as his *thy.*   there being no timber on this part of the Rochjhone sufficintly large for a Canoe and time is pracious as it is our wish to get to the U States this Season, conclude to take Gibson in a litter if he is not able to ride on down the river untill I can find a tree Sufficently large for my purpose. I had the Strongest and jentlesst Horse Saddled and placed Skins & blankets in Such a manner that when he was put on the horse he felt himself in as easy a position as when lying.   this was a fortunate circunstance as he Could go much more at his ease than in a litter.   passed Rose bud river[63] on 'Sd Side   I proceeded on about 9 miles, and halted to let the horses graze and let Gibson rest.   his leg become So numed from remaining in one position, as to render extreemly painfull to him. I derected Shields to keep through the thick timber and examine for a tree sufficently large & Sound to make a Canoe, and also hunt for Some Wild Ginger for a Poltice for Gibsons wound . . . Gibsons thy became So painfull that he could not Set on the horse after rideing about 2 hours and a half   I directed Sergt Pryor and one man to continue with him under the Shade of a tree for an hour and then proceed on to the place I Should encamp which would be in the first good [timber] . . . about 4 Miles below the place I left Sergt. Pryor with Gibson found some large timber near which the grass was tolerably good   I Encamped under a thick grove of those trees. [Camped on the north side of the Yellowstone, south of Park City, Stillwater County, Montana, the so-called Canoe Camp, where the party remained until July 24.]

63. Stillwater River, meeting the Yellowstone opposite Columbus, Stillwater County, Montana.

July 23, 1806

[CLARK] Sgt. pryor found an Indian Mockerson and a Small piece of a roab, the mockerson worn out on the bottom & yet wet, and have every appearance of haveing been worn but a fiew hours before. those Indian Signs is Conclusive with me that they have taken the 24 horses which we lost on the night of the 20th instant, and that those who were about last night were in Serch of the ballance of our horses which they could not find as they had fortunately got into a Small Prarie Serounded with thick timber in the bottom . . . I gave Sergt Pryor his instructions and a letter to Mr. Haney and directed that he G. Shannon & Windser take the remaining horses to the Mandans, where he is to enquire for Mr. H. Heney if at the establishments on the Assinniboin river to take 12 or 14 horses and proceed on to that place and deliver Mr. Heney the letter which is with a view to engage Mr. Heney to provale on some of the best informed and most influential Chiefs of the different bands of Sieoux to accompany us to the Seat of our Government with a view to let them See our population and resourses &c. which I believe is the Surest garentee of Savage fidelity to any nation that of a Governmt. possessing the power of punishing promptly every aggression. Sergt. Pryor is directed to leave the ballance of the horses with the grand Chief of the Mandans untill our arival at his village also to keep a journal of his rout courses distances water courss Soil production, & animals to be particularly noted.[64] [Remained at Canoe Camp.]

July 24, 1806

[CLARK] for me to mention or give an estimate of the differant Spcies of wild animals on this river particularly Buffalow, Elk Antelopes & Wolves would be incredibable. I shall therefore be silent on the Subject further. So it is we have a great abundance of the best of meat. [Camped opposite and just below the mouth of Dry Creek in Yellowstone County, Montana.]

64. Pryor with Hall, Shannon, and Windsor were to take the horses to the Mandans and deliver a message to Hugh Heney, a North West Company trader whom the captains had met at Fort Mandan during the winter stay there. The men were defeated in that mission by having their horses stolen, probably by Crow Indians. They rejoined Clark on August 8. No journal by Pryor is known to exist.

July 25, 1806

[CLARK] at 4 P M arived at a remarkable rock Situated in an extensive bottom on the Stard. Side of the river & 250 paces from it. this rock I ascended and from it's top had a most extensive view in every direction. This rock which I shall Call Pompy's Tower[65] is 200 feet high and 400 paces in secumphrance and only axcessable on one Side which is from the N. E the other parts of it being a perpendicular Clift of lightish Coloured gritty rock on the top there is a tolerable Soil of about 5 or 6 feet thick Covered with Short grass. The Indians have made 2 piles of Stone on the top of this Tower. The nativs have ingraved on the face of this rock the figures of animals &c. near which I marked my name and the day of the month & year[66] . . . after Satisfying my Self Sufficiently in this delightfull prospect of the extensive Country around, and the emence herds of Buffalow, Elk and wolves in which it abounded, I decended and proceeded on a fiew miles. [Camped on the south side of the Yellowstone River, Yellowstone County, Montana, about two miles northeast of the village of Pompeys Pillar.]

July 30, 1806

[CLARK] Set out early this morning   at 12 miles arived at the Commencement of Shoals the Chanel on the Stard Side near a high bluff. passed a Succession of those Shoals for 6 miles the lower of which was quit across the river and appeared to have a decent of about 3 feet. here we were Compeled to let the Canoes down by hand for fear of their Strikeing a rock under water and Splitting. This is by far the wost place which I have Seen on this river from the Rocky mountains to this place a distance of 694 miles by water.   a Perogu or large Canoe would with Safty pass through the worst of those Shoals, which I call the Buffalow

---

65. Clark named the rock for little Jean Baptiste Charbonneau. The sandstone formation, now called Pompeys Pillar (after a misinterpretation of Clark's name for the rock), is in Yellowstone County, about twenty-eight miles northeast of Billings.

66. After some improvements, Clark's inscription of his name and date are still visible, the only well-documented, surviving physical evidence of the expedition along the route.

Sholes[67] from the Circumstance of one of those animals being in them. [Camped in Prairie County, Montana, opposite and a little below the mouth of Powder River.]

August 1, 1806
[CLARK] we had Showers of rain repeetedly all day at the intermition of only a fiew minits between them. My Situation a very disagreeable one. in an open Canoe wet and without a possibility of keeping my Self dry ... at 2 P. M. I was obliged to land to let the Buffalow Cross over. not with-standing an island of half a mile in width over which this gangue of Buf-falow had to pass and the Chanel of the river on each Side nearly ¼ of a mile in width, this gangue of Buffalow was entirely across and as thick as they could Swim. the Chanel on the Side of the island the[y] went into the river was crouded with those animals for ½ an hour. the other Side of the island for more than ¾ of an hour. I took 4 of the men and killed 4 fat Cows for their fat and what portion of their flesh the Small Canoes Could Carry that which we had killed a few days ago being nearly Spoiled from the wet weather. [Camped on an island in Dawson County, Mon-tana, just below the mouth of Cottonwood Creek, Wibaux County.]

August 3, 1806
[CLARK] at 8. A. M. I arived at the Junction of the Rochejhone with the Missouri, and formed my Camp imediately in the point between the two river at which place the party had all encamped the 26th of April — 1805. [Camped at the mouth of the Yellowstone in McKenzie County, North Dakota, at the campsite of April 26, 1805, as Clark notes.]

August 4, 1806
[CLARK] Musquetors excessively troublesom So much So that the men complained that they could not work at their Skins for those troublesom insects. and I find it entirely impossible to hunt in the bottoms, those in-sects being So noumerous and tormenting as to render it imposseable for a man to continue in the timbered lands and our best retreat from those insects is on the Sand bars in the river and even those Situations are only

67. In Custer County, Montana, just below the mouth of Sand Creek.

clear of them when the Wind Should happen to blow which it did to day for a fiew hours in the middle of the day. the evenings nights and mornings they are almost [un]indureable perticelarly by the party with me who have no Bears [bars or nets] to keep them off at night, and nothing to Screen them but their blankets which are worn and have maney holes. The torments of those Missquetors and the want of a Sufficety of Buffalow meat to dry, those animals not to be found in this neighbourhood induce me to deturmine to proceed on to a more eliagiable Spot on the Missouri below at which place the Musquetors will be less troublesom and Buffalow more plenty . . . wrote a note to Capt Lewis informing him of my intentions and tied it to a pole which I had Stuck up in the point. At 5 P. M Set out and proceeded on down to the 2d point which appeared to be an eligable Situation for my purpose   killed a porcupine   on this point the Musquetors were So abundant that we were tormented much worst than at the point. The Child of Shabono has been So much bitten by the Musquetor that his face is much puffed up & Swelled. [Camped at an undetermined spot in either McKenzie or Williams County, North Dakota, and in the vicinity of the camp of April 25, 1805.]

August 6, 1806

[CLARK] This morning a very large Bear of white Specis, discovered us floating in the water and takeing us, as I prosume to be Buffalow imediately plunged into the river and prosued us. I directed the men to be Still. this animal Came within about 40 yards of us, and tacked about. we all fired into him without killing him, and the wind So high that we could not pursue hi[m], by which means he made his escape to the Shore badly wounded. I have observed buffalow floating down which I suppose must have been drounded in Crossing above. [Camped below the mouth of Little Muddy River, probably in McKenzie County, North Dakota.]

August 8, 1806

[CLARK] at 8 A. M. Sergt. N. Pryor Shannon, hall & Windsor Came down the river in two Canoes made of Buffalow Skins. Sergt. Pryor informed me that the Second night after he parted with me on the river Rochejhone he arived about 4 P M on the banks of a large Creek which contained no running water.   he halted to let the horses graze dureing which time a heavy Shower of rain raised the Creek so high that Several horses which had Stragled across the Chanel of this Creek was obliged to Swim back. here he deturmined to Continue all night it being in good food for the horses. In the morning he could See no horses. in lookg about their Camp they discovered Several tracks within 100 paces of their Camp, which they pursued found where they had Caught and drove off all the horses. they prosued on five miles the Indians there divided into two parties. they Continued in pursute of the largest party five miles further finding that there was not the Smallest Chance of overtakeing them, they returned to their Camp and packed up their baggage on their backs and Steared a N. E. course to the River Rochejhone which they Struck at *pompys Tower*, there they killed a Buffalow Bull and made a Canoe in the form and shape of the mandans & Ricares . . . the night after the horses had been stolen a Wolf bit Sergt. Pryor through his hand when asleep, and this animal was So vicious as to make an attempt to Seize Windsor, when Shannon fortunately Shot him. Sergt. Pryers hand has nearly recovered. [Remained at the camp of August 7 which is difficult to determine but apparently was above Tobacco Creek, McKenzie County, North Dakota.]

August 9, 1806
[CLARK] The Squar brought me a large and well flavoured Goose berry of a rich Crimsin Colour, and deep purple berry of the large Cherry of the Current Speces which is common on this river as low as the Mandans, the engagees Call it the Indian Current.[68] [Camped approximately ten miles above Tobacco Creek, McKenzie County, North Dakota.]

August 10, 1806
[CLARK] I finished a Copy of my Sketches of the River Rochejhone. [Remained at the camp of August 9.]

August 11, 1806
[CLARK] at Meridian I set out and had not proceeded more than 2 miles before I observed a Canoe near the Shore. I derected the Canoes to land here I found two men from the illinoies Jos. Dixon, and [blank] Hand-

68. Golden currant.

cock[69] those men are on a trapping expedition up the River Rochejhone.
They inform me that they left the Illinois in the Summer 1804. the last
winter they Spent with the Tetons in Company with a Mr. *Coartong*[70]
who brought up goods to trade The tetons robed him of the greater part
of the goods and wounded this Dixon in the leg with a hard wad. The
Tetons gave Mr. *Coartong* Some fiew robes for the articles they took from
him. Those men further informed me that they met the Boat and party
we Sent down from Fort Mandan near the Kanzas river on board of
which was a Chief of the Ricaras, that he met the Yankton Chiefs with
Mr. Deurion, McClellen & Several other traders on their way down.[71]
that the Mandans and Menitarrais wer at war with the Ricaras and had
killed two of the latter. the Assinniboins were also at war with the Mandans &c and had prohibited the N W. traders from Comeing to the Missouri to trade. they have latterly killed one Trader near the Mous River[72]
and are now in wait for Mr. McKenzey[73] one of the Clerks who have been
for a long time with Menetarias. Those dificulties if true will I fear be a
bar to our expectations of having the Mandan Minetarra & Ricara Chief
to acompany us to the U. States. Tho we Shall endeavor to bring abot a
peace between Mandans Mennetaries & Ricaras and provail on Some of
their Cheifs to accompany us to the U. States. [Camped opposite Little
Knife River, in McKenzie County, North Dakota.]

August 12, 1806
[CLARK] at meridian Capt Lewis hove in Sight with the party which went
by way of the Missouri as well as that which accompanied him from Travellers rest on Clarks river;[74] I was alarmed on the landing of the Canoes
to be informed that Capt. Lewis was wounded by an accident. I found
him lying in the Perogue, he informed me that his wound was slight and
would be well in 20 or 30 days this information relieved me very much.

69. Joseph Dickson and Forrest Hancock. See also Lewis's entry of August 12.
70. Charles Courtin.
71. Pierre Dorion and Robert McClellan.
72. Souis River of Saskatchewan, North Dakota, and Manitoba.
73. Charles McKenzie.
74. Lewis and Clark reunited about six miles south of Sanish, Mountrail County, North
Dakota.

I examined the wound and found it a very bad flesh wound   the ball had passed through the fleshey part of his left thy below the hip bone and cut the cheek of the right buttock for 3 inches in length and the debth of the ball . . . I washed Capt L. wound which has become Sore and Somewhat painfull to him. [Camped near the McKenzie-Mountrail county line, North Dakota.]

CHAPTER 12

Hurrying Home

August 13 – September 23, 1806

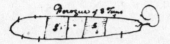

August 14, 1806

[CLARK] when we were opposit the Minetares Grand Village[1] we Saw a
number of the Nativs viewing of we derected the Blunderbuses fired Several times, Soon after we Came too at a Croud of the nativs on the bank
opposit the Village of the Shoe Indians or *Mah-har-ha's*[2] at which place I
saw the principal Chief of the Little Village of the Menitarre[3] & the principal Chief of the *Mah-har-has*.[4] those people were extreamly pleased to
See us. the Chief of the little Village of the Menetarias cried most imod-
erately, I enquired the Cause and was informed it was for the loss of his
Son who had been killed latterly by the Blackfoot Indians. after a delay
of a fiew minits I proceeded on to the *black Cats* Village[5] on the N. E. Side
of the Missouri where I intended to Encamp but the Sand blew in Such
a manner that we deturmined not to continu on that Side but return to
the Side we had left. here we were visited by all the inhabitants of this
village who appeared equally as well pleased to See us as those above. I
walked up to the Black Cats village & eate some Simnins with him, and
Smoked a pipe this Village I discovered had been rebuilt Since I left it
and much Smaller than it was; on enquirey into the Cause was informed
that a quarrel had taken place and [*NB: a number of*] Lodges had removed to the opposd Side. I had Soon as I landed despatched Shabono to

1. Hidatsa village of Menetarra.
2. Awaxawi Hidatsas of Mahawha.
3. Black Moccasin of Metaharta.
4. White Buffalo Robe Unfolded of Mahawha.
5. Mandan Black Cat's Ruptáre village.

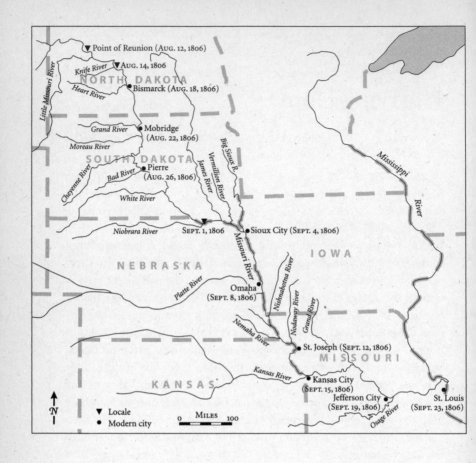

▼ Point of Reunion (Aug. 12, 1806)

Little Missouri River

Knife River

▼ Aug. 14, 1806

NORTH DAKOTA

Heart River

● Bismarck (Aug. 18, 1806)

Grand River

● Mobridge (Aug. 22, 1806)

Moreau River

SOUTH DAKOTA

Cheyenne River

Bad River

● Pierre (Aug. 26, 1806)

James River

Big Sioux R.

Vermillion River

White River

Niobrara River

▼ Sept. 1, 1806

Missouri River

● Sioux City (Sept. 4, 1806)

Mississippi River

IOWA

NEBRASKA

Platte River

Omaha (Sept. 8, 1806)

Nishnabotna River

Nodaway River

Grand River

Nemaha River

● St. Joseph (Sept. 12, 1806)

MISSOURI

KANSAS

Kansas River

● Kansas City (Sept. 15, 1806)

Jefferson City (Sept. 19, 1806)

Osage River

● St. Louis (Sept. 23, 1806)

↑N

▼ Locale
● Modern city

0 MILES 100

The Expedition's Route, August 13–September 23, 1806

the Minetarras inviting the Chiefs to visit us, & Drewyer down to the lower Village of the Mandans to ask Mr. Jessomme to Come and enterpret for us.[6] Mr. Jessomme arived and I spoke to the chiefs of the Village informing them that we Spoke to them as we had done when we were with them last and we now repeeted our envitation to the principal Chiefs of all the Villages to accompany us and to the U States &c. the Black Cat Chief of the Mandans, Spoke and informed me that he wished to Visit the United States and his Great Father but was afraid of the *Sciox* who were yet at war with them and had killed Several of their men Since we had left them, and were on the river below and would Certainly kill him if he attempted to go down. I indeavered to do away with his objections by informig him that we would not Suffer those indians to hurt any of our red Children who Should think proper to accompany us, and on their return they would be equally protected, and their presents which would be very liberal, with themselves, Conveyed to their own Country at the expence of the U. States &c. . . . The Great Chif of all the Menitarres the one eye[7] Came to Camp also Several other Chiefs of the different Villages. [Camped apparently on the west side of the Missouri in Mercer County, North Dakota, and below Mitutanka village.]

[ORDWAY] Capt. Lewis fainted as Capt. Clark was dressing his wound, but Soon came too again.

August 15, 1806
[CLARK] after assembling the Chiefs and Smokeing one pipe, I informed them that I Still Spoke the Same words which we had Spoken to them when we first arived in their Country in the fall of 1804 . . . the great Chief of the Menetaras Spoke, he Said he wished to go down and See his great father very much, but that the Scioux were in the road and would most certainly kill him or any others who Should go down they were bad people and would not listen to any thing which was told them. when he

---

6. Charbonneau went back to Menetarra and Drouillard downriver to Mitutanka, the village farthest south in the Mandan-Hidatsa complex, to get Jusseaume to interpret the Mandan language.

7. One Eye, or Le Borgne, of Menetarra.

Saw us last we told him that we had made peace with all the nations below, Since that time the Seioux had killed 8 of their people and Stole a
number of their horses. he Said that he had opened his ears and followed
our Councils, he had made peace with the Chyennes and rocky mountains indians, and repieted the same objecctions as mentioned.   that
he went to war against none and was willing to receive all nations as
friends . . . being informed by one of our enterpreters that the 2d Chief of
the Mandans Comonly Called the little Crow intended to accompany us
down, I took Charbono and walked to the Village to See this Chief and
talk with him on the Subject. he told me he had deturmined to go down,
but wished to have a council first with his people which would be in the
after part of the day. I smoked a pipe with the little Crow and returned to
the boat. Colter one of our men expressed a desire to join Some trappers
who offered to become Shearers with and furnish traps &c.   the offer
a very advantagious one, to him, his Services Could be dispenced with
from this down and as we were disposed to be of Service to any one of our
party who had performed their duty as well as Colter had done, we agreed
to allow him the prvilage provided no one of the party would ask or expect a Similar permission to which they all agreeed that they wished
Colter every Suckcess and that as we did not wish any of them to Seperate untill we Should arive at St. Louis they would not apply or exect it
&c. . . . we gave Jo Colter Some Small articles which we did not want and
Some powder & lead.   the party also gave him Several articles which will
be usefull to him on his expedittion.[8] This evening Charbono informed
me that our back was scercely turned before a war party from the two
menetarry villages followed on and attacked and killed the Snake Indians
whome we had Seen and in the engagement between them and the Snake
indians they had lost two men one of which was the Son of the principal
Chief of the little village of the menitarras. [Remained at the camp below
Mitutanka village.]

August 16, 1806
[CLARK] as our Swivel Could no longer be Serveceable to us as it could
not be fireed on board the largest Perogue, we Concluded to make a pres-

8. Colter joined Dickson and Hancock.

ent of it to the Great Chief of the Menetaras (the One Eye) with a view to ingratiate him more Strongly in our favour I had the Swivel Charged and Collected the Chiefs in a circle around it and adressed them with great ceremoney . . . I then a good deel of Ceremony made a preasent of the Swivel to the *One Eye* Chief and told him when he fired this gun to re-member the words of his great father which we had given him . . . [the] Chief appeared to be much pleased and conveyed it immediately to his village &c. [Remained at the camp below Mitutanka village.]

[CLARK, WEATHER REMARKS] Northern lights Seen last night.

August 17, 1806
[CLARK] Settled with Touisant Chabono for his Services as an enterpreter the pric of a horse and Lodge purchased of him for public Service in all amounting to 500$ 33⅓ cents . . . at 2 oClock we left our encampment af-ter takeing leave of Colter who also Set out up the river in Company with Messrs. Dickson & Handcock. we also took our leave of T. Chabono, his Snake Indian wife and their Son Child who had accompanied us on our rout to the pacific Ocean in the Capacity of interpreter and interpretes. T. Chabono wished much to accompany us in the Said Capacity if we could have provailed the Menetarre Chiefs to dcend the river with us to the U. States, but as none of those chiefs of whoes language he was Con-versant would accompany us, his Services were no longer of use to the U' States and he was therefore discharged and paid up. we offered to convey him down to the Illinois if he Chose to go, he declined proceeding on at present, observing that he had no acquaintance or prospects of makeing a liveing below, and must continue to live in the way that he had done. I of-fered to take his little Son a butifull promising Child who is 19 months old to which they both himself & wife wer willing provided the Child had been weened. they observed that in one year the boy would be Sufficiently old to leave his mother & he would then take him to me if I would be so freindly as to raise the Child for him in Such a manner as I thought proper, to which I agreeed &c. we droped down to the *Big white Cheifs* Mandan Village[9] ½ a mile below on the South Side, all the Indians proceeded on

9. Mitutanka.

down by land. and I walked to the lodge of the Chief whome I found Sorounded by his friends the men were Setting in a circle Smokeing and the womin Crying. he Sent his bagage with his wife & Son . . . to the Canoes provided for them. after Smoking one pipe, and distributing Some powder & lead which we had given him, he informed me that he was ready and we were accompd to the Canoes by all the Village . . . we then Saluted them with a gun and Set out and proceeded on to *Fort Mandan* where I landed and went to view the old works the houses except one in the rear bastion was burnt by accident, Some pickets were Standing in front next to the river. [Camped near Hensler, Oliver County, North Dakota.]

August 18, 1806

[CLARK] I set my self down with the big white man Chiefe and made a number of enquiries into the tredition of his nation as well as the time of their inhabiting the number of Villages the remains of which we see on different parts of the river, as also the cause of their evacuation. he told me his nation first Came out of the ground where they had a great village. a grape vine grew down through the Earth to their village and they Saw light Some of their people assended by the grape vine upon the earth, and Saw Buffalow and every kind of animal also Grapes plumbs &c. they gathered Some grapes & took down the vine to the village, and they tasted and found them good, and deturmined to go up and live upon the earth, and great numbers climbed the vine and got upon earth men womin and children. at length a large big bellied woman in climbing broke the vine and fell and all that were left in the Village below has remained there ever Since (The Mandans beleive when they die that they return to this village) Those who were left on earth made a village on the river below and were very noumerous &c. he Said that he was born [*NB: about 40 years*] in the Village Opposit to our Camp and at that time his nation inhabited 7 villages as large as that and were full of people, the Sieoux and Small pox killed the greater part of them and made them So weak that all that were left only made two Small villages when Collected, which were built near the old Ricaras village above. their troubles with the Scioux & Pawnees or Ricaras Compelled them to move and build a village where they now live. [Camped a little south of Bismarck, Burleigh County, North Dakota.]

August 19, 1806

[CLARK] Capt. Lewis'es wounds are heeling very fast, I am much in hope of his being able to walk in 8 or 10 days. [Camped about ten miles below the previous camp still in Burleigh County, North Dakota.]

August 20, 1806

[CLARK] I observe a great alteration in the Corrent course and appearance of this pt. of the Missouri.   in places where there was Sand bars in the fall 1804 at this time the main Current passes, and where the current then passed is now a Sand bar   Sand bars which were then naked are now covered with willow Several feet high.   the enteranc of Some of the Rivers & Creeks Changed. [Camped below the mouth of Spring Creek, Campbell County, South Dakota.]

August 21, 1806

[CLARK] a man of about 32 years of age was intreduced to me as 1st Chief of the nation [Arikara]   this man they Call the grey eyes or [blank]   he was absent from the Nation at the time we passed up, the man [Kakawissassa] whome we had acknowledged as the principal chief informed me that the Grey eyes was a greater Chief than himself and that he had given up all his pretentions with the Flag and Medal to the Grey eyes . . . [Grey Eyes] made a very animated Speach in which he mentioned his williness of following the councels which we had given them that they had Some bad young men who would not listen to the Councels but would join the Seioux, those men they had discarded and drove out of their villages, that the Seioux were the Cause of their Missunderstanding &c. that they were a bad peoples.   that they had killed Several of the Ricaras Since I Saw them. That Several of the chiefs wished to accompany us down to See their great father, but wished to see the Chief who went down last Sumer return first,[10] he expressed Some apprehention as to the Safty of that Chiefs in passing the Sieoux. [Camped apparently on Ashley Island, between Campbell and Corson Counties, South Dakota.]

10. The Arikara chief Piaheto died at Washing-ton DC (see September 12, 1806).

August 22, 1806

[CLARK] my worthy friend Capt Lewis is recovering fast, he walked a little to day for the first time. I have discontinud the tent in the hole the ball came out. [Camped about six miles southeast of Mobridge, Walworth County, South Dakota.]

August 26, 1806

[CLARK] as we were now in the Country where we were informed the Sceoux were assembled we were much on our guard deturmined to put up with no insults from those bands of Seioux, all the arms &. in perfect order. [Camped about four miles above the mouth of Medicine Creek, Lyman County, South Dakota.]

August 27, 1806

[CLARK] we discover the first Signs of the wild turkey . . . My friend Capt Lewis hurt himself very much by takeing a longer walk on the Sand bar . . . than he had Strength to undergo, which Caused him to remain very unwell all night. [Camped on an island at the lower end of the Grand Detour, Lyman and Buffalo Counties, South Dakota.]

August 29, 1806

[CLARK] from this eminance I had a view of a greater number of buffalow than I had ever Seen before at one time. I must have Seen near 20,000 of those animals feeding on this plain. I have observed that in the country between the nations which are at war with each other the greatest numbers of wild animals are to be found. [Camped some miles south of White River, in Lyman County, South Dakota.]

[ORDWAY] we Save all the buffaloe horns we can find to take to the States as they would make excelent kife and fork handles &c.

August 30, 1806

[CLARK] I told those Indians [Tetons] that they had been deef to our councils and ill treated us as we assended this river two years past, that they had abused all the whites who had visited them since. I believed them to be bad people & Should not Suffer them to cross to the Side on

which the party lay, and directed them to return with their band to their
Camp, that if any of them come near our camp we Should kill them certainly . . . 7 of them halted on the top of the hill and blackguarded us, told
us to come across and they would kill us all &c. of which we took no notice.   we all this time were extreamly anxious for the arival of the 2 fields
& Shannon whome we had left behind, and were Some what consd. [con-
cerned] as to their Safty.   to our great joy those men hove in Sight at
6 P. M. [Camped between Gregory and Charles Mix Counties, South
Dakota.]

September 1, 1806
[CLARK] about two miles below the Quicurre,[11] 9 Indians ran down the
bank and beckened to us to land, they appeared to be a war party, and I
took them to be Tetons and paid no kind of attention to them further
than an enquirey to what tribe they belonged, they did not give me any
answer, I prosume they did not understand the man who Spoke to them
as he Spoke but little of their language.   as one Canoe was yet behind we
landed in an open Commanding Situation out of Sight of the indians deturmined to delay untill they Came up.   about 15 minits after we had
landed Several guns were fired by the indians, which we expected was at
the three men behind. I calld out 15 men and ran up with a fill deturmi-
nation to Cover them if possible let the number of the indians be what
they might. Capt Lewis hobled up on the bank and formed the remainder of the party in a Situation well calculated to defend themselves and
the Canoes &c.   when I had proceeded to the point about 250 yards I discovered the Canoe about 1 mile above & the indians where we had left
them. I then walked on the Sand beech and the indians came down to
meet me   I gave them my hand and enquired of them what they were
Shooting at, they informed me that they were Shooting off their guns at
an old Keg which we had thrown out of one of the Canoes and was floating down.   those Indians informed me they were Yanktons. [Camped in
Yankton County, South Dakota, opposite the party's camp of August 28–
September 1, 1804, called Calumet Bluff, in Cedar County, Nebraska.]

11. Niobrara River.

September 3, 1806

[CLARK] at half past 4 P. M we Spied two boats & Several men, our party peyed their Ores and we Soon landed on the Side of the Boats the men of these boats Saluted us with their Small arms I landed & was met by a Mr. James Airs[12] from Mackanaw by way of Prarie Dechien and St. Louis. this Gentleman is of the house of Dickson & Co: of Prarie de Chian who has a Licence to trade for one year with the Sieoux he has 2 Batteaux loaded with Merchendize for that purpose. This Gentleman receved both Capt. Lewis and my Self with every mark of friendship he was himself at the time with a chill of the agu on him which he has had for Several days. our first enquirey was after the President of our country and then our friends and the State of the politicks of our country &c. and the State Indian affairs to all of which enquireys Mr. Aires gave us as Satisfactory information as he had it in his power to have Collected in the Illinois which was not a great deel ... this Gentleman informed us of maney Changes & misfortunes which had taken place in the Illinois amongst others the loss of Mr. Cady Choteaus house and furniture by fire.[13] for this misfortune of our friend Choteaus I feel my Self very much Concernd &c. he also informed us that Genl. Wilkinson was the governor of the Louisiana and at St. Louis. 300 of the american Troops had been Contuned on the Missouri a fiew miles above it's mouth, Some disturbance with the Spaniards in the Nackatosh Country is the Cause of their being Called down to that Country, the Spaniards had taken one of the U, States frigates in the Mediteranean, Two British Ships of the line had fired on an American Ship in the port of New York, and killed the Capts. brother.[14] 2 Indians had been hung in St. Louis for murder and several others in jale.[15] and that Mr. Burr & Genl. Hambleton fought a Duel, the latter was killed

12. James Aird, a trader out of Mackinac and Prairie du Chien, Wisconsin, was employed by Robert Dickson.

13. Jean Pierre Chouteau's house in St. Louis had burned on February 15, 1805.

14. The area west of Natchitoches, Louisiana, was disputed between the United States and the Spanish government in Mexico. The Spanish fired on the U.S. frigate *President* in the fall of 1804, while the British assaulted the American merchant ship *Richard* in April 1806, killing one seaman.

15. Two Kickapoo Indians were hanged in December 1805.

&c.[16]   I am happy to find that my worty friend Capt L's is so well as to walk about with ease to himself &c. [Camped at an undetermined spot in either Union County, South Dakota, or Dakota County, Nebraska, several miles north of Sioux City.]

September 4, 1806

[CLARK] as we were in want of Some tobacco I purposed to Mr. Airs to furnish us with 4 Carrots for which we would Pay the amount to any Merchant of St. Louis   he very readily agreed to furnish us with tobacco and gave to each man as much as it is necessary for them to use between this and St. Louis, an instance of Generossity for which every man of the party appears to acknowledge. Mr. Airs also insisted on our accepting a barrel of flour . . . we have yet a little flour part of what we carried up from the Illinois as high as Maria's river and buried it there untill our return &c. . . . at meridian we came too at Floyds Bluff below the Enterance of Floyds river and assended the hill, with Capt Lewis and Several men, found the grave had been opened by the nativs and left half Covered.[17] we had this grave Completely filled up, and returned to the Canoes and proceeded on. [Camped in either Woodbury County, Iowa, or Dakota County, Nebraska, at the party's Fish Camp of August 13, 1804.]

September 6, 1806

[CLARK] we met a tradeing boat of Mr. Ag. Choteaux of St Louis bound to the River Jacque to trade with the Yanktons, this boat was in Care of a Mr. Henry Delorn,[18] he had exposed all his loading and Sent out five of his hands to hunt they Soon arived with an Elk.   we purchased a gallon of whiskey of this man and gave to each man of the party a dram which is the first Spiritious licquor which had been tasted by any of them Since the 4 of July 1805. Several of the party exchanged leather for linen Shirts and

16. James Wilkinson was governor of Louisiana from 1805 to 1807, and was involved with Aaron Burr in some complicated conspiracies before the latter was killed in a duel with Alexander Hamilton.

17. It is, of course, the grave of Charles Floyd who died here on August 20, 1804.

18. "Delorn" could be any of several St. Louis traders with similar names with connections to René Auguste Chouteau.

beaver for Corse hats. [Camped between the Little Sioux and Soldier Rivers, in either Burt or Washington County, Nebraska, or Harrison County, Iowa.]

September 8, 1806

[CLARK] all being anxious to get to the River Platt to day they ply'd their orers very well, and we arived at our old encampment at White Catfish Camp. [Camped at Camp White Catfish, where the party had stayed July 22-27, 1804, near the Mills-Pottawattamie county line, Iowa.]

September 9, 1806

[CLARK] our party appears extreamly anxious to get on, and every day appears produce new anxieties in them to get to their Country and friends. My worthy friend Cap Lewis has entirely recovered   his wounds are heeled up and he Can walk and even run nearly as well as ever he Could. the parts are yet tender &c. [Camped northeast of Peru, Nebraska, in either Nemaha County, Nebraska, or Atchison County, Missouri.]

September 12, 1806

[CLARK] Met Mr. McClellin[19] at the St. Michl. Prarie[20] we found Mr. Jo. Gravelin the Ricaras enterpreter whome we had Sent down with a Ricaras Chief in the Spring of 1805 and old Mr. Durion[21] the Sieux enterpreter, we examined the instructions of those interpreters and found that Gravelin was ordered to the Ricaras with a Speach from the president of the U. States to that nation and some presents which had been given the Ricara Cheif who had visited the U. States and unfortunately died at the City of Washington,[22] he was instructed to teach the Ricaras agriculture & make every enquirey after Capt Lewis my self and the party. [Camped at St. Joseph, Buchanan County, Missouri.]

19. Robert McClellan, already known to Lewis and Clark, was a former scout with the U.S. Army.
20. At present-day St. Joseph, Buchanan County, Missouri.
21. Pierre Dorion Sr.
22. Gravelines carried a letter from Jefferson explaining the circumstances of Piaheto's death.

[ORDWAY] Mr. McLanen informed us that the people in general in the united States were concerned about us as they had heard that we were all killed   then again they heard that the Spanyards had us in the mines &C.

September 14, 1806

[CLARK] we met three large boats bound to the Yanktons and Mahars the property of Mr. Lacroy, Mr. Aiten & Mr. Coutau all from St. Louis,[23] those young men received us with great friendship and pressed on us Some whisky for our men, Bisquet, Pork and Onions, & part of their Stores . . . our party received a dram and Sung Songs untill 11 oClock at night in the greatest harmoney. [Camped opposite Leavenworth, Leavenworth County, Kansas.]

September 15, 1806

[CLARK] passed the enterance of the Kanzas river which was very low, about a mile below we landed and Capt Lewis and my Self assended a hill which appeared to have a Commanding Situation for a fort, the Shore is bold and rocky imediately at the foot of the hill, from the top of the hill you have a perfect Command of the river, this hill fronts the Kanzas and has a view of the Missouri a Short distance above that river.   we landed one time only to let the men geather Pappaws or the Custard apple of which this Country abounds, and the men are very fond of. [Camped a short distance above the Little Blue River, in either Jackson or Clay County, Missouri.]

September 17, 1806

[CLARK] at 11 A. M. we met a Captain McClellin[24] late a Capt. of Artily of the U States Army assending in a large boat.   this gentleman an acquaintance of my friend Capt. Lewis was Somewhat astonished to See us return and appeared rejoiced to meet us.   we found him a man of information and from whome we received a partial account of the political State of

23. The boats were probably the property of Joseph La Croix, an unknown Aiten, and Charles Courtin, but it is unclear if they were the occupants.
24. John McClallen, or McClellan, not to be confused with Robert McClellan, probably knew Lewis from military service.

our Country, we were makeing enquires and exchangeing answers &c.
untill near mid night. this Gentleman informed us that we had been long
Since given out by the people of the U S Generaly and almost forgotton,
the President of the U. States had yet hopes of us; we received some civilities of Capt. McClellin, he gave us Some Buisquit, Chocolate Sugar &
whiskey, for which our party were in want and for which we made a return of a barrel of corn & much obliges to him. [Camped about four
miles above Grand River, in Saline County, Missouri.]

September 20, 1806
[CLARK] the party being extreemly anxious to get down ply their ores
very well, we Saw Some cows on the bank which was a joyfull Sight to the
party and Caused a Shout to be raised for joy   at [blank] P M we Came
in Sight of the little french Village called Charriton   the men raised a
Shout and Sprung upon their ores and we soon landed opposit to the Village. our party requested to be permited to fire off their Guns which was
alowed & they discharged 3 rounds with a harty Cheer, which was returned from five tradeing boats which lay opposit the village . . . we purchased of a Citizen two gallons of Whiskey for our party for which we
were obliged to give Eight dollars in Cash, an imposition on the part of
the Citizen. every person, both French and americans Seem to express
great pleasure at our return, and acknowledged them selves much astonished in Seeing us return. they informed us that we were Supposed to
have been lost long Since, and were entirely given out by every person &c.
[Camped at La Charette ("Charriton"), Warren County, Missouri, which
the party passed on May 25, 1804.]

September 21, 1806
[CLARK] at 4 P M we arived in Sight of St. Charles, the party rejoiced at
the Sight of this hospital village plyed thear ores with great dexterity and
we Soon arived opposit the Town, this day being Sunday we observed a
number of Gentlemen and ladies walking on the bank, we Saluted the
Village by three rounds from our blunderbuts and the Small arms of the
party, and landed near the lower part of the town. we were met by great
numbers of the inhabitants, we found them excessively polite . . . the inhabitants of this village appear much delighted at our return and seem to

Journal entry of John Ordway, September 23, 1806. Courtesy
American Philosophical Society, Philadelphia, Pennsylvania

vie with each other in their politeness to us all. [Camped at St. Charles, St. Charles County, Missouri.]

September 23, 1806
[CLARK] decended to the Mississippi and down that river to St. Louis at which place we arived about 12 oClock.   we Suffered the party to fire off their pieces as a Salute to the Town.   we were met by all the village and received a harty welcom from it's inhabitants.

[ORDWAY] much rejoiced that we have the Expedition Completed and now we look for boarding in Town and wait for our Settlement and then we entend to return to our native homes to See our parents once more as we have been So long from them.

Afterword

Contrary to some Americans' fears, the Corps of Discovery was not captured by the Spanish, nor were they killed; they arrived safely home, as we know. But what of their lives after the great adventure? About Lewis and Clark there exists much information, but for most members of the Corps we know little. Most lived obscure lives before and after their brief season of glory. Indeed, for some even the details of their expedition experience is meager. Clark made some attempt to keep up with his comrades in arms, but separation in time and distance made this nearly impossible. Two decades after the expedition he drew up a list of thirty-four members of the Corps and tried to account for each. Eighteen he either knew or thought to be dead and for five of the remainder he had no knowledge at all. We know only slightly more today.

After the expedition Lewis did not return to a satisfying personal life. His attempts to find a wife failed and he came back to a job in St. Louis alone. Clark in the meantime had married, and his bride probably took the emotional place that Lewis had previously filled. This separation from Clark was intensified by his distance from Jefferson, who on occasion scolded him for not writing and wondered when he would finish the book about the expedition. Never deeply religious, Lewis had no reserves of spiritual commitment to fall back on and find solace when problems mounted and demons set in.

In recognition of their accomplishments Lewis and Clark were given posts of standing and responsibility. The president appointed Lewis governor of Upper Louisiana, with its capital at St. Louis, and he placed Clark in charge of Indian affairs for the same district. The governorship was to be the just reward for a national hero, but in contrast to his success as an explorer Lewis encountered a multitude of frustrations in the job. Perhaps he was not meant to be a deskbound administrator. He did not help matters when he left the office unattended while he lingered in the East after the expedition. Lewis was also burdened with an enemy in his office, an administrative assistant with a political appointment who was writing negative reports of Lewis to officials in Washington.

Notable among Lewis's difficulties as governor were attempts to return the Mandan chief Big White to his home. Expedition sergeant Pryor, now an army ensign, led the first attempt to restore the chief in 1807. He was turned back by an attack from some Arikara Indians who were angered by the death of their own chief in Washington. In the fight Shannon, another member from the Corps, suffered a wound that cost him a leg. It was not until 1809 that a private fur trading company, receiving a substantial payment under Lewis's signature, succeeded in getting Big White back to his people. Washington officials refused to honor some of Lewis's expenditures in this effort. A new executive in the White House was less obliging than Jefferson might have been. This was, in a sense, the final insult for Lewis in the unhappy ordeal of his governorship. Personal financial problems also loomed. It appears he took to drinking heavily in this period and was in a state of severe depression when he set out for Washington to straighten out his affairs. On the journey he died at Grinder's Stand, a way station on the Natchez Trace in Tennessee, on October 11, 1809, apparently by putting a pistol to his head and breast.

While some historians have suggested that he was murdered, available evidence strongly supports the belief that he committed suicide. In fact, he attempted twice earlier to kill himself along the way. His eventual fate inevitably attracts the attention of amateur psychoanalysts seeking the roots of his emotional problems. But knowledge of his childhood is scant and there is no evidence of psychological turmoil during the expedition. On the trail he functioned effectively as a cool and capable leader under numerous trying circumstances. Moreover, neither Clark nor Jefferson, the persons who knew him best, seemed to have doubted his suicide. Clark's reaction was to write, "I fear, O! I fear the weight of his mind has over come him." And Jefferson later noted that he was subject to "hypochondriac affections," perhaps meaning that he suffered bouts of depression. Suicide remains the most acceptable explanation for his death.

Jefferson had expected Lewis to prepare a full account of the expedition after his return. Although the captain had begun efforts in that direction, he had written not a single word for publication. To Clark now fell the task of bringing the results of their labors into print. Having small confidence in his own literary abilities, Clark arranged with Nicholas Biddle, a Philadelphia literary figure, to become the expedition's ghostwriter. Using the captains' journals and that of Sergeant Ordway, and in extensive consultation with Clark and with Shannon, Biddle produced a narrative account of the expedition in two volumes. Final publication was further delayed until 1814 by the failure of the initial publisher. Two years later Clark himself was still trying to get a copy.

Clark was to survive his friend by nearly thirty years. He is so established in history as joint commander of the famous expedition that it is easy to forget that the greater part of his career was spent in St. Louis as a federal agent of Indian affairs. The captain was an effective and conscientious officer in that position, promoting the best interests of his Indian wards and gaining the respect of his white contemporaries. All the while he had to balance a changing disposition in Washington toward Native Americans as Jeffersonian paternalism was succeeded by Jacksonian pressures. Western travelers were eager to visit Clark's home, to view his museum of frontier curiosities, and perhaps to hear him recount expedition adventures. He was married twice, first to Julia Hancock of Fincastle, Virginia, for whom Clark named the Judith River in Montana in the summer of 1805. He died on September 1, 1838, at the St. Louis home of his eldest son, Meriwether Lewis Clark.

For most other members of the Corps of Discovery the end of the expedition meant a return to their previous obscurity. Many of them dropped completely out of sight. Patrick Gass, promoted to sergeant to replace the deceased Floyd, produced his own account of the expedition. Heavily edited by a Virginia bookseller, Gass's book beat that of his leaders into publication, coming out in 1807. First in print and last to die, Gass survived until 1870, longer than any other member of the party whose fate is known. John Colter gained some independent fame for his later adventures. He is best known for his exploration and description of today's Yellowstone Park, but his tales of hot springs and geysers led to jokes about "Colter's Hell." His escape, naked, from the Blackfeet Indians near the Three Forks of the Missouri has become a western legend. Settling in Missouri, Colter died in 1813 of jaundice.

That expert hunter, interpreter, and woodsman Drouillard returned to the wilderness interior on fur trading ventures. He died in 1810 at the Three Forks at the hands of the Blackfeet, his foes at the Two Medicine River incident. Pryor was in and out of military service; he participated in

the Battle of New Orleans in 1815. Afterward he became a trader among
the Osage Indians, married an Osage woman, and died among that tribe
in 1831. Shannon received a government pension for the loss of his leg. He
later studied law and practiced his profession in Kentucky before moving
to Missouri to become a state senator; he died in 1836.

Journalist and top sergeant Ordway apparently returned to his home
in New Hampshire, later settled in Missouri, and was dead by 1817. Information about the trustworthy Field brothers, Joseph and Reubin, is
vague. Joseph apparently died less than a year after the return of the expedition, while Reubin settled in Kentucky and died by 1823. York received his freedom in 1811 and operated a freight business for a time in
Tennessee and Kentucky; he may have died in 1832 on his way to see Clark
in St. Louis. About the rest of this "band of brothers" we know little —
their stories long lost and forgotten, like those of so many other common
foot soldiers.

Charbonneau lived on among the Mandans and Hidatsas, much of the
time, thanks to Clark's affection for him, working as a government interpreter and agent. A train of notable visitors used his interpreting services
at the Upper Missouri villages through the years. After Clark's death in
1838, accounts of the man quickly faded and he was dead by at least 1843,
but of unknown causes or whereabouts. His child and the baby of expedition, Jean Baptiste, became a fur trader and a noted guide. Clark cared
for him as a child as he had promised, seeing to his upbringing and education. As a young man Jean Baptiste joined Prince Paul Wilhelm of
Württemberg, who was on a scientific journey in America, and returned
with him to Europe. He came back to America in 1829, afterward associ-
ating with some of the most famous frontiersmen of his day. In the 1840s
he served as alcalde of the San Luis Rey Mission in California, then followed the gold rush north. He died in 1866 in southeastern Oregon while
traveling to another gold discovery.

Of the fate of Sacagawea there are two versions. One story, now dis-
credited, has her living to the 1880s on the Wind River Shoshone Reservation in Wyoming, with Jean Baptiste joining her and dying there also.
In truth, there is little doubt that she died of fever at Fort Manuel in South
Dakota in December 1812. Despite her limited but useful contributions to
the expedition, geographic landmarks have been named for her; markers,

monuments, and memorials have been placed in her honor; and numerous literary and artistic works have given her a prominence that competes even with that of the captains.

The journey was over—the expedition not simply completed, it was magnificently accomplished. The Lewis and Clark expedition is one of the great stories in American history. Everyone knows of the two captains' trek across the continent with their band of intrepid explorers. And who has not heard of Sacagawea, the young Shoshone woman who accompanied the party with her newborn baby strapped to her back? The journey is filled with tales of high drama: of tense encounters with natives; of hair-raising river crossings and precipitous mountain trails; of hunger, thirst, and bodily fatigue. Less well known are the scientific endeavors—the constant activities of observing, considering, collecting, and recording. The records are marvels of geographic revelations, natural history studies, and ethnographic investigations. The expedition remains for all time a story of endurance, discovery, and achievement.

The expedition was preeminently a geographic endeavor. Jefferson made clear at the outset that the discovery of a practical route across the continent was the principal objective of the mission. In fact, the explorers were seeking the elusive all-water route across the continent, the fabled Northwest Passage. By following the Missouri River to its headwaters, then crossing mountains and deserts to the sea, Lewis and Clark were able to lay out the general topographic features of the West and minutely delineate their avenue of travel. The men proved that an easy path to the Western Ocean did not exist and that crossing the continent would be lengthy and difficult. Yet, in reaching the coast, the expedition laid an important claim to the Oregon country. This claim, plus the purchase of the Louisiana Territory, played an important part in the eventual settlement of the West.

Lewis and Clark's vision of the West was colored by images before the exploration. The leaders' geographic preconceptions hindered some of their work, but they were willing to reorder their ideas in the face of topographic realities. Nonetheless, they persisted with some unchanged notions about certain incorrect theories. They returned, for instance, still believing in a "height of land," from which flowed many of the great streams of the West. During their trip the captains may have relied not only on a geography of sight, but also on a geography of imagination. More important, however, was their actual field work. The men displayed an amazing ability to make accurate decisions in the face of the unknown—sometimes without the aid of helpful Indian advice. Keen geographic intuition and wilderness lore served them well on several occasions, the correct determination at the Marias River being only one example.

An important part of the captains' geographic assignment included mapping the unknown. All the attention given to securing the most accurate maps of the West before the explorers' departure fixes cartography as a principal purpose of the expedition. The men were exploring new possessions acquired under the Louisiana Purchase; thus, mapping became important in determining the boundaries and dimensions of the new lands. Moreover, accurate maps of lands beyond the purchase would serve as devices to further American territorial ambitions. To know the lands was ultimately to possess them.

Clark was the principal mapmaker. He is the author of all but a few of the nearly 200 maps from the expedition. Clark's maps are masterfully executed and are models of field cartography. Working with crude and unreliable instruments and with no apparent training, Clark did an exceptional job, and his drafting abilities have been universally admired. Later generations of explorer-mapmakers followed his example. Clark's mapping accomplished two major objectives: he skillfully plotted the route of the Corps of Discovery and he provided a view of peripheral areas based on the best native information available. Clark's great map of the West, published with the first account of the expedition in 1814, alone justified his efforts. It was the beginning of a new generation of accurate maps of the American West—maps that were based on actual field sightings and acute topographic inference. It has been called a cartographic achievement.

Lewis's scientific studies in Philadelphia before the expedition proved profitable on the trip. Especially noteworthy were the captain's accomplishments in the biological sciences. Lewis, and occasionally Clark, were the first to describe in detail a wide range of characteristic plant and animal species of the West. Previous discoveries and reports of species before them do not detract from their contributions to understanding the range, habits, and physical characteristics of many known species, such as the grizzly bear, buffalo, and beaver. Because of various mischances the results of their work did not see full publication for a century after the expedition, so that Lewis's priority of discovery was not adequately recognized until the last few decades.

Jefferson has been criticized for not sending a naturalist on the expedition. However, there were few trained naturalists in America at the time and Lewis was nearly their equal. Moreover, not many available naturalists could have stood up to the rigors of wilderness travel. Lewis was blessed with those qualities most important in a naturalist: an unquenchable curiosity, keen observational powers, and a systematic approach to understanding the natural world. For example, when Lewis counted eighteen tail feathers on the western blue grouse he recalled that the familiar ruffed grouse had exactly the same number. One has only to look at Lewis's discourses on the animals of the West to understand that Jefferson did not err. The captain's botanical writings are equally impressive, especially his precise ecological distinctions.

Among expedition accomplishments must be counted the health and well-being of the party. Lewis and Clark were their own physicians. For twenty-eight months they doctored themselves and their party. Starting out in the company of "robust, healthy young men," the captains nonetheless had to face ordinary human ills—abscesses and boils, dysentery, malaria, pleurisy, and rheumatism. Injuries and accidents were recurring events—bruises and dislocations from spills and falls, frostbite, and snakebites. Contagious diseases troubled the party as well; colds and venereal disease were not uncommon ailments. The captains' choice of bleeding and purging as routine remedies was the period's accepted practice. Lewis also had some medicinal knowledge, gained partly from his mother who grew and dispensed vegetable drugs. During the continental crossing Lewis occasionally concocted a strong brew of local plants for his own and others' relief.

More important than the captains' limited medical knowledge was the care and concern they accorded their men. As Jefferson would observe, Lewis was "careful as a father of those committed to his charge." At the end of the trip Lewis could happily report that they had returned in good health. In fact, during the entire expedition Floyd was the only member of the party to die, and his death from a ruptured appendix could not have been averted under the best medical care of the day.

In line with Jefferson's lengthy instructions regarding Indians, the captains spent much time in carrying out these responsibilities. In councils under brush arbors and around campfires where the pipe of peace was passed, the captains worked hard to establish good relations between the natives and the young republic they represented. We should not discount the important effects of the individual friendships and mutual admiration that developed, be it a Hidatsa chief's regard for Shields's handiwork in iron, Lewis's praise of Yelleppit's hospitality, the Nez Perces' admiration for Clark's medical knowledge, or the simple joys of dance under Indian drum and expedition fiddle.

The explorers established peaceful contact with most of the Indian tribes that they met. Meetings with Indians were generally cordial and mutually beneficial. Presents were exchanged and information was shared. At times, indeed, the party's success and well-being depended upon the goodwill and assistance of the natives, who provided them with food, horses, and guidance through unknown and difficult country. Indians were often helpful in describing the way ahead and providing information about distant lands. In fact, there was only one episode of violence between the explorers and Indians during the whole twenty-eight months; some other moments of extreme tension ended without bloodshed. Yet, even the difficulties with the Sioux and the Blackfeet did not result in bitterness, though later relations between these tribes and whites caused friction, war, and death.

Working among a diversity of tribes, linguistic groups, and cultural settings, from nomadic horsemen and buffalo hunters of the Great Plains to riverine villagers and salmon catchers of the Pacific Coast, the captains faced a formidable task. Simply to pass through this multitude of humanity was job enough, but to catalog, study, and understand them all appears impossible. And so it was to some extent. These tribes had their own views of such matters as trade relations, intertribal associations and conflicts, and internal tribal politics. Many of the subtleties of these attitudes were not noticed or were misunderstood by the American leaders. The captains were not totally unbiased observers able to obtain accurate and systematic cultural information, but they did rise above cultural relativism and were not nearly as ethnocentric as some of their contemporaries. As well as they could for their time and circumstance the captains took a detached, descriptive, and scientific view of Native Americans. Lewis and Clark were transitional figures between the hit-and-miss ethnographers of the early nineteenth century and the trained ethnologists of later decades.

A final and essential legacy of the expedition are the diaries which were so meticulously written and carefully preserved during the transcontinental crossing. The journals of Lewis and Clark are a national treasure. Besides describing the natural resources and native peoples of the West, the diaries also contain myriad scientific observations. Moreover, they are a genuinely interesting account of expedition events in themselves. Had the captains and four enlisted men not kept daily journals of their activities — recording events, observations, and impressions in more than one million words — many of their important discoveries might be lost. Charged with an incredible array of responsibilities, one stands in awe of the range, depth, and constancy of the men's journal-keeping labors. This abridged volume represents but a small portion of the great effort.

The expedition is enshrined in the imagination of Americans as a heroic feat of geographical exploration, which it was, but not as the major contribution to science that it was intended to be. Only in the twentieth century has the breadth of Lewis and Clark's accomplishments in so many areas been truly appreciated. Continued attention to the achievements of the Corps of Discovery can only increase the esteem it so richly deserves. It remains for all time our American epic.

Index

cucumber, mock-, 179, 179n2
Cul-te-ell, 305
cups, 126, 152, 320, 358
curlews, 148, 148n8, 178
currant, buffalo, 122, 122n17
currant, golden, 181, 181n5, 361, 361n37, 434, 434n68
currant, purple. See currant, wild black
currant, red. See currant, squaw
currant, red flowering, 360, 360n34
currant, squaw, 169
currant, swamp, 181, 181n6
currant, Western red, 165, 165n40
currant, wild black, 120, 169, 181
currants, 167, 211
Cuskalah (and similar spellings), 299, 301–2
Cut Bank Creek, lvii, 408, 408n25,
Cut Nose, liv, 374, 387, 390, 396
Cutssahnim (and similar spellings) Indians. See Yakama Indians

Dalles of the Columbia River. See Columbia River, The Dalles of the
Dame, John, 7
dances: Camp Chopunnish, 389; Fort Mandan, 86, 91, 107; Indian, 370, 460; Marias River, 152; Potlatch River, 259; Shoshones, 212, 236–37; Upper Portage Camp, 168, 174
Deapolis site, xxiv, 74, 74n61
Dearborn, Henry, 183n11
Dearborn River, 182–83, 183n11
deer: abundance, 116–19, 122, 138, 368, 419; as food, 28, 121, 308, 361; habitat, 332; killed, 30, 72, 84, 88, 97, 197, 218, 222, 240, 242, 254, 275, 310, 324, 344, 427; mentioned, 14, 128; observed, 134, 162; scarcity, 22, 213, 215, 351; search for, 294; signs, 244, 282, 295; spleen used for fishing, 154, 154n20
deer, black-tailed. See deer, mule
deer, Columbian black-tailed, 289, 289n6

deer, mule (black-tailed): described, 128; as food, xlviii; habitat, 332; hunted, xlv, lii; killed, 142; mentioned, xxiii, 55, 55n19; scarcity, 213
Delashshelwilt, 341–42
Del Nord River. See Rio Grande River
Delorn, Henry, 447, 447n18
Deschamps, Jean Baptiste, 6, 9, 11
Deschutes River, 270, 270n19, 366, 373, 373n50
Dickson, Joseph, 423, 434, 435n69, 440–41, 440n8
Dickson, Robert, 446n12
Dismal Swamp, 239, 239n35
Divide Creek, 426
dock, Mexican, 179, 179n4
dog (Lewis's). See Seaman
Dog Creek, 361
dogs: as food, xl, xli, xlv, lii, 49, 60, 259, 272, 308, 309–10, 348, 351, 361, 372; habitat, 332; and Indians, 28, 124, 208, 241, 335, 371; purchased, 261, 359, 368, 369; traded, 318, 348; travois, 63, 63n36, 117
dog's-tooth-violet, 392
dogwood, Nuttall's, 355, 355n21
dogwood, red osier (red wood), 120, 120n14, 167, 177, 348, 348n3, 402, 402n7
Dollar Creek, 251
dollars, 79, 387
Dolphees Island, 65, 65n43
Dorion, Pierre Jr., 48, 48n2
Dorion, Pierre Sr., 14, 14n30, 48, 48n2, 435, 435n71, 448, 448n21
Dorion Island No. 2 (Cedar Island), 56, 56nn21–22
Double Ditch site, 73, 73n57
dove, mourning, 383, 383n64
drawers, 302. See also clothing
Drouillard, George: accidents, 115, 403; accompanies Clark, 298n27; accompanies Lewis, lvii, 119n12, 147, 153n17, 195, 202, 286, 294, 398, 401n1, 405; af-

ter expedition, 455; attacked by bear,
142–43, 404; and Blackfeet, lviii, 410,
413–14, 455; death, 455; delayed, 395;
duties, 9, 11, 131; guide, 393; guns, 344;
hunting, 16, 28, 124–25, 181, 196, 217,
218, 229, 296, 303, 318, 403; and Indians, 206, 229–30, 335; interpreter,
xviii, 213; listed, 109; and Marias
River, lvii, 406, 406n21; medical
problems, 28; mentioned, xxix, 15, 39,
45n1, 358n30, 367, 389; returns, 3,
11n22, 31, 47, 199, 342, 387, 396, 404;
robbed, 230; scouting, 203, 408;
search for, 411; sent out, 30, 37, 199,
205, 220–21, 406, 439n6; trading, 455;
votes, 292
drum, freshwater, 40, 40n90
Ducett, Mr., 3
duck, black. See coot, American
duck, brown. See teal
duck, canvasback. See canvasback
duck, mallard. See mallard
duck, merganser. See merganser
duck, red-headed. See merganser
duck, wood, 194n29, 194
duck, black and white. See bufflehead
duckinmallard. See mallard
ducks, 283, 295, 355, 419. See also
bufflehead; canvasback; coot, American; mallard; merganser; teal
Dugout Coulee, 407
Duquette, François, 1, 2n4

eagle, bald, 121, 308, 308n44, 419
eagle, black, 158, 158n28
eagle, golden, 112, 112n3, 419, 419n41
Eagle Creek, 142
Eagle Rock, 182, 182n8
eagles, 355, 390
Eagles Feather. See Piaheto
East Gallatin River, lix
Echelute (and similar spellings). See
Wishram-Wasco Indians
Ecola Creek, 314, 318, 318n60

elderberry, red, 295, 295n20, 357
Eldorado Creek, 394, 395, 396
elk: abundance, 72, 116, 118, 122, 138, 419,
430; behavior, 119; dried, 355; as food,
xlviii, 121, 302, 306, 308, 325, 328, 336,
347, 361; habitat, 332; horns, 325, 420;
hunted, xlv, lii, 300, 332; killed, 84, 97,
142, 196, 296, 306, 310, 318, 329, 343–
44, 421, 447; marrow and tallow, 299,
306; mentioned, 142, 396; observed,
134; scarcity, 213, 215, 324, 337, 351, 370;
signs, 22, 244, 282, 295; skins, 254–55,
304, 316, 322, 341, 347, 352, 396; stolen,
li, 335, 342; tongue, 306; traded, 304,
316, 347, 352
Elkhorn River, 31, 31n74
Elk Island, 56
elms, 28, 33, 71, 120, 420
Eneshur (and similar spellings) Indians.
See Tenino Indians
engagés (French boatmen): hired, xviii;
information from, 32, 151, 323, 434;
listed, 6–7; Missouri River known by,
xix; sent to St. Louis, 109; tobacco,
348n3. See also Frenchmen
Eoote-lash-schute (and similar
spellings). See Flathead Indians
ermine. See weasel, long-tailed
espontoon, 124, 124n20, 130, 149, 157, 159
"Estimate of Eastern Indians," xxix
"Estimate of Western Indians," xlix
eulachon, xlviii, 335, 335n92, 336n93,
337–38, 340, 358
Evans, John Thomas, 16n35

feathers, 265, 390
felons. See medical problems, fingers
Femme Osage Creek, 4, 4n11
fern, western bracken, xlviii, 322, 322n62
fiddle: and Indians, liv, 236, 259, 268,
367, 369, 374, 389; and members of
the party, 120, 174, 460. See also
Cruzatte, Pierre; Gibson, George
Fidler, Peter, 150, 150n13

Hairy Horn, 98
Haley's Bay. *See* Baker Bay
Hall, Hugh: accompanies Clark,
424n48; courts-martial, 19, 70; disciplined, 1, 20; and Indians, 433–34;
listed, 6, 109; medical problems, 338;
returns, 430n64, 433; sent out,
430n64; votes, 292
Hamilton, Alexander, 446, 447n16
Hamilton Creek, 278, 278n42
Hamilton Island, 278, 278n43
Hancock, Forrest, 423, 434–35, 435n69,
440–41, 440n8
Hancock, Julia, 139n46, 455
handkerchiefs: gifts, 235, 253, 255, 264,
267, 411; mentioned, 243, 291, 341;
traded, 224
hare. *See* jackrabbits
hatchets, 272
hats, 79, 303, 316, 325, 341, 421, 448. *See
also* clothing
haw, black, 295, 323
hawks, 355
hawthorn, black, 360, 360n33
Hay. *See* Pocasse
Hayden Creek, 213n10
Hayden Island, 282, 282n54, 352,
352n13
hazelnuts, 14, 14n28
Heart River, xxv, 72, 72n55, 105
Hébert, Charles, 7
hemlock, mountain, 246, 246n56
hemlock, western, 328, 328n76
hemlocks, 380
Heney, Hugh, 89, 89n33, 399, 399n99,
430, 430n64
heron, great blue, 338, 338n98
hickory, 177
Hidatsa Indians: and Arikaras, lxi, 97,
435, 439; and Assiniboines, 103, 104–
5; and bear, 115; and Blackfeet, 437;
and buffalo, 103; camp of, 113; and
Charbonneau, xxvii; chiefs, 104, 233,
437; councils, 79; customs, xxv, 101,

117–18, 311, 311n46; gifts, 79, 85;
horses, 103, 236–37; hunting, 114; information from, xxv, xxxii, 95, 126,
136, 136n42, 145n1; language, 82,
424n48; and Mandans, xxv, 82, 82n16,
85, 102, 109; mentioned, xxvi, 94, 138,
138n45, 215n14, 220–21, 226, 376, 456,
460; and Nez Perces, 375, 375n53; population, xxiv, 82; prairie fire set by,
103; relations with party, xliv; and
Sacagawea, 221, 225; and Shoshones,
xxxvi, lx, 79, 79n8, 95, 194, 215, 236,
440; and Sioux, 74, 74n58, 83, 85, 97;
speeches to, 78–79; viewed by Lewis
and Clark, xxv; villages, xxv, lx; visits,
93, 97, 102, 104; visit Washington, 439;
war, xxv, 95, 97, 233–34; women, 93,
95, 225
Hidatsa Indians, Awatixa, xxv, 78, 78n5
Hidatsa Indians, Awaxawi, xxv; and
Arikaras, 83; and Assiniboines, 104–5;
chiefs, 104; historical sketch, 104–5;
and Mandans, 105, 109; mentioned,
102; name, 104; population, 105; and
Sioux, 105; villages, 77, 77n3; visits, 89,
89n29
Hidatsa Indians, Hidatsa Proper: and
Cheyennes, 440; chiefs, 78n6, 439;
and Sioux, 439; villages, xxv, 78, 78n6,
437, 437n1
Highwood Mountains, 136, 136nn42–
43, 154, 154n18
Hohots Ilppilp, 374, 376–77, 383, 387,
389, 389n78
holly, mountain, 295, 330
honeysuckle, 120, 167
honeysuckle, orange, 392, 392n83
honeysuckle, western trumpet, 250,
250n72
Hooke, Moses, xvii
Horned Weasel, 85
hornets, 385
Horse Prairie Creek, 203, 203n1, 203n3,
220, 235

Miller Island, 270, 270n20
Minetares of Fort de Prairie Indians. *See*
   Atsina Indians
Minitari (and similar spellings) Indians.
   See Hidatsa Indians
mink, 332
Mississippi River, xviii, 56, 205, 330,
   370–71, 452
Missouri, camps in: Andrew County,
   24; Atchison County, 27, 448; Boone
   County, 12–13; Buchanan County,
   22–23, 448; Carroll County, 15; Chari-
   ton County, 15; Cole County, 12;
   Cooper County, 13; Franklin County,
   4–5; Gasconade County, 9; Holt
   County, 24–25; Howard County, 13;
   Jackson County, 17–18; Lafayette
   County, 16–17; Osage County, 11;
   Platte County, 20–21; Saline County,
   13–14, 450; St. Charles County, 1–4,
   452; St. Louis County, 1; Warren
   County, 5, 450
Missouria Indians: chiefs, xx, 33; customs, 25, 206; diet, 126, 130, 181; gifts,
   xx, 33; historical sketch, 22; information from, 32; mentioned, 22n53, 37,
   265, 310; and Otoe Indians, 15, 34;
   population, 15, 34; trade, 84, 84n21;
   villages, 65–66; visits, xx–xxi, 33
Missouri River: accidents, 4–5; bluffs,
   112, 141–42; camp at, 143, 147, 439;
   character, 145–46, 203–5; descent of,
   lix, 398; described, 21, 36, 56, 113–14,
   116, 118, 120, 135–38, 141–43, 151, 157–
   58, 184–85, 443; explored, 145, 145n2,
   147, 147n2, 147n5, 148–49, 151–52,
   154–57; fishing, 49; and Indians, xxii,
   227, 234–35, 241; journey up, xviii,
   xix–xx; maps, xix, 16n35, 330, 404;
   mentioned, xxiv, xlii, 120, 136–37,
   142n51, 151–52, 159n29, 199, 205–6,
   212, 214, 242, 288, 330–31, 342, 351, 384,
   417n38; name, 147; and Platte River,
   29, 29n70; route, 399, 399n99; species,

123, 169, 178, 384–85; timber, 17, 28,
   33, 137; viewed, 449. *See also* Missouri
   River, Big Bend of the; Missouri River,
   Great Falls of the; Missouri River,
   Three Forks of the; Missouri
   River, White Cliffs of the
Missouri River, Big Bend of the, 56,
   56n20, 443
Missouri River, Great Falls of the: accidents, 405; arrival at, 155; cache at,
   lvii, 162, 165, 165n38; camp at, 157, 406,
   409; described, xxxiii, 154–56; explored, 157–59; Indian guides, 388–
   89; mentioned, xxxvii, lvi, 412; noise
   heard at, 174, 174n52, 177; portage,
   xxxiii–xxxiv, lvi–lvii, 157, 161, 161n31,
   162n32, 165–72, 398, 406, 406n19;
   route to, 401, 401n2
Missouri River, middle fork. *See* Madison River
Missouri River, north or southwest
   fork. *See* Jefferson River
Missouri River, south or southeast fork.
   See Gallatin River
Missouri River, Three Forks of the: arrival at, xxxiv, 187, 187n18; and Colter,
   455; described, 187; and Indians,
   xxxvii; latitude, 194, 194n26; mentioned, lvi, 427, 455; return, lix,
   395n93, 399, 399n99
Missouri River, White Cliffs of the,
   xxxii, 141, 141n49
Mitutanka village: camp at, 439, 440;
   mentioned, xxiv, 74–77, 74n61, 78,
   439, 440; visits, 439, 439n6, 441, 441n9
moccasins: damaged, 187; found, 430;
   gifts, 208, 302, 389, 389n78; and Indians, 241, 260, 377; lost, 171, 200; making, xlvi, 103, 148, 173, 231; mended,
   168, 247; mentioned, 140, 325, 396;
   number, 340
Moniteau Creek, 12, 12n23, 13, 13n25
Montana, camps in, xxx–xxxi; Beaverhead County, 197, 201, 205–8, 212,